A Student's Guide to

BAYESIAN STATISTICS

Sara Miller McCune founded SAGE Publishing in 1965 to support the dissemination of usable knowledge and educate a global community. SAGE publishes more than 1000 journals and over 800 new books each year, spanning a wide range of subject areas. Our growing selection of library products includes archives, data, case studies and video. SAGE remains majority owned by our founder and after her lifetime will become owned by a charitable trust that secures the company's continued independence.

Los Angeles | London | New Delhi | Singapore | Washington DC | Melbourne

A Student's Guide to
BAYESIAN STATISTICS

Ben Lambert

Los Angeles | London | New Delhi
Singapore | Washington DC | Melbourne

Los Angeles | London | New Delhi
Singapore | Washington DC | Melbourne

SAGE Publications Ltd
1 Oliver's Yard
55 City Road
London EC1Y 1SP

SAGE Publications Inc.
2455 Teller Road
Thousand Oaks, California 91320

SAGE Publications India Pvt Ltd
B 1/I 1 Mohan Cooperative Industrial Area
Mathura Road
New Delhi 110 044

SAGE Publications Asia-Pacific Pte Ltd
3 Church Street
#10-04 Samsung Hub
Singapore 049483

Editor: Jai Seaman
Editorial assistant: Alysha Owen
Production editor: Ian Antcliff
Copyeditor: Sarah J. Duffy
Proofreader: Neville Hankins
Marketing manager: Susheel Gokarakonda
Cover design: Bhairvi Gudka
Typeset by: C&M Digitals (P) Ltd, Chennai, India
Printed in the UK

© Ben Lambert 2018

First published 2018

Library of Congress Control Number: 2017942214

British Library Cataloguing in Publication data

A catalogue record for this book is available from the British Library

ISBN 978-1-4739-1635-7
ISBN 978-1-4739-1636-4 (pbk)

At SAGE we take sustainability seriously. Most of our products are printed in the UK using responsibly sourced papers and boards. When we print overseas we ensure sustainable papers are used as measured by the PREPS grading system. We undertake an annual audit to monitor our sustainability.

For Mum and Dad

CONTENTS

ONLINE RESOURCES

A Student's Guide to Bayesian Statistics is supported by online resources to aid study and help you get to grips with everything Bayesian. These are available at https://study.sagepub.com/lambert.

Watch and learn! Over sixty **author videos** provide definitions, tips, and examples surrounding the key topics of each chapter.

Test yourself! **Answers to the in-text problem sets** will help you check your work and identify areas where you might need more practice.

ACKNOWLEDGEMENTS

Some book acknowledgements are perfunctory; more a product of custom than an actual need to acknowledge the real contribution of others. Not in this case. I very much owe the contents of these pages to the efforts of others. This section is my insufficient effort to recognise the altruism of those people.

I first would like to thank those who helped me to write, shuffle, and remove the words in the various drafts of this book. In the book's initial phase, Heather Harrington and Paul Kirk graciously provided me with useful feedback. My dad, Jean-Michel Johnston and Fergus Cooper benevolently gave up far too much time to reading various drafts of this work; your feedback has been invaluable in shaping this work. The Stan software forum has been an extremely useful source of information and the developers' answers to my Stan-related questions has helped to shape the second half of this book. Singling out a few Stan people, I would like to thank Bob Carpenter, Michael Betancourt and Andrew Gelman.

At SAGE, I would first like to thank Katie Metzler (and, although not a Sager, Nick Allum) who helped start the process of getting this book made. Much of what is written here within is due to my collection of editors, including Katie, Mila Steele, Jai Seaman, and the rest of the editorial/copy-editing team, including Alysha Owen, and Sarah Duffy. I'd also like to give special thanks to Ian Antcliff for putting up with my (unreasonable) demands! Thank you all for your efforts in bringing this publication to realisation.

Academically I have been spoiled. In both my jaunts at Oxford, I have had people who have inspired me, or nudged me in the right direction if (as can occasionally happen) I temporarily veered off course. Through the past thirteen years, Roman Walczak at Somerville College has done both of these things and more of the latter than anyone should have to. More recently, Ace North, Charles Godfray, Helen Byrne, Dave Gavaghan, Thomas Churcher, Astrid Iversen and Armand Leroi have taken academic custody of me, and I appreciate your guardianship and guidance. The best parts of this book are due to your efforts. Any weak parts (although I hope these are few) are due to my inability to follow through on what you have taught me.

Friends are part of my family. You have seen me at my worst and you (for some illogical reason) are still here. You are constant and strong when I am fickle and weak. Mine when I'm a 'yours'. Morzine, when I should have been in Chatel. In no particular order, thank you to Tony Marsden, Chris Sherwood, Doug Abbott, Sion Colley, Michael Beare, Tom Westcott, Joe Newell, Richard Greenberg, Jean-Michel Johnston, Fergus Cooper, Joanna Raisbeck, Hazel Tubman, Ed Youngson, Chris Page and Oli Jackson. One day, when I no longer live in a bedsit, I will host a night in your honour.

Charlotte King you, more than anyone else, know the rough road this book has taken to reach its current state. Without you, this work would be all chapter and no book. I cannot hope to repay your infinite patience and compassion in any meaningful way. For now, words will have to suffice, I'm afraid. Maybe once this book tops the best sellers' list you'll allow me to pay for your half of dinner. Whilst I hate to tag this on here, but it fits best, I also owe your parents - Judith and Michael King. The origin of your kindness is not some great genetic mystery.

Claire Wheeler, whilst you probably wouldn't let me tell you this, I owe you a lot. Much more than I have ever given you credit for. It isn't some miracle that the past three years have been pacific and bloody cracking. It was you. I have treated you badly. You deserve much better. From summer picnics in University Parks, to holidays in my natural geography ("the tropics"), to kaizen in my music tastes, to listening to my whining and incoherent babbling, you have made my life much better to live. For this I will always feel lucky, and truly thankful.

Matthew, Louise, Catherine, Nigel, Dec, Hannah and Tom. Guys, you've always been so good to me. It's not possible to summarise in few words the unwavering support you've provided me with over the past 32 years. You'll have to take my word for it when I say a hearty, yet insufficient, "thank you". I'm really excited at the prospect of (hopefully) spending more time with you all over the coming years; in particular, with Dec, Hannah and Tom. I'm continually impressed by how the three of you seem mature beyond your years (much more mature than your uncle at that/this age!), and I'm in no doubt you will all lead fantastic and worthwhile lives.

Mum and Dad. This book is for you, really. You've been through a lot with me. Much more than I imagine you expected to go through. For this, I am sorry, and I am forever thankful at your unfailing support and compassion for me. You've taught me many things, many of which, I believe are somewhat uncommon for parents to convey onto children: A sense of humour, an ability to produce occasional wit, and a recognition of the need to laugh at oneself were, I think, bequeathed from you to me. I sometimes lament my ability to follow basic social conventions and blindly follow rules. I do now recognise, however, that this extra liberty, which I seem to (perhaps overly) enjoy, is a privilege as well as a character flaw, and something that provides me with opportunities that I would otherwise not be granted. Writing this book is one of these opportunities which, I believe, arose because I never feel the pressure to do what is entirely expected of me; something which, I think, you taught me. Thank you both for all of this and the important, yet all-too-often, selfishly ignored support and guidance you have given me through the years.

To the readers, I thank you for persisting. I hope that this book brings you as close to Bayes as my Mum was as a child, when she visited her family doctor who happened to have set up practice in Thomas Bayes' former house in Tunbridge Wells.

ABOUT THE AUTHOR

 Ben Lambert is a researcher at Imperial College London where he works on the epidemiology of malaria. He has worked in applied statistical inference for about a decade, formerly at the University of Oxford, and is the author of over 500 online lectures on econometrics and statistics. He also somewhat strangely went to school in Thomas Bayes' home town for many years, Tunbridge Wells.

1

Chapter contents

HOW BEST TO USE THIS BOOK

THE PURPOSE OF THIS BOOK

This book aims to be a friendlier introduction to Bayesian analysis than other texts available out there. Whenever we introduce new concepts, we keep the mathematics to a minimum and focus instead on the intuition behind the theory. However, we do not sacrifice content for the sake of simplicity and aim to cover everything from the basics up to the advanced topics required for applied research. Overall, this book seeks to plug a gap in the existing literature (see Figure 1.1).

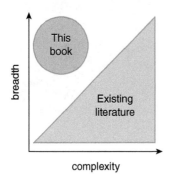

Figure 1.1   This book's niche.

To help readers along the way, we have developed a number of interactive elements which are accessible through the book's website, as well as example code for readers to peruse and, if they so desire, to run themselves. We also supplement key ideas with videos, which approach topics from different angles, and examples.

At the end of each chapter, there are problem sets, which allow the student to build up practical experience of Bayesian analysis. Whenever appropriate these problem sets will also be supplemented with video material.

 WHO IS THIS BOOK FOR?

This book is for anyone who has ever tried and failed at statistics, particularly Bayesian statistics.

The text is aimed at anyone who has completed high school mathematics and wants to conduct Bayesian inference on real-world data. We assume no previous knowledge of probability (which is central to Bayesian analysis) and devote the entirety of Chapter 3 to this topic. We do not require that the student be versed in Frequentist statistics, as we aim to build an alternative and complementary path to a shared goal. After Chapter 2 we refrain from frequent comparisons between these two approaches.

While we start at the beginning of statistical inference, we hope to provide a guide of practical use for the types of analysis encountered in real life.

 PREREQUISITES

Knowledge of the following is strongly recommended to allow the reader to get the most out of this book:

* **Algebra:** Manipulation of symbolic expressions is widespread throughout the text.
* **Products and summations:** These are mainly used for writing down likelihood and log-likelihood functions.

There is some differentiation in this book, although it is fairly limited and used mostly in sections concerning maximum likelihood. A note on integration: At early stages of this book's development, it contained many integrals. In teaching this material, we have realised that students can be discouraged by the sight of these mathematical behemoths. Fortunately, since modern Bayesian inference relies on computational sampling rather than hard calculation (see Part IV), an intimate knowledge of integrals is no longer essential. In this book, we keep the use of integrals to a minimum, apart from mainly those cases where we provide a motivation for Markov chain Monte Carlo (MCMC).

The only other prerequisite concerns the practical application of Bayesian analysis. Knowledge of the open source statistical software R [29] would be useful. We do not classify this item with those above, because we use only the basic functionality of this language and also document any use of this language thoroughly. This language is widely used for statistical analysis and, because of its popularity, there are excellent free online resources that can be used to learn it. Here we list just a few of the available resources:

- Coursera (www.coursera.org) has a number of great lecture courses with associated problem sets available for learning R. We recommend the courses by Roger Peng at Johns Hopkins University.
- Try R (http://tryr.codeschool.com) is a short interactive introductory lesson on the basics of R.
- Data Camp's free Introduction to R (www.datacamp.com/courses/free-introduction-to-r) provides 4 hours of interactive lectures on the basics of R.
- The R Guide (http://cran.r-project.org/doc/contrib/Owen-TheRGuide.pdf) is a nice written guide to R.

While none of these are essential, if you have difficulty following the examples in this text, we recommend that you try the above resources.

 **BOOK OUTLINE**

We have written this text to make each chapter as self-contained as possible. While, at times, the reader may feel that this makes the text repetitive, this approach has two purposes: first to help keep topics self-contained, but also because we believe that some ideas are worth encountering, and re-encountering, at different points along the way in learning about Bayes.

The book is divided into five parts:

- Part I: An introduction to Bayesian inference
- Part II: Understanding the Bayesian formula
- Part III: Analytic Bayesian methods
- Part IV: A practical guide to doing real-life Bayesian analysis: Computational Bayes
- Part V: Hierarchical models and regression

Part I provides an introduction to the purpose of statistical inference, then compares and contrasts the Bayesian and Frequentist approaches to it. Bayesian inference is based on probability distributions. Hence, it is imperative to understand these types of mathematical object. The latter half of this part is devoted to this topic. Part II introduces the reader to the constituent elements of the Bayesian inference formula, and in doing so provides an all-round introduction to the practicalities of doing Bayesian inference. Part III aims to equip the reader with knowledge of the most practically relevant probability distributions for Bayesian inference. These objects come under two categories (although some distributions fall into both): prior distributions and likelihood distributions. Knowledge of these distributions is essential for understanding existing research papers and books which use Bayesian statistics, as well as necessary to conduct Bayesian inference in practice. The rest of this part is concerned with introducing the reader to 'nice' combinations of distributions, which allow for a pen-and-paper deduction of quantities of interest. This is important as a stepping stone to computational methods, but also because these types of model are a good place to start before implementing more nuanced models. Part IV introduces the reader to the modern methods of undertaking Bayesian analysis, through computational Markov chain Monte Carlo. This part provides an intuitive explanation of some of the most important algorithmic tools used in computational methods. It also introduces the reader to the statistical programming language that we use for many applied examples in this text: Stan. This part is essential reading for anyone who wants to conduct serious real-world Bayesian analysis of data. Assuming this computational knowledge, Part V introduces the reader to an important Bayesian paradigm known as hierarchical models. It also provides an in-depth introduction to Bayesian regression modelling for linear and generalised linear models.

Each chapter has two introductory summaries: the chapter mission statement and chapter goals. The former is usually a one- or two-sentence summary of the material to be covered in the chapter. The goals section is more detailed and links together material encountered in previous chapters. At the end of each chapter, there are also two summary sections: a chapter summary and short list of chapter outcomes. These provide the reader with a description of the skills acquired as well as a perspective on the material's position within the book's overall goals.

1.5 ROUTE PLANNER - SUGGESTED JOURNEYS THROUGH BAYESLAND

In the style of most good guide books, we suggest itineraries that offer routes through select parts of Bayesland. These journeys are meant to be shortish paths towards gaining a better understanding of particular elements of Bayesian statistics. Like most short trips they are not as all-encompassing as a more prolonged stay, but can nonetheless be useful and fun in their own right. We offer the following trips through Bayesland, which the reader can choose based on their time constraints, goals and pre-existing knowledge:

- **The long-weekender (introductory)** provides a short introduction to the principles of Bayesian inference. Chapter 2 introduces you to the theory behind statistical inference and provides a gentle comparison between Bayesian and Frequentist approaches. If you have extra time, and knowledge of probability distributions, then try your hand at Chapter 7.
- **The 2-week basic package trip (introductory)**, consisting of Parts I and II, provides a full introduction to Bayesian statistics from the ground up.

- **The 2-week refresher (intermediate)** aims to provide a good grounding in Bayesian inference for someone with some experience in statistics. Read Chapter 2 to get your bearings. Depending on your knowledge of the Bayesian formula, Part II can be either read or left behind. Part III should be read almost in full, as this will get you up to speed with many of the tools necessary to understand research papers. To this end, you can probably avoid reading Chapter 11, on objective Bayes.
- **The Bayes summer 1-weeker (intermediate)** is a short course that provides some background information for anyone who wants to use Bayesian inference in their own work. Read Chapters 8 and 9 to get an idea of some of the distributional tools which are available to us and how they can be used. Next read Chapter 12, which explains some of the issues with analytical Bayesian inference and a motivation for Markov chain Monte Carlo.
- **The 3-week full practical swing (intermediate-expert)** is if you are happy with your knowledge of the Bayesian inference formula and the distributions used in Bayesian analysis, and you want to skip ahead to Part IV, which introduces computational methods. This introduces you to the motivation behind computational sampling and provides an introduction to Stan, which is the statistical language used in this text to do sampling via MCMC. If you have time, then you may want to progress to Part V, where there are more applied examples that use Stan.
- **The 'I need to do Bayesian analysis now' 3-day leg (intermediate-expert)** is tailored to those practitioners who need to carry out Bayesian data analysis *fast*. The most likely audience here consists of those in research, either academic or corporate, who have existing knowledge of Bayesian statistics. Skip ahead to Chapter 16, on Stan. After this, it is useful to know about hierarchical models, so we recommend reading Chapter 17, followed by the rest of Part V.
- **A 3-week Bayes ocean master (intermediate-expert)** is for those who want to learn as much about applied Bayesian methods as time allows, but also want to gain experience in practically applying Bayesian statistics. Read all of Part IV.
- **A 2-week modelling masterclass (expert)** is for you if you know all the basics, have used Stan before, and want to see these applied to carrying out real-life data analysis. Read all of Part V.

1 ○ 6   VIDEO

Whenever the reader sees the following signpost, there is a video available to supplement the main text:

Video

By following the web address indicated, the user can watch the video.

The videos are not meant to replace reading of the text. They are supplementary and aim to address topics through alternative approaches and with different examples.

This video describes the syllabus covered in this book.

1●7 PROBLEM SETS

The reader can test their knowledge using the problem sets at the end of each chapter. The problems cover mostly the practical application of Bayesian data analysis, although there are also more theoretical questions. We have tried to make these as fun as possible! They include many examples which we think demonstrate well certain aspects of Bayesian inference and could be used as jumping-off points for mini student projects. The examples often include real data sets that we believe are interesting to analyse and provide hands-on insight into what it is like to do Bayesian statistics in the field.

1●8 R AND STAN

Modern Bayesian data analysis uses computers. Luckily for the student of Bayesian statistics, the most up-to-date and useful software packages are open source, meaning they are freely available to use. In this book, we use solely this type of software.

The most recent, and powerful, software to emerge is Stan, developed by Andrew Gelman et al. [8, 34]. The language of this software is not difficult to understand, and the code is easier to write and debug than its competition. Stan allows a user to fit complex models to data sets without having to wait an age for the results. It is now the de facto choice of modelling software for MCMC for most researchers who use Bayesian statistics. This is reflected in terms of both the number of papers that cite Stan and the number of textbooks that use Stan as their programming language of choice. This popularity matters. It means that the language is here to stay, and will likely continue to improve. It also means that there is an active user forum (which is managed by Stan developers) where you can often find answers to issues by searching through the question bank or, failing a resolution, ask a question yourself. In short, if you run into issues with your code or have trouble with the sampling, then there are a range of places you can go to find a solution (covered in detail in Chapter 16).

Stan is usually run through another piece of 'helper' software. While a number of alternatives are available, we choose to use R because it is open source and widely used. This means that anyone with a modern computer can get their hands dirty in Bayesian analysis. Its popularity is important since the code base is well maintained and tested.

Whenever appropriate, particularly in Part IV onwards, we include snippets of code in R and Stan. These are commented thoroughly, which should be self-explanatory.

1●9 WHY DON'T MORE PEOPLE USE BAYESIAN STATISTICS?

Many are discouraged from using Bayesian statistics for analysis due to its supposed difficulty and its dependence on mathematics. We argue that this is, in part, a weakness of the existing literature on the subject, which this book seeks to address. It also highlights how many books on Frequentist statistics sweep their inherent complexity and assumptions under the carpet, to make their texts easier to digest. This means that for many practitioners it seems that the path of least resistance is to forge ahead with Frequentist tools.

Because of its dependence on the logic of probability, Bayesian statistics superficially appears mathematically complex. What is often lost in introductory texts on Bayesian theory is the intuitive explanations behind the mathematical formulae. Instead, here we consciously choose to shift the emphasis towards the intuition behind the theory. We focus on graphical and illustrative explanations rather than getting lost in the details of the mathematics, which is not necessary for much of modern Bayesian analysis. We hope that by doing so, we shall lose fewer casualties to the mathematical complexity and redress the imbalance between Frequentist and Bayesian analyses.

On first appearances, the concept of the *prior* no doubt leads many to abandon ship early on the path to understanding Bayesian methodologies. This is because some view this aspect of Bayesian inference as wishy-washy and hence a less firm foundation on which to build an analysis. We cover this concept in detail in Chapter 5, which is fully devoted to this subject, where we hope to banish this particular thorn in the side of would-be Bayesian statisticians.

The reliance on computing, in particular simulation, is also seen to inflate the complexity of Bayesian approaches. While Bayesian statistics is reliant on computers, we should recognise that, nowadays, the same is true for Frequentist statistics. No applied statistician does research using only pen and paper. We also argue that the modern algorithms used for simulation in Bayesian inference are straightforward to understand and, with modern software, easy to implement. Furthermore, the added complexity of simulation methods is compensated for by the straightforward extension of Bayesian models to handle arbitrarily complex situations. Like most things worth studying, there is a slight learning curve to become acquainted with a language used to write modern Bayesian simulations. We hope to make this curve sufficiently shallow by introducing the elements used in these computational applications incrementally.

1 ○ 10   WHAT ARE THE TANGIBLE (NON-ACADEMIC) BENEFITS OF BAYESIAN STATISTICS?

Bayesian textbooks often heavily emphasise the academic reasons for choosing a Bayesian analysis over Frequentist approaches. Authors often neglect to promote the more tangible, everyday benefits of the former. Here we list the following *real* benefits of a Bayesian approach:

- **Simple and intuitive model testing and comparison.** The prior and posterior predictive distributions allow for in-depth testing of any particular aspect of a model, by comparing data simulated from these distributions with the real data.
- **Straightforward interpretation of results.** In Frequentist analyses, the confidence interval is often taken to be a simple measure of uncertainty. As we shall see in Section 7.7.1, this is not the case, and interpretation of this concept is not straightforward. By contrast, Bayesian credible intervals have a more common sense interpretation which better aligns with the view that they quantify the uncertainty inherent in estimation.
- **Full model flexibility.** Modern Bayesian analyses use computational simulation to carry out analyses. While this might appear excessive when compared to Frequentist statistics, a benefit is that Bayesian models can be easily extended to encompass a data-generating process of any complexity. This is in contrast to Frequentist approaches, where the intrinsic difficulty of analysis often scales with the complexity of the model chosen.

- **Less important to remember mathematical formulae and statistical tests, and less opportunity for misuse of tests.** For someone attempting to learn Frequentist inference, there are considerable barriers to entry. There are a range of mathematical and statistical results (with somewhat random names) that are necessary to know in order to do inference. The assumptions behind each of these results are typically not self-evident, particularly when using statistical software for inference. This means that there is ample opportunity for their misuse. In Bayesian inference, by contrast, we typically build models from the ground up, starting with our assumptions about a process. While this might appear repetitive at times, this approach means that we do not need a working knowledge of disparate statistical tests. It also means that there is less opportunity to misuse Bayesian models since we explicitly state our assumptions as part of the model building process.
- **The best predictions.** Leading figures, both inside and outside of academia, use Bayesian approaches for prediction. An example is Nate Silver's correct prediction of the 2008 US presidential election results [32].

SUGGESTED FURTHER READING

A good book should leave the reader wanting more. Due to the finiteness of this text, we recommend the following books, articles and websites. These are not necessarily all on Bayesian statistics but fall under the wider categories of statistical inference and learning. We also provide a score of the complexity of these texts to help guide your choice:

- *Bayesian Data Analysis* **(intermediate-expert):** A masterpiece produced by the master statisticians Andrew Gelman and Donald Rubin, among others. This is the most all-encompassing and up-to-date text available on applied Bayesian data analysis. There are plenty of examples of Bayesian analysis applied to real-world data that are well explained [14]. However, the mathematical and statistical knowledge assumed by this book can be intimidating, especially if you are just starting out in the world of inference.
- *Data Analysis Using Regression and Multilevel/Hierarchical Models* **(master):** Another belter from Andrew Gelman along with co-author Jennifer Hill, this takes the reader through numerous examples of regression modelling and hierarchical analysis. The text is not solely limited to Bayesian analysis and covers Frequentist methods as well. Again, the level for this text is probably too high for a student not well versed in statistics.
- *Mastering Metrics* **(introductory):** This is a great back-to-basics book on causal inference by the masters of econometrics Josh Angrist and Jörn-Steffen Pischke. It is an exhibition of the five main methods for conducting causal inference using Frequentist statistics in the social sciences: regression, matching, instrumental variables, differences-in-differences and regression discontinuity design. This is a readable text and is suitable for anyone wanting to learn about economic policy evaluation.
- *Mostly Harmless Econometrics* **(master-of-metrics):** Another by Josh Angrist and Jörn-Steffen Pischke, this thorough and mathematically detailed text takes the reader through most of those methods used in Frequentist causal inference today. Its small size is deceptive; it is not one to read over a single weekend. However, it is worth persisting with this book, as the nuggets that await the determined reader are worth their weight in gold. Also see Gelman's review of this book, which provides an interesting critique of the text.

PART I
AN INTRODUCTION TO BAYESIAN INFERENCE

PART I MISSION STATEMENT

The purpose of this part is twofold: first to introduce the reader to the principles of inference, and second to provide them with knowledge of probability distributions, which is essential to Bayesian inference.

PART I GOALS

Chapter 2 introduces the reader to the aims of statistical inference, along with the differences in philosophy and approach used by Frequentists (also known as Classicists) and Bayesians in pursuit of this shared goal. Both Frequentist and Bayesian approaches aim to assess the evidence for a hypothesis using a sample of data. However, it is usually much easier to calculate the inverse – the probability of the data given the hypothesis. Therefore, in order to assess the evidence for a hypothesis, a process of *inversion* is required. There are two predominant ways of undertaking this inversion: Frequentists use a rule of thumb, which is arbitrary but has historical consensus; by contrast, Bayesians use Bayes' rule – the only method consistent with the logic of probability.

One of the differences in approach is the Bayesian insistence on describing uncertainty explicitly through probability distributions. The resultant theory is more elegant, as well as more practically useful, than Frequentist inference. To fully appreciate this elegance, it is necessary to have a good working knowledge of probability distributions and their manipulations, which is provided by Chapter 3.

2

Chapter contents

THE SUBJECTIVE
WORLDS OF
FREQUENTIST AND
BAYESIAN STATISTICS

2.1 CHAPTER MISSION STATEMENT

At the end of this chapter, the reader will understand the purpose of statistical inference, as well as recognise the similarities and differences between Frequentist and Bayesian inference. We also introduce the most important theorem in modern statistics: Bayes' rule.

2.2 CHAPTER GOALS

As data scientists, we aim to build predictive models to understand complex phenomena. As a first approximation, we typically disregard those parts of the system that are not directly of interest. This deliberate omission of information makes these models *statistical* rather than deterministic because there are some aspects of the system about which we are uncertain. There are two distinct approaches to statistical modelling: Frequentist (also known as Classical inference) and Bayesian inference. This chapter explains the similarities between these two approaches and, importantly, indicates where they differ substantively.

Usually, it is straightforward to calculate the probability of obtaining different data samples if we know the process that generated the data in the first place. For example, if we know that a coin is fair, then we can calculate the probability of it landing heads up (the probability equals 1/2). However, we typically do not have perfect knowledge of these processes, and it is the goal of statistical inference to derive estimates of the unknown characteristics, or *parameters*, of these mechanisms. In our coin example, we might want to determine its bias towards heads on the basis of the results of a few coin throws. Bayesian statistics allows us to go from what is known – the *data* (the results of the coin throw here) – and extrapolate backwards to make probabilistic statements about the parameters (the underlying bias of the coin) of the processes that were responsible for its generation. In Bayesian statistics, this inversion process is carried out by application of Bayes' rule, which is introduced in this chapter. It is important to have a good understanding of this rule, and we will spend some time throughout this chapter and Part II developing an understanding of the various constituent components of the formula.

2.3 BAYES' RULE - ALLOWING US TO GO FROM THE EFFECT BACK TO ITS CAUSE

Suppose that we know that a casino is crooked and uses a loaded die with a probability of rolling a 1, that is $\frac{1}{3} = 2 \times \frac{1}{6}$, twice its unbiased value. We could then calculate the probability that we roll two 1s in a row:

$$Pr(1,1 \,|\, \text{crooked casino}) = \frac{1}{3} \times \frac{1}{3} = \frac{1}{9}. \tag{2.1}$$

Here we use *Pr* to denote a probability, with the comma here having the literal interpretation of *and*. Hence, *Pr*(1, 1) is the probability we obtain a 1 on the first roll *and* a 1 on the second. (Don't worry if you don't fully understand this calculation, as we will devote the entirety of the next chapter to working with probabilities.) In this case, we have presupposed a cause – the casino being crooked – to derive the probability of a particular effect – rolling two consecutive 1s. In other words, we have calculated $Pr(\text{effect} | \text{cause})$. The vertical line, $|$, here means *given* in probability, so $Pr(1, 1 | \text{crooked casino})$ is the probability of throwing two consecutive 1s given that the casino is crooked.

Until the latter half of the seventeenth century, probability theory was chiefly used as a method to calculate gambling odds, in a similar vein to our current example. It was viewed as a dirty subject, not worthy of the attention of the most esteemed mathematicians. This perspective began to change with the intervention of the English Reverend Thomas Bayes, and slightly later and more famously (at the time at least), with the work done by the French mathematician Pierre Simon Laplace (see 'Bayes' rule or the Bayes–Price–Laplace rule?' below for a short history of Bayes' rule). They realised that it is possible to move in the opposite direction – to go from effect back to cause:

$$Pr(\text{effect} | \text{cause}) \xrightarrow{\text{Bayes' theorem}} Pr(\text{cause} | \text{effect}). \tag{2.2}$$

In order to take this leap, however, it was necessary to discover a rule, which later became known as Bayes' rule or theorem. This can be written:

$$Pr(\text{cause} | \text{effect}) = \frac{Pr(\text{effect} | \text{cause}) \times Pr(\text{cause})}{Pr(\text{effect})}. \tag{2.3}$$

In the casino example, this formula tells us how to invert the original probability $Pr(1, 1 | \text{crooked casino})$ to obtain a more useful quantity as a patron of said casino – $Pr(\text{crooked casino} | 1, 1)$. In words, this is the probability that the casino is crooked *given* that we rolled two 1s. We do not show how to carry out this calculation now, and instead delay this until we learn about probability in Chapter 3. However, this process where we go from an effect back to a cause is the essence of inference. Bayes' rule is central to the Bayesian approach to statistical inference. Before we introduce Bayesian inference, though, we first describe the history of Bayes' rule.

Bayes' rule or the Bayes–Price–Laplace rule?

In 1748, the Scottish philosopher David Hume dealt a serious blow to a fundamental belief of Christianity by publishing an essay on the nature of cause and effect. In it, Hume argues that '*causes and effects are discoverable, not by reason, but by experience*'. In other words, we can never be certain about the cause of a given effect. For example, we know from experience that if we push a glass off the side of a table, it will fall and shatter, but this does not prove that the push caused the glass to shatter. It is possible that both the push and the shattering are merely correlated events, reflecting some third, and hitherto unknown, ultimate cause of both. Hume's argument was unsettling to Christianity because God was traditionally known as the First Cause of everything. The mere fact that the world exists was seen as evidence of a divine creator that caused it to come into existence. Hume's argument meant that we can never deal with *absolute* causes; rather, we must make do with *probable* causes. This weakened the link between a divine creator and the world that we witness and, hence, undermined a core belief of Christianity.

(Continued)

Around this time the Reverend Thomas Bayes of Tunbridge Wells (where this book's author grew up!) began to ponder whether there might be a mathematical approach to cause and effect.

Thomas Bayes was born around 1701 to a Presbyterian minister, Joshua Bayes, who oversaw a chapel in London. The Presbyterian Church at the time was a religious denomination persecuted for

not conforming to the governance and doctrine of the Church of England. Being a *non-conformist*, the young Bayes was not permitted to study for a university degree in England and so enrolled at the University of Edinburgh, where he studied theology. After university, Bayes was ordained as a minister of the Presbyterian Church by his clergyman father and began work as an assistant in his father's ministry in London. Around 1734, Bayes moved south of London to the wealthy spa resort town of Tunbridge Wells and became minister of the Mount Sion chapel there.

Around this time, Bayes began to think about how to apply mathematics, specifically probability theory, to the study of cause and effect (perhaps invigorated by the minerals in the spa town's cold water). Specifically, Bayes wanted a mathematical way to go from

Bayes: c.1701-1761

an effect back to its cause. To develop his theory, he proposed a thought experiment: he imagined attempting to guess the position of a ball on a table. Not perhaps the most enthralling of thought experiments, but sometimes clear thinking is boring. Bayes imagined that he had his back turned to the table, and asks a friend to throw a cue ball onto its surface (imagine the table is big enough that we needn't worry about its edges). He then asks his friend to throw a second ball, and report to Bayes whether it landed to the left or right of the first. If the ball landed to the right of the first, then Bayes reasoned that the cue ball is more likely to be on the left-hand side of the table, and vice versa if it landed to its left. Bayes and his friend continue this process where, each time, his friend throws subsequent balls and reports which side of the cue ball his throw lands. Bayes' brilliant idea was that, by assuming all positions on the table were equally likely a priori, and using the results of the subsequent throws, he could narrow down the likely position of the cue ball on the table. For example, if all throws landed to the left of the cue ball, it was likely that the cue ball would be on the far right of the table. And, as more data (the result of the throws) was collected, he became more and more confident of the cue ball's position. He had gone from an effect (the result of the throws) back to a probable cause (the cue ball's position)!

Bayes' idea was discussed by members of the Royal Society, but it seems that Bayes himself perhaps was not so keen on it, and never published this work. When Bayes died in 1761 his discovery was still languishing between unimportant memoranda, where he had filed it. It took the arrival of another, much more famous, clergyman to popularise his discovery.

Richard Price was a Welsh minister of the Presbyterian Church, but was also a famous political pamphleteer, active in liberal causes of the time such as the American Revolution. He had considerable fans in America and communicated regularly with Benjamin Franklin, John Adams and Thomas Jefferson. Indeed, his fame and adoration in the United States reached such levels that in 1781, when Yale University conveyed two degrees, it gave one to George Washington and the other to Price. Yet today, Price is primarily known for the help that he gave his friend Bayes.

Price: 1723-1791

When Bayes died, his family asked his young friend Richard Price to examine his mathematical papers. When Price read Bayes' work on cause and effect he saw it as a way to counter Hume's attack on causation (using an argument not dissimilar to the Intelligent Design hypothesis of today), and realised it was worth publishing. He spent two years working on the manuscript – correcting some mistakes and adding references – and eventually sent it to the Royal Society with a cover letter of religious bent. Bayes for his (posthumous) part of the paper did not mention religion. The Royal Society eventually published the manuscript with the secular title, 'An Essay towards solving a Problem in the Doctrine of Chances'. Sharon McGrayne – a historian of Bayes – argues that, by modern standards, Bayes' rule should be known as the Bayes–Price rule, since Price discovered Bayes' work, corrected it, realised its importance and published it.

Given Bayes' current notoriety, it is worth noting what he did not accomplish in his work. He did not actually develop the modern version of Bayes' rule that we use today. He just used Newton's notation for geometry to add and remove areas of the table. Unlike Price, he did not use the rule as proof for God, and was clearly not convinced by his own work since he failed to publish his papers. Indeed, it took the work of another, more notable, mathematician to improve on Bayes' first step, and to elevate the status of inverse probability (as it was known at the time).

Pierre Simon Laplace was born in 1749 in Normandy, France, into a house of respected dignitaries. His father, Pierre, owned and farmed the estates of Maarquis, and was Syndic (an officer of the local government) of the town of Beaumont. The young Laplace (like Bayes) studied theology for his degree at the University of Caen. There, his mathematical brilliance was quickly recognised by others, and Laplace realised that maths was his true calling, not the priesthood. Throughout his life, Laplace did important work in many fields including analysis, differential equations, planetary orbits and potential theory. He may also have even been the first person to posit the existence of black holes – celestial bodies whose gravity is so great that even light can't escape. However, here, we are most interested in the work he did on inverse probability theory.

Laplace: 1749–1827

Independently of Bayes, Laplace had already begun to work on a probabilistic way to go from effect back to cause, and in 1774 published 'Mémoire sur la probabilité des causes par les évènemens', in which he stated the principle':

Si un évènement peut être produit par un nombre n de causes différentes, les probabilités de l'existence de ces causes prises de évènement, sont entre elses comes les probabilités de l'évènement prises de ces causes, et la probabilité de l'existence de chacune d'elles, est égale á la probabilité de l'évènement prise de cette cause, diviseé par la somme de toutes les probabilités de l'évènement prises de chacune de ces causes.

This translates as (Laplace (1986)):

If an event can be produced by a number n of different causes, then the probabilities of these causes given the event are to each other as the probabilities of the event given the causes, and the probability of the existence of each of these is equal to the probability of the event given the cause, divided by the sum of all the probabilities of the event given each of these causes.

(Continued)

This statement of inverse probability is only valid when the causes are all equally likely. It was not until later than Laplace generalised this result to handle causes with different prior weights.

In 1781, Price visited Paris and told the Secretary of the French Royal Academy of Sciences, the Marquis of Condorcet, about Bayes' discovery. This information eventually reached Laplace and gave him confidence to pursue his ideas in inverse probability. The trouble with his theory for going from an effect back to a cause was that it required an enormous number of calculations to be done to arrive at an answer. Laplace was not afraid of a challenge, however, and invented a number of incredibly useful techniques (for example, generating functions and transforms) to find an approximate answer. Laplace still needed an example application of his method that was easy enough for him to calculate, yet interesting enough to garner attention. His chosen data sample was composed of babies. Specifically, his sample comprised the numbers of males and females born in Paris from 1745 to 1770. This data was easy to work with because the outcome was binary – the child was recorded as being born a boy or girl – and was large enough to be able to draw conclusions from it. In the sample, a total of 241,945 girls and 251,527 boys were born. Laplace used this sample and his theory of inverse probability to estimate that there was a probability of approximately 10^{-42} that the sex ratio favoured girls rather than boys. On the basis of this tiny probability, he concluded that he was as 'certain as any other moral truth' that boys were born more frequently than girls. This was the first practical application of Bayesian inference as we know it now. Laplace went from an effect – the data in the birth records – to determine a probable cause – the ratio of male to female births.

Later in his life, Laplace also wrote down the first modern version of Bayes' mathematical rule that is used today, where causes could be given different prior probabilities. He published it in his "Théorie analytique des probabilités" in 1820 (although he probably derived the rule around 1810-1814):

$$P = \frac{Hp}{S.Hp};$$

ce qui donne les probabilités des diverses causes, lorsqu'elles ne sont pas toutes, également possible á priori.

On the left-hand side, P denotes the posterior probability of a given cause given an observed event. In the numerator on the right-hand side, H is the probability of an event occurring given that cause, p, is the a priori probability of that cause. In the denominator, $S.$ denotes summation (the modern equivalent of this is Σ) over all possible causes, and H and p now represent the corresponding quantities to those in the numerator, but for each possible cause. Laplace actually presented two versions of the rule – one for discrete random variables (as we show above) and another for continuous variables. The typesetting he used for the continuous case, however, did not allow him to write limits on integrals, meaning that the numerator and denominator look the same.

History has been unfair to Laplace and Price. If they were alive today, the theory would, no doubt, be known as the Bayes-Price-Laplace rule. We hope by including this short biographical section that this will encourage you, in your own work, to give credit to others where it is due. We, in particular, would like to thank Sharon McGrayne for her excellent book, *The theory that would not die: how Bayes' rule cracked the enigma code, hunted down Russian submarines, & emerged triumphant from two centuries of controversy*, that served as an invaluable reference to this section, and we encourage others to read it to learn of the tempestuous history of Bayesian inference [26].

THE PURPOSE OF STATISTICAL INFERENCE

How much does a particular drug affect a patient's condition? What can an average student earn after obtaining a college education? Will the Democrats win the next US presidential election? In life, we develop theories and use these to make predictions, but testing those theories is not easy. Life is complicated, and it is often impossible to exactly isolate the parts of a system which we want to examine. The outcome of history is determined by a complex nexus of interacting elements, each of which contributes to the reality that we witness. In the case of a drug trial, we may not be able to control the diets of participants and are certainly unable to control for their idiosyncratic metabolisms, both of which could impact the results we observe. There are a range of factors which affect the wage that an individual ultimately earns, of which education is only one. The outcome of the next US presidential election depends on party politics, the performance of the incumbent government and the media's portrayal of the candidates.

In life, noise obfuscates the signal. What we see often appears as an incoherent mess that lacks any appearance of logic. This is why it is difficult to make predictions and test theories about the world. It is like trying to listen to a classical orchestra which is playing on the side of a busy motorway, while we fly overhead in a plane. Statistical inference allows us to focus on the music by separating the signal from the noise. We will hear 'Nessun Dorma' played!

Statistical inference is the logical framework which we can use to trial our beliefs about the noisy world against *data*. We formalise our beliefs in models of *probability*. The models are probabilistic because we are ignorant of many of the interacting parts of a system, meaning we cannot say with certainty whether something will, or will not, occur. Suppose that we are evaluating the efficacy of a drug in a trial. Before we carry out the trial, we might believe that the drug will cure 10% of people with a particular ailment. We cannot say which 10% of people will be cured because we do not know enough about the disease or individual patient biology to say exactly whom. Statistical inference allows us to test this belief against the data we obtain in a clinical trial.

There are two predominant schools of thought for carrying out this process of inference: Frequentist and Bayesian. Although this book is devoted to the latter, we will now spend some time comparing the two approaches so that the reader is aware of the different paths taken to their shared goal.

THE WORLD ACCORDING TO FREQUENTISTS

In Frequentist (or Classical) statistics, we suppose that our sample of data is the result of one of an infinite number of exactly repeated experiments. The sample we see in this context is assumed to be the outcome of some probabilistic process. Any conclusions we draw from this approach are based on the supposition that events occur with probabilities, which represent the long-run frequencies with which those events occur in an infinite series of experimental repetitions. For example, if we flip a coin, we take the proportion of heads observed in an infinite number of throws as defining the probability of obtaining heads. Frequentists suppose that this probability actually exists, and is fixed for each set of coin throws that we carry out. The sample of coin flips we obtain for a fixed and finite number of throws is generated as if it were part of a longer (that is, infinite) series of repeated coin flips (see the left-hand panel of Figure 2.1).

In Frequentist statistics the data are assumed to be *random* and results from *sampling* from a fixed and defined *population* distribution. For a Frequentist the noise that obscures the true signal of the real population process is attributable to *sampling variation* – the fact that each sample we pick is slightly different and not exactly representative of the population.

We may flip our coin 10 times, obtaining 7 heads even if the long-run proportion of heads is $\frac{1}{2}$. To a Frequentist, this is because we have picked a slightly odd sample from the population of infinitely many repeated throws. If we flip the coin another 10 times, we will likely get a different result because we then pick a different sample.

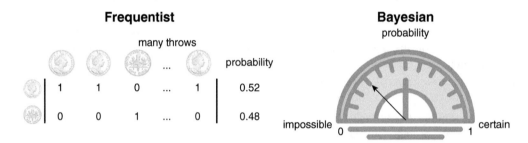

Figure 2.1　The Frequentist (left) and Bayesian (right) approaches to probability.

2.6　THE WORLD ACCORDING TO BAYESIANS

Bayesians do not imagine repetitions of an experiment in order to define and specify a probability. A probability is merely taken as a measure of certainty in a particular belief. For Bayesians the probability of throwing a 'heads' measures and quantifies our underlying belief that before we flip the coin it will land this way.

In this sense, Bayesians do not view probabilities as underlying laws of cause and effect. They are merely abstractions which we use to help express our uncertainty. In this frame of reference, it is unnecessary for events to be repeatable in order to define a probability. We are thus equally able to say, 'The probability of a heads is 0.5' or 'The probability of the Democrats winning the 2020 US presidential election is 0.75'. Probability is merely seen as a scale from 0, where we are certain an event will not happen, to 1, where we are certain it will (see the right-hand panel of Figure 2.1).

A statement such as 'The probability of the Democrats winning the 2020 US presidential election is 0.75' is hard to explain using the Frequentist definition of a probability. There is only ever one possible sample – the history that we witness – and what would we actually mean by the 'population of all possible US elections which happen in the year 2020'?

For Bayesians, probabilities are seen as an expression of subjective beliefs, meaning that they can be updated in light of new data. The formula invented by the Reverend Thomas Bayes provides the only logical manner in which to carry out this updating process. Bayes' rule is central to Bayesian inference whereby we use probabilities to express our uncertainty in parameter values after we observe data.

Bayesians assume that, since we are witness to the data, it is *fixed*, and therefore does not vary. We do not need to imagine that there are an infinite number of possible samples, or that our data are the undetermined outcome of some random process of sampling. We never perfectly know the value of an unknown parameter (for example, the probability that a coin lands heads up). This epistemic uncertainty (namely, that relating to our lack of knowledge) means that in Bayesian inference the parameter is viewed as a quantity that is probabilistic in nature. We can interpret this in one of two ways. On the one hand, we can view the unknown parameter as truly being fixed in some absolute sense, but our beliefs are uncertain, and thus we express this uncertainty using probability. In this perspective, we view the sample as a noisy representation of the signal and hence obtain different results for each set of coin throws. On the other hand, we can suppose that there is not some definitive true, immutable probability of obtaining a heads, and so for each sample we take, we unwittingly get a slightly different parameter. Here we get different results from each round of coin flipping because each time we subject our system to a slightly different probability of its landing heads up. This could be because we altered our throwing technique or started with the coin in a different position. Although these two descriptions are different philosophically, they are not different mathematically, meaning we can apply the same analysis to both.

2○7   DO PARAMETERS ACTUALLY EXIST AND HAVE A POINT VALUE?

For Bayesians, the parameters of the system are taken to vary, whereas the known part of the system – the data – is taken as given. Frequentist statisticians, on the other hand, view the unseen part of the system – the parameters of the probability model – as being fixed and the known parts of the system – the data – as varying. Which of these views you prefer comes down to how you interpret the parameters of a statistical model.

In the Bayesian approach, parameters can be viewed from two perspectives. Either we view the parameters as truly *varying*, or we view our knowledge about the parameters as imperfect. The fact that we obtain different estimates of parameters from different studies can be taken to reflect either of these two views.

In the first case, we understand the parameters of interest as varying – taking on different values in each of the samples we pick (see the top panel of Figure 2.2). For example, suppose that we conduct a blood test on an individual in two consecutive weeks, and represent the correlation between the red and white cell count as a parameter of our statistical model. Due to the many factors that affect the body's metabolism, the count of each cell type will vary somewhat randomly, and hence the parameter value may vary over time. In the second case, we view our uncertainty over a parameter's value as the reason we estimate slightly different values in different samples. This uncertainty should, however, decrease as we collect more data (see the middle panel of Figure 2.2). Bayesians are more at ease in using parameters as a means to an end – taking them not as real immutable constants, but as tools to help make inferences about a given situation.

The Frequentist perspective is less flexible and assumes that these parameters are constant, or represent the average of a long run – typically an infinite number – of identical experiments. There are occasions when we might think that this is a reasonable assumption. For example, if our parameter represented the probability that an individual taken at random from the UK population has dyslexia, it is reasonable to assume that there is a *true*, or fixed, *population* value of the parameter in question. While the Frequentist view may be reasonable here, the Bayesian view can also handle this situation. In Bayesian statistics these parameters can be assumed fixed, but that we are uncertain of their value (here the true prevalence of dyslexia) before we measure them, and use a probability distribution to reflect this uncertainty.

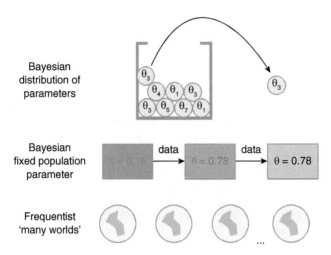

Figure 2.2 The Bayesian (top and middle) and Frequentist perspectives on parameters. In the top panel, the urn holds a large number of parameter values – a population distribution – that we sample from each time we pick a new sample. These parameters, in turn, determine the data that we obtain in our sample. The middle panel shows the Bayesian view where the uncertainty about a parameter's true value (shown in the box) decreases as we collect more data. The bottom panel represents the Frequentist view where parameters represent averages across an infinite number of exactly repeated experiments (represented by the many worlds).

But there are circumstances when the Frequentist view runs into trouble. When we are estimating parameters of a complex distribution, we typically do not view them as actually existing. Unless you view the Universe as being built from mathematical building blocks,[1] then it seems incorrect to assert that a given parameter has any deeper existence than that with which we endow it. The less restrictive Bayesian perspective here seems more reasonable.

The Frequentist view of parameters as a limiting value of an average across an infinity of identically repeated experiments (see the bottom panel of Figure 2.2) also runs into difficulty when we think about one-off events. For example, the probability that the Democrat candidate wins in the 2020 US election cannot be justified in this way, since elections are never rerun under the exact same conditions.

2○8 FREQUENTIST AND BAYESIAN INFERENCE

The Bayesian inference process is the only logical and consistent way to modify our beliefs to account for new data. Before we collect data we have a probabilistic description of our beliefs, which we call a *prior*. We then collect data, and together with a model describing our theory, Bayes' formula allows us to calculate our post-data or *posterior* belief:

$$\text{prior} + \text{data} \xrightarrow{\quad model \quad} \text{posterior}. \tag{2.4}$$

For example, suppose that we have a prior belief that a coin is fair, meaning that the probability of it landing heads up is ½. We then throw it 10 times and find that it lands heads up every time; this is our data. Bayes' rule tells us how to combine the prior with the data to result in our updated belief that the coin is fair. Ignore for the moment that we have not explained the meaning of this mysterious prior, as we shall introduce this element properly in Section 2.9.2.

---

[1]See [37] for an interesting argument for this hypothesis.

In inference, we want to draw conclusions based purely on the rules of probability. If we wish to summarise our evidence for a particular hypothesis, we describe this using the language of probability, as the 'probability of the hypothesis given the data obtained'. The difficulty is that when we choose a probability model to describe a situation, it enables us to calculate the 'probability of obtaining our data given our hypothesis being true' – the opposite of what we want. This probability is calculated by accounting for all the possible samples that could have been obtained from the population, if the hypothesis were true. The issue of statistical inference, common to both Frequentists and Bayesians, is how to invert this probability to get the desired result.

Frequentists stop here, using this inverse probability as evidence for a given hypothesis. They assume a hypothesis is true and on this basis calculate the probability of obtaining the observed data sample. If this probability is small, then it is assumed that it is unlikely that the hypothesis is true, and we reject it. In our coin example, if we throw the coin 10 times and it always lands heads up (our data), the probability of this data occurring given that the coin is fair (our hypothesis) is small. In this case, Frequentists would reject the hypothesis that the coin is fair. Essentially, this amounts to setting $Pr(\text{hypothesis}|\text{data}) = 0$. However, if this probability is not below some arbitrary threshold, then we do not reject the hypothesis. But Frequentist inference is then unclear about what probability we should ascribe to the hypothesis. Surely it is non-zero, but exactly how confident are we in it? In Frequentist inference we do not get an accumulation of evidence for a particular hypothesis, unlike in Bayesian statistics.

In reality, Frequentist inference is slightly different to what we described. Since the probability of obtaining any one specific data sample is very small, we calculate the probability of obtaining a range of possible samples to obtain a more usable probability. In particular, Frequentists calculate the probability of obtaining a sample as extreme as, or more extreme than, the one actually obtained, assuming a certain hypothesis to be true. For example, imagine we have a hypothesis that people's heights are normally distributed with a mean of 1.55m and a standard deviation of 0.3m. Then suppose we collect a sample of one individual with a height of 2.5m. To test the validity of the hypothesis, Frequentists calculate the probability of obtaining a height greater than, or equal to, 2.5m, assuming the hypothesis to be true. However, we did not actually witness an individual with a height greater than 2.5m. In Frequentist inference we must invent fictitious samples to test a hypothesis!

Bayes' formula allows us to circumvent these difficulties by inverting the Frequentist probability to get the 'probability of the hypothesis given the *actual* data we obtained'. In our heights example, this would be the probability that the mean population height is 1.55m and has a standard deviation of 0.3m given that our data consists of a single individual of height 2.5m. In Bayesian inference, there is no need for an arbitrary threshold in the probability in order to validate the hypothesis. All information is summarised in this (posterior) probability and there is no need for explicit hypothesis testing. However, to use Bayes' rule for inference, we must supply a prior – an additional element compared to Frequentist statistics. The prior is a probability distribution that describes our beliefs in a hypothesis before we collect and analyse the data. In Bayesian inference, we then update this belief to produce something known as a posterior, which represents our post-analysis belief in the hypothesis.

The next few, albeit silly, examples illustrate a difference in methodology but also, perhaps more significantly, in philosophy between the two different approaches.

2.8.1 The Frequentist and Bayesian murder trials

Assume you find yourself in the unfortunate situation where you are (hopefully falsely) accused of murder, and face a trial by jury. A complication in the tale is that you personally have a choice over the method used by the jury to assign guilt: either Frequentist or Bayesian. Another unfortunate twist is that the legal system of the country starts by presuming guilt rather than innocence.

Let's assume that security camera footage indicates you were in the same house as the victim – Sally – on the night of her demise.

If you choose the Frequentist trial, your jurors start by specifying a model based on previous trials, which assigns a probability of your being seen by the security camera if you were guilty. They use this to make the statement that 'If you did commit the murder, then 30% of the time you would have been seen by the security camera' based on a hypothetical infinity of repetitions of the same conditions. Since $Pr(\text{you were seen by the camera} \mid \text{guilt})$ is not sufficiently unlikely (the p value is not below 5%), the jurors cannot reject the null hypothesis of guilt, and you are sentenced to life in prison.

In a Bayesian trial, the jury is first introduced to an array of evidence, which suggests that you neither knew Sally nor had any previous record of violent conduct, being otherwise a perfectly respectable citizen. Furthermore, Sally's ex-boyfriend is a multiple offending-violent convict on the run from prison after being sentenced by a judge on the basis of Sally's own witness testimony. Using this information, the jury sets a prior probability of the hypothesis that you are guilty equal to $\frac{1}{1000}$ (don't worry about what is meant by a 'prior' as we devote all of Chapter 5 to this purpose). The jury then uses the same model as the Frequentists which indicates that 30% of the time you would have been seen by the camera if you were guilty. However, the jury then coolly uses Bayes' rule and concludes that the probability of your committing the crime is $\frac{1}{1000}$ (see Section 2.13.1 for a full description of this calculation). Based on this evidence, the jury acquits you, and you go home to your family.

2.8.2 Radio control towers

In a hypothetical war, two radio control workers, Mr Pearson (from the county of Frequentland) and Mr Laplace (from the county of Bayesdom), sit side by side and are tasked with finding an enemy plane that has been spotted over the country's borders. They will each feed this information to the nearest air force base(s), which will respond by sending up planes of their own. There are, however, two different air forces – one for each county. Although the air forces of Frequentland and Bayesdom share airbases, they are distinct, and only respond to Mr Pearson's and Mr Laplace's advice, respectively. The ongoing war, though short, has been costly to both allies, and they each want to avoid needless expenditure while still defending their territory.

Mr Pearson starts by inputting the plane's radar information into a computer program that uses a model of a plane's position which has been calibrated against historical enemy plane data. The result comes out instantly:

> The plane is most likely 5 miles North of the town of Tunbridge Wells.

Without another moment's thought, Mr Pearson radios the base of Tunbridge Wells, telling them to scramble all 10 available Frequentist fighter jets immediately. He then gets up and makes himself a well-earned coffee.

Mr Laplace knows from experience that the enemy has used three different flight paths to attack in the past. Accordingly, he gives these regions a high probability density in his prior for the plane's current location and feeds this into the same computer program used by Mr Pearson. The output this time is different. By using the optional input, the program now outputs a map with the most likely regions indicated, rather than a single location. The highest posterior density is over the region near Tunbridge Wells, where Mr Pearson radioed, although the map suggests there are two other towns which might also be victims of the plane's bombing. Accordingly, Mr Laplace radios to Tunbridge Wells, asking them to send up four jets, and to the other two towns, asking them to send up two jets each. At the end of all this, Mr Laplace remains seated, tired but contented that he has done his best for his own.

The enemy bomber turned out to be approaching Berkstad, one of the towns which Mr Laplace radioed. The Bayesdom jets intercept the encroaching plane and escort it out of allied airspace. Mr Laplace is awarded a medal in honour of his efforts. Pearson looks on jealously.

BAYESIAN INFERENCE VIA BAYES' RULE

Bayes' rule tells us how to update our prior beliefs in order to derive better, more informed, beliefs about a situation in light of new data. In Bayesian inference, we test hypotheses about the real world using these posterior beliefs. As part of this process, we estimate characteristics that interest us, which we call *parameters*, that are then used to test such hypotheses. From this point onwards we will use θ to represent the unknown parameter(s) which we want to estimate.

The Bayesian inference process uses Bayes' rule to estimate a probability distribution for those unknown parameters after we observe the data. (Don't worry if you don't know what is meant by a *probability distribution* since we shall devote the entirety of Chapter 3 to this purpose.) However, it is sufficient for now to think of probability distributions as a way to represent uncertainty for unknown quantities.

Bayes' rule as used in statistical inference is of the form:

$$p(\theta \mid data) = \frac{p(data \mid \theta) \times p(\theta)}{p(data)},\tag{2.5}$$

where we use p to indicate a probability distribution which may represent either probabilities or, more usually, probability densities (see Section 3.3.2 for a description of their distinction). We shall now spend the next few sections describing, in short, the various elements of expression (2.5). This will only be a partial introduction since we spend the entirety of Part II on an extensive discussion of each of the constituent components.

2.9.1 Likelihoods

Starting with the numerator on the right-hand side of expression (2.5), we come across the term $p(data \mid \theta)$, which we call the *likelihood*, which is common to both Frequentist and Bayesian analyses. This tells us the probability of generating the particular sample of data if the parameters in our statistical model were equal to θ. When we choose a statistical model, we can usually calculate the probability of particular outcomes, so this is easily obtained. Imagine that we have a coin that we believe is fair. By *fair*, we mean that the probability of the coin landing heads up is $\theta = \frac{1}{2}$. If we flip the coin twice, we might suppose that the outcomes are independent events (see Section 3.4), and hence can calculate the probabilities of the four possible outcomes by multiplying the probabilities of the individual outcomes:

$$Pr(H,H \mid \theta = \tfrac{1}{2}) = Pr(H \mid \theta = \tfrac{1}{2}) \times Pr(H \mid \theta = \tfrac{1}{2}) = \frac{1}{2} \times \frac{1}{2} = \frac{1}{4}$$

$$Pr(H,T \mid \theta = \tfrac{1}{2}) = Pr(H \mid \theta = \tfrac{1}{2}) \times Pr(T \mid \theta = \tfrac{1}{2}) = \frac{1}{2} \times \frac{1}{2} = \frac{1}{4}$$

$$(2.6)$$

$$Pr(T,H \mid \theta = \tfrac{1}{2}) = Pr(T \mid \theta = \tfrac{1}{2}) \times Pr(H \mid \theta = \tfrac{1}{2}) = \frac{1}{2} \times \frac{1}{2} = \frac{1}{4}$$

$$Pr(T,T \mid \theta = \tfrac{1}{2}) = Pr(T \mid \theta = \tfrac{1}{2}) \times Pr(T \mid \theta = \tfrac{1}{2}) = \frac{1}{2} \times \frac{1}{2} = \frac{1}{4}.$$

(Don't worry if you don't understand the logic in the above, as we devote the whole of Chapter 4 to understanding likelihoods.)

2.9.2 Priors

The next term in the numerator of expression (2.5) $p(\theta)$, is the most controversial part of the Bayesian formula, which we call the prior distribution of θ. It is a probability distribution which represents our pre-data beliefs across different values of the parameters in our model, θ. This appears, at first, to be counterintuitive, particularly if you are familiar with the world of Frequentist statistics, which does not require us to state our beliefs explicitly (although we always do implicitly, as we explain in Section 2.10). Continuing the coin example, we might assume that we do not know whether the coin is fair or biased beforehand, so suppose all possible values of $\theta \in [0, 1]$ – which represents the probability of the coin falling heads up – are equally likely. We can represent these beliefs by a continuous uniform probability density on this interval (see the black line in Figure 2.3). More sensibly, however, we might believe that coins are manufactured in a way such that their weight distribution is fairly evenly distributed, meaning that we expect that the majority of coins are reasonably fair. These beliefs would be more adequately represented by a prior similar to the one shown by the red line in Figure 2.3.

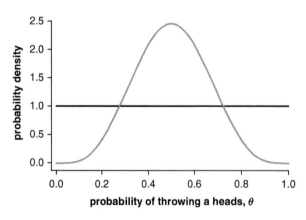

Figure 2.3 Two different prior distributions: a uniform prior, where we believe all values of θ (corresponding to the probability of throwing a heads) are equally likely (black line), and another where we believe that the coin is most likely fair before we throw it (red line).

The concept of priors will be covered in detail in Chapter 5.

2.9.3 The denominator

The final term on the right-hand side of expression (2.5) in the denominator is $p(data)$. This represents the probability of obtaining our particular sample of data if we assume a particular model and prior. We will mostly postpone discussion of this term until Chapter 6 when we understand better the significance of likelihoods and priors. However, for our purposes here it suffices to say that the denominator is fully determined by our choice of prior and likelihood function. While it appears simple, this is deceptive, and it is partly the difficulty with calculating this term that leads to the introduction of computational methods that we discuss in Part IV.

The concept of the denominator will be covered in detail in Chapter 6.

2.9.4 Posteriors: the goal of Bayesian inference

The posterior probability distribution $p(\theta|data)$ is the main goal of Bayesian inference. For example, we might want to compute the probability distribution representing our post-experimental beliefs of the inherent bias, θ, of a coin, given that it was flipped 10 times and it landed heads up 7 times. If we use Bayes' rule, assuming the likelihood model specified in Section 2.9.1, and the uniform prior shown in Figure 2.3 (black line), then the result is the posterior distribution shown as the grey line in Figure 2.4. Here, the peak of the distribution occurs at $\theta = 0.7$, which corresponds exactly with the percentage of 'heads' obtained in the experiment.

The posterior distribution summarises our uncertainty over the value of a parameter. If the distribution is narrower, then this indicates that we have greater confidence in our estimates of the parameter's value. More narrow posterior distributions can be obtained by collecting more data. In Figure 2.4, we compare the posterior distribution for the previous case where 7 out of 10 times the coin landed heads up with a new, larger, sample where 70 out of 100 times the same coin comes up heads. In both cases, we obtained the same ratio of heads to tails, resulting in the same peak value at $\theta = 0.7$. However, in the latter case, since we have more evidence to support our claim, we end up with greater certainty about the parameter value after the experiment.

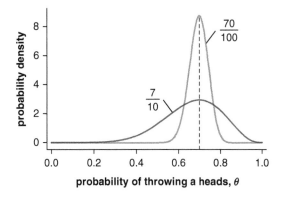

The posterior distribution is also used to predict future outcomes of an experiment and for model testing. However, we leave discussion of these until Chapter 7.

IMPLICIT VERSUS EXPLICIT SUBJECTIVITY

One of the major arguments levied against Bayesian statistics is that it is *subjective* due to its dependence on the analyst specifying

Figure 2.4 Posterior distributions for θ – the probability that a coin landing heads up when flipped. The grey line represents the posterior probability distribution function (PDF) resulting from a data sample where 7 out of 10 times the coin came up heads. The red line is the posterior probability distribution function for the case where 70 out of 100 times the coin came up heads. Both of the posteriors assume a binomial likelihood and uniform prior (don't worry if these mean nothing to you as we will introduce these concepts in Chapters 4 and 5).

their pre-experimental beliefs through priors. This experimenter prejudice towards certain outcomes is said to bias the results away from the types of fair, objective outcomes resultant from a Frequentist analysis.

We argue that *all* analyses involve a degree of subjectivity, which is either explicitly stated or, more often, implicitly assumed. In a Frequentist analysis, the statistician typically selects a model of probability which depends on a range of assumptions. These assumptions are often justified explicitly, revealing their suggestive nature. For example, the simple *linear regression model* is often used, without justification, in applied Frequentist analyses. This model makes assumptions about the relationships between the dependent and independent variables that may, or may not, be true. In a Bayesian approach, we more typically build our models from the ground up, meaning that we are more aware of the assumptions inherent in the approach.

In applied research, there is a tendency among scientists to choose data to include in an analysis to suit one's needs, although this practice should really be discouraged (see [20]). The choice of which data points to include is subjective, and the underlying logic behind this choice is more often than not kept opaque from the reader.

A further source of subjectivity is the way in which models are checked and tested. In analyses, both Frequentist and Bayesian, there is a need to exercise (subjective) judgement in suggesting a methodology which will be used in this process. We would argue that Bayesian analysis allows greater flexibility and a more suitable methodology for this process because it accounts for the inherent uncertainty in our estimates.

In contrast to the examples of subjectivity mentioned above, Bayesian priors are explicitly stated. This makes this part of the analysis openly available to the reader, meaning it can be interrogated and debated. This transparent nature of Bayesian statistics has led some to suggest that it is honest. While Frequentist analyses hide behind a fake veil of objectivity, Bayesian equivalents explicitly acknowledge the subjective nature of knowledge.

Furthermore, the more data that is collected, (in general) the less impact the prior exerts on posterior distributions. In any case, if a slight modification of priors results in a different conclusion being reached, it must be reported by the researcher.

Finally, comparing the Frequentist and Bayesian approaches to the pursuit of knowledge, we find that both approaches require a subjective judgement to be made. In each case, we want to obtain $p(\theta\,|\,data)$ – the probability of the parameter or hypothesis under investigation, given the data set which has been observed. In Frequentist hypothesis testing we do not calculate this quantity directly, but use a rule of thumb. We calculate the probability that the data set would, in fact, have been more extreme than those we actually obtained assuming a null (the given, default) hypothesis is true. If the probability is sufficiently small, typically less than a cut-off of 5% or 1%, then we reject the null. This choice of threshold probability – known as a statistical test's *size* – is completely arbitrary, and subjective. In Bayesian statistics, we instead use a subjective prior to invert the likelihood from $p(data\,|\,\theta) \rightarrow p(\theta\,|\,data)$. There is no need to accept or reject a null hypothesis and consider an alternative since all the information is neatly summarised in the posterior. In this way we see a symmetry in the choice of Frequentist test size and Bayesian priors; they are both required to invert the likelihood to obtain a posterior.

2 ○ 11   CHAPTER SUMMARY

This chapter has focused on the philosophy of statistical inference. Statistical inference is the process of inversion required to go from an effect (the data) back to a cause (the process or parameters). The trouble with this inversion is that it is generally much easier to do things the other way round: to go from a cause to an effect. Frequentists and Bayesians start by defining a forward probability model that can generate data (the effect) from a given set of parameters (the cause). The method that they each use to run this model in reverse and determine the probability for a cause is different. Frequentists assume that if the probability of generating the data (actually data as extreme as or more extreme than that obtained) from a particular cause is small, then the cause is rejected; the probability of that cause is concluded to be zero. The set of all non-rejected causes then forms a confidence interval that contains the actual cause with some measure of certainty. Bayesians instead carry out the inversion formally using Bayes' rule. This results in an accumulation of evidence for each cause, rather than a binary 'yes' or 'no' as for the Frequentist case.

Frequentists and Bayesians also differ in their view on probabilities. Frequentists view probabilities as the frequency at which an event occurs in an infinite series of experimental repetitions. In this sense Frequentists view probabilities as fixed laws that actually exist independent of the individual analyst. Because they are fixed, it does not make sense to update them. Similarly, in the Frequentist viewpoint, it does not make sense to define probabilities for one-off events, where an infinite series of experimental reproductions is not possible. Bayesians take a more general view on probabilities. They see probabilities as measuring the strength of an individual's underlying belief in the likelihood of some outcome. For Bayesians probabilities are only defined in relation to a particular analyst and are hence, by their very nature, subjective. Since probabilities measure beliefs, they can be updated in light of new data. The only correct way to update probabilities is through Bayes' rule, which Bayesians use to do statistical inference. Because Bayesian probabilities measure a subjective belief in an outcome, they can be used for all categories of events, from those that could in some way be infinitely repeated (for example, coin flips) or one-off events (for example, the outcome of the 2020 US presidential election).

One argument that is often levied against Bayesian approaches to inference is that they are subjective, in contrast to the objectivity of Frequentism. We argued that all analytical approaches to inference are inherently subjective at some level. Beginning with the data selection process, the analyst often makes a subjective judgement of which data to include. The choice of a specific probability model is also inherently subjective and is typically justified by making assumptions about the data-generating process. In Frequentist inference the choice of the threshold probability for null hypothesis testing is also arbitrary and inherently depends on the analyst. Bayesian inference has priors, which should always be explicitly stated in an analysis. That priors are explicitly stated means that they can be debated and interrogated in a transparent fashion. While priors are inherently subjective, this does not mean they cannot be informed by data. In fact, in analyses that are repeated at different points in time, it often makes sense to use the posterior of a previous analysis as a prior for a new one (see Chapter 7).

In this chapter, we also introduced Bayes' rule for inference and discussed briefly its constituent parts. The Bayesian formula is the central dogma of Bayesian inference. However, in order to use this rule for statistical analyses, it is necessary to understand and, more importantly, be able to manipulate probability distributions. The next chapter is devoted to this cause.

2.12 CHAPTER OUTCOMES

The reader should now be familiar with the following concepts:

- the goals of statistical inference
- the difference in interpretation of probabilities for Frequentists versus Bayesians
- the differences in the Frequentist and Bayesian approaches to inference

2.13 APPENDIX

2.13.1 The Frequentist and Bayesian murder trials

In the Bayesian trial the probability of guilt if you are seen by the security camera on the night of the murder is:

$$p(guilt \mid security\ camera\ footage) = \frac{p(security\ camera\ footage \mid guilt) \times p(guilt)}{p(security\ camera\ footage)}$$

$$= \frac{\dfrac{30}{100} \times \dfrac{1}{1000}}{\dfrac{30}{100} \times \dfrac{999}{1000} + \dfrac{30}{100} \times \dfrac{1}{1000}} \tag{2.7}$$

$$= \frac{1}{1000}.$$

In the above equation we assume that the security camera is hidden, and hence a murderer does not change their behaviour to avoid being seen, meaning that the probability of being seen by the security camera in each case is 30%. We have also assumed that the footage is itself uninformative about the motivations of an individual; it is merely indicative of a person's location at a given time. In other words, we are supposing that criminals and innocents cannot be differentiated by their actions on the video.

2.14 PROBLEM SETS

Problem 2.1 The deterministic nature of random coin throwing

Suppose that, in an idealised world, the ultimate fate of a thrown coin – heads or tails – is deterministically given by the angle at which you throw the coin and its height above a table. Also in this ideal world, the heights and angles are discrete. However, the system is chaotic[2] (highly sensitive to initial conditions), and the results of throwing a coin at a given angle and height are shown in Table P2.1.

---

[2]The authors of the following paper actually experimentally tested this and found it to be the case, "The three-dimensional dynamics of the die throw", Chaos, Kapitaniak et al. (2012).

Problem 2.1.1 Suppose that all combinations of angles and heights are equally likely to be chosen. What is the probability that the coin lands heads up?

Problem 2.1.2 Now suppose that some combinations of angles and heights are more likely to be chosen than others, with the probabilities shown in Table P2.2. What are the new probabilities that the coin lands heads up?

Problem 2.1.3 We force the coin-thrower to throw the coin at an angle of 45 degrees. What is the probability that the coin lands heads up?

Problem 2.1.4 We force the coin-thrower to throw the coin at a height of 0.2m. What is the probability that the coin lands heads up?

Problem 2.1.5 If we constrained the angle and height to be fixed, what would happen in repetitions of the same experiment?

Problem 2.1.6 In light of the previous question, comment on the Frequentist assumption of exact repetitions of a given experiment.

Problem 2.2 Objections to Bayesianism

Table P2.1 The results of a coin throw from a given angle and height above a table.

Angle (degrees)	Height above table (m)				
	0.2	0.4	0.6	0.8	1
0	T	H	T	T	H
45	H	T	T	T	T
90	H	H	T	T	H
135	H	H	T	H	T
180	H	H	T	H	H
225	H	T	H	T	T
270	H	T	T	T	H
315	T	H	H	T	T

Table P2.2 The probability that a given person throws a coin at a particular angle and at a certain height above a table.

Angle (degrees)	Height above table (m)				
	0.2	0.4	0.6	0.8	1
0	0.05	0.03	0.02	0.04	0.04
45	0.03	0.02	0.01	0.05	0.02
90	0.05	0.03	0.01	0.03	0.02
135	0.02	0.03	0.04	0.00	0.04
180	0.03	0.02	0.02	0.00	0.03
225	0.00	0.01	0.04	0.03	0.02
270	0.03	0.00	0.03	0.01	0.04
315	0.02	0.03	0.03	0.02	0.01

The following criticisms of Bayesian statistics are raised in an article by Gelman [4]. Provide a response to each of these.

Problem 2.2.1 'As scientists we should be concerned with objective knowledge rather than subjective belief.'

Problem 2.2.2 'Subjective prior distributions don't transfer well from person to person.'

Problem 2.2.3 'There's no good objective principle for choosing a noninformative prior ... Where do prior distributions come from, anyway?'

Problem 2.2.4 A student in a class of mine: 'If we have prior expectations of a donkey and our dataset is a horse then Bayesians estimate a mule.'

Problem 2.2.5 'Bayesian methods seem to quickly move to elaborate computation.'

Problem 2.3 Model choice

Suppose that you have been given the data contained in `subjective_overfitShort.csv` and are asked to find a 'good' statistical model to fit the (x,y) data.

Problem 2.3.1 Fit a linear regression model using least squares. How reasonable is the fit?

Problem 2.3.2 Fit a quintic (powers up to the fifth) model to the data. How does its fit compare to that of the linear model?

Problem 2.3.3 You are now given new data contained within `subjective_overfitLong.csv`. This contains data on 1000 replications of the same experiment, where the x values are held fixed. Using the least squares fits from the first part of this question, compare the performance of the linear regression model with that of the quintic model.

Problem 2.3.4 Which of the two models do you prefer, and why?

3

Chapter contents

PROBABILITY – THE NUTS AND BOLTS OF BAYESIAN INFERENCE

CHAPTER MISSION STATEMENT

In Bayesian statistics, we formulate models in terms of entities called *probability distributions*. This chapter provides an introduction to all things related to probability, starting with the interpretation and manipulation of these distributions.

3⊙2 CHAPTER GOALS

There are some ideas which we know are true, and others which we know are false. But for most ideas, we cannot be sure either way – in these cases, we say we are uncertain. And the correct way to quantify our uncertainty is by using the language of probability. In this vein, Bayesian inference uses probability theory to allow us to update our uncertain beliefs in light of data.

This chapter takes a step away from Bayesian inference to focus on probability distributions, assuming the reader has no previous knowledge of them. (If you feel confident with interpreting and using probability distributions, then you can either skim or skip this chapter.) To understand these abstract objects, we first explicitly define what is meant by probability distributions. This exercise is also useful since Bayesian inference attempts to invert a *likelihood* – itself not a valid probability distribution – to obtain a valid probability distribution that we call a posterior. We also discuss why the distinction between likelihoods and probabilities is important. We then explain how to manipulate probability distributions in order to derive quantities of interest. We start with simple one-dimensional distributions and work up to more adventurous examples, typical of the variety encountered in Bayesian inference. We finish with a derivation of the Bayesian formula from the law of conditional probability.

3⊙3 PROBABILITY DISTRIBUTIONS: HELPING US TO EXPLICITLY STATE OUR IGNORANCE

▶

Random variables and probability distributions

Before we look out of the window in the morning, before we get our exam results, before the cards are dealt, we are uncertain of the world that lies in wait. To plan, and make sense of things, we want to use a suitable framework to describe the uncertainty inherent in a range of situations. Using a particular framework to explicitly state our thoughts illuminates our thought process, and allows others to interrogate our assumptions.

The mathematical theory of probability provides a logic and language which is the only completely consistent framework to describe situations involving uncertainty. In probability theory, we describe the behaviour of *random variables*. This is a statistical term for variables that associate different numeric values with each of the possible outcomes of some random process. By *random* here we do not mean the colloquial use of this term to mean something that is entirely unpredictable. A random process is simply a process whose outcome cannot be perfectly known ahead of time (it may nonetheless be quite predictable). So for a coin flip, we may create a random variable X that takes on the value 1 if the coin lands heads up or 0 for tails up. Because the coin flip can produce only a countable number of outcomes (in this case two), X is a discrete random variable. By contrast, suppose we measure the weight of an individual, Y. In this case Y is a continuous random variable, because in principle it can take on any positive real number.

▶

What is a probability distribution?

3.3.1 What makes a probability distribution valid?

Imagine that we enter a lottery, where we select a number from 1 to 100, to have a chance of winning $1000. We suppose that in the lottery only one ball is drawn and it is fair, meaning that all numbers are equally likely to win. Although we have not stated this world view in mathematical notation, we have without realising it formulated a valid probability distribution for the number drawn in the lottery (see the left-hand panel of Figure 3.1).

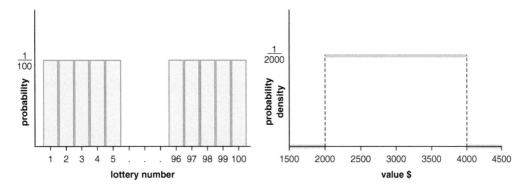

Figure 3.1   Probability distributions representing (left) the chance of winning a lottery and (right) the value of a second-hand car.

The outcome of the lottery example is a discrete probability distribution since the variable we measure – the winning number – is confined to a finite set of values. However, we could similarly define a probability distribution where our variable may equal one value from an infinite number of possible values across a spectrum. Imagine that, before test driving a second-hand car, we are uncertain about its value. From seeing pictures of the car, we might think that it is worth anywhere from $2000 to $4000, with all values being equally likely (see the right-hand panel of Figure 3.1).

The aforementioned cases are both examples of valid probability distributions. So what are their defining properties?

- All values of the distribution must be real and non-negative.
- The sum (for discrete random variables) or integral (for continuous random variables) across all possible values of the random variable must be 1.

In the discrete lottery case, this is satisfied since $Pr(X) = 1/100 \geq 0$ and:

$$\frac{1}{100} + \frac{1}{100} + \ldots + \frac{1}{100} = \sum_{i=1}^{100} \frac{1}{100} = 1. \tag{3.1}$$

For the continuous case of the second-hand car example, the right-hand graph in Figure 3.1 indicates that $p(v) = 1/2000 \geq 0$ for $2000 \leq v \leq 4000$, but how do we determine whether this distribution satisfies the second requirement for a valid probability distribution? To do this we could do the continuous equivalent of summation, which is integration. However, we want to

An introduction to discrete probability distributions

avoid doing this (difficult) maths if possible! Fortunately, since integration is essentially just working out an area underneath a curve, we can calculate the integral by appealing to the geometry of the graph shown in the right-hand panel of Figure 3.1. Since this is just a rectangular shape, we calculate the integral by multiplying the base by its height:

$$area = \frac{1}{2000} \times 2000 = 1. \tag{3.2}$$

An introduction to continuous probability distributions

So for the second-hand car example, we also have a valid probability distribution. Although it may seem that this definition is arbitrary or, perhaps, well-trodden territory for some readers, it is of *central* importance to Bayesian statistics. This is because Bayesians like to work with and produce *valid* probability distributions. This is because only valid probability distributions can be used to describe uncertainty. The pursuit of this ideal underlies the majority of all methods in applied Bayesian statistics – analytic and computational – and hence its importance cannot be overstated!

3.3.2 Probabilities versus probability densities: interpreting discrete and continuous probability distributions

The discrete probability distribution for the lottery shown in the left-hand panel of Figure 3.1 is straightforward to interpret. To calculate the probability that the winning number, X, is 3, we just read off the height of the relevant bar, and conclude that:

$$Pr(X = 3) = \frac{1}{100}. \tag{3.3}$$

In the discrete case, to calculate the probability that a random variable takes on any value within a range, we sum the individual probabilities corresponding to each of the values. In the lottery example, to calculate the probability that the winning number is 10 or less, we just sum the probabilities of it being {1, 2, 3, 4, 5, 6, 7, 8, 9, 10}:

$$Pr(X \le 10) = Pr(X = 1) + Pr(X = 2) + Pr(X = 3) + ... + Pr(X = 9) + Pr(X = 10)$$

$$= \frac{1}{100} + \frac{1}{100} + \frac{1}{100} + ... + \frac{1}{100} + \frac{1}{100} = \frac{1}{10}. \tag{3.4}$$

To calculate the probability that the value of the second-hand car is \$2500, we could simply draw a vertical line from this value on the horizontal axis up to the distribution function's value, and conclude that $Pr(value = \$2500) = 1/2000$ (see the right-hand panel of Figure 3.1). However, using this logic, we would also deduce that the probabilities of the value of the car being {\$2500, \$2500.10, \$2500.01, \$2500.001} are all $1/2000$. Furthermore, we could deduce the same probability for an infinite number of possible values, which if summed together would yield infinity.

There is evidently something wrong with our method for interpreting continuous distributions. If we reconsider the test values {\$2500, \$2500.10, \$2500.01, \$2500.001}, we reason that these are all equally unlikely and belong to a set of an infinite number of potential values that we could draw. This means that, for a continuous random variable, we always have $Pr(\theta = number) = 0$, to avoid an infinite sum. Hence, when we consider $p(\theta)$ for a continuous random variable, it turns out we should interpret its values as *probability densities*, not probabilities.

We can use a continuous probability distribution to calculate the probability that a random variable lies within an interval of possible values. To do this, we use the continuous analogue of a sum, an *integral*. However, we recognise that calculating an integral is equivalent to calculating the area under a probability density curve. For the car example, we can calculate the probability that the car's value lies between \$2500 and \$3000 by determining the rectangular area underneath the graph shown in Figure 3.2 between these two points on the horizontal axis:

$$Pr(2500 \leq value \leq 3000) = \underbrace{\frac{1}{2000}}_{\text{height}} \times \underbrace{500}_{\text{base}} = \frac{1}{4}. \tag{3.5}$$

In expression (3.5), we use Pr to explicitly state that the result is a *probability*, whereas $p(value)$ is a probability density.

A quick note on terminology: Often theorists use probability *mass* to handle discrete distributions, where the distribution's values are directly interpretable as probabilities, and probability *densities* to handle continuous distributions. Unlike their discrete sisters, continuous distributions need to be integrated to yield a probability. We mostly eschew the *mass* terminology as we find it counterproductive to differentiate between the two types of distributions since Bayes' rule handles them in the same way.

Discrete versus continuous probability distributions: a (wet) river crossing

Imagine that you wish to cross a fast-flowing river to reach friends on the other side. Unbeknownst to you, a rather devious park ranger has arranged six stepping stones which guarantee that a person attempting to cross the river will suffer a wet fate. Since you are certain to have a damp walk home, the only uncertainty is exactly where along the stepping stone route you will fall. Your friends (schadenfreunde) are anticipating this outcome and have assigned probabilities of your falling when attempting to reach each

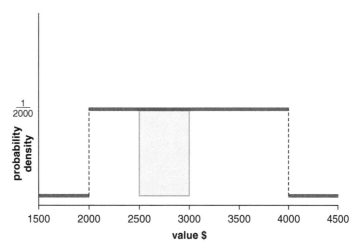

Figure 3.2 We calculate the probability that the second-hand car's value lies between \$2500 and \$3000 by integrating the probability density function between these bounds. This amounts to finding the corresponding area under the graph.

individual stone; the higher the stone, the more probable you will fall into the water from it (see the top panel of Figure 3.3). In this case, there are only six outcomes to the crossing: you fall from one of stones 1, 2, 3, 4, 5 or 6. Thus, each of these *discrete* outcomes is associated with its own non-zero probability.

By contrast, imagine that the malevolent omnipotent ranger has, instead, arranged a bridge across the river. Again, they have ensured that you will *definitely* fall while attempting to navigate the path. This, of course, *seems* like divine intervention, perhaps even the playing out of the laws of physics, but your cheeky friends believe in a probabilistic order behind this façade of arbitrariness, and assign probabilities to each of the outcomes. This time, however, since there are no longer a finite number of possible places where you can fall, there is, in fact, a continuum consisting of an infinite number of possibilities. For example, you could fall from a point 5m from the bank, or 5.000001m from the bank. Clearly, here we cannot assign a positive probability to all of these possible outcomes, since then the total probability would sum to infinity. Instead, your friends choose to specify probabilities across intervals of the bridge length, again deciding that the higher the bridge, the greater the probability of your falling (see the middle panel of Figure 3.3). To determine the quantity of interest – the probability of falling across a small interval – we must now multiply our quantity – called a probability *density* – by the small length of bridge interval we choose. Here we use a small interval so that we can assume that the probability density is unchanging across its length. Also, notice that a probability density has no meaning without a corresponding length scale. In this case, the density has units of probability/metre.

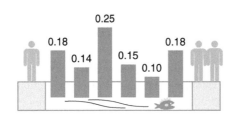

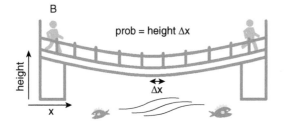

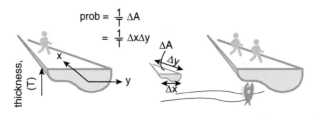

Figure 3.3   Top: crossing a river on discrete stepping stones, where the stone heights represent probabilities. Middle: crossing via a bridge whose height (*B*) is a probability density, which can be used to calculate the probability of falling over a short length (Δ*x*). Bottom: crossing on thin ice – the reciprocal of the thickness of the ice (*F*) can be used to create a probability density that represents the probability of falling through across a small area (Δ*A*). The area is calculated by multiplying its width (Δ*x*) by its length (Δ*y*).

Finally, imagine that it is winter and the surface of the river is frozen, allowing you to choose your own path across. Again, we imagine that our cunning (increasingly deified) ranger has determined that you will fall at some point in your attempted crossing. Your friends realise that the ice is thinner in some places than others and, hence, it is more likely that you will fall in those places. We can characterise a given point in your path by its distance across the river – the y direction – together with the transverse distance along the bank – called the x direction. Using this information your friends construct a probability density which is defined by these two coordinates and is *inversely* related to the thickness of the ice. Again, we realise that there are an infinite number of different places where you could fall, for example at the point (1.1m, 3.2m) or (1.1000001m, 3.2000000001m) across. Clearly, for our density to make sense it must have units of probability/ m^2. To calculate the quantity of interest – a probability of falling within a small area – we multiply the value of the probability density by the corresponding surface area (see the bottom panel of Figure 3.3).

To close our discussion of the differences between probabilities and probability densities, we realise that for densities we must supply a volume, which provides the exchange rate to convert it into a probability. Note that the word *volume* is used for its analogy with three-dimensional solids, where we calculate the mass of an object by multiplying the density by its volume. Analogously, here we calculate the *probability mass* of an infinitesimal volume:

$$probability\ mass = probability\ density \times volume. \tag{3.6}$$

However, here a volume need not correspond to an actual three-dimensional volume in space, but to a unit of measurement across a parameter range of interest. In the above examples we use a length then an area as our volume unit, but in other cases it might be a volume, a percentage or even a probability.

Probability zero versus impossibility

We have reasoned that for continuous distributions, Pr(a value) $= 0$. However, does this mean it is impossible to obtain any individual value? If you answered 'yes' here, then how can we hope to obtain a sample of numbers from our distribution, since they are all individually impossible? The apparent paradox at hand is subtle, but important nonetheless. While a full explanation of this issue requires a knowledge of *measure theory*, we attempt a more heuristic explanation.

When we say an event is impossible, it has a probability of zero. When we use the word *impossible* we mean that the event is not within our space of potential outcomes. Imagine the event that you simultaneously conclude both of the following about a ball withdrawn from an urn of many balls:

- The ball is entirely white, and
- The ball is entirely black.

Philosophically, we could argue that such an event is impossible, and does not belong to the set of possible outcomes, meaning it has a probability of zero.

Imagine a sample of numbers from a standard normal distribution. Here the purely imaginary number i does not belong to the set of possible outcomes and hence has zero probability. Conversely, consider attempting to guess exactly the number that we sample from a standard normal distribution. Clearly, obtaining the number 3.142 here is possible – it does not lie outside of the range of the distribution – so it belongs to our potential outcomes. However, if we multiply our probability density by the volume corresponding to this single value, then we get zero because the volume element is of zero width. So we see that events that have a probability of zero can still be possible.

So events that are impossible have zero probability. However, the converse is not true: some events that are of zero probability are still possible. If this does not make sense to you, then remember that probabilities are just units of measurement. For a Bayesian, they measure subjective points of view, so, clearly, an event that we assign zero probability to can still happen. For a Frequentist, they measure the frequency at which an outcome occurs in an infinite series of identical trials. In our normal distribution example imagine counting the number of times we sample a value of 3.142. We could then enumerate the ratio: *#successes* / *#trials* (where a success is sampling a value of 3.142). While for an infinite sample size we might obtain this value a few times, clearly the denominator will dominate (go to infinity) and we obtain a probability of zero.

The good news: Bayes' rule does not distinguish between probabilities and probability densities

While it is important to understand that probabilities and probability densities are not the same types of entity, the good news for us is that Bayes' rule is the same for each. So we can readily write:

$$Pr(\theta = 1 \mid X = 1) = \frac{Pr(X = 1 \mid \theta = 1)Pr(\theta = 1)}{Pr(X = 1)}, \tag{3.7}$$

when the data, X, and the parameter θ are discrete, and hence Pr denotes a probability. Alternatively, we can write Bayes' rule as:

$$p(\theta = 1 \mid X = 1) = \frac{p(X = 1 \mid \theta = 1)p(\theta = 1)}{p(X = 1)} \tag{3.8}$$

when the data and parameter are continuous and p denotes a probability density. We will more commonly use the latter representation since for the majority of interesting models the parameters will be continuous.

3.3.3 The mean of a distribution

A popular way of summarising a distribution is by its *mean*, which is a measure of central tendency for a distribution. More intuitively, a mean, or *expected value*, of a distribution is the long-run average value that would be obtained if we sampled from it an infinite number of times.

The method to calculate the mean of a distribution depends on whether it is *discrete* or *continuous* in nature. However, the concept is essentially the same in both cases. The mean is calculated as a weighted sum (for discrete random variables) or integral (for continuous variables) across all potential values of the random variable where the weights are provided by the probability distribution. This results in the following expressions for the mean of a discrete and continuous variable, respectively:

$$\mathbb{E}(X) = \sum_{\text{All } \alpha} \alpha Pr(X = \alpha),$$

$$\mathbb{E}(X) = \int_{\text{All } \alpha} \alpha p(\alpha) d\alpha.$$

(3.9)

In the two expressions in (3.9), α is any one of the discrete set, or continuum, of possible values for the random variable X, respectively. We use Pr in the first expression in (3.9) and p in the second, to indicate these are probabilities and probability densities, respectively.

We now use the first expression of (3.9) to calculate the mean winning number from the lottery example introduced in Section 3.3.1:

$$\mathbb{E}(X) = \sum_{\alpha=1}^{100} \alpha Pr(X = \alpha)$$

$$= 1 \times \frac{1}{100} + 2 \times \frac{1}{100} + 3 \times \frac{1}{100} + \ldots + 99 \times \frac{1}{100} + 100 \times \frac{1}{100}$$

$$= 50\tfrac{1}{2}.$$

(3.10)

We also demonstrate the long-run nature of the mean value of $50\tfrac{1}{2}$ by computationally simulating many plays of the lottery (see Figure 3.4). As the number of games played increases, the running mean becomes closer to this value.

We now use the second expression of (3.9) to calculate the expected (or mean) value of the second-hand car. This amounts to integrating the curve $v \times \frac{1}{2000}$ between \$2000 and \$4000. The region bounded by this curve and the axis can be broken up into triangular and rectangular regions (see Figure 3.5), and so we calculate the total area by summing the individual areas:

$$\text{area} = \underbrace{2000 \times 1}_{A} + \underbrace{0.5 \times 2000 \times 1}_{B} = \$3000.$$

(3.11)

If we had a business buying (and selling) second-hand cars, we might keep a record of the prices we paid for cars over time. If the value of all cars we buy can be represented by the same uniform distribution then the average price we pay should eventually approach the mean of \$3000 (see Figure 3.6).

If you understand the process used to produce Figures 3.4 and 3.6, then you already understand the basis behind modern computational Bayesian statistics. However, if you do not, fear not; we devote Part IV of the book to this purpose.

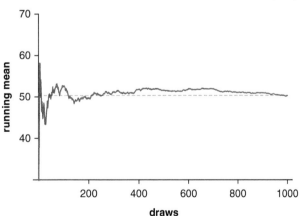

Figure 3.4 Playing a computational lottery. As the number of games played increases, the sample mean approaches the true mean of $50\tfrac{1}{2}$. This quantity corresponds to the mean winning number that would be drawn from a lottery where the possible numbers are the integers from 1 to 100, each of which is equally likely.

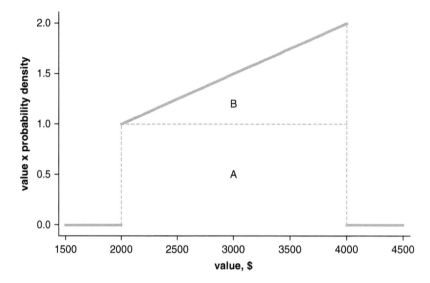

Figure 3.5   Calculating the mean of the second-hand car distribution (shown in Figure 3.2) by finding the area under the graph representing the PDF times the car's value. We can do this by splitting up the area into a triangle and a rectangle, and summing their respective areas.

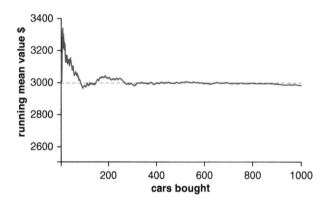

Figure 3.6   The running mean value of cars we have bought over our long career. Eventually, the sample mean approaches the true mean of $3000.

3.3.4 Generalising probability distributions to two dimensions

Life is often more complex than the examples encountered thus far. We often must reason about the outcomes of a number of processes, whose results may be interdependent. We begin by considering the outcome of two measurements to introduce the mechanics of two-dimensional probability distributions. Fortunately, these rules do not become more complex when generalising to higher dimensional problems. This means that if the reader is comfortable with the following examples, then they should understand the majority of calculations involving probability distributions. In Bayesian statistics, being familiar with the manipulations of probability distributions is essential, since the output of the Bayesian formula – the posterior probability distribution – is used to derive all post-experiment conclusions. As such, we will devote some time to introducing two examples, which we will use to describe and explain the manipulations of two-dimensional probability distributions.

Matt's horses: a two-dimensional discrete probability example

Imagine that you are a horse racing aficionado and want to quantify the uncertainty in the outcome of two separate races. In each race there are two horses from a particular stable, called A and B. From their historical performance over 100 races, you notice that both horses often react the same way to the racing conditions. When horse A wins, it is more likely that, later in the day, B will also win, and vice versa, with similar interrelations for the losses; when A finds conditions tough, so does B. Wanting to flex your statistical muscle, you represent the historical race results by the two-dimensional probability distribution shown in Table 3.1.

Table 3.1   A probability distribution indicating the historical performance of two horses, A and B, that race in separate events.

		A	
		0 (lose)	1 (win)
B	0 (lose)	$\frac{30}{100}$	$\frac{10}{100}$
	1 (win)	$\frac{10}{100}$	$\frac{50}{100}$

Does this distribution satisfy the requirements for a valid probability distribution? To check, we apply the rules described in Section 3.3.1. Since all the values of the distribution are real and non-negative, this satisfies our first requirement. Since our distribution is composed of two discrete random variables, we must sum over the possible values of both to test if it is normalised:

$$\sum_{i=0}^{1}\sum_{j=0}^{1} Pr(X_A = i, X_B = j) = \frac{30}{100} + \frac{10}{100} + \frac{10}{100} + \frac{50}{100} = 1. \tag{3.12}$$

In expression (3.12) X_A and X_B are random variables which represent the race for horses A and B, respectively. Notice that since our situation considers the outcome of two random variables, we must index the probability, $Pr(X_A, X_B)$, by both. Since the probability distribution is a function of two variables, we say that it is two-dimensional.

How can we interpret the probability distribution shown in Table 3.1? The probability that both horses lose (and hence both their random variables equal 0) is just read off from the top-left entry in the table, meaning $Pr(X_A = 0, X_B = 0) = \frac{30}{100}$. We ascribe a smaller likelihood of heterogeneous outcomes, $Pr(X_A = 0, X_B = 1) = \frac{10}{100}$ or $Pr(X_A = 1, X_B = 0) = \frac{10}{100}$, since based on historical data we believe that the horses react similarly to the racing conditions. The most likely outcome is that both horses win with $Pr(X_A = 1, X_B = 1) = \frac{50}{100}$.

2D discrete distributions: an introduction

Foot length and literacy: a two-dimensional continuous probability example

Suppose that we measure the foot size and literacy test scores for a group of individuals. Both of these variables can be assumed to be continuous, meaning that we represent our strength of beliefs by specifying a two-dimensional probability distribution across a continuum of values. Since this distribution is two-dimensional we need three dimensions to plot it – two dimensions for the variables and one dimension for the probability density (see the left-hand plot of Figure 3.7). These three-dimensional plots are, however, a bit cumbersome to deal with, and so we prefer to use

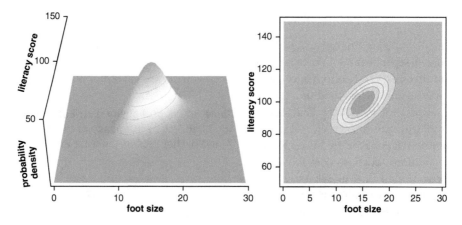

Figure 3.7 Left: the probability density (vertical axis) as a function of foot size and literacy scores (the other two axes). Right: the same distribution shown as a contour plot. The contour lines and shading from the right-hand plot correspond to those in the left-hand plot.

contour plots to graph two-dimensional continuous probability distributions (see the right-hand plot of Figure 3.7). In contour plots, we mark the set of positions where the value of the probability density function is constant, as contour lines. The rate of change of the gradient of the function at a particular position in parameter space is, hence, determined by the local density of contour lines.

We could verify that the distribution shown in the left-hand plot of Figure 3.7 is valid by showing that the volume underneath the left-hand surface is 1, by integration. However, to avoid overcomplicating things, you will have to take our word for it.

2D continuous distributions: an introduction

Notice that in the right-hand plot of Figure 3.7, the contour lines are diagonally oriented. This means that there is a positive correlation between foot size and scores on the literacy test; as an individual's foot size increases, so does their literacy score, on average. Why might this be so? Our sample of individuals here consists of children of various ages. Age is positively correlated with both foot size and literacy!

Table 3.2 The marginal distributions of A and B (shown below and to the right of the joint density values, respectively), achieved by summing the values in each column or row, respectively.

3.3.5 Marginal distributions

		A		
		0 (lose)	**1 (win)**	$Pr(X_B)$
B	**0 (lose)**	$\dfrac{30}{100}$	$\dfrac{10}{100}$	$\dfrac{40}{100}$
	1 (win)	$\dfrac{10}{100}$	$\dfrac{50}{100}$	$\dfrac{60}{100}$
	$Pr(X_A)$	$\dfrac{40}{100}$	$\dfrac{60}{100}$	

Although in the horse racing example there are two separate races, each with an uncertain outcome, we can still consider the outcome of one race on its own. Suppose, for example, that we witness only the result for A. What would be the probability distribution that describes this outcome?

What is a marginal probability distribution? A discrete example

To calculate this, we must *average* out the dependence of the other variable. Since we are interested only in the result of A, we can sum down the column values for B to give us the *marginal*[1] distribution of A, which is shown at the bottom of Table 3.2.

Hence, we see that the marginal probability of A winning is 0.6. This value is calculated by considering the two possible ways that this event can occur:

$$Pr(X_A = 1) = Pr(X_A = 1, X_B = 0) + Pr(X_A = 1, X_B = 1)$$

$$= \frac{10}{100} + \frac{50}{100} \tag{3.13}$$

$$= \frac{60}{100}.$$

In expression (3.13) to calculate the probability that A wins, we sum the probability that A wins and B loses with the probability that both win.

So to calculate the probability of a single event we just sum the probabilities of all the potential ways this can happen. This amounts to summing over all potential states of the other variable. Mathematically we can write down this rule for a two-dimensional probability distribution as:

Discrete marginal probability distributions

$$Pr(A = \alpha) = \sum_{\beta} Pr(A = \alpha, B = \beta). \tag{3.14}$$

In expression (3.14), α and β refer to the specific values taken on by the random variables A and B, respectively. We can use expression (3.14) for the horses example to calculate the probability that B loses:

$$Pr(X_B = 0) = \sum_{\alpha=0}^{1} Pr(X_B = 0, X_A = \alpha)$$

$$= Pr(X_B = 0, X_A = 0) + Pr(X_B = 0, X_A = 1) \tag{3.15}$$

$$= \frac{30}{100} + \frac{10}{100} = \frac{40}{100}.$$

For continuous random variables we use the continuous analogue of a sum, an integral, to calculate the marginal distribution because the other variable can now equal any of a continuum of possible values:

$$p_A(\alpha) = \int_{\text{All } \beta} p_{AB}(\alpha, \beta) \mathrm{d}\beta \tag{3.16}$$

In expression (3.16), $p_{AB}(\alpha, \beta)$ represents the joint probability distribution of random variables A and B, evaluated at $(A = \alpha, B = \beta)$. Similarly, $p_A(\alpha)$ represents the marginal distribution of random variable A, evaluated at $A = \alpha$. Although it is somewhat an abuse of notation, for simplicity, from now on we write $p_{AB}(\alpha, \beta)$ as $p(A, B)$ and $p_A(\alpha)$ as $p(A)$.

What is a marginal probability distribution? A continuous example

---

[1]Marginal distributions are thus called because, for discrete random variables, they are obtained by summing a row or column of a table and placing the result in its margins.

In the foot size and literacy test example, suppose we want to summarise the distribution for literacy score, irrespective of foot size. We can obtain this distribution by 'integrating out' the dependence on foot size:

$$p(score) = \int_0^{30} p(score, FS)dFS. \tag{3.17}$$

Continuous marginal probability distributions

The result of carrying out the calculation in (3.17) is the distribution shown in the right-side graph in Figure 3.8. We have rotated this graph to emphasise that it is obtained by summing (really, integrating) across the joint density at each individual value of literacy score. Similarly, we can obtain the marginal distribution for foot size by integrating the joint density with respect to literacy score. The resultant distribution is shown in the bottom graph of Figure 3.8.

Another way to think about marginal densities is to imagine walking across the landscape of the joint density, where regions of greater density represent hills. To calculate the marginal density for a literacy score of 100 we walk along the horizontal line that corresponds to this score and record the number of calories we burn in walking from $FS = 0$ to $FS = 30$. If the path is relatively flat, we burn fewer calories and the corresponding marginal density is low. However, if the path includes a large hill, we burn a lot of energy and the marginal density is high.

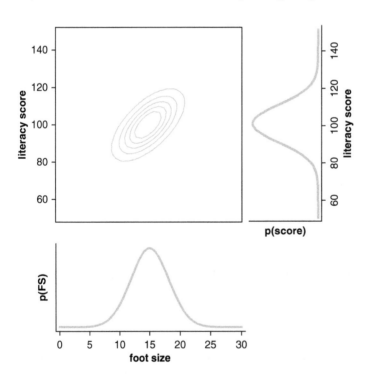

Marginal distribution by sampling

An alternative approach to estimating the marginal distribution of literacy test score is by *sampling* from the joint distribution of literacy score and foot size. But what is sampling, and why does this help us determine the marginal distribution?

Even if we do not know what sampling means, we have all done it at one stage or another in our lives. An example is

Figure 3.8   Top left: the joint density of foot size and literacy test scores. Right: the marginal density of literacy scores. Bottom left: the marginal density of foot size.

throwing a die and recording the number that results. Each number we record is an *independent* sample from the discrete probability distribution that describes the outcome from throwing the die. One way to understand this distribution is to throw the die a large number of times and record the frequency of each outcome.

While it may seem counterintuitive, we can also understand a continuous distribution by sampling from it. In particular, if we can generate independent samples from the joint distribution of literacy score and foot size, we can estimate the marginal distribution for each variable. To estimate these marginal distributions we ignore the observations of the variable not directly of interest and draw a histogram of the remaining samples (see Figure 3.9). While not exact, the shape of this histogram is a good approximation of the marginal distribution if we have enough samples.

This has been a very quick introduction to using sampling to understand distributions. Because of this, we have skimmed over many of the details. What is an independent sample? Why does sampling mean we can avoid doing sums (for discrete variables) or integrals (for continuous variables)? For now, it suffices to say that sampling is behind most modern computational methods used for applied research in Bayesian statistics. Rather than provide a complete exposition of this method now, we wait until Part IV (after we know a little more about the underlying theory) before doing so.

Venn diagrams

An alternative way to think about marginal distributions is using Venn diagrams. In a Venn diagram, the area of a particular event indicates its probability, and the rectangular area represents all the events that can possibly happen, so it has an area of 1. In Figure 3.10, we specify the events of horses A and B winning as sub-areas in the diagram, which we refer to as A and B respectively. These areas overlap, indicating a region of joint probability where $Pr(X_A = 1, X_B = 1)$. Using this diagram, it is straightforward to calculate the marginal probability of A or B winning: we find the area of the elliptic shapes A or B, respectively. Considering A, when we calculate the area of its ellipse, we implicitly calculate the sum:

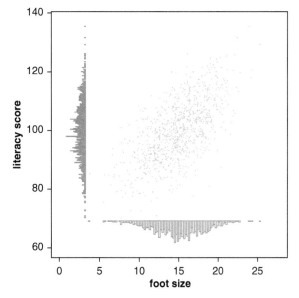

Figure 3.9 Sampling from the joint distribution of literacy score and foot size to estimate the marginal distribution for literacy score (the histogram on the left) and foot size (the histogram at the bottom). In this case, we use 1000 samples from the joint distribution of foot size and literacy scores.

$$Pr(A) = Pr(A, B) + Pr(A, not\ B).$$
(3.18)

In expression (3.18), the terms on the right-hand side correspond to the overlap region and the remaining part of A (where B does not occur), respectively.

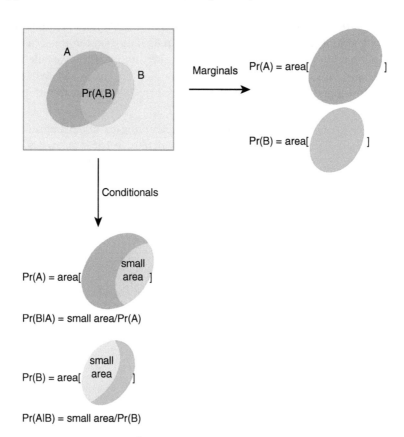

Figure 3.10   A Venn diagram showing the marginal and conditional distributions for the horse racing example. Note that here the labels A and B refer to the events that horse A wins or horse B wins, respectively. So $Pr(A,B)$ is used as a shorthand for $Pr(X_A = 1, X_B = 1)$.

3.3.6 Conditional distributions

What is a conditional probability distribution?

We sometimes receive only partial information about a system which is of interest to us. In the horse racing example, we might observe the result of only one horse race, and use this to update the probability that the other horse will win. Alternatively, in the foot size and literacy example, we might measure an individual's foot size and then want to estimate their literacy score.

In probability, when we observe one variable and want to update our uncertainty for another variable, we are seeking a conditional distribution. This is because we compute the probability distribution of one uncertain variable, conditional on the known value of the other(s).

In each case, we have reduced some of the uncertainty in the system by observing one of its characteristics. Hence, in the two-dimensional examples described above, the conditional distribution is one-dimensional because we are only now uncertain about one variable.

Luckily, it is straightforward to obtain the probability of one variable, conditional on the value of the other:

$$p(A \mid B) = \frac{p(A,B)}{p(B)}. \tag{3.19}$$

In expression (3.19), $p(A \mid B)$ refers to the probability (or probability density) of A occurring, given that B has occurred. On the right-hand side of this expression, $p(B)$ is the *marginal* distribution of B, and $p(A,B)$ is the joint probability that A and B both occur.

For the horses example, suppose that we observe that horse A wins. To calculate the probability that B also wins, we use (3.19):

$$
\begin{aligned}
Pr(X_B = 1 \mid X_A = 1) &= \frac{Pr(X_A = 1, X_B = 1)}{Pr(X_A = 1)} \\[2mm]
&= \frac{Pr(X_A = 1, X_B = 1)}{Pr(X_A = 1, X_B = 0) + Pr(X_A = 1, X_B = 1)} \\[2mm]
&= \frac{\dfrac{50}{100}}{\dfrac{10}{100} + \dfrac{50}{100}} \\[2mm]
&= \frac{5}{6}.
\end{aligned}
\tag{3.20}
$$

In the above, we used expression (3.14) to calculate the denominator, $Pr(X_A = 1)$. Table 3.3 shows another way to conceive of this calculation. When we observe that A wins, we reduce our solution space to only the middle column (highlighted). Therefore, we renormalise the solution space to have a total probability of 1 by dividing each of its entries by its sum of probabilities $\left(\frac{60}{100}\right)$, yielding the conditional probabilities shown in the right-hand column.

The Venn diagram in Figure 3.10 shows another way to interpret conditional distributions. If we observe that B wins, our event space collapses to

Table 3.3 Calculating the conditional probabilities (rightmost column) of horse B winning (lower-right cell) and losing (upper-right cell) given that we observe that horse A wins. To do so, we only consider the probabilities in the highlighted column, and divide these by the overall probability that A wins $\left(\frac{60}{100}\right)$.

		A		
		0	**1**	$Pr(X_B \mid X_A = 1)$
B	**0**	$\dfrac{30}{100}$	$\dfrac{10}{100}$	$= \dfrac{10}{100} / \dfrac{60}{100} = \dfrac{1}{6}$
	1	$\dfrac{10}{100}$	$\dfrac{50}{100}$	$= \dfrac{50}{100} / \dfrac{60}{100} = \dfrac{5}{6}$
	$Pr(X_A)$	$\dfrac{40}{100}$	$\dfrac{60}{100}$	

An introduction to discrete conditional probability distributions

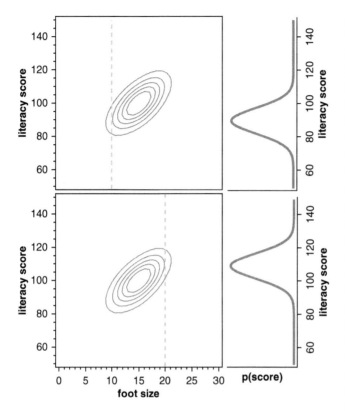

only the area specified by *B*. The conditional probability, $Pr(X_A = 1 | X_B = 1)$, is then given by the ratio of the area of overlap to the total area of *B*. This makes intuitive sense, since this is the only way that A can win, given that B has already won.

We can also use (3.19) to calculate the conditional distribution of literacy scores for individuals after we measure their foot size. The only difference with the discrete example is that we must now integrate to calculate the marginal probability for foot size. Figure 3.11 shows the conditional distributions traced out when we measure an individual's foot size to be 10cm (in the top panel) and 20cm (in the lower panel). The dashed lines show the new event space since we now have no uncertainty over foot size in each of the cases. Therefore, the heights traversed on the

Figure 3.11 Calculating the conditional density for literacy test score (right-hand panels) after we measure an individual's foot size to be 10cm (top-left-hand panel) and 20cm (bottom-left-hand panel). The dashed lines indicate the new event space in each case.

walk along these lines of constant foot size indicate the relative probability of different values of literacy scores.

3●4 INDEPENDENCE

If there is a relationship between two random variables, we say that they are *dependent*. This does not necessarily mean *causal* dependence, as it is sometimes supposed, in that the behaviour of one random variable affects the outcome of another. It just means that the outcome of the first is informative for predicting the second.

An introduction to continuous conditional probability distributions

An example of dependent variables can be illustrated using the colour and suit of a playing card. If we are told that the colour of a playing card is red, then our other variable, suit, is constrained to be either hearts or diamonds. In this case, knowing the value of the first variable, colour, allows us to narrow down the list of outcomes of the second variable, suit (see Figure 3.12). This would not be the case if, instead, we considered the suit of the card and its value. Since all suits have the same range of cards from 2 to Ace, knowing the suit of the card is uninformative of its value. The suit and card value are hence independent variables.

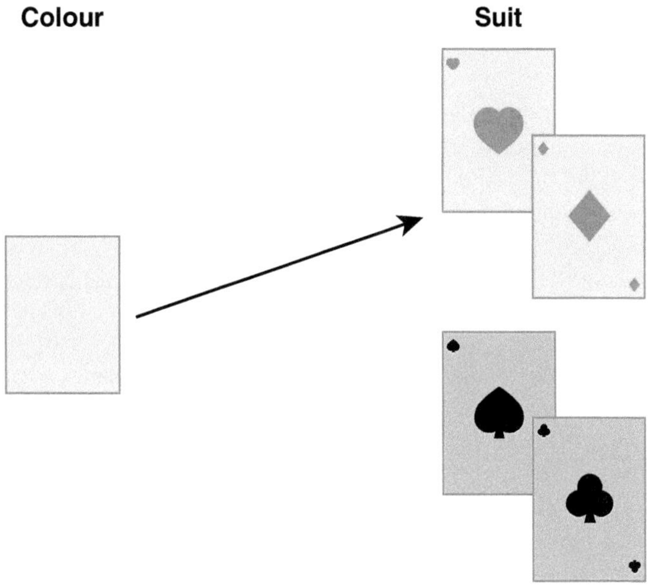

If two events, A and B, are *disjoint*, then if one occurs, the other cannot. In this case, it is often mistakenly believed that the variables are *independent*, although this is not true (see the left-hand panel of Figure 3.13). In this case, knowledge that event A has occurred provides significant information about whether B will. If A occurs, then we know for certain that B cannot.

In contrast, if two events are independent, then knowledge of B provides no additional information on A. Mathematically, this means that the conditional probability of A is equal to its marginal:

$$Pr(A \mid B) = Pr(A). \tag{3.21}$$

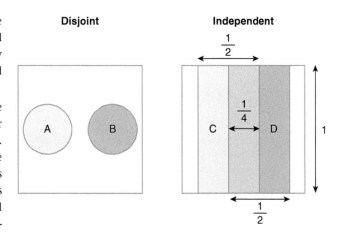

Colour **Suit**

Figure 3.12 Knowledge of the colour of a card provides information about the suit of the card. The colour and suit of a card are dependent variables.

This makes intuitive sense, since knowing that B has occurred does not affect the probability that A occurs (see the right-hand panel of Figure 3.13).

We now provide a toy example to describe what it means for two events to be independent. We do this partly because we think it helps to explain this concept, but also because this approach will prove useful when discussing more complex concepts (for example, the Kullback–Leibler divergence and mutual information) later on. Imagine that we have two

Figure 3.13 Venn diagrams representing the probability space for left: disjoint events (A and B) and right: independent events (C and D). The lengths indicated in the right-hand panel indicate $Pr(C) = Pr(C|D) = 1/2$.

types of object, a ball and a cube, and each object can be coloured either red or grey. Suppose that in an urn, hidden from our view, there are three balls and three cubes and that, for each object type, one of them is red and the other two are grey (see the left-hand panel of Figure 3.14). A friend of ours will reach into the urn and grab an object at random, and we want to describe the probability of each of the outcomes. Before a ball is drawn, we know that $Pr(\square)=\frac{1}{2}$ and $Pr(O)=\frac{1}{2}$. We also know that $Pr(red)=1/3$ and $Pr(grey) = 2/3$. Suppose that we wear a blindfold, and our friend reaches into the urn and takes out an object. She then says the object is a ball. What now is the probability that it is red? Well, since there are three balls and one of them is red (see the middle panel of Figure 3.14) then $Pr(red|O) = 1/3$. In other words, this is unchanged from the situation when we were entirely ignorant of the object. Similarly, suppose our friend had told us that she had pulled out a grey object. What would be the probability that it is a cube? Since four objects are grey and two of them are balls (see the right-hand panel of Figure 3.14), again our probability remains the same at $Pr(\square|grey) = 1/2$. In other words, knowing one property about the object does not help us predict the other one, in line with expression (3.21). This means that the shape of the object and its colour represent independent outcomes.

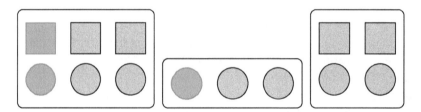

Figure 3.14 Left: the six objects in an urn. Middle: the possible outcomes if we know the object is a ball. Right: the possible outcomes if we know the object is coloured grey.

Using the conditional probability rule given in expression (3.19), we use this to rewrite expression (3.21) as:

$$\frac{Pr(A,B)}{Pr(B)} = Pr(A).$$

(3.22)

In other words, the ratio of the joint probability A and B occurring to the marginal probability of B is the same as the overall probability of A (see the right-hand panel of Figure 3.13). The most common expression to describe independent events is obtained by multiplying both sides of expression (3.22) by its denominator:

$$p(A,B) = p(A) \times p(B)$$

(3.23)

where here for generality we use 'p' to represent either a probability (for discrete A and B) and a probability density (for continuous A and B).

To provide a more concrete example, consider again the results of two horse races. Imagine that now there are two horses, C and D, which come from separate stables and race on consecutive days. The probability distribution shown in Table 3.4 is based on the historical race results of both horses. We can use this table to test whether the outcomes of the two races are independent using expression (3.23). If the event that C wins and the event that D wins are independent, then their joint probability should equal the product of the marginal probabilities:

Table 3.4 The joint probability distribution for horses C and D (four central cells). The marginal distribution of horses C and D are achieved by summing the values in each column or row, respectively.

		C		
		0	**1**	$Pr(X_D)$
D	**0**	0.2	0.3	**0.5**
	1	0.2	0.3	**0.5**
	$Pr(X_C)$	**0.4**	**0.6**	

$$Pr(X_C = 1, X_D = 1) = 0.3$$

$$= Pr(X_C = 1) \times Pr(X_D = 1) \tag{3.24}$$

$$= 0.6 \times 0.5 = 0.3,$$

which is true. To determine whether the variables X_C and X_D are independent we should use the above method to check that the above holds true for the three other joint outcomes in Table 3.4. We leave it as an exercise to the reader to demonstrate this is the case.

3○5   CENTRAL LIMIT THEOREMS

We choose statistical models to approximate some aspect of the real world, yet the choice of a particular model can appear arbitrary. Therefore, any concrete results that help to determine our choice of model are most welcome. Imagine that we are modelling the mean IQ test score in a particular school. Suppose, also, that IQ scores are constrained to lie in the range [0,300], and we believe that an individual is equally likely to attain any score across this range – in formal terms, the individual's score is 'uniformly distributed over this range' (this isn't a particularly good model, but try to suspend your disbelief for now). We also suppose that individuals' scores are independent of one another.

To start, imagine that we have a sample of two individuals and want to describe the distribution of the mean of their scores. If the individual test scores are uniformly distributed, we might then suppose that their average is also uniformly distributed. But is this actually true? Begin by considering the extremes: there is only one way to obtain a mean test score of 300; both individuals must score 300. Similarly, to obtain a mean of 0, both individuals must score 0. By contrast, consider a mean of 150. This could result from a number of individual score combinations, for example $(score_A, score_B) = : (150,150), (100,200), (125,175)$. Intuitively, there are many more ways to obtain moderate values for the sample mean than there are for the extremes.

This central tendency of the sample mean increases along with sample size, since extreme values then require more individual scores to be simultaneously extreme, which is less likely. This effect is visible in Figure 3.15; however, we also see another impact on the probability distribution for the mean: as our sample size increases, the distribution is an increasingly good fit to the normal distribution. This approximation, it turns out, becomes exact in the limit of an infinite sample size and is known as the *central limit theorem (CLT)*. For practical purposes, however, the approximation is generally reasonable if the sample size is above about 20 (see right-hand panel of Figure 3.15).

There are, in fact, a number of central limit theorems. The above CLT applies to the average of independent, identically distributed random variables. However, there are also central limit theorems that apply far less stringent conditions. This means that whenever an output is the result of the sum or average of a number of largely independent factors, then it may be reasonable to assume it is normally distributed. For example, one can argue that an individual's intelligence is the result of the average of a number of factors, including parenting, genetics, life experience and health, among others. Hence, we might assume that an individual's test score picked at random from the population is normally distributed.

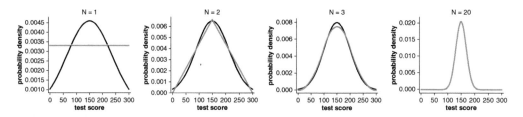

Figure 3.15 The central limit theorem in action: as we increase the sample size (left to right), the probability distribution for the sample mean (red lines) approaches a normal with the same mean and standard deviation (black lines).

3○6 A DERIVATION OF BAYES' RULE

Bayes' rule dictates the correct way to go from a conditional probability to its inverse. It is crucial to Bayesian inference because it allows us to go from 'the probability of the data given a hypothesis' to the desired 'the probability of the hypothesis given the data'. In this section, we derive Bayes' rule from first principles. First, we rewrite the conditional probability formula expression (3.19) for the probability that event A occurs given that B occurs:

$$Pr(A \mid B) = \frac{Pr(A,B)}{Pr(B)}. \tag{3.25}$$

However, we could also swap the order of A and B, resulting in the probability that B occurs given that A occurs:

$$Pr(B \mid A) = \frac{Pr(B,A)}{Pr(A)}, \tag{3.26}$$

where $Pr(A,B)$ is the joint probability that both A and B occur. This is exactly the same as the reverse: the probability of B and A coinciding, given by $Pr(B,A)$. We can, therefore, rearrange (3.26) to obtain this joint probability:

$$Pr(A,B) = Pr(B \mid A) \times Pr(A). \tag{3.27}$$

We can use expression (3.27) to decompose the probability of both A and B occurring into two steps. First, for this joint event to happen, A must happen, with probability, $Pr(A)$. We then require that B occurs given that A has already occurred, with probability $Pr(B|A)$. We finally substitute expression (3.27) into the numerator of expression (3.25) to yield the famous Bayesian formula:

$$Pr(A|B) = \frac{Pr(B|A) \times Pr(A)}{Pr(B)}. \tag{3.28}$$

Importantly, the Bayesian formula explains how to convert $Pr(B|A)$ to its inverse $Pr(A|B)$, which is central to Bayesian statistics.

3.6.1 The intuition behind the formula

If we multiply both sides of expression (3.28) by $Pr(B)$, this produces an alternative statement of Bayes' rule:

$$Pr(A|B) \times Pr(B) = Pr(B|A) \times Pr(A) \quad [= Pr(A,B)]. \tag{3.29}$$

In expression (3.29) we include the joint distribution in square brackets because of the logic described above. Expression (3.29) indicates that there are two ways of arriving at this joint probability (see Figure 3.16). The first way is given by the left-hand side and is due to A occurring, with probability $Pr(A)$, followed afterwards by B, with probability $Pr(B|A)$. An equivalent way for both A and B to occur is given by the right-hand side of Figure 3.16. Here B occurs first, with probability $Pr(B)$, followed by A given that B has occurred, with probability $Pr(A|B)$.

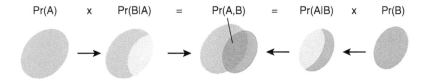

Figure 3.16   The two ways of arriving at the joint probability that both A and B occur: $Pr(A,B)$. When rearranged, the above equations can be used to derive Bayes' rule.

3.6.2 Breast cancer screening

To gain experience in using Bayes' rule, we now describe a practical application of it. Suppose that we are a clinician specialising in breast cancer. Out of all women aged 40 who participate in screenings, roughly 1% of them will have breast cancer at the time of testing. The screening process is fairly robust, and for those women with breast cancer the tests indicate a positive result 80% of the time. However, there is also a risk of false positives, and 10% of women without breast cancer also test positive.

Suppose that a 40-year-old woman has been screened, and tested positive for cancer. What is the probability that she has the disease?

To answer this question, we must calculate the conditional probability: $Pr(cancer \mid +ve)$. In other words, the probability that she has breast cancer given that she has tested positive. To compute this probability we first summarise the relevant information in the language of probability: $Pr(cancer) = 0.01$, $Pr(+ve \mid cancer) = 0.8$ and $Pr(+ve \mid no\,cancer) = 0.1$. How do we use this information to produce the quantity of interest? Bayes' formula to the rescue! That is:

$$Pr(cancer \mid +ve) = \frac{Pr(+ve \mid cancer) \times Pr(cancer)}{Pr(+ve)}, \tag{3.30}$$

where the only element that is not readily available is $Pr(+ve)$, the probability that an individual tests positive. There are two ways an individual can test positive: either they have cancer and the test shows a true positive; or they are disease free and the test is a false positive:

$$Pr(+ve) = \underbrace{Pr(+ve, cancer)}_{true\,positive} + \underbrace{Pr(+ve, no\,cancer)}_{false\,positive}$$

$$= Pr(+ve \mid cancer) \times Pr(cancer) + Pr(+ve \mid no\,cancer) \times Pr(no\,cancer) \tag{3.31}$$

$$= 0.8 \times 0.01 + 0.1 \times 0.99$$

$$= 0.11.$$

Using this result, we can now calculate our desired probability:

$$Pr(cancer \mid +ve) = \frac{0.8 \times 0.01}{0.107} \tag{3.32}$$

$$\approx 0.08.$$

This seems extremely small – even though the woman in the clinic tests positive she only has an 8% probability of having the disease. To understand this result, we imagine two pools of individuals: those with the disease and those without. Since the risk of breast cancer is 1%, the size of the disease-free group (the other 99%) is about 100 times bigger. So, while a high proportion of those individuals with cancer test positive, the number of people is still relatively few (see the left-hand side of Figure 3.17). Whereas even though only a small proportion of people test positive in the disease-free group, their number dwarfs the true positives (see the right-hand side of Figure 3.17). Until relatively recently, unfortunately, the probabilities we assumed in this analysis were indicative of actual clinical outcomes.

Breast cancer example use of Bayes rule

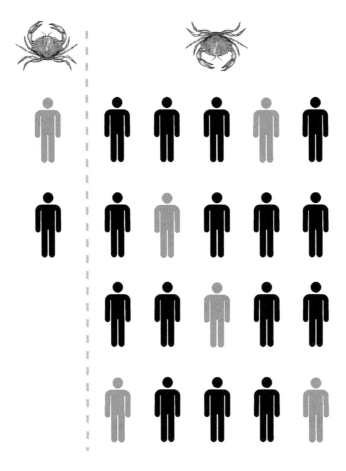

Figure 3.17   The number of 40-year-old women with breast cancer (left, under the normal crab) is small compared with the number that do not have the disease (right, under the upturned crab). This means that, even though a high proportion of the women with cancer will test positive (red shading), this number is small compared with the false positives – the women without the disease who also test positive.

3○7   THE BAYESIAN INFERENCE PROCESS FROM THE BAYESIAN FORMULA

In Bayesian statistics, we use probability distributions to describe all components of our system. Our starting point is Bayes' rule (for a continuous random variable):

$$p(A \mid B) = \frac{p(B \mid A) \times p(A)}{p(B)}. \tag{3.33}$$

In statistics, we aim to estimate a number of parameters, which from now on we call θ. We can think of these parameters as levers that we can pull to change the behaviour of a statistical model.

These parameters can be thought of as real (such as the proportion of individuals in a given population with a disease) or mere abstractions (such as the degrees of freedom of a Student-t distribution).

In Bayesian statistics, we update our beliefs about a parameter after we observe a sample of data. Being Bayesians, we represent these beliefs by a probability distribution, which we write as $p(\theta \mid data)$. If we associate A with θ and B with the data, we use expression (3.33) to write:

$$p(\theta \mid data) = \frac{p(data \mid \theta) \times p(\theta)}{p(data)}. \tag{3.34}$$

This is Bayes' rule as we use it for inference. But what exactly do the terms on the right-hand side of expression (3.34) mean? We devote Part II to answering this question.

3○8 CHAPTER SUMMARY

In Bayesian statistics, we describe uncertainty using probability distributions. In this chapter, we introduced the reader to two flavours of such objects: discrete and continuous probability distributions. For the discrete case, the values of the distribution function can be interpreted as probabilities since there are only a finite number of discrete values where these distributions are defined. However, for continuous probability distributions, the probability of any one value is zero because there are an infinite number of any such values. Instead, the value of a continuous probability distribution is interpreted as a density. To convert this to a probability, we multiply the density by a volume. Mathematically this amounts to integrating the probability density function with respect to the measure.

In this chapter, we also introduced marginal distributions. These are obtained by summing (for discrete variables) or integrating (for continuous variables) joint distributions. We also introduced conditional distributions. These are the probability distributions that represent our updated state of knowledge after observing part of a system. In Section 3.3.6 we described how to calculate these objects using the law of conditional probability. In Bayesian inference, we aim to obtain a conditional probability distribution – the posterior – which is the probability distribution that represents our uncertainty over parameter values after we observe a data sample.

In this chapter we introduced the concept of statistical independence: Two events are statistically independent if the knowledge that event A occurs does not affect our belief that B occurs. This is a key concept in statistical modelling since independence implies we can calculate the overall probability of a data set by simply multiplying together the probabilities for each of the individual data points. In Bayesian statistics, we make extensive use of this result to calculate our likelihood function in a range of different settings.

It is often difficult to justify a specific choice of probability model, particularly for complex systems. The central limit theorem sometimes provides such a justification. The central limit theorem states that, whatever process generates our data, the sample mean always behaves as if it is normally distributed for large enough sample sizes. This means that for all processes that can be considered as an average, we can use the normal distribution as our probability model.

If you do not feel fully confident with probability distributions, do not worry, since we will have ample opportunity to work with these mathematical objects in the next part of the book. There we discuss the various elements of the central formula of Bayesian inference: Bayes' rule.

 **CHAPTER OUTCOMES**

The reader should now be familiar with the following concepts:

- the conditions satisfied for valid probability distributions, for discrete and continuous random variables
- the difference between probability (mass) and probability density
- the mean of a distribution
- two-dimensional probability distributions
- marginal and conditional distributions
- statistical independence
- the central limit theorem
- the Bayesian formula

 **PROBLEM SETS**

Problem 3.1 Messy probability density

Suppose that a probability density is given by the following function:

$$f(X) = \begin{cases} 1, & \text{if } 0 \le X < 0.5, \\ 0.2, & \text{if } 0.5 \le X < 1, \\ 0.8(X-1), & \text{if } 1 \le X < 2, \\ 0, & \text{otherwise.} \end{cases} \tag{3.35}$$

Problem 3.1.1 Demonstrate that the above density is a valid probability distribution.

Problem 3.1.2 What is the probability that $0.2 \le X \le 0.5$?

Problem 3.1.3 Find the mean of the distribution.

Problem 3.1.4 What is the median of the distribution?

Problem 3.2 Keeping it discrete

Suppose that the number of heads obtained, X, in a series of N coin flips is described by a binomial distribution:

$$Pr(X = K \mid \theta) = \binom{N}{K} \theta^K (1-\theta)^{N-K}, \tag{3.36}$$

where $\binom{N}{K} = \frac{N!}{K!(N-K)!}$ is the binomial coefficient and θ is the probability of obtaining a heads on any particular throw.

Problem 3.2.1 Suppose that $\theta = 0.5$ (that is, the coin is fair). Calculate the probability of obtaining 5 heads in 10 throws.

Problem 3.2.2 Calculate the probability of obtaining fewer than 3 heads.

Problem 3.2.3 Find the mean of this distribution. (You can either derive the mean of this distribution or take it as given that $\mathbb{E}(X) = N\theta$.)

Problem 3.2.4 Suppose I flip another coin with $\theta = 0.2$. What is the probability that I get more than 8 heads?

Problem 3.2.5 What is the probability that I obtain fewer than 3 heads in 10 flips of the first coin, and more than 8 heads with the second?

Problem 3.3 Continuously confusing

Suppose that the time that elapses before a particular component on the Space Shuttle fails can be modelled as being exponentially distributed:

$$p(t \mid \lambda) = \lambda e^{-\lambda t}, \tag{3.37}$$

where $\lambda > 0$ is a rate parameter.

Problem 3.3.1 Show that the above distribution is a valid probability density.

Problem 3.3.2 Find the mean of this distribution.

Problem 3.3.3 Suppose that $\lambda = 0.2$ per hour. Find the probability that the component fails in the first hour of flight.

Problem 3.3.4 What is the probability that the component survives for the first hour but fails during the second?

Problem 3.3.5 What is the probability that the component fails during the second hour given that it has survived the first?

Problem 3.3.6 Show that the probability of the component failing during the $(n+1)$th hour given that it has survived n hours is always 0.18.

Problem 3.4 The boy or girl paradox

The boy or girl paradox was first introduced by Martin Gardner in 1959. Suppose we are told the following information:

Problem 3.4.1 Mr Bayes has two children. The older child is a girl. What is the probability that both children are girls?

Problem 3.4.2 Mr Laplace has two children. At least one of the children is a girl. What is the probability that both children are girls?

Problem 3.5 Planet Scrabble

On a far-away planet suppose that people's names are always two letters long, with each of these letters coming from the 26 letters of the Latin alphabet. Suppose that there are no constraints on individuals' names, so they can be composed of two identical letters, and there is no need to include a consonant or a vowel.

Problem 3.5.1 How many people would need to be gathered in one place for there to be a 50% probability that at least two of them share the same name?

Problem 3.5.2 Suppose instead that the names are composed of three letters. Now how many people would need to be gathered in one place for there to be a 50% probability that at least two of them share the same name?

Problem 3.6 Game theory

A game show presents contestants with four doors: behind one of the doors is a car worth $1000; behind another is a forfeit whereby the contestant must pay $1000 out of their winnings thus far on the show. Behind the other two doors there is nothing. The game is played as follows:

1   The contestant chooses one of four doors.
2   The game show host opens another door, always to reveal that there is nothing behind it.
3   The contestant is given the option of changing their choice to one of the two remaining unopened doors.
4   The contestant's final choice of door is opened, to their delight (a car!), dismay (a penalty), or indifference (nothing).

Assuming that:

•   the contestant wants to maximise their expected wealth, and
•   the contestant is risk-averse,

what is the optimal strategy for the contestant?

Problem 3.7 Blood doping in cyclists

Suppose, as a benign omniscient observer, we tally up the historical cases where professional cyclists either used or did not use blood doping, and either won or lost a particular race. This results in the probability distribution shown in Table P3.1.

Problem 3.7.1 What is the probability that a professional cyclist wins a race?

Problem 3.7.2 What is the probability that a cyclist wins a race, given that they have cheated?

Problem 3.7.3 What is the probability that a cyclist is cheating, given that they win?

Now suppose that drug testing officials have a test that can accurately identify a blood-doper 90% of the time. However, it incorrectly indicates a positive for clean athletes 5% of the time.

Problem 3.7.4 If the officials care only about the proportion of people correctly identified as dopers, should they test all the athletes or only the winners?

Table P3.1 The historical probabilities of behaviour and outcome for professional cyclists.

	Lost	Won
Clean	0.70	0.05
Doping	0.15	0.10

Problem 3.7.5 If the officials care five times as much about the number of people who are falsely identified as they do about the number of people who are correctly identified as dopers, should they test all the athletes or only the winners?

Problem 3.7.6 What factor would make the officials choose the other group? (By factor, we mean the number 5 in the previous problem.)

Problem 3.8 Breast cancer revisited

Suppose that the prevalence of breast cancer for a randomly chosen 40-year-old woman in the UK population is about 1%. Further suppose that mammography has a relatively high sensitivity to breast cancer, where in 90% of cases the test shows a positive result if the individual has the disease. However, the test also has a rate of false positives of 8%.

Problem 3.8.1 Show that the probability that a woman tests positive is about 9%.

Problem 3.8.2 A woman tests positive for breast cancer. What is the probability she has the disease?

Problem 3.8.3 Draw a graph of the probability of having a disease, given a positive test, as a function of (a) the test sensitivity (true positive rate) (b) the false positive rate, and (c) the disease prevalence. Draw graphs (a) and (b) for a rare (1% prevalence) and a common (10% prevalence) disease. What do these graphs imply about the relative importance of the various characteristics of medical tests?

Problem 3.8.4 Assume the result of a mammography is independent when retesting an individual (probably a terrible assumption!). How many tests (assume a positive result in each) would need to be undertaken to ensure that the individual has a 99% probability that they have cancer?

Problem 3.8.5 Now we make the more realistic assumption that the probability of testing positive in the nth trial depends on whether positive tests were achieved in the $(n-1)$th trials, for both individuals with cancer and those without. For a cancer status $\kappa \in \{C, NC\}$:

$$p(n+|(n-1)+,\kappa) = 1 - (1 - p(+|\kappa))e^{-(n-1)\epsilon}, \tag{3.38}$$

where $n+$ denotes testing positive in the nth trial, $p(+|\kappa)$ and $\epsilon \geq 0$ determine the persistence in test results. Assume that $p(+|C) = 0.9$ and $p(+|NC) = 0.08$. For $\epsilon = 0.15$ show that we now need at least 17 positive test results to conclude with 99% probability that a patient has cancer.

PART II

UNDERSTANDING THE BAYESIAN FORMULA

PART II MISSION STATEMENT

This part introduces the reader to the elements of the Bayesian inference formula: the likelihood, the prior, the denominator and the posterior.

PART II GOALS

In this book, we discuss how to model phenomena whose constituent processes we do not fully know, or understand. This uncertainty means that we include random variability as part of our models. This randomness means that these models are *probabilistic* in nature. The most important choice in such analyses is the specific probability model to use. In Bayesian inference, these probability models are called *likelihoods* because (somewhat confusingly) they do not behave as valid probability distributions in this context. In Chapter 4 we discuss this conceptual confusion. We also explain how to choose a likelihood for any circumstance.

In Bayesian inference, we describe uncertainty using probability distributions. Bayes' rule describes how to convert the likelihood – itself, not a valid probability distribution – into a posterior probability distribution. To carry out this conversion we must specify a probability distribution known as a *prior*, which we discuss in Chapter 5. This distribution is a measure of our pre-data beliefs about the parameters of the likelihood function. Priors are, without doubt, the most controversial part of Bayesian inference, although, as we argue in Chapter 5, this criticism is unwarranted.

The final part of the formula – the denominator – is fully determined by our choice of likelihood and prior. However, this predetermination does not mean it is simple to calculate, and we see in Chapter 6 that the difficulty in evaluating this term motivates the computational methods we introduce in Part IV.

The goal of Bayesian inference is to calculate the posterior probability distribution for the parameters which interest us. This distribution is the starting point for drawing conclusions and making decisions. It is thus important to understand why this part of Bayes' formula is so useful, and we devote Chapter 7 to this purpose.

4

Chapter contents

LIKELIHOODS

4⊙1 CHAPTER MISSION STATEMENT

At the end of this chapter, the reader will know how to choose a likelihood that is appropriate for a given situation. Further, the reader will understand how maximum likelihood estimation works:

$$p(\theta \mid data) = \frac{p(data \mid \theta) \times p(\theta)}{p(data)}. \tag{4.1}$$

4⊙2 CHAPTER GOALS

The first and most important choice in a Bayesian (or Frequentist) analysis is which probability model to use to describe a given process. Probability models are characterised by a set of parameters which, when varied, generate a range of different system behaviours. If the model choice is appropriate, we should be able to tune these parameters so that the model's behaviour mimics the behaviour of the real-world system that we are investigating. When we fix the parameter values and use our model to generate data, the resultant distribution of the data behaves as a valid probability distribution (see Section 3.3). However, in Bayesian inference, we wish to determine a posterior belief in each set of parameter values. This means that in Bayesian inference we instead hold the data constant, and vary the parameter values. Confusingly, in this context, our probability model no longer behaves as a valid probability distribution. In particular, the distribution no longer sums (for discrete distributions) or integrates (for continuous distributions) to 1. To acknowledge this distinction in Bayesian inference, we avoid using the term *probability distribution* in favour of *likelihood*. In this chapter, we devote considerable discussion to this distinction as it is crucial to Bayesian inference.

When starting out in statistical inference, it can seem bewildering to choose a likelihood function that is appropriate for a given situation. In this chapter, we use a number of case studies to explain how to choose a likelihood. This process should begin with the analyst listing the various assumptions about the data generating process. The analyst should then search through the list of probability distributions provided in Chapter 8 and select one (or a number) that satisfy these conditions. The model selection process does not stop here, however. After a model is fitted to the data it is important to check that the results are consistent with the actual data sample (see Chapter 10) and, if necessary, adjust the likelihood.

Frequentist inference also proceeds from a likelihood function. Instead of using Bayes' rule to convert this function into a valid probability distribution, Frequentists determine the parameter values that maximise the likelihood. Accordingly, these parameter estimates are known as *maximum likelihood* estimators and, because they maximise the likelihood, they are the values of model parameters that result in the greatest probability of achieving the observed data sample. Bayesian posterior distributions can be viewed as a weighted average of the likelihood and the prior. This means that it can be helpful to know where the maximum likelihood peak occurs to make sense of the shape of the posterior distribution. We devote the last part of this chapter to maximum likelihood inference.

4⊙3 WHAT IS A LIKELIHOOD?

In all statistical inference, we use an idealised model to approximate a real-world process that interests us. This model is then used to test hypotheses about the world. In Bayesian statistics, the evidence for a particular hypothesis is summarised in a posterior probability distribution. Bayes' magic rule explains how to compute this posterior probability distribution:

$$p(\theta \mid data) = \frac{p(data \mid \theta) \times p(\theta)}{p(data)}. \tag{4.2}$$

To understand this rule we first need to know what is meant by the numerator term, $p(data \mid \theta)$, which Bayesians call a *likelihood*.

What does this mean in simple, everyday language? Imagine that we flip a coin and record its outcome. The simplest model to represent this outcome ignores the angle the coin was thrown at, and its height above the surface, along with any other details. Because of our ignorance, our model cannot perfectly predict the behaviour of the coin. This uncertainty means that our model is *probabilistic* rather than *deterministic*. We might also suppose that the coin is fair, so the probability of the coin landing heads up is given by $\theta = \frac{1}{2}$. Furthermore, if the coin is thrown twice, we assume that the result of the first flip does not affect the result of the second. This means that the results of the first and second coin flips are *independent* (see Section 3.4).

We can use our model to calculate the probability of obtaining two heads in a row:

$$Pr(H,H \mid \theta, Model) = Pr(H \mid \theta, Model) \times Pr(H \mid \theta, Model)$$

$$= \theta \times \theta = \theta^2 \tag{4.3}$$

$$= \left(\frac{1}{2}\right)^2 = \frac{1}{4},$$

where *Model* represents the set of assumptions that we make in our analysis. In this book, we generally omit this term on the understanding that it is implicit. We can also calculate the corresponding probabilities for all possible outcomes for two coin flips. The most heads that can occur is 2, and the least is 0 (if both flips land tails up). Figure 4.1 displays the probabilities for each possible outcome. The most likely number of heads is 1 since this can occur in two different ways – either the first coin lands heads up and the second lands tails up, or vice versa – whereas the other possibilities

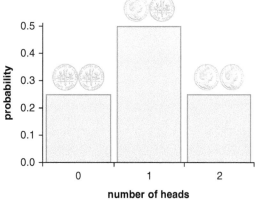

Figure 4.1 The probabilities of each outcome for a fair coin that is flipped twice.

(all heads or no heads) can occur in only one way. The discrete distribution shown in Figure 4.1 is a valid probability distribution (see Section 3.3.1) because:

- The individual event probabilities are all non-negative.
- The sum of the individual probabilities is 1.

When we assume a particular value of θ and vary the data (in this case the number of heads obtained), the collection of resultant probabilities forms a probability distribution. So why do Bayesians insist on calling $p(data|\theta)$ a *likelihood*, not a *probability*?

4●4　WHY USE *LIKELIHOOD* RATHER THAN PROBABILITY?

Why is a likelihood not a probability distribution?

When we hold the parameters of our model fixed, for example when we held the probability of a coin landing heads up at $\theta = \frac{1}{2}$, the resultant distribution of possible data samples is a valid probability distribution. So why do we call $p(data|\theta)$ in Bayes' rule a *likelihood*?

This is because in Bayesian inference we do not keep the parameters of our model fixed. In Bayesian analysis, the data are fixed and the parameters vary. In particular, Bayes' rule tells us how to calculate the posterior probability density for any value of θ. Consider flipping a coin whose inherent bias, θ, is unknown beforehand. In Bayesian inference, we use a sample of coin flip outcomes to estimate a posterior belief in any value of θ (perhaps ending up with something similar to Figure 4.2). To obtain $p(\theta|data)$ we must compute $p(data|\theta)$ in the numerator of Bayes' rule for each possible value of θ. Suppose that we flip our coin twice and obtain one head and one tail. We can use our model to calculate the probability of this data for any value of θ:

$$Pr(H,T|\theta) + Pr(T,H|\theta) = \theta(1-\theta) + \theta(1-\theta)$$

(4.4)

$$= 2\theta(1-\theta).$$

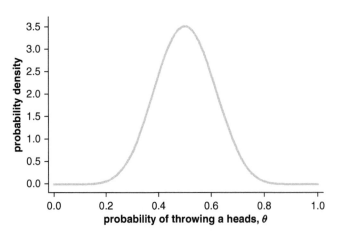

Figure 4.2 An example posterior distribution for the probability of obtaining heads in a coin flip.

This result yields the probability for a fixed data sample (one head and one tail) as a function of θ. We can graph the value of expression (4.4) as a function of this parameter. It might appear that Figure 4.3 is a continuous probability distribution, but looks can deceive. While all the values of the distribution are non-negative, if we calculate the area underneath the curve in Figure 4.3 we obtain:

$$\int_0^1 2\theta(1-\theta)\,\mathrm{d}\theta = \frac{1}{3},$$　(4.5)

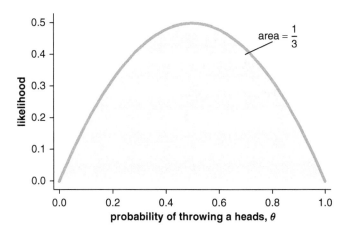

Figure 4.3 The likelihood function when we flip a coin twice and obtain a single heads. The area under this function is also indicated to illustrate that this is not a valid probability density.

which does not equal 1. Thus our distribution is not a valid probability distribution. Hence, when we vary θ, $p(data|\theta)$ is not a valid probability distribution. We thus introduce the term *likelihood* to describe $p(data|\theta)$ when we vary the parameter, θ. Often the following notation is used to emphasise that a likelihood is a function of the parameter θ with the data held fixed:

$$\mathcal{L}(\theta\,|\,data) = p(data\,|\,\theta). \tag{4.6}$$

The duality of meaning for likelihoods and probability distributions: the equivalence principle

We call the above the *equivalence relation* since a likelihood of θ for a particular data sample is equivalent to the probability of that data sample for that value of θ. In this book, we mainly use the right-hand notation as this is most typical in the literature, under the implicit assumption that this term is not a probability distribution in Bayesian statistics.

We now provide another example to underscore the difference between likelihoods and probabilities. Continuing with our coin flipping example, we can calculate the probability of all possible numbers of heads, X, from two coin flips:

$$Pr(X = 0\,|\,\theta) = Pr(T,T\,|\,\theta) = Pr(T\,|\,\theta) \times Pr(T\,|\,\theta) = (1-\theta)^2$$

$$Pr(X = 1\,|\,\theta) = Pr(H,T\,|\,\theta) + Pr(T,H\,|\,\theta) = 2 \times Pr(T\,|\,\theta) \times Pr(H\,|\,\theta) = 2\theta(1-\theta) \tag{4.7}$$

$$Pr(X = 2\,|\,\theta) = Pr(H,H\,|\,\theta) = Pr(H\,|\,\theta) \times Pr(H\,|\,\theta) = \theta^2.$$

Further, suppose (somewhat artificially) that the probability of obtaining heads on a particular throw is confined to one of six discrete values: $\theta \in \{0.0, 0.2, 0.4, 0.6, 0.8, 1.0\}$. Using this information we compute the various probabilities of each possible outcome, which are displayed in Table 4.1.

In tabular form, we can see the effect of varying the data (moving along each row) and contrast it with the effect of varying θ (moving down each column). If we hold the parameter fixed – regardless

Table 4.1 The probabilities/likelihoods for two coin flips, where the probability of heads (θ) is confined to the discrete values: {0.0, 0.2, 0.4, 0.6, 0.8, 1.0}. X is the number of heads we obtain in two throws of the coin.

Probability of coin landing heads up, θ	Number of heads, X			
	0	1	2	Total
0.0	1.00	0.00	0.00	1.00
0.2	0.64	0.32	0.04	1.00
0.4	0.36	0.48	0.16	1.00
0.6	0.16	0.48	0.36	1.00
0.8	0.04	0.32	0.64	1.00
1.0	0.00	0.00	1.00	1.00
Total	2.20	1.60	2.20	

of the value of θ – and vary the data by moving along each row, the values sum to 1, meaning that this is a valid probability distribution. By contrast, when we hold the number of heads fixed and vary the parameter θ, by moving down each column the values do not sum to 1. When θ varies we do not have a valid probability distribution, meriting the use of the term *likelihood*.

In Bayesian inference, we always vary the parameter and hold the data fixed (we only obtain one sample). Thus, from a Bayesian perspective, we use the term *likelihood* to remind us that $p(data \mid \theta)$ is not a probability distribution.

WHAT ARE MODELS AND WHY DO WE NEED THEM?

All models are wrong. They are idealised representations of reality that result from making assumptions which, if reasonable, may recapitulate some behaviours of a real system. In an article titled 'Why Model?', Joshua Epstein argues that in life we automatically build *implicit* mental models [11]. Before we go to bed at night, we set an alarm for the next morning on the basis of a model. We imagine an idealised – model – morning when it takes us 15 minutes to wake up after the alarm sounds, which we hope gives us enough time to prepare for the day ahead. Whenever we go to the doctor, they use an internalised biological model of the human body to advise on the best course of treatment for a particular ailment. Whenever we hear expert opinions on TV about the outcome of an upcoming election, the pundits use mental models of society to explain the results of current polls. As is the case with all models, some are better than others. Hopefully, the models a doctor uses to prescribe medicine are better than those used by TV pundits![1]

We inevitably use implicit models. Epstein argues, however, that there are many benefits to explicitly stating our models. These include:

- To predict.
- To explain.
- To guide data collection.
- To discover new questions.
- To bound outcomes to plausible ranges.
- To illuminate uncertainties.

---

[1]For a great discussion of the performance of TV pundits, read [21].

- To challenge the robustness of prevailing theory through perturbations.
- To reveal the apparently simple (complex) to be complex (simple).

There are, of course, other reasons to build models, but we think this list covers most cases. Whenever we build a model, whether it is statistical, biological or sociological, we should ask: What do we hope to gain by building this model, and how can we judge its success? Only when we have answers to these basic questions should we proceed to model building.

4●6 HOW TO CHOOSE AN APPROPRIATE LIKELIHOOD

Bayesians are acutely aware that their models are wrong. At best, these simple abstractions can explain some aspect of real behaviour; at worst, they can be very misleading. Before we use a model to make decisions in the real world, we require it to be able to explain key characteristics of the system's behaviour for the past and present. With this in mind we introduce the following framework for building a model:

1   Write down the real-life behaviour that the model should be capable of explaining.
2   Write down the assumptions that it is believed are reasonable to achieve step 1.
3   Search Chapter 8 for probability models that are based on these assumptions. If necessary, combine different models to produce a resultant model that encompasses all assumptions.
4   After fitting the model to data, test its ability to explain the behaviour identified in step 1. If unsuccessful, go back to step 2 and assess which of your assumptions are likely violated. Then choose a new, more general, probability model that encompasses these new assumptions.

To illustrate the above framework we now consider a few example scenarios.

4.6.1 Example: an individual's disease status

Suppose you work for the state as a healthcare analyst who wants to estimate the prevalence of a certain disease. Also, imagine (unrealistically) that we begin with a sample of only one person, for whom we have no prior information. Let the disease status of that individual be denoted by the binary random variable X, which equals:

$$X = \begin{cases} 0, & \text{No disease} \\ 1, & \text{Disease.} \end{cases} \tag{4.8}$$

The goal of our analysis is to estimate a probability, θ, that a randomly chosen individual has the disease. We now calculate the probability of each outcome for our sample of one individual:

$$Pr(X = 0 | \theta) = (1 - \theta)$$

$$Pr(X = 1 | \theta) = \theta. \tag{4.9}$$

Note the similarity between these probabilities and those from the coin flipping example in the previous section. One model can often be used in a multitude of different settings.

Example likelihood model: waiting times between epidemics

We want to write down a single rule which yields either of the expressions in (4.9), dependent on whether $X = 0$ or $X = 1$. This can be achieved by the following expression:

$$Pr(X = \alpha \mid \theta) = \theta^\alpha (1 - \theta)^{1-\alpha}, \tag{4.10}$$

where $\alpha \in \{0,1\}$ is the numeric value of the variable X. Expression (4.10) is known as a *Bernoulli* probability density.

Although this rule for calculating the probability of a particular disease status appears complex, it reduces to either of the expressions in (4.9) if the individual is disease-positive or -negative, respectively:

$$Pr(X = 0 \mid \theta) = \theta^0 (1 - \theta)^1 = (1 - \theta)$$

$$Pr(X = 1 \mid \theta) = \theta^1 (1 - \theta)^0 = \theta. \tag{4.11}$$

These two likelihood functions are graphed in the bottom-left panel of Figure 4.4. The top-left panel of Figure 4.4 shows that, for a fixed value of θ, the sum (in the figure, the vertical sum) of the two probabilities always equals 1, and so expression (4.10) is a valid discrete probability density. By contrast, when we hold the data X fixed and vary θ, the distribution is continuous, and the area under the curve is not 1 (bottom-right panel of Figure 4.4), meaning expression (4.10) is a likelihood.

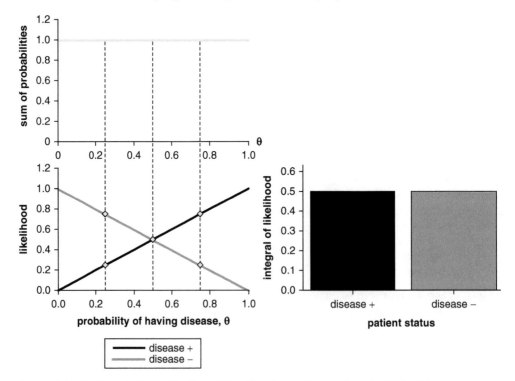

Figure 4.4 Bottom left: the likelihood function for a disease-free individual (red) or a disease-positive individual (black). Top left: holding θ fixed and summing the probabilities of each outcome equals 1. Bottom right: integrating the likelihood across $\theta \in [0,1]$, we obtain 0.5 in each case.

4.6.2 Example: disease prevalence of a group

Now imagine that instead of a solitary individual, we have a sample of N individuals, and want to develop a model that yields the probability of obtaining Z disease cases in this sample.

To choose a model, we must first make some simplifying assumptions. We assume that one individual's disease status does not influence the probability that another individual in the sample has the disease. This would not be reasonable if the disease were contagious, and if the individuals in the sample came from the same neighbourhood or household. This assumption is called statistical *independence* (see Section 3.4). We also assume that all individuals in our sample are from the same population. If we knew that some individuals came from different geographic regions, with heterogeneous prevalence rates, we might abandon this assumption. Combining these two assumptions, we say in statistical language that our data sample is composed of *independent* and *identically distributed* observations, or alternatively we say that we have a *random sample*.

With our two assumptions, we can formulate a model for the probability of obtaining Z disease-positive individuals in a total sample size of N. We first consider each person's disease status individually, meaning we can reuse expression (4.10). Then by assuming independence, we obtain the overall probability by multiplying together the individual probabilities. For $N = 2$, this means we obtain the probability that the first person has disease status X_1 *and* the second person has status X_2:

$$Pr(X_1 = \alpha_1, X_2 = \alpha_2 \mid \theta_1, \theta_2) = Pr(X_1 = \alpha_1 \mid \theta_1) \times Pr(X_2 = \alpha_2 \mid \theta_2)$$

$$= \theta_1^{\alpha_1}(1-\theta_1)^{1-\alpha_1} \times \theta_2^{\alpha_2}(1-\theta_2)^{1-\alpha_2},$$

(4.12)

where we have assumed that each individual has a different predisposition to having the disease denoted by θ_1 and θ_2, respectively. By assuming identically distributed observations, we can set $\theta_1 = \theta_2 = \theta$:

$$Pr(X_1 = \alpha_1, X_2 = \alpha_2 \mid \theta) = \theta^{\alpha_1}(1-\theta)^{1-\alpha_1} \times \theta^{\alpha_2}(1-\theta)^{1-\alpha_2} = \theta^{\alpha_1+\alpha_2}(1-\theta)^{2-\alpha_1-\alpha_2},$$ (4.13)

where we obtained the resulting line by using the exponent rule $a^b \times a^c = a^{b+c}$ for the components θ and $(1-\theta)$, respectively. For our sample of two individuals, we can now calculate the probability of obtaining Z cases of the disease. We first realise that:

$$Z = X_1 + X_2.$$ (4.14)

We then use expression (4.13) to generate the respective probabilities:

$$Pr(Z = 0 \mid \theta) = Pr(X_1 = 0, X_2 = 0 \mid \theta) = \theta^{0+0}(1-\theta)^{2-0-0} = (1-\theta)^2$$

$$Pr(Z = 1 \mid \theta) = Pr(X_1 = 1, X_2 = 0 \mid \theta) + Pr(X_1 = 0, X_2 = 1 \mid \theta) = 2\theta(1-\theta)$$ (4.15)

$$Pr(Z = 2 \mid \theta) = Pr(X_1 = 1, X_2 = 1 \mid \theta) = \theta^{1+1}(1-\theta)^{2-1-1} = \theta^2.$$

We want to determine a single rule for calculating the probability of any possible value of Z. To do this, we recognise that the above can be rewritten as:

$$Pr(Z = 0 \mid \theta) = \theta^0 (1 - \theta)^2$$

$$Pr(Z = 1 \mid \theta) = 2\theta^1 (1 - \theta)^1 \tag{4.16}$$

$$Pr(Z = 2 \mid \theta) = \theta^2 (1 - \theta)^0.$$

In all the above expressions we notice a common term $\theta^\beta (1 - \theta)^{2-\beta}$, where $\beta \in \{0,1,2\}$ represents the number of disease cases found. This suggests that we can write down a single rule of the form:

$$Pr(Z = \beta \mid \theta) \sim \theta^\beta (1 - \theta)^{2-\beta}. \tag{4.17}$$

The only problem with matching expression (4.17) to those expressions in (4.16) is the factor of 2 in the middle expression of (4.16). To resolve this issue we realise that when a quadratic is expanded we obtain:

$$(x + 1)^2 = x^2 + 2x + 1 \tag{4.18}$$

where the numbers $\{1,2,1\}$ are the coefficients of $\{x^2, x^1, x^0\}$, respectively. This sequence of numbers appears in early secondary school maths classes and is known as either the binomial expansion coefficients or simply ${}^nC_r$. The expansion coefficients are typically written in compact form:

$$\binom{2}{\beta} = \frac{2!}{(2 - \beta)! \beta!}, \tag{4.19}$$

where $!$ means factorial and $\beta \in \{0,1,2\}$. Using this notation we can write the probability distribution of disease count for our sample of two individuals:

$$Pr(Z = \beta \mid \theta) = \binom{2}{\beta} \theta^\beta (1 - \theta)^{2-\beta}. \tag{4.20}$$

This likelihood function is illustrated in Figure 4.5 for the three possible numbers of disease cases. We now extend the analysis to N individuals. First, suppose we have a sample size of 3. If we assume that the individuals are independent and identically distributed, then the four probabilities are:

$$Pr(Z = 0 \mid \theta) = Pr(X_1 = 0 \mid \theta)Pr(X_2 = 0 \mid \theta)Pr(X_3 = 0 \mid \theta)$$

$$Pr(Z = 1 \mid \theta) = 3Pr(X_1 = 1 \mid \theta)Pr(X_2 = 0 \mid \theta)Pr(X_3 = 0 \mid \theta)$$

$$\tag{4.21}$$

$$Pr(Z = 2 \mid \theta) = 3Pr(X_1 = 1 \mid \theta)Pr(X_2 = 1 \mid \theta)Pr(X_3 = 0 \mid \theta)$$

$$Pr(Z = 3 \mid \theta) = Pr(X_1 = 1 \mid \theta)Pr(X_2 = 1 \mid \theta)Pr(X_3 = 1 \mid \theta).$$

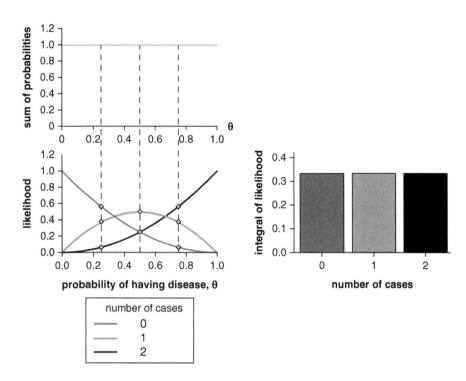

Figure 4.5 Bottom left: the likelihood function for each possible disease outcome for a sample of two individuals. Top left: when we hold θ constant and vary the data, the sum of probabilities equals 1. Bottom right: when we vary the parameter and hold the data constant, the result does not integrate to 1.

Again we recognise a pattern in the coefficients of each expression {1,3,3,1}, which corresponds exactly to the polynomial coefficients for the expansion of $(x+1)^3$. Hence we can write the likelihood using binomial expansion notation:

$$Pr(Z = \beta \mid \theta) = \binom{3}{\beta} \theta^\beta (1-\theta)^{3-\beta}. \tag{4.22}$$

We recognise a pattern in the likelihoods of expressions (4.20) and (4.22), meaning that for a sample size of N, the likelihood is given by:

$$Pr(Z = \beta \mid \theta) = \binom{N}{\beta} \theta^\beta (1-\theta)^{N-\beta}, \tag{4.23}$$

which is known as the *binomial* probability distribution.

If we had data we could test the model's assumptions by calculating the model-implied probability of this outcome. For example, suppose previous analyses estimate $\theta = 1\%$. Suppose also that we collect a sample of 100 individuals and find that 10 are disease-positive. We then calculate the probability of obtaining 10 or more disease cases using expression (4.23):

$$Pr(Z \geq 10 \mid \theta = 0.01) = \sum_{Z=10}^{100} \binom{100}{Z} 0.01^Z (1-0.01)^{100-Z} = 7.63 \times 10^{-8}, \qquad (4.24)$$

where we summed over all disease cases from 10 to 100, to obtain the probability of getting a result as bad as, or worse than, what we actually obtained. This is a Frequentist hypothesis test, which we will later avoid, but for now it seems a reasonable way of assessing our model.

The probability of generating our data using our model is extremely small. What does this tell us? There is something wrong with our model. It could be that the actual disease prevalence is much higher than the 1% we assumed. The assumption of independence could also be violated, for example if we sampled households rather than individuals. It is difficult to diagnose what is specifically wrong with our model without further information. However, it does suggest that we should adjust one or more of our assumptions and reformulate the model to take these into account. We must never simply accept that a model is correct. A model is only as good as its ability to recapitulate real-life data, which is lacking in this case.

4.6.3 Example: intelligence test scores for a group of people

Suppose that we are modelling the intelligence test scores for a group of individuals, where test score is measured on a continuous scale from 0 to 200. We have no information on individual characteristics to help predict individual scores. There are many factors that affect an individual's performance on this test, such as their schooling, parental education, 'innate' ability, and so on. If we assume that an individual's score is a sort of average of all these factors, then the central limit theorem might apply (see Section 3.5) and we can use a normal distribution to model the test score of an individual, X:

$$p(X = \alpha \mid \mu, \sigma) = \frac{1}{\sqrt{2\pi\sigma^2}} e^{-\frac{(\alpha-\mu)^2}{2\sigma^2}}, \qquad (4.25)$$

where μ and σ are the population mean and standard deviation, respectively. Since this distribution is continuous, we write p rather than Pr, to indicate it is a probability density (see Section 3.3.2).

Now consider a sample of N individuals. If we assume that one individual's test score does not help to predict another's, then our data are independent. If we also assume that all individuals are drawn from the same population, we have a random sample (see Section 4.7). We can then calculate the joint probability density for a sample of N individuals by taking the product of the individual densities:

$$p(X_1 = \alpha_1, X_2 = \alpha_2, ..., X_N = \alpha_N \mid \mu, \sigma) = \prod_{i=1}^{N} \frac{1}{\sqrt{2\pi\sigma^2}} e^{-\frac{(\alpha_i-\mu)^2}{2\sigma^2}}, \qquad (4.26)$$

which we could then use to calculate a probability of obtaining a sample as extreme as ours if we were so inclined. However, we leave further discussion of this model until Section 4.8.

4●7   EXCHANGEABILITY VERSUS RANDOM SAMPLING

We introduced the concept of a random sample to develop a probability model for the disease status of patients (Section 4.6.2) and the intelligence of a group of people (Section 4.6.3). This term is just a shorthand for an independent and identically distributed sample of data. Often, however, Bayesians assume a (slightly) weaker condition that still means the overall likelihood is the product of individual likelihoods in many situations.

Suppose that we have a sequence of random variables representing the height of three individuals: $\{H_1, H_2, H_3\}$. If this sequence is equally as likely as the reordered sequence, $\{H_2, H_1, H_3\}$, or any other possible reordering, then the sequence of random variables is said to be *exchangeable*.

The assumption of random sampling is stronger than that of exchangeability, meaning that any random sample is automatically exchangeable. However, the converse is not necessarily true. An example of this is drawing balls without replacement from an urn containing three red and three blue balls. The probability of obtaining the sequence *RBR* is given by:

$$Pr(RBR) = \frac{3}{6} \times \frac{3}{5} \times \frac{2}{4} = \frac{3}{20}. \tag{4.27}$$

The sequence of random variables representing the outcome of this sampling is exchangeable since any permutation of this sequence is equally likely:

$$Pr(BRR) = \frac{3}{6} \times \frac{3}{5} \times \frac{2}{4} = \frac{3}{20}$$

$$Pr(RRB) = \frac{3}{6} \times \frac{2}{5} \times \frac{3}{4} = \frac{3}{20}. \tag{4.28}$$

However, this sequence of random variables is not a random sample. The probability distribution for the first ball drawn is different to that for the second. For the first draw, there are six balls in total, with equal numbers of each. However, for the second draw there are only five balls, and, dependent on the first draw, there may be either more red balls or blue balls remaining.

Sometimes we cannot assume to have a random sample of observations for similar reasons to the urn example. However, a brilliant theory originally developed by Bruno de Finetti means a sample behaves as a random sample so long as it is exchangeable. Technically, this requires an infinite sample of observations, but for a reasonably large sample, this approximation is reasonable. Often we do have a random sample and so need not worry about any of this. However, due to this theorem, we can still write down an overall likelihood as the product of individual likelihoods, so long as the observations are exchangeable.

Maximum
likelihood
estimation:
another
example

4○8   MAXIMUM LIKELIHOOD: A SHORT INTRODUCTION

In Section 4.6 we assumed we knew the prevalence of disease, θ, in the population. In reality, we rarely know such a thing. Indeed, it is often the main focus of statistical modelling to estimate such parameters. The Frequentist approach to estimation is known as the method of *maximum likelihood*, which we introduce in this section.

The principle of maximum likelihood estimation is simple. First, we assume a likelihood using the logic described earlier in this chapter. We then calculate the parameter values that *maximise* the likelihood of obtaining our data sample. We now use some examples to illustrate this process.

4.8.1 Estimating disease prevalence

Consider our disease prevalence example again. Suppose in a random sample of 100 individuals, 10 are disease-positive, meaning the overall likelihood is given by:

$$\mathcal{L}(\theta \mid X = 10, N = 100) = \binom{100}{10} \theta^{10}(1-\theta)^{90}. \tag{4.29}$$

Remember that since we vary θ and hold the data constant, expression (4.29) is a *likelihood,* not a probability. We then calculate the value of θ which maximises the likelihood. To maximise a function, we need to find the point at which its gradient is 0 – in other words, where the function stops either increasing or decreasing. The correct way to do this is by differentiation.

We could differentiate expression (4.29) and set the derivative equal to 0, and rearrange the resultant equation for θ. However, it is simpler to first take the *log* of this expression, before we differentiate it. We can do this because the properties of the log transformation ensure that the function is maximised at the same value of θ (see Figure 4.6):

$$l(\theta \mid X = 10, N = 100) = \log\left(\mathcal{L}(\theta \mid X = 10, N = 100)\right) = \log\binom{100}{10} + 10 \log(\theta) + 90 \log(1-\theta), \tag{4.30}$$

where $l(\theta \mid data)$ is the *log-likelihood*. We obtained expression (4.30) by using the log rules:

$$\log(ab) = \log(a) + \log(b)$$
$$\log(a^b) = b \log(a). \tag{4.31}$$

We now differentiate the log-likelihood and set the derivative to zero:

$$\frac{\partial l}{\partial \theta} = \frac{10}{\hat{\theta}} - \frac{90}{1-\hat{\theta}} = 0 \tag{4.32}$$

and obtain the maximum likelihood *estimate,* $\hat{\theta} = 1/10$ (see Figure 4.7).

This estimator makes sense intuitively. The value of the parameter which maximises the likelihood of obtaining our data sample occurs when the population disease prevalence exactly matches the diseased proportion in our sample. In general, if we observe a number β of disease-positive individuals in a sample size of N, then the maximum likelihood estimator equals the diseased proportion in our sample:

$$\hat{\theta} = \frac{\beta}{N}. \qquad (4.33)$$

4.8.2 Estimating the mean and variance in intelligence scores

This example describes to the reader how maximum likelihood estimation works with continuous data. Suppose that we collect a random sample of two individuals with test scores {75,71} and model the scores using a normal likelihood, $\mathcal{L}$:

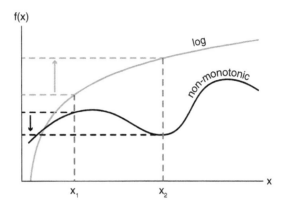

Figure 4.6 The log function versus an unspecified non-monotonic function. The log function is monotonically increasing, meaning that as x increases, the function value always increases. For the other function, increases in x do not necessarily cause increases in the function value; it is non-monotonically increasing. The monotonicity of the log-likelihood means that the function will be maximised at the same input value as the original likelihood.

$$\mathcal{L}(\mu,\sigma \mid X_1 = 75, X_2 = 71) = \frac{1}{\sqrt{2\pi\sigma^2}} e^{-\frac{(75-\mu)^2}{2\sigma^2}} \times \frac{1}{\sqrt{2\pi\sigma^2}} e^{-\frac{(71-\mu)^2}{2\sigma^2}}. \qquad (4.34)$$

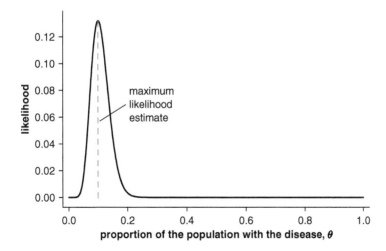

Figure 4.7 The likelihood function described in Section 4.8.1 as a function of disease prevalence, θ, when we obtain 10 disease-positive individuals out of a sample of 100 people. The dashed line indicates the maximum likelihood estimate $\hat{\theta} = 1/10$.

We then take the log of this expression (see Section 4.8.1):

$$l(\mu,\sigma \mid X_1 = 75, X_2 = 71) = 2 \log\left(\frac{1}{\sqrt{2\pi\sigma^2}}\right) - \frac{(75-\mu)^2}{2\sigma^2} - \frac{(71-\mu)^2}{2\sigma^2}. \tag{4.35}$$

We now differentiate expression (4.35) with respect to both variables, holding the other constant, setting each derivative equal to 0:

$$\frac{\partial l}{\partial \mu} = \frac{(75-\hat{\mu})}{\hat{\sigma}^2} + \frac{(71-\hat{\mu})}{\hat{\sigma}^2} = 0$$

$$\frac{\partial l}{\partial \sigma^2} = -\frac{1}{\hat{\sigma}^2} + \frac{(75-\hat{\mu})^2 + (71-\hat{\mu})^2}{2\hat{\sigma}^4} = 0. \tag{4.36}$$

The solution of the top equation in (4.36) is $\hat{\mu} = (71+75)/2 = 73$, which if substituted into the bottom, yields:

$$\hat{\sigma}^2 = \frac{1}{2}\left[(75-73)^2 + (71-73)^2\right] = 4. \tag{4.37}$$

Technically we should check that our parameter estimates do not correspond to a minimum (since this would also have a zero gradient). To do this we could graph the likelihood or check that the second derivative is negative. Notice that the maximum likelihood estimators of the population mean and variance are here the *sample mean* and *sample variance* (actually a slightly biased estimate of the sample variance). This holds for a sample of N individuals where the maximum likelihood estimators are:

$$\hat{\mu} = \frac{1}{N}\sum_{i=1}^{N} X_i = \bar{X}$$

$$\hat{\sigma}^2 = \frac{1}{N}\sum_{i=1}^{N}(X_i - \bar{X})^2 = s^2. \tag{4.38}$$

4.8.3 Maximum likelihood in simple steps

In the above examples, we followed the same procedure each time to obtain maximum likelihood estimates of parameters. These steps were:

1   Find the density of a single data point.
2   Calculate the joint probability density of all data points, by multiplying the likelihood from the individual data points together (if the data are independent).
3   Take the log of the joint density to produce the log-likelihood function.
4   Maximise the log-likelihood by differentiation.

4.8.4 Inference in maximum likelihood

We now know how to calculate point estimates of parameters using the method of maximum likelihood. However, at the moment we are unable to make any conclusions about the population.

This is because we do not know whether our estimated value is due to picking a weird sample or because it is close to the true value. Frequentists tackle this issue by examining the likelihood function near the maximum likelihood point estimate. If the likelihood is strongly peaked near the maximum likelihood estimate (see the black line in Figure 4.8), then this suggests that only a small range of parameters could generate a similar likelihood. In this case, we are fairly confident in our estimates. By contrast, if the likelihood is gently peaked near the maximum likelihood estimate (see the red line in Figure 4.8), then a large range of parameter values could yield similar values for the likelihood. We are now less confident in our estimates. We measure the peakedness in the likelihood by calculating the magni-

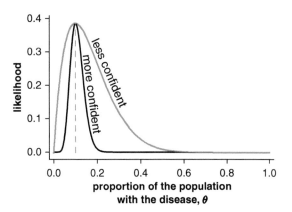

Figure 4.8   Two likelihood functions resulting in the same maximum likelihood estimates of parameters (dashed line). The likelihood shown by the solid black line is more strongly peaked than the one shown by the solid red line, meaning that we are more confident in the estimate.

tude of its second derivative at the maximum likelihood estimates. This is because the first derivative represents the gradient, whereas the second derivative represents the rate of change of the gradient – a measure of curvature. The more curved the likelihood, the more confident we are in our estimates and any conclusions drawn from them. Note, however, that the Frequentist inference is not based on valid probability distributions, since we infer based on likelihoods. This contrasts with Bayesian inference that relies on probability distributions.

4○9   CHAPTER SUMMARY

We often have information for only a few of the factors that influence the outcome of a process. Because of this informational incompleteness, we cannot build deterministic models of a situation and, instead, use probabilistic models. These probabilistic models are at the centre of Bayesian inference, and enter Bayes' formula as the likelihood.

In this chapter, we explained the distinction between likelihoods and probability distributions. When we hold the model parameters fixed and vary the data, the object describes a valid probability distribution. By contrast, in Bayes' rule (and maximum likelihood estimation) we vary the parameters and hold the data fixed. In this circumstance, the object does not behave as a valid probability distribution, and hence we call it a *likelihood*.

To choose a likelihood for a given situation, we start by writing down assumptions about the data-generating process. Some of these are fairly objective: for example, the outcome is either discrete or continuous. Others are more contentious: for example, assuming that the data are statistically independent. We then search for a probability model that satisfies these assumptions.

Any likelihood function has parameters. By changing these parameters we change the behaviour of the data-generating process. In maximum likelihood estimation, we find the value for the parameters that maximises the likelihood of obtaining our observed data sample. In Frequentist inference, we determine the uncertainty in our estimates by examining the curvature of the likelihood near the maximum likelihood estimates. We recognise, however, that this situation is not ideal because we make inferences based on a likelihood, that is by definition, not a valid probability distribution. Bayes' rule tells us how we can convert a likelihood – itself, not a valid probability distribution – to a posterior probability distribution for parameters. To do this, though, we must specify a prior distribution. In Chapter 5 we discuss the meaning of these distributions, and how to choose one in practice.

4.10 CHAPTER OUTCOMES

The reader should now be familiar with the following concepts:

- the difference between likelihoods and probability distributions
- how to choose a likelihood for a given situation
- maximum likelihood estimation and how to carry out inference in this framework

4.11 PROBLEM SETS

Problem 4.1 Blog blues

Suppose that visits to your newly launched blog occur sporadically. Imagine you are interested in the length of time between consecutive first-time visits to your homepage. You collect the time data for a random sample of 50 visits to your blog for a particular time period and day, and you decide to build a statistical model to fit the data.

Problem 4.1.1 What assumptions might you make about the first-time visits?

Problem 4.1.2 What might be an appropriate probability model for the time between visits?

Problem 4.1.3 Using your chosen probability distribution from the previous part, algebraically derive the maximum likelihood estimate (MLE) of the mean.

Problem 4.1.4 You collect data from Google Analytics that contains the time (in minutes) between each visit for a sample of 50 randomly chosen visits to your blog. The data set is called `likelihood_blogVisits.csv`. Derive an estimate for the mean number of visits per minute.

Problem 4.1.5 Graph the log-likelihood near the MLE. Why do we not plot the likelihood?

Problem 4.1.6 Estimate 95% confidence intervals around your estimate of the mean visit rate.

Problem 4.1.7 What does this interval mean?

Problem 4.1.8 Using your maximum likelihood estimate, what is the probability you will wait:

(a) 1 minute or more,
(b) 5 minutes or more,
(c) half an hour or more

before your next visit?

Problem 4.1.9 Evaluate your model.

Problem 4.1.10 Can you think of a better model to use? What assumptions are relaxed in this model?

Problem 4.1.11 Estimate the parameters of your new model, and hence estimate the mean number of website visits per minute.

Problem 4.1.12 Use your new model to estimate the probability that you will wait:

(a) 1 minute or more,
(b) 5 minutes or more,
(c) half an hour or more

before your next visit.

Problem 4.2 Violent crime counts in New York counties

In data file `likelihood_NewYorkCrimeUnemployment.csv` is a data set of the population, violent crime count and unemployment across New York counties in 2014 (openly available from the New York Criminal Justice website).

Problem 4.2.1 Graph the violent crime count against population size across all the counties. What type of relationship does this suggest?

Problem 4.2.2 A simple model here might be to assume that the crime count in a particular county is related to the population size by a Poisson model:

$$crime_i \sim Poisson(n_i\theta), \qquad\qquad (4.39)$$

where $crime_i$ and n_i are the crime count and population in county i. Write down an expression for the likelihood.

Problem 4.2.3 Find the maximum likelihood estimators of the parameters.

Problem 4.2.4 By generating fake data, assess this model.

Problem 4.2.5 What are the assumptions of this model? And do you think that these hold in this case?

Problem 4.2.6 Suggest an alternative model and estimate its parameters by maximum likelihood.

Problem 4.2.7 Evaluate this new model.

5

Chapter contents

PRIORS

CHAPTER MISSION STATEMENT

At the end of this chapter, the reader will know what is meant by a prior and the different philosophies that are used to understand and construct them:

$$p(\theta \mid data) = \frac{p(data \mid \theta) \times p(\theta)}{p(data)}.$$

(5.1)

 CHAPTER GOALS

Bayes' rule tells us how to convert a likelihood – itself, not a valid probability distribution – into a posterior probability distribution for parameters, which can be used for inference. The numerator of Bayes' rule tells us we must multiply the likelihood by a weighting of each parameter value, which is known as the *prior*. Priors are, without doubt, the most controversial aspect of Bayesian statistics, with opponents criticising their inherent subjectivity. In this chapter, we hope to convince the reader that not only is subjectivity inherent in all statistical models – both Frequentist and Bayesian – but the explicit subjectivity of priors is more transparent than the implicit subjectivity abound elsewhere.

This chapter will also explain the differing interpretations which are ascribed to priors. The reader will come to understand the different approaches to constructing prior distributions and how they can be chosen to be weakly informative or otherwise to contain informative pre-experimental insights from data or opinion.

Finally, we use a few examples to illustrate how changes to the prior affect the shape of the posterior. However, the reader will appreciate that if significant data are available, then the conclusions drawn are typically insensitive to the initial choice of prior.

Inevitably, this chapter is slightly more philosophical and abstract than other parts of this book, but we hope that the examples given are sufficiently concrete to ensure its practical use.

 WHAT ARE PRIORS AND WHAT DO THEY REPRESENT?

Chapter 4 introduced the concept of a likelihood and how this can be used to derive Frequentist estimates of parameters using the method of maximum likelihood. This presupposes that the parameters in question are immutable, fixed quantities that actually exist and can be estimated by methods that can be repeated, or imagined to be repeated, many times (see Section 2.7). As Gill (2007) indicates, this is unrealistic for the vast majority of social science research [17].

It is simply not possible to rerun elections, repeat surveys under exactly the same conditions, replay the stock market with exactly matching market forces or re-expose clinical subjects to identical stimuli. Furthermore, since parameters only exist because we have invented a model, we should be suspicious of any analysis which assumes they have a single 'true' value.

For Bayesians, the data are treated as fixed and the parameters vary. We know that the likelihood – however useful – is not a valid probability distribution. Bayes' rule tells us that to calculate the posterior probability distribution we must combine a likelihood with a prior probability distribution over parameter values. But what does it actually mean for a parameter to have a probability distribution?

Gelman et al. (2013) suggest that there are two different interpretations of parameter probability distributions: the subjective *state of knowledge* interpretation, where we use a probability distribution to represent our uncertainty over a parameter's true value; and the more objective *population* interpretation, where the parameter's value varies between different samples we take from a population distribution [14]. In both viewpoints, the model parameters are not viewed as static, unwavering constants as in Frequentist theory (see Section 2.7).

If we adopt the state of knowledge viewpoint, the prior probability distribution represents our pre-data uncertainty for a parameter's true value. For example, imagine that a doctor gives their probability that an individual has a particular disease before the results of a blood test become available. Using their knowledge of the patient's history, and their expertise on the particular condition, they assign a prior disease probability of 75% (see the left-hand panel of Figure 5.1). Alternatively, imagine we want to estimate the proportion of the UK population that has this disease. Based on previous analyses we probably have an idea of the underlying prevalence, and uncertainty in this value. In this case, the prior is continuous and represents our beliefs for the prevalence (see the right-hand panel of Figure 5.1).

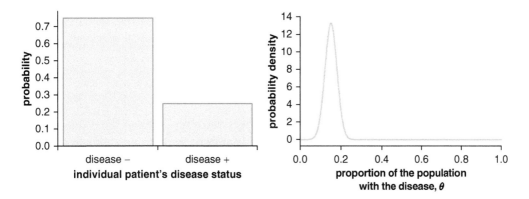

Figure 5.1   Left: a prior representing a doctor's probability that they ascribe to an individual having a given disease. Right: a prior representing our uncertainty in disease prevalence in a population.

Adopting the population perspective, we imagine the value of a parameter is drawn from a population distribution, which is represented by our prior. Imagine the process of flipping a coin. If we knew the angle at which it is tossed, the height from which it is thrown above the surface and other relevant physical properties, we could exactly determine the side on which the coin would fall. We could then hypothetically enumerate the (infinitely) many angles and heights of the coin throw, and for each set determine whether the coin will land heads up or down. Each time we throw the coin, we implicitly choose an angle and height from the set of all possible combinations, which exactly determines the outcome of the toss. Some ranges of the angle and the height will be chosen more frequently than others, although the coin will likely land 'heads up' roughly half the time. However, we regard this choice of angle and height as a realisation from a population distribution of all possible sets.

For the disease prevalence example, we imagine the observed data sample is partly determined by the characteristics of the subpopulations from which the individuals were drawn. The other variability is sampling variation within those subpopulations. Here we can view the individual subpopulation characteristics as drawn from an overall population distribution of parameters, representing the entirety of the UK.

The prior is always a valid probability distribution and can be used to calculate prior expectations of a parameter's value. For example, we could use the prior probability distribution in the right-hand panel of Figure 5.1 for the proportion of diseased individuals and would estimate a pre-experimental mean of approximately 15% prevalence.

5.3.1 Why do we need priors at all?

A question we might ask is: Why do we need priors at all? Can't we simply let the data speak for itself, without the need for these subjective beasts?

Bayes' rule is really only a way to update our initial beliefs in light of data:

$$\text{initial belief} \xrightarrow{\text{Bayes' rule + data}} \text{new beliefs.} \tag{5.2}$$

Viewed in this light, it is clear that we must specify an initial belief, otherwise we have nothing to update! Unfortunately, Bayes does not tell us how to formulate this initial belief, but fear not, in this chapter we describe the process of prior determination.

5.3.2 Why don't we normalise the likelihood by assuming a unity prior?

Another question that can be asked is: Why can't we simply let the prior weighting be constant across all values of θ? In other words, set $p(\theta) = 1$ in the numerator of Bayes' rule, resulting in a posterior that takes the form of a normalised likelihood:

$$p(\theta \,|\, data) = \frac{p(data \,|\, \theta)}{p(data)}. \tag{5.3}$$

This would surely mean we can avoid choosing a prior and, hence, thwart attempts to denounce Bayesian statistics as more subjective than Frequentist approaches. So why do we not do just that?

There is a pedantic, mathematical, argument against this, which is that $p(\theta)$ must be a valid probability distribution to ensure that the posterior is similarly valid. If our parameter is unbounded and we choose $p(\theta) = 1$ (or in fact any positive constant), then the integral (for a continuous parameter) is $\int_{-\infty}^{+\infty} p(\theta)d\theta = \infty$, and so $p(\theta)$ is not a valid probability distribution. Even if the prior is not a valid probability distribution, the resultant posterior can sometimes satisfy the properties of one. However, take care using these distributions for inference, as they are not technically probability distributions, because Bayes' rule requires us to use a valid prior distribution. Here the posteriors should be viewed, at best, as limiting cases when the parameter values of the prior distribution tend to ±∞.

Example of how an improper prior leads to an improper posterior

Another perhaps more persuasive argument is that assuming all parameter values are equally probable can result in nonsensical resultant conclusions being drawn. As an example, suppose we want to determine whether a coin is fair, with an equal chance of both heads and tails occurring, or biased, with a very strong weighting towards heads. If the coin is fair, $\theta = 1$, and if it is biased, $\theta = 0$. Imagine that coin is flipped twice, with the result $\{H,H\}$.

Figure 5.2 illustrates how assuming a uniform prior results in a strong posterior weighting towards the coin being biased. This is because, if we assume that the coin is biased, then the probability of obtaining 2 heads is high. Whereas, if we assume that the coin is fair, then the probability of obtaining this result is only $\frac{1}{4}$. The maximum likelihood estimate (which coincides with the posterior mode due to the flat prior) is hence that the coin is biased. By ignoring common sense – that the majority of coins are likely unbiased – we obtain an unreasonable result.

Of course, we hope that by collecting more data, in this case throws of the coin, we would be more confident in the conclusions drawn from the likelihood. However, Bayesian analysis allows us to achieve such a goal with a smaller sample size, by including other relevant information.

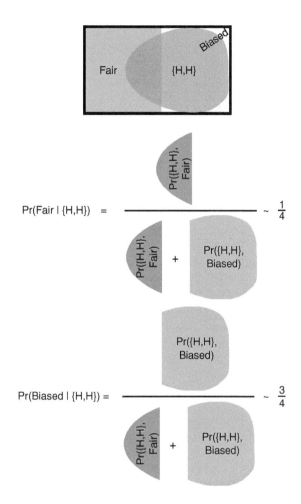

Figure 5.2   The top box illustrates the outcome of the coin toss along with its possible causes according to our prior beliefs: with probability 1/2 the coin is fair, and with probability 1/2 the coin is biased. Using Bayes' rule, we assign a high posterior probability to the coin being biased.

5 ⊙ 4   THE EXPLICIT SUBJECTIVITY OF PRIORS

Opponents of Bayesian approaches to inference criticise the subjectivity involved in choosing a prior. However, all analysis involves a degree of subjectivity, particularly the choice of a statistical model. This choice is often viewed as objective, with little justification for the underlying assumptions necessary to arrive there. The choice of prior is at least explicit, leaving this aspect of Bayesian modelling subject to the same academic examination to which any analysis should be subjected. A word that is sometimes used by protagonists of Bayesian methods is that the approach is more *honest* due to the explicit statement of assumptions. The statement of pre-experimental biases actually forces the analyst to self-examine and perhaps also reduces the temptation to manipulate the analysis to serve one's own ends.

5●5   COMBINING A PRIOR AND LIKELIHOOD TO FORM A POSTERIOR

Thus far this chapter has given more attention to the philosophical and theoretical underpinnings of Bayesian analysis. Now we illustrate the mechanics behind Bayes' formula, specifically how changes to the prior affect the posterior distribution. The following examples introduce an illustrative method, known as *Bayes' box* (described in detail in [35] and [6]), which provides intuition about Bayes' rule that is important for applied work.

5.5.1 The fish game

Imagine a bowl of water covered with a cloth, containing five fish, each of which is either red or white. We want to estimate the total number of red fish in the bowl after we pick out a single fish, and find it to be red. Before we pulled the fish out from the bowl, we had no strong belief in there being a particular number of red fish and so suppose that all possibilities (0 to 5) are equally likely, and hence have the probability of $\frac{1}{6}$ in our discrete prior. Our model for the likelihood of Y red fish is simple: it is based on the assumption that that all fish are equally likely to be picked (irrespective of colour). Further, suppose that the random variable $X \in \{0,1\}$ indicates whether the sampled fish is white or red. The analogy with the disease status of an individual described in Section 4.6.1 is evident, hence we choose a Bernoulli likelihood:

$$Pr(X = 1 | Y = \alpha) = \frac{\alpha}{5}, \tag{5.4}$$

where $\alpha \in \{0,1,2,3,4,5\}$ represents the possible numbers of red fish in the bowl, and $X = 1$ indicates that the single fish we sampled is red.

We illustrate the mechanics of Bayes' rule using the Bayes' box shown in Table 5.1. We start by listing the possible numbers of red fish in the bowl in the leftmost column. In the second column, we then specify our prior probabilities for each of these numbers of red fish. In the third column, we calculate the likelihoods for each of these outcomes using expression (5.4). In the fourth column, we then multiply the prior by the likelihood (the numerator of Bayes' rule), which when summed yields $Pr(X = 1) = \frac{1}{2}$; the denominator of Bayes' rule that normalises the numerator to yield the posterior distribution is shown in the fifth column. For a mathematical description of this process, see Section 5.10.1.

The Bayes' box illustrates the straightforward mechanism of Bayes' rule for the case of discrete data. We also note that when we sum the likelihood over all possible numbers of red fish in the bowl – in this case, our parameter – this equals 3, demonstrating again that a likelihood is not a valid probability distribution. We also see that at a particular parameter value, if either the prior or the likelihood is 0, as for the case of zero red fish being in the bowl (impossible since we sampled a red fish), then this ensures that the posterior distribution is 0 at this point. The posterior is also displayed graphically in Figure 5.3. To explain its shape we resort to Bayes' rule:

$$p(\theta | data) = \frac{p(data | \theta) \times p(\theta)}{p(data)}$$

$$\propto \underbrace{p(data | \theta)}_{\text{likelihood}} \times \underbrace{p(\theta)}_{\text{prior}}, \tag{5.5}$$

where we obtained the second line because the denominator contains no θ dependence (see Chapter 6). Viewed in this light, the posterior is a sort of weighted (geometric) average of the likelihood and the prior. Because, in the above example, we specify a uniform prior, the posterior's shape is entirely determined by the likelihood.

Table 5.1 A Bayes' box showing how to calculate the posterior distribution for the fish bowl example. Here we assume that, before drawing a single red fish out of the bowl, all possible numbers of red fish are equally likely (by adopting a uniform prior).

Number of red fish	Prior	Likelihood	Prior × Likelihood	Posterior $= \dfrac{Prior \times Likelihood}{p(data)}$
0	1/6	0	0	0
1	1/6	1/5	1/30	1/15
2	1/6	2/5	1/15	2/15
3	1/6	3/5	1/10	3/15
4	1/6	4/5	2/15	4/15
5	1/6	1	1/6	5/15
Total	**1**	**3**	*Pr(1 red fish) = 1/2*	**1**

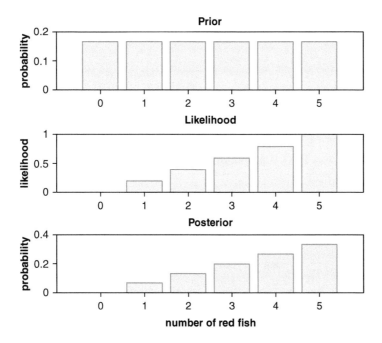

Figure 5.3 The prior, likelihood and posterior distributions for the fish example. The prior in the top panel gives uniform weighting to all possible numbers of red fish. This is then multiplied by the likelihood (in the middle panel) which, when normalised, yields the posterior distribution shown in the bottom panel.

Table 5.2 A Bayes' box showing how to calculate the posterior distribution for the fish bowl example. Here we use a prior with more weight towards moderate numbers of red fish.

Number of red fish	Prior	Likelihood	Prior × Likelihood	Posterior $= \dfrac{Prior \times Likelihood}{p(data)}$
0	1/12	0	0	0
1	1/6	1/5	1/30	1/15
2	1/4	2/5	1/10	1/5
3	1/4	3/5	3/20	3/10
4	1/6	4/5	2/15	4/15
5	1/12	1	1/12	1/6
Total	1	3	Pr(1 red fish) = 1/2	1

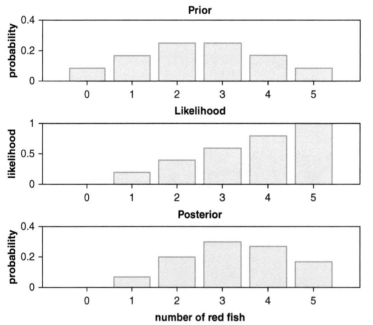

Imagine that we believe that the game-maker likes fish of all colours, and tends to include comparable numbers of both fish, so we modify our prior accordingly (see Table 5.2 and Figure 5.4). Again, because the posterior is essentially a weighted average of the likelihood and prior, this new prior results in a posterior that is less extreme, with a stronger posterior weighting towards more moderate numbers of red fish in the bowl.

5.5.2 Disease proportions revisited

Suppose that we substitute our fish bowl from Section 5.5.1 for a

Figure 5.4 The prior, likelihood and posterior distributions for the fish example. The prior in the top panel gives a higher weighting to more comparable numbers of red and white fish. This is then multiplied by the likelihood (in the middle panel) which, when normalised, yields the posterior distribution shown in the bottom panel.

Table 5.3 A Bayes' box for the discretised version of the disease model.

θ	Prior	Likelihood	Prior × Likelihood	Posterior
0.00	0.09	0.00	0.00	0.00
0.10	0.09	0.06	0.01	0.07
0.20	0.09	0.20	0.02	0.22
0.30	0.09	0.27	0.02	0.30
0.40	0.09	0.21	0.02	0.23
0.50	0.09	0.12	0.01	0.13
0.60	0.09	0.04	0.00	0.04
0.70	0.09	0.01	0.00	0.01
0.80	0.09	0.00	0.00	0.00
0.90	0.09	0.00	0.00	0.00
1.00	0.09	0.00	0.00	0.00
Total	**1.00**	**0.91**	$Pr(Z = 3 \mid N = 10) = \mathbf{0.08}$	**1.00**

sample of 100 individuals taken from the UK population. We assume the independence of individuals within our sample and also that they are from the same population, and are therefore identically distributed. We want to conclude about the overall proportion of individuals within the population with a disease, θ. Suppose that in a sample of 10 there are 3 who are disease-positive, meaning we have a binomial likelihood (see Section 4.6.2) of the form:

$$Pr(Z = 3 \mid \theta) = \binom{10}{3} \theta^\beta (1 - \theta)^{10-3}. \tag{5.6}$$

Before we collect the data, we suppose that all values of θ are equally likely and so use a uniform prior. Since the parameter of interest is now continuous, it appears that we cannot use Bayes' box, as there would be infinitely many rows (corresponding to the continuum of possible θ values) to sum over. However, we can still use it to approximate the shape of the posterior if we discretise the prior and likelihood at 0.1 intervals across the [0,1] range for θ (see Table 5.3).

The method to calculate the exact continuous posterior is identical to that in the discretised Bayes' box of Table 5.3, except now we multiply two functions – one for the prior, the other for the likelihood. As expected, the general shape of the posterior is the same for the continuous and discretised versions of the posterior (compare the left- and right-hand panels of Figure 5.5). The impact of using a flat prior is that the posterior is peaked at the same value of θ as the likelihood.

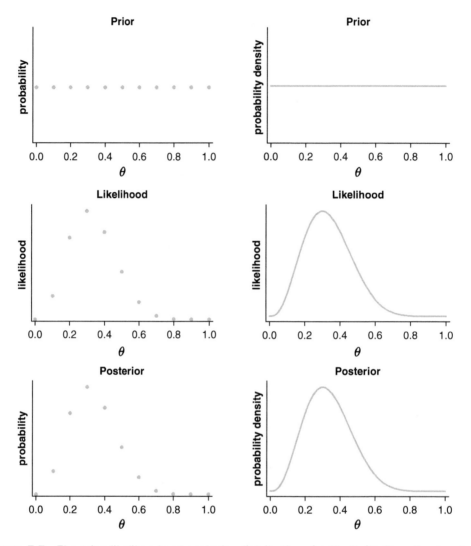

Figure 5.5 The prior, likelihood and posterior distributions for the (left) discretised and (right) continuous disease proportion model. Each value of θ along the prior curve (top panel) is multiplied by the corresponding value of likelihood (middle) to calculate the numerator of Bayes' rule. The numerator is then normalised to produce the posteriors shown in the bottom panel.

5 O 6 CONSTRUCTING PRIORS

There are a number of different methodologies and philosophies for constructing a prior density. In this section, we consider how priors can be engineered to be relatively uninformative, weakly informative or alternatively to combine pre-experimental knowledge in a logical manner.

5.6.1 Uninformative priors

When there is a premium placed on the objectivity of analysis, as is true in regulatory work (drug trials, public policy and the like), then the use of uninformative priors is desired. For example, if we were uncertain about the proportion of individuals in a population with a particular disease, then we might specify a uniform prior. The use of a prior that has a constant value, $p(\theta) = constant$, is attractive because, in this case:

$$p(\theta \mid data) = \frac{p(data \mid \theta) \times p(\theta)}{p(data)}$$

$$\propto p(data \mid \theta) \times p(\theta) \tag{5.7}$$

$$\propto p(data \mid \theta),$$

and the shape of the posterior distribution is determined by the likelihood function. This is seen as a merit of uniform priors since they 'let the data speak for itself' through the likelihood. This is used as the justification for using a flat prior in many analyses.

The flatness of the uniform prior distribution is often termed *uninformative*, but this is misleading. Assuming the same model as described in Section 5.5.2, the probability that one individual is disease-positive is θ, and the probability that two randomly chosen individuals both have the disease is θ^2. If we assume a flat prior for θ, then this implies the decreasing prior for θ^2 shown by the red line in Figure 5.6. Furthermore, considering the probability that in a sample of 10 individuals all are diseased, a flat prior for θ implies an even more accentuated prior for this event (dashed line in Figure 5.6). For the mathematical details of these graphs, see Section 5.10.2.

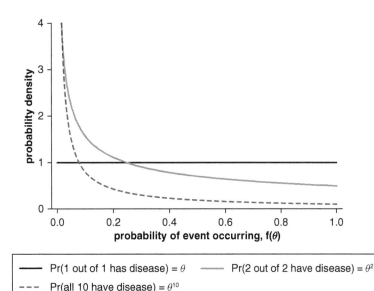

So even though a uniform prior for an event appears to convey no information, it actually confers quite considerable information about other events. This aspect of choosing flat priors is swept under the carpet for most analyses because we usually care most about the particular event (parameter) for which we create a prior. All priors contain some information, so we prefer the use of the terms *vague* or *diffuse* to represent situations where a premium is placed on drawing conclusions based only on observed data.

Figure 5.6 The probability density of obtaining a sample composed of only diseased individuals, for sample sizes of 1, 2 and 10, assuming a flat prior for θ, the underlying proportion of the population with the disease. Here f(θ) represents the three different functions of θ shown in the legend.

Legend:
Pr(1 out of 1 has disease) = θ Pr(2 out of 2 have disease) = θ^2
Pr(all 10 have disease) = θ^{10}

There are methods for constructing priors that aim to limit the information contained within them to avoid colouring the analysis with pre-experimental prejudices. We leave a discussion of these methods until Chapter 11, where we argue that these methods are usually not helpful for real-life analysis. More seriously, we argue that these methods (and the resultant priors they construct) actually miss the point – no analysis is objective. True Bayesians recognise this and realise that a real benefit of the Bayesian approach is the possibility to include information based on previous experiences.

While uniform priors are straightforward to specify for a bounded parameter – as in the previous example, where $\theta \in [0,1]$, or in the case of discrete parameters – we run into issues with parameters which have no predefined range. For example, imagine we aim to estimate the mean, μ, time of onset of lung cancer for individuals who develop the disease after they begin to smoke. If we remove all background cases (assumed not to be caused by smoking), then μ has a lower bound of 0. However, there is no obvious point at which to draw an upper bound. A naive solution is to use a prior for $\mu \sim U(0,\infty)$. This solution, although at first appearing reasonable, is not viable for two reasons: one statistical, the other practical. The statistical reason is that $\mu \sim U(0,\infty)$ is not a valid probability density, because any non-zero constant value for the density implies infinite total probability because the μ axis stretches out for ever. The common sense argument is that it is impossible for humans to develop the disease after 250 or 2500 years! The finiteness of human lifespan dictates that we choose a more appropriate prior. A better choice of prior would be a density that ascribes zero probability to negative values of μ allocates most weight towards values of μ that we believe are most reasonable, such as the prior indicated by the red line shown in Figure 5.7. While many analyses assume a discontinuous uniform prior of the type shown by the grey line in Figure 5.7, we discourage their usage (see Section 5.7.1), due to the arbitrary, and often nonsensical, lower and upper bounds. There are also good computational reasons for using gentler, less discontinuous priors, which we discuss in Section 11.7. These types of prior are what Gelman terms *weakly informative*.

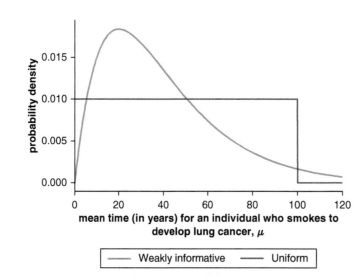

Figure 5.7   **Two prior distributions for the average time before the onset of lung cancer after a patient begins smoking.**

5.6.2 Informative priors

In Section 5.6.1 we discussed priors that give a strong weight to recent data and aim to minimise the impact of pre-existing beliefs. There are, however, occasions when it is essential to include significant information in the prior: to incorporate previously collected data, or the results of a former analysis, to include data from another source or to account for theoretical considerations.

In cases where data are available from previous studies, the construction of a prior can proceed by a method known as *moment-matching*. Suppose that we obtain the data shown in Figure 5.8 for SAT scores of past participants of a particular class, which we want to use to form a prior for scores for a future class. We might assume that the test scores could be modelled as having come from a normal distribution. We characterise normal distributions by two parameters: their mean, μ, and standard deviation, σ. In moment-matching a normal prior to this previous data, we choose the mean and standard deviation to equal their sample equivalents, in this case $\mu = 998$ and $\sigma = 145$, respectively (indicated by the red line in Figure 5.8).

While this simple methodology produces priors that closely approximate pre-experimental data sets, it was an arbitrary choice to fit the first two moments (the mean and the standard deviation, respectively) of the sample. We could have used, for instance, the skewness and kurtosis (skewness measures how symmetric a distribution is, and kurtosis quantifies how fat its tails are; these relate to the third and fourth moments of a distribution, respectively). Also, moment-matching is not Bayesian in nature and can often be difficult to apply in practice. When we discuss hierarchical models in Chapter 17, we will learn about a purer Bayesian method that can be used to create prior densities.

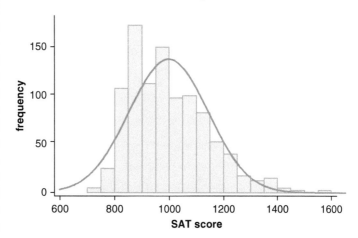

Figure 5.8 The SAT scores for past students of a class. The mean and standard deviation of a hypothetical sample are 998 and 145, respectively, which are used to fit a normal distribution to the data whose PDF is shown in red.

5.6.3 Eliciting priors

A different sort of informative prior is sometimes necessary, which is not derived from prior data, but from expert opinions. These priors are often used in clinical trials, where clinicians are interviewed before the trial is conducted. However, a considerable amount of research in the social sciences also uses these types of priors. There are many methods to create priors from subjective views (see [17] for a detailed discussion). Here we use a simple example to illustrate how such methods can work in practice.

Suppose that we ask a sample of economists to provide estimates of the 25th and 75th percentiles, $wage_{25}$ and $wage_{75}$, of the wage premium that one extra year of college education commands on the job market. If we assume a normal prior for the data, then we can relate these two quantiles back to the corresponding quantiles of a standardised normal distribution for each expert:

$$z_{25} = \frac{wage_{25} - \mu}{\sigma} \tag{5.8}$$

$$z_{75} = \frac{wage_{75} - \mu}{\sigma},$$

(5.9)

where z_{25} and z_{75} are the 25th and 75th percentiles of the standard normal distribution, respectively. These two simultaneous equations could be solved for each expert, giving an estimate of the mean and standard deviation of a normal variable. These could then be averaged to determine the mean and standard deviation across all the experts. A better method relies on linear regression. Expressions (5.8) and (5.9) can be rearranged to give the following:

$$wage_{25} = \mu + \sigma z_{25}$$

$$wage_{75} = \mu + \sigma z_{75}.$$

(5.10)

We recognise that each equation represents a straight line $y = mx + c$ in $(z, wage)$ space where in this case $c = \mu$ and $m = \sigma$. If we fit a linear regression line to the data from the whole panel, the values of the y intercept and gradient hence estimate the mean and standard deviation (see Figure 5.9).

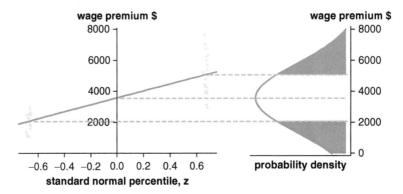

Figure 5.9 Regressing hypothetical 25th and 75th percentiles on the corresponding percentiles from a standard normal distribution (left) yields estimates of the mean and standard deviation of a normal distribution (right). The horizontal dashed lines indicate the position of the estimated 25th (lower), 50th (middle) and 75th (top) percentiles of the distribution of annual wage premiums. Note that jitter has been added to the left-hand plot x coordinates to allow the points to be resolved.

5○7   A STRONG MODEL IS LESS SENSITIVE TO PRIOR CHOICE

Returning to the disease prevalence example in Section 5.5.2, we now examine the effects of using an informative prior on the analysis. Suppose that we choose a prior which suggests that the prevalence of a disease within the population is high (see the top row of Figure 5.10). If we have a sample composed of 10 individuals and find that one person in our sample tests positive for the disease, the posterior is located roughly equidistant between the peaks of the prior and likelihood functions (see the left-hand column of Figure 5.10). If the sample size increases to 100, holding constant the percentage of individuals who are disease-positive (now 10 individuals), the posterior peak is much closer to the position of the likelihood peak (see the middle column of Figure 5.10). If the sample size increases further, still maintaining the percentage of individuals with the disease in the sample, the posterior appears indistinguishable from the likelihood (see the rightmost column of Figure 5.10).

Figure 5.10 shows that the effect of the prior on the posterior density decreases as we collect more data. By contrast, the influence of the likelihood – the effect of current data – increases along with sample size. To explain this, remember that the posterior is essentially a weighted average of the likelihood and prior:

$$p(\theta \mid data) \propto \underbrace{p(data \mid \theta)}_{\text{likelihood}} \times \underbrace{p(\theta)}_{\text{prior}}. \tag{5.11}$$

Because the above is a product, its behaviour is determined by whichever of the terms is smallest. In the extreme, if either the likelihood or the prior is zero, then the above ensures that the posterior is also zero. In general, as the amount of data we collect increases, the likelihood of that data becomes smaller (intrinsically there are many more different ways in which a larger data set could be generated) and more peaked. This means that the posterior peak becomes increasingly closer to the likelihood peak.

In Bayesian analysis, when we collect more data our conclusions become less affected by priors. The use of a prior allows us to make inferences in small sample sizes by using pre-experimental knowledge of a situation, but in larger samples the effect of prior choice declines. In all cases,

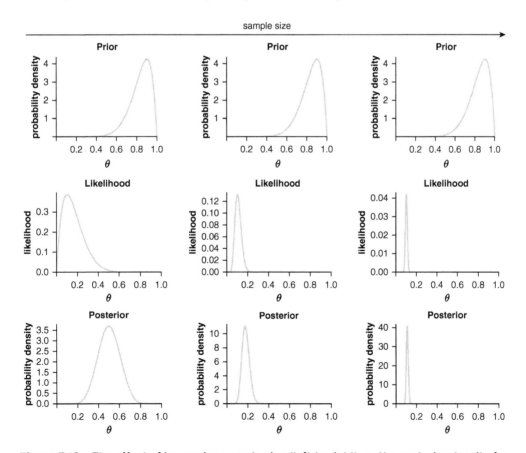

Figure 5.10 The effect of increasing sample size (left to right) on the posterior density for the prevalence of a disease in a population (bottom panels). Left: $N = 10$. Middle: $N = 100$. Right: $N = 1000$. All three have the same proportion of disease cases in the sample (10%).

we have an obligation to report whenever the conclusion of an analysis is sensitive to the form of prior that is specified. Alternatively, a field called *sensitivity analysis* actually allows a range of priors to be specified and combined to produce a single posterior.

5.7.1 Caveat: zero priors always affect the posterior

Suppose that we strongly believe that the world is flat – so much so that we give the probability that the world is non-flat a prior probability of zero. We then collect data on star movements in the night sky and calculate the likelihood of obtaining these results by assuming either a flat or non-flat world, finding overwhelming support in favour of the non-flat world. However, using Bayes' rule here, the posterior probability of the world being non-flat equals zero, since it is the product of a zero-valued prior and a finite likelihood. Clearly, choosing a zero prior has (wrongly) dictated the ultimate inferential result!

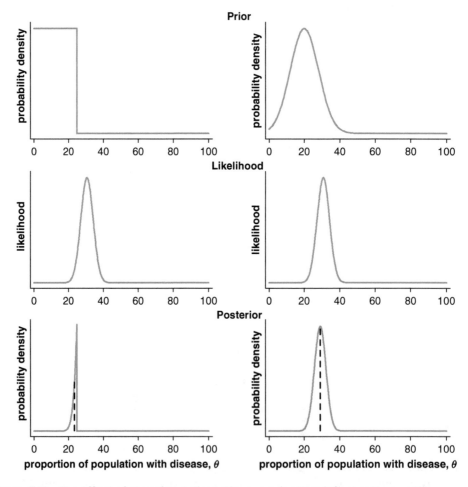

Figure 5.11 The effect of choosing a discontinuous prior (top-left panel) or weakly informative one (top-right panel) on the posterior distribution for the disease prevalence (bottom panels). Choosing a smoother prior with some weight towards higher values of disease prevalence (top-right panel) results in a less skewed mean (shown by black dashed line). In both cases, the data, and hence likelihood, are assumed to be the same.

Alternatively, suppose that we wish to estimate the prevalence of a common disease in a particular developing country. We speak with the Minister for Health of the country in question, who says that he is 'morally certain' that the prevalence of a disease is lower than 25%. As such, we decide to use a zero-valued prior for values of prevalence greater than this value (see the top-left panel of Figure 5.11). We then collect sample data on disease transmission for families across the country, resulting in a likelihood that is peaked nearer 30%. Multiplying together the prior and the likelihood to get the posterior, we notice that we end up with a rather ugly distribution with a kink in it. Apart from poor aesthetics, this posterior indicates unrealistic estimates of the mean level of disease prevalence that lie quite a distance away from the maximum likelihood value.

Choosing a zero-valued prior across a parameter range always results in a corresponding zero posterior probability. For most cases, the type of discontinuous prior shown in the top-left panel of Figure 5.11 should be discouraged, and smoother, less definitive distributions chosen instead (see the top right-hand panel for an example of one). Remember that priors should represent our subjective viewpoints of the likelihood of a given event. Choosing a zero-valued prior for such an event means that, from our perspective, it is impossible. For most circumstances, we are not nearly this sure, and we should be more cautious in our certainty. That is not to say we should not use highly informative priors – just that we should use smoother, more mathematically friendly distributions. There are also computational benefits to using these types of priors, but we leave this discussion until after we have covered more theory (see Section 11.7).

 CHAPTER SUMMARY

We now know that a prior is a probability distribution that represents our pre-data knowledge about a particular situation. We also understand the importance of selecting a valid prior density and the need to carefully test and interpret a posterior that results from using an improper prior. Further, we understand that when we want to draw conclusions solely from the data, a vague prior may be most appropriate. This contrasts with situations when we wish to use previous data or expert knowledge to help us draw conclusions, in which case we specify a more informative prior. In all cases, however, we recognise that we must be aware of the sensitivity of our inferences to the choice of prior. We also realise that as the number of data points increases or a better model is chosen, then the posterior density is less sensitive to the choice of prior.

We are now nearly in a position to start doing Bayesian analysis. All that we have left to cover is the denominator of Bayes' rule. This element appears benign at first sight but is actually where the difficulty lies in Bayesian approaches to inference. For this reason, we devote the next chapter to studying this final part of Bayes' rule.

 CHAPTER OUTCOMES

The reader should now be familiar with the following concepts:

- why we need priors for Bayesian analysis
- the need to use valid priors to ensure valid posterior probability distributions result
- Bayes' box for discrete parameters

- how Bayes' rule combines a prior and a likelihood to yield a posterior
- the difference between vague and informative priors
- how expert knowledge can be encoded in priors
- the influence of collecting more data on the shape of the posterior distribution

 APPENDIX

5.10.1 Bayes' rule for the fish problem

In this case application of the discrete form Bayes' rule results in:

$$Pr(Y = \alpha \mid X = 1) = \frac{Pr(X = 1 \mid Y = \alpha) \times Pr(Y = \alpha)}{Pr(X = 1)}$$

$$= \frac{Pr(X = 1 \mid Y = \alpha) \times Pr(Y = \alpha)}{\sum_{\alpha=0}^{5} Pr(X = 1 \mid Y = \alpha) \times Pr(Y = \alpha)}$$

(5.12)

$$= \frac{\dfrac{\alpha}{5} \times \dfrac{1}{6}}{\sum_{\alpha=0}^{5} \dfrac{\alpha}{5} \times \dfrac{1}{6}}$$

5.10.2 The probabilities of having a disease

We assume that the probability an individual has a disease is θ, and specify a uniform prior on this probability, $p(\theta) = 1$. We calculate the probability that out of a sample of two individuals, $p(Y) = p(\theta^2)$, by applying the change of variables rule:

$$p(Y) = p(\theta(Y)) \times |\theta'(Y)|.$$

(5.13)

In (5.13), $\theta(Y) = Y^{1/2}$ is the inverse of $Y = \theta^2$, and θ' means the derivative with respect to Y. Hence we derive the probability density for two individuals to have the disease:

$$p(Y) = \frac{1}{2\sqrt{Y}}.$$

(5.14)

5⬤11 PROBLEM SETS

Problem 5.1 Dodgy coins

Suppose there are three coins in a bag. The first coin is biased towards heads, with a 75% probability of a heads occurring if the coin is flipped. The second is fair, so a 50% chance of heads occurring. The third coin is biased towards tails, and has a 25% probability of coming up heads. Assume that it is impossible to identify which coin is which from looking at or touching them.

Problem 5.1.1 Suppose we put our hand into the bag and pull out a coin. We then flip the coin and find it comes up heads. Let the random variable $C = \{1,2,3\}$ denote the identity of the coin, where the probability of heads is $(0.75, 0.50, 0.25)$, respectively. Obtain the likelihood by using the equivalence relation (that a likelihood of a parameter value given data is equal to the probability of data given a parameter value), and show that the sum of the likelihood over all parameter values is 1.5.

Problem 5.1.2 What is the maximum likelihood estimate of the coin's identity?

Problem 5.1.3 Use Bayes' rule to prove that:

$$Pr(C = c \,|\, X = H) \propto Pr(X = H \,|\, C = c) \times Pr(C = c),$$ (5.15)

where $c = 1,2,3$.

Problem 5.1.4 Assume that since we cannot visually detect the coin's identity we use a uniform prior $Pr(C = c) = \frac{1}{3}$ for $c = 1,2,3$. Use this to complete Table P5.1 (known as a Bayes' box) and determine the (marginal) probability of the data.

Table P5.1   A Bayes' box for the coins example.

Parameter	Likelihood	Prior	Likelihood × Prior	Posterior
C	$Pr(X = H \,|\, C = c)$	$Pr(C = c)$	$Pr(X = H \,|\, C = c) \times Pr(C = c)$	$Pr(C = c \,|\, X = H)$
1				
2				
3			$Pr(X = H) =$	

Problem 5.1.5 Confirm that the posterior is a valid probability distribution.

Problem 5.1.6 Now assume that we flip the same coin twice, and find that it lands heads up on both occasions. By using a table similar in form to Table P5.1, or otherwise, determine the new posterior distribution.

Problem 5.1.7 Now assume that you believe that the tails-biased coin is much more likely to be drawn from the bag, and thus specify a prior: $Pr(C = 1) = 1/20$, $Pr(C = 2) = 5/20$ and $Pr(C = 3) = 14/20$. What is the posterior probability that $C = 1$ now?

Problem 5.1.8 Continuing on from the previous example, calculate the posterior mean, maximum a posteriori (MAP) and maximum likelihood estimates. Does the posterior mean indicate much here?

Problem 5.1.9 For the case when we flip the coin once and obtain $X = H$, using the uniform prior on C, determine the posterior predictive distribution for a new coin flip with result $\tilde{X}$, using the expression:

$$Pr(\tilde{X} \,|\, X = H) = \sum_{c=1}^{3} Pr(\tilde{X} \,|\, C) \times Pr(C \,|\, X = H).$$ (5.16)

Problem 5.1.10 (Optional) Justify the use of the expression in the previous question.

Problem 5.2 Left-handedness

Suppose that we are interested in the prevalence of left-handedness in a particular population.

Problem 5.2.1 We begin with a sample of one individual whose dexterity we record as $X = 1$ for left-handed, $X = 0$ otherwise. Explain why the following probability distribution makes sense here:

$$Pr(X \mid \theta) = \theta^X (1 - \theta)^{1-X}, \tag{5.17}$$

where θ is the probability that a randomly chosen individual is left-handed.

Problem 5.2.2 Suppose we hold θ constant. Demonstrate that under these circumstances the above distribution is a valid probability distribution. What sort of distribution is this?

Problem 5.2.3 Now suppose we randomly sample a person who happens to be left-handed. Using the above function calculate the probability of this occurring.

Problem 5.2.4 Show that when we vary θ the above distribution does not behave as a valid probability distribution. Also, what sort of distribution is this?

Problem 5.2.5 What is the maximum likelihood estimator for θ?

6

Chapter contents

THE DEVIL IS IN THE DENOMINATOR

6●1   CHAPTER MISSION STATEMENT

At the end of this chapter, the reader will recognise the importance of the denominator term, $p(data)$, in Bayes' rule. Furthermore, the reader will appreciate that it is partly the complexity of calculating this term that motivates the move away from exact Bayesian inference, towards the sampling methodology that we discuss in Part IV:

$$p(\theta \mid data) = \frac{p(data \mid \theta) \times p(\theta)}{p(data)}. \tag{6.1}$$

6●2   CHAPTER GOALS

Bayesian inference uses probability distributions, called *posteriors*, to make inferences about the world at large. To be able to use these powerful tools, however, we must ensure they are valid probability distributions. The denominator of Bayes' rule, $p(data)$, is a number that ensures that the posterior distribution is a *valid* probability distribution by normalising the numerator term.

There is, however, another interpretation of the denominator. Before we get the data, it is a probability distribution that represents our beliefs over all possible data samples. To obtain the denominator we marginalise out all parameter dependence in the numerator. The seeming simplicity of the previous statement belies the fact that, for most circumstances, this calculation is complicated and practically intractable. In this chapter, we will learn why this difficulty arises, as well as a basic appreciation of how modern computational methods sidestep this issue. We will leave the details of how these methods work in practice to Part IV, but this chapter lays the foundations for this later study.

6●3   AN INTRODUCTION TO THE DENOMINATOR

6.3.1 The denominator as a normalising factor

We know from Chapter 4 that the likelihood is not a valid probability density, and hence we reason that the numerator of Bayes' rule – the likelihood multiplied by the prior – is similarly not one. The numerator satisfies the first condition of a valid probability density – its values are non-negative. However, it falls down on the second test – its sum or integral (dependent on whether the parameters are discrete or continuous) across all parameter values does not typically equal 1.

A natural way to normalise the numerator is to divide it by the value of this sum or integral. The denominator of Bayes' rule, $p(data)$, is this normalising factor. Notice that it does not contain the parameter, θ. This is because $p(data)$ is a *marginal* probability density (see Section 3.3.5), obtained by summing or integrating out all dependence on θ. This parameter independence of the denominator ensures that the influence of θ on the shape of the posterior distribution is solely due to the numerator (see Section 6.5).

Why is it difficult to calculate the denominator of Bayes' rule in practice?

There are two varieties of Bayes' rule which we will employ in this chapter, which use slightly different (although conceptually identical) versions of the denominator. When θ is a discrete parameter, we sum over all possible parameter values to obtain a factor that normalises the numerator:

$$Pr(data) = \sum_{\text{All}\theta} Pr(data,\theta)$$

$$= \sum_{\text{All}\theta} Pr(data\,|\,\theta) \times Pr(\theta). \tag{6.2}$$

We leave multiple-parameter inference largely to Part IV, although we discuss how this complicates matters considerably in Section 6.4. The multivariate method proceeds in similar fashion to expression (6.2), except that the single sum is replaced by a number of summations, one for each of the number of parameters in the model.

For continuous parameters we use the continuous analogue of the sum – an integral – to calculate a denominator of the form:

$$p(data) = \int_{\text{All}\theta} p(data,\theta)\mathrm{d}\theta$$

$$= \int_{\text{All}\theta} p(data\,|\,\theta) \times p(\theta)\mathrm{d}\theta. \tag{6.3}$$

Bayes box
example
of the
denominator

Similarly, for multiple-parameter systems, the single integral is replaced by a multiple integral. Next, we use examples to demonstrate how to use expressions (6.2) and (6.3) in Sections 6.3.2 and 6.3.3, respectively.

6.3.2 Example: individual patient disease status

Imagine that we are a medical practitioner and want to calculate the probability that a patient has a particular disease. We use θ to represent the two possible outcomes:

$$\theta = \begin{cases} 0, & \text{disease negative} \\ 1, & \text{disease positive}. \end{cases} \tag{6.4}$$

Taking account of the patient's medical history, we specify a prior probability of $\frac{1}{4}$ that they have the disease. We subsequently obtain data from a diagnostic test and use this to re-evaluate the probability that the patient is disease-positive. To do this we choose a probability model (likelihood) of the form:

$$Pr(test\ positive\,|\,\theta) = \begin{cases} \dfrac{1}{10}, & \theta = 0 \\[2mm] \dfrac{4}{5}, & \theta = 1, \end{cases} \tag{6.5}$$

where we implicitly assume that the probability of a negative test result equals 1 minus the positive test probabilities. Also, since $Pr(test\ positive\,|\,\theta = 0) > 0$ we are assuming that false positives do occur.

Suppose that the individual test result is positive for the disease. We can now use expression (6.2) to calculate the denominator of Bayes' rule in this case:

$$Pr(test\ positive) = \sum_{\theta=0}^{1} Pr(test\ positive\,|\,\theta) \times Pr(\theta)$$

$$= Pr(test\ positive\,|\,\theta = 0) \times Pr(\theta = 0) + Pr(test\ positive\,|\,\theta = 1) \times Pr(\theta = 1) \tag{6.6}$$

$$= \frac{1}{10} \times \frac{3}{4} + \frac{4}{5} \times \frac{1}{4} = \frac{11}{40}.$$

The denominator is a valid probability density, meaning that we can calculate the counter-factual $Pr(test\ negative) = 1 - Pr(test\ positive) = \frac{29}{40}$. We need to be careful with interpreting this last result, however, since it did not actually occur; $Pr(test\ negative)$ is our model-implied probability that the individual will test negatively before we carry out the test and obtain the result.

We then use Bayes' rule to obtain the posterior probability that the individual has the disease, given that they test positive:

$$Pr(\theta = 1\,|\,test\ positive) = \frac{Pr(test\ positive\,|\,\theta = 1) \times Pr(\theta = 1)}{Pr(test\ positive)} = \frac{\frac{4}{5} \times \frac{1}{4}}{\frac{11}{40}} = \frac{8}{11}. \tag{6.7}$$

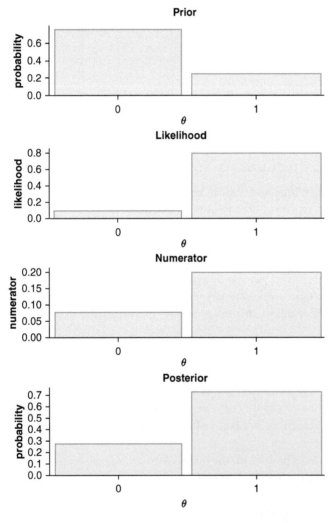

In this case, even though we began with a fairly optimistic belief – a probability that the individual has the disease of $\frac{1}{4}$ – the strength of the data has shone through, and we are now fairly confident in the alternative (see Figure 6.1 for a graphical depiction of this change of heart). Bayesians are fickle by design!

6.3.3 Example: the proportion of people who vote for the Conservative Party in a UK general election

Suppose that we work for a pollster and aim to estimate the proportion of voters, θ, who have voted for the Conservative Party in the UK, on the basis of exit poll data. Also, suppose that Conservatives are relatively unpopular at the time of the election, and we assume that, at most, 45% of the electorate will vote for them, meaning we choose a uniform prior of the form shown in the top panel of Figure 6.2. While we do not favour the

Figure 6.1 The Bayesian inference process illustrated for the disease example described in the text: the prior (top panel) is multiplied by the likelihood (second from top), resulting in the numerator (second from bottom), which is then normalised by the denominator, to yield the posterior distribution (bottom).

use of these types of uniform prior (see Section 5.7.1), we use it again to highlight its effects on the posterior. The data comprise voter preferences from 100 individuals who were surveyed when leaving a particular polling station. To simplify the analysis, we assume that there are only two political parties, and all voters must choose between either of these two options. We assume that the polling station chosen is representative of the electorate as a whole, and voters' choices are independent of one another. In this situation, we use a binomial likelihood function (see Section 4.6.2):

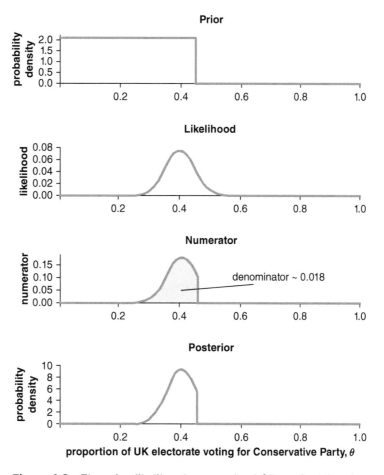

Figure 6.2   The prior, likelihood, numerator (of Bayes' rule) and posterior distributions for the Conservative Party voting example.

$$Pr(Z = \beta \mid \theta) = \binom{100}{\beta}\theta^{\beta}(1-\theta)^{100-\beta}, \tag{6.8}$$

where Z is a random variable that represents the number of individuals voting Conservative in the sample and $\beta \in [0,100]$ is the variable's specific value. We assume that, in this case, 40 people out of the sample of 100 voted for the Conservatives, resulting in the likelihood shown in the second-from-top panel in Figure 6.2, which is peaked at the maximum likelihood estimate of $\hat{\theta} = 40\%$.

We calculate the denominator by integrating the numerator of Bayes' rule (likelihood times prior) over $\theta \in [0,1]$ (which amounts to finding the area under the numerator curve shown in Figure 6.2):

$$Pr(Z = 40) = \int_{0}^{1} \underbrace{Pr(Z = 40 \mid \theta)}_{\text{likelihood}} \times \underbrace{p(\theta)}_{\text{prior}} d\theta$$

$$= \int_{0}^{0.45} \binom{100}{40}\theta^{40}(1-\theta)^{60} \times \frac{20}{9} d\theta \tag{6.9}$$

$$\approx 0.018.$$

In the above, we assumed that since $p(\theta) = 0$ for $\theta > 0.45$, we can restrict the integral to only the region below that value (the factor $\frac{20}{9}$ is the uniform density for $0 \le \theta \le 0.45$). The value $Pr(Z = 40) \approx 0.018$ is obtained by numerically integrating the second line.

After calculating the denominator, we use it to normalise the product of the prior and the likelihood, resulting in the posterior distribution seen in Figure 6.2. The effect of truncating the uniform distribution at $\theta = 0.45$ is to artificially truncate the posterior distribution at this value. Because of this, summary measures of centrality of the posterior will be skewed towards the left of the peak, which is undesirable.

6.3.4 The denominator as a probability distribution

An alternative view of the denominator is as a probability distribution for the data before we observe it – in other words, the *probability distribution for a future data sample given our choice of model*. Here *model* encompasses both the likelihood and the prior. The denominator is actually a *marginal* probability density that is obtained by integrating the joint density $p(data,\theta)$ across all θ:

$$
\begin{aligned}
p(data) &= \int_{\text{All}\theta} p(data \mid \theta) \times p(\theta) \mathrm{d}\theta \\
&= \int_{\text{All}\theta} p(data,\theta) \mathrm{d}\theta \,,
\end{aligned}
\tag{6.10}
$$

where we have assumed that the parameter(s) is continuous. We obtained the second line from the first by using the conditional probability formula introduced in Section 3.3.6:

$$
p(data \mid \theta) = \frac{p(data,\theta)}{p(\theta)}.
\tag{6.11}
$$

We are thus able to characterise the joint density of the data and the parameter, $p(data, \theta)$. This joint density is a function of both the data and θ, and so is a valid probability distribution. This contrasts with the numerator in Bayesian inference (which is not a valid probability distribution), where we vary θ but hold the data constant. We can draw the joint density for the disease example in Section 6.3.2 as the discrete distribution shown in Table 6.1. We also show (in the rightmost column) the discrete probability distribution for $p(data)$, obtained by marginalising the joint distribution.

Table 6.1 The derivation of the joint density of test result and disease status (shown at the bottom) for the example described in the text. Each column of the likelihood – corresponding to a given disease status – is multiplied by the corresponding prior value, resulting in the joint density. By summing the joint density across the different disease statuses of the patient, we obtain p(data).

		Disease status		
	Test Results	Negative	Positive	
Likelihood	0 (Negative)	0.90	0.20	
	1 (Positive)	0.10	0.80	
		×	×	
Prior		0.75	0.25	
		=	=	
	Test Results			p(data)
Joint density	0 (Negative)	0.675	0.05	**0.725**
	1 (Positive)	0.075	0.20	**0.275**

THE DIFFICULTY WITH THE DENOMINATOR

The previous examples illustrate that the denominator of Bayes' rule is obtained by summing (for discrete variables) or integrating (for continuous variables) the joint density $p(data,\theta)$ across the range of θ. We have seen how this procedure works when there is a single parameter in the model. However, in most real-life applications of statistics, the likelihood is a function of a number of parameters. For the case of a two-parameter discrete model, the denominator is given by a double sum:

$$p(data) = \sum_{\text{All} \theta_1} \sum_{\text{All} \theta_2} p(data,\theta_1,\theta_2).$$

(6.12)

And for a model with two continuous parameters, we must do a double integral:

$$p(data) = \int_{\text{All} \theta_1} \int_{\text{All} \theta_2} p(data,\theta_1,\theta_2) d\theta_1 d\theta_2.$$

(6.13)

While the two-parameter expressions (6.12) and (6.13) may not look more intrinsically difficult than their single-parameter counterparts in expressions (6.2) and (6.3), respectively, this aesthetic similarity is misleading, particularly for the continuous case. While in the discrete case it is possible to enumerate all parameter values and hence – by brute force – calculate the exact value of $p(data)$, for continuous parameters the integral may be difficult to calculate. This difficulty is amplified the more parameters our model has, rendering analytic calculation of the denominator practically impossible for all but the simplest models.

As an example, imagine we are modelling high school test scores of individuals within schools, and use a model where test $score_{ij}$ for an individual i within school j is normally distributed:

$$score_{ij} \sim N\left(\mu_j,\sigma_j\right),$$

(6.14)

where μ_j and σ_j are the mean and standard deviation of test scores within school j. If we have 100 schools in our data set, then the denominator term is an integral of the form:

$$p(data) = \int_{\mu_1}\int_{\sigma_1} \cdots \int_{\mu_{100}}\int_{\sigma_{100}} \underbrace{p(data \mid \mu_1,\sigma_1,...,\mu_{100},\sigma_{100})}_{\text{likelihood}} \times \underbrace{p(\mu_1,\sigma_1,...,\mu_{100},\sigma_{100})}_{\text{prior}}$$

$$d\mu_1 d\sigma_1...d\mu_{100}d\sigma_{100},$$

(6.15)

where $p(data \mid \mu_1,\sigma_1,...,\mu_{100},\sigma_{100})$ is the likelihood, which equals the product of individual normal densities (one for each of the schools); $p(\mu_1,\sigma_1,...,\mu_{100},\sigma_{100})$ is a prior distribution that we do not specify explicitly, but suppose incorporates dependence between the parameters from each school.

(Don't worry if you think expression (6.15) looks hideously complicated – that is actually our point in displaying it!) The above integral is 200-dimensional, which is impossible to exactly calculate. Furthermore, any approximate numerical scheme that uses a deterministic method to estimate the above integral, for example Gaussian quadrature, will also fail to work.

So it looks like we are stuck! For relatively complex problems we simply cannot calculate the denominator of Bayes' rule. This means we cannot normalise the numerator and, in doing so, transform it into a valid probability distribution.

In fact, even if we could calculate the denominator of Bayes' rule, we would still have difficulties. A common summary measure of a posterior distribution is the posterior mean. Suppose for our school test example we want to calculate the posterior mean of μ_1, which represents the mean test score for school 1. In this case, we would want to calculate the integral:

$$\mathbb{E}(\mu_1 \mid data) = \int_{\mu_1}\int_{\sigma_1} \cdots \int_{\mu_{100}}\int_{\sigma_{100}} \mu_1 \underbrace{p(\mu_1,\sigma_1,...,\mu_{100},\sigma_{100} \mid data)}_{\text{posterior}}$$

$$d\mu_1 d\sigma_1 ... d\mu_{100} d\sigma_{100},$$

(6.16)

where we have multiplied the posterior by μ_1 to find the posterior mean of this parameter. Since this integral is also 200-dimensional, we will have the same problems as we did for the denominator. This means that, in most circumstances, we cannot exactly calculate the mean, variance or any other summary measure of the posterior for that matter!

So for relatively complex models, it seems that we are in trouble. This issue originates from the inherent complexity of integrating multidimensional probability distributions, not just the difficulty in calculating the denominator term of Bayes' rule.

6⊙5   HOW TO DISPENSE WITH THE DIFFICULTY: BAYESIAN COMPUTATION

If a model has more than about three parameters, then it is difficult to calculate any of the integrals necessary to do applied Bayesian inference. However, all is not lost. In these circumstances, we can take a different route. There are two solutions to the difficulty:

- Use priors conjugate to the likelihood (see Chapter 9).
- Abandon exact calculation, and opt to sample from the posterior instead (see Part IV).

Using conjugate priors still allows exact derivation of the posterior distribution (and usually most summary measures) by choosing a mathematically 'nice' form for the prior distribution. This simplifies the analysis since we can simply look up tabulated formulae for the posterior, avoiding the need to do any maths.

However, in real-life applications of Bayesian statistics, we often need to stray outside this realm of mathematical convenience. The price we pay for a wider choice of priors and likelihoods is that we must stop aspiring for exact results. For example, we cannot hope to exactly calculate the posterior mean, standard deviation and any uncertainty intervals for parameters. However, it happens that, in these circumstances, we can sample from the posterior and then use sample summary statistics to describe the posterior. We leave a full description of these computational methods to Part IV, but to provide a clue as to where we are heading, we write the posterior density as:

$$p(\theta \mid data) = \frac{p(data \mid \theta) \times p(\theta)}{p(data)}$$

$$\propto p(data \mid \theta) \times p(\theta),$$

(6.17)

where we obtained the second line because $p(data)$ is independent of θ – it is a constant that we use to normalise the posterior. Therefore, the numerator of Bayes' rule tells us everything we need to know about the *shape* of the posterior distribution, whereas the denominator merely tells us about its *height*. Fortunately, we only require information on the shape of the posterior to generate samples from it. This forms the basis of all modern computational methods (see Part IV).

6⊙6 CHAPTER SUMMARY

In this chapter, we introduced two interpretations of the denominator. Before we observe data, it is a probability distribution that represents our beliefs over possible data samples. After we obtain a particular sample of data, this probability distribution collapses to a single number that normalises the numerator of Bayes' rule, to ensure the posterior is a valid probability distribution.

Once we have specified a likelihood and a prior, the denominator term is fully determined. To calculate it, we 'marginalise out' all parameter dependence in the numerator of Bayes' rule (the product of the likelihood and prior). For discrete models, this is often not problematic because the marginalisation involves a summation, which is computationally tractable (unless the model has many parameters). However, for continuous models, the marginalisation involves calculating a multidimensional integral. For more than a few parameters this integral cannot be exactly calculated, or even well approximated, using deterministic numerical integration methods. Since most applied Bayesian analyses have more than a handful of continuous parameters, this means that we are usually unable to exactly calculate the posterior distribution.

In fact, even if we could calculate the posterior we would still run into trouble. Typically, we want to summarise the posterior distribution by calculating its mean or, instead, intervals of uncertainty. To calculate these summaries exactly requires calculation of integrals as difficult as those required to calculate the denominator.

There are two methods to avoid this difficulty. One of these approaches is to use priors that are *conjugate* to the likelihood (see Chapter 9). This choice ensures that the posterior is of the same distributional form as the prior, albeit with different parameter values. Fortunately, however, the formulae for these posterior parameters have been tabulated by others, meaning we can avoid doing any calculations ourselves. Unfortunately, for all but the simplest problems, conjugacy is not a feasible solution. An alternative approach is to *sample* from the posterior distribution. We then use the properties of the sample to approximate for the corresponding properties of the posterior distribution. We shall see in Part IV that this forms the basis of most modern computational approaches to applied Bayesian analysis.

In this chapter, we did not discuss how the denominator can be used to compare the predictive fit of different models. In this guise, the denominator is typically known as the *marginal likelihood* of the data. We prefer to leave discussion of marginal likelihoods until Chapter 10, where we compare this approach with other (better) methods to assess a model's predictive power.

Now that we understand the three ingredients of Bayes' rule, we suppose that we can turn the handle and produce the posterior probability distribution – the goal of Bayesian inference. In Chapter 7 we turn our attention to discussing the various uses of this object.

6●7 CHAPTER OUTCOMES

The reader should now be familiar with the following concepts:

- the denominator as a probability distribution over possible data samples, before we actually observe the data
- the denominator as a normalising factor
- the difficulty with computing the denominator and other multidimensional integrals that arise in Bayesian inference for models with continuous parameters

6●8 PROBLEM SETS

Problem 6.1 Too many coin flips

Suppose we flip two coins. Each coin i is either fair ($Pr(H) = \theta_i = 0.5$) or biased towards heads ($Pr(H) = \theta_i = 0.9$); however, we cannot visibly detect the coin's nature. Suppose we flip both coins twice and record each result.

Problem 6.1.1 Suppose that we specify a discrete uniform prior on both θ_1 and θ_2. Find the joint distribution of the data and the coins' identity.

Problem 6.1.2 Show that the above distribution is a valid probability distribution.

Problem 6.1.3 We flip each coin twice and obtain for coin 1 $\{H,H\}$ and coin 2 $\{H,T\}$. Assuming that the result of each coin flip is independent of the previous result, write down a likelihood function.

Problem 6.1.4 What are the maximum likelihood estimators of each parameter?

Problem 6.1.5 Calculate the marginal likelihood of the data (that is, the denominator of Bayes' rule).

Problem 6.1.6 Hence calculate the posterior distribution, and demonstrate that this is a valid probability distribution.

Problem 6.1.7 Find the posterior mean of θ_1. What does this signify?

Problem 6.1.8 Now suppose that away from our view a third coin is flipped, and denote $Z = 1$ for a heads. The result of this coin affects the bias of the other two coins that are flipped subsequently, so that:

$$Pr(\theta_i = 0.5 \,|\, Z) = 0.8^Z 0.1^{1-Z}. \tag{6.18}$$

Suppose we again obtain for coin 1 $\{H,H\}$ and for coin 2 $\{H,T\}$. Find the maximum likelihood estimators (θ_1, θ_2, Z). How do the inferred biases of coin 1 and coin 2 compare to the previous estimates?

Problem 6.1.9 Calculate the marginal likelihood for the coin if we suppose that we specify a discrete uniform prior on Z, that is $Pr(Z = 1) = 0.5$.

Problem 6.1.10 Suppose we believe that the independent coin flip model (where there is no third coin) and the dependent coin flip model (where the outcome of the third coin affects the biases of the two coins) are equally likely a priori. Which of the two models do we prefer?

Problem 6.2 Coins combined

Suppose that we flip two coins, each of which has $Pr(H) = \theta_i$ where $i \in \{1,2\}$, which is unknown. If their outcomes are both the same then we regard this as a success; otherwise a failure. We repeatedly flip both coins (a single trial) and record whether the outcome is a success or failure. We do not record the result of flipping each coin. Suppose we model the number of failures, X, we have to undergo to attain n successes.

Problem 6.2.1 Stating any assumptions that you make, specify a suitable probability model here.

Problem 6.2.2 We obtain the data in `denominator_NBCoins.csv` for the number of failures to wait before five successes occur. Suppose that we specify the priors $\theta_1 \sim U(0,1)$ and $\theta_2 \sim U(0,1)$. Calculate the denominator of Bayes' rule. (*Hint*: use a numerical integration routine.)

Problem 6.2.3 Draw a contour plot of the posterior. Why does the posterior have this shape?

Problem 6.2.4 Comment on any issues with parameter identification for this model and how they might be rectified.

Problem 6.2.5 Now suppose that we have three coins instead of two. Here we regard a success as all three coins showing the same result. Using the same data as before, attempt to calculate the denominator term. Why is there a problem?

Problem 6.2.6 Assuming a denominator term equal to 3.64959×10^{-169}, estimate the posterior mean of θ_1.

7

Chapter contents

THE POSTERIOR – THE GOAL OF BAYESIAN INFERENCE

7○1   CHAPTER MISSION STATEMENT

This chapter introduces posterior distributions and the approaches used to summarise these objects. We then discuss how the posterior distribution can be used for forecasting:

$$\boxed{p(\theta \,|\, data)} = \frac{p(data \,|\, \theta) \times p(\theta)}{p(data)}. \tag{7.1}$$

7○2   CHAPTER GOALS

In Chapters 4 to 6, we explained how the various elements of Bayes' rule combine to produce a posterior probability distribution for a model's parameters. Calculating the posterior distribution is the focus of Bayesian analysis. This probability distribution can be used to yield estimates of parameters that interest us, to forecast and to test a model's foundations. In this chapter, we examine these topics and demonstrate some of the ways in which posterior distributions are used in practice.

Bayes' rule is the recipe for combining our pre-data beliefs with information from our data sample to produce an updated set of beliefs. This process involves first choosing a likelihood function (see Chapter 4). Likelihoods have parameters that, when varied, produce a range of different system behaviours. Even before we collect data, previous experience dictates that some of those behaviours are more probable than others. We quantify these pre-data preferences using a prior probability distribution (see Chapter 5). Once a likelihood and a prior are selected, Bayes' rule requires calculation of a denominator term to ensure that the posterior is a valid probability distribution (see Chapter 6). In this chapter, we explain intuitively how the shape of the likelihood and prior influences the shape of the posterior.

In policy making, we may require point estimates of parameters in order to make decisions. In Bayesian inference, we are free to choose which point estimates we use to summarise the posterior distribution. In this chapter, we discuss these options and argue that the posterior mean or median are superior choices to the mode. Point estimates of parameters can be misleading, particularly if there is considerable uncertainty associated with them. Even when policy makers demand a point estimate, we prefer to provide a measure of uncertainty in a parameter's value. Again, in Bayesian inference, there are a range of options available to us, and we discuss these in this chapter. We also compare these Bayesian *credible* intervals with Frequentist *confidence* intervals.

We may want to make predictions about a current, or future, state of the world using a model. This process is trivial in Bayesian statistics. We just estimate the *posterior predictive distribution* – itself a straightforward extension of the posterior, which we introduce in Section 7.8. In Chapter 10 we shall see that the posterior predictive distribution is also an essential part of Bayesian model checking.

7○3   EXPRESSING PARAMETER UNCERTAINTY IN POSTERIORS

Unlike looking out of the window to determine the weather, getting exam results, or playing a hand at blackjack, in inference we typically do learn the true state of the world. The uncertainty here is in both the present and future. Partly because we can only imperfectly explain the world today, we are unable to perfectly predict the state of the world tomorrow.

We represent our ignorance, or uncertainty, in a parameter's value through probability distributions. For example, suppose that we want to estimate the proportion of individuals who will vote for the Democrats in an upcoming election. We might, on the basis of past exit poll surveys, calculate the posterior probability distribution shown in Figure 7.1.

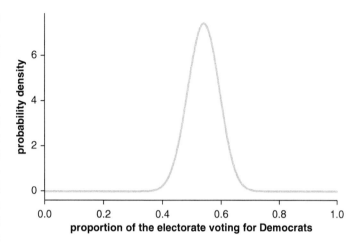

Figure 7.1 A probability distribution representing our uncertainty over the proportion of the electorate that will vote for the Democrats in an upcoming election.

How can we interpret the probability distribution shown in Figure 7.1? And further, how can we use it to express our uncertainty to a non-mathematician?

Often we describe a distribution by its summary characteristics. For example, we often want to know the *mean* value of a parameter. This is essentially a weighted mean (where the weights are provided by the values of the probability density function). If we have the mathematical formula for the distribution shown in Figure 7.1, we calculate this by the following integral (see Section 3.3.3):

$$\mathbb{E}[\theta \mid data] = \int_0^1 p(\theta \mid data)\theta \, d\theta = 54\%, \tag{7.2}$$

where in this case we have not provided the function $p(\theta)$ so you cannot do the above calculation yourselves. However, note that the point estimate of the proportion of individuals intending to vote for the Democrats coincides roughly with the peak of Figure 7.1.

A point estimate is dangerous to use without some measure of our confidence in the value. One useful measure of uncertainty is a parameter's variance:

$$var(\theta \mid data) = \int_0^1 p(\theta \mid data)(\theta - (\mathbb{E}[\theta \mid data])^2) \, d\theta. \tag{7.3}$$

It is usually easier to understand an uncertainty if it is expressed in the same units as the mean, which we obtain by taking the square root of the variance, which yields a standard deviation of 5.3% for the distribution shown in Figure 7.1. A larger standard deviation indicates that we believe a wider range of outcomes are possible. In this case, a wider standard deviation means we are less certain that the proportion voting for the Democrats in the actual election will actually be 54%.

An alternative way to summarise uncertainty is by specifying an interval rather than a point estimate. In Section 7.7 we compare and contrast the Frequentist and Bayesian approaches to interval estimation.

7.4 BAYESIAN STATISTICS: UPDATING OUR PRE-DATA UNCERTAINTY

In Bayesian statistics, the posterior distribution combines our pre-existing beliefs with information from observed data to produce an updated belief, which is used as the starting point for all further analyses. To calculate it we must choose a likelihood function (see Chapter 4) that determines the influence of the data on the posterior. This function is characterised by its parameters, which affect the behaviour of our model system. In Bayesian inference, these parameters are assigned priors that represent our pre-data beliefs across the range of parameter values (see Chapter 5). The priors and likelihoods are then combined in a certain way – using Bayes' rule – to yield the posterior distribution:

$$\text{likelihood} + \text{prior} \xrightarrow{\text{Bayes' rule}} \text{posterior}. \tag{7.4}$$

The posterior is the synthesis of past experience and information from observed data and represents our updated state of knowledge. The uncertainty in the posterior is usually (although not always) reduced compared to the prior because the data allows us to better understand the world.

The next section illustrates this process with the example of determining a ship's location in stormy weather.

7.4.1 Example: Bayesian coastguard

Imagine you are stationed in a radio control tower at the top of a steep cliff in the midst of a stormy night. The tower receives a distress call over the radio from a ship – *The Frequentasy* – which has engine trouble somewhere in the bay. It is your job to direct a search helicopter to rescue the poor sailors.

While you have received a radio communication that the ship is in trouble, its GPS is not working, and so the sailors do not know their location. However, you know the ship must be somewhere within 25km of the tower since this is the maximum range of the radio. Accordingly, you represent this view with the prior shown in the left-hand panel of Figure 7.2. Unfortunately, the search area covered by this prior is far too wide for a rescue crew to find the flagging ship before it sinks.

In an attempt to improve the odds, you radio the ship and ask that the crew switch on their emergency transmitter. After radioing a number of times you eventually receive a weak signal, which you feed into the computer. The computer uses Bayes' rule to produce the posterior probability density for the ship's location shown in the middle panel of Figure 7.2.

The issue is that the posterior still indicates a large uncertainty in the ship's position, and searching for the troubled vessel would again take too long. Luckily for the crew, however, another nearby radio station has also picked up the signal, and they share this information with you.

You use your previous posterior as a prior for a new analysis, where the observed data sample is the information received from the other radio station. Using the Bayesian computer you obtain a new posterior for the ship's location shown in the right-hand panel of Figure 7.2. Since there is only a small area of high density, you direct the rescue helicopter to this region, and it finds the captain and crew in time.

Figure 7.2 Searching for a distressed ship in a storm. Left: a contour plot of the prior probability of the ship's location. Middle: a contour plot of the posterior density for the ship's location after we receive its distress signal. Right: a contour plot of the posterior density for the ship's location after we incorporate information received from the other control tower.

We began with a wide prior since we were very unsure of the ship's location. We then fed the data from the ship's emergency transmitter, along with our prior, into the computer – which used Bayes' rule – to provide an updated estimate of the ship's location. This posterior was used as a prior for a new analysis that used data from the other radio tower. The Bayesian computer then produced a more accurate estimate of the ship's location. This example illustrates a key feature of Bayesian inference: the more data we collect (in general), the better precision we obtain in our posterior.

While we did not show this, Bayesian inference also satisfies a property known as *data order invariance*. This means that we could have obtained the final posterior in one of two ways: the incremental process we used above, where we used Bayes' rule twice; and using the posterior from the first step as a prior for the second step, where we use the new data. Alternatively, we could use Bayes' rule once using the initial prior, and a data set comprising both radio signals, and we would obtain the same final posterior representing our uncertainty over the ship's location. Note that this logic assumes that the ship does not move between receipt of the first and second radio signals, otherwise data order invariance would not apply.

7·5 THE INTUITION BEHIND BAYES' RULE FOR INFERENCE

In any application of Bayesian analysis, it is important to understand how changes to the prior and/or data affect the posterior. While this might appear like a difficult problem given the complexity of probability distributions, in this section we use an example to illustrate how to determine the influence of these two components on the posterior distribution for any applied analysis. This means that, for most circumstances, we can predict how changes to our model or data will influence our inferences before we actually estimate the posterior.

Suppose that we model the proportion of individuals who have a disease within a population, θ. We start by collecting a sample of 10 individuals and choose a binomial model to explain the numbers of individuals with the disease, X (see Section 4.6.2). Suppose that we find that two individuals in our sample are disease-positive. We can use Bayes' rule to write down an expression for the posterior diseased proportion:

Explaining
the intuition
behind
Bayesian
inference

$$p(\theta \mid X = 2, N = 10) = \frac{p(X = 2 \mid \theta, N = 10) \times p(\theta)}{p(X = 2 \mid N = 10)}$$

$$\propto \underbrace{p(X = 2 \mid \theta, N = 10)}_{\text{likelihood}} \times \underbrace{p(\theta)}_{\text{prior}},$$

(7.5)

where we obtained the second line from the first because the denominator is independent of θ.

To investigate how changes in the prior distribution $p(\theta)$ affect the posterior, we use expression (7.5). This tells us that the posterior is a sort of weighted geometric average[1] of the likelihood and prior. This means that the posterior peak will be situated somewhere between the peaks of the likelihood and prior, so any changes to the prior will be mirrored by changes in the posterior (see Figure 7.3).

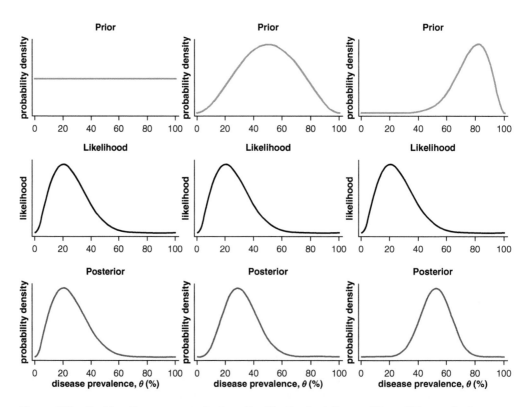

Figure 7.3 For the disease example described in the text the position of the posterior peak (bottom panels) reflects movements in the prior (top panels) for a fixed data sample (ensuring a fixed likelihood; middle panels).

---

[1] A geometric average of a sample is the product of the individual data points, all raised to the power of $1/n$, where n is the sample size. It is typically used in statistics to determine a central measure of data, when an outcome depends strongly on small (or zero) values of the data points.

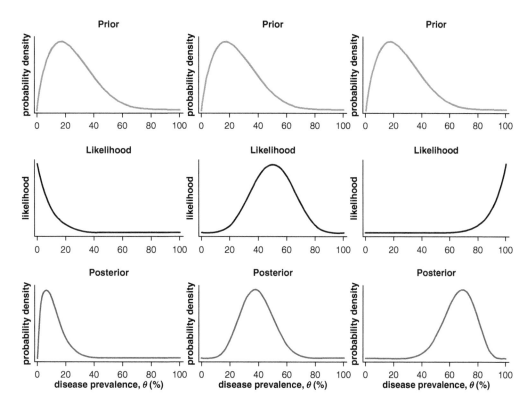

Figure 7.4 For the disease example described in the text the position of the posterior peak (bottom panels) reflects changes to the data through the likelihood (middle panels) for a fixed prior (top panels). The columns represent the inference process when we obtain $X = 0$ (left column), $X = 5$ (middle) and $X = 10$ (right) diseased individuals out of a sample size of 10.

Similarly, any changes to the data will cause changes in the likelihood which, in turn, affects the posterior (see Figure 7.4). As we increase the numbers of disease-positive individuals, from $X = 0$ (left column) to $X = 5$ (middle column) to $X = 10$ (right column), we see that the likelihood shifts to the right and, correspondingly, the posterior peak shifts to give more weight to higher disease prevalences. In these instances, the posterior peak lies about midway between the peaks of the likelihood and prior.

We can also demonstrate how the posterior changes as we increase the sample size, yet maintain the proportion of disease-positive individuals in our sample at 20% (see Figure 7.5). As the sample size increases, the likelihood function becomes narrower and much smaller in value, since the probability of generating a larger data set with any particular characteristics diminishes. Since the posterior is related to the product of the likelihood and prior, it is sensitive to small values of either part. This means that as the sample size increases, and the likelihood function becomes smaller and narrower, the position of the posterior shifts towards the location of the likelihood peak.

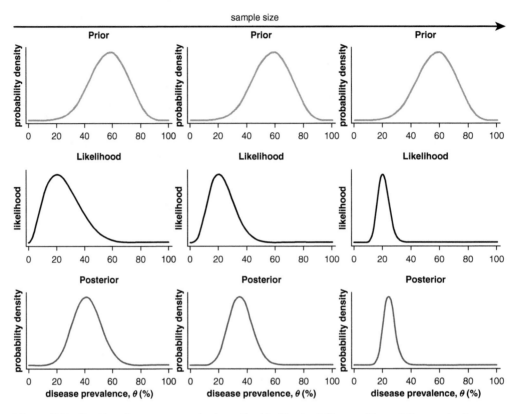

Figure 7.5 For the disease example described in the text the position of the posterior peak (bottom panels) approaches the peak of the likelihood function as the sample size increases (left to right). In the left, middle and right columns, the sample size is 10, 20 and 100, respectively.

7.6 POINT PARAMETER ESTIMATES

While we can estimate the full posterior distribution for a parameter, we are often required to present point estimates. This is sometimes to facilitate direct comparison with Frequentist approaches, but more often it is to allow policy makers to make decisions. We argue that, even if we are asked to provide a single estimated value, it is crucial that we provide a corresponding measure of uncertainty.

There are three predominant point estimators in Bayesian statistics:

- the posterior mean
- the posterior median
- the maximum a posteriori (MAP) estimator

The posterior mean is just the expected value of the posterior distribution. For a univariate continuous example, this is calculated by an integral:

$$\mathbb{E}[\theta \mid data] = \int_{\text{All }\theta} \theta \times p(\theta \mid data) \, d\theta. \tag{7.6}$$

For the discrete case, we replace the above integral with a sum (see Section 3.3.3). For multivariate posteriors, the calculation is more difficult and involves a number of integrals or sums.

The posterior median is the point of a posterior distribution where 50% of probability mass lies on either side of it. The MAP estimator is simply the parameter value that corresponds to the highest point in the posterior and consequently is also referred to as the posterior mode (see Figure 7.6).

While each of these three estimators can be optimal in different circumstances, we believe that there is a clear hierarchy among them. At the top of the hierarchy is the posterior mean. This is our favourite for two reasons: first, it typically yields sensible estimates which are representative of the central position of the posterior distribution; second, and more mathematically, this estimator makes sense from a measure-theoretic perspective, since it accounts for the measure. (Don't worry about this last point too much; we just wanted to mention it for completeness.) Next down the hierarchy is the posterior median. This is usually pretty close to the mean (see Figure 7.6) and is often indicative of the centre of the posterior distribution. It is sometimes preferable to use a median if the mean is heavily skewed by extrema, although the choice between the two estimators depends on circumstance. At the bottom of the hierarchy, we have the MAP estimator. Proponents argue that the simplicity of this estimator is a benefit. It is simple to calculate because the denominator does not depend on the parameter (see Chapter 6), meaning that, to find the posterior mode, we can simply find the parameter value that maximises the numerator. However, its simplicity is misleading. The mode of a distribution often lies away from the bulk of probability mass and is hence not a particularly indicative central measure of the posterior. This estimator also does not make sense mathematically because it is based on the density, which depends on the particular parameterisation in question. The bottom line is that you should not use the MAP estimator unless you have a very good reason for doing so.

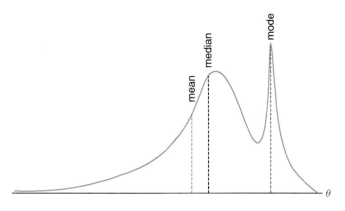

Figure 7.6 The mean, median and mode (MAP) for a skewed, multimodal posterior distribution.

7 O 7 INTERVALS OF UNCERTAINTY

This section describes the Frequentist and Bayesian approaches to parameter uncertainty intervals. While the two approaches both yield intervals that express uncertainty, we argue that the Bayesian *credible interval* is more easily interpreted than the Frequentist *confidence interval*.

7.7.1 Failings of the Frequentist confidence interval

The mainstay of the Frequentist estimation procedure is the confidence interval. In applied research, these intervals often form part of the main results of a paper. For example:

From our research, we concluded that the percentage of penguins with red tails, *RT*, has a 95% confidence interval of 1% ≤ *RT* ≤ 5%.

This is often incorrectly taken as having an implicit meaning: 'There is a 95% probability that the true percentage of penguins with red tails lies in the range of 1% to 5%.' However, what it actually captures is uncertainty about the interval we calculate, rather than the parameter in question.

In the Frequentist paradigm we imagine taking repeated samples from a population of interest, and for each of the fictitious samples, we estimate a confidence interval (see Figure 7.7). A 95% confidence interval means that across the infinity of intervals that we calculate, the true value of the parameter will lie in this range 95% of the time.

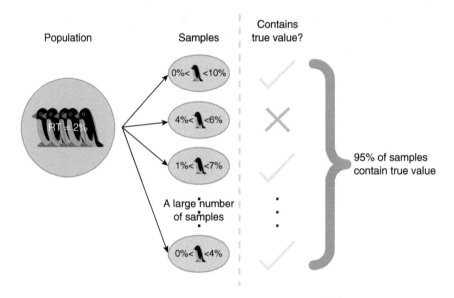

Figure 7.7   The Frequentist confidence interval for the penguin example described in the text. For each possible sample we can draw from the population, we can calculate a 95% confidence interval. Across all these samples, the Frequentist confidence interval will contain the true parameter value 95% of the time.

In reality, we draw only one sample from the population and have no way of knowing whether the confidence interval we calculate actually contains the true parameter value. This means that for 95% of our fictitious samples, the confidence intervals we calculate will contain the true parameter value, but for 5% of samples, the confidence intervals will be nonsense!

A confidence interval indicates uncertainty about the interval we obtain, rather than a statement of probability about the parameter of interest. The uncertainty is quantified in terms of all the samples we could have taken, not just the one we observe.

7.7.2 Credible intervals

Bayesian credible intervals, in contrast to confidence intervals, describe our uncertainty in the location of the parameter values. They are calculated from the posterior density. In particular, a 95% credible region satisfies the condition that 95% of the posterior probability lies in this parameter range. The statement

> From our research, we concluded that the percentage of penguins with red tails, RT, has a 95% credible interval of 0% ≤ RT ≤ 4%

can be interpreted straightforwardly as 'From our research, we conclude that there is a 95% probability that the percentage of penguins with red tails lies in the range $0\% \leq RT \leq 4\%$.'

An arbitrary credible interval of $X\%$ can be constructed from the posterior density by finding a region whose area is equal to $X / 100$.

In contrast to the Frequentist confidence interval, a credible interval is more straightforward to understand. It is a statement of confidence in the location of a parameter. Also, in contrast to the Frequentist confidence intervals, the uncertainty here refers to our inherent uncertainty in the value of the parameter, estimated using the current sample, rather than an infinite number of counterfactual samples.

There are usually a large number of regions which represent an $X\%$ credible interval. For example, all three of the posterior intervals shown in Figure 7.8 are 50% credible intervals. To reduce the number of possible credible intervals, there are industry standards that are followed in most applied research. We introduce two of the most frequently used metrics now, using a treasure hunting example. In doing so, we provide some logic for choosing between these two summary measures.

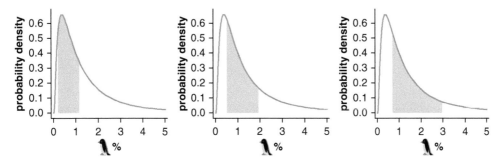

Figure 7.8 Three examples of 50% credible intervals for a parameter representing the proportion of penguins with red tails.

Treasure hunting: the central posterior and highest density intervals

Imagine that you (as a pirate) are told by a fortune teller that a treasure of gold worth $1000 is buried somewhere along the seashore of an island. Further, imagine that the mystic has gone to the trouble of using their past experience, and observed data, to produce the posterior density for the location of the treasure along the seashore, which is shown in Figure 7.9.

Suppose that you want to find the gold with 70% certainty, and maximise your profit in doing so. To reach this level of confidence in plundering the gold, you can choose between the two 70% credible intervals shown in Figure 7.9: on the left, the *central posterior interval* and on the right, the *highest density interval*.

Both of these intervals have the same area, so we are equally likely to find the gold in either. So which one should we choose?

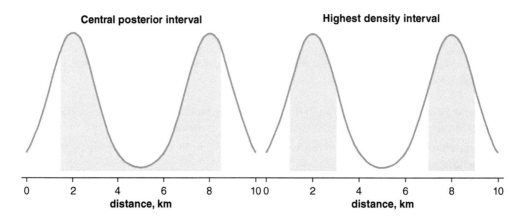

Figure 7.9 The two main types of Bayesian uncertainty interval: the central posterior interval (left) and the highest density interval (right), representing our uncertainty in the treasure's position along the seashore (horizontal axis). In both cases, the curves indicate the posterior probability density function. Note that here the seashore is curvy since we are discussing an island, but we can nonetheless represent the distance along it on a linear scale, as we have done here.

The central posterior interval spans the range of 1.5km to 8.5km along the beach. Suppose that the cost to hire a digger to excavate 1km of coastline is $100. This means that to 'dig up' this interval would cost $700.

The highest density interval spans two non-contiguous regions, given by 1km to 3km and 7km to 9km. Each has a cost of $200 to excavate, meaning a total cost of $400. We hence pick the highest density region and cross our fingers.

If, instead, it was costly to drive a digger a given distance (without digging), then we might change our minds and favour the contiguous region of the central posterior interval over the highest density interval. However, in most practical (non-pirate) situations, the most sensible thing to do is to report the highest density interval.

To calculate the upper and lower bounds of an $X\%$ central posterior interval, we find the $(100 - X) / 2$ and $X + (100 - X) / 2$ quantiles of the posterior distribution. This results in an interval that is centred on the median parameter value.

To calculate the $X\%$ highest density interval, we find the set of values which encompasses this percentage of the posterior probability mass, with the property that the probability density in this set is never lower than outside.

For a unimodal, symmetric distribution, the central posterior density and highest density intervals will be the same. However, for more complex distributions, this may not be true (see Figure 7.9).

7.7.3 Reconciling the difference between confidence and credible intervals

It is easy to jump on the Bayesian bandwagon and favour credible intervals, dismissing Frequentist confidence intervals as misleading. However, in doing so, we are guilty of zealotry. The two concepts really just represent different measures of uncertainty. As we explained in Section 2.5,

Frequentists view data sets as one of an infinite number of exactly repeated experiments, and hence design an interval which contains the true value X% of the time across all these repetitions. The Frequentist confidence interval represents uncertainty in terms of the interval itself. By contrast, Bayesians view the observed data sample as fixed and assume the parameter varies, and hence calculate an interval where X% of the parameter's estimated probability mass lies.

Explaining the difference between confidence and credible intervals

The main problem with the Frequentist confidence interval is that it is often interpreted incorrectly as a credible interval. It is not necessarily a problem with the concept itself. It just depends on your personal preference, and situation, which you find more useful. The following example hopefully makes this difference in perspective clearer.

The interval ENIGMA

Suppose that at the outbreak of war, we are employed as code breakers in hut 8 at Bletchley Park. By monitoring enemy communications we can identify the source of the message, although not its contents. The source of the message is one of a submarine, boat, tank or aircraft. The messages contain details of the next domestic target of the enemy and can be one of dams, ports, towns or airfields; however, these messages are encrypted and hence this information cannot be determined before the attack occurs.

Fortunately, previous code breakers have decoded a large proportion of messages, and for each attack destination have calculated the historical proportions of communications from each source that resulted in an attack on that particular destination (see Table 7.1). We also know from experience that the proportion of attacks on each destination is roughly similar.

Table 7.1 The historical communication frequencies (rows) resulting in attacks for each of the different destinations (columns).

| | Attack destination | | | |
Communication method	Dam	Port	Town	Airfield
Submarine	73%	50%	50%	13%
Boat	9%	25%	25%	16%
Tank	0%	25%	25%	66%
Aircraft	18%	0%	0%	5%
Total	100%	100%	100%	100%

Our job is to predict the next attack destination after we find out the specific mode of communication. Since there is uncertainty over the attack destination, our confidence intervals consist of groups of attack destinations. These intervals are discrete because our parameter (the attack destination) is discrete. To avoid unnecessary defence expenditure, we are told to use the most narrow intervals that provide at least 75% coverage.

Feeding the historical data into a 'statistics machine' and pressing a button that says 'Frequentist confidence intervals' results in the uncertainty intervals shown in Table 7.2. Note that, in all cases, the sum of the probabilities in each column exceeds the 75% threshold. This is because Frequentists suppose that the parameter is fixed (the attack destination) and imagine the data (the communication mode) varies across an infinite number of repeated samples. So their intervals are constructed to ensure that, for every fixed value of the parameter (the attack destination), the true attack destination lies within the specified sets at least 75% of the time, across all possible data samples (the communication modes).

Table 7.2 Frequentist confidence intervals calculated from data shown in Table 7.1. Confidence intervals greater than or equal to 75% are surrounded by square brackets. Note that the attack destination (the parameter) is a discrete categorical outcome, and so the intervals here are not continuous (as the above might be seen to represent). Also note that the above intervals are not necessarily unique in ensuring that 75% coverage is attained.

	Attack destination				
Communications method	Dam	Port	Town	Airfield	Credibility
Submarine	[73%	50%	50%]	13%	**93%**
Boat	[9%	25%	25%	16%]	**100%**
Tank	0%	25%	25%	[66%]	**57%**
Aircraft	18%	0%	0%	5%	**0%**
Coverage	**82%**	**75%**	**75%**	**82%**	

We next press the button corresponding to 'Bayesian credible intervals' and obtain the results shown in Table 7.3. Bayesians assume that the parameter (the attack destination) is uncertain, whereas the data (the communication mode) is fixed. They, therefore, ensure that, whatever the mode of communication, the interval contains the true attack destination at least 75% of the time. This corresponds to ensuring that the sum of probabilities in each row exceeds 75%.

Table 7.3 Bayesian credible intervals calculated from data shown in Table 7.1. Credible intervals greater than or equal to 75% are surrounded by square brackets. Note: Credibility is calculated by dividing the sum of interval values in each row by the row's total. Note that the attack destination (the parameter) is a discrete categorical outcome, and so the intervals here are not continuous (as the above might be seen to represent). Also note that the above intervals are not necessarily unique in ensuring that 75% coverage is attained.

	Attack destination				
Communication method	Dam	Port	Town	Airfield	Credibility
Submarine	[73%	50%	50%]	13%	**93%**
Boat	[9%	25%	25%]	16%	**79%**
Tank	0%	25%	[25%	66%]	**78%**
Aircraft	[18%]	0%	0%	5%	**78%**
Coverage	**100%**	**75%**	**100%**	**66%**	

The difference between these two measures is subtle. In fact, as is often the case, the intervals overlap considerably. But which should we choose? Using the Frequentist confidence intervals, we are assured that whatever attack location the enemy chooses, our interval will contain the true attack destination at least 75% of the time. However, a Bayesian would criticise the confidence interval for the case when an aircraft sends the message since this is an empty interval. This is clearly nonsensical since we know that one of the locations is about to be attacked. This error would be foolhardy if attacks coordinated by aircraft are particularly costly. A Frequentist would argue that since, at most, aircraft communications happen 18% of the time (for dams), this is not something to worry about.

A Bayesian would also criticise the Frequentist confidence intervals, since for a given communication mode, what is the use in worrying about all the other communication modes? We are not uncertain about the communication mode.

A Frequentist would argue that, for attacks on airfields, the Bayesian confidence intervals correctly predict this as the attack destination only 66% of the time. Again, if these types of attack are particularly costly, then this interval might not be ideal. A Bayesian would argue that, assuming a uniform prior, this type of attack happens only 25% of the time and so is not worth worrying about. Further, for every mode of communication, our credible intervals are guaranteed not to be nonsense, in contrast to the Frequentist confidence interval.

FROM POSTERIOR TO PREDICTIONS BY SAMPLING

You might be wondering how to do forecasting using a posterior distribution. Suppose, for example, that we want to use the posterior distribution shown in Figure 7.1 to forecast the outcome of the upcoming US election. How do we do this? While we delay a complete discussion of this until Chapter 10, we now briefly outline what is involved in this process. There are two sources of uncertainty in prediction: first, we do not know the true value of the parameters; and second, there is sampling variability. The first of these sources of uncertainty is represented by the posterior. The second is represented by our choice of likelihood (see Chapter 4). To account for both these sources of variation, we typically derive an approximate distribution that represents our uncertainty over future data by iterating the following steps:

1 Sample $\theta_i \sim p(\theta \mid data)$, that is the posterior distribution.
2 Sample $data'_i \sim p(data \mid \theta_i)$, that is the sampling distribution (likelihood).

By repeating these steps a large number of times (keeping each sampled data value), we eventually obtain a reasonable approximation to the *posterior predictive distribution*. This distribution represents our uncertainty over the outcome of a future data collection effort, accounting for our observed data and model choice.

As an example, suppose that we estimate the prevalence of a particular disease in the UK population using a sample of 10 individuals, where we find that $X = 1$ individual is disease-positive. We use a binomial distribution to explain disease prevalence θ in the sample (see Section 4.6.2) which, along with a uniform prior for the prevalence, results in a posterior shown in the right-hand panel of Figure 7.10. We then follow the steps above to generate an approximate posterior predictive distribution, which forecasts the number of disease-positive individuals in a future sample of the same size. In each iteration, i, we collect a paired sample (θ_i, X_i). We first independently sample a value of disease prevalence from the posterior $(\theta_i \sim p(\theta \mid X = 1, N = 10))$.

The posterior predictive distribution by sampling

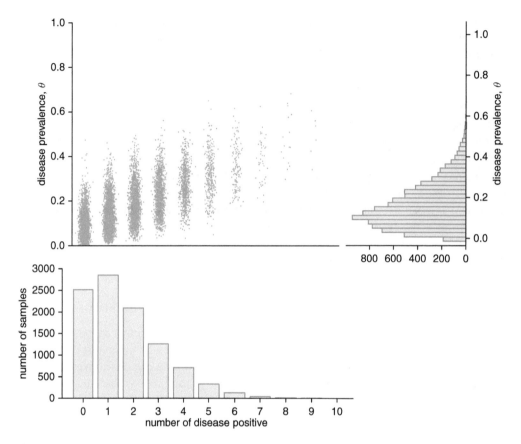

Figure 7.10 Constructing an approximate posterior predictive distribution. Top: the pairs of (X_i, θ_i) sampled in our iterative routine. Right: the marginal distribution of disease prevalences, θ, sampled from the posterior. Bottom: the posterior predictive distribution. Note that we have added horizontal jitter to the number of disease cases in the top-left graph to make it easier to see the individual samples; the actual number is a discrete count, not continuous as it appears.

We then use this disease prevalence to characterise our binomial sampling distribution and use it to independently sample a number of disease cases ($X_i \sim p(X \mid \theta_i, N = 10)$). The set of all samples for the number of disease-cases, X_i, forms our posterior predictive distribution. This distribution is peaked at $X = 1$ (see the bottom panel of Figure 7.10) and has an 80% predictive interval of zero to four cases.

Because of the two sources of uncertainty included in our model – the parameter uncertainty and sampling variability – the uncertainty of the Bayesian predictive distribution is typically greater than the Frequentist equivalent. This is because the Frequentist approach to forecasting typically makes predictions based on a point estimate of a parameter (typically the maximum likelihood value). By ignoring any uncertainty in the parameter's value, the Frequentist approach produces predictive intervals that are overly confident.

One of the uses for posterior predictive distributions is to make forecasts, but these distributions also have another important use: to check the validity of a model's assumptions. These so-called *posterior predictive checks* are essential to the Bayesian modelling process, and we discuss these at length in Chapter 10.

 CHAPTER SUMMARY

In this chapter, we completed our tour of Bayes' rule. Perhaps the most important part of this chapter is Section 7.5, where we saw that the posterior distribution is essentially a weighted average of the position of the likelihood (representing the effect of the data) with that of the prior (representing our pre-data beliefs). This intuition for the mechanics of Bayesian inference is essential, particularly when we move on to more complex models.

We also discussed how the posterior distribution can be used to produce summary estimates of parameters. We argued that, in terms of point estimates, the posterior mean or median are typically preferable to the MAP estimator, because the former are better indications of the location of the bulk of posterior probability mass. We also discussed how to use the posterior to produce uncertainty intervals known as *credible intervals*. We then compared and contrasted these with the analogous Frequentist concept, known as *confidence intervals*, and reasoned that in many cases the Bayesian formulation is more straightforward and intuitive.

Finally, we described how the posterior distribution can be used to forecast by estimating *posterior predictive distributions*. These probability distributions are typically estimated in Bayesian inference by sampling. These distributions encompass two types of uncertainty: first, our uncertainty in the value of the parameters (quantified by the posterior); and second, in the data-generating process itself (quantified by the likelihood). By including our epistemic uncertainty in parameter values as part of a forecast, this Bayesian approach provides a better quantification of uncertainty than the equivalent from Frequentist methods.

To build a good statistical model in Bayesian inference, we must know the essential building blocks of an analysis. Part III is concerned with acquainting the reader with these essential ingredients of Bayesian analyses: the probability distributions that can be used for likelihoods or priors. We shall also see that posterior predictive distributions have a crucial role to play in model building, due to their use in model checking (see Chapter 10).

 CHAPTER OUTCOMES

The reader should now be familiar with the following concepts:

- expressing post-data uncertainty in a parameter's value through posterior probability distributions
- the differences between Frequentist confidence intervals and Bayesian credible intervals
- summary measures of centrality: posterior mean and median, and the MAP estimator (including the issues with the latter)
- how to estimate the posterior predictive distribution by sampling and how to use this for forecasting data in a future experiment

7 ● 11   PROBLEM SETS

Problem 7.1 Googling

Suppose you are chosen, for your knowledge of Bayesian statistics, to work at Google as a search traffic analyst. Based on historical data, you have the data shown in Table P7.1 for the actual word searched and the starting string (the first three letters typed in a search). It is your job to help make the search engine faster by reducing the search space for the machines to look up each time a person types.

Table P7.1   The columns give the historic breakdown of the search traffic for three topics (Barack Obama, baby clothes and Bayes) by the first three letters of the user's search.

	Barack Obama	Baby clothes	Bayes
Bar	50%	30%	30%
Bab	30%	60%	30%
Bay	20%	10%	40%

Problem 7.1.1 Find the minimum coverage confidence intervals of topics that are at least at 70%.

Problem 7.1.2 Find most narrow credible intervals for topics that are at least at 70%.

Now we suppose that your boss gives you the historic search information shown in Table P7.2. Further, you are told that it is most important to correctly suggest the actual topic as one of the first auto-complete options, *irrespective* of the topic searched.

Table P7.2   The historic search traffic broken down by topic

	Barack Obama	Baby clothes	Bayes
Search volume	60%	30%	10%

Problem 7.1.3 Do you prefer confidence intervals or credible intervals in this circumstance?

Problem 7.1.4 Now assume that it is most important to pick the correct actual word across all potential sets of three letters, which interval do you prefer now?

Problem 7.2 GDP versus infant mortality

The data in `posterior_gdpInfantMortality.csv` contains the GDP per capita (in real terms) and infant mortality across a large sample of countries in 1998.

Problem 7.2.1 A simple model is fitted to the data of the form:

$$M_i \sim N(\alpha + \beta GDP_i, \sigma).$$

$$(7.7)$$

Fit this model to the data using a Frequentist approach. How well does the model fit the data?

Problem 7.2.2 An alternative model is:

$$\log(M_i) \sim \mathcal{N}(\alpha + \beta \log(GDP)_i, \sigma). \tag{7.8}$$

Problem 7.2.3 Construct 80% confidence intervals for (α, β).

Problem 7.2.4 We have fitted the log–log model to the data using Markov chain Monte Carlo. Samples from the posterior for (α, β, σ) are contained within the file `posterior_posteriorsGdpInfantMortality.csv`. Using this data, find the 80% credible intervals for all parameters (assuming these intervals to be symmetric about the median). How do these compare with the confidence intervals calculated above for (α, β)? How does the point estimate of σ from the Frequentist approach above compare?

Problem 7.2.5 The following priors were used for the three parameters:

$$\alpha \sim \mathcal{N}(0, 10),$$

$$\beta \sim \mathcal{N}(0, 10), \tag{7.9}$$

$$\sigma \sim \mathcal{N}(0, 5), \quad \sigma \geq 0.$$

Explain any similarity between the confidence and credible intervals in this case.

Problem 7.2.6 How are the estimates of parameters (α, β, σ) correlated? Why?

Problem 7.2.7 Generate samples from the prior predictive distribution. How do the minimum and maximum of the prior predictive distribution compare with the actual data?

Problem 7.2.8 Generate samples from the posterior predictive distribution, and compare these with the actual data. How well does the model fit the data?

Problem 7.3 Bayesian neurosurgery

Suppose that you are a neurosurgeon and have been given the unenviable task of finding the position of a tumour within a patient's brain, and cutting it out. Along two dimensions (vertical height and left–right axis) the tumour's position is known with a high degree of confidence. However, along the remaining axis (front–back) the position is uncertain and cannot be ascertained without surgery. However, a team of brilliant statisticians has already done most of the job for you, generating samples from the posterior for the tumour's location along this axis which you will find in the data file `posterior_brainData.csv`.

Suppose that the more brain that is cut, the more the patient is at risk of losing cognitive functions. Additionally, suppose that there is uncertainty over the amount of damage done to the patient during surgery. As such, three different surgeons have differing views on the damage caused:

Surgeon 1: Damage varies quadratically with the distance the surgery starts away from the tumour.

Surgeon 2: There is no damage if tissue cut is within 0.0001 mm of the tumour; for cuts further away there is a fixed damage.

Surgeon 3: Damage varies linearly with the absolute distance the surgery starts away from the tumour. (Hard – use the fundamental theorem of calculus for this part of the question.)

Problem 7.3.1 Under each of the three regimes above, find the best position along this axis to cut.

Problem 7.3.2 Which of the above loss functions do you think is most appropriate, and why?

Problem 7.3.3 Which loss function might you choose to be most robust to any situation?

Problem 7.3.4 Following on from the previous point, which type of posterior point measure might be most widely applicable?

Problem 7.3.5 Using the data, estimate the loss under the three different regimes, assuming that the true loss $L(\hat{\theta},\theta) = (\hat{\theta}-\theta)^3$.

PART III

ANALYTIC BAYESIAN METHODS

PART III MISSION STATEMENT

This part of the book aims to familiarise the reader with the nuts and bolts of *analytic* Bayesian inference, that is the subset of analyses where an exact posterior distribution can be calculated, often using pen and paper. This begins with Chapter 8, where we introduce the most useful distributions for applied analyses. We then introduce the concept of a conjugate prior in Chapter 9, which allows us to carry out exact Bayesian inference under special circumstances. We then shift focus to model testing and comparison in Chapter 10, before a final chapter on some of the attempts to make Bayesian statistics objective.

PART III GOALS

Up until now, we have built our knowledge of the tools necessary to undertake a Bayesian analysis, first by learning the calculus of probability, then by introducing the various elements of the Bayesian formula. In applied Bayesian analysis, we must choose two parts of the Bayesian formula: the likelihood and the prior. This gives us considerable freedom, and it pays to be familiar with the available options. Chapter 8 introduces some of the most common distributions used for likelihoods and priors in a non-mathematical way. More than previous chapters, it is also supplemented with a number of videos, which may be useful as a complementary source of information.

Before considering the fully unconstrained analyses we describe in Part IV, we next introduce the reader to a special subset of problems where exact Bayesian analysis is possible and can be conducted using only pen and paper. While confining ourselves to this class of problems is restrictive, knowledge of this type of analysis is a useful pedagogic step (towards unconstrained analysis), and will also allow the reader to understand much of the literature.

We argue that an important part of Bayesian inference is the flexibility it provides us in model testing. Unlike Frequentist analysis, where a standard array of tests is used, somewhat mechanically, to test models, we believe Bayesians are freer to decide the way to test their model. This added flexibility may appear onerous since we must make another choice, but we argue that it is ultimately beneficial in refining and choosing between models. Bayesians recognise that the worth of a model depends on its ultimate intended use, and recognise this when deciding how to evaluate a particular model. Chapter 10 provides an introduction to this aspect of Bayesian analysis. It also provides an introduction to the various measures used to score the predictive power of a model.

Chapter 11 provides a short summary of the various attempts to make Bayesian analysis objective. We argue that these attempts are somewhat misguided, since any analysis is subjective, but it is nonetheless important to be acquainted with these methods, to understand the existing literature.

8

Chapter contents

AN INTRODUCTION TO DISTRIBUTIONS FOR THE MATHEMATICALLY UNINCLINED

CHAPTER MISSION STATEMENT

At the end of this chapter, the reader should be familiar with the likelihood and prior distributions used in many applied analyses.

 CHAPTER GOALS

Often texts on Bayesian analysis assume a familiarity with probability distributions that is appropriate for statistics fanatics, but not for the occasional user of Bayesian inference. The absence of this presumed knowledge makes it difficult to penetrate the literature and makes Bayesian inference appear more difficult than it actually is. The aim of this chapter is to redress the balance, by introducing the commonly used distributions, highlighting their interrelationships, and the types of situation when they could be employed. We hope that, by using practical examples, we can turn an otherwise dry subject into something more palatable for bedtime reading.

Generally, there are two classes of distributions: those that can be used for likelihoods and those that can be used for priors. However, there is considerable overlap between these groupings (particularly for continuous distributions), meaning that we will often encounter the distributions twice.

It is important to remember that all distributions are related to one another (see Section 8.3). Knowledge of these interrelations is illuminating and practically useful since it makes it easier to remember them.

Throughout the chapter, there are considerable interactive elements. It is hoped that the reader will take the opportunity to use this material to gain hands-on experience. In particular, there are videos which take the reader through some of the basic properties, and uses of, the distributions.

At the end of the chapter is Figure 8.33, a tree diagram that helps guide a reader to choose a likelihood. While not exhaustive, it is hoped that this tree will nonetheless be a useful starting point in an analysis.

It should be stressed that this chapter, perhaps more than some of the others, need not be read in its entirety. While we recommend reading all of Section 8.4, it is not necessary to read the entirety of Section 8.5. There is much to be gained from persevering but, to avoid boredom, it may be better to refer to the relevant section in the event that you encounter a hitherto unknown distribution, either in reading this book or in applied work.

 THE INTERRELATION AMONG DISTRIBUTIONS

This chapter introduces the reader to a multitude of different distributions, and one could be forgiven for becoming overwhelmed by the sheer number of them. However, it is important to remember that the distributions are all related to one another. The nexus of resultant connections is not merely academic – it is informative when choosing a distribution for an analysis, as well as for recollection. While it is not expected that the reader will remember all of the connections between the distributions, it is hoped that exposure to the graph shown in Figure 8.1 is nevertheless worthwhile. We strongly encourage the student to refer back to this graph when reading this chapter, as it may help with the understanding.

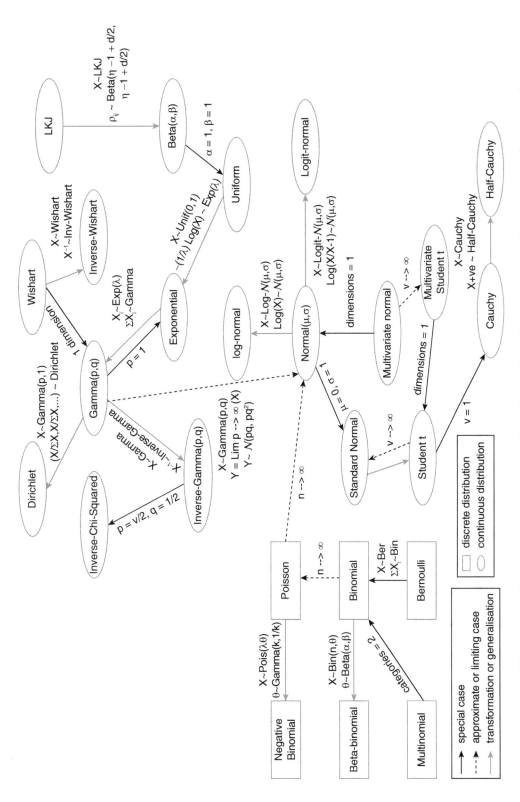

Figure 8.1 Some of the interrelations among common statistical distributions. Discrete distributions are shown in rectangular boxes and continuous ones in ovals. Black lines indicate that the resultant is a special case of the former, dashed lines indicate approximate or limiting cases, and red lines indicate that the latter can be made by a transformation of the former. Note that the relationships shown here are not exhaustive.

DISTRIBUTIONS FOR LIKELIHOODS

The first class of distributions that we encountered in Part II were those used for likelihood functions. These likelihood models should satisfy our assumptions about the system under examination. They also define the parameters that we will infer. Specifying an appropriate likelihood is the most important decision in Bayesian inference. To help make these decisions, it is essential to have an appreciation of possible likelihood distributions. While there are an infinite number of these available, we believe that the distributions we present here are the most commonly used in applied analyses.

8.4.1 Bernoulli

Distribution checklist:

- ✓ Discrete data
- ✓ A single trial
- ✓ *Only* two trial outcomes: *success* and *failure* (These do not need to literally represent successes and failures, but this shorthand is typically used.)

Example uses: to model the outcome of flipping a coin, a single clinical trial or a presidential election.

Imagine that we are interested in the outcome of a single horse race. For simplicity, we suppose that we only care whether the horse wins or loses, not its position in the field, should it not come first. Any position after first we deem a loss. We use the random variable, X, which associates the following numerical values with each of the outcomes:

$$X = \begin{cases} 0, \ horse \ wins \\ 1, \ horse \ loses. \end{cases} \tag{8.1}$$

We assume that the outcome of a single race is influenced by a latent probability of the horse winning, $0 \le \theta \le 1$. We do not actually witness this probability, and after the discussion in Chapter 2, we are not sure it really exists. In the Frequentist paradigm, θ is the proportion of races that the horse has won historically (and would win in total, if we continued racing for ever). For Bayesians, θ merely gauges our subjective confidence in the event of the horse winning (see Section 2.6).

We can now calculate the probability of the two distinct possible outcomes. The probability that the horse wins is just $p(win) = \theta$, meaning that the probability of a loss is $p(loss) = 1 - \theta$. In the left-hand panel of Figure 8.2, we show this probability distribution for two different values of θ. As we increase this parameter, the horse is more likely to win and, hence, the distribution gives more weight to this outcome.

We can also write down the likelihood of each outcome. Remember that a likelihood is not a valid probability density, and is found by holding the data (here the race outcome) constant while varying the parameters.

Suppose that the horse had a good meal of carrots this morning and wins by a country mile. By the equivalence relation, the likelihood of this event is given by $L(\theta \mid X = 1) = p(X = 1 \mid \theta) = \theta$ (see the red line in the right-hand panel of Figure 8.2).

An introduction to the Bernoulli and binomial distributions

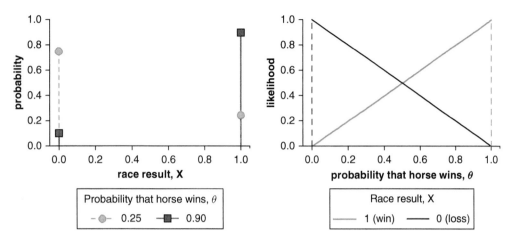

Figure 8.2 Left: the Bernoulli probability distribution for two different values of θ. Right: the Bernoulli likelihoods for the two possible outcomes of the horse race, where the maximum likelihood estimates are shown as dashed lines in each case.

Alternatively, if our horse spent the night in the midst of night-mares and loses, then the likelihood is given by $L(\theta \mid X = 1) = 1 - \theta$ (see the black line in the right-hand panel of Figure 8.2). The maximum likelihood estimates in each case are given by $\hat{\theta} = 1$, if the horse wins, and $\hat{\theta} = 0$, if it loses.

We can write down a single expression that yields the likelihood, or probabilities (dependent on viewpoint), for both possible outcomes:

$$Pr(X = k \mid \theta) = \theta^k (1 - \theta)^{(1-k)}. \tag{8.2}$$

This distribution is known as the *Bernoulli*, after the famous Swiss mathematician Jakob Bernoulli, who first discovered it in the late seventeenth century. Among his modest achievements, Bernoulli proved the Law of Large Numbers, did important work on differential equations, and discovered the fundamental mathematical constant e. Bernoulli chose a graph of a logarithmic spiral for his gravestone. When he died in 1705, however, the spiral inscribed by stonemasons was an Archimedean spiral. We can forgive him for turning (or perhaps spiralling) in his grave!

Properties:

notation: $X \sim Ber(\theta)$ (8.3a)

PMF: $Pr(X = k \mid \theta) = \theta^k (1 - \theta)^{1-k}$ (8.3b)

mean: $\mathbb{E}[X] = \theta$ (8.3c)

variance: $var[X] = \theta(1 - \theta)$ (8.3d)

8.4.2 Binomial

Distribution checklist:

- ✓ Discrete data
- ✓ A fixed number of total trials
- ✓ Each trial has two possible outcomes (see the Bernoulli; often called *successes* and *failures*)
- ✓ Trial outcomes are independent
- ✓ Probability of success is the same in each trial
- ✓ The outcome is the aggregate number of successes

Example uses: to model the aggregate outcome of clinical drug trials, to estimate the proportion of the population voting for each political party using exit poll data (where there are only two political parties).

Suppose that we have data from a number of Bernoulli events. For example, imagine that we have a sample of 10 willing students who have chosen to undertake a clinical trial that lasts for 1 week. At the start, the students are infected with a flu virus by an injection. Halfway through the experiment, they are given an experimental drug that is thought to help the immune system fight the infection. At the end of the week, the consulting physician records the number of volunteers who still show flu-like symptoms and those who do not. Since it usually takes a patient about 2 weeks to recover from this particularly nasty version of the flu virus, any recoveries during the week are deemed to be due to the drug. To build a statistical model of these outcomes, we need some assumptions. In particular, we assume that the students' data are independent and identically distributed. This might be violated if, for example, some of the volunteers have asthma, and hence are unlikely to be cured by the wonder drug. We create a random variable, X, representing the outcome of the trial for a single volunteer, which equals 1 if the trial is successful (the volunteer is no longer symptomatic), and 0 if not.

We record the aggregate number of successes across all 10 volunteers. Here, it makes sense to create another helper random variable, $0 \leq Z \leq 10$, which represents the aggregate outcome of the overall trial:

$$Z = \sum_{i=1}^{10} X_i. \tag{8.4}$$

After the drug trial, we find that five volunteers successfully recovered from the virus during the week. We reason that the following outcomes could have led to this aggregate result: $\boldsymbol{X} = \{1, 1, 1, 1, 1, 0, 0, 0, 0, 0\}$, where the first five volunteers appeared to react well to the treatment. Feeling satisfied, we present our results to the pharma company executives who developed the drug. They look slightly perturbed and say that $\boldsymbol{X} = \{1,0,1,0,1,0,1,0,1,0\}$ could also have been possible. Realising our mistake, we see that there are a large number of individual trial outcome combinations that are consistent with the aggregate result that five individuals recovered. Thankfully, we realise that the number of such combinations is given by the binomial ^nC_r formula (see Section 4.6.2), meaning that there are $\binom{10}{5} = 252$ possible individual outcome combinations consistent with this aggregate outcome.

With this realisation, we can write down the likelihood. Since we assumed that the individual trial outcomes were *independent*, we can calculate the overall probability by multiplying together the individual probabilities, accounting for the 252 possible combinations:

$$Pr(Z = 5 \mid \theta) = 252 \times Pr(X_1 = 1 \mid \theta)...Pr(X_5 = 1 \mid \theta)Pr(X_6 = 0 \mid \theta)...Pr(X_{10} = 0 \mid \theta)$$

$$= 252 \times \theta^5 (1 - \theta)^5$$

(8.5)

where θ is the probability that an individual recovers over the course of the week.

As for the Bernoulli case, we would like a compact way of writing the likelihood to cover any eventuality. In general, suppose that the number of volunteers is given by n, and the probability of individual treatment success is θ, where we find k successes in our sample:

$$Pr(Z = k \mid n, \theta) = \binom{n}{k} \theta^k (1 - \theta)^{n-k}.$$

(8.6)

This is known as the *binomial* distribution.

If we hold n constant and increase the probability of success, θ, the discrete probability distribution shifts to the right as expected (see the left-hand panel of Figure 8.3).

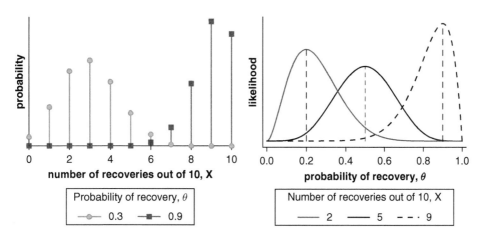

Figure 8.3 Left: the discrete probability distribution for the number of successful trials. Right: the binomial likelihood functions for three different study outcomes, where the maximum likelihood estimates are shown as vertical dashed lines in each case.

For our current example, where 5 out of 10 individuals recovered, we find that the maximum likelihood estimator of θ occurs when $\theta = \frac{1}{2}$ so that it equals the proportion of individuals that recovered in the sample (see the black line in the right-hand panel of Figure 8.3).

If the drug were less effective and only two patients recovered, the likelihood would shift leftwards, peaking now at $\theta = \frac{1}{5}$ (see the grey line in the right-hand panel of Figure 8.3). By contrast, if the patients responded well, and 9 out of 10 recovered during the week, then the likelihood would shift rightwards (see the dashed line in the right-hand panel of Figure 8.3).

Properties:

notation: $X \sim \mathcal{B}(n,\theta)$ (8.7a)

PMF: $Pr\left(X=k\,|\,\theta\right)=\dbinom{n}{k}\theta^k(1-\theta)^{n-k}$ (8.7b)

mean: $\mathbb{E}\left[X\right]=n\theta$ (8.7c)

variance: $var\left[X\right]=n\theta(1-\theta)$ (8.7d)

8.4.3 Poisson

Distribution checklist:

✓ Count of discrete events
✓ Individual events occur at a given rate and independently of other events
✓ Fixed amount of time or space in which the events can occur

Example uses: estimating the failure rate of artificial heart valves, estimating the prevalence of violent crimes in different districts, approximating the binomial which is, itself, being used to explain the prevalence of autism in the UK.

Suppose that we want to estimate the rate at which new outbreaks of Legionella disease[1] occur world-wide. Public health officials have the count of Legionella outbreaks that have occurred each year, X, for a number of years. We assume that the outbreaks appear spontaneously and independently of one another, at a mean rate of λ per year. A probability distribution function that satisfies this condition is:

$$Pr(X=k\,|\,\lambda)=\frac{\lambda^k}{k!}e^{-\lambda},$$ (8.8)

▶

An introduction to the Poisson distribution

which is known as the *Poisson* distribution, after the prominent French mathematician Siméon Denis Poisson born in the late eighteenth century. Apart from his work on probability theory, Poisson made major contributions to the study of planetary motion and to the theory of attraction (including his famous partial differential equation that is used to calculate gravitational or electric fields). He was clearly a man of few non-academic interests and was famously quoted as saying, 'Life is good for only two things: doing mathematics and teaching.' Not perhaps the best man to go to Ibiza with then, we suspect!

This discrete Poisson probability distribution is shown for different values of λ in the left-hand panel of Figure 8.4. We can see that as we increase λ, the distribution shifts rightwards.

To graph the likelihood we vary the mean number of outbreaks that occur per year, λ, and hold the data sample constant. The likelihood is shown for three different data samples (each of the same sample size) in the right-hand panel of Figure 8.4. In this plot, we can see that increasing the mean number of disease outbreaks that we obtain in our sample leads to a rightward shift

---

[1]A nasty disease carried by bacteria that thrive in warm water, named for its first reported occurrence among conference attendees at a Philadelphia convention of the American Legion.

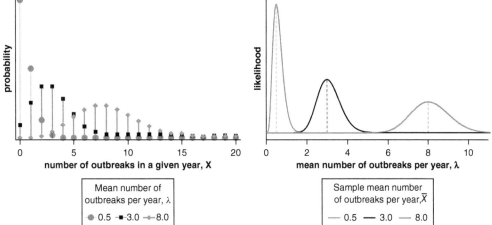

Figure 8.4   Left: the Poisson distribution for different values of λ. Right: the Poisson likelihood functions for the Legionella example corresponding to three different data samples, with the maximum likelihood estimators shown in each case (dashed lines). For the Poisson likelihood calculation, the data consisted of a sample of size 10.

in the likelihood function. For the Poisson distribution, the maximum likelihood estimate is given by the sample mean.

The Poisson distribution is defined only for non-negative integer data, which makes it ideal for modelling the count of event occurrences. The mean rate λ is not constrained to the integers, however, and can equal any non-negative real value. This distribution is based on the assumption that the individual events (the entities being counted) occur independently of each other. In our Legionella example, this assumption would be violated if there were an issue with the data collection that meant some of the outbreaks were not, in fact, new outbreaks, and were caused when the infection spread from another outbreak.

Notice that, in the properties listed below, the mean and variance of this distribution are the same, and equal λ. This limits the use of this distribution to circumstances when the data sample satisfies these properties, at least approximately. However, when we cover the negative binomial (Section 8.4.4) we shall see that the addition of an extra parameter, which governs the degree of overdispersion in the data, allows the extra flexibility required to handle data with a variance that exceeds the mean.

Properties:

notation: $X \sim Poisson(\lambda)$ (8.9a)

PMF: $Pr(X = k \mid \lambda) = \dfrac{\lambda^k}{k!} e^{-\lambda}$ (8.9b)

mean: $\mathbb{E}[X] = \lambda$ (8.9c)

variance: $var[X] = \lambda$ (8.9d)

8.4.4 Negative binomial

Distribution checklist:

✓ Count of discrete events
✓ Non-independent events; it is sometimes said that the events can exhibit contagion, meaning that if one event occurs, it is more likely that another will also occur
✓ Can model a data-generating process where the variance exceeds the mean
✓ Fixed amount of time or space in which the events can occur

Example uses: everything the Poisson can do and more, to model the number of measles cases that occur on an island, or the number of banks that collapse in a financial crisis.

We sometimes want to model the count of events which occur in clumps, either in time or in space. This clumping behaviour results when the occurrence of one event makes it more likely that another will also occur.

Suppose that we work as epidemiologists, this time modelling the occurrence of flu over a winter season in three small villages, Socialville, Commuterville and Academicville, all of the same size. To keep things simple, we imagine that, in each village, the magnitude of the outbreak is determined by a parameter θ. If this number was known, we assume that the numbers of flu cases, X, can be modelled by a Poisson distribution:

$$X \mid \theta \sim Poisson(\lambda\theta). \tag{8.10}$$

θ can be thought of as measuring the strength of social interactions between the villagers, and λ measures the underlying rate of infection common to all social interactions. In Studentville, $\theta = 1.35$, because people spend their time getting drunk and going to parties. In Commuterville, $\theta = 1$, because people spend most of their time with the families, and only go outside to work. In

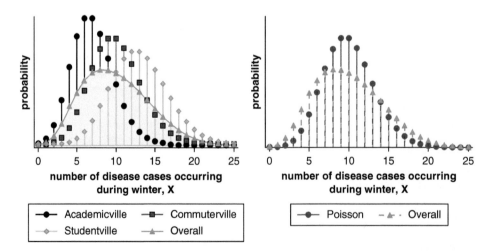

Figure 8.5 Left: the probability distribution for the number of flu cases for each of the towns and the average number of flu cases overall. Right: a comparison of the overall distribution with a Poisson distribution (grey circles) of the same mean.

Academicville, $\theta = 0.65$, because the villagers mostly stay in their houses (writing papers). Across all villages the mean number of cases is $\lambda(1.35 + 1 + 0.65)/3 = \lambda$. Here we take $\lambda = 10$.

Considering now the occurrence of the disease, Studentville gets the most flu cases, because people are most likely to become infected and then pass on the illness to others (red diamond distribution shown in the left-hand panel of Figure 8.5). In Commuterville, because people have contact with one another only when at work, the number of flu cases is, in general, fewer than in Studentville (grey square distribution shown in the left-hand panel of Figure 8.5). Finally, in Academicville, only a few people get sick because most people are complete hermits (black circle distribution shown in the left-hand panel of Figure 8.5). We can model the average number of disease cases across all three villages by averaging across all the village-specific distributions (see the red triangle distribution shown in the left-hand panel of Figure 8.5). The resultant distribution should have an overall mean of 10. However, due to the added uncertainty associated with the intra-village uncertainty, the distribution is wider than a simple Poisson (see the right-hand panel of Figure 8.5).

Suppose that we now want to predict the number of flu cases across a large number of equally sized villages. Imagine that we do not collect data on the social networks in the various villages but we can assume that the strength of social interactions across the villages varies according to $\theta \sim \Gamma(\kappa, 1/\kappa)$ (see Section 8.4.9 for a full explanation of the gamma distribution). This assumption means that the average level of θ across all villages is 1. This implies that the mean number of flu cases across all villages is λ. If the villages were all equally sociable, then $\theta = 1$ in each of them,

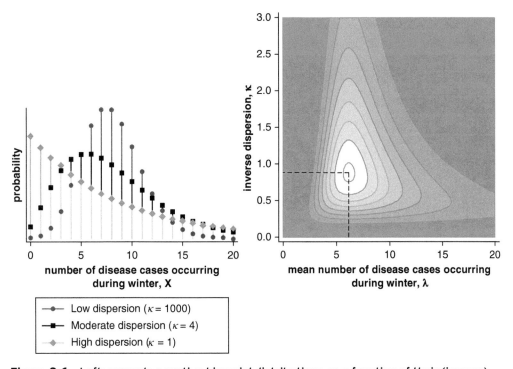

Figure 8.6 Left: example negative binomial distributions as a function of their (inverse) dispersion κ for the disease example discussed in the text. All three cases have a mean of 8. Right: a contour plot of the likelihood surface for the data sample {0, 5, 0, 5, 8, 10, 15}, with the maximum likelihood estimates indicated by dashed lines. The parameter κ here represents the inverse dispersion, with smaller values indicating less dispersion.

resulting in the overall distribution being described by a *Poisson(λ)* distribution, with a variance of λ. However, because of the variance in θ across the villages, we obtain a variance in cases given by:

$$\lambda + \frac{\lambda^2}{\kappa} \geq var(X_{poisson}) = \lambda,$$

(8.11)

which would exceed the variance in overall numbers of individuals with flu if all the towns were identical.

More generally, we see that this distribution has a variance that is greater than that of the Poisson distribution. This extra flexibility comes at a cost of extra complexity because the distribution is characterised by two parameters rather than one. The parameter κ quantifies the degree of dispersion in the data. Note, however, it is an inverse measure of dispersion – the larger its value, the smaller the variability (see the left-hand panel of Figure 8.6). The inflated variance of this distribution compared to the Poisson means that it is sometimes called the *overdispersed* Poisson. However, its more common name is the *negative binomial*.

We can also calculate the likelihood function for the negative binomial distribution although, now, because this distribution has two parameters – λ (the mean) and κ (a measure of the inverse width of the distribution) – we need three dimensions to display it fully (two dimensions for the parameters, another one for the function's value). Instead, we use a contour plot to display the likelihood surface (see the right-hand plot of Figure 8.6). It happens that the maximum likelihood estimator of λ equals the sample mean in the data, and because the data sample has a large variance we estimate a low value of κ.

This distribution has three commonly used parameterisations, each of which we describe below.

Properties:

Here κ represents the inverse dispersion.

notation: $X \sim NB(\lambda, \kappa)$

(8.12a)

PMF: $Pr(X = y | \lambda, \kappa) = \frac{\Gamma(y + \kappa)}{y! \Gamma(\kappa + 1)} \left(\frac{\lambda}{\lambda + \kappa} \right)^y \left(\frac{\kappa}{\lambda + \kappa} \right)^\kappa$

(8.12b)

mean: $\mathbb{E}[X] = \lambda$

(8.12c)

variance: $var[X] = \lambda + \frac{\lambda^2}{\kappa}$

(8.12d)

Here κ represents the dispersion.

notation: $X \sim NB(\lambda, \kappa)$

(8.13a)

PMF: $Pr(X = y | \lambda, \kappa) = \frac{\Gamma\left(y + \frac{1}{\kappa}\right)}{y! \Gamma\left(\frac{1}{\kappa} + 1\right)} \left(\frac{\lambda}{\lambda + \frac{1}{\kappa}} \right)^y \left(\frac{\frac{1}{\kappa}}{\lambda + \frac{1}{\kappa}} \right)^{\frac{1}{\kappa}}$

(8.13b)

mean: $\mathbb{E}[X] = \lambda$

(8.13c)

variance: $var[X] = \lambda + \lambda^2 \kappa$

(8.13d)

This final parameterisation is probably the most common. Here we suppose that we have an experiment consisting of a sequence of Bernoulli trials, each of which can either be a success (with probability θ) or failure. The negative binomial is the probability distribution over the number of failures that would be obtained before r successes occur.

notation: $X \sim NB(r,\theta)$	(8.14a)
PMF: $Pr(X = y \mid r,\theta) = \binom{r+y-1}{r-1}(1-\theta)^y \theta^r$	(8.14b)
mean: $\mathbb{E}[X] = \dfrac{r(1-\theta)}{\theta}$	(8.14c)
variance: $var[X] = \dfrac{r(1-\theta)}{\theta^2}$	(8.14d)

Be careful: Γ in the above distributions is the gamma function, not the gamma distribution.

8.4.5 Beta-binomial

Distribution checklist:

✓ Discrete data
✓ Multiple trials with a fixed number of total trials
✓ Each trial has two possible outcomes (which are often referred to as *successes* and *failures*)
✓ Overall data we measure is the aggregate number of successes
✓ Probability of success varies across trials

Example uses: everything the binomial can do and more, to estimate breast cancer prevalence across heterogeneous patient groups, or to determine the number of votes for the Republican Party with a sample composed of data across many states.

The beta-binomial is to the binomial what the negative binomial is to the Poisson. By assuming that there is heterogeneity in the probability of success, this leads to a variance that exceeds that of the basic binomial. This is another example of an overdispersed distribution. As the following example illustrates, overdispersion results when there is heterogeneity across groups.

Imagine that we want to quantify the efficacy of a drug, which aims to cure depression. We conduct a number of separate trials, where in each case a drug is given to a number of individuals diagnosed with depression, and we record the number of recoveries. For an individual group, we might assume that the number of successes, X, can be modelled by a binomial distribution: $X \sim \mathcal{B}(n,\theta)$. Here n represents the sample size, and θ is the probability of recovery for an individual patient.

Suppose that we replicate our drug trial for two patient groups, each comprising 10 individuals. The groups differ in the seriousness of their condition: in one, the individuals have *mild* depression; in the other, the individuals are diagnosed with a more *severe* version of the disorder. We suppose that the drug is most efficacious for the mild group, so that the drug's success probability is greater, $\theta_{mild} > \theta_{severe}$. Suppose that we create a sample of individuals of size 10, where five individuals were drawn from the mild group and the other five from the severe group. The probability distribution for the combined sample would then be the average of a binomial distribution for the mild group

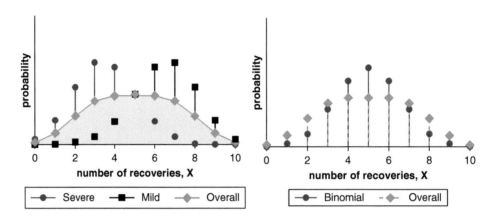

Figure 8.7   Left: binomial distributions for the number of recoveries from depression after taking the drug for the two groups and overall. Right: a comparison of the overall distribution with a binomial distribution with the same mean. In all cases, the sample size is 10.

and another binomial distribution for the severe group (see the left-hand panel of Figure 8.7). Because of the heterogeneity among individuals in the combined sample, there is more uncertainty than would be present for a homogeneous sample, where the outcome can be adequately described by a binomial distribution (see the right-hand panel of Figure 8.7 and the problem set at end of the chapter).

More generally, consider a sample of a number of individuals, where each individual has a different response to the drug, manifesting in individual-specific success probabilities that are

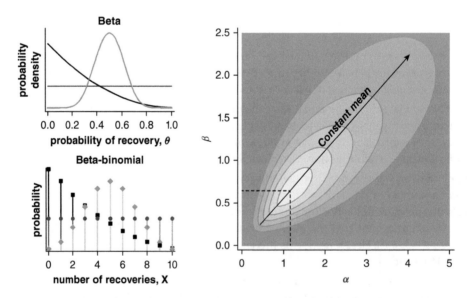

Figure 8.8   Top-left: the beta distribution for three different sets of parameter values. Lower-left: the beta-binomial distribution for the corresponding parameter values. Right: the likelihood contour plot for the following numbers of successes across five different studies: {1,10,8,3,8,9}. The dashed lines show the maximum likelihood estimates of the parameters, and the arrow shows the combinations of parameter values which result in the same mean. The sample size is 10 in all cases.

drawn from an overarching beta distribution, $\theta \sim beta(\alpha, \beta)$. In this case, the aggregate number of individuals that recover from depression in the sample is given by a *beta-binomial* distribution. The variance of this distribution exceeds that of the binomial distribution (see problem set at the end of the chapter), which is useful whenever a sample is composed of individuals of considerable heterogeneity.

In the left-hand panels of Figure 8.8 we illustrate how changes to α and β affect the distribution for θ (top panel) which, in turn, are reflected by corresponding changes in the probability distribution for the data (bottom panel). In the right-hand panel of the figure we also show a contour plot of the likelihood in (α, β) space for a given sample of data. In this plot we notice that there is significant correlation between our estimates. This is because the mean of the beta-binomial depends on the ratio of these parameter values. For example, for a sample size of 10, if $\alpha = 1$ and $\beta = 1$ we obtain a mean of 5. If, instead, we use $\alpha = 2$ and $\beta = 2$, we also obtain the same mean. Therefore, it is unsurprising that we find it difficult to separately identify these parameters since different combinations of them can result in the same mean (indicated by the arrow in the right-hand panel of Figure 8.8).

> *Properties:*
>
> PMF: $Pr(X = y \mid n, \alpha, \beta) = \binom{n}{y} \dfrac{B(y + \alpha, n + \beta - y)}{B(\alpha, \beta)}$ (8.15a)
>
> mean: $\mathbb{E}[X] = \dfrac{n\alpha}{\alpha + \beta}$ (8.15b)
>
> variance: $var[X] = \dfrac{n\alpha\beta(\alpha + \beta + n)}{(\alpha + \beta)^2(\alpha + \beta + 1)}$ (8.15c)

Here $B(a,b) = \int_0^1 t^{a-1}(1-t)^{b-1}\, dt$ and is known as the beta function.

8.4.6 Normal

Distribution checklist:

- ✓ Continuous data
- ✓ Unbounded outcomes, at least *practically* unbounded, for example the weight of adults aged 30 (This is bounded by zero, since weight cannot be negative, but this bound is never approached by data.)
- ✓ Outcome is the result of a large number of additive factors

Example uses: to model the error in regression models, to describe the intelligence of individuals, as an approximation to the binomial distribution when the sample size is large and the probability of success is close to $\frac{1}{2}$, as an approximation to the Poisson distribution when its mean is large.

The normal is the most commonly occurring distribution in nature (hence its name). This is because of the central limit theorem (see Section 3.5), which predicts its occurrence whenever there are a large number of additive factors that produce an outcome.

Imagine that we want to explain the distribution of body temperatures among people. We might imagine that measurements of body temperature depend on a number of factors: the amount of

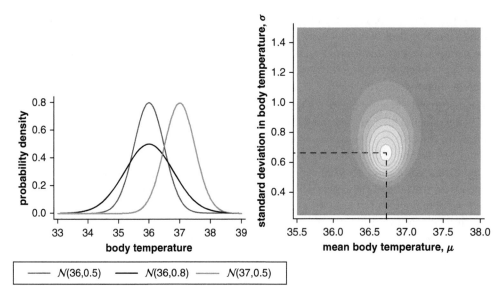

Figure 8.9   Left: the normal probability density functions for three different sets of (μ, σ). Right: a contour plot of the normal likelihood for a sample of body temperatures: {36.4, 37.2, 35.8, 36.4, 37.1, 35.6, 36.4, 37.6, 37.5, 37.1}. The maximum likelihood estimates are shown by dashed lines. All temperatures are given in degrees centigrade.

exercise taken before the appointment, the outside temperature, how much water the person has drunk, as well as genetic and other physiological characteristics. When we have no information on these individual-specific factors, we might invoke the central limit theorem and suppose that body temperatures are normally distributed within a population.

This distribution is specified by two parameters: μ, its mean, and σ, its standard deviation. Changing these has the expected outcome of translating the position of the peak, and changing the distribution's width, respectively (see the left-hand panel of Figure 8.9).

Suppose that we measure the body temperature of 10 participants. Since the distribution is specified by two unknown parameters, the likelihood function corresponds to a surface, and it is easiest to understand by looking at contour plots (see the right-hand panel of Figure 8.9). Unsurprisingly, the maximum likelihood estimates of the mean and standard deviation (dashed lines) essentially correspond to their sample equivalents.

Properties:

---

notation: $X \sim N(\mu, \sigma)$ (8.16a)

PDF: $p(x \mid \mu, \sigma) = \dfrac{1}{\sqrt{2\pi\sigma^2}} e^{-\frac{(x-\mu)^2}{2\sigma^2}}$ (8.16b)

mean: $\mathbb{E}[X] = \mu$ (8.16c)

variance: $var[X] = \sigma^2$ (8.16d)

8.4.7 Student-*t*

Distribution checklist:

- ✓ Continuous data
- ✓ Unbounded outcomes, or, at least, *practically* unbounded
- ✓ Outcome is the outcome of a large number of additive factors
- ✓ Data sample composed of heterogeneous individuals

Example uses: same uses as normal and more, for example to model stock returns.

Like the binomial and Poisson, the normal distribution has an overdispersed cousin – the Student-*t* distribution – which can be used to handle data sets with greater variability. Like some other cases, this distribution can be shown to be equivalent to a mixture of other, simpler, distributions. In particular, the Student-*t* distribution is a mixture of individual normal distributions with differing variances.

Suppose that we measure the mean test score for a standardised arithmetic test for two neighbouring schools: Privilege High, where the times are easy and the fees extortionate; and Danum Comprehensive, where schooling is free and kids of all abilities attend. We suppose that, controversially, a local newspaper has done some research and determined that the mean test scores are the same across both schools. However, Privilege High has a lower variance in test scores than Danum Comprehensive. Since a student's test score is likely the result of a combination of factors including work ethic, family education and brilliance in maths, a normal distribution may be a reasonable approximation for the distribution of test scores for a number of individuals (see Section 8.4.6).

Suppose that we are employed by the local education authority who wants us to develop a model for the combined schools' test scores, to help them decide whether to merge the schools. We can think of the resultant distribution as an average of the school-specific distributions, meaning that its head will rise, its shoulders will fall and its tails will fatten (see the left-hand panel of Figure 8.10). The distribution for the combined schools will have a greater variability in test results than a normal distribution of the same mean would allow (see the right-hand panel of Figure 8.10). This variability is not necessarily borne out in the variance of the distribution, but will be evident in higher-order moments (for example, the fourth moment, often used to compute the kurtosis, which represents the 'fatness' of a distribution's tails).

Imagine that we are now combining the data from a large number of schools, each with the same mean arithmetic score, but differing variances. If we suppose that the school-level variances are distributed as $\sigma^2 \sim Inv\text{-}\Gamma(v/2, v/2)$ then the distribution across all schools is a *Student-t* distribution[2] with v degrees of freedom.[3] Unsurprisingly, this distribution can encompass a larger amount of variation than is possible with a normal distribution.

---

[2]Named after the pseudonym used by William Sealy Gosset, a Guinness brewery worker. Remarkable, as this is perhaps the first but not last time that statistics and alcohol were found to mix well!

[3]While 'degrees of freedom' suggests that v is discrete, it is not. Any positive real value is allowed for this input of the Student-*t* distribution.

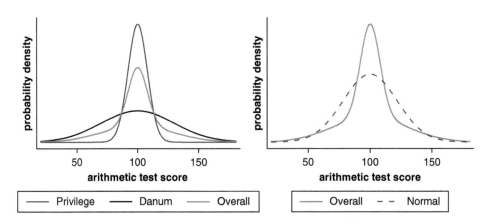

Figure 8.10 Left: the distribution of test scores for each school and overall (imagine merging the two schools – a nightmare for Privilege High parents!). Right: a comparison of the combined school's distribution and a normal distribution with the same mean and standard deviation.

As we increase v, the variance of the inv-gamma distribution decreases and the distribution of test scores becomes closer in shape to a normal distribution (this is a consequence of the central limit theorem discussed in Section 3.5). Figure 8.11 illustrates how changes to the parameters σ and v, which characterise this distribution, affect its shape.

Now suppose that we have a sample of six test scores by randomly picking individuals from the combined list of students across all schools. Since we have three unknown parameters in our distribution, the likelihood function is three-dimensional, which is not easy to plot in our paltry three spatial dimensions (since we need a fourth dimension to represent the value of the likelihood function). However, we can use pairwise contour plots of the variables to illustrate the marginal distributions of the likelihood surface (see Figure 8.12). These indicate little correlation between the estimates of the mean of the distribution with either of the parameters σ and v (bottom panels) because the contours of constant likelihood in the bottom panels are horizontal with respect to each of these. However, since both of these latter parameters affect the

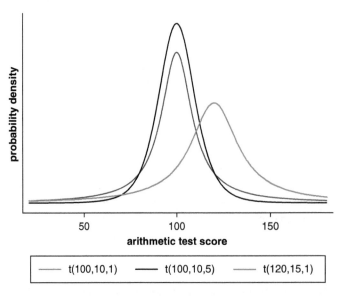

Figure 8.11 Student-t distributions drawn for three parameter sets of (μ, σ, v).

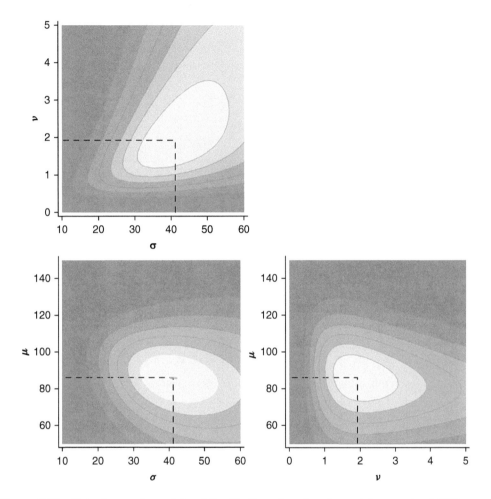

Figure 8.12 Pairwise contour plots of the likelihood surface for a data sample of {124, 97, 34, −101, 120, 67}. The dashed lines indicate the positions of the maximum likelihood estimates of the parameters. In each of the plots, the remaining variable is set at its maximum likelihood estimated value.

variability of the Student-t distribution, the likelihood surface indicates a correlation between estimates of these two parameters (top-left panel of Figure 8.12). Intuitively, there is not enough information in the data to differentiate between the effects of σ and v.

When $v = 1$ the Student-t distribution has very fat tails and is sometimes called the *Cauchy* distribution (see Section 8.5.2). However, this choice of v has a cost – the mean and variance no longer exist. However, in circumstances where there are occasionally very extreme observations, this distribution is a robust choice. In fact, in the popular book *The Black Swan*, Nassim Taleb strongly advocates the use of this type of sampling distribution to account for rare (black swan) events [36].

Properties:

PDF: $p(x \mid \mu, \sigma, v) = \dfrac{\left(\dfrac{v}{v + \frac{(x-\mu)^2}{\sigma^2}} \right)^{\frac{v+1}{2}}}{\sqrt{v}\, \sigma\, B\left(\dfrac{v}{2}, \dfrac{1}{2} \right)}$ (8.17a)

mean: $\mathbb{E}[X] = \mu$, *if* $v > 1$; otherwise does not exist   (8.17b)

variance: $var[X] = \dfrac{v\sigma^2}{v-2}$, *if* $v > 2$; otherwise does not exist   (8.17c)

8.4.8 Exponential

Distribution checklist:

✓ Continuous, non-negative data
✓ Often used to measure the amount of time or space between events that occur independently, and at a constant rate through time or space

Example uses: to estimate failure rates for artificial heart valves, to determine the distance between appearances of new plant species in a study area.

Suppose that we work for the World Health Organization and want to model the time between new outbreaks of Ebola. We define these epidemics as those not caused by contagion from existing outbreaks, and suppose that the source of each new outbreak is the result of a single transfer of the virus from an animal (most likely bats) to a human. We assume that these crossover events occur independently of one another, and at a constant rate through time. In this circumstance, an *exponential* model for the times between outbreaks is likely a good choice. This distribution has the following probability density function:

$$p(x \mid \lambda) = \lambda e^{-\lambda x}. \qquad\qquad (8.18)$$

This distribution depends on a single parameter λ, which is actually the same parameter that characterises the mean of a Poisson process over some predefined time length (see Section 8.4.3). For our current example, suppose that the time scale is measured in years. In this case, the number of Ebola outbreaks that occur per year is given by a *Poisson*(λ) distribution. As we increase λ, more outbreaks occur, with a shorter time between consecutive epidemics (see the left-hand panel of Figure 8.13).

Suppose that we measure the mean amount of time, in years, between consecutive outbreaks across three different 10-year periods. Graphing the likelihood for each of these separate data samples (see the right-hand panel of Figure 8.13), we find that, in each case, the maximum likelihood estimate of the parameter is the reciprocal of the mean amount of time between the emergence of consecutive epidemics.

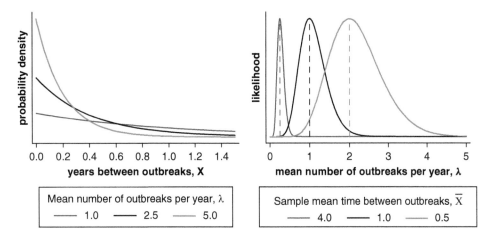

Figure 8.13   Left: the exponential probability distribution for three values of λ, which corresponds to the number of Ebola outbreaks per year. Right: the likelihood function for three data samples with differing sample mean times between consecutive outbreaks. The dashed vertical lines indicate the maximum likelihood estimates of the parameters in each case. In all cases, our sample constituted 10 observations. Note that the likelihood functions have been scaled to be comparable with one another.

Properties:

notation: $X \sim Exp(\lambda)$	(8.19a)
PDF: $p(x\mid\lambda) = \lambda e^{-\lambda x}$	(8.19b)
mean: $\mathbb{E}[X] = \dfrac{1}{\lambda}$	(8.19c)
variance: $var[X] = \dfrac{1}{\lambda^2}$	(8.19d)

8.4.9 Gamma

Distribution checklist:

✓ Continuous, non-negative data
✓ Greater flexibility than the exponential, but more complex
✓ Can be used to model the time taken for n independent events to occur

Example uses: to estimate the time taken for the nth diode in a computer to fail, or to model daily rainfall amounts.

Suppose that we work for a company which organises lotteries in a city, and that for a particular lottery game, there is always a single jackpot winner. During one night in the holiday season, the company organises a 'bonanza' night, where there are three different games. People can enter all three, although they can win only one of them. The unusual twist in the lotteries run by this

An
introduction
to the
gamma
distribution

company is that the jackpot amount decreases with time after the prize draw. Further, suppose that the time taken for a jackpot winner to claim their prize is thought to be exponentially distributed from the moment the winning numbers are announced, with a rate $\lambda = 1$ per day. The company wants to know what the aggregate reaction time is across all three players. So if one player takes 1 day, another 2 and the last 3, the aggregate reaction time is 6 days.

The combined reaction time is given by the sum $X = \sum_{i=1}^{3} T_i$, where T_i is the time taken for person i to claim their winnings. For one person, it is most likely that they will come forward immediately, as the exponential density is highest at 0. However, for all three people, it is unlikely that they all claim their prize instantly, and the maximum density for the aggregate reaction time hence lies away from 0 (see the left-hand panel of Figure 8.14). Assuming that all three prize winners act independently of one another, the mean time taken for all three to come forward is the sum of the means for each person (1 day), producing an aggregate mean reaction time of 3 days. The aggregate time distribution, in this case, is described by a *gamma* distribution with *scale* parameter equal to 3 and *shape* parameter equal to 1; symbolically, $X \sim \Gamma(3, 1)$.

The distribution shifts further rightwards if we, instead, consider a night with five lotteries, rather than three (see the left-hand panel of Figure 8.14). Now the distribution for the aggregate reaction time has a mean of 5.

Imagine that the maximum jackpot value declines, resulting in people with less incentive to claim their prize so that now $\lambda = 0.5$ per day. For each individual there is now greater uncertainty in the time taken to claim, meaning that the aggregate distribution across all three people is much wider. Also, because people have less incentive to claim, the distribution for the aggregate reaction time shifts rightwards (see the right-hand panel of Figure 8.14). Now the aggregate density is a $X \sim \Gamma(3, 0.5)$ distribution for a night where three lotteries are played. As before, if we consider a night with five lotteries, the distribution shifts further to the right, and is more extreme than the corresponding distribution for the case of $\lambda = 1$ per day.

Suppose that we collect data on the collective time taken (in days) for three people to claim their prizes. To examine the shape of the likelihood surface for this sample, we again use a contour plot (see the left-hand panel of Figure 8.15). The mean of the distribution equals the ratio α / β of the

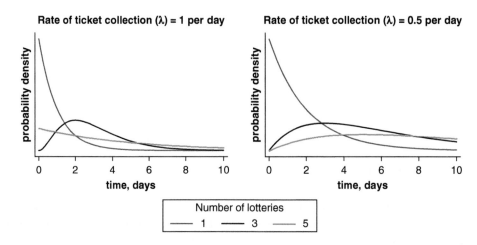

Figure 8.14 The distribution for aggregate lottery claim times for $\lambda = 1$ per day (left) and $\lambda = 0.5$ per day (right), as a function of the number of lotteries played (coloured lines).

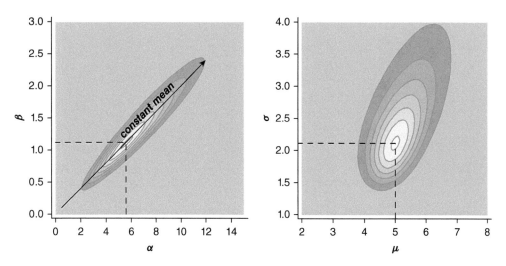

Figure 8.15 A contour plot of the likelihood surface for two different parameterisations of the gamma distribution – left: using the (α, β) formulation, and right: using the (μ, σ) formulation. The dashed lines indicate the maximum likelihood estimates of the parameters in each case. The arrow in the left-hand panel indicates the combinations of parameter values that result in the same mean (5). The sample of data we used here was {5.5, 7.5, 2.25, 1.75, 8.1, 4.9, 6.0, 4.1, 4.9, 5.0}.

parameters (with the $\Gamma(\alpha, \beta)$ parameterisation), resulting in a strong positive correlation between them. A given mean can be obtained in a number of different ways. For example, a mean of 2 can be obtained from $\alpha = 2$ and $\beta = 1$, or $\alpha = 4$ and $\beta = 2$. We illustrate combinations of parameter values that result in the same mean by the arrow in the left-hand panel of Figure 8.15. This strong correlation can be problematic for inference, both theoretically (since it may be difficult to identify both parameters) and practically (many Markov chain Monte Carlo (MCMC) methods will be slow to converge here).

In the right-hand panel of Figure 8.15, we show the likelihood surface for the same data, but with the $\Gamma(\mu, \sigma)$ parameterisation (see properties below). Using this alternative parameterisation has, to some extent, decreased the correlation between the two parameters, which now represent the mean (μ) and standard deviation (σ). We find that in some circumstances this latter parameterisation is preferable (we also prefer it because it is more intuitive).

This distribution has three parameterisations:

Properties:

notation: $X \sim \Gamma(\alpha, \beta)$	(8.20a)
PDF: $p(x \mid \alpha, \beta) = \dfrac{\beta^{\alpha}}{\Gamma(\alpha)} x^{\alpha-1} e^{-\beta x}$	(8.20b)
mean: $\mathbb{E}[X] = \dfrac{\alpha}{\beta}$	(8.20c)
variance: $var[X] = \dfrac{\alpha}{\beta^{2}}$	(8.20d)

notation: $X \sim \Gamma(\kappa, \theta)$ (8.21a)

PDF: $p(x \mid k, \theta) = \dfrac{1}{\Gamma(k)\theta^k} x^{k-1} e^{-\frac{x}{\theta}}$ (8.21b)

mean: $\mathbb{E}[X] = k\theta$ (8.21c)

variance: $var[X] = k\theta^2$ (8.21d)

notation: $X \sim \Gamma(\mu, \sigma)$ (8.22a)

PDF: $p(x \mid \mu, \sigma) = \dfrac{\left(\dfrac{\sigma^2}{\mu}\right)^{-\frac{\mu^2}{\sigma^2}} e^{-\frac{\mu x}{\sigma^2}} x^{\frac{\mu^2}{\sigma^2}-1}}{\Gamma\left(\dfrac{\mu^2}{\sigma^2}\right)}$ (8.22b)

mean: $\mathbb{E}[X] = \mu$ (8.22c)

variance: $var[X] = \sigma^2$ (8.22d)

8.4.10 Multinomial

Distribution checklist:

- ✓ Discrete data
- ✓ Multiple trials with a fixed number of total trials
- ✓ Trial outcomes are independent
- ✓ Each trial has $k \geq 2$ outcomes
- ✓ Individual outcome probabilities are not determined by a factor that varies systematically across individuals
- ✓ Probability of obtaining each category is the same in each trial
- ✓ Overall data we record is the aggregate number of outcomes in each category
- ✓ Generalisation of the binomial to handle an arbitrary number of outcome categories

Example uses: modelling political party affiliation across a group of people (for example, Republican, Democrat Independent, or none), or explaining the choice of treatment sought for back pain (for example, osteopath, acupuncture, physiotherapy, surgery or none).

Suppose that we work for the Department of Health and want to build a model to explain the prevalence of blood types for a sample of people drawn from the wider US population. For simplicity, we suppose that there are only three blood types: *A*, *B* and *O*. We assume that our sample of *n* people is randomly sampled from the US population.

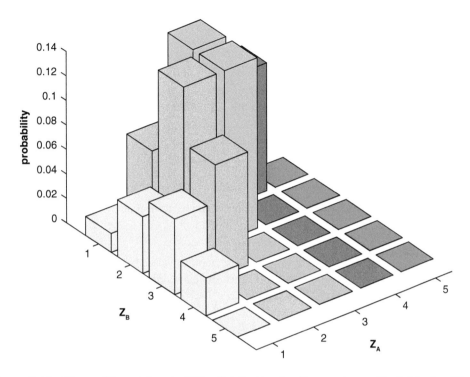

Figure 8.16 The multinomial probability distribution for the numbers of individuals with blood types A and B, where the underlying proportion of the population with each type is given by $p_A = \frac{1}{2}, p_B = \frac{1}{3}, p_O = \frac{1}{6}$.

Let's consider how we might design a distribution to cope with the three categories of blood types. Before we consider a sample of n individuals we first create a model for a single individual. The probabilities of the individual having each blood type are equal to the proportions of each type in the population, which we call $\boldsymbol{p} = (p_A, p_B, p_O)$. We now create a set of binary random variables for a single individual, $\{X_A, X_B, X_O\}$, each of which equals 1 only if that person has the respective blood type. For example, if a person has blood type A then $X_A = 1$, $X_B = 0$, and $X_O = 0$. For a given individual the sum across all of these binary indicators is always 1 (since a person can have only one blood type). We would like our distribution to return the respective probabilities for each of the blood types, in other words $Pr(X_i = x_i, X_{-i} = 0 \mid \boldsymbol{p}) = p_i$, where $i \in \{A, B, O\}$ and X_{-i} represents the other two random variables. For example, the probability that a randomly sampled individual has blood type A is $Pr(X_A = 1, X_B = 0, X_O = 0 \mid \boldsymbol{p}) = p_A$. We can achieve this behaviour from a *categorical* distribution (the generalisation of the Bernoulli to more than two categories):

$$Pr(X_A = x_A, X_B = x_B, X_O = x_O \mid \boldsymbol{p}) = p_A^{x_A} p_B^{x_B} p_O^{x_O}. \tag{8.23}$$

With our distribution for a single individual designed, we can use this to construct a distribution for the aggregate blood type counts for a sample of n individuals. If our data consists of a random sample from the population, the overall distribution function will be proportional to the product of the individual categorical distribution functions, each of the form above. We now define new random variables, which equal the aggregate numbers of people in our sample with each blood type, $Z_i = \sum_{j=1}^{n} X_i^j$, where $i \in \{A,B,O\}$. So, for example, $Z_O = 5$ means that we found five individuals with blood type O in our sample. The overall distribution function has the form:

$$Pr(Z_A = z_A, Z_B = z_B, Z_O = z_O \mid \boldsymbol{p}) = \frac{n!}{z_A! z_B! z_O!} p_A^{z_A} p_B^{z_B} p_O^{z_O} \tag{8.24}$$

where $n! / z_A! z_B! z_O!$ is the multiple-category version of the ^nC_r term that we had for the binomial case, and equals the number of combinations of individual blood types that result in the same aggregate counts of people with each blood type in our sample.

In Section 8.5.1 we will see a trick that allows us to graph this distribution and its likelihood, as a function of all three blood types. However, since there are only three categories, only two of the variables are free to vary for a given sample size. This simplification means that we can draw the probability distribution in two dimensions.

Figure 8.16 shows the probability distribution across Z_A and Z_B, with $Z_O = 5 - Z_A - Z_B$ for a sample size of five, where the population blood type proportions are $p_A = \frac{1}{2}, p_B = \frac{1}{3}, p_O = \frac{1}{6}$. The density for this distribution is zero for all points above the line $Z_A + Z_B = 5$ since this would constitute a sample size greater than five.

Figure 8.17 shows the likelihood surface in (p_A, p_B) space for a combined data sample comprising three separate studies of individuals' blood types, where there are five individuals in each study. The likelihood surface is shown as a lower triangle in this space, because to the right of the main diagonal the sum of probabilities exceeds 1. Since all of the samples we pick have a high proportion of blood type B, the contours of high likelihood are squashed into the upper-left-hand corner of the graph.

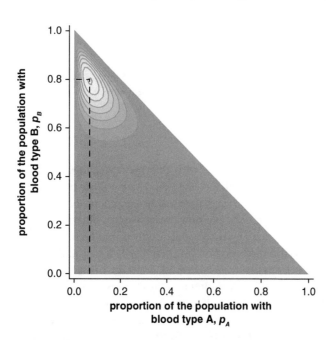

Figure 8.17 A contour plot of the multinomial likelihood across (p_A, p_B) space. The data sample we collect consists of three different samples of individuals' blood types, each of size 5: (p_A, p_B, p_O) = (1,3,1),(0,4,1),(0,5,0), for the numbers of individuals with blood types A, B and O respectively. The dashed lines show the maximum likelihood estimates of p_A and p_B (the estimate for the proportion with blood type O is given by $\hat{p}_O = 1 - \hat{p}_A - \hat{p}_B$).

Properties:

PMF: $Pr(Z_1 = z_1, Z_2,..., Z_k = z_k \mid p_1, p_2,..., p_k) = \dfrac{n!}{z_1! z_2! ... z_k!} p_1^{z_1} p_2^{z_2} ... p_k^{z_k}$ (8.25a)

mean: $\mathbb{E}[X_i] = n p_i$ (8.25b)

variance: $var[X_i] = n p_i (1 - p_i)$ (8.25c)

8.4.11 Multivariate normal and multivariate Student-t

The following is somewhat more advanced (at least mathematically) than the preceding distributions. Unless you are in need of multivariate models and have a grasp of vectors, and matrices, then it can be left until required.

Distribution checklist:

✓ Multivariate distribution: used to specify likelihoods for *vectors of random variables*
✓ Continuous, unconstrained data
✓ Parameterised by two distinct parts: a vector of mean parameters; and a matrix of parameters that describes the covariances between pairs of random variables
✓ Use multivariate Student-t distribution to allow for more uncertainty in the data-generating process

Example uses: to describe gene expression magnitudes for multiple genes, to model test scores for members of a family, or to explain temperature variation in neighbouring villages.

Imagine you get a job at a prestigious hedge fund as an analyst. Your manager gives you your first task: to model the risk of a portfolio containing the stocks of two different companies in a particular industry sector. You are told that, if both stocks have a daily loss of 10% or greater, then the portfolio goes bankrupt. Further, your boss tells you that a risk of $\frac{1}{1000}$ for bankruptcy is acceptable, but no more. If the risk is below this threshold the hedge fund will buy the stocks, otherwise it will wait for a better opportunity.

You obtain the historical daily stock returns for the past year (shown in the left-hand panel of Figure 8.18). Looking at the historical returns, you notice that when one increases, the other tends to increase as well. You plan to use a model that will account for this covariance in stock returns. Bearing this in mind, you do some research and decide to use a *multivariate normal* distribution to model the returns of the two stocks, r:

$$r \sim \mathcal{N}(\mu, \Sigma).$$ (8.26)

In expression (8.26), the bold typeface for parameters indicates that we are dealing with vectors and matrices, rather than scalar quantities. For our two stock example, μ is a vector of length 2, where the two elements correspond to the mean returns for each of the two stocks (which can be different from one another). Σ is a *covariance* matrix, which for our example is written explicitly as:

$$\Sigma = \begin{bmatrix} \sigma_1^2 & \rho \sigma_1 \sigma_2 \\ \rho \sigma_1 \sigma_2 & \sigma_2^2 \end{bmatrix},$$ (8.27)

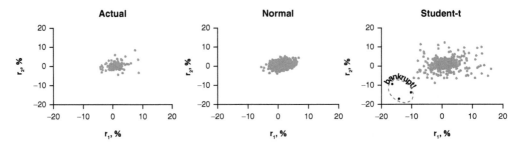

Figure 8.18　Left: the actual daily stock returns for two different stocks, from all days of trading in the last year. Middle: 1000 simulated data points from a bivariate normal fit to the data. Right: 1000 simulated data points from a bivariate Student-*t* distribution fit to the data. The days on which the portfolio would go bust are shown in black.

where σ_1^2 and σ_2^2 represent the variances in the returns of stock 1 and 2, respectively; ρ is the correlation in the daily stock returns of the two companies. So overall in our model, there are five parameters. Contour plots of the probability density for a bivariate normal distribution with different values of ρ are shown in the top row of Figure 8.19.

You fit the bivariate normal to the data using maximum likelihood and use the fitted model to simulate 1000 replicate daily returns, resulting in the data points shown in the middle panel of Figure 8.18. Feeling happy that none of the samples are in the danger zone, you go to your boss and tell her to invest. Your boss, being an analytical person, asks you to show her your model basis and reasoning. When you explain the model and show her the graph of simulated stock returns, she quickly realises that something is amiss: 'Why is there more variability in the actual returns than we see in your fake data? I think you should go away and rethink your model.'

Feeling ashamed, you retreat to your desk and realise the error of your ways. How could you have fallen into the trap of so many before and used a distribution that allows insufficient uncertainty in the data-generating process? You do a quick bit of Googling and find that the *multivariate Student-t* distribution is a more robust alternative to the multivariate normal (see the bottom row of Figure 8.19).

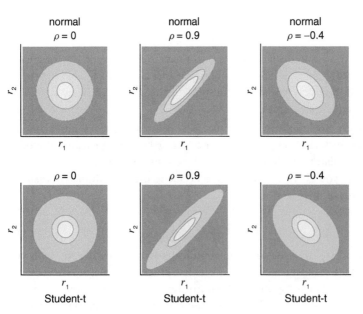

Figure 8.19　Top: a contour plot of the two-dimensional multivariate normal density. Bottom: a contour plot of the two-dimensional Student-*t* density, with $\nu = 3$, using the same covariance matrix as for the normal case.

You fit a bivariate Student-*t* distribution to the data and then, as before, you simulate 1000 pairs of stock returns. To your shock, there are now a number of points in the danger area (see the right-hand plot of Figure 8.18). What's more, because there is more than one point that would cause the portfolio to go bankrupt, the modelled risk exceeds the threshold of $\frac{1}{1000}$. You slink over to your boss and tell her, 'Sorry – here are the results. We shouldn't invest.' She recognises that people make mistakes and that your new work is of much better quality than before, and says, 'That's better. Go to lunch. We need you in a meeting in half an hour.'

This cautionary tale should have conveyed the seriousness of ensuring that your modelling choices sufficiently account for extreme data. In situations where there is evidence of this type of behaviour in the real data, and some would argue even if there is not (see Mandelbrot's *Misbehaviour of Markets* [25] and Taleb's *The Black Swan* [36]), there is an argument for replacing normal distributions with Student-*t* distributions. The Student-*t* gives much more weight to the tails of the distribution and hence is much better equipped to handle extreme variation in the data.

The multivariate normal has the properties shown below. Here k is the number of elements of X; in our example, $k = 2$, because we consider the returns of two stocks.

Properties:

notation: $\boldsymbol{X} \sim N(\mu, \Sigma)$ $\hspace{4cm}$ (8.28a)

PDF: $p(\boldsymbol{x} \mid \mu, \Sigma) = (2\pi)^{-\frac{k}{2}} |\Sigma|^{-\frac{1}{2}} e^{-\frac{1}{2}(\boldsymbol{x}-\mu)'\Sigma^{-1}(\boldsymbol{x}-\mu)}$ $\hspace{1.5cm}$ (8.28b)

mean: $\mathbb{E}[\boldsymbol{X}] = \mu$ $\hspace{6cm}$ (8.28c)

variance: $var[\boldsymbol{X}] = \Sigma$ $\hspace{5.5cm}$ (8.28d)

The multivariate Student-*t* distribution's properties are shown below.

Properties:

notation: $\boldsymbol{X} \sim t_\nu(\mu, \Sigma)$ $\hspace{5cm}$ (8.29a)

PDF: $p(x \mid \mu, \Sigma, \nu) = \dfrac{\Gamma\left(\dfrac{\nu+k}{2}\right)}{\Gamma(\nu/2)\nu^{\frac{\nu}{2}}\pi^{\frac{\nu}{2}} |\Sigma|^{-\frac{1}{2}} \left[1 + \dfrac{1}{\nu}(x-\mu)'\Sigma^{-1}(x-\mu)\right]^{(\nu+k)/2}}$ $\hspace{1cm}$ (8.29b)

mean: $\mathbb{E}[\boldsymbol{X}] = \mu$, if $\nu > 1$; otherwise does not exist $\hspace{1cm}$ (8.29c)

variance: $var[\boldsymbol{X}] = \dfrac{\nu}{\nu-2}\Sigma$, if $\nu > 2$; otherwise does not exist $\hspace{1cm}$ (8.29d)

8○5 PRIOR DISTRIBUTIONS

The first step in a Bayesian analysis is choosing a likelihood function. The second step is choosing prior distributions to set on the parameters that characterise the behaviour of the likelihood functions (see Chapter 5). In a similar vein to the likelihoods, there are also a large range of distributions available to us to use as priors. Here, we focus on some of the most common choices used in applied research for prior distributions.

There are a number of different categories of parameters in likelihood functions: probabilities and proportions, which are constrained to lie between 0 and 1; location parameters, for example the mean; shape parameters, for example variances, which are non-negative; and more exotic entities like simplexes or covariance matrices.

While we will re-encounter some of the distributions we met in Section 8.4, we believe the difference in focus here is sufficient to merit these repetitions.

8.5.1 Distributions for probabilities and proportions

It is common to encounter parameters that are naturally constrained to lie between 0 and 1. Examples include probabilities and proportions. In these cases, it is important to use priors that are appropriate for this purpose, since a poor choice can lead to nonsensical values which lie outside of the [0,1] range.

Uniform

Prior checklist:

✓ Continuous parameters
✓ Parameters bounded between a and b, where for the case of probabilities, and proportions, $a = 0$ and $b = 1$

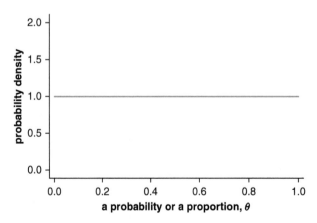

Figure 8.20 The continuous uniform distribution with bounds equal to [0,1].

A common choice of uninformative (although in Section 5.6.1 we argued for calling these vaguely informative) priors for variables constrained to lie between 0 and 1 is the continuous uniform prior (see Figure 8.20). This choice of prior might be warranted if there is an emphasis on 'objective' analysis; for example, when undertaking an analysis of a clinical trial for a new drug.

We argue that the uniform distribution bounded between 0 and 1 is superseded by the beta distribution (see p. 173) since the uniform is a special case of this more flexible distribution. However, since many analyses still use this distribution, it is worth knowing about it.

Properties:

notation: $\theta \sim U(a,b)$ (8.30a)

PDF: $p(\theta \mid a,b) = \dfrac{1}{b-a}$ where $a < b$ (8.30b)

mean: $\mathbb{E}[X] = \dfrac{1}{2}(a+b)$ (8.30c)

variance: $var[X] = \dfrac{1}{12}(b-a)^2$ (8.30d)

Beta

Prior checklist:

✓ Continuous parameters
✓ Parameters bounded between 0 and 1
✓ Encompasses a wide range of priors, ranging from vaguely informative to strongly informative
✓ $beta(1,1)$ equivalent to a $U(0,1)$ distribution

A beta distribution is a more flexible version of the uniform distribution for parameters con-strained to lie between 0 and 1. There are a number of reasons why we prefer to use a beta distribution over a uniform distribution. Importantly, this distribution encompasses a range of priors, ranging from vaguely informative (grey line in the left-hand panel of Figure 8.21) to more strongly informative (black line).

To provide an example use of a beta prior, consider obesity rates in the UK. We know that the per-centage of people who are obese is less than 50%, so it does not make sense to specify a prior here that gives equal weight to all values between 0 and 1. In this case, we might specify a $beta(2,10)$

An introduction to the Beta distribution

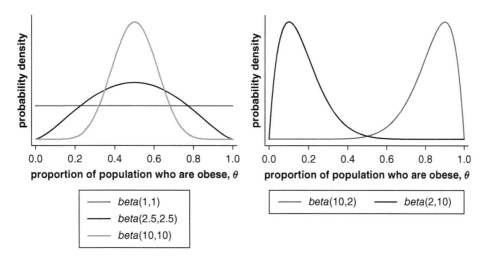

Figure 8.21 Left: three symmetric beta distributions centred on $\theta = \frac{1}{2}$. Right: two non-symmetric beta distributions.

prior, for example (black line in the right-hand panel of Figure 8.21). This prior gives most weight to an obesity rate between 5% and 30% and so could be a reasonable choice here.

The beta distribution also has the property that it is *conjugate* to some useful distributions, and so allows analytic calculation of the posteriors in these cases. (Don't worry if this talk of conjugacy has gone over your head, as we devote the entirety of Chapter 9 to discussing this concept.)

> *Properties:*

$$\text{notation: } \theta \sim beta(\alpha, \beta) \tag{8.31a}$$

$$\text{PDF: } p(\theta \mid \alpha, \beta) = \frac{\theta^{\alpha-1}(1-\theta)^{\beta-1}}{B(\alpha, \beta)} \tag{8.31b}$$

$$\text{mean: } \mathbb{E}[\theta] = \frac{\alpha}{\alpha + \beta} \tag{8.31c}$$

$$\text{variance: } var[\theta] = \frac{\alpha\beta}{(\alpha + \beta)^2(\alpha + \beta + 1)} \tag{8.31d}$$

Logit-normal

Prior checklist:

- ✓ Continuous parameters
- ✓ Parameters bounded between 0 and 1
- ✓ Encompasses a wide range of priors, ranging from weakly informative to strongly informative

In life, there are often multiple choices that result in a similar outcome. In statistical inference, it is no different – there are two commonly used distributions to model probabilities and proportions (discounting the uniform since it is a special case of the beta distribution): the beta distribution and the logit-normal. Here we continue with the obesity example from the beta distribution section. The idea behind the logit-normal is to allow an unconstrained variable to vary according to a normal distribution, then transform it to lie between 0 and 1, using a *logistic* transform:

$$a \sim \mathcal{N}(\mu, \sigma)$$

$$\theta = \frac{1}{(1 + e^{-a})}. \tag{8.32}$$

A large set of prior distributions is possible with this parameterisation (see Figure 8.22). However, care must be taken to ensure that the prior does not place too much weight near 0 or 1, which can happen if we choose σ to be high (red line in Figure 8.22).

This distribution is useful because its multivariate analogue is a generalisation of the Dirichlet distribution (that we cover next) which allows for correlation between probabilities.

Properties:

notation: $\theta \sim logit\text{-}N(\mu,\sigma)$ (8.33a)

PDF: $p(\theta \mid \mu,\theta) = \dfrac{1}{\sqrt{2\pi}\,(1-\theta)\theta\sigma}\exp\left(-\dfrac{(\log(\theta/1-\theta)-\mu)^2}{2\sigma^2}\right)$ (8.33b)

mean: $\mathbb{E}[\theta] = $ no analytic expression   (8.33c)

variance : $var[\theta] = $ no analytic expression   (8.33d)

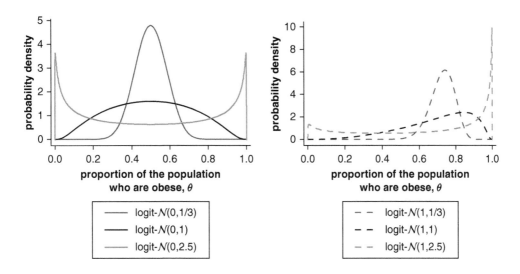

| logit-N(0,1/3) |
| logit-N(0,1) |
| logit-N(0,2.5) |

| logit-N(1,1/3) |
| logit-N(1,1) |
| logit-N(1,2.5) |

Figure 8.22 Left: $logit\text{-}N(0,\sigma)$ densities across different values of σ. Right: $logit\text{-}N(1,\sigma)$ densities for the same values of σ.

Dirichlet

Prior checklist:

✓   Vector of continuous parameters
✓   Sum of parameters equals 1
✓   Encompasses a wide range of priors, ranging from weakly informative to strongly informative

Imagine that we want to estimate the proportions of individuals who will vote for each of the three political parties: Republican, Democrat and Liberal. If people are obligated to vote (and cannot spoil their ballot paper) the sum of the proportions of individuals voting for each of the parties must equal 1. Accordingly, we need a model that satisfies this constraint.

We start by considering the case where there are only two political parties: Republican and Democrat. We can represent the possible voting proportions as points along a line (see the left-hand panel of Figure 8.23) of length 1. If we consider the leftmost point on the line, this represents the case where nobody votes Republican and everyone votes Democrat, with the rightmost point being the exact opposite. At the mid point, 50% vote Republican and 50% vote Democrat.

Now, considering three political parties, we can represent all feasible combinations of voting proportions as those points that lie within an equilateral triangle of height 1. Here the axes corresponding to the proportions voting for each party extend from each vertex to the opposite midpoint of each edge (see the right-hand panel of Figure 8.23). This triangular representation can be justified by imagining a three-dimensional space defined by axes that represent the proportions voting for each party, (p_R, p_D, p_L). The set of allowable points corresponds to the plane defined by $p_R + p_D + p_L = 1$, where all probabilities must be greater than or equal to 0. This set of points corresponds to an equilateral triangle-shaped plane in this space.

The Dirichlet distribution is characterised by k parameters, $\alpha_1, \alpha_2, ..., \alpha_k$, which can be thought of as weights for each category. For our three-party example, we start by specifying a *Dirichlet*(2,2,2) prior on the proportions, (p_R, p_D, p_L). This prior gives equal weight to all three categories, with the result that the distribution has a broad peak towards the centre of the equilateral triangle (see the left-hand panel of Figure 8.24). If we instead specify a *Dirichlet*(5,5,5) prior, this results in a prior that again gives most weight to equal proportions voting for each party. In this case, however, by specifying higher weights we assert that we are more confident in a three-way equal split, with the resultant prior distribution now being more strongly peaked in the centre of the triangle. Finally, if we specify a *Dirichlet*(4,2,2) distribution, this gives a higher prior weight to individuals voting for the Republican Party. The peak of the resultant prior distribution is hence in the corner that corresponds to the top of the p_R axis.

This distribution allows for a large range of prior distributions for the individual category proportions. The marginal distribution for an individual category proportion is a beta distribution, meaning that we can, for example, specify a uniform distribution for a given category proportion, or instead choose a prior that is more informative about it.

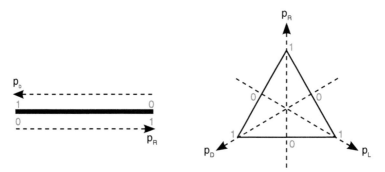

Figure 8.23 Left: the feasible region for probabilities for two categories. Right: the feasible region for probabilities for three categories.

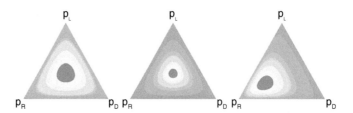

Figure 8.24 The Dirichlet distribution for $(\alpha_R, \alpha_D, \alpha_L)$ equal to (2,2,2), (5,5,5) and (4,2,2), in the left, middle and right plots, respectively.

However, the Dirichlet distribution is not fully flexible, because it cannot allow for an arbitrary correlation structure between the category proportions. For example, a Dirichlet prior distribution might be inappropriate for the analysis of a survey which asked participants' percentage of travel by train, bike, car or other. Individuals who prefer to travel by train might also like biking, since these are more carbon-friendly modes of transport than cars, meaning that we believe there could be a positive correlation between the train and bike categories (and a negative correlation of each of these with the car category). The Dirichlet distribution could not handle this set of correlations. However, it turns out that the multivariate equivalent of the logit-normal is capable of allowing such relationships between category probabilities.

> **Properties:**

> notation: $(p_1, p_2, \ldots, p_k) \sim Dir(\alpha_1, \alpha_2, \ldots, \alpha_k)$ $\qquad$ (8.34a)
>
> where: $\sum_{i=1}^{k} p_i = 1$ $\qquad$ (8.34b)
>
> PDF: $p(\theta \mid \alpha_1, \alpha_2, \ldots, \alpha_k) = \frac{1}{B(\alpha)} \prod_{i=1}^{k} \theta_i^{\alpha_i - 1}$ $\qquad$ (8.34c)
>
> where $B(\alpha) = \frac{\prod_{i=1}^{k} \Gamma(\alpha_i)}{\Gamma\left(\sum_{i=1}^{k} \alpha_i\right)}$ $\qquad$ (8.34d)
>
> and $\alpha = (\alpha_1, \alpha_2, \ldots, \alpha_k)$ $\qquad$ (8.34e)
>
> mean: $\mathbb{E}[\theta_i] = \frac{\alpha_i}{\sum_{i=1}^{k} \alpha_i}$ $\qquad$ (8.34f)
>
> variance: $var[\theta_i] = \frac{\alpha_i \left(\sum_{j=1}^{k} \alpha_j - \alpha_i\right)}{\left(\sum_{j=1}^{k} \alpha_j\right)^2 \left(\sum_{j=1}^{k} \alpha_j + 1\right)}$ $\qquad$ (8.34g)

8.5.2 Distributions for means and regression coefficients

In some probability models for continuous data, for example the normal distribution, the distribution is characterised by a location parameter – the mean – and a scale parameter – the variance, standard deviation or some other measure of distributional width. Interest usually focuses on the location parameter, for example the mean proportion of the electorate that votes Republican, the average success rate for a new drug or the median stock returns. Alternatively, in linear regression models, the interest usually centres on the estimation of regression coefficients, which are multiplied by the independent variables to yield the mean (usually of a normal distribution). This section is devoted to showcasing some of the more popular choices of priors for these types of parameters.

Normal

Prior checklist:

✓   Continuous unconstrained, or practically unconstrained, parameters
✓   Encompasses a wide range of priors, ranging from weakly informative to strongly informative

We already saw in Section 8.4.6 that we can use a normal distribution for likelihoods under a wide range of situations; however, here we detail its use for an altogether different purpose: specifying prior distributions.

For example, consider the problem of trying to estimate the global mean sea temperature using a sample of many worldwide temperature measures. We might suppose that a range of factors contribute to the temperature θ_i that we measure at location i: time of year, geography and measurement error, for example. This multitude of factors might justify the use of a normal distribution for the likelihood (see Section 8.4.6):

$$\theta_i \sim N(\mu, \sigma). \tag{8.35}$$

This distribution is characterised by two parameters – its mean μ and its standard deviation σ. From experience we know that the mean sea temperature is likely in the range of 10–22 degrees Celsius, although it varies by location, and from year to year. In this circumstance, we might specify a weakly informative normal prior for μ with a mean of 16 degrees and a standard deviation of 10.

Properties: See Section 8.4.6.

Student-*t*

Prior checklist:

✓ Continuous unconstrained, or practically unconstrained, parameters
✓ Robust version of the normal, allowing for a greater range of parameter values

In Section 8.4.7 we suggested using the Student-*t* distribution in circumstances when there is more variation in the data than can be accounted for by the normal distribution. Similarly, we advocate using the Student-*t* distribution for a prior when we wish to allow a wider range of parameter values, a priori, than is possible with a normal distribution.

To be clear, it is possible to set the parameters of a normal distribution so that its variance is the same as that of a Student-*t* distribution (so long as v > 2). However, the nature of that variance will not be the same (see the left-hand panel of Figure 8.25). Whereas the normal is more evenly spread about its centre,

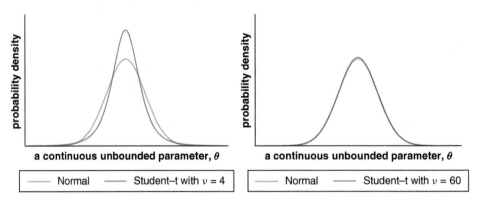

Figure 8.25   Comparing normal and Student-*t* distributions with the same mean and standard deviation for low (left) and high (right) values of the Student-*t*'s degrees of freedom, v.

the Student-t distribution is sharply peaked, with less weight on its shoulders and more on its tails. The difference in shape between these distributions is controlled by a parameter, v, called the degrees of freedom. As we increase this parameter, there is a greater correspondence between the normal and Student-t distributions, and in the limit that $v \to \infty$ they are the same (see the right-hand panel of Figure 8.25).

Properties: See Section 8.4.7.

Cauchy

Prior checklist:

✓ Continuous unconstrained, or practically unconstrained, parameters
✓ Robust version of the Student-t and normal distributions, allowing for a greater range of parameter values
✓ A special case of the Student-t distribution where $v = 1$

Imagine that we are building a model to help understand the effect of a new microfinance scheme on the wages of individuals in an unspecified country. Apart from the scheme, there are a number of factors that also influence a person's wage: education, social status and health, for example. Based on previous analyses we assume that the relationship between wage and the amount borrowed using the microfinance scheme is linear:

$$wage_i = \alpha + \beta finance_i + \epsilon_i, \tag{8.36}$$

where $\epsilon \sim \mathcal{N}(\mu, \sigma)$ represents the myriad of other factors influencing wage, $finance_i$ represents the amount borrowed through the scheme over a given time period, and $wage_i$ is the amount of income earned over the same period. We assume that both the variables are standardised (have mean equal to 0 and standard deviation equal to 1), meaning that β is the average increase in wage (in standard deviations) for a 1 standard deviation increase in the amount borrowed. Suppose proponents of micro-finance schemes argue that they typically have a positive impact on wages, by allowing individuals the freedom to devote more time to producing a specialist good or service. Those in opposition perhaps argue that the moral hazard it induces can lead people to make worse choices, and

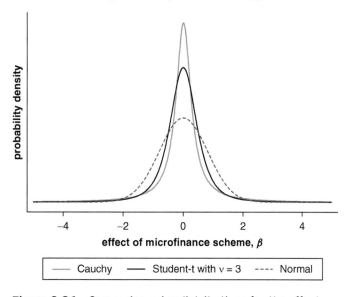

Figure 8.26 Comparing prior distributions for the effect of a microfinance scheme on income. The normal and Student-t distributions shown both have variances equal to 0.64; for the Cauchy distribution the mean and variance do not exist.

hence detrimentally affects income. After reading these views we imagine that we are quite uncertain about the impact of our microfinance scheme, and want to allow a wide range of possibilities, including positive and negative values of β, before we do our analysis.

In this case, we may choose to specify a prior distribution that is wider than a normal or Student-t distribution (with more than 1 degree of freedom), instead choosing the fatter-tailed *Cauchy* (see Figure 8.26). This distribution actually corresponds to a Student-t distribution with 1 degree of freedom. The Cauchy is named after the mercurial French mathematician Augustin Louis Cauchy, who lived during the nineteenth century in post-revolutionary France. While Cauchy is rightly famous for his work on complex analysis, this distribution's naming is an example of Stigler's Law of Eponymy – that a scientific discovery is never named after its original discoverer – since much of the initial work on this distribution was done by others, including the brilliant French mathematicians Fermat and Poisson. Before its current naming, the distribution was actually known by the mysterious title, 'The Witch of Agnesi', named after an Italian mathematician, Maria Gaetana Agnesi, who published work on it. It is likely that 'witch' is actually a mistranslation of the Italian word *versiera*, meaning 'adversary of God' or 'she-devil'. Either way, the name is quite apt since its properties mean the distribution can behave in quite an unholy manner. In particular, the tails are so fat that the distribution has no mean or variance. This may look confusing, especially since the distribution is symmetric about its median. However, drawing repeated samples from this distribution is illuminating, as the running mean does not converge! Whether these costs are more than compensated for by its added robustness depends on the circumstances. It is recommended that this distribution be used only for those situations where we want to allow a large prior range for the parameter value. In other, less extreme cases, the Student-t distribution (with degrees of freedom greater than 1) or the normal distribution will most likely suffice.

> *Properties:*

> PDF: $p(\theta \mid \theta_0, \gamma) = \dfrac{1}{\pi\gamma\left(\dfrac{(\theta-\theta_0)^2}{\gamma^2}+1\right)}$ (8.37a)
>
> *mean:* $\mathbb{E}[\theta] =$ does not exist (8.37b)
>
> *variance:* $var[\theta] =$ does not exist (8.37c)
>
> *median:* $median[\theta] = \theta_0$ (8.37d)

Multivariate normal and multivariate Student-*t*

The following is somewhat more (at least mathematically) advanced than the preceding distributions. Unless you are in need of multivariate models and have a grasp of vectors and matrices, then it can be left unread until required.

Prior checklist:

- ✓ Multivariate distribution: used to specify priors for a number of parameters simultaneously
- ✓ Continuous unconstrained, or practically unconstrained, parameters
- ✓ Mostly useful in hierarchical models, although can be used in non-hierarchical settings

Imagine that we want to evaluate how the size of a house, S, and its number of bedrooms, B, affect the price it sells at, P. Based on graphs of the data we assume a linear relationship between the predictors and the price at which a house is sold:

$$P_i = \alpha + \beta_1 S_i + \beta_2 B_i + \epsilon_i, \tag{8.38}$$

where $i \in \{1,...,N\}$ indicates individual cases in our sample of houses. Before we start our analysis we might suppose that there will be some correlation in the estimated effects of the variables S_i and B_i. Intuitively, since larger houses tend to have more bedrooms, we expect that if we give more weight to the effect of size, then we will have to give less weight to bedrooms for the house price to remain the same. We could choose independent priors for the parameters β_1 and β_2, but these would not represent our beliefs of their interrelation. Forgetting α for now, in this circumstance, we might specify a prior of the following form:

$$\begin{pmatrix} \beta_1 \\ \beta_2 \end{pmatrix} \sim \mathcal{N}\left[\begin{pmatrix} \mu_1 \\ \mu_2 \end{pmatrix}, \begin{pmatrix} \sigma_1^2 & \rho\sigma_1\sigma_2 \\ \rho\sigma_1\sigma_2 & \sigma_2^2 \end{pmatrix} \right] \tag{8.39}$$

Here $\rho < 0$ captures our pre-analysis belief that these estimates should be negatively correlated, μ_1, μ_2 are the prior mean effect sizes and σ_1^2, σ_2^2 are the prior variances. To allow greater freedom in the estimates of the parameters, we could instead use a multivariate Student-t distribution (see Section 8.4.11).

Properties: See Section 8.4.11.

8.5.3 Distributions for non-negative parameters

There is a wide class of parameters that are naturally constrained to be non-negative in value. Examples include variances and a range of other parameters, including the mean of a Poisson distribution, the shape parameter of a gamma, and so on. Although with Stan MCMC software it is possible to use an unbounded continuous distribution coupled with explicit bounds on parameter

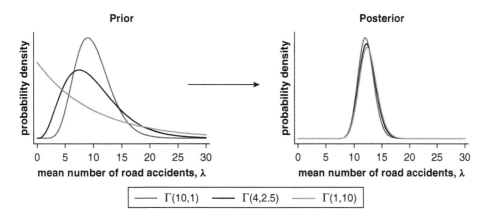

Figure 8.27   Left: three prior distributions for $\lambda \sim \Gamma(\alpha, \beta)$ where in all cases the mean is 10. Right: the resultant posterior distributions for the corresponding prior case for the following sample of data: {17, 6, 11, 13, 16}.

values, it is often preferable to set a prior distribution that naturally has support (also called positive density) on the positive real numbers only. This section introduces those distributions that are constrained to the positive real numbers.

Gamma

Prior checklist:

- ✓ Continuous parameters constrained to be non-negative
- ✓ Typically allows lower uncertainty than the inverse-gamma or half-Cauchy

Suppose that we want to build a statistical model for the count, X_i, of road accidents occurring on a given day, i, in a particular (small) geographic area, to help allocate emergency service resources. If the weather is similar over the days when data collection took place, then a reasonable model here might be the Poisson distribution: $X_i \sim Poisson(\lambda)$. Historically, we know that the number of incidents per day has a mean near 10, although there is some variance around this value. In this circumstance, we might specify a gamma prior for λ, partly because of its mathematical convenience (due to its conjugacy; see Chapter 9), but also because this distribution can represent our reasonably confident prior beliefs. In the left-hand panel of Figure 8.27, we show three possible gamma prior distributions, each with a mean of 10. While these example prior distributions encompass a range of possible prior beliefs, after we collect five data points, the resultant posterior distributions are very similar (see the right-hand panel of Figure 8.27). Even though we have only a modest amount of data, changes to the prior have minimal effect on the posterior; the information from the data swamps our prior beliefs.

Properties: See Section 8.4.9.

Half-Cauchy, inverse-gamma, inverse-χ^2 and uniform

Prior checklist:

- ✓ Continuous parameters constrained to be non-negative
- ✓ Often used for variances and shape parameters (parameters which govern the curvature of a distribution rather than its central position)
- ✓ Variants can be used to specify vaguely informative priors
- ✓ For vaguely informative priors we recommend using a half-Cauchy over the alternatives

Suppose that we want to build a statistical model to describe the length, L, of fully grown adult male crocodiles. Since size is determined by a range of factors (genetics, climate, local competitors), we invoke the central limit theorem and suppose that a normal sampling model is appropriate: $L \sim N(\mu,\sigma)$. Further, imagine that our study is novel, being the first attempt to describe the lengths of these animals, so previous data are scarce.

Suppose that our primary purpose of the analysis is to focus on the parameter μ, which represents the mean length of the male members of the species, thought to be around 4.5 from previous observational evidence. The other parameter, σ, gives the spread of the crocodile lengths about the population mean, and in this circumstance is considered a nuisance parameter, since it is not the primary purpose of estimation. Nevertheless, in Bayesian inference, we must set a prior for this parameter.

There are two related distributions that are commonly used to specify priors on the normal variance which have nice mathematical properties (in particular, conjugacy; see Section 9.5): the inv-gamma and the inv-χ^2. The latter is a special case of the former, although since both are used in the literature, we consider them separately here. Both of these distributions are derived from the bit after the *inverse* in their names. An inv-$\Gamma(\alpha,\beta)$ is simply the distribution of ζ^{-1} where $\zeta \sim \Gamma(\alpha,\beta)$. In words, we imagine sampling a value, ζ, from a gamma distribution, then taking $1/\zeta$. If we took enough

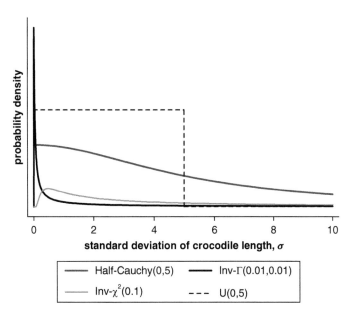

Figure 8.28 The probability density functions for distributions often used as priors for standard deviation parameters.

samples we would obtain a histogram that has the shape of an inv-$\Gamma(\alpha,\beta)$. The inv-χ^2 distribution is derived from the χ^2 distribution (not discussed in this book, but is a special case of the gamma distribution) in the same way as the inv-gamma, although is a simpler distribution, parameterised by a single input parameter. Both of these distributions are often used to specify vaguely informative priors for variance parameters. For the inv-gamma, a vaguely informative prior is obtained by choosing small values for each of its inputs; for the inv-χ^2, a vaguely informative prior is obtained by specifying small parameter values.

Another distribution popularised by Andrew Gelman is the *half-Cauchy* distribution, which is a truncated version of a Cauchy distribution (see Section 8.5.2) constrained to have zero density for negative parameter values.

A final alternative sometimes used for vaguely informative priors is a continuous uniform distribution over some non-negative (and finite) set. An issue with using this distribution is setting its upper bound, which is necessary to ensure that the distribution is a valid probability density. These sorts of priors can also prove troublesome with MCMC, meaning that the samplers often take much longer to converge than weakly informative alternatives (see Part IV).

In Figure 8.28 we compare the probability density functions for the priors that we discussed in this section. For the prior for the variance parameter, we prefer to use the half-Cauchy distribution due to its gentle-sloping nature, which means it does not allocate probability mass to areas of parameter space that are infeasible (see [13] for a more quantitative argument for the half-Cauchy).

Properties: We list properties only for our preferred distribution – the half-Cauchy – and refer the reader to Table 8.1 for the properties of the inv-gamma and inv-χ^2. The continuous uniform distribution is discussed in Section 8.5.1.

$$PDF: \ p(\theta \mid a,b) = \frac{2b}{\left(b^2 + (\theta - a)^2\right)\left(2\tan^{-1}\left(\frac{a}{b}\right) + \pi\right)}, \ if \ \theta > 0 \tag{8.40a}$$

$$mean: \ \mathbb{E}[\theta] = \text{does not exist} \tag{8.40b}$$

$$variance: var[\theta] = \text{does not exist} \tag{8.40c}$$

Log-normal

Prior checklist:

✓ Continuous parameters constrained to be non-negative
✓ Possible parameter values could exist across a wide range

Imagine again that we want to build a model for the counts of traffic accidents, X_l, this time for a location with considerable variability in weather. Due to this variability, we might choose a negative binomial likelihood (see Section 8.4.4): $X \sim NB(\mu,\kappa)$. We use the particular form of the distribution, where $var[X] = \lambda + \lambda^2 / \kappa$, where κ represents the inverse dispersion, and in the limit $\kappa \to \infty$ this distribution becomes the Poisson.

If we did not have access to historical counts of the local traffic incidents, then we might suppose that a large range of κ values is possible. In the left-hand panel of Figure 8.29 we show that increases in κ up until 40 have a considerable effect on the resultant sampling distribution. Hence, we want to use a prior distribution that allows this much variation in the parameter value.

A *log-normal* distribution satisfies this requirement. Mathematically, this means that we set a normal prior distribution for the log of κ, $log(\kappa) \sim \mathcal{N}(\mu,\sigma)$.

Because we effectively set a prior on $log(\kappa)$ this distribution has a density that can span across a wide range of possible values, although care must be taken when using it, as it is extremely sensitive to its input parameters (see the variance's dependence on μ and σ in the properties

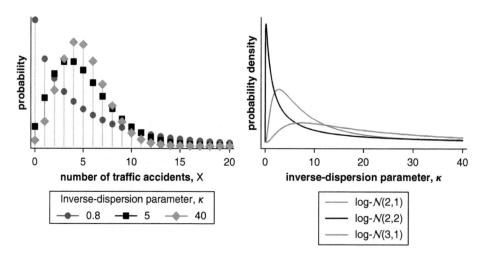

Figure 8.29 Left: negative binomial probability distributions, each with the same mean, for different values of κ. Right: possible log-normal prior distributions for κ, each with values of (μ,σ).

section below). If you decide to use this distribution as a prior, we advocate plotting its density at the chosen parameter values to ensure it looks as you expect it to (see example of the log-normal probability distributions displayed in the right-hand panel of Figure 8.29).

Properties:

---

notation: $\theta \sim \log\text{-}\mathcal{N}(\mu, \sigma)$ (8.41a)

PDF: $p(\theta \mid \mu, \sigma) = \dfrac{e^{-\frac{(\mu - \log(\theta))^2}{2\sigma^2}}}{\sqrt{2\pi}\sigma\theta}$ (8.41b)

mean: $\mathbb{E}[\theta] = e^{\mu + \frac{\sigma^2}{2}}$ (8.41c)

variance: $var[\theta] = \left(e^{\sigma^2} - 1\right)e^{2\mu + \sigma^2}$ (8.41d)

8.5.4 Distributions for covariance and correlation matrices

There are circumstances, particularly for hierarchical models, where it is necessary to specify priors for covariance and correlation matrices. The distributions that can be used as priors for these objects are quite different to those that we have discussed thus far, because they describe objects that are highly constrained. As such, the following section is more advanced than those previous to it.

There are two basic choices for covariance and correlation matrices. Up until recently, the usual choice was to opt for Wishart or inverse-Wishart distributions for these matrices due to their nice conjugacy properties (see Chapter 9). However, Stan gives us the freedom to choose non-conjugate alternatives. The most popular of these is a recently described distribution known as the LKJ distribution, which is more flexible than the Wishart varieties [23]. We cover this distribution first because we believe that, in many cases, it should replace the Wishart distributions that were commonly used before. However, there are still analyses that hinge on the conjugacy properties of the Wishart distributions, so we cover these subsequently.

LKJ

Prior checklist:

✓ Prior distribution for correlation matrices. Can also be used as a prior for covariance matrices by specifying an independent prior for a vector of scale parameters that multiply the correlation matrix.
✓ By their nature, the parameters of these matrices are constrained (the matrices must be positive definite; see below)
✓ Mostly useful in hierarchical models, although can be used in non-hierarchical settings
✓ A better alternative to the inv-Wishart and Wishart for many circumstances (apart from when conjugacy is required for computational efficiency reasons)

Suppose that we want to model the comorbidity (the coincidental presence of the condition in a patient) of a number of distinct psychological conditions: major depression, schizophrenia, obsessive compulsive disorder and anorexia. Before our analysis, we do not know whether a patient that suffers from one of these disorders is more likely to suffer from another. There is also uncertainty regarding the underlying rates of these conditions. Suppose that we have a sample of 1000 patients' scores on diagnostic tests for each of the conditions. For each patient we thus have four scores, one for each of the conditions, which we choose to model using a normal likelihood (see Section 8.4.11):

$$d \sim \mathcal{N}(\mu, \Sigma), \tag{8.42}$$

where d is a vector of length 4, and its elements are each patient's test scores for major depression, schizophrenia, obsessive compulsive disorder and anorexia, respectively. The four-element vector, μ, represents the mean test scores for each of these disorders in the population and Σ is a 4×4 covariance matrix representing the variances (on the diagonals) and covariances (off-diagonals) in the performance across the tests.

If we specify independent priors for the mean vector and covariance matrix, then we can consider the latter on its own. This, however, means that we need a prior distribution for covariance matrices, meaning that we need to associate a probability density with each admissible covariance matrix. It is important to emphasize the word *admissible* in the previous sentence. There are an infinite number of 4×4 matrices, but not many of these can be covariance matrices. So what are the properties of a covariance matrix?

- The diagonal terms are variances and so must be positive.
- The off-diagonal terms can be positive or negative, representing positive or negative covariance, respectively.
- There is symmetry between the off-diagonal elements since, for example, the covariance between depression and anxiety must be the same and vice versa.
- For two elements of the vector, the square of their covariances must be less than the product of their variances.

These conditions are satisfied if a matrix is *positive definite* and symmetric. These requirements greatly reduce the number of admissible covariance matrices, and we must take care when constructing an appropriate prior distribution. Fortunately, we do not actually need to construct such a distribution, because the work has already been done for us by the authors of [23]. To use their method we first decompose our covariance matrix as follows [8]:

$$\Sigma = \tau \Omega \tau', \tag{8.43}$$

where τ is a vector representing the variance scales of each variable and Ω is a *correlation* matrix. Correlation matrices are similar to covariance matrices, but with the additional requirement that the diagonal elements are all 1 (the correlation of anything with itself). We can use a weakly informative non-negative prior (see Section 8.5.3) for each of the elements of τ, and, to keep things simple, we assume it is independent of the prior on Ω. We now use the LKJ distribution (named in honour of the names of the authors of [23]) for our prior on the correlation matrix:

$$\Omega \sim LKJ(\eta) \propto |\Omega|^{\eta-1}, \tag{8.44}$$

where $|\Omega|$ represents the determinant of the correlation matrix Ω. This is a distribution over admissible correlation matrices and hence applies only if the matrices are symmetric, positive definite and have unit diagonals.

But what does this distribution actually look like? And how does the parameter η affect it? Here we describe some of the ways to visualise these distributions but refer the interested reader to [38] for a more thorough exposition of these methods (from which we borrow a few suggestions).

It is helpful for our purposes to ascribe some meaning to the determinant of a covariance matrix. This is sometimes referred to as the *generalised variance*, which captures the overall freedom of the system to vary. If the off-diagonal elements are 0, then the system is free to vary, and has a higher generalised variance (and a high determinant). In our example, this would correspond to each of the mental health conditions being determined mostly by outside factors that do not influence one another, resulting in low pairwise correlation for the test scores. Here the system that we study – a person's score on the four diagnostic tests – has a high generalised variance because it is possible that a person may score highly for one of the tests, and none of the others (since they are independently determined). This means that our sample (at least in terms of individuals' psychological states) will comprise individuals with considerable heterogeneity. There may be people with just depression, those with both depression and anorexia, those with all four disorders, and so on.

In contrast, if the off-diagonal elements increase, the variance of the system in one direction is not free of another (since the two covary), meaning that there is less generalised variance overall (and a lower determinant). In our example, this would mean that there is considerable co-occurrence of all of the conditions, resulting in high pairwise correlations. Here there is low generalised variance because, if a person has one mental disorder, it is likely that they will have the others as well. Or, if they do not have one condition, it is likely that they will have none of the others. The sample of individuals here, therefore, comprises mostly two types of people – those with all four disorders and those with none of them.

Similarly, we can think of the determinant of a correlation matrix as a kind of *generalised correlation*, having a maximum of 1 (where all the elements are independent) and a minimum of 0 (where everything is the same). The LKJ distribution gives a positive density to all possible values of generalised correlation, but, dependent on the value of η, will favour some areas of this spectrum more than others.

If $\eta = 1$, then expression (8.44) gives equal weight to all admissible correlation matrices (of any determinant). But what does the distribution of 'admissible correlation matrices' actually look like? For a 2×2 correlation matrix, the only choice is for the off-diagonal element, ρ_{12} (the correlation between depression and schizophrenia if we only considered the first two disorders), which must lie between -1 and 1. Since all values of ρ_{12} result in valid correlation matrices, the distribution of allowable correlation matrices has ρ_{12} values that are uniformly distributed between -1 and 1. For a 3×3 matrix, we are more constrained in our choice of ρ_{12} since there are two other free parameters to choose, ρ_{13} and ρ_{23}, which overall must ensure that the matrix is symmetric and positive definite. Choosing ρ_{12} to be close to 0 results in more admissible correlation matrices since this places fewer restrictions on the other two parameters, resulting in a distribution that is peaked at $\rho_{12} = 0$. For higher-dimensional matrices, it is harder to construct a positive definite matrix due to the numerous interactions between its elements, meaning that there is a lower density for more extreme values of ρ_{12} (see the middle panel of Figure 8.30). In our example, this prior specification would mean that we have an a priori belief that each of the conditions most likely occurs independently of the others, but we do not discount the possibility of there being comorbidity between pairs of the disorders.

When $\eta > 1$, the distribution gives more weight to those correlation matrices with higher determinants; in other words, those matrices that have greater generalised correlation and, hence, are closer to the identity matrix. This means that each of the correlation terms, for example ρ_{12} and ρ_{23}, are constrained to be close to zero (see the right-hand panel of Figure 8.30). Therefore, in our example, by setting $\eta > 1$ in our prior, we would be implicitly assuming that there is little co-occurrence between the four disorders; they present independently of one another.

In contrast, if $\eta < 1$, there is greater weight given to those matrices with smaller determinants. These correspond to correlation matrices with lower generalised correlation because the correlation of each variable with another one is typically non-zero. The result of this is that, compared with the $\eta = 1$ case, weight is reallocated from ρ_{12}, $\rho_{23} = 0$ towards either –1 and 1. For example, when $\eta = 0.1$ and $\mathbf{\Omega}$ is 4×4 dimensional, the LKJ marginal probability density of either ρ_{12} or ρ_{23} is roughly uniform between –1 and 1 (see the left-hand panel of Figure 8.30). In our example, by specifying $\eta < 1$ we would implicitly be giving quite a lot of weight towards there being co-occurrence of all of the conditions. In other words, we believe that it is quite possible that an individual who has depression will also have anxiety.

Importantly, we note that in the three regimes of η that we consider, both the marginal distributions of correlation terms (the histograms above or to the side of the main plots in Figure 8.30) and the joint distributions of correlation terms (the main density plots in Figure 8.30) are well behaved. For example, when $\eta = 0.1$, the marginal distribution looks roughly uniform for each of the correlation parameters, which is mirrored by the two-dimensional joint density (see the left-hand panel of Figure 8.30). This is different to the behaviour of the inv-Wishart distribution (and, to a lesser extent, the Wishart distribution), where examining the marginal densities alone can give a misleading impression of the joint distribution, which can have quite unexpected and, generally, undesirable properties.

In summary, the LKJ distribution encompasses a wide variety of prior beliefs for a correlation matrix. Its distribution function is stated in terms of a function of the determinant of the correlation matrix. By varying η we can give greater prior weights to those matrices closer to the identity (where there is little correlation between elements of the data vector), or alternatively towards correlation matrices

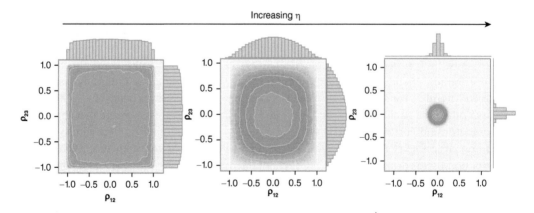

Figure 8.30   The joint distribution (the main density plots) and marginal distribution (histograms above and to the side of the main plots) of ρ_{12} and ρ_{23} resulting from sampling the LKJ distribution for three different values of η: $\eta = 0.1$ (left), $\eta = 1$ (middle) and $\eta = 100$ (right). In all cases, the plots were generated using 500,000 samples from an LKJ distribution for a 4×4 correlation matrix. Note that the individual points in the joint density plots represent samples and the shading indicates a high local density of samples.

with strong pairwise correlation. Finally, when combined with a suitable prior distribution for a set of scale parameters, the LKJ distribution can be used to specify priors for covariance matrices.

> *Properties:*

> *notation*: $\Omega \sim \text{LKJ}(\nu)$ — (8.45a)
>
> *covariance matrix decomposition*: $\Sigma = \tau\Omega\tau'$ — (8.45b)
>
> *PDF*: $p(\Omega|\eta) \propto |\Omega|^{\eta-1}$ where $\Omega \in$ correlation matrices — (8.45c)
>
> *marginal*: $\rho_{ij} \sim beta\left(\eta - 1 + \dfrac{d}{2}, \eta - 1 + \dfrac{d}{2}\right)$ over $(-1, 1)$ — (8.45d)
> where d is the number of rows of Ω [18,23].

Wishart and inverse-Wishart

Prior checklist:

✓   Prior distributions for covariances matrices
✓   By their nature, these matrices are constrained (the matrices must be positive definite)
✓   Mostly useful in hierarchical models, although can be used in non-hierarchical settings
✓   Conjugate to multivariate normal likelihoods
✓   Represent quite restrictive correlations between parameters. A better prior to use in many applied settings is the LKJ distribution
✓   Gamma distribution is a special case of the Wishart distribution and the inv-gamma distribution is a special case of the inv-Wishart distribution

In the past, the most frequently used prior distributions for covariance matrices were the inv-Wishart and Wishart distributions, in order of importance. While we prefer the LKJ matrix for most settings, there are times when conjugacy is useful, mostly for reasons of computational speed, and so we discuss the Wishart family here.

We continue with our example from the LKJ section on the prevalence of four mental health conditions: depression, schizophrenia, obsessive compulsive disorder and anorexia. Recall that we had assumed a multivariate normal distribution for the scores, $\boldsymbol{d}$, of individuals on separate diagnostic tests of four different mental health disorders:

$$\boldsymbol{d} \sim N(\mu, \Sigma).\qquad(8.46)$$

In Chapter 9 we will discuss the conjugacy properties of the inv-Wishart and Wishart distributions and for now just focus on the behaviour of these as we vary their input parameters. Considering first the inv-Wishart:

$$\Sigma \sim W^{-1}(\Psi, \nu),\qquad(8.47)$$

we see that this distribution is parameterised by two parameters: Ψ, a scale matrix, and ν, the degrees of freedom. The probability distribution function for an inv-Wishart is much more complicated than for the LKJ case and so we do not explain its behaviour from first principles. Instead, we describe the behaviour of the inv-Wishart distribution as we vary ν, assuming an identity scale matrix, Ψ (which makes all variables exchangeable [38]), by independently sampling from this distribution.

When v is small, the marginal distributions for the partial correlations ρ_{12} and ρ_{23} are each fairly uniform between −1 and 1 (see the histograms in the top-left-hand panel of Figure 8.31). In our example, this would correspond to our believing that there could be strong pairwise correlations between the scores of individuals for two different mental health disorders. However, unlike in the LKJ case which also results in uniform marginal densities (see the left-hand panel of Figure 8.30), the joint density is much more complex for the inv-Wishart (see the top-left-hand panel of Figure 8.31). Specifically, it allocates considerable weight to the corners of parameter space, for example in the upper-left corner of the joint density, where $\rho_{12} = -1$ and $\rho_{23} = 1$. In our example this would correspond to our having a belief that there is a strong negative correlation between the occurrence of depression and schizophrenia, but a strong positive correlation between schizophrenia and obsessive compulsive disorder. While this might be reasonable, we recognise that this distribution also gives the same weight to the exact opposite case, where there is a strong positive correlation between the occurrence of depression and schizophrenia, but a strong negative correlation between schizophrenia and obsessive compulsive disorder (corresponding to the bottom-left-hand corner of the joint density). It seems odd for us to specify a prior distribution that gives equal weight to these completely opposing views!

As we increase v, we obtain a distribution that favours diagonal matrices (see the bottom-left-hand panel of Figure 8.31). In our case, this corresponds to the four disorders occurring independently of one another in a patient.

Remember that the Wishart family are distributions over *covariance* matrices, not *correlation* matrices like the LKJ. This means that these distributions also determine what the variance of each element of the data vector should be. When v is low, the inv-Wishart allows considerable variance in the score of individuals for each of the mental health disorders (see the top-right-hand panel of Figure 8.31; note it has a log scale). When we increase v, we indicate that there is much lower variability in the scores on these diagnostic tests (see the bottom-right-hand panel of Figure 8.31). We find it cumbersome to have a single parameter that changes both the covariances and variances of the elements in our data vector, $\boldsymbol{d}$. Instead, we prefer to use an LKJ distribution to determine the correlation structure of our correlation matrix, and an independent prior on a vector of positive weights (τ in expression (8.43)), which multiplies the correlation matrix to yield a covariance matrix. Our choice of prior for the weight vector then influences the scale of the elements of $\boldsymbol{d}$, independently from their covariances.

Next we consider the behaviour of the Wishart distribution:

$$\Sigma \sim W(\Psi, v). \tag{8.48}$$

Although this distribution is typically used as a prior for the inverse of the covariance matrix (because of its conjugacy properties), we are free in Stan nonetheless to use this distribution as a prior for a covariance matrix. Again, we assume that Ψ equals the identity matrix, and examine the effects of changes in v. As an aside, the inv-Wishart distribution is obtained by first sampling $\boldsymbol{C} \sim W(\Psi, v)$, then inverting $\boldsymbol{X} = \boldsymbol{C}^{-1}$ (hence the name *inverse*). The Wishart distribution also turns out to be the sampling distribution for covariance matrices, where the data has been generated by sampling from multivariate normals.

The Wishart distribution is, in general, better behaved than its inverse sister. In particular, the joint distribution for the correlation of partial correlations ρ_{12} and ρ_{23} is less complex for low values of v (see the top-left-hand panel of Figure 8.32). This means that the marginal distributions for the partial correlations are more reflective of the joint distribution, meaning that we specify a prior belief with fewer unexpected, and often inconsistent, relationships. Again, as we increase v, we obtain covariance matrices which are closer to being diagonal (see the lower-left-hand panel of Figure 8.32). In contrast to the inv-Wishart, the variances (the diagonal terms of our matrix) increase when we increase v (compare the top and lower panels of Figure 8.32). This is unsurprising since, as we described in the previous paragraph, to sample from the inv-Wishart distribution we take the inverse of matrices sampled from the Wishart distribution.

In summary, we advise using the LKJ distribution over the Wishart family of distributions to model covariance and correlation matrices. This is because, while the Wishart family have been

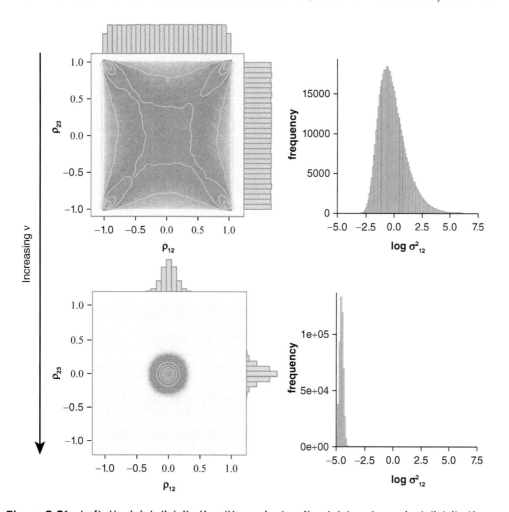

Figure 8.31 Left: the joint distribution (the main density plots) and marginal distribution (histograms above and to the side of the main plots) of ρ_{12} and ρ_{23} resulting from sampling the inv-Wishart distribution for two different values of v: $v = 5$ (top panels) and $v = 100$ (lower panels). Right: the distribution for the variances corresponding to these two values of v. In all cases, the plots were generated using 500,000 samples from an inv-Wishart distribution for a 4×4 covariance matrix. Note that the individual points in the joint density plots represent samples and the shading indicates a high local density of samples. Also, note that the scales of the right-hand plots are logarithmic.

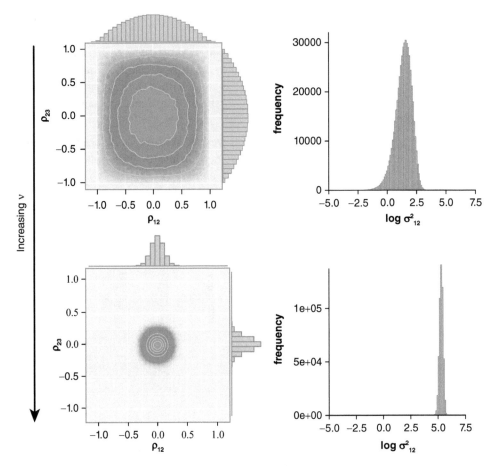

Figure 8.32 Left: the joint distribution (the main density plots) and marginal distribution (histograms above and to the side of the main plots) of ρ_{12} and ρ_{23} resulting from sampling the Wishart distribution for two different values of ν: $\nu = 5$ (top panel) and $\nu = 100$ (lower panel). Right: the distribution for the variances corresponding to these two values of ν. In all cases, the plots were generated using 500,000 samples from a Wishart distribution for a 4×4 covariance matrix. Note that the individual points in the joint density plots represent samples and the shading indicates a high local density of samples. Also, note that the scales of the right-hand plots are logarithmic.

used historically (mainly due to their conjugacy with the multivariate normal), their use can be highly restrictive, and can result in inconsistent prior beliefs.

Inverse-Wishart properties:

notation: $\Sigma \sim W^{-1}(\Psi, \nu)$ (8.49a)

PDF: $p(\Sigma \mid \Psi, \nu) = \dfrac{|\Psi|^{\frac{\nu}{2}}}{2^{\frac{\nu d}{2}} \Gamma_d\left(\frac{\nu}{2}\right)} |\Sigma|^{-\frac{(\nu+d+1)}{2}} e^{\frac{-tr(\Psi\Sigma^{-1})}{2}}$ (8.49b)

mean: $\mathbb{E}(\Sigma) = \dfrac{1}{\nu - d - 1} \Psi, \ \nu > d + 1$ (8.49c)

where $\nu > d + 1$, and d is the number of rows of Σ

Wishart properties:

notation: $\Sigma \sim W^{-1}(\Psi, \nu)$ (8.50a)

PDF: $p(\Sigma \mid \Psi, \nu) = \dfrac{|\Sigma|^{\frac{\nu - d - 1}{2}} e^{\frac{-tr(\Psi^{-1}\Sigma)}{2}}}{2^{\frac{\nu d}{2}} |\Psi|^{\frac{\nu}{2}} \Gamma_d\left(\dfrac{\nu}{2}\right)}$ (8.50b)

mean: $\mathbb{E}(\Sigma) = \nu \Psi$ (8.50c)

8 ○ 6   CHOOSING A LIKELIHOOD MADE EASY

Figure 8.33 shows a tree diagram that gives a simple way of choosing a likelihood that is appropriate for a given circumstance. While, of course, this diagram is not exhaustive, and should not be followed blindly, it is hoped that it will nonetheless be useful as a starting point.

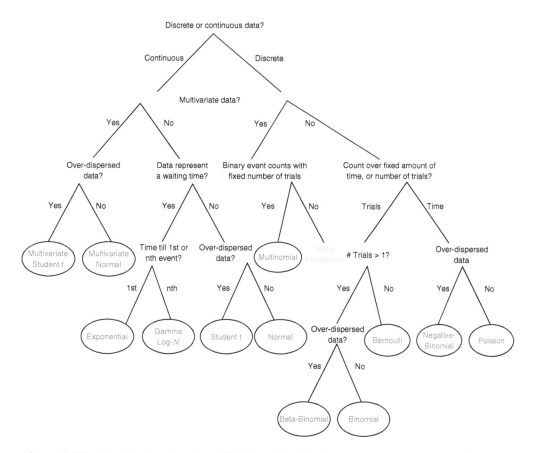

Figure 8.33   A guide for choosing a likelihood. Circled text represents an appropriate choice of distribution. The uncircled 'Many Possibilities' indicates that there are many multivariate discrete distributions possible here.

8.7 TABLE OF COMMON LIKELIHOODS, THEIR USES AND POSSIBLE PRIORS

The properties of the various distributions encountered in this chapter are summarised in Table 8.1. For an interactive guide to the distributions, take a look at: https://study.sagepub.com/lambert

8.8 CHAPTER SUMMARY

The reader should now have a good idea of the array of likelihood and prior distributions which are available to us; however, this chapter was not meant to be all-encompassing. It is almost inevitable that in applied analysis the reader will find circumstances when none of the distributions we discussed here will be appropriate. It is hoped, however, that this chapter provides some guidance for where to look in the literature. It is also often the case that a suitable distribution can be constructed using the distributions that we discussed in this chapter as building blocks.

One of the most important decisions when choosing a likelihood and prior is how much variability to allow for. We have stressed the benefits of the robust versions of sampling distributions (for example, the negative binomial to the Poisson and the Student-*t* distribution to the normal) and similarly for choices for priors (again, the Student-*t* distribution to the normal and the LKJ to the Wishart distribution). However, how should one decide on just how robust to make a model? We shall postpone some of this discussion until Chapter 10, where we will see there is a general methodology to help us to make these decisions. But it would be remiss not to mention in passing an important cost of using more robust models: they are typically more complex and can significantly lengthen the time taken for modern computational samplers to run (see Part IV). This cost must be balanced against the needs of the situation, although we advise to always err on the side of robustness.

We have, in passing, mentioned conjugate priors. This is a set of conditions that make it possible to calculate some posterior distributions by hand, without the need to appeal to a computer for sampling. In many circumstances using conjugate priors can be limiting, but these models can nonetheless be useful starting points for an analysis. This class of priors also helps us to build further our intuition for the mechanics of Bayesian inference. In Chapter 9 we discuss these conjugate beasts.

8.9 CHAPTER OUTCOMES

The reader should now be familiar with the following concepts:

- the sampling distributions (likelihoods from a different perspective) that can be chosen, which encompass discrete and continuous random variables, as well as multivariate outcomes
- the robust versions of sampling distributions that allow greater variability
- prior distributions to use for:
    - probabilities and proportions
    - means and regression coefficients
    - non-negative parameters for scale and shape
    - covariance and correlation matrices

- the robust versions of priors that allow a wider possible range of parameter values

Table 8.1 Common choices for likelihoods, their uses and possible priors.

Note, for the prior and likelihood columns, NA does not mean that a distribution cannot be used as such – just that this is uncommon practice.

Distribution	Range	Mean	Variance	Over-dispersed sister(s)	Likelihood example uses	Prior example uses	Preferred distribution
Bernoulli	[0,1]	θ	$\theta\,(1-\theta)$	NA	Infection status of single individual	NA	NA
Beta	[0,1] continuous	$\dfrac{\alpha}{(\alpha+\beta)}$	$\dfrac{\alpha\beta}{(\alpha+\beta)^2\,(\alpha+\beta+1)}$	NA	Proportion of individuals with a disease in a population	Probability of obtaining a 'heads' on a coin flip	NA
Beta-binomial	[0,1,2,3,...,n]	$n\,\dfrac{\alpha}{\alpha+\beta}$	$n\,\alpha\beta\,\dfrac{(\alpha+\beta+n)}{(\alpha+\beta)^2\,(\alpha+\beta+1)}$	NA	Count of bank failures across Europe	NA	NA
Binomial	[0,1,2,3,...,n]	$n\,\theta$	$n\,\theta(1-\theta)$	Beta-binomial	Infection status count of n individuals	NA	NA
Categorical	$[0,1]^k$	θ_i	$p_i\,(1-p_i)$	NA	Blood type of one individual	NA	NA
Cauchy	[−inf,inf] = R	Undefined	Undefined	NA	Individual stock returns	Mean wealth	NA
Dirichlet	Unit simplex, e.g. probability vectors	$E(\theta_i)=\dfrac{\alpha_i}{\Sigma\alpha_i}$	$var(\theta_i)=\dfrac{\alpha_i\,(\Sigma\alpha_i-\alpha_i)}{(\Sigma\alpha_i)^2\,(\Sigma\alpha_i+1)}$	Multivariate logit-normal	Probabilities of having a range of non-overlapping diseases	Probabilities of having a range of non-overlapping diseases	NA
Exponential	[0,inf] = R+	$\dfrac{1}{\lambda}$	$\dfrac{1}{\lambda^2}$	Gamma	Time before mutation arises in a population	Variance in phenotype in a population	NA
Gamma	[0,inf] = R+	$\dfrac{\alpha}{\beta}$	$\dfrac{\alpha}{\beta^2}$	NA	Daily rainfall amount	Variance in rainfall amount	NA

(Continued)

Table 8.1 (Continued)

Distribution	Range	Mean	Variance	Over-dispersed sister(s)	Likelihood example uses	Prior example uses	Preferred distribution
Half-Cauchy	[0,inf] = R+	Undefined	Undefined	NA	–	Variance in stock returns	NA
Inverse-chi-squared	[0,inf] = R+	$\frac{1}{(\nu-2)}$, for $\nu>2$	$\frac{2}{(\nu-2)^2(\nu-4)}$	NA	–	Variance of disease prevalence	Half-Cauchy
Inverse-gamma	[0,inf] = R+	$\frac{\beta}{(\alpha-1)}$	$\frac{\beta^2}{(\alpha-1)^2(\alpha-2)}$, for $\alpha>2$	NA	–	Variance of disease prevalence	Half-Cauchy
Inverse-Wishart	Space of covariance matrices	$(\nu-\kappa-1)^{-1}S$	No simple expression	NA	Covariance of stock returns	Covariance of stock returns	LKJ
LKJ	Space of correlation matrices	No analytic solution	No analytic solution	NA	Correlation of stock returns	Correlation matrix representing relationship between different gene expression levels	NA
Logit-normal	[0,1] continuous	No analytic solution	No analytic solution	NA	–	Probability of developing a particular disease	NA
Log-normal	[0,inf] = R+	$Exp\left(\mu+\frac{\sigma^2}{2}\right)$	$Exp(2\mu+\sigma^2)(-1+Exp(\sigma^2))$	NA	Wealth of individuals	Overdispersion parameter for a negative binomial	NA
Multinomial	$[0,1,2,3,....n]^k$	$n p_i$	$n p_i (1-p_i)$	Dirichlet-multinomial	Blood type counts of n individuals	NA	NA

Distribution	Range	Mean	Variance	Over-dispersed sister(s)	Likelihood example uses	Prior example uses	Preferred distribution
Multivariate normal	R^n	μ	Σ	Multivariate Student-t	Gene expression concentrations across multiple genes	Regression coefficients	NA
Multivariate Student-t	R^n	μ, for $v>1$	$\frac{v}{(v-2)}\Sigma$, for $v>2$	NA/Cauchy ($v=1$)	Stock returns of many companies	Mean stock returns	NA
Negative binomial	[0,1,2,3,...inf]	λ	$\lambda + \frac{\lambda^2}{\kappa}$	NA	Number of cars passing a traffic light in one hour	NA	NA
Normal	[-inf,inf] = R	μ	σ^2	Student-t/Cauchy	Error in regression models	Regression coefficient	NA
Poisson	[0,1,2,3,...inf]	λ	λ	Negative binomial	Count of number of component failures per week	Negative binomial	NA
Student-t	[-inf,inf] = R	μ, for $v>1$	$\frac{v}{(v-2)}$, for $v>2$	NA/Cauchy ($v=1$)	Individual stock returns	Mean stock return	NA
Uniform	[a,b] continuous	$\frac{(a+b)}{2}$	$\frac{(b-a)^2}{12}$	NA	Failure point along a railway track	Probability of a railway failure on a given day	NA
Wishart	Space of covariance matrices	vS	No simple expression	NA	Covariance of stock returns	Covariance of stock returns	LKJ

 **PROBLEM SETS**

Problem 8.1 Drug trials

Suppose that we are testing the efficacy of a certain drug which aims to cure depression, across two groups, each of size 10, with varying levels of the underlying condition: *mild* and *severe*. We suppose that the success rate of the drug varies across each of the groups, with $\theta_{mild} > \theta_{severe}$. We are comparing this with another group of 10 individuals, which has a success rate equal to the mean of the other two groups, $\theta_{homogeneous} = (\theta_{mild} + \theta_{severe})/2$.

Problem 8.1.1 Calculate the mean number of successful trials in each of the three groups.

Problem 8.1.2 Compare the mean across the two heterogeneous groups with that of the single group of 10 homogeneous people.

Problem 8.1.3 Calculate the variance of outcomes across each of the three groups.

Problem 8.1.4 How does the variance across both heterogeneous studies compare with that of a homogeneous group of the same sample size and same mean?

Problem 8.1.5 Now consider the extension to a large number of trials, where the depressive status of each group is unknown to the experimenter, but follows $\theta \sim beta(\alpha, \beta)$. Calculate the mean value of the beta distribution.

Problem 8.1.6 Which combinations of α and β would make the mean the same as that of a single study with success probability θ?

Problem 8.1.7 How does the variance change, as the parameters of the beta distribution are changed, so as to keep the same mean of θ?

Problem 8.1.8 How does the variance of the number of disease cases compare to that of a single study with success probability θ?

Problem 8.1.9 Under what conditions does the variance in disease cases tend to that from a binomial distribution?

Problem 8.2 Political partying

Suppose that in polls for an upcoming election there are three political parties that individuals can vote for, denoted by $\{A, B, C\}$, respectively.

Problem 8.2.1 If we assume independence among those individuals who are polled then what likelihood might we choose?

Problem 8.2.2 In a sample of 10 individuals we find that the numbers who intend to vote for each party are $(n_A, n_B, n_C) = (6, 3, 1)$. Derive and calculate the maximum likelihood estimators of the proportions voting for each party.

Problem 8.2.3 Graph the likelihood in (p_A, p_B) space.

Problem 8.2.4 If we specify a *Dirichlet(a,b,c)* prior on the probability vector $\boldsymbol{p} = (p_A, p_B, p_C)$ the posterior distribution for a suitable likelihood is given by a *Dirichlet(a + n_A, b + n_B, c + n_C)*. Assuming a *Dirichlet(1,1,1)* prior, and for the data given, find the posterior distribution and graph it in (p_A, p_B) space.

Problem 8.2.5 How do the posterior means compare with the maximum likelihood estimates?

Problem 8.2.6 How does the posterior shape change if we use a *Dirichlet(10,10,10)* prior?

Problem 8.2.7 How does the posterior shape change if we use a *Dirichlet(10,10,10)* prior but have data $(n_A, n_B, n_C) = (60, 30, 10)$?

9

Chapter contents

CONJUGATE PRIORS

9◉1   CHAPTER MISSION STATEMENT

At the end of this chapter the reader should appreciate that, under special circumstances, it is possible to specify 'conjugate priors' that allow exact calculation of a posterior density.

9◉2   CHAPTER GOALS

Bayesian analysis requires us to compute the denominator of Bayes' rule to exactly calculate the posterior. For most realistic models of phenomena, this is usually a bridge too far, since this involves calculating a high-dimensional integral, which is practically intractable. However, there is a class of models – pairs of likelihoods and priors – where this calculation is possible. Furthermore, previous researchers have tabulated the formulae for the posterior probability distribution functions that result from particular combinations of likelihoods and priors, meaning that we do not need to do any maths at all! The priors that result in these nice posterior properties are referred to as *conjugate*. By choosing a prior that is conjugate to a given likelihood, the resultant posteriors are actually in the same family of distributions as the priors themselves, making it even easier to remember and use this class of models.

Choosing conjugate priors is usually overly restrictive, but can nevertheless be a useful starting point before moving on to more realistic models, which are typically estimated by computational sampling (see Part IV). Additionally, because many texts assume a basic understanding of conjugate priors, it is important to be familiar with their use.

This chapter is deliberately kept short for three reasons. First, we believe that a few indicative examples can provide sufficient insight into how to use conjugate priors. Second, the whole point of using conjugate priors is that we do not need to do the maths – so why learn it! Third, the use of conjugate priors is typically restrictive and now less important with computational sampling.

9◉3   WHAT ARE CONJUGATE PRIORS AND WHY ARE THEY USEFUL?

Suppose that we run a restaurant and want to build a model for the number of people who have food allergies in a particular sitting, X, in order to inform the buying of ingredients. If we assume that the allergy status of one person is independent of everyone else's then a reasonable choice is a binomial sampling model (see Section 4.6.2), $X \sim \mathcal{B}(n,\theta)$, where n is the number of people in a sitting and θ is the probability that a randomly chosen individual has an allergy. We can write the binomial likelihood as:

$$Pr(X = k \,|\, \theta,n) = \binom{n}{k}\theta^k(1-\theta)^{n-k}$$

$$\propto \theta^k(1-\theta)^{n-k}.$$

(9.1)

What is a conjugate prior?

Since the beta distribution is defined over the [0,1] interval and can represent a range of prior beliefs (see Section 8.5.1), we use a beta prior for θ (see Section 8.5.1). The beta distribution's probability density function (PDF) can be written as:

$$p(\theta \mid \alpha, \beta) = \frac{\theta^{\alpha-1}(1-\theta)^{\beta-1}}{B(\alpha, \beta)}$$

$$\propto \theta^{\alpha-1}(1-\theta)^{\beta-1},$$

(9.2)

where $B(\alpha, \beta)$ is a beta function, which is not dependent on θ.

We notice that expression (9.1) for the sampling distribution and expression (9.2) for the prior both contain a term of the form $\theta^a(1-\theta)^b$. When we use Bayes' rule to calculate the posterior, we are required (in the numerator) to multiply together the likelihood and the prior, resulting in:

$$p(\theta \mid data) \propto p(data \mid \theta) \times p(\theta)$$

$$\propto \theta^k (1-\theta)^{n-k} \times \theta^{\alpha-1}(1-\theta)^{\beta-1}$$

(9.3)

$$= \theta^{k+\alpha-1}(1-\theta)^{n-k+\beta-1}$$

$$= \theta^{\alpha'-1}(1-\theta)^{\beta'-1},$$

where $\alpha' = \alpha + k$ and $\beta' = \beta + n - k$. In this case, the posterior PDF has exactly the same θ dependence as the beta prior's PDF. Furthermore, since the prior is a valid probability distribution, the posterior must also be one. This means that, because the posterior PDF has the same functional form (in terms of θ) as a beta distribution's functional form, it must actually be one. Alternatively, if we actually do the denominator calculation in Bayes' rule, we find it equals $B(\alpha', \beta')$, meaning that the posterior PDF is a beta distribution, although with different parameters to the prior. Here we say that the beta prior is *conjugate* to the binomial likelihood since the posterior is also a beta distribution.

OK, let's step away from the maths for a minute and examine what happens to the beta posterior as we include data from our restaurant (see the left-hand panels of Figure 9.1). If there are more allergy sufferers in our sample the likelihood shifts to the right, which is, in turn, mirrored by the $beta(\alpha + k, \beta + n - k)$ posterior. Alternatively, if we maintain the same number of people with allergies in our sample and adjust our priors, the posterior now moves in accordance with the prior (see the right-hand panels of Figure 9.1).

So we see that using a binomial likelihood with a beta prior leads to a beta posterior, and that the behaviour of the estimated posterior behaves as we would expect it to intuitively. However, we are yet to define what is meant by a conjugate prior. We can describe conjugacy through the following flow diagram, which represents the Bayesian inference process:

$$prior \xrightarrow{\text{likelihood}} posterior.$$

(9.4)

In the allergy example, this process is described by:

$$beta \xrightarrow{\text{binomial}} beta'.$$

(9.5)

So, we specified a beta prior, and the data, through the binomial likelihood, updated our beliefs and resulted in a beta posterior (albeit with different parameters, hence why *beta'* is used above).

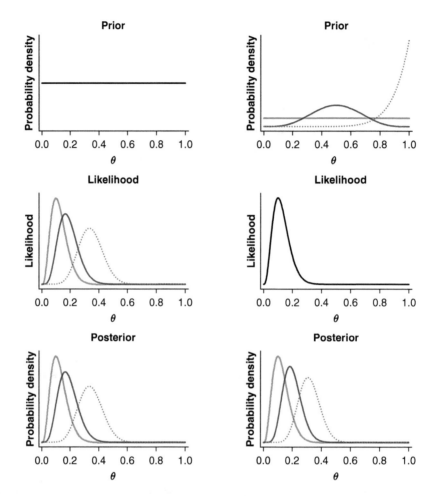

Figure 9.1   The effect of different numbers of individuals with allergies (left) and priors (right) on the posterior distribution. In all cases, the sample size was 30.

Conjugate priors are always defined relative to a particular likelihood and means that both the prior and the posterior come from the same family of distributions. Diagrammatically, we have that for a specified likelihood, L, and a prior distribution from a particular family, $f \in F$:

$$f \xrightarrow{\ L\ } f',$$

(9.6)

where $f' \in F$ is another member of the same family of distributions. For example, if we feed a gamma prior into our Bayesian updating rule, we should get a gamma posterior out (as is the case for a Poisson likelihood). If we feed a normal prior in, we should get a normal posterior out (for particular normal likelihoods), and so on.

For all conjugate prior examples, we can write down a mechanistic rule using our flow diagram for how to update our prior beliefs in light of data. In our example above:

$$beta(\alpha, \beta) \xrightarrow{\text{binomial likelihood with } (n,k)} beta(\alpha + k, \beta + n - k). \tag{9.7}$$

By using this simple rule we can avoid doing any maths since we can just substitute our numbers into the above formula (which we can look up in Table 9.1) to yield the posterior PDF. This really is Bayesian statistics made easy!

9 ○ 4 GAMMA-POISSON EXAMPLE: COUNTING CARS

As another example, imagine that we work for a department for transport and want to build a model that predicts the number of cars, Y, that approach a particular intersection over a certain period of the day. Here we might use a Poisson likelihood if we believe that the cars arrive independently of one another (see Section 8.4.3). We can write down the likelihood in this case as:

$$
\begin{aligned}
Pr(Y = \mathbf{y} \mid \lambda) &= \prod_{i=1}^{n} \frac{\lambda^{y_i} e^{-\lambda}}{y_i!} \\
&= \frac{\lambda^{\sum_{i=1}^{n} y_i} e^{-n\lambda}}{\prod_{i=1}^{n} y_i!} \\
&\propto \lambda^{n\bar{y}} e^{-n\lambda},
\end{aligned}
\tag{9.8}
$$

where $\mathbf{y}$ represents a data vector comprising the numbers of cars that approached the intersection over n samples, and we have used $n\bar{y} = \sum_{i=1}^{n} y_i$.

If we use a gamma prior to describe our prior preferences (see Section 8.4.9), we can write down its PDF in the following form:

$$
\begin{aligned}
p(\lambda \mid \alpha, \beta) &= \frac{\beta^\alpha \lambda^{\alpha-1} e^{-\beta\lambda}}{\Gamma(\alpha)} \\
&\propto \lambda^{\alpha-1} e^{-\beta\lambda}.
\end{aligned}
\tag{9.9}
$$

Again, we notice a common term in both the likelihood and prior expressions (this time $\lambda^a e^{-b\lambda}$). This means that when we multiply the two terms together in the numerator of Bayes' rule, we obtain a posterior PDF given by:

$$
\begin{aligned}
p(\lambda \mid k) &\propto \lambda^{n\bar{y}} e^{-n\lambda} \times \lambda^{\alpha-1} e^{-\beta\lambda} \\
&= \lambda^{n\bar{y}+\alpha-1} e^{-(\beta+n)\lambda} \\
&= \lambda^{\alpha'-1} e^{-\beta'\lambda},
\end{aligned}
\tag{9.10}
$$

where $\alpha' = \alpha + n\bar{y}$ and $\beta' = \beta + n$. Again, since the dependence on the parameter λ is the same in both the posterior and prior PDFs, and because the prior is a valid probability distribution, the posterior must be from the same family of distributions – in this case a gamma distribution. Writing down the updating rule for this example, we find that:

$$gamma(\alpha,\beta)\xrightarrow{\text{Poisson likelihood with}(n,\bar{y})} gamma(\alpha+n\bar{y},\beta+n).\tag{9.11}$$

Note that this rule is only correct for the form of gamma distribution parameterised as in expression (9.9). If we used a different parameterisation of the gamma prior, we would need to adjust the rule accordingly.

Let's now apply this rule to our example of cars arriving at an intersection. Suppose that we collect hourly counts of the number of cars that arrive at two different intersections. We use the above rule to calculate the posteriors in each of these cases (see the left-hand plots of Figure 9.2). We see that increases in the average number of cars in the sample leads to an increase in α', resulting in a shift rightwards in the posterior, in accordance with the likelihood. Similarly, if we change the prior parameters (α,β), this leads to changes in (α',β') for the posterior, resulting in a corresponding shift in the posterior (see the right-hand panel of Figure 9.2).

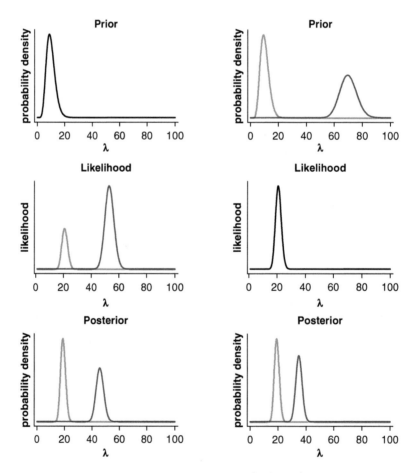

Figure 9.2   The effect of (left) different samples and (right) different priors on the posterior distribution for the car example described in the text. The prior shown in the top-left-hand panel is a Γ (10,1) distribution. The data sample in the right-hand columns had a mean of 21. In all cases the sample size is 5.

9○5 NORMAL EXAMPLE: GIRAFFE HEIGHT

Suppose that we are modelling the average height of adult male giraffes in a particular nature reserve. Since the height of a giraffe is the result of a multitude of different factors – both genetic and environmental – we might use a normal likelihood (see Section 8.4.6). Furthermore, we assume that the heights of the individual giraffes in our sample, $\mathbf{z} = \{z_1, z_2, ..., z_n\}$, are independent of one another, resulting in a likelihood of the form:

$$p(\mathbf{z} \mid \mu, \sigma) = \prod_{i=1}^{n} \frac{1}{\sqrt{2\pi\sigma^2}} \exp\left(-\frac{(z_i - \mu)^2}{2\sigma^2}\right)$$

$$\propto (\sigma^2)^{-\frac{n}{2}} \exp\left(-\frac{1}{2\sigma^2} \sum_{i=1}^{n} (z_i - \mu)^2\right).$$

(9.12)

To construct a conjugate prior, we reason from previous examples that its functional form must be similar to the likelihood. This means that we require a prior distribution of the form:

$$p(\mu, \sigma^2) \propto (\sigma^2)^a \times \exp\left(-\frac{1}{2\sigma^2} c(\mu - b)^2\right).$$

(9.13)

We could separate the prior using the law of conditional probability into $p(\mu, \sigma^2) = p(\sigma^2) \times p(\mu \mid \sigma^2)$, where we have:

$$p(\sigma^2) \propto (\sigma^2)^a$$

$$p(\mu \mid \sigma^2) \propto \exp\left(-\frac{1}{2\sigma^2} c(\mu - b)^2\right).$$

(9.14)

This prior structure turns out to be reasonable for a range of circumstances. The following priors have the above structure [14] (see Section 8.5.3 for a discussion of the first):

$$\sigma^2 \sim Inv\text{-}\chi^2(v_0, \sigma_0^2)$$

$$\mu \mid \sigma^2 \sim \mathcal{N}(\mu_0, \sigma^2 / \kappa_0).$$

(9.15)

Gelman et al. [14] label the joint prior specified by these assumptions as an $\mathcal{N}-Inv\text{-}\chi^2(\mu_0, \sigma_0^2 \kappa_0; v_0, \sigma_0^2)$ distribution, in other words a normal inverse chi-squared distribution. Multiplying together the normal likelihood function and our chosen prior PDF, we obtain the numerator of Bayes' rule, which dictates the functional form of the posterior density. We will not go into the maths here, but it is possible to derive the parameters (see [14]) of the posterior $\mathcal{N}-Inv\text{-}\chi^2$ distribution, which are:

$$\mu' = \frac{\kappa_0}{\kappa_0 + n} \mu_0 + \frac{n}{\kappa_0 + n} \bar{z}$$

$$\kappa' = \kappa_0 + n$$

$$v' = v_0 + n$$

$$v'\sigma'^2 = v_0\sigma_0^2 + (n-1)s^2 + \frac{\kappa_0 n}{\kappa_0 + n}(\bar{z} - \mu_0)^2.$$

(9.16)

Table 9.1 Some of the most common likelihood–prior conjugate pairs. For the normal case where both parameters are unknown, consult Section 9.5 for the update rules.

Likelihood	Prior	Posterior
Bernoulli	Beta(α,β)	Beta($\alpha + \sum_{i=1}^{n} X_i, \beta + n - \sum_{i=1}^{n} X_i$)
Binomial	Beta(α,β)	Beta($\alpha + \sum_{i=1}^{n} X_i, \beta + \sum_{i=1}^{n} N_i - \sum_{i=1}^{n} X_i$)
Poisson	Gamma(α,β)	Gamma($\alpha + \sum_{i=1}^{n} X_i, \beta + n$)
Multinomial	Dirichlet($\boldsymbol{\alpha}$)	Dirichlet($\alpha + \sum_{i=1}^{n} \mathbf{X}_i$)
Normal (known σ^2)	Normal (μ_0, σ_0^2)	$N\left(\dfrac{1}{\frac{1}{\sigma_0^2} + \frac{n}{\sigma^2}} \left(\dfrac{\mu_0}{\sigma_0^2} + \dfrac{\Sigma x_i}{\sigma^2} \right), \left(\dfrac{1}{\sigma_0^2} + \dfrac{n}{\sigma_0^2} \right)^{-1} \right)$
Normal (known μ)	Inv-gamma (α, β)	Inv-gamma $\left(\dfrac{\alpha + n}{2}, \dfrac{\beta + \Sigma (X_i - \mu)^2}{2} \right)$

While the expressions above are perhaps bewildering, there is intuition in the results. The posterior mean giraffe height μ' is a weighted average of the prior mean and the mean from the data, with more weight given to the data for larger samples. The posterior variance parameter σ'^2 is a weighted average of the prior variance for σ^2, the data sample variance s^2 and a third term which represents the difference between the prior mean and the sample mean.

Note that here we have assumed that both parameters of the likelihood are unknown beforehand. In some circumstances, one of (μ, σ^2) may be known, and simpler conjugate priors can be found (see Table 9.1).

9○6 TABLE OF CONJUGATE PRIORS

Since this information is widely available online (see, for example, https://en.wikipedia.org/wiki/Conjugate_prior), we give the conjugate prior update rules for only a few common cases in Table 9.1.

9○7 THE LESSONS AND LIMITS OF A CONJUGATE ANALYSIS

Using conjugate priors means that there is no need to actually do any of the maths ourselves, as we can stand on the shoulders of past giants and use their tabulated results. All we need to do is plug our numbers into these convenient formulae, and then we can exactly derive a form of the posterior distribution which is a weighted average of the prior and likelihood, as we expect.

While the use of conjugate priors makes Bayesian statistics easy, it can limit us. These limits are quickly approached when we need greater modelling flexibility, which is especially the case when using hierarchical models (see Part V).

Continuing with the giraffe heights example, suppose that we fit a normal distribution to our sample, first by the method of maximum likelihood (see Chapter 4) to give us an initial insight

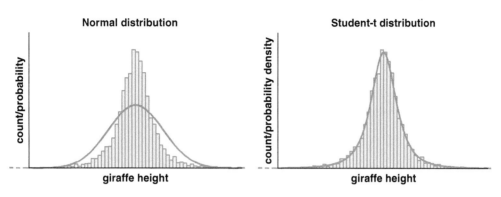

Figure 9.3 Fitting giraffe height data using (left) a normal distribution and (right) a Student-*t* distribution. The curves indicate the maximum likelihood fits of each distribution to the data (shown in red).

into the problem. We then compare the fitted normal distribution's PDF with the actual data sample, and find that it has insufficient variability to explain the data (see the left-hand panel of Figure 9.3). Instead, we decide to use the Student-*t* distribution since we know that it is a more robust alternative to the normal distribution (see Section 8.4.7). This time the maximum likelihood estimates of the parameters of this distribution represent a much better fit to the data (see the right-hand panel of Figure 9.3).

We now want to use what we have learned to do full Bayesian inference using our giraffe heights data. We know that the normal likelihood has a conjugate prior (a normal–inv-χ^2 distribution) meaning that we could derive an exact form for the posterior distribution. However, our pre-Bayesian analysis has hinted that a normal likelihood is not fit for purpose here and so we want to use a Student-*t* distribution instead. As such, we consult Table 9.1 to look for the conjugate prior to a Student-*t* distribution. Alas! There is no corresponding entry. This means that simply choosing a more appropriate sampling distribution has made it impossible to use a conjugate prior. This leaves us with a choice. Either we stay with a normal likelihood, which we know to be inadequate, or we abandon the conjugate-ship and use computational methods (see Part IV). There is only one correct answer here – we should not allow our analysis to be determined by the complexity of choosing a more appropriate distribution, and should use Markov chain Monte Carlo. Of course, we can use the normal distribution, with its normal–inv-χ^2 conjugate prior, to gain some understanding of the problem, but the Student-*t* distribution will ultimately be more satisfactory.

9⊙8 CHAPTER SUMMARY

The reader should now understand how choosing a *conjugate* prior can help to simplify Bayesian inference. However, this simplicity comes at a cost! In most real-life examples of inference, the constraint of choosing likelihood–prior conjugate pairs is too restrictive and can lead us to use models that inadequately capture the variability in the data. However, there are circumstances when conjugate pairs are appropriate, but, as always, we need to check the suitability of our chosen modelling framework before drawing any conclusions.

Bayesians happen to have at their disposal powerful and flexible ways of checking the adequacy of their models. We now concentrate on this underused and, perhaps, most important aspect of Bayesian modelling.

9 O 9 CHAPTER OUTCOMES

The reader should now be familiar with the following concepts:

- the definition of a conjugate prior
- how to use Table 9.1 to find a conjugate prior for a particular likelihood as well as write down (not calculate!) the posterior PDF
- the limits of conjugate priors and the need for computational methods

9 O 10 PROBLEM SETS

Problem 9.1 The epidemiology of Lyme disease

Lyme disease is a tick-borne infectious disease spread by bacteria of species *Borrelia*, which are transmitted to ticks when they feed on animal hosts. While fairly common in the United States, this disease has recently begun to spread throughout Europe.

Imagine you are researching the occurrence of Lyme disease in the UK. As such, you begin by collecting samples of 10 ticks from fields and grasslands around Oxford, and counting the occurrence of the *Borrelia* bacteria.

Problem 9.1.1 You start by assuming that the occurrence of *Borrelia* bacteria in one tick is independent of that in other ticks. In this case, why is it reasonable to assume a binomial likelihood?

Problem 9.1.2 Suppose the number of *Borrelia*-positive ticks within each sample i is given by the random variable X_i, and that the underlying prevalence (among ticks) of this disease is θ. Write down the likelihood for sample i.

Problem 9.1.3 Suppose that in your first sample of size 10 you find $X_1 = 1$ case of *Borrelia*. Graph the likelihood here and hence (by eye) determine the maximum likelihood estimate of θ.

Problem 9.1.4 By numerical integration show that the area under the likelihood curve is about 0.09. Comment on this result.

Problem 9.1.5 Assuming that $\theta = 10\%$, graph the probability distribution (also known as the sampling distribution). Show that, in contrast to the likelihood, this distribution is a valid probability distribution.

Problem 9.1.6 (Optional) Now assume that you do not know θ. Use calculus to show that the maximum likelihood estimator of the parameter, for a single sample of size 10 where you found X ticks with the disease, is given by:

$$\hat{\theta} = \frac{X}{10}.$$ (9.17)

(*Hint*: maximise the log-likelihood rather than the likelihood.)

Problem 9.1.7 A colleague mentions that a reasonable prior to use for θ is a *beta*(a,b) distribution. Graph this for $a = 1$ and $b = 1$.

Problem 9.1.8 How does this distribution change as you vary a and b?

Problem 9.1.9 Prove that a *beta*(a,b) prior is conjugate to the binomial likelihood, showing that the posterior distribution is given by a *beta*$(X + a, 10 - X + b)$ distribution.

Problem 9.1.10 Graph the posterior for $a = 1$ and $b = 1$. How does the posterior distribution vary as you change the mean of the beta prior? (In both cases assume that $X = 1$.)

Problem 9.1.11 You now collect a larger data set (encompassing the previous one) that has a sample size of 100 ticks in total, of which you find 7 carry *Borrelia*. Find and graph the new posterior using the conjugate prior rules for a *beta*$(1,1)$ prior and binomial likelihood.

Problem 9.1.12 You collect a second data set of 100 ticks, this time finding that 4 carry the disease. Find and graph the new posterior (across both data sets) using the conjugate prior rules for a *beta*$(1,1)$ prior and binomial likelihood. How does it compare to the previous one?

Problem 9.1.13 Now we will use sampling to estimate the posterior predictive distribution for a sample size of 100, using the posterior distribution obtained from the entire sample of 200 ticks (11 of which were disease-positive). To do this we will first sample a random value of θ from the posterior: so $\theta_i \sim p(\theta \mid X)$. We then sample a random value of the data X by sampling from the binomial sampling distribution $X_i \sim \mathcal{B}(100, \theta_i)$. We repeat this process a large number of times to obtain samples from this distribution. Follow the previous rules to produce 10,000 samples from the posterior predictive distribution, and then graph it using a histogram.

Problem 9.1.14 Does our model fit the data?

Problem 9.1.15 Indicate whether you expect this model to hold across future sampling efforts.

Problem 9.1.16 If we assume a uniform prior on θ, the probability that a randomly sampled tick carries Lyme disease, what is the shape of the prior for θ^2? (This is the probability that 2/2 ticks carry Lyme disease.) (*Hint*: do this either using Jacobians (hard-ish), or by sampling (easy-ish).)

Problem 9.2 Epilepsy

In the data file `conjugate_epil.csv` there is a count of seizures for 112 patients with epilepsy who took part in a study [2]. Assume that the underlying rate of seizures is the same across all patients, and that the event of a seizure occurring is independent of any other seizures occurring.

Problem 9.2.1 Under these assumptions what model might be appropriate for this data?

Problem 9.2.2 Write down the likelihood for the data.

Problem 9.2.3 Show that a gamma prior is conjugate to this likelihood.

Problem 9.2.4 Assuming a $\Gamma(4, 0.25)$ prior (with a parameterisation such that it has mean of 16), find the posterior distribution, and graph it.

Problem 9.2.5 Find or look up the posterior predictive distribution, and graph it.

Problem 9.2.6 Comment on the suitability of the model to the data.

Problem 9.3 Light speed

The data file `conjugate_newcomb.csv` provides Simon Newcomb's (1882) measurements of the passage time (in millionths of a second) it took light to travel from his lab to a mirror on the Washington Monument, and back again. The distance of the path travelled is about 7.4km. The primary goal of this experiment is to determine the speed of light, and to quantify the uncertainty of the measurement. We assume there are a multitude of factors that additively result in measurement error for the passage time.

Problem 9.3.1 Why might a normal distribution be appropriate here?

Problem 9.3.2 Write down the likelihood for all the data.

Problem 9.3.3 Derive the maximum likelihood estimators of all parameters.

Problem 9.3.4 Based on the likelihood function, what functional form for the prior $p(\mu, \sigma^2)$ would make it conjugate?

Problem 9.3.5 Assuming a decomposition of the prior $p(\mu, \sigma^2) = p(\sigma^2) \times p(\mu \mid \sigma^2)$, what priors might we use?

Problem 9.3.6 (Difficult) Using these priors, find the parameters of the posterior distribution.

Problem 9.3.7 Comment on the suitability of the model to the data. (You can use the MLEs here, or, if you are feeling ambitious, the full posterior predictive distribution.)

10

Chapter contents

EVALUATION OF MODEL FIT AND HYPOTHESIS TESTING

CHAPTER MISSION STATEMENT

At the end of this chapter, the reader will grasp the powerful methods that a Bayesian has at their disposal to evaluate the fit of their models to data as well as to select between different models.

10○2   CHAPTER GOALS

Models are interpretations of real life, and are, necessarily, reduced versions of it. However, a good model can, despite its simplicity, suggest valuable strategies for navigating the real world. This begs us to ask, 'What is a good model?' Such a model should incorporate just enough realism so that we trust its outputs, while being simple enough to allow interpretation and extrapolation. But how in practice can we determine whether our model meets these criteria?

The Bayesian testing framework which allows us to judge the fit of a model to data is known as *posterior predictive checks* (PPCs). The idea behind this umbrella of methods is simple. If the model is a good fit to the data, then fake data that we generate from the fitted model should look indistinguishable from the real thing. In practice, this is not usually fully attainable, so, instead, we choose a model that captures the characteristics of the data most important to us. This means that we are free to choose which features of the data to use to assess the fit of a model to data, and this choice, hence, becomes an important part of Bayesian model checking. The beauty of PPCs is that they allow us to understand the ways in which a model is good and the ways in which it is deficient. Examining models through this multidimensional lens is more rewarding than more commonly used evaluation criteria and easier to understand.

In the scientific process, we often encode different hypotheses in each of our models. To determine which, if any, of the hypotheses best represents the data, we hence want to identify the most predictive model. Recently, criteria have been introduced that estimate a model's predictive capability in a more Bayesian spirit than the more conventionally used AICs or DICs (if you don't know these, don't worry – we cover them in this chapter). Towards the end of this chapter, we introduce these relatively new additions to the modeller's arsenal and discuss their use. This section is inevitably a little more mathematically advanced than those preceding it, although we endeavour to focus on the intuitive nature of the maths, rather than dwell on the algebraic details.

 POSTERIOR PREDICTIVE CHECKS

10.3.1 Recap – posterior predictive distributions

We discussed how to estimate the posterior predictive distribution in Section 7.8, but we briefly review this process now, as it is crucial to what follows. If we fit a Bayesian model to data, x, we obtain the posterior distribution, $p(\theta \mid x)$. We can then use this distribution to generate samples from the posterior predictive distribution, which is a probability distribution over possible values of future data x'. In particular, we iterate the following:

1   Sample $\theta_i \sim p(\theta \mid x)$: that is, sample a parameter value from the posterior distribution.
2   Sample $x'_i \sim p(x' \mid \theta_i)$: that is, sample a data value from the sampling distribution conditional on the parameter value from the previous step.

For clarity, we have termed $p(x'|\theta_i)$ a sampling distribution rather than a likelihood because we hold the parameter fixed at θ_i. This two-stage process reflects the two sources of uncertainty that we have: the uncertainty in the parameter value (reflected in the posterior distribution) and the uncertainty due to sampling variation (reflected by the sampling distribution).

If the two above steps are iterated a sufficient number of times, then the resultant histogram of our data samples approaches the shape of the exact posterior predictive distribution, were we to calculate it by integration. For the majority of cases, we estimate the posterior predictive distribution by sampling since the high-dimensional integrals involved are often intractable.

10.3.2 Graphical PPCs and Bayesian p values

Now that we understand the methodology for calculating the posterior predictive distributions, we can discuss PPCs. In doing so, we need to discuss what is meant by a *good* model.

It does not make sense to talk of an unconditionally good model. Since a statistical model is always a simplification of reality, it will not reproduce real life exactly. Typically, models are good at reproducing some aspects of the real world, but worse at others. Usually, when we build a model, we plan to use it for a particular purpose. Hence, a good model is one that can account for the variation in data that is pertinent to this specific purpose.

In Bayesian analyses, we leverage the power of the posterior predictive distribution to test whether our model can replicate the behaviours that are most important to its eventual use. Specifically, we use these distributions to generate fake data samples, which we then compare to the real thing. These comparative tests are what constitute PPCs. We interpret the data that we generate from the posterior predictive distributions as being the data sample that we might collect tomorrow if the data-generating process remained the same as it is today.

Graphical visualisations are a great way to test the performance of our model. By visually comparing key aspects of the simulated and actual data samples, we can quickly determine if our model is reasonable. The choice of visualisations tests our creativity and familiarity with the problem at hand, but definitely gets easier with more experience in PPCs. Graphical PPCs are an important first step in testing a model's performance, but they may become cumbersome if we want to carry out many of these tests across a large number of replicates. Instead, a numerical measure of a model's coherence with the data is often used, which is known as a *Bayesian* p *value*.

Both of these concepts are better explained through application, and we have created the following examples to convey their use and usefulness. It is not possible to be exhaustive here since the range of possible tests is essentially infinite, but the following should provide a flavour of the different types of tests that we can apply in practice. Note also that the 'real' data used in the following examples is not actually real but created to aid with understanding PPCs.

What is a posterior predictive check and how is it useful?

Amazon staff hiring

Imagine that we work as part of Amazon's logistics team and are tasked with building a statistical model to describe the weekly UK order volume. The company has helpfully collected data on the weekly orders in the UK over the past year (see the top-left panel of Figure 10.1). We might then ask: What eventualities would we want our model to be able to handle?

Suppose that our model is to be used for planning the number of staff to hire in UK warehouses next year. In this case, we want to hire sufficient staff numbers to handle those weeks with the highest order volumes, with some confidence that we can meet the demand. Perhaps we are content if our model can generate the maximum order volume that we see in the real data in at least 20% of simulated scenarios, since we believe that last year's maximum is relatively unlikely to be reached this year. However, we are constrained by costs and so we do not want this probability to exceed 80% – this would correspond to our being overly cautious about next year's demand. We fit an (unspecified) model to the data and then use it to generate samples from the posterior predictive distribution.

In Figure 10.1 we show the actual order data from last year (in black), along with 15 fake yearly samples (grey and red) that were generated from the posterior predictive distribution of our model. We colour those sets in grey that produce at least one observation that exceeds the highest order volume from the actual data, and those in red if they fail to do so.

We find that $\frac{5}{15}$ of the fake data sets have a maximum that exceeds the highest order volume from last year's data. Since this lies between 20% and 80%, we conclude that for this particular application (planning staff allocation) we are reasonably confident in our model's capability.

The proportion of cases where the maximum of our fake data sample maximum exceeds the maximum of the actual data set is referred to as a Bayesian p value, by analogy with Frequentist hypothesis tests. However, we should take care not to interpret it in the same way. In contrast to Frequentist p values, we need to be aware of either low or high values of this statistic. In our example, if $p < 20\%$, then the model does not generate enough extreme observations. Whereas if $p > 80\%$, then the model is, for our purposes, overly cautious with uncertainty.

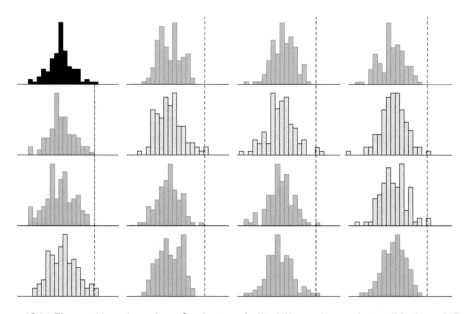

Figure 10.1   The weekly order volume for Amazon in the UK over the past year (black) and 15 simulated yearly data sets from the posterior predictive distribution of our model. The dashed line in each case indicates the value of the highest weekly order volume from the real data. If the sample has at least a single data point whose value exceeds this maximum, then the graph is shown in grey, and red otherwise. Note that in those red cases above, some appear to have a maximum greater than the actual, but this is a result of binning the data.

As this example indicates, it is usually best to start with graphical checks of a model's performance, then move onto p values. The danger of starting right away with a p value is that you will not fully understand the source of your model's problems resulting in erroneous conclusions.

Mosquito lifetime

Mosquito lifetime is an important determinant of malaria transmission, so knowledge about this characteristic is much sought after. One of the ways of determining the lifetime of mosquitoes in the wild is to use so-called mark–release–recapture experiments. In this method a large number of mosquitoes are marked with a fluorescent dye and are then released into the wild. By capturing batches of mosquitoes over time and counting the number of marked mosquitoes recaptured, this provides a way of gauging mortality (plus migration technically). The faster the marked mosquito count decays, the faster the mosquitoes are dying.

Suppose that we carry out one of these experiments, and obtain the data series shown in Figure 10.2, indicating the number of recaptured marked mosquitoes since release (on day 0). Since we know the number of mosquitoes we released, we use a binomial regression model (where time is the independent variable), where mosquito death reduces the number of marked mosquitoes we expect to capture over time. This model assumes that individual recapture events are independent of one another (see Section 8.4.2). After setting priors on the relevant distribution parameters, we estimate the posterior and use it to generate samples from the posterior

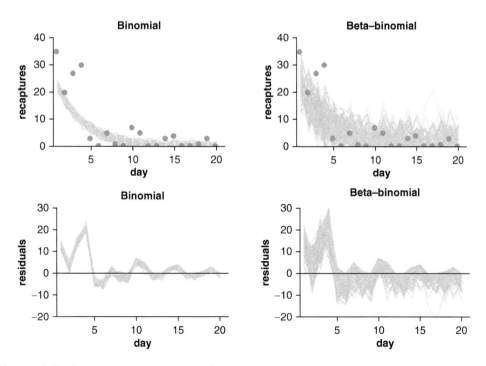

Figure 10.2   Top: the real recaptures of marked mosquitoes (red dots) versus simulations from the posterior predictive distribution (lighter red lines) for the binomial (left) and the beta-binomial (right) models. Bottom: residuals from the simulated data versus actual for both model types over time.

predictive distribution (see top-left panel of Figure 10.2). It is evident from this graph that the binomial sampling model does not capture the variation in the data across all time points (the real data points frequently lie outside of the simulated lines).

A reason for this discrepancy could be that we assumed that captures of the individual mosquitoes were independent. In practice, we might expect that mosquitoes respond similarly to weather conditions – making them all more or less likely to be captured at a given point in time. Similarly, if they exist in swarms, they may be easier to catch en masse, again violating the independence assumption. In these circumstances, we might change our likelihood to a beta-binomial distribution since this allows for non-independent events. We find that this model is a better fit to the data since only a small proportion of the actual data points lies outside of the bulk of samples from the posterior predictive distribution (see the top-right panel of Figure 10.2). We would hence be more confident in making any inferences about mosquito longevity using the results from the beta-binomial model.

Another way of displaying this data is to look at the residuals over time. In the bottom panels of Figure 10.2 we see that both models under-predict the number of mosquitoes recaptured on the first few days. This could be because immediately after release the mosquitoes behave differently, meaning that they are easier to recapture. A future iteration of this model might directly model this behaviour, by introducing a parameter which inflates the recapture probability for the first few days following the release.

Snow days

Suppose that we work for the New York City Council, which is responsible for planning road gritting during the winter. As such, we wish to build a model capable of reproducing realistic sequences of days in which the average temperature falls below freezing (and, hence, the roads need gritting). Suppose that we have the data from the previous April (see the top-left panel of Figure 10.3) and want to build a model to generate possible weather patterns for the coming April, to help inform policy making.

We begin by modelling the probability of a freeze occurring on a day t, $X_t = 1$, as an independent Bernoulli process (see Section 8.4.1):

$$X_t \sim Ber(\theta), \tag{10.1}$$

where θ is the probability that a freeze occurs on any given day in April. We fit the model to the real data and use it to generate fake data samples from the posterior predictive distribution. In planning the gritting, it is particularly important to have knowledge of the persistence in freezing conditions as this affects the buying of the salt and the hiring of temporary workers. A measure of persistence is to calculate the length of the longest run of freezing days which occurs in the data. We show this measure for the real and fake data samples in Figure 10.3, shading those data samples grey that have a maximum freezing spell duration equal to, or longer than, that of the real data.

We find that the model cannot reproduce this aspect of the real data particularly well, because in only 1 case out of 15 fake data samples (see Figure 10.3) was the simulated duration of the longest run of freezing days greater than the corresponding quantity from the real data, resulting in $p = \frac{1}{15} \approx 6\%$. Since p is small, we conclude that we need to change our model. In particular,

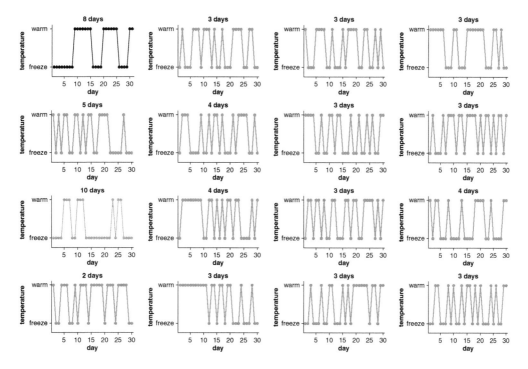

Figure 10.3 The real data set (black) and 15 fake samples from the Bernoulli model. Above each plot, we display the length of the longest freezing spell that occurs in that data sample. If the fake data has a maximum freezing spell duration that exceeds that of the real data, then we colour the graph grey, and red otherwise.

we want to choose a new model that better accounts for autocorrelation in the state of the weather. For example, we might use a model incorporating a persistent latent process, which represents the predisposition to freezing.

Word distributions within topics

Google is interested in automatically decomposing corpuses of text into a set of constituent topics to allow it to better understand the nature of the content that is within them. This, in turn, means Google can build better algorithms for its search engines (see [27]). If the corpus of text can be represented by a group of documents (where each document might correspond to a single website, for example) then Google might want to understand the differing mixes of topics that are represented in each document. For example, a website called 'exotic-animals.com' may devote much of its content to discussing cool facts about animals, although it may also devote some attention to wildlife conservation activities; a website called 'pet-funeral.com' will probably spend less time discussing animals facts, and none to conversation activities, and much of its content will be about the funereal services offered to grieving pet owners. The most popular way to estimate the topic content of documents is using a method known as Latent Dirichlet Allocation (LDA) [5]. We do not go into the detail of this method, but nonetheless believe that this example nicely illustrates the use of a PPC. The assumptions of LDA are that each document is composed of a small number of topics, with each word's creation being attributable to one of these topics. Importantly, the distribution of words within each topic is assumed to be the same multinomial probability distribution (see Section 8.4.10), independent of the particular document in question [5].

We can test the validity of this independence assumption by an appropriate PPC. Specifically, if we look at the frequencies of words that belong to a particular topic, then the independence assumption indicates that this distribution should not vary across documents. As an example, imagine that we have seven different documents and examine the frequency of the word *kitchen*, which belongs to the *house* topic which concerns descriptions of people's houses. In LDA, we do not assume that the percentage of the topics within each document is the same; however, within a certain topic, this model assumes that the distribution of word frequencies is the same.

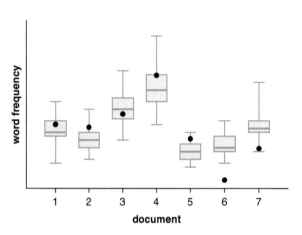

Figure 10.4 Frequencies of the word *kitchen* across seven different documents (black dots), with simulations from the posterior predictive distributions for the LDA model shown as box and whisker charts.

To test this we use the posterior predictive distribution for our fitted LDA model to generate samples of text for each document; we then count the occurrence of the word *kitchen* across the different documents (see Figure 10.4). We see that, for some of the documents, the actual frequency of the word lies outside of the bounds of the fake data samples (notably documents 2, 5, 6 and 7), which leads us to question the assumption of independence. It is possible to allow for greater variance in the word distribution by incorporating extra document-level multinomial variance, using Dirichlet compound distributions [27], or to add extra covariates that might explain this systematic variation [5].

Bacterial infection

Suppose that we are working in a lab at the Centre for Disease Control and are trying to understand why some of our samples often become contaminated with a particular species of bacteria. First, we graph the infection status of the 16 samples by the order they were pipetted (see the top-left panel of Figure 10.5). We next decide to use an independent Bernoulli likelihood for the infection status of each sample, supposing that the source of the infection is airborne, meaning that all samples are equally likely to become contaminated. We then generate fake data sets from the posterior predictive distribution of the fitted model. Deciding that an important aspect of the data to recreate is the number of infected samples, we evaluate whether the recreated samples have a number of infected samples greater than the real.

Doing so, we find that 6 out of 15 fake data samples have more infected samples than the true number, resulting in $p = \frac{6}{15} = 40\%$. Confident that we have created a model that adequately

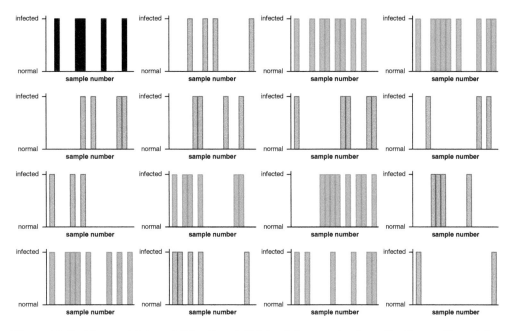

Figure 10.5   The real data set (black) and 15 fake data samples from the Bernoulli model. If the number of infected samples in the fake data set exceeds the real, then we colour the graph red, and grey otherwise.

simulates the real data, we go to the lab manager and tell her that the source of the infection is airborne. She looks at us with consternation. This is surprising to her, since the bacteria species that are colonising the samples is not known to travel through the air. She advises that we go back and repeat the laboratory experiment to see if our airborne model stands up to the test.

Demoralised at the lack of confidence in our ability, and not excited by the prospect of redoing the experiment, we go back and repeat it. In three repeats, with 16 samples in each, we find {0,7,15} samples are infected. We then assess the model's capability using the previous PPC. Although the middle case, where seven samples are infected, is produced in the fake data, the extremes are not. Something is amiss with our model!

We go back to our desk and start to rethink things. Suddenly we realise the error of our ways. We were graphing the infection status of our original sample by the order the tubes were filled, but this is not the way the tubes are organised during the experiment – they are in a 4 × 4 array. We then graph the infection status of the samples in this fashion (see Figure 10.6). When viewed in this light, we see that all of the infected samples were actually next to one another – it looks like, rather than transmission through the air, the bacteria simply 'crawl' from one tube to its neighbours. To test this hypothesis, we generate fake data samples from the original Bernoulli model and compare the number of separate infected blocks in these with the original. By an 'infected block' we mean a single contiguous collection of neighbouring samples that are all infected with the bacteria. For example, the panel second from the top and second from the left of Figure 10.6 shows a sample where there are two separate infected blocks.

In Figure 10.6 we see that only 1 sample out of 15 had a single block of infection, resulting in $p = \frac{1}{15} = 7\%$. Since this value is quite low we conclude that the original model is not a good fit to

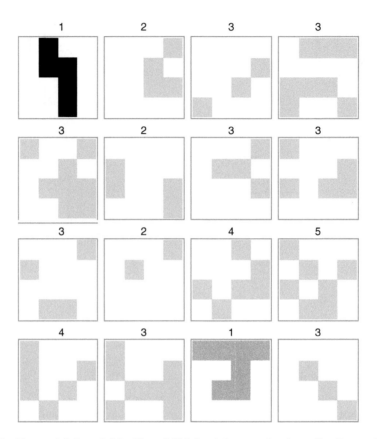

Figure 10.6 The real data set (black) and 15 fake data samples from the Bernoulli model. If the number of separate blocks of infection (count displayed above each panel) exceeds that of the real, then we colour the graph red, and grey otherwise. Note that here we assume that diagonal touching does not constitute a contact.

the data. Examination of the experimental repeats also illustrates a similar result – they each only have a single block of infection. To account for the spread of the infection, we need a model that allows for a spatial covariance in infection status.

We go back to the supervisor and tell her we were wrong before; the infection is not airborne and is spread simply by contact. She is pleased we have come to this conclusion ourselves, albeit after a little prodding.

This example demonstrates that it is imperative to use the correct visualisation for our data (the example was inspired by an example in [14]). Misleading visualisations lead to false conclusions being drawn, as we saw here. The example also demonstrates that it is essential to use a PPC that is appropriate for the particular situation. Again, using the wrong form of PPC leads to incorrect conclusions.

10○4   WHY DO WE CALL IT A *p VALUE*?

As discussed earlier, we can generate simulations from the posterior predictive distribution, y_{sim}, and statistics, $T(y_{sim}, \theta)$, calculated on the fake data samples to capture some key aspect of the data-generating process. We then generate a Bayesian p value by comparing the simulated data test statistic with its value on the actual data, $T(y,\theta)$ [14]:

$$p = Pr(T(y_{sim},\theta) > T(y,\theta)\,|\,y) \tag{10.2}$$

where the probability is calculated by, first, comparing the real and fake data statistics for each fake data sample that we generate from the posterior predictive distribution, and then, second, we count the number of fake data samples where the simulated statistic exceeds the actual, which equals p. This differs from the Frequentist p value because here we do not condition on the parameter value θ and, instead, allow for its variation in accordance with the posterior distribution. This is due to a difference in perspective, where Bayesians regard the data as fixed and the parameter to vary, whereas Frequentist statisticians see the converse (see Chapter 2).

The quantity p is a probability, although unlike Frequentist p values it is not Pr(hypothesis is true | data). It is simply a measure of model (mis)fit. So unlike Frequentist p values, values near 0 or 1 indicate a discrepancy between the model and the data; values of $p = 0.5$ are the ideal. Typically, p values lower than 5%–10% or higher than 90%–95% are chosen as thresholds to indicate significant misfit. However, these are only rules of thumb. The thresholds that we choose should ultimately be governed by the model's intended use.

10.5 STATISTICS MEASURING PREDICTIVE ACCURACY: AIC, DIC, WAIC AND LOO-CV

10.5.1 Out-of-sample prediction and overfitting

We build statistical models to explain the variation in a data sample because we believe that the insight this gives us applies to wider circumstances. One way to measure the wider applicability of a statistical model is to evaluate its predictive power on out-of-sample data. By fitting our model to one sample of data and then using it to predict data in another, we hope to produce an unbiased measure of a model's capacity to generalise. The problem is that we generally do not have access to out-of-sample data. (If we did, we would usually include this as part of our sample!) One way out of this issue is to use the same sample twice: once to fit the statistical model and again to test its predictive power. The trouble with this approach is that we bias the odds in our favour and leave ourselves susceptible to *overfitting*.

Overfitting is a statistician's equivalent of cheating on a test in high school. If we steal the test beforehand, we can work away – textbook in hand – to write down the answers to the test before we take it. Unsurprisingly, when we take the test we perform well, artificially well, in fact. However, if we take another test – written by, for example, a teacher from another school – we would perform badly. In this case, our learning is overfit. We perform well in one particular application, the test that we have learned beforehand, but our performance generalises poorly to other tests. In this case, the performance on the first test is biased upwards and does not actually represent our inherent knowledge of the subject matter. The second test performance – because it is independent of the first – more adequately represents our state of knowledge or, more likely, lack thereof. We would do better to actually learn the material, and then our performance on the first test should be more similar to that on the second. Our new model of learning would generalise much better to out-of-sample data.

What is true of high school tests is also true of statistical models. If we try hard enough we can build a model that predicts a given data set perfectly, by adding layer upon layer of additional complexity. In producing a more complex model, we make more extreme assumptions about the data-generating process that may or, more likely, may not, be true. When we obtain a fresh data set, these assumptions are tested and often found wanting, meaning that the model is terrible for prediction.

In machine learning (a statistical framework for developing the most predictive models), overfitting is avoided by splitting a data set into a *training* set and a *cross-validation* set. The models are fitted to the training set, which is then assessed by its performance on an independent cross-validation set.

While we would ideally carry out this sort of partitioning in statistical inference (in fact, one measure we discuss, LOO-CV, does exactly this), often the computational task of refitting a model on many data sets makes it prohibitive to do so. Also, the nature of the data can make it difficult to decide on an appropriate data split. Among other reasons, these two issues have led to a demand for other measures of model predictive capability, which can be calculated without the need for re-estimation on a cross-validation set.

What is meant by overfitting?

These measures are, at best, approximations to the cross-validation ideal [15]. They aim to correct for the bias inherent in trying to assess a model's performance on the same data set which was used to fit the model in the first place. Over the next few sections we introduce the most popular of these measures.

10.5.2 How to measure a model's predictive capability?

If we obtain new data $y^{new} = \{y_1^{new}, y_2^{new}, ..., y_n^{new}\}$ there are a few different ways we might measure the fit of a model. A popular way of summarising the discrepancy between the model's predictions $y^{pred} = \{y_1^{pred}, y_2^{pred}, ..., y_n^{pred}\}$ and the real data y^{new} is to measure the mean squared error (MSE):

$$\text{MSE} = \frac{1}{n}\sum_{i=1}^{n}(y_i^{new} - y_i^{pred})^2. \tag{10.3}$$

This measure is easy to calculate but does not have any theoretical justification (apart from when a normal likelihood is used), which limits its scope. A more theoretically justified Bayesian measure would be to use the posterior predictive distribution (see Section 10.3.1) to measure a model's ability to predict new data. In particular, we could choose a model with the highest posterior probability of generating the new data, $p(y^{new}|y)$.

Since the log function is a monotonic transformation, the score obtained by using the logarithm of the posterior predictive distribution will mirror the posterior predictive distribution. We favour using the log form because of its connection with a concept called the Kullback–Leibler (KL) divergence, which is a measure of the difference between the true density and the estimated one. If we maximise the log of the posterior predictive distribution, this is equivalent to estimating the posterior predictive density with the lowest KL divergence from the true density (see Section 10.5.3). The scoring function hence used is:

$$prediction\ accuracy = \log\left[p(y^{new}|y)\right], \tag{10.4}$$

which can also be written as:

$$prediction\ accuracy = \log \int_{All\,\theta} p(\mathbf{y^{new}} \mid \theta) p(\theta \mid \mathbf{y}) d\theta$$

$$= \log \left[E_{posterior} \left(p(\mathbf{y^{new}} \mid \theta) \right) \right],$$

(10.5)

where $E_{posterior}$ denotes the expectation with respect to the posterior distribution.

10.5.3 The ideal measure of a model's predictive accuracy

This section is fairly mathematically involved, with a few integrals making an appearance. (If you don't fancy this mathematical odyssey, then feel free to skip ahead to Section 10.5.4, as this section is not crucial to understanding the rest of the material in this chapter.)

For simplicity, imagine that we start by considering a single new data point, y^{new}, which amounts to replacing $\mathbf{y^{new}}$ (a vector) by y^{new} (a scalar) in expression (10.4). Usually, we do not have access to this extra data, and so the new data y^{new} is unknown. If we knew the true distribution $f(y)$ for a single new data point, we could evaluate the expectation of expression (10.4), which Gelman et al.[14] call the expected log predictive density (*elpd*):

$$elpd = E_f \left(\log \left[p(y^{new} \mid \mathbf{y}) \right] \right)$$

$$= \int_{y^{new} \in Y} f(y^{new}) \log \left[p(y^{new} \mid \mathbf{y}) \right] dy^{new},$$

(10.6)

where E_f denotes expectation under the true data distribution $f(y)$. This measure quantifies how close the estimated posterior predictive distribution, $p(y^{new} \mid \mathbf{y})$, is to the true distribution, $f(y)$. Accordingly, expression (10.6) is maximised when the estimated distribution equals the true one (see Figure 10.7).

While expression (10.6) appears abstract, it is actually full of intuition. A useful concept here is the Kullback–Leibler divergence ($KL \geq 0$), which is a measure of discrepancy between two distributions (see Figure 10.9 below). For two continuous distributions, $p(x)$ and $q(x)$, we can quantify the 'distance' of $q(x)$ from $p(x)$ (the measure is not symmetric) by the following:

▶

The ideal measure of a model's predictive fit

$$KL(p \to q) = \int_{x \in X} p(x) \log \left[\frac{p(x)}{q(x)} \right] dx.$$

(10.7)

If the distributions are the same (that is, $q(x) = p(x)$), then we have:

$$KL = \int_{x \in X} p(x) \log[1] dx$$

$$= 0.$$

(10.8)

Interestingly, the KL divergence can be related back to Morse code. This code was optimised for the English language. This is why the most common letter in English, e, has the shortest Morse code equivalent (.) whereas a less common letter, q, has a longer representation (–.-). We can think about these letter frequencies in English text as being governed by a distribution, *p*. The KL divergence tells us the informational penalty, in terms of the length of Morse messages

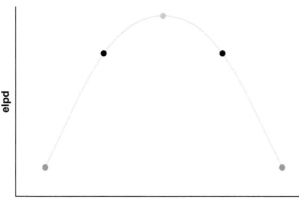

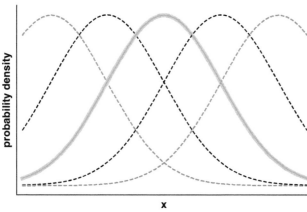

Figure 10.7   The expected log predictive density (*elpd*) (top) as a function of the estimated posterior predictive density (bottom). The true distribution – *f(y)* in expression (10.6) – is shown as the bold curve, and example estimated posterior predictive distributions – $p(y^{new}|y)$ in expression (10.6) – are shown as dashed lines.

versus the optimum that we would pay if we used the same code to transmit messages in Spanish, which has letters with a different frequency *q*. This is why the KL divergence is not a symmetric measure; the inefficiencies from going English–Spanish are not the same as Spanish–English since in both cases we are comparing the inefficient code with code optimised to the target language. We can also think of the letter frequencies in a Scrabble game as being optimised to help people make the most number of words in their particular language. The KL divergence associated with using an English board to play Scrabble in Spanish would measure something like the reduction in average length of words used versus using a Spanish board. So, in general, we can think about the KL divergence as measuring some sort of informational penalty in going from something optimised to distribution *p* to code for another distribution *q*.

We can further explain the meaning of the KL divergence using a simple example. Suppose there are 10 objects in an urn we call *p*, and we can reach in and randomly draw out one of these objects. In the urn, there is one red ball and nine grey cubes. Imagine that there is another urn, which we call *q*, which also has 10 objects but with a hitherto unknown frequency of red balls and grey cubes. We then play a game with a friend – we agree to pay a friend £1 if they reach into urn *q* and draw out a grey cube and they will pay us £9 if they draw out a red ball. We decided the rules of the game on the basis of the object frequencies in urn *p*, because these rules ensure that the game is fair since $\frac{9}{10}$ of the time they will draw out a grey cube, and we will pay them £1, but $\frac{1}{10}$ of the time they will pick a red ball and we will win £9. This means that if we play the game long enough, each of our average winnings will be zero. Hence, if the distribution of objects in urn *q* is the same as *p* then we expect to make no money on any given play of the game; in this case, the KL divergence of *q* from *p* is zero (see Figure 10.8). However, if there are more red balls in *q* than there are in *p*, then we expect

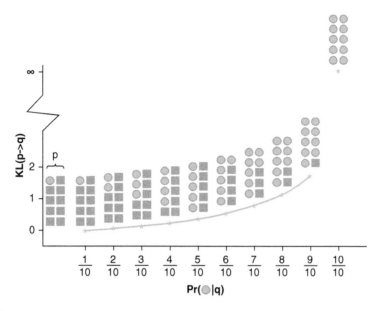

Figure 10.8   The KL divergence for urn *p* (left) as a function of the number of balls (circles) in urn *q* (shown above the line) which also contains 10 objects.

to make a profit in the long run. Therefore, on a given play of the game, we expect to make a profit. Our confidence in whether we will make a profit, however, depends on the number of balls in the urn. The KL divergence provides a gauge of our confidence, and hence increases

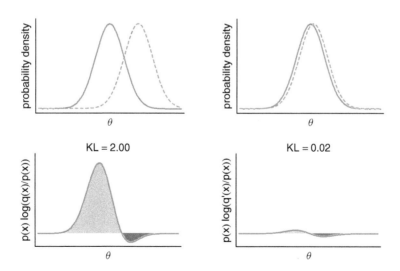

Figure 10.9   Top: a distribution $p(x)$ (full curve) against two distributions: $q(x)$ and $q'(x)$ (both dashed). Bottom: the products, $p(x)\log(q(x)/p(x))$ and $p(x)\log(q'(x)/p(x))$, which are then integrated (see expression (10.7)) to yield the KL divergence from $p(x)$ to the other distributions, which are shown in each case. The light and dark grey areas show regions that contribute positively and negatively to the integral's value.

with the numbers of balls in the urn (see graph in Figure 10.8). When all of the objects are balls, we are certain that we will win on any given play of the game. In this case, the KL divergence of p from q is infinite.

We can use expression (10.7) to calculate the KL divergence between our posterior predictive distribution, $p(y^{new} | y)$, and the *true* distribution of new (and old) data, $f(y)$:

$$KL = \int_{y^{new} \in Y} f(y^{new}) \log\left[\frac{f(y^{new})}{p(y^{new} | y)}\right] dy^{new}$$

$$= \int_{y^{new} \in Y} f(y^{new}) \log\left[f(y^{new})\right] dy^{new} - \int_{y^{new} \in Y} f(y^{new}) \log\left[p(y^{new} | y)\right] dy^{new},$$

(10.9)

where the first term in the final line of (10.9) is fixed because we have no choice over the true data distribution $f(y)$. However, we do have a choice over p in the second term, since we are choosing between models with different posterior predictive distributions. Thus, to minimise the KL divergence between the true distribution and the posterior predictive distribution, we should pick the model with the posterior predictive distribution that maximises the second term (maximises, because of the minus sign in front of it).

A quick comparison between the second term of expressions (10.9) and (10.6) for *elpd* reveals that they are the same. If we choose a model to maximise *elpd*, we also minimise the KL divergence between our posterior predictive distribution and the true data distribution.

If we then consider the *elpd* for our n new data points, taken one at a time, we have what Gelman et al. [14] call the expected log pointwise predictive density (*elppd*):

$$elppd = \sum_{i=1}^{n} E_f\left(\log\left[p(y_i^{new} | y)\right]\right).$$

(10.10)

The pointwise measure defined in (10.10) is preferable to using the full joint predictive distribution $E_f\left(\log\left[p(y^{new} | y)\right]\right)$ because it enables a range of expressions representing out of sample error to be calculated from it [14].

10.5.4 Estimating out-of-sample predictive accuracy from in-sample data

As we discussed previously, attempts to estimate out-of-sample predictive accuracy using data that was used to fit the model are, at best, approximations. They can also be misleading if attempts are not made to correct for the selection bias caused by fitting a model to the same data used to test its predictive capability. For overfit models (see Figure 10.10), if these sources of bias are not corrected for, there will be a large gap between the actual out-of-sample predictive capability of a model versus the amount we estimate from within the sample.

Ultimately, we would like a measure of predictive accuracy that approximates the *elppd* defined in expression (10.10), given that we do not have new data, y^{new}, nor the true density of a single data point $f(y^{new})$. All the methods (with the exception of LOO-CV) use the same data that was used to estimate a model as a proxy for the future data and f, resulting in an overstatement of its predictive capability. To correct for this over-optimistic gauge of a model's predictive capability,

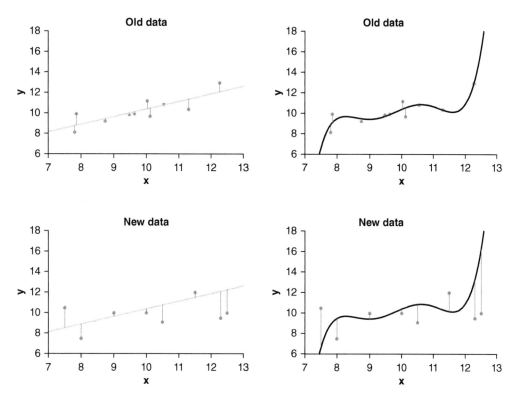

Figure 10.10 Top: the fit of a linear model (left) and non-linear model (right) to data. Bottom: the performance of each model when applied to a new data set – the non-linear model does not generalise to new data as well as the linear one.

a bias correction is made in each method. There are a number of different approaches to do this, although, as we suggest in the following sections, we recommend using only WAIC or LOO-CV, as these are the most Bayesian of methods currently in wide use.

10.5.5 AIC

The most common method for evaluating a model's predictive accuracy and for choosing between non-nested models is the Akaike Information Criterion (AIC). This method comes from Frequentist statistics and, hence, does not use the posterior distribution to evaluate the average log-likelihood, but instead uses the maximum likelihood point estimate, meaning that $E_{posterior}(p(y_i | \theta)) \rightarrow p(y_i | \hat{\theta})$. Since this method uses only point estimates, it is inherently non-Bayesian.

The next step is to correct for the upward bias in estimation of predictive accuracy due to fitting the model to the same data that is used to evaluate its fit. To do this an assumption is made, based on the asymptotic normal approximation for a posterior distribution [14], where subtracting the number of parameters k from the log predictive density corrects for the increase in accuracy due to heightened model complexity:

Evaluating
model fit
through AIC,
DIC, WAIC
and LOO-CV

$$\widehat{elpd}_{AIC} = \log\left[p(\mathbf{y} \,|\, \hat{\theta}_{mle}) \right] - k. \tag{10.11}$$

This results in an estimate of *elpd* denoted $\widehat{elpd}_{AIC}$. AIC – like all the other measures that we consider – attempts to correct for the problem of overfitting, in this case by penalising additional model complexity through k. AIC is actually given by –2 times expression (10.11), meaning that we seek to minimise this criterion.

This attempt at bias reduction is akin to using a kitchen knife to do surgery. In all but the simplest of operations, this is not a great idea. In particular, for more complex models (particularly hierarchical ones), the effective number of parameters is not necessarily given by k. A more nuanced (and Bayesian) approach is needed.

10.5.6 DIC

The Deviance Information Criterion (DIC) [33] is a more Bayesian alternative to AIC. It uses the posterior mean point estimate, $\hat{\theta}_{Bayes}$, rather than the maximum likelihood estimate, as the point at which to evaluate the log-likelihood. It then subtracts a data-dependent term which captures the overfitting bias more effectively than the k term in AIC [14]:

$$\widehat{elpd}_{DIC} = \log\left[p(\mathbf{y} \,|\, \hat{\theta}_{Bayes}) \right] - k_{DIC}, \tag{10.12}$$

where the bias correction term is given by:

$$k_{DIC} = 2var_{posterior}\left(\log[p(\mathbf{y}\,|\,\theta)]\right), \tag{10.13}$$

where $var_{posterior}$ is the variance with respect to the posterior distribution. More complex models have more parameters, with higher posterior uncertainty for each of its parameter values. This increased uncertainty in the parameter values means there is more variability in the log-likelihood – our measure of model fit – meaning that we penalise these models more heavily.

DIC, like AIC, is again defined as –2 times $\widehat{elpd}_{DIC}$, meaning that we aim to minimise this quantity. We usually use computational sampling to approximate the integrals required to exactly calculate the posterior mean and variance in log probability (see Chapter 12), since, for all but the most simple examples, these are analytically intractable.

10.5.7 WAIC

Both the aforementioned methods use point estimates to estimate the predictive accuracy of the model, followed by a post-hoc correction to account for overfitting. The correction for AIC is rigid and data-independent, where we simply subtract the number of fitted parameters, and is based on asymptotic normality conditions unlikely to be achieved in most circumstances. The correction for DIC is more nuanced and uses both the posterior distribution and the data to derive the bias term.

However, both of these measures ignore the uncertainty in the parameter estimates when estimating the predictive accuracy. In this sense, these estimates are still Frequentist in nature. The Watanabe–Akaike Information Criterion or Widely Applicable Information Criterion (there is no consensus over the meaning of this acronym) improves on this by incorporating posterior uncertainty in the estimation of predictive accuracy. In correspondence with expression (10.10), we consider each of the n data points separately. Considering a single data point y_i, we can take the log of the average value of the likelihood across the posterior distribution:

$$\widehat{lpd} = \log\left[E_{posterior}\left(p(y_i \mid \theta)\right)\right],\tag{10.14}$$

where $E_{posterior}$ is the expectation with respect to the posterior distribution. If we sum corresponding terms for each of the n points, and include a bias correction term, we obtain an estimate of the expected log pointwise predictive density (*elppd*):

$$\widehat{elppd} = \sum_{i=1}^{n}\log\left[E_{posterior}\left(p(y_i \mid \theta)\right)\right] - k_{WAIC},\tag{10.15}$$

where:

$$k_{WAIC} = \sum_{i=1}^{n} var_{posterior}(\log p(y_i \mid \theta)).\tag{10.16}$$

Expression (10.16) makes the dependence of the bias correction on the parameter uncertainty in the posterior more explicit and is recommended by Gelman et al. [14] due to its similarity with the cross-validation ideal. Again, to be on the same scale as AIC and DIC, we multiply expression (10.15) by –2 to yield the WAIC, which we aim to minimise.

Note that in practice we typically use sampling rather than integration to evaluate the various integrals involved in expressions (10.15) and (10.16) (see Chapter 16).

10.5.8 LOO-CV

As we discussed previously, the ideal measure of a model's predictive accuracy would be to split a data set into a training set and a cross-validation set. The model is then fitted (trained) on the training set, and its predictive performance gauged on the independent cross-validation set. The use of this independent cross-validation set circumvents the issue of selection bias, and allows us to be more confident in our estimates of the model's out-of-sample predictive capability.

While the use of training and cross-validation sets provides a better measure of predictive accuracy in principle, there are practical concerns which limit its use. Here, we consider a method known as leave-one-out cross-validation (LOO-CV), where we use a single data point to test the model's predictive power, y_{cv}, and use the rest of the sample, Y_{train}, to train the model. Ideally, this process is iterated n times (where n is the size of the data sample) so that each data point in the sample is used once, and once only, as the single cross-validation datum in one of the iterations. This can be extremely expensive computationally speaking, particularly if the data set is large. Also, if the data are structured, for example in the case of a time series, it may be difficult to estimate the model with gaps in the data series.

In each iterate of LOO-CV we evaluate the log posterior predictive density (across all samples from our posterior distribution):

$$lpd = \log\left[p(y_i \mid Y_{-i})\right],\tag{10.17}$$

where $\boldsymbol{Y}_{-i}$ denotes the training data vector with all data points included apart from y_i. If this process is iterated n times, we can estimate the overall expected log pointwise predictive density by summing the individual *lpd* [14]:

$$\widehat{elppd} = \sum_{i=1}^{n} \log\left[p(y_i \mid \boldsymbol{Y}_{-i}) \right]. \tag{10.18}$$

Estimates of *elppd* by this method may understate the predictive accuracy of the full model because the training sample consists of only $n - 1$ data points rather than the full sample [14]. So a corrective term can be added for completeness; however, in practice this term is small (particularly for large data sets), so it can usually be ignored.

In using LOO-CV to choose between models, we also run the risk of overfitting. This is because, if we use LOO-CV to select a model, we will likely pick one that fits both the signal and noise in the cross-validation set. This is well documented in the machine-learning literature and merits the use of a third data set called the *test* set, which is used only once to evaluate a model.

10.5.9 A practical summary of measures of predictive accuracy in simple terms

We have now introduced the theoretical ideal measure of a model's predictive accuracy and the various methods used to approximate this. Ultimately, we would like a measure that is Bayesian as well as a reasonable approximation for the out-of-sample predictive accuracy of a given model. While AIC and DIC are commonly used, they are not fully Bayesian in nature. WAIC is fully Bayesian as well as being closer to the ideal measure of a model's out-of-sample predictive accuracy. However, this method, like AIC and DIC, estimates out-of-sample predictive accuracy from within the same sample that was used to originally fit the model, meaning that post-hoc bias corrections are required to correct for overfitting. LOO-CV partitions the sample into a training set, which is used to fit the model, and a single cross-validation data point, which is used to estimate out-of-sample predictive accuracy. Since this method uses an independent data set to assess the predictive accuracy, it avoids the need to correct for the overfitting bias inherent in the other methods. In this respect, this method is the closest, and cleanest, approximation to the ideal measure of out-of-sample predictive accuracy.

However, there is a penalty to LOO-CV, in that it requires repeated estimation on each of the n training and cross-validation set pairs, which may be computationally infeasible for complex models. Also, both LOO-CV and WAIC require a partitioning of the data sample into subsamples, which may not be straightforward for situations where the data are structured (for example, in time series, panel or network data). AIC and DIC do not require such a partitioning and hence are more amenable in these circumstances.

Figure 10.11 shows the general hierarchy of all the measures. For a reader unsure about which of the measures to use, we argue that WAIC and LOO-CV, being fully Bayesian, would be the best choices. Better still, there is a great R package called *loo* by Vehtari, Gelman and Gabry, which allows estimation of LOO-CV and WAIC using existing simulation draws from the posterior by a method known as Pareto Smoothed Importance Sampling (PSIS) [40]. This actually makes it a lot easier to estimate LOO-CV, negating the computational difficulty or time issues inherent in exactly calculating it. Another great thing about the *loo* package is that it also outputs estimates of the standard errors of the measures, which are helpful when trying to decipher whether a model is actually better than another or is just due to noisy measurements.

While WAIC and LOO-CV require the separation of the sample into n partitions, it should be said that these individual subsamples do not necessarily have to be individual data points. If a structured data set can be broken up into these bigger blocks more easily than at the individual data point level, then we suggest using these in the expressions that we presented for WAIC and LOO-CV.

In Chapter 16, where we introduce Stan, we describe how to computationally estimate the various measures of predictive accuracy that we discuss here. The use of sampling makes things considerably easier for us, and we need not remember the various formulae that we introduced here. However, this does not mean that the aforementioned is not worthwhile – it is important to understand the provenance of the various measures of model predictive accuracy.

Finally, this section would not be complete without a nod to the masters. For a more thorough perspective on measures of model predictive accuracy, see [14] and [15], which served as invaluable references for this section.

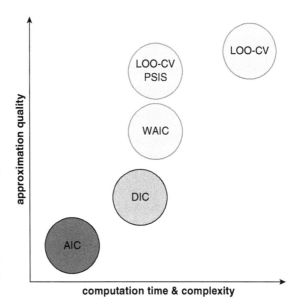

Figure 10.11 Assessing the different measures used to evaluate the out-of-sample predictive accuracy of a model as a function of computational time and complexity (horizontal axis) and approximation quality (vertical axis). The more red the colour, the more Bayesian the method. The idea for this diagram came from a discussion on the Stan User Group forum, in particular, due to suggestions from Michael Betancourt.

10○6 MARGINAL LIKELIHOODS AND BAYES FACTORS

An alternative approach to choosing between models is to use Bayes' rule, except allowing the choice of model to correspond to a parameter in itself. In particular, we can compare:

$$\frac{Pr(\text{model}_1 \mid data)}{Pr(\text{model}_2 \mid data)} = \underbrace{\frac{p(data \mid \text{model}_1)}{p(data \mid \text{model}_2)}}_{\text{Bayes factor}} \times \frac{Pr(\text{model}_1)}{Pr(\text{model}_2)}, \tag{10.19}$$

where the left-hand side expression is the ratio of the posterior probabilities for each of the models. To compute this ratio, we must calculate a term known as a *Bayes factor* (first term on the right) and the ratio of prior preferences for each of the models (second term on the right).

On first glance, this application of Bayes' rule seems to allow us to automatically choose between models. However, there are a number of issues with this approach.

First, it requires us to specify a prior belief in each of the models. While this might seem like an unfair criticism, given that we use priors in other parts of a Bayesian analysis, in our experience it

Introducing Bayes factors and marginal likelihoods

can be difficult to choose sensible probabilities here. We usually want to choose models that are more parsimonious, and so want our prior preferences over the model choice to reflect this, but just how much should we penalise model complexity? We believe there is no obvious answer to this question without appealing to the various measures mentioned earlier in this chapter and we prefer their approach.

Second, to calculate the Bayes factor we are required to calculate the *marginal likelihood* or denominator for each model (see Chapter 6), $p(data \,|\, model_i)$, where $i \in \{1,2\}$. However, we already know this is a difficult task for all but the most simple of models because it involves calculating a high-dimensional integral. In fact, it is this difficulty that partly motivates our decision to avoid exact calculation and do sampling instead (see Part IV). That said, some methods do exist to calculate marginal likelihoods, such as Annealed Importance Sampling (see [28]). However, these methods are not straightforward to implement and their convergence to the correct calculation value can be painfully slow.

Another concern is the sensitivity of Bayes factors to the particular choice of prior distribution, even if the posterior is relatively insensitive. This is particularly true if we choose between models that use vaguely informative priors. This sensitivity can be justified by examining the calculation of the marginal likelihood itself:

$$p(data \,|\, model) = \int \underbrace{p(data \,|\, \theta, model)}_{\text{likelihood}} \times \underbrace{p(\theta \,|\, model)}_{\text{prior}} \, d\theta. \qquad (10.20)$$

We calculate expression (10.20) by finding the area under the graph of the likelihood multiplied by the prior. The likelihood is generally (for a large enough sample) very small across most areas of parameter space, meaning that there is a narrow region of overlap between the high-density regions of the likelihood and the prior. This means that the bulk of the marginal likelihood's value – determined by integrating the product of the likelihood and prior – comes from a narrow region of parameter space. In this context, changes to the prior that have relatively little effect on the posterior can have a large impact on the product of the prior and likelihood in this narrow region, causing significant fluctuations in the marginal likelihood.

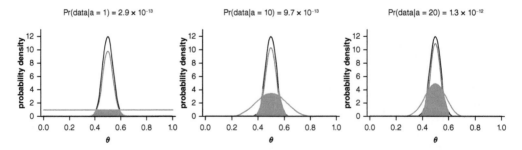

Figure 10.12 The prior (red), likelihood (black) and posterior (grey) for a data sample with the value of the marginal likelihood shown above each diagram. The likelihood was a binomial distribution with a sample size of 10; the prior was a *beta(a,a)* distribution; the data sample was {3, 3, 3, 4, 4, 4, 5, 5, 5, 6, 6, 6, 7, 7, 7}. In all cases, we indicate the region where both the likelihood and prior have high values (as red shading) which represent the bulk of the contribution to the marginal likelihood integral. Note that the likelihood function has been scaled up to allow comparison with the prior.

As an example, imagine that we model a data sample as being generated from a binomial distribution of sample size 10, and use a *beta(a,a)* prior to represent our pre-experimental beliefs for the probability parameter. In Figure 10.12 we show how changes in the prior parameter *a* cause little change to the shape of the posterior distribution, yet significantly affect the value of the marginal likelihood.

CHOOSING ONE MODEL OR A NUMBER OF THEM?

Gelman et al. [14] imagine that there are basically two different circumstances when models are compared. The first is when a model is expanded and made more complex, meaning that the original model is nested within the second. In this circumstance, it seems logical to use criteria – perhaps both PPCs and the aforementioned measures of predictive accuracy – to ask whether the additional complexity is sufficiently compensated for by the better fit of the model to the data. For either answer to this question, it probably makes sense to go ahead with a single model.

The second example is where we compare models that are not necessarily nested within one another. This is frequently the case when building regression models, where we choose which of the predictor variables to include and which to omit. We strongly disagree with the Frequentist perspective that there exists one true model; all models are really just interpretations, and it does not make sense to suppose that one interpretation is correct over all others. In light of this, it makes sense not to choose one particular model, but to construct a larger model that encompasses all of the smaller models within it. Machine learning algorithms frequently use this type of methodology, and often it is the method with the best predictive accuracy.

In the scientific process, we often encapsulate differing hypotheses about the world in separate models. In this context, it is often the explicit aim of the analysis to select the best-fitting model and, in doing so, choose the hypothesis that best represents the data-generating process. We believe that in these settings, it usually makes most sense to determine a single, best-performing, model. However, a hierarchy of performance across a number of models is also valuable as it can suggest which flavours of hypotheses are performing worse than others.

10.8 SENSITIVITY ANALYSIS

Models are interpretations of reality. Posteriors are derived by assuming that those interpretations are true. The uncertainty described by a posterior distribution, and posterior predictive distributions, is likely downwardly biased because it ignores the variability in the choice of model. Usually, a number of models can describe a given situation equally well. If we ignore this source of uncertainty, then we do ourselves an injustice because of our intellectual overconfidence. In situations where there exists considerable uncertainty over the choice of model, it can be sensible to model this epistemic uncertainty explicitly, rather than merely discuss it. When we conduct a statistical analysis, we usually have a few questions that we will use our models to address. It is our duty to check that the answers to those questions do not vary as we use one from the list of feasible models.

Imagine that we want to develop a model for rainfall in an area that will be used to help architects plan the construction of a dam. Unfortunately, we have only the past 100 days of rainfall available to use to build a model (see the left-hand panel of Figure 10.13). Here, we are interested in building a model that generates realistic patterns of wet and dry days. We will then use this to investigate the maximum number of rainy days that we are likely to encounter in reality since this information is crucial to decide the height and thickness of the dam.

We consult the literature and find two models that might be appropriate in this circumstance. One is a two-state Markov model, consisting of dry days and wet days, with probabilities of transitioning between these states. The other model is slightly more complex, having three states: dry, wet and persistently wet. In both models, dry days occur when there is no recorded rainfall. In the first model, a wet day occurs when there is non-zero rainfall, and, in the latter, it is defined as a wet day following a dry one. The persistently wet state occurs when there are two consecutive wet days.

Suppose that we fit both of these models to the data and find that both perform similarly across a raft of tests, even when accounting for the extra complexity of the three-state model. However, when we simulate rainfall series from each, we find that the three-state model assigns a greater probability to longer spells of wet days (see the right-hand panel of Figure 10.13). In this circumstance, we should probably err on the side of caution, and tell the architects about the results of the three-state model, since the two models differ considerably in their answers to the important question.

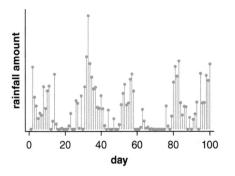 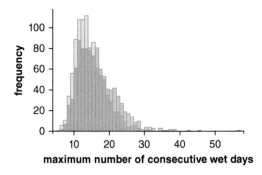

Figure 10.13   Left: the past 100 days of rainfall. Right: the maximum number of consecutive rainy days using simulations from the simple rainfall model (dark shading) and the more complex one (light shading).

A sensitivity analysis is more important the fewer data we have, or the more uncertainty there is surrounding the choice of model. It is also imperative to conduct such an analysis when there is an inherent sensitivity of decisions to the conclusions of the models at hand.

There are a number of ways in which changes in a model's conclusions can be tested for sensitivity to modelling assumptions. We list here some of the most common methods, although recognise that this list is not exhaustive:

- Use robust prior and likelihood distributions as opposed to narrower ones.
- Consider different classes of likelihoods.
- Consider the effects of different priors.
- Within a particular model class, compare simple models with more complex ones.

Rather than choosing a particular model, a nice way to incorporate this uncertainty in the modelling process is to create a hierarchical model, of which the individual models are particular cases (see Chapter 17). This naturally allows the data to dictate the amount of weight to lend to each model, rather than the extreme case of using only one of them.

 CHAPTER SUMMARY

The reader should now understand how to critically assess a Bayesian model and choose between different models. Posterior predictive checks (PPCs) are used to compare the fit of a given model to some aspect of the sample data, and statistical measures like WAIC and LOO-CV are used to compare models in terms of their out-of-sample predictive accuracy.

You may be wondering why we need both of these approaches. This is because the purpose of these two frameworks is different, although complementary. PPCs assess the fit of your model to the data at hand, whereas WAIC and LOO-CV assess the fit of your model to out-of-sample data. The trouble with blindly using PPCs to construct a model is that this can result in an overly complex model, which is overfit to the sample of data on which it was estimated. We guard against this overfitting by using WAIC and LOO-CV. In reality, these two different frameworks should be used in tandem throughout the modelling process; we would not want to choose a model with a good predictive accuracy but failed to represent some key aspect of variation seen in the data. It can also be useful to combine aspects of PPCs with measures of predictive accuracy. For example, we could partition our data set into a training and cross-validation set, and see how a model fitted to the former performs on PPCs on the latter.

We are now ready to describe in Part IV how to do modern Bayesian inference using computers. However, before we do, we turn our attention to a backwater of Bayesian statistics, concerning attempts to make it more objective. While we do think that there is an issue with any method that suggests that one analysis is more objective than another, it is important to understand them since these methods are sometimes used in applied Bayesian statistics today.

10 10 CHAPTER OUTCOMES

The reader should now be familiar with the following concepts:

- how to evaluate a model's fit to data using PPCs
- Bayesian p values
- the theoretical ideal measure of a model's predictive accuracy through log posterior predictive probabilities and the problems with achieving this ideal in practice
- WAIC and LOO-CV as the most Bayesian and preferred methods to estimate a model's out-of-sample predictive performance
- the Bayes factor way of choosing between competing models and the problems inherent with this method
- the importance of conducting a sensitivity analysis

10○11 PROBLEM SETS

Problem 10.1 WHO's reported novel disease outbreaks

Suppose that you are interested in modelling the number of outbreaks of novel diseases that the WHO reports each year. Since these outbreaks are of new diseases, you assume that you can model the outbreaks as *independent* events, and hence decide to use a Poisson likelihood, $X_t \sim Poisson(\lambda)$, where X_t is the number of outbreaks in year t, and λ is the mean number of outbreaks.

Problem 10.1.1 You decide to use a $\Gamma(3,0.5)$ prior for the mean parameter (λ) of your Poisson likelihood (where $\Gamma(\alpha,\beta)$ is defined to have a mean of α/β). Graph this prior.

Problem 10.1.2 Suppose that the number of new outbreaks over the past 5 years is $X = (3,7,4,10,11)$. Using the conjugate prior rules for a Poisson distribution with a gamma prior, find the posterior and graph it. (*Hint*: look at Table 9.1.)

Problem 10.1.3 Generate 10,000 samples from the posterior predictive distribution, and graph the distribution. To do this we first independently sample a value λ_i from the posterior distribution, then sample a value of X from a $Poisson(\lambda_i)$ distribution. We carry out this process 10,000 times. (*Hint*: use R's `rgamma` and `rpois` functions to draw (pseudo-)independent samples from the gamma and Poisson distributions, respectively.)

Problem 10.1.4 Compare the actual data with your 10,000 posterior predictive samples. Does your model fit the data?

Problem 10.1.5 (Optional) Can you think of a better posterior predictive check to carry out on the data?

Problem 10.1.6 The WHO issues a press release stating that the number of novel disease outbreaks for this year was 20. Use your posterior predictive samples to test whether your model is a good fit to the data.

Problem 10.1.7 By using your previously determined posterior as a prior, update your posterior to reflect the new datum. Graph the PDF for this new distribution.

Problem 10.1.8 Generate posterior predictive samples from your new posterior and use it to test the validity of your model.

Problem 10.1.9 Would you feel comfortable using this model to predict the number of disease outbreaks next year?

Problem 10.2 Sleep-deprived reactions

These data are from a study described in Belenky et al. [2] that measured the effect of sleep deprivation on cognitive performance. Eighteen subjects were chosen from a population of interest (lorry drivers) who were restricted to 3 hours of sleep during the trial. On each day of the experiment their reaction time to a visual stimulus was measured. The data for this example is contained in `evaluation_sleepstudy.csv` and consists of three variables, *Reaction*, *Days* and *Subject ID*, which measure the reaction time of a given subject on a particular day.

A simple model that explains the variation in reaction times is a linear regression model of the form:

$$R(t) \sim N(\alpha + \beta t, \sigma), \qquad\qquad (10.21)$$

where $R(t)$ is the reaction time on day t of the experiment across all observations.

Problem 10.2.1 By graphing all the data, critically assess the validity of the model for the data.

Problem 10.2.2 Graph the data at the individual subject level using R's *lattice* package, or otherwise. What does this suggest about assuming a common β across all participants?

Problem 10.2.3 The above model has been fitted to the data using MCMC, with 2000 samples from the posterior distribution for (α, β, σ) contained in the file `evaluation_sleepPosteriors.csv`. Generate samples from the posterior predictive distribution, and visualise them in an appropriate way.

Problem 10.2.4 How does the posterior predictive data compare with the actual data?

Problem 10.2.5 How (if at all) do the posterior predictive checks suggest we need to change our model?

Problem 10.3 Discoveries data

Problem 10.3.1 The file `evaluation_discoveries.csv` contains data on the numbers of 'great' inventions and scientific discoveries in each year from 1860 to 1959 [1]. The aim of this problem is for you to build a statistical model that provides a reasonable approximation to this series. As such, you will need to choose a likelihood, specify a prior on any parameters, and go through and calculate a posterior. Once you have a posterior, you will want to carry out posterior predictive checks to see that your model behaves as desired.

Problem 10.4 Marginal likelihood of voting

Suppose that we collect survey data where respondents are asked to indicate for whom they will vote in an upcoming election. Each poll consists of a sample size of 10 and we collect the following data on the number voting for a particular candidate for 20 such polls: {2, 7, 4, 5, 4, 5, 6, 4, 4, 4, 5, 6, 5, 7, 6, 2, 4, 6, 6, 6}. We model each outcome as having been obtained from a $X_i \sim \mathcal{B}(10, \theta)$ distribution.

Problem 10.4.1 Find the posterior distribution where we specify $\theta \sim beta(a, 1)$ as a prior. Graph how the posterior changes for $a \in [1, 10]$.

Problem 10.4.2 Graph the marginal likelihood as a is increased between 1 and 10 (just use integer values).

Problem 10.4.3 Calculate the Bayes factor where we compare the model when $a = 1$ to that when $a = 10$. Hence comment on the use of Bayes factors as a method for choosing between competing models.

11

Chapter contents

MAKING BAYESIAN
ANALYSIS OBJECTIVE?

11 O 1   CHAPTER MISSION STATEMENT

At the end of this chapter, the reader should understand the principles behind popular attempts to make Bayesian inference less dependent on priors, giving most weight to the likelihood.

11 O 2   CHAPTER GOALS

As we discussed in Chapter 2, there really is no such thing as an *objective* analysis. For most real-world applications of statistical inference, there will be aspects of the chosen modelling framework for which there is less consensus, and hence can be deemed *subjective*. Critics of the Bayesian method ignore this aspect of data analysis and object to the fact that it uses subjective *priors*. The (misdirected) criticism for priors has motivated attempts that aim to reduce the influence of this aspect of the Bayesian formula. These methods aim to maximise the effect of the current data (through the likelihood) on the posterior density. This type of approach is sometimes warranted if there is a premium placed on the objectivity of the analysis, for example in clinical drug trials. However, we argue that in most circumstances, the use of weakly informative priors is a more sensible approach, avoiding the mathematical and computational difficulties of the methodologies that we describe in this chapter.

Unlike many of the other chapters, this one is not necessarily essential for those wanting to do applied Bayesian analysis and can be skipped with little impact on what follows. It is included mainly because methods to make Bayesian statistics objective had interest historically, but also because some researchers still persist with these approaches.

11 O 3   THE ILLUSION OF THE UNINFORMATIVE UNIFORM PRIOR

Suppose that we want to build a statistical model to describe the prevalence of obesity in a given population. We start by considering a sample of size 2, where each individual is randomly sampled from the population. We assume that the probability a given individual has the condition is given by θ. Wanting to limit the effect of previous results or experimenter prejudices, we choose to assign a uniform prior for θ over the range [0,1].

This prior assigns the same weight to all allowed values of this parameter and hence appears uninformative. However, imagine that, instead, we consider a hypothesis based on whether, or not, both individuals in our sample have the disorder. We denote $\phi = \theta^2$ as the probability that this event occurs. We can now ask: If we assume a flat prior on θ, what does this imply about our belief in the new event?

To answer this, we need to know a little about how a change of variable impacts a probability density. Suppose that we are changing from a variable x, with a probability density function given by $f_X(x)$, to a new variable $y = g(x)$, and we want to find the density $f_Y(y)$. It turns out that we can apply the following rule (using what is known as a *Jacobian* transform):

$$f_Y(y) = f_X(g^{-1}(y))g'^{-1}(y)$$

$$= f_X(g^{-1}(y))\left|\frac{dx}{dy}\right|,$$

(11.1)

where $g^{-1}(y)$ is the inverse transform of g and $g'^{-1}(y)$ is its derivative. Applying this to our example, we have that $\phi = g(\theta) = \theta^2$, meaning that $g^{-1}(\phi) = \sqrt{\phi}$ and $d\theta / d\phi = \frac{1}{2}\phi^{\frac{1}{2}}$. Now, using expression (11.1), we obtain the following probability density for the new event:

$$f_\Phi(\phi) = f_\theta(\sqrt{\phi})\frac{1}{2}\phi^{-\frac{1}{2}}$$

$$= 1 \times \frac{1}{2}\phi^{-\frac{1}{2}} \tag{11.2}$$

$$= \frac{1}{2}\phi^{-\frac{1}{2}}.$$

We obtain the second line of (11.2) from the first by using the uniform prior that we specified (hence independent of the function argument). Figure 11.1 below illustrates that, while this prior is uniform for the probability that one individual is obese, it is considerably different for the event that both people have the condition. It is downward-sloping, implying that before we collect the data, we believe that this event is relatively unlikely, with more than 70% of the prior weight assigned to values of $\phi < \frac{1}{2}$.

In one frame of reference we may specify a prior whose nature in another frame is completely different. Thus, it not usually the case that an uninformative prior for one event is also uninformative for another.

This would seem to put a spanner in the works of finding a prior that is objectively uninformative since we have found that the nature of a prior depends on the viewpoint. However, we shall see in the next section that if we redefine our notion of uninformative, we can construct such priors in special circumstances.

The illusion of uninformative priors

11 O 4   JEFFREYS PRIORS

11.4.1 Another definition of *uninformative*

An alternative view of what is meant by an uninformative prior was presented by an Englishman called Harold Jeffreys in the mid twentieth century. Jeffreys was a man of many talents. At Cambridge University he taught mathematics and then moved on to geophysics, before becoming a professor of astronomy! Along with his contribution to probability theory, he made major contributions to quantum physics, as well as being the first to propose the idea that the earth's core is liquid. The one blemish on an otherwise stellar career was that Jeffreys did not believe in plate tectonics up until his death (which seems unfortunate given the literal mountains of evidence for this).

We now introduce the concept of a Jeffreys prior. We know from expression (11.1) that if we define a prior in terms of one parameter θ, we can derive the implied prior density for a transformed parameter $\phi = g(\theta)$ using:

$$p(\phi) = p(\theta)\left|\frac{d\theta}{d\phi}\right|. \tag{11.3}$$

An introduction to Jeffreys priors
(3 videos)

Jeffreys said that a prior is uninformative if we can calculate it using the above rule, or directly through the function $p(.)$, and get the same result irrespective of the choice of parameter.

For a uniform distribution $p(\theta) = 1$, if we use expression (11.1), we obtain $p(\phi) = p(\theta^2) = 1/2\sqrt{\phi}$.

However, if we approach the problem from the other side, and substitute directly in for ϕ, we get $p(\phi) = 1 \neq 1/2\sqrt{\phi}$. Clearly, this distribution does not satisfy the requirements set out by Jeffreys.

Jeffreys managed to find the general form of a prior that satisfied his condition:

$$p(\theta) \propto I(\theta)^{\frac{1}{2}} = \left[-\mathbb{E}\left[\frac{\partial^2 \log(p(y \mid \theta))}{\partial \theta^2} \right] \right]^{\frac{1}{2}}, \tag{11.4}$$

where $I(\theta)$ is the information matrix, which indicates the curvature of the likelihood surface at a given point, and is used in maximum likelihood inference (see Section 4.8.4).

We can see that a prior that has the form of expression (11.4) satisfies his parameter invariance condition. Considering a parameter transformation $\theta \rightarrow \phi$:

$$p(\phi) = \left[-\mathbb{E}\left[\frac{\partial^2 \log(p(y \mid \phi))}{\partial \phi^2} \right] \right]^{\frac{1}{2}}$$

$$= \left[-\mathbb{E}\left[\frac{\partial^2 \log(p(y \mid \theta))}{\partial \theta^2} \right]\left(\frac{d\theta}{d\phi}\right)^2 \right]^{\frac{1}{2}} \tag{11.5}$$

$$= p(\theta)\left| \frac{d\theta}{d\phi} \right|.$$

This is of the same form as that in the probability transformation rule given in (11.1). To obtain the second line of (11.5) from the first we used the chain rule of differentiation twice (since we differentiate the expression twice) here, $\partial / \partial \phi = (d\theta / d\phi)(\partial / \partial \theta)$.

Now that we have shown that Jeffreys prior works, let's apply it to the obesity example that we introduced in Section 11.3. We did not introduce a likelihood before since our discussion concerned only priors, but now this is necessary because Jeffreys prior requires that we use it to calculate the information matrix. A sensible likelihood to describe whether an individual is obese, $Y \in \{0,1\}$, is the Bernoulli, since we believe that the data are independent. To derive the information matrix (which is actually a scalar quantity here because there is only a single parameter) for this particular case, we first write down the probability mass function:

$$Pr(Y = y \mid \theta) = \theta^y (1-\theta)^{1-y}, \tag{11.6}$$

which we then log to obtain the log-likelihood:

$$\log[Pr(Y = y \mid \theta)] = y\log(\theta) + (1-y)\log(1-\theta). \tag{11.7}$$

We then differentiate this expression to obtain the first derivative:

$$\frac{\partial \log[p(Y = y \mid \theta)]}{\partial \theta} = \frac{y}{\theta} - \frac{1-y}{1-\theta}, \tag{11.8}$$

which we differentiate again to yield the second derivative of the log-likelihood:

$$\frac{\partial^2 \log[p(Y = y \mid \theta)]}{\partial \theta^2} = -\frac{y}{\theta^2} - \frac{1-y}{(1-\theta)^2}. \tag{11.9}$$

We then take the expectation of expression (11.9) to yield the information matrix:

$$I(\theta) = -\mathbb{E}\left(\frac{\partial^2 \log[p(Y = y \mid \theta)]}{\partial \theta^2}\right)$$

$$= \frac{\theta}{\theta^2} + \frac{1-\theta}{(1-\theta)^2}$$

$$= \frac{1}{\theta} + \frac{1}{1-\theta} \tag{11.10}$$

$$= \frac{1}{\theta(1-\theta)},$$

where we used $\mathbb{E}(y) = \theta$ for a Bernoulli density, to arrive at the final answer. It is now straightforward to find Jeffreys prior using expression (11.4):

$$p(\theta) \propto I(\theta)^{\frac{1}{2}}$$

$$= \theta^{-\frac{1}{2}}(1-\theta)^{-\frac{1}{2}} \tag{11.11}$$

$$\sim beta\left(\frac{1}{2}, \frac{1}{2}\right),$$

where we obtained the last line by noticing that the θ dependence is of the same form as a $beta\left(\frac{1}{2}, \frac{1}{2}\right)$ density, meaning that the prior must be such a distribution.

The Jeffreys prior in this case is shown in Figure 11.1 alongside a uniform density. We notice that this Jeffreys prior is inversely proportional to the standard deviation of the Bernoulli, which is given by $\theta^{\frac{1}{2}}(1-\theta)^{\frac{1}{2}}$ (see the left-hand panel of Figure 11.2). This makes intuitive sense since the posteriors are least affected by data where $\theta = \frac{1}{2}$ (the posterior is not very peaked), compared to the more extreme values of θ where the likelihood exerts a strong effect (the posterior is more peaked). The likelihood exerts a strong effect at more extreme values of θ because the standard deviation is much lower near these points. The Jeffreys prior gives more weight to posteriors in

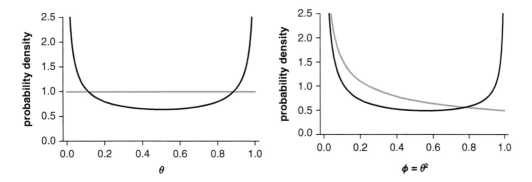

Figure 11.1 Left: a uniform prior (red) and Jeffreys prior (black) for a Bernoulli probability parameter, which represents the probability that an individual is obese. Right: the implied priors for the probability of the event that both people are obese in corresponding colours. Note that the left and right black priors are not the same shapes.

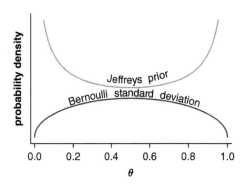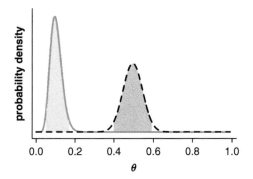

Figure 11.2   Left: the Jeffreys prior (a $beta\left(\frac{1}{2},\frac{1}{2}\right)$ density; grey) versus Bernoulli standard deviation (black). Right: posteriors assuming a Jeffreys prior for X = 10 (red) and X = 50 (black) in a sample size of 100.

this circumstance because it is less likely that these data sets would have arisen by chance (see the right-hand panel of Figure 11.2). The Jeffreys prior here simply tries to align with the likelihood as much as possible.

Importantly, Jeffreys prior does not mean that a prior in one frame of reference 'looks' the same in any other frame of reference. The analysis of Section 11.3 hopefully showed that this sort of prior is not possible. What it means is more subtle than this. It means that if two individuals use different parameterisations for a given distribution, but both use Jeffreys priors, then we can get from the posterior of one individual to the other's, by applying the Jacobian transformation. So the invariance property of Jeffreys priors is really about Jeffreys' posterior distribution. We actually find the word *invariance* misleading here. The posteriors do change under a change of parameters, and so are not invariant in this sense. Jeffreys priors just ensure that the posterior transforms in a way that is nice as determined by the Jacobian transformation.

11.4.2 Being critical of Jeffreys priors

While Jeffreys' idea is interesting theoretically, it has two issues that limit its practical use:

1   It is not simple to extend Jeffreys prior to multi-parameter models.
2   Jeffreys priors are improper for many models.

Various workarounds have been proposed for the first of these issues, but the second is more problematic since we have to be careful when using improper priors to ensure that the resultant 'posterior' density is itself valid.

We believe that it is important not to obsess about the use of uninformative priors. As we shall see, weakly informative priors and hierarchical models can help guard against some of the issues raised by critics of Bayesian inference. Furthermore, often the difference in posteriors resulting from Jeffreys priors versus vaguely informative priors is minimal. Indeed, Figure 11.3 shows that there is little difference in the posteriors for our Bernoulli example, whether we use a Jeffreys prior or uniform prior.

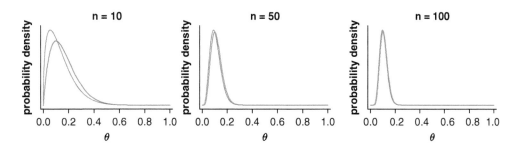

Figure 11.3 The posteriors resulting from using a uniform prior (red) versus a Jeffreys prior (grey) for different sample sizes, where in each case the proportion of obese cases is 10%.

11 ○ 5 REFERENCE PRIORS

A more recent approach to defining uninformative distributions was given by Bernardo in 1979 [2]. His idea was to choose a prior distribution that maximised some measure of discrepancy (for example, the KL divergence) between the prior distribution and the posterior. By choosing a prior to maximise the discrepancy, this should allow the data to exert the maximal effect on the posterior.

Does this involve getting the data and then working backwards to find the prior from a given posterior? No, since this would invalidate the whole Bayesian inference process by using the data to obtain the prior. However, before we obtain the data, we can take expectations of the KL divergence over the data distribution, giving us a prior without recourse to using our data.

So suppose that we have some data x and a sufficient statistic $t(x)$. A sufficient statistic is a quantity that, if calculated from the sample, provides exactly the same information about parameter values as the entire sample. This means that the posterior distribution is the same whether we condition on the sample or the summary statistic $p(\theta|x) = p(\theta|t(x))$. To derive reference priors we want to maximise the KL divergence from the prior to the posterior:

$$\text{KL} = \int_{\theta \in \Theta} p(\theta \mid t) \log \left[\frac{p(\theta \mid t)}{p(\theta)} \right] d\theta, \tag{11.12}$$

over choice of $p(\theta)$. However, we do not know $t(x)$ before we collect the data, and so we maximise the expected KL divergence over the distribution of $t(x)$:

$$\text{E}_t \left(\int_{\theta \in \Theta} p(\theta \mid t) \log \left[\frac{p(\theta \mid t)}{p(\theta)} \right] d\theta \right) = \int_{t \in T} p(t) \int_{\theta \in \Theta} p(\theta \mid t) \log \left[\frac{p(\theta \mid t)}{p(\theta)} \right] d\theta dt,$$

$$= \int_{t \in T} \int_{\theta \in \Theta} p(\theta, t) \log \left[\frac{p(\theta, t)}{p(\theta) p(t)} \right] d\theta dt, \tag{11.13}$$

where the bottom line of expression (11.13) is actually the *mutual information* between t and θ, which is a measure of their dependence.

The mutual information between variables is a measure of how much extra information is conveyed by their joint density versus considering only their marginal densities. For example, for independent variables x and y, their mutual information is 0 because $\log(p(x,y)/p(x)p(y)) = \log(p(x)p(y)/p(x)p(y)) = \log(1) = 0$. This is because no additional

An introduction to reference priors

An introduction to the concept of a sufficient statistic

information is obtained by considering both variables together – by definition, knowing the value of one of the variables is uninformative for the other one.

We can further explain the meaning of mutual independence using a simple example. Imagine that there are 16 objects in an urn, and that we can reach in and randomly draw an object out. The objects can either be cubes or balls, and they can either be coloured red or grey (see Figure 11.4). If there are equal numbers of red balls, red cubes, grey balls and grey cubes then the shape and colour of an object are independent, meaning that the mutual information between the shape and colour of an object is zero (see the middle case in Figure 11.4). This is because knowing the colour of an object does not help us to predict its shape. For example, before we draw out an object we know that $\frac{1}{2}$ of them are cubes. Suppose that (with our backs turned) a friend draws out an object and tells us that it is red. For the independent case, we know that $\frac{1}{2}$ of red objects are cubes and the other $\frac{1}{2}$ are balls. In other words, the probability of drawing a cube is unchanged, and remains at $\frac{1}{2}$. In contrast, if the urn contains only red balls and grey cubes then the mutual information is maximised (see the top-right-hand case in Figure 11.4). This is because, now, if we know the colour of the object we can perfectly predict its shape.

To construct reference priors it makes sense to maximise the mutual information between the summary statistic and the parameter because this maximises their dependence. In turn, this ensures that we have the maximal transfer of information from the sample to our posterior distribution. To choose $p(\theta)$ to maximise expression (11.13) we need to use a mathematical approach known as the *calculus of variations*. For some fairly simple situations this can be done, but for most circumstances, the difficult calculations involved are sufficient to thwart even the most ardent objectivists.

What is meant by entropy in statistics?

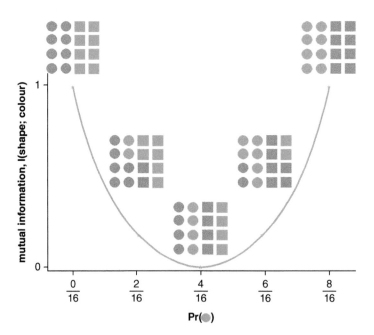

Figure 11.4   The mutual information between the shape and colour of objects in an urn as a function of their joint distribution, while we hold their marginal distributions constant (that is, the probability of drawing a cube is always $\frac{1}{2}$, the probability of drawing a red object is always $\frac{1}{2}$).

An introduction to mutual information

Again, we reason that, although interesting theoretically, the practical importance of this area of statistics is insufficient to merit its use, particularly when there is a reasonable amount of data available. Indeed, in Figure 11.5 we show that for a sample modelled as being exponentially distributed, if we have a sample size of 100, then the posterior distributions resultant from using either the reference prior or a weakly informative prior are virtually indistinguishable. We also argue that, in many circumstances, seeking an objective answer is suboptimal, since using an informative prior distribution helps to reduce the variance in estimates. We have encountered many problems that would not be soluble using Frequentist statistics, but the injection of prior information (often from other analyses) allowed us to estimate quantities that interest us.

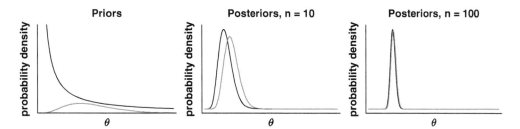

Figure 11.5   Left: The reference prior for the exponential distribution (black) and a $\Gamma(4,2)$ prior (red). The effects of each prior on posterior distributions with sample sizes (middle) $n = 10$ and (right) $n = 100$. The data samples were randomly drawn from $X \sim Exp(\frac{1}{2})$. Note here that the reference prior distribution ($p(\theta) = 1/\theta$) is improper.

11 O 6   EMPIRICAL BAYES

Another attempt to make Bayesian analysis less dependent on the subjective whims of the investigator is called *empirical Bayes,* a type of analysis which explicitly uses data to estimate priors. We regard this approach as an approximation to full hierarchical modelling (which we cover in Part V) and also an invalidation of the Bayesian methodology, since we use the data to determine our priors. However, since occasionally this approach is used in applied research we use an example to illustrate the mechanism behind this method.

Here we adapt an example originally given by George Casella [9]. Suppose that we have the results of a drug trial, which are represented by a continuous variable X_i, where i indexes a patient who has taken the drug. Furthermore, suppose that the results for a particular patient are subject to variance around a patient-specific mean θ_i:

$$X_i \sim \mathcal{N}(\theta_i, \sigma_0).$$ (11.14)

There is variance around θ_i because there is a multitude of factors that influence the drug's effect on a patient: diet, physical stress, time of day, and so on. Next, we assume that there is a population distribution that dictates the between-patient variability:

$$\theta_i \sim \mathcal{N}(\mu, \sigma_1).$$ (11.15)

Expression (11.15) indicates that we expect there to be variability in the effect of the drug across patients. This variability could, for example, be due to genetics. However, while we believe that there will be between-patient variability, we still think that the effects of the drug will be similar across patients. This similarity is implicitly included in the previous expression because we assume that there is a mean μ effect of the drug that is common to all patients.

The model that we have discussed thus far is exactly the sort of hierarchical model that we will explore more thoroughly in Part V (so don't worry if you find it a little hard going now). In hierarchical Bayesian modelling, the parameters (μ, σ_1) are assigned priors, and we obtain posteriors for them. The empirical Bayesian approach, by contrast, uses the data to estimate point values of these parameters and then uses these to estimate the values of θ_i.

If we assume that the parameters (μ, σ_1) are fixed, given as prior parameters, then we can calculate the posterior distribution for θ_i:

$$p(\theta_i \mid X_i) = \frac{p(X_i \mid \theta_i) p(\theta_i)}{p(X_i)}$$

$$= \frac{p(X_i \mid \theta_i) p(\theta_i)}{\int_{-\infty}^{+\infty} p(X_i \mid \theta_i) p(\theta_i) \mathrm{d}\theta_i},$$

(11.16)

where $p(\theta_i) = N(\mu, \sigma_1)$ and $p(X_i \mid \theta_i) = N(\theta_i, \sigma_0)$ in a small abuse of notation. We can actually calculate the posterior mean of θ_i, and obtain:

$$\mathrm{E}_{\text{posterior}}(\theta_i) = \mu \frac{\sigma_0^2}{\sigma_0^2 + \sigma_1^2} + X_i \frac{\sigma_1^2}{\sigma_0^2 + \sigma_1^2},$$

(11.17)

where, as the sampling variance (σ_0^2) increases, we give more weight to our prior μ. Expression (11.17) is the non-hierarchical Bayes point estimator of θ_i, the drug efficacy in a particular patient. In the hierarchical Bayesian approach we specify priors for (μ, σ_1), which are used to estimate their respective posteriors. The empirical Bayes estimators do not go quite this far and, instead, estimate point values for these parameters. As such, we can think of the empirical Bayes estimator as lying somewhere along the spectrum between non-hierarchical and hierarchical models. In calculating the denominator of the expression in the first line of (11.16), we would have calculated the marginal data distribution: $X_i \sim N(\mu, \sigma_0^2 + \sigma_1^2)$. Empirical Bayesians use this distribution to calculate point estimates of the population-level parameters using a Frequentist technique called the *method of moments* [9]:

$$\hat{\mu} = \bar{X}$$

(11.18)

$$\frac{\sigma_0^2}{\sigma_0^2 + \hat{\sigma}_1^2} = \frac{(n-3)\sigma_0^2}{\sum_{i=1}^{n}(X_i - \bar{X})^2},$$

where we matched the first and second moments (the mean and variance of the marginal data distribution, respectively), and have assumed that σ_0^2 is fixed. The empirical Bayesian estimator of θ_i is then calculated by substituting the above estimates into expression (11.17) yielding the empirical Bayes estimator:

$$\hat{\theta}_i^{EB} = \bar{X} \frac{(n-3)\sigma_0^2}{\sum_{i=1}^{n}(X_i - \bar{X})^2} + X_i \left[1 - \frac{(n-3)\sigma_0^2}{\sum_{i=1}^{n}(X_i - \bar{X})^2} \right].$$

(11.19)

So, while we have not assigned priors to the population-level parameters (μ, σ_1^2), we have nonetheless estimated them, albeit through a Frequentist method. We find this half-Bayesian/

half-Frequentist methodology convoluted, and instead prefer to employ the full hierarchical Bayesian models that we will describe in Part V, which allow us to obtain posteriors for all parameters in a model. Nonetheless, a number of popular methods use empirical Bayes estimators, and so it pays to be aware of these methods.

11 ○ 7   A MOVE TOWARDS WEAKLY INFORMATIVE PRIORS

We have argued that all analyses are inherently subjective, and so any attempts to make Bayesian inference, or any other analysis, objective are inherently flawed. We have also reasoned that if we have at least a moderately sized data sample, the use of uninformative priors typically results in little difference in the estimated posterior distributions anyway. There are also times – particularly when we move to computational methods – when the use of 'uninformative' priors can cause issues for an analysis. First, the posterior densities that we estimate may have non-zero support in unrealistic areas of parameter space; second, the computational methods may take considerably longer to converge than if we used more reasonable priors.

Gelman terms priors that sit between those that are maximally uninformative and those that are strongly informative, *weakly informative*. These typically incorporate more uncertainty than priors constructed using all of our pre-analysis knowledge, but less variability than entirely ignorant priors. Most people automatically use a variety of weakly informative priors, so this news is not necessarily controversial. However, we believe that by explicitly discussing these priors it will encourage their continued use.

How should we set weakly informative priors in practice? The following provides some guidance:

- Allow considerable uncertainty in priors, such that the range of feasible parameter values is wider than we would expect, but not unreasonable. For example, for parameters in a regression with standardised variables, use $\beta \sim N(0,10)$ rather than $\beta \sim N(0,1000)$.
- Use smooth distributions for parameters, rather than discontinuous ones. For example, use a long-tailed Cauchy distribution rather than a uniform distribution over some finite scale.
- Avoid using those distributions that give too much weight to areas of unrealistic parameter values. For example, instead of using an inv-gamma use a half-Cauchy for a prior on a variance parameter.

What is meant by a 'weakly informative' prior and why are they useful?

Some of these lessons are hard to learn before applying Bayesian analysis, which is where we head to next.

11 ○ 8   CHAPTER SUMMARY

This chapter has given the reader some insight into a few of the methods used to try and make Bayesian inference less dependent on subjective priors. We believe that the fear of subjectivity is inherently misplaced because all statistical analyses require us to choose models from a range of reasonable modelling options. We also argued that the effects of using non-informative prior distributions are slight versus weakly informative priors, particularly when there are moderate amounts of data.

Before we take the plunge into a discussion of the modern methodologies that are used to do Bayesian inference, we provide a carrot to entice the sceptical reader to proceed. Most critics of Bayesian analysis object to the use of prior distributions due to their inherent subjectivity. However, some of these issues can be relegated, if not dismissed, if we choose a more abstract model which assigns priors on the prior parameters themselves. These hierarchical models provide much more freedom than is available through non-hierarchical equivalents. They allow the data much more freedom to determine the structure of the model, and typically place less emphasis on an analyst's beliefs. The use of hierarchical models also helps to avoid a whole range of estimation pathologies, for example overfitting.

However, these hierarchical models are typically not amenable to exact estimation using pen and paper. Nor, for that matter, are the majority of interesting non-hierarchical models, since they require greater flexibility than is provided by using conjugate prior–likelihood pairs. It transpires that, while we may not be able to exactly calculate posteriors, we can still obtain samples from them through computational methods. The use of these computational methods, in contrast to what is often believed, actually makes it easier and less mathematically onerous to do Bayesian analysis in practice. Even better, masters of Bayes have made things a lot easier for us by coding up these methods into simple-to-implement statistical languages. While it may be fairly straightforward to implement a particular model in one of these languages, pitfalls still await those who do not fully understand the underlying algorithms. Fortunately, however, these methods are full of intuition, which we hope to confer on the reader in Part V.

 CHAPTER OUTCOMES

The reader should now be familiar with the following concepts:

* Jeffreys' definition of non-informative priors and his solution
* the limitations of Jeffreys priors
* the framework behind reference priors and reasons for their practical limitations
* empirical Bayes estimates as half-Bayesian/half-Frequentist beasts lying somewhere in the spectrum between non-hierarchical and hierarchical Bayesian models

 PROBLEM SETS

Problem 11.1 Jeffreys prior for a normal likelihood

Suppose that we are modelling the result of a medical test, which to a suitable approximation can be regarded as being continuous and unbounded. We suppose that a normal probability model is a reasonable sampling model to use here, $X_i \sim N(\mu,\sigma)$, where μ is unknown but σ is known (perhaps based on the results of many previous tests).

Problem 11.1.1 Write down the likelihood for a single observation.

Problem 11.1.2 Find the information matrix (here a scalar).

Problem 11.1.3 Hence calculate the information matrix for a sample of N observations.

Problem 11.1.4 State Jeffreys prior for μ.

Problem 11.1.5 Is Jeffreys prior proper here?

Problem 11.2 The illusion of uninformative priors revisited

Suppose that θ represents the probability that one randomly chosen individual has a particular disease.

Problem 11.2.1 Suppose that we start by assigning a uniform prior on θ. Use sampling to estimate the prior distribution that in a sample of two, one person has the disease and the other does not. Hence comment on the assumption that a uniform prior is uninformative.

Problem 11.2.2 Assume instead that we ascribe a uniform prior to the probability that two out of two individuals have the disease. What is the implicit prior distribution for the probability that one individual has the disease?

PART IV

A PRACTICAL GUIDE TO DOING REAL-LIFE BAYESIAN ANALYSIS: COMPUTATIONAL BAYES

PART IV MISSION STATEMENT

This part aims to introduce the reader to Bayesian inference in practice. We start by introducing the most popular algorithms that underlie computational attempts to sample from posterior distributions. Fortunately for us, for many purposes, we need not code up these algorithms ourselves, since others have already produced software which implements efficient versions of these algorithms. In Chapter 16 we provide a thorough introduction to the most advanced of these languages, Stan, providing a base which should allow the reader to start to code up their own models.

PART IV GOALS

We are now familiar with the range of distributions which we have at our disposal for both the likelihood and prior. In Chapter 9 we illustrated how, in certain special circumstances, we can compute posteriors exactly, by choosing priors that are conjugate to the likelihood in question. While this can be a useful starting point, our ultimate method of analysis should not be dictated solely by the ease of calculation. In most real-world circumstances, using conjugate priors is too restrictive. However, we shall see in Chapter 12 that choosing a non-conjugate prior causes difficulties in calculating the posterior, meaning that, in most cases, it is impossible to calculate an exact posterior.

Fortunately for us, all is not lost if we abandon the goal of exact calculation of the posterior and choose, instead, to sample from it. Sampling from a distribution provides a window onto its properties, which allows us to understand its nature. It allows us to estimate those characteristics – the mean, variance and quantiles – that we usually want as outputs from a Bayesian analysis. But what is sampling and why is it helpful? It is easiest to describe sampling through an example than it is to define it formally. Imagine throwing a die. If we knew the exact physical properties of the die, the way people tend to throw it and the surface on which it lands, we could in principle determine the probability distribution underlying the result of throwing a die. However, an alternative approach is to estimate the probability distribution simply by throwing it a large number of times and enumerating the number of times it lands on each of the six numbers. Although approximate, this throwing (an example of sampling) should yield accurate estimates of the underlying probability distribution if we use enough samples.

The type of sampling described in the die example is what is termed *independent* sampling. Here the value obtained on one throw of the die does not depend on what was obtained on previous throws. In Bayesian statistics, we are unfortunately unable (for most interesting cases) to independently sample from the posterior, and instead have to resort to something known as *dependent* sampling. In dependent sampling, the value that we sample next *depends* on the current value. Rather than throwing the die, imagine tilting a surface on which it sits in some random orientation. Now, the value that we obtain on the next 'tilt' of the die will depend on which number is currently face up. Because of this dependence, using this tilting method means that it takes more samples to accurately estimate the die's probability distribution. That is, many more samples than would be required by the (independent) throwing. This relative inefficiency is reflected in the vast majority of dependent sampling routines. Independent sampling is always the gold standard.

The type of dependent sampling that is most frequently used in computational Bayesian inference is *Markov chain Monte Carlo* (MCMC), first invented for use in physics in the mid twentieth century. In MCMC, we undertake a random walk through posterior space, where each step represents a sample from the posterior. In Chapter 12 we shall see that this technique provides a framework capable of handling the majority of Bayesian models that we encounter in reality. However, MCMC is not without its pitfalls. In particular, the question of how many samples are needed to adequately represent our posterior distribution is fraught with danger and rife with opportunities for misuse. This makes understanding the algorithms behind MCMC, and the methods used to judge Markov chains' convergence (to the desired posterior), pivotal, and we shall devote significant time to this issue.

Three of the most frequently-used algorithms in Bayesian inference are Random Walk Metropolis, Gibbs sampling, and Hamiltonian Monte Carlo. We start by introducing Random Walk Metropolis in Chapter 13 since this is the simplest of the three to understand. In fact, Random Walk Metropolis is a special case of Gibbs sampling (and vice versa, as it turns out), which we introduce in Chapter 14. Gibbs sampling is the algorithm implemented in the BUGS and JAGS languages, which have been popular for applied Bayesian analyses in the past. Gibbs sampling is a powerful technique which is sufficiently general to be applied in a large range of circumstances. However, there are still cases where it is limiting. For example, Gibbs sampling can be slow to converge in larger hierarchical models, where there often exists strong correlation in the posterior.

A more recently invented way of sampling from the posterior is Hamiltonian Monte Carlo (HMC), which represents less of a random walk through parameter space and more of a directed one. This direction allows for efficient sampling from the posterior distribution, meaning that we are able to tackle bigger, more complex problems. Stan [34], a programming language created by Andrew Gelman and his colleagues at Columbia, implements a faster cousin of HMC, called the 'No-U-Turn Sampler' (NUTS), in a fast and extremely sensible manner. Stan is more similar to conventional programming languages than JAGS (and BUGS), making its learning curve less steep and extending its potential use. We introduce HMC and NUTS in Chapter 15 before we introduce Stan in Chapter 16.

12

Chapter contents

LEAVING CONJUGATES BEHIND: MARKOV CHAIN MONTE CARLO

12◯1   CHAPTER MISSION STATEMENT

By the end of this chapter, the reader should understand the problems with attempting to calculate posterior distributions (and any posterior summaries) by exact calculation, and how sampling can help us sidestep the problem.

12◯2   CHAPTER GOALS

Bayes' rule dictates that we sum (for discrete parameters) or integrate (for continuous parameters) the product of the likelihood and prior, across all parameter ranges, in order to estimate its denominator. This denominator term is essential since it normalises the posterior distribution, ensuring that it is a valid probability density. For problems involving continuous parameters, this multidimensional integral is practically intractable. In Section 12.3 we see that, even if we could calculate the exact posterior density, we typically want to calculate its moments. To calculate these we must calculate additional integrals, which are as difficult to compute as the denominator itself.

This means that in order to conduct Bayesian analysis in practice, we need to change tactics somewhat, and abandon the relative comfort of exact calculation in favour of an alternative approach. While in many circumstances we are unable to exactly calculate the posterior distribution, it turns out we are nonetheless able to sample from it.

In life, we use sampling unwittingly to gain an understanding of various entities: we do not know whether we like a particular food before we try a bit of it; when voters are quizzed in exit polls, these represent a sample from the overall population; a dice manufacturer rolls its produce a large number of times to check that they sufficiently mimic the behaviour of (theoretical) unbiased dice. In all cases, we use sampling to understand an object that is hitherto uncertain to us. Sampling from a distribution is no different conceptually.

While we are able to sample from a posterior, the sampling is somewhat different to that of the dice example. Whereas it is possible to independently sample dice, we typically cannot generate independent samples from the posteriors, the experimental ideal. Instead, we must use dependent samples, where the next sample value depends on the value of the current sample. Markov chain Monte Carlo (MCMC) is a type of dependent sampling algorithm, which we introduce in Section 12.9. As one might expect, dependent sampling results in a correlation between consecutive samples. This correlation means that the incremental informational value of each new sample is less than would be obtained from an independent sampler, where each sampled value does not depend on the previous value. This means that we need more dependent samples to characterise our posterior than would be necessary from an independent sampler. We quantify the difference in sampling efficiency between the independent sampler ideal and the dependent sampler we use in practice, through the concept of *effective sample size*. The effective sample size is the number of samples of an independent sampler that would provide the same amount of information about the posterior as our actual MCMC sample size.

Whenever we use sampling we need to take sufficient samples to yield a faithful representation of the posterior. In most cases, it is difficult to determine what constituents an adequate sample since, for the vast majority of cases, we do not know the posterior we are trying to sample – this is the reason for doing sampling in the first place! In Section 13.9, we advocate using a number of

Markov chains, since this provides better insight into convergence to the posterior than is possible when using a single chain. Specifically, this method works by monitoring the convergence of the sampling distribution of each chain to all the others. Although this method is not foolproof, it is currently the best available approach for judging whether our sampling distribution has converged to the posterior.

12.3 THE DIFFICULTY WITH REAL-LIFE BAYESIAN INFERENCE

Bayes' rule gives us the recipe for calculating a posterior probability density:

$$p(\theta \mid data) = \frac{p(data \mid \theta)p(\theta)}{p(data)}. \tag{12.1}$$

As an example, imagine that we count the number of secondary bovine spongiform encephalopathy (BSE) cases (also known as 'mad cow disease') originating from a particular infected cow. Further suppose that we use a Poisson distribution for our likelihood in this case (see Section 8.4.3), with a mean parameter λ. We expect that the mean could take a large range of possible values, and hence specify a log-$\mathcal{N}(1,1)$ prior for λ, which allows significant pre-data uncertainty.

To calculate the posterior, Bayes' rule tells us that we need to calculate the denominator, $p(data)$, which we obtain by multiplying the likelihood and prior, and then integrating over θ (for continuous parameter problems):

$$p(data) = \int\limits_{\text{All }\theta} p(data \mid \theta) \times p(\theta)\mathrm{d}\theta. \tag{12.2}$$

In our mad cow disease example this involves calculating the following integral:

$$p(\boldsymbol{x}) = \int\limits_0^\infty \left(\prod_{i=1}^N \frac{\lambda^{x_i}\exp(-\lambda)}{x_i!} \right) \times \frac{1}{\lambda\sqrt{2\pi}}\exp\left(-\frac{(\log(\lambda)-1)^2}{2} \right)\mathrm{d}\lambda, \tag{12.3}$$

where N is the number of data points, and $\boldsymbol{x}$ is the sample of data we obtained. While our model is not conceptually challenging, we have nevertheless arrived at an expression that is, at least, difficult to work out.

Furthermore, suppose that we manage to calculate expression (12.3), and hence obtain an analytic expression for $p(\lambda \mid \boldsymbol{x})$. At this point, we might want to summarise the posterior, by its mean. From Chapter 3 we know that calculating the mean of a continuous distribution involves an integral which, in this case, is of the form:

$$\mathbb{E}(\lambda|\boldsymbol{x}) = \int\limits_0^\infty \lambda\, p(\lambda \mid \boldsymbol{x})\mathrm{d}\lambda$$

$$= \int\limits_0^\infty \lambda\, \frac{p(\boldsymbol{x} \mid \lambda) \times p(\lambda)}{p(\boldsymbol{x})}\mathrm{d}\lambda. \tag{12.4}$$

The above integral is similar to expression (12.3), except with an additional λ out in front. Since the original integral was tricky to calculate, we expect that calculating the above integral is going to be similarly difficult.

So even though we are dealing with a situation of quite modest complexity – we can explain the situation and model in a couple of lines – we nevertheless found that the calculations involved in calculating the posterior and its mean are difficult to undertake. This difficulty only becomes exacerbated as the complexity of the model increases. As an example, consider replacing the Poisson distribution in the mad cow model with a negative binomial (parameterised by a mean λ_i and a dispersion parameter κ; see Section 8.4.4). To determine the posterior mean, we must now compute a double integral:

$$\mathbb{E}(\lambda|\boldsymbol{x}) = \int_0^\infty\!\!\int_0^\infty \lambda\, p(\lambda,\kappa\mid\boldsymbol{x})\, \mathrm{d}\kappa\mathrm{d}\lambda. \tag{12.5}$$

The difficulty with real life Bayesian inference: high multi-dimensional integrals (and sums)

As you might expect, a double integral is considerably harder to calculate than a single one, so the above is going to be tricky. In general, as the dimensionality of a model increases (the number of free parameters), we see an exponential-like increase in the difficulty of calculating the requisite integrals. Clearly, exact calculation of the posterior is going to be difficult for all but the most simple of examples.

There are a number of methods proposed to derive approximate versions of the posterior. In the next section, we survey a few of these methods as a stepping stone to MCMC sampling later on in the chapter.

12 O 4 DISCRETE APPROXIMATION TO CONTINUOUS POSTERIORS

The denominator for continuous parameter problems is typically (for univariate models) harder to calculate than for discrete parameter models, where we can usually calculate:

$$p(data) = \sum_{\theta=\theta_1}^{\theta_p} p(data\mid\theta)\times p(\theta). \tag{12.6}$$

Expression (12.6) is relatively easy to calculate because modern computers can evaluate each of the p terms (each one corresponding to one of the finite number of possible θ values) in the sum, and then add them together, in the blink of an eye. This ease carries over into formulae for the moments[1] of these distributions, where, for example, we can calculate the posterior mean value of θ through:

$$\mathbb{E}(\theta\mid data) = \sum_{\theta=\theta_1}^{\theta_p} \theta\times p(\theta\mid data). \tag{12.7}$$

So if we had a way of converting our continuous parameter problems into discrete versions, we could then calculate an approximate posterior. This discretisation process is an approximation, where we suppose that our prior and likelihood exist only at a finite set of points on a grid, resulting

---

[1]Moments are summaries of probability distributions, such as the mean (the first moment) and variance (second moment).

in a posterior that is also discrete. This is exactly what we did when we used Bayes' box to calculate the posterior for a discretised version of the disease prevalence example described in Section 5.5.2.

Suppose that we continue with our mad cow disease problem, using again a Poisson likelihood and a log-N prior. We can then use the value of our prior and likelihood at only even integer values of λ, to produce a discretised posterior by Bayes' rule (see Figure 12.1). The quality of the posterior approximation improves as we use a finer grid (compare the middle and right panels of Figure 12.1). Furthermore, we can use our discretised posterior to calculate the posterior mean, once again using Bayes' box (see Table 12.1).

We can also estimate discrete versions of posteriors for models with more than a single parameter by discretising the prior and likelihood along the range of each parameter. Again, consider we use a negative binomial likelihood for the mad cow case count, where we assign log-normal priors on both the mean and dispersion parameters. In this case, calculating the integral that corresponds to the denominator is more difficult than for the Poisson case, but we can still gain insight into the posterior by discretising the problem (see Figure 12.2).

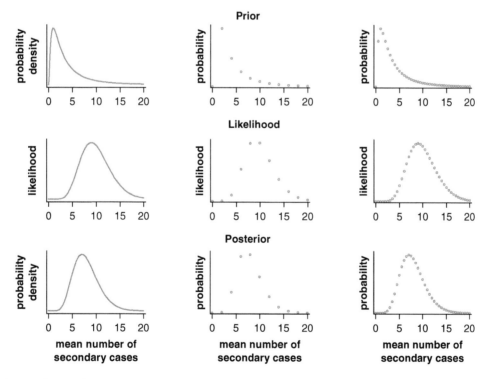

Figure 12.1 Left: the exact prior, likelihood and posterior for the mad cow example using the Poisson model. Middle and Right: discrete prior, likelihood and posterior (= likelihood × prior divided by their sum) for the same problem, at intervals of 2 units (middle) and 0.5 units (right). In all cases, the likelihood and posterior are calculated assuming that we have data consisting of a single sample, where we found that seven secondary cases of BSE originated from an infected cow.

Table 12.1   A Bayes' box illustrating the calculation of the posterior and the posterior mean for the mad cow example where we have discretised the parameter lambda into a grid. Here we assume that we have data consisting of a single sample, where we found that seven secondary cases of BSE originated from an infected cow.

λ (mean number of BSE cases)	Prior	Likelihood	Prior × Likelihood	Posterior	λ × Posterior
0	0.000	0.000	0.000	0.000	0.000
2	0.468	0.000	0.000	0.002	0.004
4	0.228	0.060	0.014	0.301	1.204
6	0.120	0.138	0.016	0.365	2.192
8	0.069	0.140	0.010	0.212	1.698
10	0.042	0.090	0.004	0.084	0.840
12	0.027	0.044	0.001	0.026	0.316
14	0.018	0.017	0.000	0.007	0.099
16	0.013	0.006	0.000	0.002	0.027
18	0.009	0.002	0.000	0.000	0.007
20	0.007	0.001	0.000	0.000	0.002
	1.00	0.50	$Pr(X = 7) = 0.045$	1.000	$\mathbb{E}[\lambda \mid x = 7] = 6.39$

While this discretisation procedure works well for relatively simple problems, it quickly becomes unwieldy as the number of parameters involved increases. Comparing Figure 12.1 with Figure 12.2, we see that, even though we only have one more parameter, there has been a dramatic increase in the number of grid points that we require to estimate the posterior. In fact, for linear increases in the number of model parameters, there are exponential increases in the number of grid points we need. Suppose that we discretise each parameter in our model using 10 grid points. For a model with a single parameter, this means we need to do 10 calculations. For a model with two parameters, we must do $10 \times 10 = 100$ calculations. For a model with 20 parameters, this requires $10^{20} = 100,000,000,000,000,000,000$ calculations! This methodology clearly becomes impractical as the complexity of the model increases. We say that it suffers from *the curse of dimensionality*, a term used to explain problems in a method that arise only as the dimensionality increases (here dimensionality is the number of parameters in our model).

The problem with discrete approximation to integrals or probability densities

12 O 5   THE POSTERIOR THROUGH QUADRATURE

Rather than discretising the entire prior, likelihood and posterior space, we could attempt to determine approximate values for the integrals involved in Bayesian inference, for example those involved in calculating the denominator or the posterior mean. In numerical quadrature, integrals

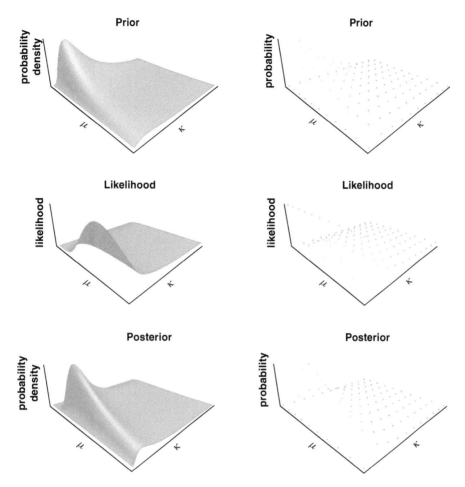

Figure 12.2   Left: the exact prior, likelihood and posterior for the mad cow example using the negative binomial model. Right: discrete prior, likelihood and posterior (= likelihood × prior divided by their sum) for the same problem. In all cases, the likelihood and posterior are calculated assuming that we have data consisting of a single sample, where we found that seven secondary cases of BSE originated from an infected cow.

are approximated by discretising the function being integrated into a finite set of function values, summing these together and then multiplying by a type of weighting function.

A crude quadrature method is to discretise a function over a range and assume that its value between consecutive grid points is constant. A univariate integral is then approximated by summing the areas of individual rectangles. In Figure 12.3, we see that this rule allows accurate evaluation of the denominator of our univariate mad cow example for even sizeable interval widths.

However, once again this method suffers from the curse of dimensionality. As the number of parameters increases, we are required to discretise our function across an exponentially increasing number of points, as part of any quadrature method to evaluate an integral. Numerical quadrature is also not the answer it seems.

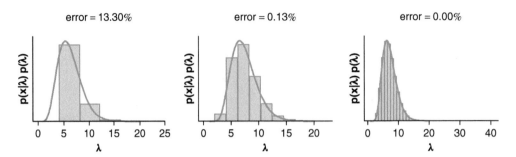

Figure 12.3 Rectangular quadrature in action: as the interval width decreases (left to right panels), there is a corresponding reduction in the percentage error in estimating the denominator (errors shown above each plot).

12⬤6   INTEGRATING USING INDEPENDENT SAMPLES: AN INTRODUCTION TO MONTE CARLO

Often in applied Bayesian analyses, we want to estimate models with hundreds or thousands of parameters. Neither discretisation nor quadrature is feasible in these circumstances. Evidently, to handle models of arbitrary complexity, indexed by the number of parameters, we need a new approach. Fortunately, such an approach exists, but it requires a change of perspective, where we abandon the use of brute force to directly calculate posterior densities and posterior summaries, such as the mean. We instead estimate these quantities, indirectly, through sampling.

Suppose that we have a black box containing a die with an unknown number of sides, which may, or may not, be fair. However, fortunately for us, there is a tiny window in the top of the box. Each time we shake the box, we can look through this window and see the number that results from the throw. Suppose that we play a game where we pay $X for the chance to win the amount of money that shows on the top of the box. For example, if we pay $5 and throw a 7, we win $2. If instead we throw a 1, we lose $4. If we were left in a room with the box for long enough, could we work out a fair amount to pay for such a bet?

In this example, a fair amount to pay would correspond to the mean of the die since in this circumstance our expected winnings are zero. How can we estimate the mean of the die? Suppose that we shake the box and record the number which shows through the window after each shake. We then repeat this process – shaking and recording – a large number of times. Clearly, we can estimate the mean of the die if we just average the numbers we obtain across all of our throws. There is, of course, the question: Just how many throws do we need to be confident in our estimate? But let's leave answering this question until later.

So, to recap, if we sample from our black box die a large number of times, and then take the sample mean of the resultant throws, this allows us to estimate the true mean of the die. While this might not appear revolutionary, remember that the mean of a discrete distribution is given by:

$$\mathbb{E}(X) = \sum_{i=1}^{k} x_i \times Pr(X = x_i),$$ (12.8)

where, here, X represents the value on each side of the die, and k is the number of sides. The amazing thing is that, by throwing the die, we have estimated the result of the calculation in expression (12.8), even though we have no idea of the number of sides, nor the individual face probabilities!

Furthermore, let's suppose that we increase the number of sides of our die so it now has an infinite number of faces. Further, suppose that each face corresponds to a single real value between 0 and 1, with all of the real values between these limits covered. (We realise that this is a strange die, and not strictly possible due to Cantor's arguments, but bear with us.) Now after we shake our box, one of these real numbers appears at the top. To estimate the mean of the die, we again iterate shaking the box and recording the die's value.[2] Since we are considering a continuous random variable, we have now essentially estimated the *integral*:

$$E(X) = \int_0^1 x \times p(x)dx.$$

(12.9)

Again, this is without any knowledge of the underlying probability distribution $p(x)$, representing the uncertainty inherent in throwing this bizarre die. This is the sort of maths that we would always like to do if we could.

In general, if we can repeatedly generate independent samples from a continuous probability distribution, $X_i \sim p(x)$, we can estimate its mean by the following formula:

$$E(X) = \int_{-\infty}^{\infty} x \times p(x)dx$$

$$\approx \frac{1}{n}\sum_{i=1}^{n} X_i \, ,$$

(12.10)

where n is the number of samples. The above is really just a grandiose way of saying that we take the mean of all our samples. While this method might seem limited in scope, in that we can only calculate the mean of a given distribution, it turns out that the above is a specific example of a more general rule. If we can generate samples from a given probability distribution, $X_i \sim p(x)$, we can estimate the expectation of any function, $g(X)$, by:

$$E(g(X)) = \int_{-\infty}^{\infty} g(x) \times p(x)dx$$

$$\approx \frac{1}{n}\sum_{i=1}^{n} g(X_i) \cdot$$

(12.11)

So we just take the mean of our function $g( )$ applied to each of the points in our sample. The above might appear a bit purposeless until we realise that we can manipulate it to allow us to estimate the variance of a distribution by:

$$var(X) = E(X^2) - \left[E(X)\right]^2$$

$$\approx \frac{1}{n}\sum_{i=1}^{n} X_i^2 - \left[\frac{1}{n}\sum_{i=1}^{n} X_i\right]^2.$$

(12.12)

---

[2]Technically, for this to work we require that there is a valid probability distribution over the sides, which has a finite first moment, but let's not get caught up in this issue here.

The class of method that relies on computational random sampling is known as *Monte Carlo* methods. Monte Carlo methods were first used in the 1930s by the Italian nuclear physicist Enrico Fermi who was studying neutron diffusion. Fermi would go on to work on the Manhattan Project to build the world's first nuclear bomb, and has been called the 'architect of the nuclear age'. It was not until 1949, however, that the Polish–American mathematician Stan Ulam (who also worked on the Manhattan Project, and after whom the Stan MCMC software is named) together with the Greek–American physicist Nicholas Metropolis (whose MCMC method we shall encounter in Chapter 13) in 1949 published the first public document on Monte Carlo simulation (see "The Monte Carlo method", *Journal of American Statistical Association*). Metropolis was also the man who coined the phrase 'Monte Carlo simulation' for these methods, and refers to the Monte Carlo Casino in Monaco, where Ulam's uncle would gamble away money borrowed from his relatives. Nuclear bombs and casinos – who says that beauty can't have ugly origins?

Although you can start to see that this method may have some promise, the best is yet to come. So long as we can generate independent samples from a multidimensional probability distribution, $\mathbf{X_i} \sim p(\mathbf{x})$, where $X_i = (X_{1i}, X_{2i}, ..., X_{ki})$, then we can approximate multidimensional integrals as simply as we did for the univariate case:

$$E(g(\mathbf{X})) = \int_{-\infty}^{\infty} \int_{-\infty}^{\infty} ... \int_{-\infty}^{\infty} g(\mathbf{x}) p(\mathbf{x}) dx_k ... dx_2 dx_1$$

(12.13)

$$\approx \frac{1}{n} \sum_{i=1}^{n} g(\mathbf{X_i}).$$

Importantly, we have found a methodology whose complexity appears insensitive to the dimensionality of the probability distribution we use; we could have chosen k above to be 10, 1000 or 1,000,000, and the method would still work the same.

How to do integration by sampling

Can we use sampling to approximate the integrals involved in Bayesian inference? The answer is yes, but it turns out that, for all but the easiest of problems, we need to modify our method a bit since, in general, we are not able to generate independent samples from a posterior distribution. Before we discuss this modification, we first show how to use independent sampling to estimate the denominator of our mad cow example.

12.6.1 Mad cows revisited

Since today most software packages come equipped with pseudo-random-number generators capable of generating independent samples from a wide range of univariate distributions, we can use independent sampling to estimate the denominator in our mad cow example. Remember that here we had trouble calculating:

$$p(\mathbf{x}) = \int_0^{\infty} \left(\prod_{i=1}^{N} \frac{\lambda^{x_i} \exp(-\lambda)}{x_i!} \right) \times \frac{1}{\lambda \sqrt{2\pi}} \exp\left(-\frac{(\log(\lambda)-1)^2}{2} \right) d\lambda,$$

(12.14)

$$= \int_0^{\infty} p(\mathbf{x} \mid \lambda) p(\lambda) d\lambda.$$

However, Section 12.6 suggested that we can estimate the above integral, so long as we can generate independent samples, $\lambda_i \sim p(\lambda)$ (where $p(\lambda)$ is a log-$\mathcal{N}$ prior distribution), using the following:

$$E(p(\boldsymbol{x}\,|\,\lambda) = \int_{0}^{\infty} p(\boldsymbol{x}\,|\,\lambda)p(\lambda)\mathrm{d}\lambda$$

$$\approx \frac{1}{n}\sum_{i=1}^{n} p(\boldsymbol{x}\,|\,\lambda_i),$$

(12.15)

where in expression (12.15) we calculate the mean value of the likelihood across the n samples of λ_i from our prior. Figure 12.4 shows that as we increase the sample size, the above estimator rapidly converges to the true value of the denominator integral. Although we do not show it, we could use the same framework to estimate the mean of the posterior, again exploiting the fact that in this example we can generate independent samples from the prior.

In Bayesian analysis we do not typically use samples from the prior to explicitly estimate the denominator term, as we have done here. There is a good reason for this. In particular, this approach can be extremely slow to converge on the correct value. We shall see in Section 12.9 that we instead choose another route to the posterior, which avoids explicit calculation of the denominator, yet still allows us to generate samples from it. These samples are then used to summarise the posterior distribution.

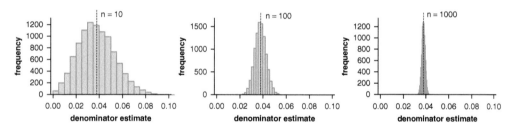

Figure 12.4 Using independent sampling to estimate the denominator in the mad cow example: as the number of independent samples increases (left to right), there is an improvement in the accuracy of estimating the true denominator value (dashed lines). In this case, we assume a Poisson likelihood and priors as described in the text and assume that we have data consisting of a single sample, where we found that seven secondary cases of BSE originated from an infected cow. The histograms show counts of estimates of the denominator obtained at each sample size across 10,000 repetitions.

12○7 WHY IS INDEPENDENT SAMPLING EASIER SAID THAN DONE?

Let's take a step away from Bayes' rule for a minute to discuss how computers actually generate seemingly random samples from a particular distribution. Many users of statistical software take for granted the fact that computers are able to, almost instantaneously, produce an arbitrarily long list of independent samples from a range of distributions. Since computers are deterministic machines they cannot yet generate truly random numbers,[3] and instead rely on seed values that completely determine the sequence of numbers that pseudo-random-number generators (PRNGs)

---

[3]A possible caveat to this is quantum-based random-number generators; see http://arxiv.org/pdf/1004.1521v2. pdf.

output. Typically, statistical software uses these PRNGs to produce sequences of numbers that behave, in some ways, as if they are random samples from a given distribution. If the software user does not specify the seeds explicitly, the seed is often determined by a rapidly changing input, such as the internal clock of a computer, meaning that consecutive samples from a given distribution are different and have a veneer of randomness. The appearance of randomness is attained because of the chaotic nature of the algorithms that produce the outputs. By 'chaotic' here we mean that small changes in the input seed can have a large effect on the outputted value.

Rather than going into depth about how PRNGs work (see the problem set at the end of the chapter for this), let's suppose we have at our disposal a random-number generator that is capable of producing independent random samples from a continuous uniform distribution between 0 and 1 (see Section 8.5.1). How can we use such a generator to produce independent samples from another distribution, for example an exponential?

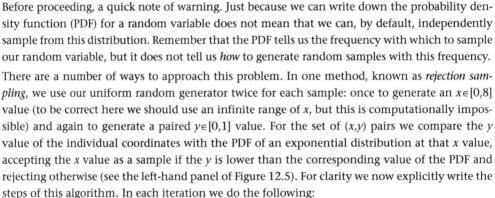

Doing
independent
sampling
by rejection
sampling

Before proceeding, a quick note of warning. Just because we can write down the probability density function (PDF) for a random variable does not mean that we can, by default, independently sample from this distribution. Remember that the PDF tells us the frequency with which to sample our random variable, but it does not tell us *how* to generate random samples with this frequency.

There are a number of ways to approach this problem. In one method, known as *rejection sampling*, we use our uniform random generator twice for each sample: once to generate an $x \in [0,8]$ value (to be correct here we should use an infinite range of x, but this is computationally impossible) and again to generate a paired $y \in [0,1]$ value. For the set of (x,y) pairs we compare the y value of the individual coordinates with the PDF of an exponential distribution at that x value, accepting the x value as a sample if the y is lower than the corresponding value of the PDF and rejecting otherwise (see the left-hand panel of Figure 12.5). For clarity we now explicitly write the steps of this algorithm. In each iteration we do the following:

1   Generate pairs of samples x~U(lower,upper) and y~U(0,1), where (lower,upper) are chosen to correspond (to a good approximation) to the range of the distribution of interest (in the above example, the exponential distribution).
2   For each data point (x,y), if y < PDF(x) then accept the x value as a sample from the distribution, otherwise reject it. Here, PDF corresponds to the PDF of the distribution of interest.

It is evident from the right-hand plot of Figure 12.5 that rejection sampling is pretty wasteful since only a small proportion of the initial samples are accepted. Furthermore, this inefficiency increases exponentially with the number of parameters in our distribution, meaning that for most Bayesian models we should not use rejection sampling. Can we design a better way of generating exponential samples from a uniform generator? Yes we can, with a bit of thought.

If we could draw samples from an exponential distribution, and then work out the exponential cumulative density function (CDF)[4] value for each of those points, what would the sample of CDF values look like? We know it would be bounded between 0 and 1 since all CDFs bounded by these values, but what about the distribution? Those samples that are most extreme will be squashed the most – towards 0 or 1 dependent on the nature of the extremity. In fact, samples will be moved an amount that depends on the distance that they lie from the middle of the sample, with those

---

[4]A CDF is a function that indicates the probability that a random variable is less than, or equal to, a given value For example, for a uniform distribution between 0 and 1, CDF(0) = 0, and CDF(1) = 1.

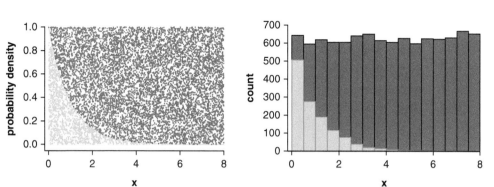

Figure 12.5 Using rejection sampling to generate samples from an exponential distribution with rate parameter equal to 1. Left: independent $(x,y) \sim (U(0,8),U(0,1))$ samples and the exponential PDF (red line). The points are coloured red if they are accepted (if the PDF at that x value exceeds the y value) and grey otherwise. Right: a stacked histogram for accepted (red) and rejected (grey) points.

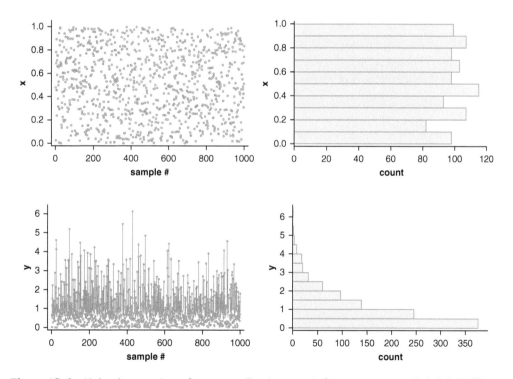

Figure 12.6 Using inverse transform sampling to sample from an exponential distribution with rate parameter equal to 1. Top-left: 1000 samples generated from a $U(0,1)$ distribution, arranged in the order that they were generated. Bottom-left: the samples that result from transforming the samples in the top-left panel using the exponential inverse-CDF, with red lines showing the amount they were moved by the transform. Right: histograms show the sampling distribution for both sets: original (top-right) and transformed (bottom-right).

around the median not moving much at all. The CDF transform changes the nature of variation until the distribution looks homogeneous overall, resulting in a uniform distribution. So why does this help us? Well, if we run the whole process in reverse, creating uniform samples, and then taking the exponential inverse-CDF transform of these, we should get samples that are exponentially distributed. Figure 12.6 shows how this method works for our exponential example. This method is known as *inverse transform sampling*. For clarity we now define the algorithm for inverse transform sampling explicitly. In each iteration we do the following:

1   Sample $x \sim U(0,1)$.
2   Generate $y = CDF^{-1}(x)$.

The resultant samples for y form samples from our distribution of interest (in the above example, the exponential distribution).

This new method is clearly better than rejection sampling since it has an efficiency of 100%. For each sample we obtain from the uniform distribution, we can produce a sample from the exponential distribution. However, it is not without a catch. To do this type of sampling, we must be able to calculate the inverse-CDF, which is typically not possible for complex distributions. This issue only becomes worse the more parameters that are in a model. Furthermore, in Bayesian statistics, we are generally unable to compute the posterior, meaning that we cannot implement inverse transform sampling.

Doing independent sampling by inverse transform sampling

It is hoped that this section has conveyed the non-triviality of drawing computational independent samples from a particular distribution. This difficulty motivates the sidestep that we take in Bayesian inference by moving from independent to dependent sampling (see Section 12.9).

12●8   IDEAL SAMPLING FROM A POSTERIOR USING ONLY THE NUMERATOR OF BAYES' RULE

Before we discuss how we sample from the posterior in practice, let's pause a second to think about what these samples should look like. Consider two points in posterior space, θ_A and θ_B, each representing different parameter values (bear in mind that the parameter here usually represents a vector). If the ratio of the posterior at the two points is given by:

$$\frac{p(\theta_A \mid data)}{p(\theta_B \mid data)} = \frac{3}{1}, \qquad\qquad (12.16)$$

then, intuitively, we want our sampler to generate random samples three times as often from the point θ_A as for the point θ_B. This is because this is what a PDF actually represents – the frequency that we will sample a particular value in an infinite sample of observations (this was the underlying premise behind rejection sampling; see Figure 12.5). Hence, we can use the histogram of many samples from a distribution to proxy for its PDF (see Figure 12.7). We have done this frequently throughout this book, but it is worth now making this point explicit. We also see from Figure 12.7 that this histogram representation works for both positive and zero values of the PDF. If the value of a PDF is zero at any point, then we want our sampler to generate zero samples at that point. Note, however, that we did not need the absolute height of the posterior to dictate that we generate zero samples at this point – we could have used its relative height versus all other points (which would have also been zero in this case) to calibrate our sampler. The same goes for any other location we pick – we can use the relative density of a given point versus all others to determine its sampling frequency.

Therefore, we want a sampling methodology that produces samples across parameter space in accordance with the relative heights of the posterior. This is an important point underlying all of the MCMC methods that we discuss in this book, so it is worth repeating: to determine the frequency of samples at a given point in parameter space, we do not need the absolute values of the PDF at that point, so long as we know its value relative to other parameter values. How does this help

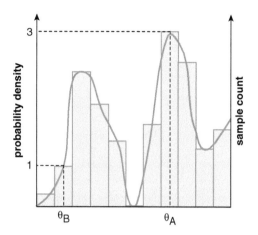

Figure 12.7 A PDF (full line) and its histogram representation obtained from sampling from the distribution.

us in Bayesian statistics? Well, it turns out that, while we cannot generally calculate the absolute posterior PDF value at a given point (since this requires knowledge of the denominator), we can nonetheless determine its value relative to other points. To explain this, consider our points θ_A and θ_B again, and calculate the ratio of the posterior density at the two parameter values:

$$\frac{p(\theta_A \mid data)}{p(\theta_B \mid data)} = \frac{\dfrac{p(data \mid \theta_A) \times p(\theta_A)}{p(data)}}{\dfrac{p(data \mid \theta_B) \times p(\theta_B)}{p(data)}}$$

$$= \frac{p(data \mid \theta_A) \times p(\theta_A)}{p(data \mid \theta_B) \times p(\theta_B)},$$

(12.17)

where we have used Bayes' rule to obtain the right-hand side of the first line of expression (12.17). Thus we see that here the problem denominator term has cancelled. Now everything in the bottom line of expression (12.17) is known; we just have the likelihoods and priors at each of the two points. Thus knowledge of the *un-normalised* posterior (the numerator of Bayes' rule) suffices to tell us the relative sampling frequency at each point in parameter space versus all others. In theory, we could then calculate the sampling frequency at all points in parameter space since, for each point, we could calculate the ratio of the PDF value compared to all other points.

However, how can we do this in practice? Does this require us to do an infinite number of calculations for each parameter value to determine the ratio of its posterior density versus all other points? One way forward might be to partition parameter space into a finite number of points, and then calculate the ratio for only those points within a given partition. However, we have already seen in Section 12.4 that as the number of parameters grows, we soon have too many calculations to carry out. Clearly, we need a different way of using the relative posterior density to sample from the posterior, which we discuss in the next section.

12.8.1 The un-normalised posterior: a window onto the real deal

Let's consider why the un-normalised posterior tells us everything that we need to know about the posterior. Revisiting Bayes' rule we can write it as:

$$p(\theta \mid data) = \frac{p(data \mid \theta) \times p(\theta)}{p(data)}$$

$$\propto p(data \mid \theta) \times p(\theta).$$

(12.18)

Thus, all the shape of the posterior is determined by the numerator, since the denominator does not contain any θ dependence. It turns out that, if we can generate samples with a distribution of the same shape as the posterior, then we can still calculate all the properties that we want. The mean and variance can both be estimated, including any other posterior summary.

To explain why knowledge of just the numerator of Bayes' rule suffices for our purposes, imagine a family of landscapes, each of similar shape, but of scales different to the previous (see Figure 12.8). Each surface represents the posterior shape for different values of the normalising denominator term. Only one of these surfaces will actually be at the correct height, when the surface encloses a volume equal to 1. However, if all we need is the relative heights of the posterior at one point versus another, the un-normalised density gives us all the geographical features of the actual posterior landscape; nothing is lost!

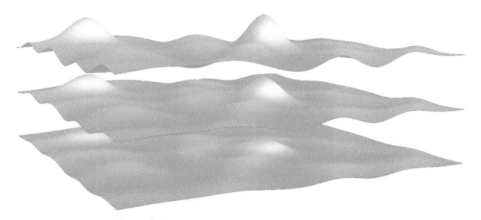

Figure 12.8 A family of distributions corresponding to possible posterior geometries, each for different values of the denominator. Note that the correct distribution corresponds to the case when the volume enclosed by the surface is 1.

12○9 MOVING FROM INDEPENDENT TO DEPENDENT SAMPLING

Let's recap. We would ideally like to draw independent samples from our posterior distribution in order to understand it. Also, if we could do this, it would mean we can avoid calculating the difficult multidimensional integrals necessary to calculate its properties exactly. But why is independent sampling difficult?

The problem is twofold here. First, calculating the denominator of Bayes' rule is typically very difficult, particularly for high-dimensional problems. Second, even if we did know the value of the denominator, and hence had an expression for the posterior density, it is usually impossible to generate independent samples from it. Neither of the strategies we discussed in Section 12.7 – rejection sampling and inverse transform sampling – can be used to generate samples from the posterior distributions we encounter in Bayesian inference: rejection sampling is too inefficient, especially for multi-parameter settings; inverse transform sampling is unusable since we are generally unable to calculate the posterior CDF and are definitely unable to invert it. Once more in our winding path towards practical applications of Bayesian inference, we are required to change direction. (Don't worry, however, this is the final time. We're nearly there – just bear with us.)

We learned in Section 12.8 that we do not actually need the denominator to calculate the relative height of the posterior at one point versus all others. However, does this mean that to reproduce an accurate global posterior density we need to compute an unfeasibly large number of ratios?

It turns out that using dependent sampling is a way out of these problems – the impossibility of generating independent samples and the practical intractability of computing the ratio of the PDF value at a single point versus all others. What does dependent sampling mean? It means that the next sample value *depends* on the current sample value.

Why we typically use dependent sampling to sample from the posterior

In the simplest form of dependent sampling (Random Walk Metropolis), we essentially do a type of random walk through posterior space. At each point in parameter space, we randomly determine a proposed stepping location and then, based on the height of the PDF at the proposed location, we either accept or reject the proposal. If the proposed location is higher than our current position, we accept the proposal and move there. If the height is lower, however, we only accept the proposal probabilistically, with a probability that depends on how much lower the proposed location is than our current position. If we do not accept the proposal we remain at our current location for the next sample. If we repeat this process a large number of times, we hope to have surveyed much of posterior space, with areas sampled in direct proportion to their height. Thus, ideally, our simple dependent sampler will have replicated the behaviour of the optimal sampler that we discussed in Section 12.8 – at least at a conceptual level, we are done!

The key to the success of this new sampling technique is that it forgets about the *global* structure of the posterior density, which is typically far too complex to contemplate, and instead focuses on *local* steps. These local steps are easy enough for us to handle since they only require us to evaluate the un-normalised posterior twice: once at our current location and once at the proposed step location. While we have not yet described how to generate a proposed step location (see Chapter 13), it suffices, for now, to say that we do it in a randomised fashion, meriting the use of Monte Carlo – an ode to the randomness of dice in casino games – in our sampler name.

The random walk through parameter space that we have described thus far represents the most simple type of dependent sampler, where the decision of where and whether to step is determined solely by the current state of the sampler (the current value and proposed value). However, we can imagine more complex samplers, where this decision depends on the history of all places that we have stepped thus far. To capture the memoryless of the algorithm, we term these samplers *Markov chains*, where the run of consecutive samples we generate forms the chain. Specifically, the Markov part of their name describes the amnesia of the stepping routine and refers to the Russian statistician Andrey Markov, born in the mid nineteenth century, who first described these objects (as part of wider work done on stochastic processes). Markov was alive during a time of great political upheaval and was not afraid to give his opinion on matters that he deemed important. In 1913 the Romanov dynasty celebrated 300 years of rule (which, in hindsight, probably was not a particularly sensible thing to celebrate at the time). Markov showed his disapproval by organising a celebration of his own – a celebration of 200 years since the Law of Large Numbers was proved! Although it was likely not such a debauched affair, we nonetheless appreciate its sentiment.

Strictly, our Markov chains should be called *1st order*, since their behaviour depends only on the current parameter value. It is possible, however, to have chains that remember the previous *m* states, but otherwise are memoryless, though these are usually less useful for Bayesian inference. Overall, this means that our sampling method is categorised as a type of MCMC.

There is a slight catch with using dependent samplers, which we discuss in Section 12.10, but before we rein in your elation we want to use an analogy to help with the intuition behind MCMC.

12.9.1 An analogy to MCMC: mapping mountains

Suppose that you are an explorer tasked with creating a contour map of a hitherto unknown mountainous area. The catch is that the area is perpetually covered in fog, and you can see only as far as your feet. You are, however, equipped with GPS that tells you your location and height above sea level.

This may seem like a daunting task. The danger of trekking through misty undiscovered mountains notwithstanding, it seems difficult to imagine how you can accomplish your task. However, you realise that there is still hope! If you take a (careful) step in a random direction, each time marking in your notebook the latitude, longitude and altitude, then you will eventually build a reasonable map of the area. It might seem like an inefficient way of attacking the problem, but there really is not much else available to you.

Of course, it would be better if you could use satellites to more fully scan or sample the heights of the area, but unfortunately, the cost of this type of mapping is prohibitive. You are on your own, it seems. You realise it is going to be quite a lot of hard work, and you get to it.

After some years in the wilderness, you emerge with your notebook, which contains sufficient measurements to (computationally) draw contour maps for the region. Although you had no access to satellites offering you a more macro view of the terrain, by taking *local* steps through space, you have managed to reconstruct such a *global* representation.

This locality of stepping and evaluation is much like an MCMC which takes local steps through parameter space, not physical space, and on the basis of many such steps estimates the overall shape of the global posterior. Of course, posterior space is usually much more complex than any physical terrain on earth. For a start, it usually has many more dimensions than physical space, but it would also be a much harder landscape to explore for other reasons. Romantically, we imagine such a terrain as encompassing huge shapeless deserts, punctuated by massive jagged peaks that dwarf their Himalayan equivalents. Edmund Hillary would truly have no chance!

12○10 WHAT IS THE CATCH WITH DEPENDENT SAMPLERS?

Effective sample size: representing the cost of dependent sampling

In Section 12.6 we used the analogy of a die in a black box to represent our posterior and the shaking of the box to represent the act of sampling. This, in turn, was used to motivate the use of sampling in general as a way of understanding a distribution – both its overall aesthetics and its properties. However, the analogy is no longer perfect for our MCMC sampling algorithm, since each time we shake the box, the result we obtain depends on the current value of the die; it is not an independent realisation. We should expect that the inherent dependence of our sampling algorithm will detrimentally affect its ability to approximate the posterior. Intuitively, this is because the informational value of each incremental sample is less than it would be for a purely independent sampler.

The manifestation of dependence for MCMC is autocorrelation in the chain of samples. In other words, the current sample value is correlated with its value in the previous sample. This correlation means that an MCMC algorithm takes many more samples to reach a reasonable approximation of the posterior than would be necessary for an independent sampler.

As an example, consider a method of throwing a die that we call *tilting*. We suppose that tilting causes a directional weighting in the next value of the die, such that following a 3, the numbers 2 and 4 are most likely. If we obtain a 4, the numbers 3 and 5 are most likely, and so on. The tilting methodology is illustrated for a six-faced die in the network graph of Figure 12.9, where the edges represent possible transitions and the edge width represents the probability of such a transition. We allow the transition probabilities to be determined by a parameter $0 \leq \varepsilon \leq 1$, where a value of 0 indicates independent sampling (where all transitions are equally likely) and a value of 1 indicates the circumstance where only consecutive transitions are allowed, meaning that there is significant dependence in the Markov chains.

We next estimate the mean of two dies: one with six faces and another with eight. The left and middle panels of Figure 12.10 show the errors in estimating the mean for each of these dies, when using independent sampling ($\varepsilon = 0$, red) or a heavily dependent sampling algorithm ($\varepsilon = 1$, black and grey). For all sample sizes, more dependence leads to a higher average predictive error. Further, the difference in predictive performance between dependent and independent sampling algorithms is greater for the die with more faces.

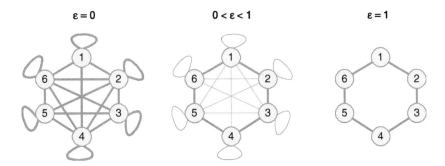

Figure 12.9 Possible transitions of for a six-faced die that is thrown by 'tilting' for three different values of transition bias, ε. The edges represent possible transitions, with thicker edges representing more probable transitions.

The right-hand panel of Figure 12.10 illustrates the concept of *effective sample size*. This is calculated by finding the independent sample size that results in the same error rate as the dependent algorithm. We find that a sample size of 40 for a dependently sampled ($\varepsilon = 1$) six-faced die produces an average error that is roughly equivalent to an independent sampler with a sample size of 20 – an effective sample size of roughly 50% of the size of the actual. For the die with eight faces, the situation is even worse: for the same number of throws as the six-faced die, the effective sample size is only 10.

Dependence in samples is typically more important for complex models. So a model with more parameters (like our eight-faced die) usually requires larger sample sizes to achieve an equivalent approximation to a posterior. For these sorts of model, it is not unusual to encounter an effective sample size that is less than 10% of the actual sample size, although this sort of slow convergence can be symptomatic of problems with a given model. This rule is not absolute, but something to bear in mind when considering different models. We will not explain how to estimate effective sample size for a given model just yet, as this is better tackled after a little more theory (see Section 13.10).

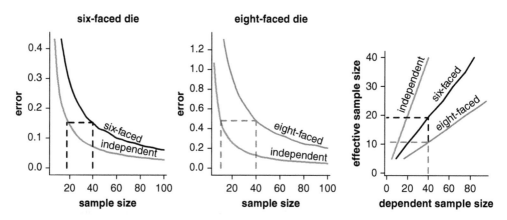

Figure 12.10 Left and middle: the average errors in estimating the mean of a fair die, with six and eight faces, respectively, across a range of sample sizes for dependent sampling (black and grey lines; $\varepsilon = 1$) and independent sampling (red lines). Right: dependent sample size versus effective sample size for six-faced (black) and eight-faced (grey) fair dice, and an independent sampler (red). The horizontal and vertical dashed lines across all plots indicate the calculation of effective sample size corresponding to an actual sample size of 40 for the dice. These estimates were produced using 10,000 iterates from the Markovian dice for each parameter set.

As a final analogy to explain the concept of effective sample sizes, imagine attempting to estimate the mean temperature in a particular tropical locale (that has no seasons). You have two options available to you: either you can use the temperature measured on consecutive days, meaning you have a run of temperature samples from day 1 to day n; or you have a list of temperatures of the same length measured at monthly intervals. The question here is: Just how many measurements of temperature do you need to accurately infer the mean temperature by each method?

In the monthly case, there may be some correlation between the temperature measured today versus a month ago – for example, a region of low pressure may sit above an area for months at a time. However, we suppose that after two months there is no longer much correlation with the temperature today. By contrast, there is considerable dependence in the daily measurements. If the temperature today is above the mean, then it is likely that the temperature tomorrow will also be high. The same goes for the next day and, to a lesser extent, the weather next week. The point is that we could easily – if we had only 30 daily measurements, corresponding to a month – infer that the mean temperature is much higher than it is in reality. If instead, we had 30 measurements that were taken at monthly intervals, this scenario is much less likely. Therefore we obtain a much better estimate of the mean temperature from the monthly measurements than we would if we used the daily ones. The monthly measurements are closer to the ideal of independent measurements than the daily measurements are. Thus, a sample size of 30 monthly observations would correspond to a higher effective sample size than for the same sample size for daily observations.

12●11 CHAPTER SUMMARY

The reader should, by now, realise the difficulty of practical Bayesian inference. The trouble is that, for most continuous parameter examples, the Bayesian denominator term requires us to calculate an intractable high-dimensional integral. Even if we could calculate this beast, our work would only just be beginning, since we usually want to calculate the distribution's summary moments, such as its mean and variance, requiring further complex integrals to be computed.

While there are a number of ways to address these difficulties, including discretising posteriors and numerical quadrature, the only method whose complexity does not scale exponentially with the dimensionality of parameter space is Monte Carlo sampling.

By drawing samples from our posterior we hope to gain an understanding of its properties. Ideally, these samples would be independent. That is, the value of the next sample does not depend on the current value. For most posteriors, however, obtaining independent samples is not possible, due to their inherent complexity, and because we cannot calculate the denominator term. A solution to both of these issues is to use dependent sampling, in the form of MCMC.

These chains do a kind of random walk through parameter space, where the path is determined by a series of decisions made using information about the posterior that is obtained by localised stepping. This locality means that we do not need to calculate any global properties of the posterior, and ensures that each of its steps is sufficiently easy to compute. This low computational burden means that MCMC methods can be used for posteriors of an arbitrary number of dimensions.

Thus far, we have been vague in our description of the way in which these Markov chains step through parameter space. Over the next three chapters, we discuss the three predominant algorithms that are used to dictate the stepping process. Burdening ourselves with the level of the algorithms may appear unnecessary, particularly if you choose not to implement the algorithms, and instead rely on probabilistic programming languages that come pre-loaded with this information. However, this knowledge is essential to understand the output of this software, and to avoid the (many) pitfalls of computational Bayesian inference. As is the case for most things in life, the devil is in the detail.

12○12 CHAPTER OUTCOMES

The reader should now be familiar with the following concepts:

- the issue with attempts to calculate the posterior, as well as its summary measures, in practice
- how discretising the density, as well as discretising the integral, through quadrature can be used to approximate the calculations involved in Bayes' rule
- how the complexity of methods based on discretisation scales too abruptly with the difficulty of the problem at hand to make these methods a practical solution
- the use of Monte Carlo sampling to estimate integrals whose complexity is relatively unaffected by model complexity
- how dependent Monte Carlo sampling can be used to sample from a posterior density by computing only the numerator of Bayes' rule: the likelihood multiplied by the prior
- the difference between the effective sample size and the actual sample size for dependent samplers

12○13 PROBLEM SETS

Problem 12.1 A fairground game

At a fairground a man advertises a gambling game that allows participants the chance to win a money prize if they pay an entrance fee. The game sequence goes like this:

- You pay £X.
- The man flips a fair coin (with an equal chance of the coin landing heads or tails up).
- If the coin lands tails up, the game ends and you walk away with nothing.
- If the coin lands heads up, he flips the coin a further two times and you receive the total number of heads across these latter two flips, H. So if the coin lands heads up twice, you receive £2; if once, you receive £1; if zero, you receive £0.
- Your winnings are given by £$(H − X)$.

Problem 12.1.1 Calculate the expected value of your winnings W if you participate, and hence determine the fair price of the game.

Problem 12.1.2 Create an R function that simulates a single run of the game, and use this to estimate the expected value of your winnings. (*Hint*: use R's `rbinom` and `ifelse` functions.)

Problem 12.1.3 Suppose that you pay £1 for each game, and start with £10 in your pocket. By using your previously created function, or otherwise, determine the expected number of games you can play before going broke.

Problem 12.1.4 Suppose you start with £10, and play the game 100 times (stopping only if your wealth is below the price of entry), each time paying £0.49. You want to insure against the risk of losing all your wealth. What is the fair price to pay for such an insurance scheme?

Problem 12.2 Independent sampling

An analysis results in a posterior with the following probability density function:

$$f(x) = \begin{cases} \dfrac{1}{1.33485} \dfrac{e^{-x^2/2}}{\sqrt{2\pi}}, & \text{if } x < 0.9735, \\ 0.186056, & \text{if } 0.9735 \le x \le 5, \\ 0, & \text{otherwise.} \end{cases} \tag{12.19}$$

Problem 12.2.1 Verify that this is a valid PDF. (Hint: see R's numerical integration function.)

Problem 12.2.2 Using independent sampling, estimate the mean and variance of this distribution.

Problem 12.2.3 Construct uncertainty intervals around your estimates of the mean.

Problem 12.2.4 Verify your previous answer by calculating the mean and variance of this distribution.

Problem 12.2.5 On the basis of the equation:

$$\mathbb{E}(X) = \int x f(x)\,dx = \int x \frac{f(x)}{g(x)} g(x)\,dx, \tag{12.20}$$

provide another way to estimate the mean.

Problem 12.2.6 Using the above method, where g is the continuous uniform distribution between 0 and 5, find an estimate of the mean.

Problem 12.2.7 How should we choose $g(x)$ to yield estimators with the lowest variance? (Difficult.)

Problem 12.3 Integration by sampling

Calculate the following integrals by sampling.

Problem 12.3.1

$$\int_{-\infty}^{\infty} \frac{x^6}{\sqrt{2\pi}} \exp\left(-\frac{x^2}{2}\right) dx \qquad\qquad (12.21)$$

Problem 12.3.2

$$\int_{1}^{\infty} \frac{x^3}{\sqrt{2\pi}} \exp\left(-\frac{x^2}{2}\right) dx \qquad\qquad (12.22)$$

Problem 12.3.3

$$\int_{1}^{\infty} \frac{x^6}{\sqrt{2\pi}} \exp\left(-\frac{x^2 - 4x}{2}\right) dx \qquad\qquad (12.23)$$

Problem 12.3.4

$$\int_{1}^{10} x^6 \frac{e^{-x^4/2}}{\sqrt{2\pi}} dx \qquad\qquad (12.24)$$

Problem 12.3.5 What is the approximate sampling distribution in using independent sampling to evaluate integrals?

Problem 12.4 Markovian coin

Consider a type of coin for which the result of the next throw (heads or tails) can depend on the result of the current throw. In particular, if a heads is thrown then the probability of obtaining a heads on the next throw is $\frac{1}{2} + \epsilon$; if instead a tails is thrown then the probability of obtaining a tails on the next throw is $\frac{1}{2} + \epsilon$. To start, we assume $0 \le \epsilon \le \frac{1}{2}$. The random variable X takes the value 0 if the coin lands tails up or 1 if it lands heads up on a given throw.

Problem 12.4.1 Find the mean of the coin, supposing it starts with probability $\frac{1}{2}$ on each side.

Problem 12.4.2 Computationally estimate the mean of the coin by simulating 10, 20 and 100 throws for $\epsilon = 0$.

Problem 12.4.3 As ϵ increases, how does the error in estimating the mean change, and why?

Problem 12.4.4 When $\epsilon = \frac{9}{20}$ calculate the effective sample size of an actual sample size of 100. How does the effective sample size depend on ϵ?

Problem 12.4.5 Now assume that $\epsilon = -\frac{9}{20}$. What is the effective sample size of an actual sample size of 100? Explain your result.

Problem 12.5 Markovian die

Consider a type of die whose next value thrown can depend on the current value. The degree of dependence is specified by a parameter $0 \le \epsilon \le 1$ (see Figure 12.9). If $\epsilon = 0$ then each separate throw of the die can be considered independent of the previous value. Another way of saying this is that each number has an equal probability of being thrown irrespective of the current value. If $\epsilon = 1$ then there is strong dependence from one throw to the next, where from a given number on a throw only neighbouring numbers are possible on the next. So $1 \to (6,2)$, $2 \to (1,3)$, and so on. If $0 < \epsilon < 1$ we suppose that there is preference towards consecutive numbers, with the preference increasing in ϵ.

For all values of ϵ we assume that both the forward and backward steps are equally likely, so $1 \to 2$ and $1 \to 6$ are of the same probability. If $0 < \epsilon < 1$, we suppose that those transitions that are not neighbours are all of the same probability (which is less than the probability of consecutive numbers).

Specifically, we define ϵ in the following way:

$$Pr(X_{n+1} \mid X_n) = \frac{1}{6}(1-\epsilon) + \frac{\epsilon}{2} 1_{X_{n+1} \in C(X_n)} \tag{12.25}$$

where $1_{X_{n+1} \in C(X_n)}$ is an indicator function which is equal to 1 if the next value of the die, X_{n+1}, is in the neighbour set $C(X_n)$ of the current value, X_n. (The above is just a fancy way of saying that we increase the probability of neighbours by an amount $\epsilon/2$ relative to the non-neighbours.)

Problem 12.5.1 Find the mean of the die across all values of ϵ, assuming it starts on a randomly selected side.

Problem 12.5.2 By simulating throws of the die, find an estimator of its mean.

Problem 12.5.3 Compute the error in estimating the mean as ϵ is varied at a sample size of 5, 10 and 100.

Problem 12.5.4 Find the effective sample size of 100 throws (when estimating the mean) for a die where $\epsilon = 1$. Comment on the effect of dependence on sampling.

Problem 12.5.5 Now suppose that the die starts always on side 2. Find the expectation of the die (not the running total, just the current value) at each time step. (Difficult.)

Problem 12.5.6 Following on from the last question, find how long we need to leave the die before we are confident we are sampling from its unconditional distribution. (By 'unconditional' here, we mean its probability distribution, disregarding its start point.) (Difficult.)

Problem 12.5.7 Carry out the above investigations but for a die with n sides. How does n affect the results?

Problem 12.6 Turning a coin into a random-number generator

Suppose you have one coin that has equal probability of landing heads up or tails up.

Problem 12.6.1 How can you use this coin to create a random variable X that has $Pr(X = 1) = \frac{1}{3}$ and $Pr(X = 0) = \frac{2}{3}$? (*Hint*: use rejection sampling.)

Problem 12.6.2 In R use a computational fair coin (namely, a Bernoulli distribution with $\theta = 0.5$) to create a random variable that is approximately distributed as a standard normal.

Problem 12.6.3 Using the answer to the previous question, create a variable that is approximately uniformly distributed between 0 and 1.

Problem 12.7 Pseudo-random-number generators

Problem 12.7.1 A particular pseudo-random-number generator is known as the linear congruential generator which generates a sequence of pseudo-randomised numbers using the relation:

$$s_t = \{as_{t-1} + b\} \bmod M, \tag{12.27}$$

where a, b and M are suitably chosen positive integers. What is the maximum period that such a sequence can have?

Problem 12.7.2 Write a function that implements the above recurrence relation and hence show that when $a = 2$, $b = 3$ and $M = 10$, where we begin with $s_0 = 5$ (the seed), the series has a period of 4.

Problem 12.7.3 Create a new function that has a maximum of 1 and a minimum of 0.

Problem 12.7.4 Use your newly created function with $a = 1229$, $b = 1$ and $M = 2048$, beginning with $s_0 = 1$, to generate 10,000 numbers between 0 and 1. Draw a histogram of the resulting sample. What sort of distribution does this look like?

Problem 12.7.5 Draw a scatter plot of pairs of consecutive samples for the previously generated series. Does this series look random?

Problem 12.7.6 Now generate a series with $a = 1597$, $b = 51,749$ and $M = 244,944$, beginning with $s_0 = 1$, to generate 10,000 numbers between 0 and 1. Draw a histogram of the resulting sample. What sort of distribution does this look like? Does a scatter plot of consecutive pairs look random?

Problem 12.7.7 Prove that inverse transform sampling works.

Problem 12.7.8 Use your most recent sequence of numbers from the linear congruential generator along with inverse transform sampling to generate pseudo-independent samples from the density $F(x) = 1 - \exp(-\sqrt{x})$.

Problem 12.7.9 Using the inverse transform method or otherwise, use your sequence linear congruential generator to generate samples from a standard normal distribution.

13

Chapter contents

RANDOM WALK
METROPOLIS

CHAPTER MISSION STATEMENT

This chapter introduces the reader to one of the most popular MCMC sampling algorithms: Random Walk Metropolis. This chapter also introduces the methods used to judge convergence of MCMC algorithms.

13⊙2   CHAPTER GOALS

In Chapter 12 we explained that although independent sampling from a posterior is generally impossible, it may be feasible to generate dependent samples from this distribution. While we are unable to exactly determine the global structure of the posterior, we can nevertheless build up a picture of it by local exploration using dependent sampling, where the next sample value depends on the current value. Although not as efficient as independent sampling, dependent sampling is easier to implement, and only requires calculation of the un-normalised posterior, avoiding the troublesome denominator term.

We also know that MCMC is typically used to do dependent sampling. It is called Monte Carlo because the decision of where to step next involves a random component. However, thus far, we have been vague about how this decision is made in practice. In this chapter we see that there are two components to this decision: in the first, we choose *where* to propose a next step from the current position; in the second, we choose *whether* we accept this step or stay where we are.

We aim to generate samples at points in parameter space whose frequency varies in proportion to the corresponding values of the posterior density. On first glance, it might appear that, whatever we select for these two components, we will eventually achieve this goal. This is not correct. If we always chose to step upwards, we would keep climbing until we reach the mode of the distribution, where we would stay forevermore. If, instead, we accepted all proposals, irrespective of their posterior height, then we would generate a uniform density of samples across all areas of parameter space.

Clearly, we need to design our stepping routine so that it is just right, sampling more from the peaks of the distribution and less from the low valleys. One of the most commonly used routines that satisfies these conditions is known as the *Random Walk Metropolis* algorithm and is the focus of this chapter. We will spend the majority of time developing an intuition of why this algorithm works and a relatively short time describing its mathematical underpinnings.

The basic Metropolis method is a general algorithm, but has limits – it can only be used (straightforwardly) to sample from an unconstrained parameter. By *unconstrained* here we mean one whose value can be any real number. This is a problem since many distributions have parameters that are constrained, either to be non-negative or to lie between particular bounds. For example, the standard deviation parameter of a normal distribution must be positive. In these circumstances the standard Metropolis algorithm does not work, so we are left with two choices: either we can transform our parameter so that its transformed value is unconstrained, and run Metropolis on the transformed parameter space; or we can switch to the *Metropolis–Hastings* algorithm. This algorithm allows constrained stepping which ensures that our Markov chains never stray outside of the correct bounds for a parameter. Fortunately, once we understand basic Metropolis, it is not much harder to grasp Metropolis–Hastings, and we shall discuss this other algorithm at this point in our learning.

An important consideration for practical MCMC is how to know when the sampling distribution has converged to the posterior distribution. You may ask: Why do we need to wait any time at all? Isn't the point of the MCMC that it will generate samples from the posterior? Well, under a wide range of conditions, it will – eventually. But how long is long enough? This depends on a number of factors: for example, where we decide to start our chains. Ideally, we would use an independent sample from the posterior as our initial chain location. However, we generally do not know the posterior, nor know how to generate an independent sample from it. This is why we started doing MCMC sampling in the first place! So, because we cannot achieve this optimality, we instead usually choose a random (and hence arbitrary) starting point, unlikely to be representative of an independent sample. This means that early samples from our Markov chains will be more representative of the random initialisation distribution than they are of the posterior. However, the good news is that, if we run our chains for long enough, they will eventually get there. But just how long do we need to wait to reach this goal? This is a difficult question, which we address in Section 13.9.

13.3 SUSTAINABLE FISHING

Suppose that David Robinson (a more fortunate cousin of Robinson Crusoe), marooned on his island, has access to four freshwater lakes of different sizes, each of which has a supply of fish. Furthermore, suppose that the amount of fish in each lake is proportional to its size. Robinson knows this and, being a sensible person, would like to ensure that he does not overfish each resource, by fishing each lake in proportion to the amount of fish it contains. Unfortunately though, Robinson drinks too much coconut toddy (an alcoholic beverage made from the sap of a coconut tree) and cannot remember the size of lakes he previously visited. We also assume that Robinson's activities do not affect the fish populations, so long as he does not massively overfish any of the lakes.

We suppose that on a given day, Robinson fishes and then camps next to a particular lake, which is connected by a series of pathways to the other lakes in a ring-like way, as shown in the left-hand panel of Figure 13.1. This means that he can travel from lake A to B, from B to C, from C to D, from D to A, as well as in the anticlockwise direction. The total number of fish in each of the lakes is shown in the right-hand panel of Figure 13.1.

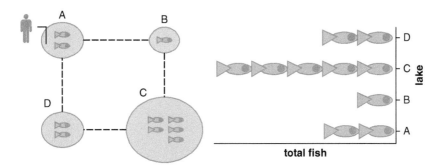

Figure 13.1 Left: the connectivity of the four lakes for the Robinson fishing example. Note that Robinson cannot actually see the fish, only the size of the lakes. Right: the total number of fish in each lake.

How can Robinson achieve his goal of fishing each lake in proportion to its fish stocks? One way is for him to flip a coin at the end of each day: if it is heads, he proposes a move in the clockwise direction (from A to B, for example); if it is tails, he proposes a move in the anticlockwise direction (from A to D, for example). He then calculates the following ratio using the proposed lake size, $S_{proposed}$, and the current lake size, $S_{current}$:

$$r = \begin{cases} 1, & \text{if } S_{proposed} \geq S_{current} \\ \dfrac{S_{proposed}}{S_{current}}, & \text{if } S_{proposed} < S_{current}. \end{cases} \tag{13.1}$$

Luckily for Robinson, he also has a solar-powered watch, which can generate a single (pseudo-)random uniform number at the end of each day, $p \sim U(0,1)$. He compares the calculated value of r with p, and moves to a new location, if $p < r$; or fishes the same lake tomorrow, if $p \geq r$.

Using this method, we computationally simulate Robinson's journey (left-hand panels of Figure 13.2) and, assuming he catches one fish per day (he retires to eat his catch after his first success), we can graph the total number of fishes caught (right-hand panels of Figure 13.2). After 50 days, the spread of fish he has caught across all lakes appears similar to the actual distribution of fish. After 500 days (bottom-right panel of Figure 13.2), the difference between sampled and actual distributions of fish is even smaller.

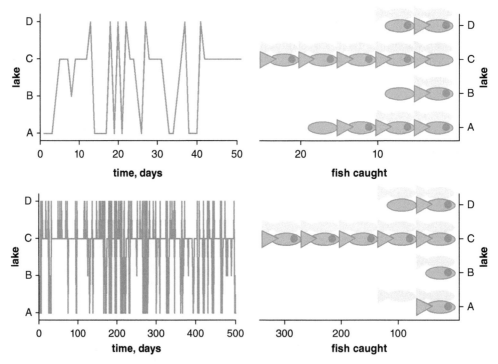

Figure 13.2 Left: the sequence of lakes (A, B, C, D) which Robinson fishes according to a Metropolis sampling routine over 50 (top) and 500 (bottom) days marooned on the island. Right: the actual number of fish he catches (red) for both time periods versus the true distribution of fish across the lakes (pink). Note the fish dimensions are not comparable between the top and bottom plots (in other words, over 500 days Robinson caught many more fish – see axes).

Our algorithm appears to have worked! Robinson has fished each pond in rough proportion to the fish stocks in each. Without knowing it, we have actually used the Random Walk Metropolis algorithm to produce a Markov chain that samples from the desired distribution. Before we more rigorously define this algorithm, let's consider another example, this time in continuous space.

 PROSPECTING FOR IRON

We are employed as a contractor for a mining company to map the amount of subterranean iron across a vast, lifeless desert. The desert is flat and uninformative of the treasures that lie underneath (see Figure 13.3). However, fortunately, we have a machine that measures the magnetic field directly underneath, which varies in direct proportion to the total amount of iron below. Suppose that the mining company has already determined that the area is rich with iron deposits and is interested only in mapping the relative abundance of deposits over the desert.

How should we approach mapping the underground iron? The simplest way would be to survey the magnetic field at, say, 1km intervals. However, even at this modest resolution, we would need to sample 1000 × 1000 = 1million points. If instead we increased the precision to 100 metres, we would then need to take 100 million samples. We'd die of thirst! There must be a quicker way to build an accurate map.

Suppose that we start in a random location in the desert and measure the magnetic field beneath. We then use a random sample from a bivariate normal distribution centred on our current location, to pick a new location to sample. We then measure the magnetic field there, and if it exceeds the value at the old site, we move to the new location and add the new (north, east) location to our list. By contrast, if the value of the magnetic field is lower than the current value, then we

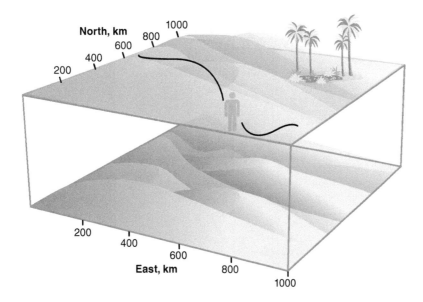

Figure 13.3   The desert above, with the iron deposits underneath. The red path shows a possible sampling path that our intrepid worker (Lawrence of Abayesia) might follow.

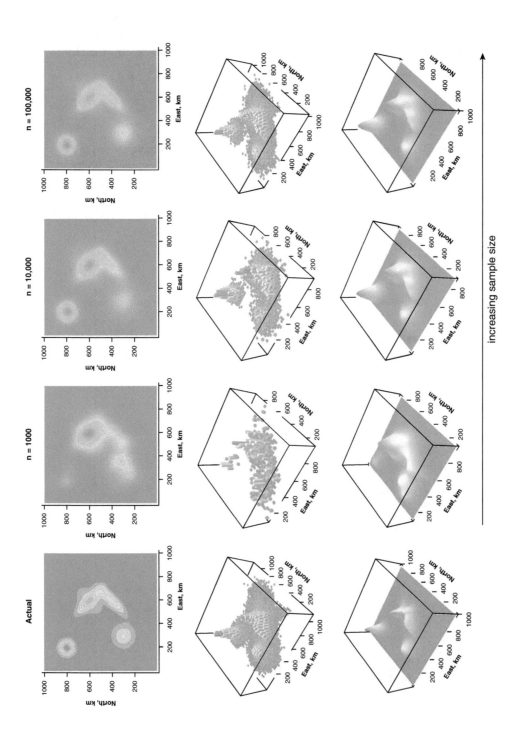

Figure 13.4 Searching for iron using the Metropolis algorithm. The left-hand column results exactly reflect the actual iron deposits, and all other panels represent the estimated deposits using samples generated by the Random Walk Metropolis algorithm with an increasing sample size (left to right). Top row: the path taken through the desert (red lines). The histogram of samples obtained using the Metropolis algorithm and the reconstructed posterior density correspond to the middle and bottom rows respectively.

only move there *probabilistically*, with a probability given by the ratio of the new value to the old. To do this we compare the ratio with a random sample from a uniform distribution, $p \sim U(0,1)$. If our ratio exceeds p, then we move there and add the new (north, east) to our current list. If it does not, then we move back to where we were, and add our previous location to our list again.

If we follow this routine a large number of times, and look at the concentration of sample points across the desert, we can obtain a map of the underground iron deposits (see Figure 13.4). While sample size obviously affects the accuracy of the map, after only 1000 samples, we have built up a rough, yet usable, map of the iron deposits below. Time to go and relax in an oasis! Note the indirect way that we built this map, using the measurements of magnetic field only to determine where next to step. The spatial density of above-ground (north, east) samples then determined the amount of iron below. This is different to the survey method where we used the measurements of the magnetic field below a given location to directly quantify the amount of deposits that lay beneath it.

13○5 DEFINING THE RANDOM WALK METROPOLIS ALGORITHM

We illustrated how the Metropolis algorithm works using two (silly) examples, but now we need to spend a little time to define it properly. (It shouldn't take too long, so bear with us; you'll be better for understanding its details.)

Imagine that we have a posterior whose density is known up to a proportion:

$$p(\theta \,|\, data) \propto p(data \,|\, \theta) \times p(\theta). \tag{13.2}$$

We would like to sample from this posterior to build an understanding of its shape and properties. For this example, imagine that θ is a one-dimensional continuous parameter, but note that the method outlined below is also applicable for models with more parameters.

We imagine that we do a random walk in posterior space, and at each point in time decide where next to step based on our current position and the shape of the posterior. We want the list of locations where we step to constitute samples from the posterior. If we have designed our stepping routine correctly, and take enough steps, we hope to build up an approximate global picture of the posterior from the local density of samples across parameter space.

If we always move to our next proposed location, irrespective of its height, we call this a *drunk-ard's random walk*. The result of this approach is uniform sampling across parameter space (see top panels of Figure 13.5). The drunkard, in a stupor, pays no attention to the posterior shape, and hence returns samples that are not indicative of the posterior terrain.

Clearly, to generate samples for locations in proportion to their posterior density, where we next decide to step should account for the height of the posterior. So, instead, we imagine a less random stepping routine where we step to a proposed location only if its height exceeds the current one. In memory of the mountaineer Edmund Hillary, we call this method a *Hillary climb*. In the bottom panel of Figure 13.5, we see that a Hillary algorithm has the opposite problem to the drunkard: they quickly ascend the posterior landscape, until they reach its peak. They then stay there for ever, resulting in a reconstructed posterior that is increasingly biased towards this mode.

Taking stock of the situation, we realise that we need an algorithm that pays just the right amount of attention to the posterior shape: too little attention, like the drunkard, and we get uniform

An introduction to the random walk Metropolis algorithm

sampling; too much, like Hillary, and we just get stuck on a mode forevermore. It turns out that, if we use the following decision-making rule, we then get the perfect balance:

$$r = \begin{cases} 1, & \text{if } p(\theta_{t+1} \mid data) \geq p(\theta_t \mid data) \\ \dfrac{p(\theta_{t+1} \mid data)}{p(\theta_t \mid data)}, & \text{if } p(\theta_{t+1} \mid data) < p(\theta_t \mid data), \end{cases} \tag{13.3}$$

where r is the probability that we accept the proposed point θ_{t+1} as our next sample value. This type of schema allows us to move both upwards and downwards in posterior space (see Figure 13.6 for a cartoon depiction of this algorithm) and ensures that we sample from a parameter location in relation to its relative height. As we discussed in Chapter 12, this rule requires only the relative height of the posterior at each step (because the denominator cancels in the ratio), meaning that we can substitute the un-normalised posterior densities for θ_t and θ_{t+1} for the corresponding full posterior densities in expression (13.3) (see Section 12.8.1 for a more thorough

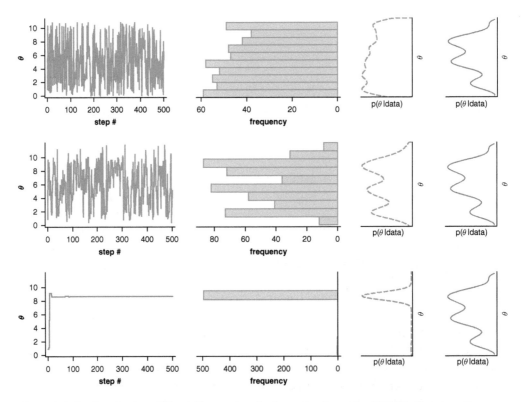

Figure 13.5 Comparing different accept-reject mechanisms for MCMC stepping. Top row: a drunkard's random walk. Middle row: a walk generated by the Metropolis algorithm. Bottom row: an example Hillary climb. The red lines (left) show the path taken by each stepping algorithm over time, the histograms (middle left) show the binned samples, and the dashed red lines (middle right) show the reconstructed posterior for each set of samples. The solid grey lines (right) show the actual posterior, assumed to be the same in each case.

explanation). This means that we can avoid the complication of calculating the denominator and instead approximate all quantities of interest from our samples.

In the middle panel of Figure 13.5, we see that this sampling routine produces paths that are someway between the extremes of the drunkard and Hillary, resulting in a reconstructed posterior that is much closer to the real thing.

We have now described the basic Metropolis recipe, but have omitted an important element: we have not yet described how we should generate the proposed location. (Don't worry, however, as this element will be fully explained in Section 13.6.)

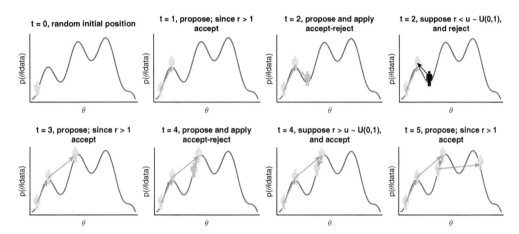

Figure 13.6   Exploring a landscape using the Random Walk Metropolis algorithm. Time here is computational runtime. Note that for two times ($t = 2$, $t = 4$), two plots are shown apiece: once for proposal, the other for accept-reject. Red figures represent accepted steps, grey figures represent proposed steps and black figures represent rejected steps.

13⊙6   WHEN DOES METROPOLIS WORK?

We now describe the conditions when the Random Walk Metropolis algorithm produces samples that are representative of the posterior. A key issue is that we would, ideally, like to initialise our Markov chain by independently sampling a start point from the posterior density. This would ensure that we immediately start to generate samples representative of the posterior. However, we cannot generate independent samples from the posterior; if we could, then we would not need to do MCMC in the first place! (See Section 12.7 for a refresher of this theory, if you need it.)

This means that in MCMC we start our Markov chains at some random points in parameter space, which will not be indicative of the posterior density. Often we may start our chains in areas of higher density so that they do not meander around in flat stretches of posterior space for too long. We then hope, by repeatedly doing Metropolis steps, that our distribution of sample values converges to the posterior distribution (see Figure 13.7)[1].

---

[1]This figure was inspired by the excellent lectures of Michael Betancourt: https://www.youtube.com/watch?v=pHsuIaPbNbY.

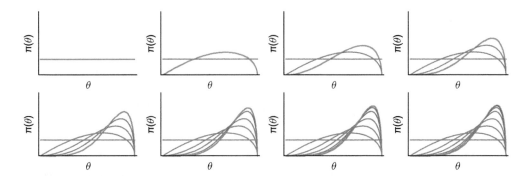

Figure 13.7 Convergence to a posterior distribution in MCMC. Here we start with a uniform distribution over possible starting values of each Markov chain (top-left), and as we repeatedly apply the transition operator, we eventually converge to a stationary distribution that is the posterior distribution (red line in bottom-right panel).

Mathematically we can firm up exactly what we mean by convergence to the posterior. If you want, you can skip Section 13.6.1 since it will be quite mathematical and not essential to what follows.

13.6.1 Mathematical underpinnings of MCMC

Suppose that we start with an arbitrary distribution for possible starting values of the chains, $\pi(\theta)$, and in each step apply a transition operator, $T(\theta'|\theta)$, representing the two steps – proposal then accept–reject – of the Metropolis algorithm, but can also represent whatever type of algorithm governs our Markov chain's transitions [10]. $T(\theta'|\theta)$ is a conditional probability distribution, often called the *transition kernel*, which specifies the probability of a chain transitioning from a parameter value θ to another value θ'. To apply this operator across all possible starting values of our parameter, we must calculate an integral:

$$\pi(\theta') = \int_{\text{All}\,\theta} d\theta\, T(\theta'|\theta)\pi(\theta), \tag{13.4}$$

where $\pi(\theta')$ is the distribution of the Markov chain values after one step. The differential $d\theta$ is put first to make the integrals easier to read. We aim to design this transition operator so that repeated application of it results in the posterior density:

$$\pi(\theta'') = \int_{\text{All}\,\theta} d\theta' T(\theta''|\theta') \int_{\text{All}\,\theta} d\theta\, T(\theta'|\theta)\pi(\theta)$$

$$\pi(\theta''') = \int_{\text{All}\,\theta} d\theta'' T(\theta'''|\theta'') \int_{\text{All}\,\theta} d\theta' T(\theta''|\theta') \int_{\text{All}\,\theta} d\theta\, T(\theta'|\theta)\pi(\theta) \tag{13.5}$$

$$\vdots$$

$$p(\theta\,|\,data) \approx \int_{\text{All}\,\theta} d\theta''' T(\theta'''\,|\,\theta'''^{-1}) \dots \int_{\text{All}\,\theta} d\theta\, T(\theta'|\theta)\pi(\theta)\,,$$

where θ'_n represents the parameter space for the nth step of the MCMC algorithm, where n is assumed to be a large integer. The consequences of this repeated application of the transition operator are illustrated graphically in Figure 13.7, where the sampling distribution of our chain shifts over time, converging towards the desired posterior distribution. We call this limiting distribution the stationary or invariant distribution.

13.6.2 Desirable qualities of a Markov chain

It turns out that, so long as we design our Markov chains so that they satisfy certain properties, we can be assured that (at least in the limit of infinitely long chains) our Markov chain sampling distribution will converge to the posterior. But what are those properties?

Mathematically proving that a Markov chain converges to the posterior is typically done in two steps [14]: the first step proves that the chain converges to a unique stationary distribution; the second proves that this stationary distribution is the posterior distribution. The first of these conditions is usually trivial, and requires that we design our Markov chain with the following properties:

- Irreducible or ergodic – this means that all parts of posterior parameter space can eventually be reached from all others by the chain (see the left-hand panel of Figure 13.8 for a counter-example).
- Aperiodic – this just means that the chain does not perfectly cycle (see the right-hand panel of Figure 13.8 for a counter-example).

These two conditions tend to be trivially satisfied by the Markov chains that we consider in Bayesian statistics, meaning that we do not need to consider them when we design our sampler. However, to ensure that the stationary distribution of a Markov chain corresponds to the posterior, we need to take care, since it would be easy to fall foul here. This design decision is the subject of Section 13.6.3.

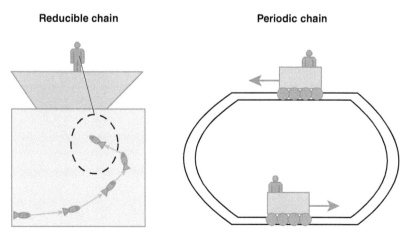

Figure 13.8 Examples of reducible (left) and periodic chains (right). Left: once the fish enters the net, it cannot escape and visit other parts of the ocean [12]. Right: a rollercoaster is constrained to (hopefully!) cycle forevermore on its track.

13.6.3 Detailed balance

Imagine that we determine where next to consider stepping using a conditional probability distribution, $J(\theta^{t+1}|\theta^t)$, which we call the *jumping* or *proposal* distribution [14]. Here θ^t corresponds to the sampled value of our parameter at a time t, in other words the current value of our Markov chain. (The jumping distribution is similar to the transition kernel we introduced in Section 13.6.1 but does not account for the accept–reject step.)

We want to design our Markov chain proposal distribution such that, if it reaches a distribution corresponding to the posterior, it stays there. In other words, the stationary distribution (the limiting distribution of the Markov chain) is the posterior distribution.

The Metropolis algorithm is characterised by a *symmetric* proposal distribution, meaning that we are as likely to propose θ_b from θ_a as we are to go in the reverse direction, to θ_a from θ_b. Mathematically, this means that $J(\theta_a|\theta_b) = J(\theta_b|\theta_a)$. In what follows, we show that this assumption is sufficient to prove that the Metropolis algorithm converges (for infinite sample sizes) to the posterior distribution.

To do this, we follow the derivation in [14] by supposing we can generate two samples from our posterior, $\theta_a \sim p(\theta|data)$ and $\theta_b \sim p(\theta|data)$, where we assume (without loss of generality) that $p(\theta_b|data) \geq p(\theta_a|data)$. We can then determine the probability density of a transition in either direction, from $\theta_a \rightarrow \theta_b$:

$$p(\theta^t = \theta_a, \theta^{t+1} = \theta_b) = p(\theta_a|data) \times J(\theta_b|\theta_a). \tag{13.6}$$

By assumption the posterior density is higher at θ_b than θ_a, and hence, using the Metropolis rule, we *deterministically* (that is, with probability 1) move to θ_b. Now consider a move in the opposite direction, from $\theta_b \rightarrow \theta_a$:

$$p(\theta^t = \theta_b, \theta^{t+1} = \theta_a) = p(\theta_b|data) \times J(\theta_a|\theta_b) \frac{p(\theta_a|data)}{p(\theta_b|data)}$$

$$= p(\theta_a|data) \times J(\theta_a|\theta_b) \tag{13.7}$$

$$= p(\theta_a|data) \times J(\theta_b|\theta_a) = p(\theta^t = \theta_a, \theta^{t+1} = \theta_b),$$

where we obtained the right-hand side of the first line of (13.7) using the Metropolis acceptance rule. The bottom line of (13.7) is obtained by assuming the symmetry of the proposal distribution, in line with the Metropolis algorithm. Thus we have proved that the joint density of a transition from $\theta_a \rightarrow \theta_b$ is the same as that for $\theta_b \rightarrow \theta_a$. This means that our Markov chain satisfies a principle called *detailed balance*, meaning that at equilibrium each transition should have a probability equal to its reverse process.

But how does this help us? Well, since we know that (repeating what we have above but in longhand notation:

$$p(\theta^t = \theta_b, \theta^{t+1} = \theta_a) = p(\theta^t = \theta_b|data) \times J(\theta_a|\theta_b)$$

$$= p(\theta^t = \theta_a|data) \times J(\theta_b|\theta_a), \tag{13.8}$$

we can determine the marginal distribution of the next value of our algorithm θ^{t+1} by integrating out $\theta^t = \theta_b$ in the above:

$$p(\theta^{t+1} = \theta_a) = \int_{\text{All } \theta_b} p(\theta^t = \theta_a \mid data) \times J(\theta_b \mid \theta_a) d\theta_b$$

$$= p(\theta^t = \theta_a \mid data) \int_{\text{All } \theta_b} J(\theta_b \mid \theta_a) d\theta_b \qquad (13.9)$$

$$= p(\theta^t = \theta_a \mid data),$$

where we obtained the final line of (13.9) by remembering that the jumping distribution is a valid probability distribution, and hence must integrate to 1. The above expression dictates that the probability density for the next step of the Markov chain is the same as the current density, which, by assumption, equals the posterior. Thus, if we reach the posterior density (which we will do asymptotically since our change is ergodic and aperiodic), then our Markov chain will stay there. This amounts to requiring that our Markov chain at equilibrium is *reversible*. This means that if we run our chain backwards we would have the same probability densities.

13.6.4 The intuition behind the accept-reject rule of Metropolis and detailed balance

Only one accept–reject rule works with the symmetric proposal distribution of the Metropolis algorithm. This dictates that we always move to a new parameter value if its posterior density is higher there, and that we only move probabilistically if its value is lower, with a probability given by the ratio of the proposed density at the new location compared to its current value. No other rule will work.

We can think of all (reasonable) rules as existing on a spectrum. At one extreme is the case where we always accept, corresponding to the drunkard's random walk we discussed in Section 13.5. At the other extreme, we have the Hillary climb, which only accepts a new parameter value if its posterior density is higher. While these are the extremes, all rules on the spectrum can be related back to the following ratio:

$$r = \begin{cases} 1, & \text{if } p(\theta_{t+1} \mid data) \geq p(\theta_t \mid data) \\ \dfrac{p(\theta_{t+1} \mid data)}{p(\theta_t \mid data)} \pm \epsilon, & \text{if } p(\theta_{t+1} \mid data) < p(\theta_t \mid data), \end{cases} \qquad (13.10)$$

where $\epsilon > 0$. Considering the + case, this means that we move towards the drunkard's walk end of the spectrum, and our sampler will give too much weight to lower posterior values. By contrast, the – case does the opposite and gives too much weight to the peaks of the posterior, as per Hillary. As Figure 13.9 illustrates, we can view the just-right Metropolis rule as being the knife-edge case on the spectrum of rules, where the 'distance' between our sampling approximation and the actual posterior goes to zero (at least for infinitely long Markov chains).

When we tune this rule just right, our Markov chain satisfies the principle of *detailed balance* when it reaches equilibrium. This means that for any two points in the stationary distribution, the probability of transition from one location to the other is the same both ways.

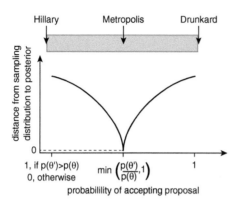

Figure 13.9 How the probability of accepting a proposal affects whether the MCMC sampling distribution converges to the posterior. Note that this is a conceptual representation and should be not interpreted quantitatively.

What is the intuition behind this seemingly innocuous result? Imagine that you work as a conservationist for a national park, where unfortunately a chemical spill has just released toxic waste into a lake (see Figure 13.10). To begin with, the chemical is relatively localised to the site where the spill occurred, which happens to be in the part of the lake not used for swimming. At this point in time, there is a net flux of the chemical from this side towards the swimming side (left-hand panel). This diffusion process continues until equilibrium, when the chemical is evenly distributed throughout the whole body of water. At this point, the flux of chemical from the non-swimming zone into the swimming zone is the same, meaning that the net flux is zero (right-hand panel). This maintains roughly the same number of chemical particles on either side of the barrier.

We can think of the chemical as representing probability mass. In the beginning, there is a considerable flow of probability from place to place, as our Markov chains traverse posterior space, uncovering new peaks and crossing undiscovered valleys. To reach equilibrium, where we have a stationary distribution, we require that the flux of probability from one place to another – like the flux of chemical particles from the swimming to the non-swimming area – is exactly balanced. Luckily enough for us as statisticians (not swimmers), this is what the principle of detailed balance exactly stipulates, ensuring that our stationary distribution stays that way.

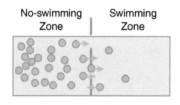 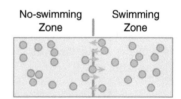

Figure 13.10 The principle of detailed balance explained through swimming. Immediately after a chemical spill (left), the chemical particles are relatively localised in the no-swimming zone, and there is a net flux of particles from this area into the swimming area. After some time, the chemical particles reach equilibrium, with roughly equal numbers of them in each zone and a net flux of zero from one zone into the other. We can think of the chemical particles as representing probability mass.

13 ○ 7　EFFICIENCY OF CONVERGENCE: THE IMPORTANCE OF CHOOSING THE RIGHT PROPOSAL SCALE

For detailed balance to be satisfied for our Metropolis algorithm, we required that the proposal distribution be symmetric. But what sorts of distribution might we actually use here? A common choice is a normal distribution centred on the current location of our Markov chain in parameter space. Since this distribution is symmetric about its mean, the probability of choosing a point

θ_a from θ_b is the same as the other way round (see Figure 13.11). Another benefit of this distribution is that it generalises well to multidimensional settings, becoming the multivariate normal.

Whatever choice of normal distribution for our proposal, so long as it is centred on the current value of the sampler, we will obtain convergence to the posterior for an infinitely long chain (see Section 13.6). However, we usually do not have an infinite amount of time to run our Markov chains, and would like them to converge as fast as possible. The only choice available to us is the standard deviation of the normal distribution, σ, so we might wonder: Does changing this parameter have any effect

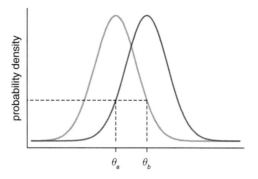

Figure 13.11 The symmetry of a normal distribution as a proposal makes it an attractive choice. Here the probability of proposing θ_a from θ_b is the same as in the opposite direction.

on the rate of convergence? Our answer would be a resounding yes!

Figure 13.12 illustrates that the rate at which Metropolis converges to the posterior distribution is highly sensitive to the Metropolis step size (characterised by the standard deviation of the normal proposal density). Using a step size that is too small (top panels of Figure 13.12) means it takes the sampler a long time to find areas of high density. Using these samples to reconstruct the posterior, we obtain a density that is highly dependent on the start location of the chain, with a bulk of probability mass away from the heart of posterior probability mass. If instead we use a step size that is too high (bottom panels of Figure 13.12), we reject the majority of proposals, since most of parameter space is low and flat, meaning that we get a highly autocorrelated chain with low numbers of effective samples (see Section 12.10 for a refresher of this concept). Only when our step size is just right (middle panels) do we obtain a Markov chain that mixes well and looks roughly like white noise (the type of noise we get when we turn on a radio that is not tuned to a station).

We can quantify how much better the just-right step size is by estimating the effective sample size of each Markov chain (see Figure 13.13). The samplers with step lengths that are either too long or too short have a large degree of autocorrelation compared with the just-right case (see the left-hand panel of Figure 13.13). The just-right case has an effective sample size of approximately 160 out of 1000 total samples (see the middle panel of Figure 13.13), much better than the too-small case ($n_{eff} \approx 4$) and the too-large one ($n_{eff} \approx 25$). However, while the autocorrelation is relatively low for the just-right Metropolis sampler, it still falls far short of the performance of the independent sampler, which would achieve an effective sample size of 1000.

The importance of step size for RWM (2D example)

The Kolmogorov–Smirnov test statistic comparing the posterior density to the sampling density is displayed in the right-hand panel of Figure 13.13. This statistic provides a simple quantification (compared to the Kullback–Leibler divergence) between the empirical and actual CDFs. The closer it is to zero, the nearer the sampling distribution is to the actual. It should not strictly be used for data where repeated samples occur, but we could not resist using it here since it is easy to interpret. This shows that the just-right sampler converges to the true posterior at a faster rate than either of the extreme step sizes. However, in the same graph, we illustrate the results for an independent sampler, and find that its convergence is considerably faster than even the best Metropolis case.

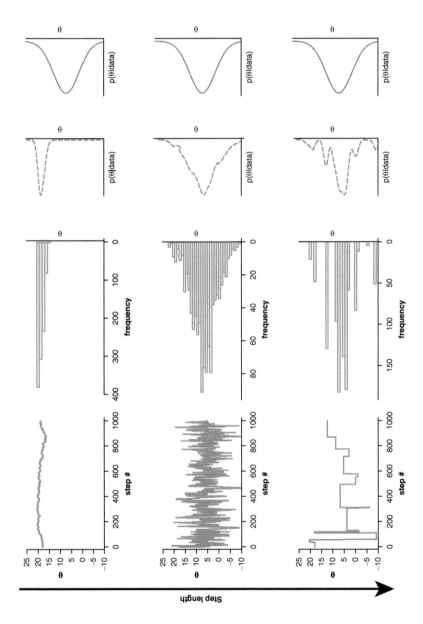

Figure 13.12 The effect of proposal step length on sampling: small steps (top row), large steps (bottom row) and medium-sized steps (middle row). Left column: the path of the sampler over time. Left-middle column: the distribution of binned samples. Right-middle column: the reconstructed posterior. Right column: the actual posterior. The samplers were all started at the same point, away from the bulk of probability mass.

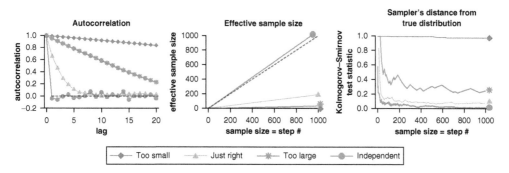

Figure 13.13   Comparing the performance of different step sizes in terms of chain autocorrelation (left), effective sample size (middle) and the distance between the sampling and posterior distribution (right) for the Metropolis sampler with various step sizes (see legend) against independent samples from the posterior (red circles). In the left and middle panels the ideal performance of a sampler is shown as a dashed grey line.

13.7.1 MCMC as finding and exploring the typical set

A nice intuition for understanding an MCMC algorithm comes from *information theory*.[2] It is common in Bayesian inference for the majority of the posterior probability to be confined to a small area of parameter space, particularly for more complex models. The rest of the posterior terrain is low and flat, meaning that if we drew independent samples from our posterior it would be very unlikely to end up here. We call the set of most likely outcomes rather loosely the *typical set*.

We can consider an ideal MCMC algorithm as being composed of two steps: finding the typical set and exploring it. We want to find the typical set since this is where the majority of the posterior probability mass sits. We do not want to concern ourselves with sampling outside this region since these parameter values would be highly unlikely. We need to explore the typical set because we want to build up an accurate map of the actual posterior density in those areas with the highest probability mass.

We can use these principles to explain further the behaviour of the Metropolis samplers with either too-small or too-large step sizes. The one that does not step far enough spends a long time finding the typical set; too long. The sampler that steps too far can find the typical set easily enough but is not very good at exploring it, since most of its proposed steps are rejected. This high rejection rate results in a rather coarse fit of the sample-reconstructed distribution to the actual posterior (see the bottom-right panels of Figure 13.12). The just-right step size sampler does reasonably well in both finding and then exploring the typical set. (However, we shall see in Chapter 15 how we can do better.)

13.7.2 Speeding up convergence: tuning the proposal distribution

What is the optimal rate of acceptance for our MCMC sampler to converge on the posterior at the fastest rate? It turns out that this depends on the type of algorithm we are implementing, but for the Metropolis algorithm an acceptance rate of 0.44 for one-dimensional models and 0.23 for models with more dimensions leads to optimal convergence as measured by a number of criteria,

---

[2]The idea to think of MCMC this way came from an excellent lecture by Michael Betancourt: https://www.youtube.com/watch?v=pHsuIaPbNbY.

across a range of target densities [30, 31]. Can we use this knowledge to help tune our Metropolis sampler dynamically as it runs? It turns out the answer to this is yes, but care is needed to ensure that we still converge to the posterior distribution.

In reality, it is often easier to split the algorithm into two stages:

1 Run a training algorithm to find the optimal proposal distribution parameters.
2 Initialise new chains and run them using a proposal distribution with tuned parameters.

An example training stage is illustrated in Figure 13.14, where we start a Metropolis Markov chain and update its proposal step size at regular intervals, in order to bring the acceptance rate closer to the ideal of 0.44 (our example is the one-dimensional example considered in Figure 13.12). We start two chains – one with a step size that is too low, the other taking steps that are too long – and then subtract a small amount (ε_t) from the step size if the acceptance rate is too low, or, conversely, we increase the step size if it is too high (ε_t decreases with MCMC iteration number t). Here both chains converge to approximately the same optimal step size. We actually used this optimal step size in a second stage of MCMC to produce the just-right panels in Figures 13.12 and 13.13.

Note that this adaptive MCMC algorithm we used here is simplistic, and many more nuanced variants are possible where, for example, we account for our distance from the ideal acceptance rate.

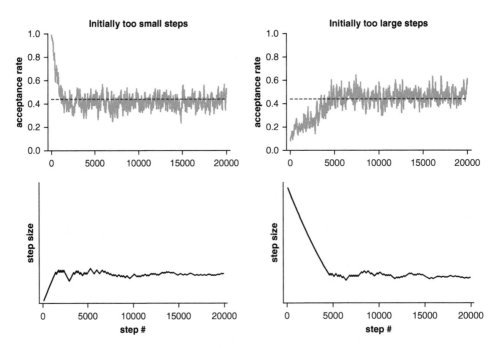

Figure 13.14 Illustrating an adaptive Metropolis Markov chain in action. Top row: the acceptance rate over time for Markov chains with different initial step lengths (left = small steps, right = large steps). Bottom row: the average step length, which is adjusted at regular intervals. If the acceptance rate is below the optimum (0.44) we decrease the step length; if it is above the optimum we increase it. The amount ε_t by which the step sizes are adjusted decays at a rate $\varepsilon_t = 0.99\,\varepsilon_{t-1}$.

13○8 METROPOLIS-HASTINGS

Suppose that we believe that the returns of a single stock X_t can be modelled by a normal sampling distribution (see Section 8.4.6):

$$X_t \sim \mathcal{N}(\mu, \sigma), \qquad\qquad\qquad (13.11)$$

where μ is the stock's mean return and σ is its standard deviation. While μ can, in theory, be negative, it is not meaningful for $\sigma < 0$, since a standard deviation must always be positive. Unfortunately, this causes problems for our Metropolis algorithm, since a symmetric proposal distribution can propose a negative value for σ. Further, when $\sigma < 0$ the normal PDF is undefined, and hence we cannot use our Metropolis update rule to determine whether to accept the step.

Naively we might think that we can simply reject all steps that propose $\sigma < 0$, and still sample from the posterior density. However, this is not the case. If we reject all steps where $\sigma < 0$, we will generate relatively few samples from areas of parameter space where σ is close to zero (see Figure 13.15). Intuitively, the areas near zero have only one side from which they can be reached – positive values of σ. This contrasts with higher parameter values which can be reached from either side. This asymmetry in neighbours means that we eventually generate too few proposals near zero.

Constrained parameters? Use Metropolis-Hastings

The Metropolis algorithm does not work when we have boundaries in parameter values. So how can we fix things? One way is to transform parameters so that they are then unconstrained, and then sample using this transformed parameter space. In our stock example, one way to transform σ would be to take its log. Since $\log(\sigma)$ can be positive or negative, we can use the Metropolis algorithm to sample from it and then re-transform back to σ space. However, because we have used a non-linear transform of variables, we need to use something called a *Jacobian* to ensure that we account for the squashing and stretching of probability mass. Although not difficult for this example, in more complex settings it can become cumbersome to use Jacobians, and instead we prefer to use the Metropolis–Hastings algorithm.

The Metropolis–Hastings algorithm is a modification that we make to the basic Metropolis algorithm to allow for an asymmetric proposal distribution. What does this mean? For a Metropolis sampler, we used a normal distribution whose mean equalled the current

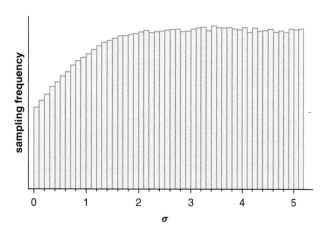

Figure 13.15 The sampling distribution that results from using simple rejection sampling to sample values for a non-negative parameter. Here we use a normal distribution as a proposal distribution, and reject any negative samples of the parameter. We assume that the posterior density is locally flat over the region we sample from.

parameter value. However, even if the mean of the proposal distribution satisfies the parameter constraints, it is possible that the proposed value will be on the wrong side of the boundary. What we need is a proposal distribution that always produces parameter values in the allowed region of parameter space. This means we need an asymmetric proposal distribution. In our σ example, we could use a log-normal distribution that naturally has support only for positive parameter values. Accordingly, we might use the following distribution as a proposal:

$$\sigma_{t+1} \sim \log\text{-}\mathcal{N}\left(\log(\sigma_t) - \frac{1}{2}d^2, d\right), \tag{13.12}$$

where σ_t is the current value of the parameter, and d characterises the step length (see Figure 13.16). The reason that we choose this parameterisation of the distribution is because it has a mean of σ_t. However, unlike the normal case, this distribution is not symmetric and allows only positive parameter values.

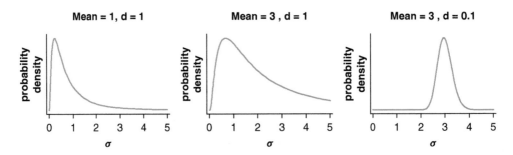

Figure 13.16   Three densities corresponding to different input values for an asymmetric proposal distribution. The distribution here is a log-$\mathcal{N}\left(\log(\sigma) - \frac{1}{2}d^2, d\right)$.

We have fixed the proposal distribution so that it will not propose negative parameter values. However, now we must correct the accept–reject rule to ensure it still produces samples from the posterior. Fortunately, this modification to the basic Metropolis accept–reject rule is simple, with the ratio r changed to:

$$r = \frac{p(\theta_{t+1} \mid data)}{p(\theta_t \mid data)} \times \frac{J(\theta_t \mid \theta_{t+1})}{J(\theta_{t+1} \mid \theta_t)}, \tag{13.13}$$

where the first part of the expression is the same as basic Metropolis, and the second is the correction due to asymmetric jumping. Here $J(\theta_t \mid \theta_{t+1})$ is the proposal probability density at θ_t if the current position of the sampler is θ_{t+1}. Note that, when $J(\theta_t \mid \theta_{t+1}) = J(\theta_{t+1} \mid \theta_t)$, the proposal distribution is symmetric, and r collapses down to the Metropolis ratio. If we use this new ratio, r, instead of the basic Metropolis one in our stepping algorithm, we are assured of asymptotic convergence to the posterior density.

13.9   JUDGING CONVERGENCE

We have discussed what it means for a Markov chain to converge to the posterior distribution. In Figure 13.13 we even measured it. If we knew the posterior distribution, then we could measure the degree of correspondence between the sampling distribution and the actual using a number of criteria. We previously used the Kolmogorov–Smirnov test statistic as an approximate measure; a better attempt might use the Kullback–Leibler (KL) measure (see Section 10.5.3 for an explanation), although there are many choices here dependent on the goals of an analysis.

In pretty much all applied examples of Bayesian inference, we do not know the posterior distribution, and hence measuring convergence is difficult. It is a bit of a Catch-22 situation. In order to decide whether our sampling algorithm converges to the posterior, we need the posterior. However, to get the posterior we need to do sampling.

We could actually use the KL divergence, but with an un-normalised posterior, recognising that a distribution that minimises this will also minimise the KL from the actual posterior. However, this calculation is difficult as it involves a nasty high-dimensional integral, although this forms the basis of some approximate methods, such as *variational Bayes*. So how can we proceed? One of the nicest ways to monitor convergence of a sampling distribution is with the methods first suggested by Andrew Gelman and Donald Rubin [16]. Like much of this book, we will explain this methodology using an analogy, and afterwards describe the approach more formally.

13.9.1 Bob's bees in a house

Imagine that there is a dark house of unknown size and shape, whose blueprints we would like to determine. Luckily, we have at our disposal a number of Bumble Bees[3] that are each fitted with a tracker that charts their location as they move. We hope that by releasing these bees and tracking their location at discrete time intervals (these locations represent samples), we can eventually reconstruct an accurate three-dimensional image of the house. Imagine that, at first, we release only a single bee. A question that occurs to us is: How long do we have to wait before we can be confident that our bee has moved throughout the whole house? We think for a second, then realise that we can use its tracker to look at its path over time. If we have been monitoring the path over some period and its distribution of locations does not appear to be changing, then does this mean that we are done?

No, it does not. Imagine that some of the doors in the house are very small, making it less likely that the bee – which we assume moves randomly throughout the building – will pass through. It is possible that our bee is temporarily stuck in a single room of the house (see the top row of Figure 13.17). When we look at the bee's path, we have the illusion that it has converged on the floor plan of the whole house because the distribution of locations does not appear to change over time. However, this is a statistical mirage; if we waited a bit longer, our bee would eventually go through the door and move around the rest of the house.

So if we wait a bit longer we may, now, in hindsight think that the bee's path represents the layout of the entire house. However, just as we are about to call our bee in for nectar, our tracker shows that the bee has moved into a completely new area, with a size that dwarfs our original estimates of the house floor space. Damn! It seems that, however long we wait, we are always destined to face this type of issue, particularly because we assume that we have no idea of the actual house size and shape.

---

[3]We first heard this example in a lecture by Bob Carpenter (https://www.youtube.com/watch?v=qQFF4tPgeWI) and thought it nicely analogises the approach that Gelman and Rubin suggested for measuring convergence, so we describe a version of it here.

Fortunately, we have read Gelman and Rubin's article, and this gives us an idea. Suppose that we can release a number of bees in random, at diverse locations throughout the house. (For this analogy to work we assume that the bees do not interact with one another; they are loner bees.) We then monitor the paths of all the bees over time. Now looking at our bees, we can see that some of them have remained in parts of the house; they have not yet passed through the small doors in order to mix with the other bees. This is now obvious to us because we can actually see that some bees' paths never cross one another (see the bottom row of Figure 13.17).

Gelman and Rubin's idea is that, if we release a sufficiently large number of such bees and monitor their paths over time, we can determine if the bees have explored the entire house. To do this we attempt to differentiate between the paths produced by the separate bees. If we cannot tell which bee has produced which path, then this is a reasonable indication that the bees have searched the whole house.

Of course, this method relies on a few things. First, how do we determine the number of bees to release to give us peace of mind that we have converged on the house's floor plan? Second, we need to ensure that we release the bees in sufficiently diverse locations throughout the house, to be relatively confident that they will eventually move through the doors to each of the rooms. But how do we determine what is 'sufficiently diverse here', particularly as we do not know the layout of the house?

These are good questions, and there are no simple rules here. In practice, maybe releasing a few dozen bees might suffice. However, this number clearly depends on the size and shape of the house. For a typical apartment, we imagine that this would be fine. For a country mansion with lots of narrow passages, then perhaps a few dozen are not enough; we need to release a few hundred! Similarly for the release strategy. We want to make sure we randomise our releases over the space of the house to give our bees a wide variety of starting locations. But it is difficult in practice to determine just how to do this. If we had rough blueprints of the house, then we could probably use this to randomly place our bees at dispersed locations in the building. In some cases, we may have such a rough approximation, but in many others, we will not. For these latter applications, we will just have to choose a suitably wide distribution from which to start our bees. We then hope that if their paths converge over time, we have arrived at an accurate representation of the house.

However, we can never be sure. There is always the chance that a room is of a sufficiently weird shape – being, for example, both long and narrow – meaning we will have to wait a long time for our bees to reach its corners. Similarly, if some of the doors are a tight squeeze for the bees, then it may take years for any of them to pass through them. (Anyone who has tried to get a trapped bee to go out through a window knows this difficulty.) This is where it helps to have an idea of the house's shape before we actually release the bees. If we have a rough idea of its architecture (for example, through maximum likelihood estimates), then we should not get so many nasty surprises when eventually we come to do the experiment. As ever, the more we educate ourselves about a problem, the more we can be confident in our results.

▶

Bob's bees: the importance of using multiple bees (chains) to judge MCMC convergence

13.9.2 Using multiple chains to monitor convergence

From the previous analogy, we hope that it is not too much of a stretch to see that running multiple Markov chains, initialised at highly dispersed parts of parameter space, is crucial. Its importance cannot be overstated, and we have seen many an unhappy student go through the following process:

1   Write model (boring).
2   Code model (even more boring).

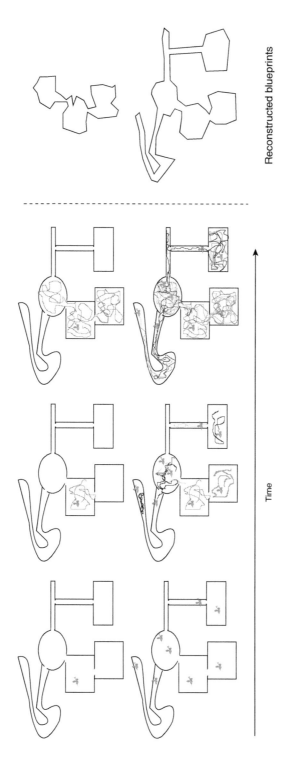

Time

Reconstructed blueprints

Figure 13.17 Using Bob's bees to reproduce blueprints of a house. The three left columns show the effect of using a single bee (top) and multiple bees (bottom) to randomly traverse the house. Right: blueprints reconstructed from the paths of the bees.

3   Run MCMC and get results (excitement!).
4   The chain looks to have converged. (More excitement - go to the pub!)
5   Tomorrow professor asks, 'How many chains did you run? Only one?! Run more!' (Trepidation, and annoyance at the professor.)
6   Rerun with multiple chains. Convergence vanishes. (Hangover reaching a breaking point.)
7   Night(s) spent in the library. (Lonely desperation.)

OK, maybe not all students of Bayes go through all of the above, but we have all at least experienced some of them. In particular, the issue of running a single chain and mistakenly believing that your chains have converged on the posterior distribution. Unfortunately, current software makes it all too easy to fall into this trap. It is also tempting at first because running more chains can take more time (although with modern hardware, which allows parallel processing, this is less of an issue). However, we reiterate the point once more: running a single chain is never a good idea. In fact, we would advocate running as many chains in parallel as is feasible. For relatively simple models, running only four to eight chains may be fine but, as the complexity of the model increases, it is often a good idea to run a few tens of chains. As we tried to make clear in the bee analogy, we can never be sure that we have reached convergence, but the more chains we run, the less likely this is to occur.

So after we have decided on the number of chains to run, how do we monitor their convergence? As we tried to explain in the bee analogy, we can be fairly confident that the chains have converged on the posterior distribution when it is impossible to – by just looking at the samples of one chain – differentiate one chain from all others. But what do we mean by 'differentiate one chain from all others'?

Imagine that we start with the path taken by each bee and look at the range of locations surveyed in a particular direction (see Figure 13.18). If the ranges of motion do not overlap across the different paths, then we clearly can still differentiate one path from the others (top panels of Figure 13.18). In this case imagine that we take the paths, and colour some random parts of them so that they correspond to the wrong bee. If the paths were originally separate, then it

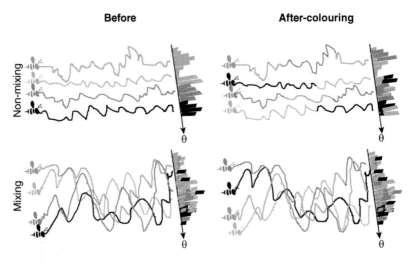

Figure 13.18 Non-mixing (top) and better mixing (bottom) of bee paths, before (left) and after (right) they are randomly recoloured. In both cases, the histogram corresponds to the number of samples at that particular distance along the axis.

should be visually obvious that we have done some fiddling. This is because there is now mixing between the resultant paths, and we can no longer resolve between the histograms. By contrast, if the paths were originally well mixed, then it is much harder to notice that we have been a-colourin' (bottom panels of Figure 13.18). Moving now back to Markov chains, this latter case, where the chains cross over one another's paths time and time again, is a much better candidate for convergence than the case where there is no mixing.

Now that we understand qualitatively how to tell whether our chains have converged, we discuss how to do it quantitatively, through a bit of simple maths.

13.9.3 Using within- and between-chain variation to estimate convergence

Going back to our bee example, how can we create a mathematical rule that allows us to differentiate between the top and bottom panels of Figure 13.18? The most common method, due to Rubin and Gelman, is to calculate the variance of samples within each chain and compare it to the between-chain variance. Intuitively, if these are about the same, then it indicates that we would find it difficult, on the basis of the sampling distribution alone, to differentiate between samples from one chain versus those from any of the others (see Figure 13.19).

So how do we calculate the within- and between-chain variances? If we imagine that our parameter space is one-dimensional – in other words, our model has only a single free parameter θ – then we could calculate the within variance, W, by [14]:

$$W = \frac{1}{m}\sum_{j=1}^{m} s_j^2, \tag{13.14}$$

where $s_j^2 = (1/n-1)\sum_{i=1}^{n}(\theta_{ij} - \bar{\theta}_j)^2$ is the estimator for the sample variance of chain j (see the left-hand panel of Figure 13.20 for a diagrammatic explanation of this calculation). Note here that we index θ by both i and j. So θ_{ij} corresponds to the ith sample from the jth chain, $\bar{\theta}_j$ is the mean sample of the jth chain, and m indicates the number of chains. In expression (13.14) we are hence just averaging the sample variances across all chains.

To calculate the between-chain variability, we want to compare the mean of each chain with that of the overall mean (see the right-hand panel of Figure 13.20). Averaging this over all the chains we obtain:

$$B = \frac{n}{m-1}\sum_{i=1}^{m}(\bar{\theta}_j - \bar{\theta})^2, \tag{13.15}$$

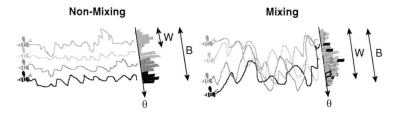

Figure 13.19 The within-path variation (*W*) versus the between-path variation (*B*) for the case of non-mixing (left) and mixing (right) paths.

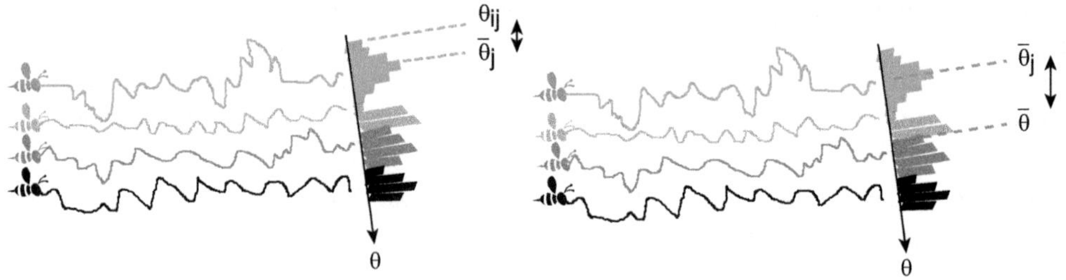

Figure 13.20 Illustrating the calculation of within- (left) and between-chain (right) variance.

where $\bar{\theta}_j$ and $\bar{\theta}$ are the jth and overall chain's sample means, respectively. The factor of n at the front of expression (13.15) is because our estimator is based on the jth chain's sample mean, which is calculated using n samples. The $m-1$ in the denominator is analogous to the $n-1$ in the sample variance formula, and is to ensure this estimator is unbiased.

This process is the same method that is used in ANOVA modelling, where variation in data is apportioned to that originating from within groups and that due to between-group sources. Gelman and Rubin's idea was to use estimators of the posterior variance – one accounting for total variance (namely, the variance from both within- and between-chain sources) and another due solely to the within-chain variation – and then take the ratio of these quantities. If our chains have converged, this ratio should be close to 1. Explicitly, they first calculate an estimator of the posterior variance by a weighted average of W and B [16]:

$$var(\hat{\theta} \,|\, data) = \frac{n-1}{n}W + \frac{1}{n}B$$

$$= W + \frac{1}{n}(B-W).$$

(13.16)

When written this way, it is apparent that if $B \to W$, or $n \to \infty$, then the above estimator $var(\hat{\theta} \,|\, data) \to W$. However, when we first start the chains, it will be the case that $B \gg W$, since we start the chains in an overdispersed position. Gelman and Rubin suggest that we calculate the ratio:

$$\hat{R} = \sqrt{\frac{W + \frac{1}{n}(B-W)}{W}},$$

(13.17)

where initially $\hat{R} \gg 1$. Their idea was that, if this ratio exceeds a threshold (in practice, a rule of thumb is to use $\hat{R} \leq 1.1$ as a cut-off), then our chains have not mixed well and we cannot assume our posterior has converged. However, as $B \to W$, then $\hat{R} \to 1$, and we are more confident in using our sampling distribution for inference.

In practice, we estimate $\hat{R}$ across all of our parameters, and we continue to run our chains until all of our parameters satisfy $\hat{R} < 1.1$.

13.9.4 Two types of non-convergence

We have said that a chain converges if its sampling distribution is stationary. However, it is easy for a chain to become stuck in a region of parameter space, and hence its distribution appears stationary. To detect this type of non-convergence, we have discussed using multiple non-interacting chains, each of which is started in some disparate part of parameter space. If one of the chains becomes stuck in a part of parameter space, we can resolve between the paths of each of the chains, and we conclude that we have not converged on the posterior distribution. We call this type of non-convergence poor *inter-chain* mixing (see the left-hand panel of Figure 13.21).

There is, however, a second scenario, where our individual chains mix with others but do not mix well with themselves, which we call poor *intra-chain* mixing (see the right-hand panel of Figure 13.21).

What do we mean by 'mix with itself', and why do we care? This type of non-convergence means that we cannot be confident that our chains have converged on the posterior because their individual sampling distributions are non-stationary. This is characterised by a chain that – if you split it in half and considered each of the halves as a separate chain – would fail to show mixing by the $\hat{R}$ measure we considered before (see Figure 13.22). In fact, this is exactly the way that Stan calculates $\hat{R}$ [8]. It splits all chains in two, then – considering the resultant half-chains as independent – calculates $\hat{R}$ using expression (13.17).

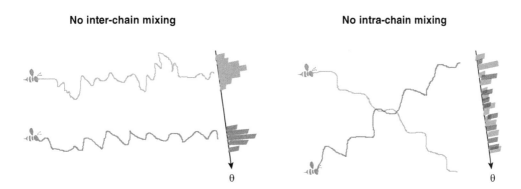

Figure 13.21 Non-convergence due to (left) no mixing between chains and (right) poor within-chain mixing.

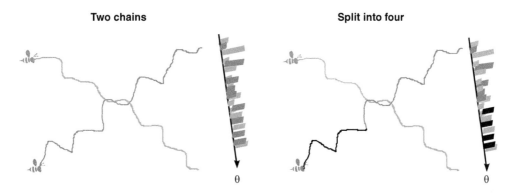

Figure 13.22 Diagnosing intra-chain non-convergence by splitting the chains on the left into two (shown on the right).

13.9.5 Warm-up

The previous sections of this chapter illustrate that our chains have not converged if $\hat{R} \gg 1$, for any of our parameters. If this is true, we need to run the chains for longer, change our algorithm, or (more often) change our model to speed up the rate of convergence. Once our chain exhibits good convergence characteristics, then, and only then, can we think of its samples as representing the posterior.

However, even after convergence diagnostics indicate convergence, the first part of the chain is nonetheless likely to reflect its starting position – which is selected in a fairly haphazard fashion – and hence is unlikely to be representative of the posterior. So we probably should not include our first few samples in our final posterior sample, but where do we draw the line? Sometimes a point where the chains reach the stationary distribution is obvious from visually inspecting the path of the chains over time (see Figure 13.23), but usually, things are less clear-cut. Following Gelman et al. [14], we recommend discarding the first half of chains that appear to have converged as a default method. The authors call this first part of the chains *warm-up*, where they have yet to converse on the posterior distribution (see the shaded area of the bottom panel in Figure 13.23).

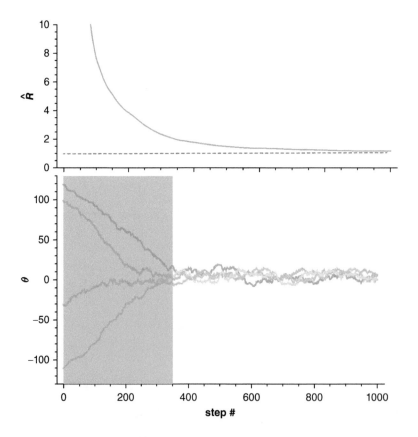

Figure 13.23 Bottom: the paths of initially dispersed chains converge over time. Top: $\hat{R}$ computed as the chains run. In this case, we would discard the first 300–400 samples (the shaded region) as warm-up.

This protocol is only a rule of thumb. There are circumstances where we can almost immediately assume our samples are representative of the posterior, and hence discarding the first half of the chains is quite conservative. There are also times when discarding the first half of chains may not be conservative enough (for example, sometimes when sampling from multimodal distributions).

13 ○ 10 EFFECTIVE SAMPLE SIZE REVISITED

In Section 12.10 we introduced the concept of an effective sample size for a dependent sampling algorithm. This concept arose from considering the action of an ideal sampling algorithm, which would independently sample from the posterior. In most cases, this level of efficiency is not realisable, and instead we have to use dependent samples – where the next sample value depends on the current value. For dependent samplers, the incremental benefit of one extra sample is less than for an individual sample from an independent sampling algorithm; intuitively, there is less new information in each further sample, since each sample is partly determined by the previous value. This reduced efficiency is crystallised in the concept of effective sample size, which estimates – fairly crudely – the number of independent samples which are equivalent to a given dependent sample size. We want to create a sampling algorithm that generates the maximum number of effective samples per second.

In our previous discussion of effective sample size, we found that the effective sample size is negatively impacted by the autocorrelation of Markov chains. Intuitively, lower autocorrelation means that our Markov chain is closer to generating independent samples. We previously used a die example to illustrate how to estimate an effective sample size. We now describe a more general method for calculating effective sample size, which we can apply to the samples outputted by MCMC algorithms. The method is more mathematical than our previous discussion, but we aim to keep the intuition central to our explanation. (If you don't feel like wading through all this maths, then you can skip ahead to the end-of-chapter summaries, since the concept is not entirely new.) We nonetheless feel it is useful to understand the mathematical basis of effective sample size estimation, if only to be able to fully appreciate the results of a Stan run.

First, imagine that we have access to truly independent samples from our posterior. In this case, we might want to determine the accuracy in estimating a particular posterior characteristic, for example its mean: $\mathbb{E}(\theta \,|\, data) = \mu$. Since our samples are independent we can use the central limit theorem (see Section 3.5 for a refresher) to derive an approximate sampling distribution of our estimator:

$$\hat{\mu} \approx \mathcal{N}\left(\mu, \frac{\sigma}{\sqrt{T}}\right), \tag{13.18}$$

where we have assumed that we are using the sample mean estimator $\left(\hat{\mu} = \frac{1}{T}\sum_{i=1}^{T}\theta_i\right)$ and that T – the sample size – is large. From expression (13.18), we see that the convergence rate is a function of $\sim 1/\sqrt{T}$. This convergence rate is the best we can hope to attain since it pertains to the independent sampling case.

One way to define the effective sample size, n_{eff}, for a dependent sampler is so that its convergence rate is proportional to $1/\sqrt{n_{eff}}$. So, for a dependent sampler, the convergence rate is a function of the square root of the effective sample size, whereas for the independent sampler it depends on the square root of the actual sample size.

Imagine that we use a single chain with T samples in our MCMC algorithm. An estimator of the posterior mean is given by $\hat{\mu} = \frac{1}{T}\sum_{t=1}^{T}\theta_t$. We want to estimate the variance of our estimator since this determines its rate of convergence. Taking the variance we obtain:

$$T^2 var(\hat{\mu}) = var\left(\sum_{t=1}^{T}\theta_t\right)$$

$$= \sum_{t=1}^{T} var(\theta \mid data) + \sum_{t=1}^{T}\sum_{\tau\geq 1}^{T} cov(\theta_t, \theta_{t-\tau}).$$

(13.19)

If our sampler produced independent samples, then the covariance terms in expression (13.19) would disappear. However, our dependent sampler produces autocorrelated samples, therefore $cov(\theta_t, \theta_{t-\tau}) = \rho_\tau var(\theta \mid data)$, where ρ_τ is the autocorrelation at a lag τ. Substituting this into expression (13.19) we obtain:

$$Tvar(\hat{\mu}) = \left(1 + 2\sum_{\tau=1}^{T}\rho_\tau\right)var(\theta \mid data),$$

(13.20)

where we have cancelled a common T term on each side of the expression. If we consider the case where we have m chains and take the limit as our sample size becomes infinite, we obtain:

$$\lim_{T\to\infty} mTvar(\hat{\mu}) = \left(1 + 2\sum_{\tau=1}^{\infty}\rho_\tau\right)var(\theta \mid data).$$

(13.21)

Comparing this with an equivalent independent sampler where $n_{eff} = mT$, we obtain:

$$\lim_{T\to\infty} n_{eff} var(\hat{\mu}) = var(\theta \mid data).$$

(13.22)

Rearranging the previous two expressions, we obtain the following expression for the effective sample size [14]:

$$n_{eff} = \frac{mT}{1 + 2\sum_{\tau=1}^{\infty}\rho_\tau}.$$

(13.23)

This expression indicates the theoretical effective sample size of a Markov chain and illustrates that as the autocorrelation increases, the number of effective samples decreases. However, how do we actually calculate the above expression, since in reality we do not have an infinite sample size and do not know ρ_τ?

There are a number of methods to do this, but they typically amount to estimating ρ_τ using some measure of the sample autocorrelation, $\hat{\rho}_\tau$. The sample autocorrelation is then substituted in for ρ_τ in expression (13.23). We also replace the infinite sum with a sum over only the first T' terms, where T' is the first odd positive integer when $\hat{\rho}_{T'+1} + \hat{\rho}_{T'+2}$ is negative [8]. This is because, due to sampling error, the higher-order estimates of sampler autocorrelation are noisy and often become negative. Stan actually uses fast Fourier transforms to calculate the sample autocorrelation simultaneously for all lags efficiently (see [1]).

13.10.1 Thinning samples to increase effective sample size

Once convergence is reached, we could make our samples look 'more independent' if we kept only every tenth, or hundredth, sample. These will naturally be less correlated than consecutive samples, meaning that they are more similar to the theoretical independent ideal. This process, where we take only every nth sample, is known as *thinning* a dependent sampler.

However, we notice that this really is just a trick – our sampler does not produce independent samples – and we are discarding information if we remove these samples from our final sample set. However, thinning can be worthwhile if we are dealing with a high-dimensional model, and computational memory is limited [14].

13 ⊙ 11   CHAPTER SUMMARY

Whoa, that was a lot of information! We began by considering the mechanics of the Random Walk Metropolis algorithm – one of the most fundamental and important methods in MCMC. We saw that its accept–reject rule for deciding whether to accept a proposed parameter value results in just the right balance of samples across the posterior landscape, sampling each point in proportion to its posterior height. By contrast, any deviations from this rule result in a sample of parameter values that does not reflect the posterior distribution. We learned that the Metropolis acceptance rule satisfies the principle of detailed balance, which ensures that the sampling algorithm converges to a unique stationary distribution which equals the posterior distribution.

We next saw that the decision of where to consider stepping next, through the proposal distribution, is crucial for the sampling efficiency of a Metropolis Markov chain. Too small a step size and our samplers will take a long time to explore the posterior space. If the steps are too large, then we hardly accept any proposals and our sampler gets stuck in areas of high density. We described the ideal behaviour of an MCMC algorithm as first finding the typical set (an area with the majority of probability mass) and then exploring it. A Markov chain with steps that are too small takes a long time to find the typical set. With larger step sizes we find the typical set quickly enough but we do not explore it well, resulting in a coarse approximation to those areas of parameter space with most probability mass.

We introduced the Metropolis–Hastings algorithm to allow us to sample from constrained parameter spaces, by using an asymmetric proposal distribution, whose support matches the posterior distribution. To allow for asymmetric stepping we were required to modify the ratio of basic Metropolis to take account of the asymmetry in jumping.

We described how judging the convergence of a given MCMC algorithm is tricky. There are no methods currently available that allow us to be certain that our algorithm has converged. However, by using a number of non-interacting chains, initialised at overdispersed locations in parameter space, we are much better able to guard against the faux convergence signals that can result from running a single chain. This method is not foolproof, however, and we should run as many chains as is feasible to minimise the risk of faux convergence. With many chains, we can compare the within-chain variation to that between them, and only have confidence in convergence when these two measures are of similar magnitude. Gelman and Rubin's $\hat{R}$ embodies this maxim and is the most widely used metric to determine Markov chain convergence. This quantity should be calculated for each of the parameters in our model, and we should be confident in convergence only if $\hat{R} \lesssim 1.1$ in all cases.

Once convergence has been obtained, we minimise the effect of the arbitrary initialisation distribution on our estimates of the posterior, by taking samples only after a so-called warm-up period (where we are confident we are sampling from the posterior). This period is not predetermined and varies dependent on the problem at hand. There are competing methods for determining the warm-up sample size, each with its own merits. However, here we favour conservatively discarding the first half of a Markov chain once convergence has been reached.

Finally, we saw that by accounting for the autocorrelation of our dependent sampler, we derived an expression for the effective sample size, which represents the equivalent number of independent samples.

It is hard to overstate the importance of understanding this chapter's content. Knowledge of the Metropolis algorithm, alongside methods to determine convergence of Markov chains, is essential to be able to undertake applied research. Equipped with this knowledge, you should also be able to critique the research of others. The Random Walk Metropolis algorithm also provides terra firma from which to attack other, faster, algorithms, particularly the Gibbs sampler in Chapter 14 and Hamiltonian Monte Carlo in Chapter 15. We shall see that these algorithms are just modified versions of the basic Metropolis and that, luckily, much of what we have learned here will also be applicable there.

13◯12 CHAPTER OUTCOMES

The reader should now be familiar with the following concepts:

- the intuition behind the Random Walk Metropolis algorithm
- the importance of the particular accept-reject rule that is used in Random Walk Metropolis, and how it helps us ensure detailed balance
- the fact that a symmetric proposal distribution results in a sampler that will converge asymptotically (in an infinite sample size) to the posterior
- the importance of tuning the proposal distribution characteristic step distance to ensure optimal exploration of the posterior density
- the use of Metropolis-Hastings to sample from posteriors with constrained parameters
- the difficulty judging whether an MCMC algorithm has converged to the posterior
- how monitoring the within- and between-chain variation, across multiple chains and initialised at wide starting locations, can help to minimise the risk of non-convergence
- the importance of a warm-up phase of MCMC to ensure that we do not produce posterior samples skewed towards the starting positions
- how increased Markov chain autocorrelation leads to smaller effective sample sizes

13◯13 PROBLEM SETS

Problem 13.1 Ticked off

Imagine once again that you are investigating the occurrence of Lyme disease in the UK. This is a vector-borne disease caused by bacteria of the species *Borrelia* which is carried by ticks. (The ticks pick up the infection by blood-feeding on animals or humans that are infected with *Borrelia*.) You decide to estimate the prevalence of these bacteria in ticks you collect from the grasslands and woodlands around Oxford.

You decide to use sample sizes of 100 ticks, out of which you count the number of ticks testing positive for *Borrelia*. You decide to use a binomial likelihood since you assume that the presence of *Borrelia* in one tick is independent of that in other ticks. Also, because you sample a relatively small area, you assume that the presence of *Borrelia* is identically distributed across ticks.

Problem 13.1.1 You specify a *beta*(1,1) distribution as a prior. Use independent sampling to estimate the prior predictive distribution (the same as the posterior predictive, except using sampling from the prior in the first step rather than the posterior), and show that its mean is approximately 50.

Problem 13.1.2 In a single sample you find that there are 6 ticks that test positive for *Borrelia*. Assuming a *beta*(1,1) prior, graph the posterior distribution, and find its mean.

Problem 13.1.3 Generate 100 independent samples from this distribution using your software's in-built (pseudo-)random-number generator. Graph this distribution. How does it compare to the PDF of the exact posterior? (*Hint*: in R the command is rbeta; in Matlab it is betarnd; in Mathematica it is RandomVariate[BetaDistribution...]; in Python it is numpy.random.beta.)

Problem 13.1.4 Determine the effect of increasing the sample size on predictive accuracy using the independent sampler to estimate the posterior mean. (*Hint*: for each sample you are essentially comparing the sample mean with the true mean of the posterior.)

Problem 13.1.5 Estimate the variance of the posterior using independent sampling for a sample size of 100. How does your sample estimate compare with the exact solution?

Problem 13.1.6 Create a proposal function for this problem that takes as input a current value of θ, along with a step size, and outputs a proposed value. For a proposal distribution here we use a normal distribution centred on the current θ value with a standard deviation (step size) of 0.1. This means you will need to generate a random θ from a normal distribution using your statistical software's in-built random-number generator. (*Hint*: the only slight modification you need to make here, to ensure that you do not get $\theta < 0$ or $\theta > 1$, is to use periodic boundary conditions. To do this we can use modular arithmetic. In particular, we set $\theta_{proposed} = \text{mod}(\theta_{proposed}, 1)$. The command for this in R is x%%1; in Matlab the command is mod(x,1); in Mathematica it is Mod(x,1); in Python it is x%1.)

Problem 13.1.7 Create the accept–reject function of Random Walk Metropolis that accepts as inputs both $\theta_{current}$ and $\theta_{proposed}$ and outputs the next value of θ.

Problem 13.1.8 Create a function that combines the previous two functions, so it takes as input a current value of $\theta_{current}$, generates a proposed $\theta_{proposed}$, and updates $\theta_{current}$ in accordance with the Metropolis accept–reject rule.

Problem 13.1.9 Create a fully working Random Walk Metropolis sampler. (*Hint*: you will need to iterate the last function. Use a uniformly distributed random number between 0 and 1 as a starting point.)

Problem 13.1.10 For a sample size of 100 from your Metropolis sampler compare the sampling distribution to the exact posterior. How does the estimated posterior compare with that obtained via independent sampling using the same sample size?

Problem 13.1.11 Run 1000 iterations, where in each iteration you run a single chain for 100 iterations. Store the results in a 1000 × 100 matrix. For each iterate calculate the sample mean. Graph the resulting distribution of sample means. Determine the accuracy of the MCMC at estimating the posterior mean.

Problem 13.1.12 Graph the distribution of the sample means for the second 50 observations of each chain. How does this result compare with that of the previous question? Why is there a difference?

Problem 13.1.13 Decrease the standard deviation (step size) of the proposal distribution to 0.01. For a sample size of 200, how does the posterior for a step size of 0.01 compare to that obtained for 0.1?

Problem 13.1.14 Increase the standard deviation (step size) of the proposal distribution to 1. For a sample size of 200, how does the posterior for a step size of 1 compare to that obtained for 0.1?

Problem 13.1.15 Suppose we collect data for a number of such samples (each of size 100), and find the following numbers of ticks that test positive for *Borrelia*: (3,2,8,25). Either calculate the new posterior exactly, or use sampling to estimate it. (*Hint*: in both cases make sure you include the original sample of 6.)

Problem 13.1.16 Generate samples from the posterior predictive distribution, and use these to test your model. What do these suggest about your model's assumptions?

Problem 13.1.17 A colleague suggests as an alternative that you use a beta-binomial likelihood instead of the binomial likelihood. This distribution has two uncertain parameters, $\alpha > 0$ and $\beta > 0$ (the other parameter is the sample size; $n = 100$ in this case), where the mean of the distribution is $n\alpha/(\alpha + \beta)$. Your colleague and you decide to use weakly informative priors of the form $\alpha \sim \Gamma(1,\frac{1}{8})$ and $\beta \sim \Gamma(10,1)$. (Here we use the parameterisation such that the mean of $\Gamma(a,b)$ is a/b.) Visualise the joint prior in this case.

Problem 13.1.18 For this situation your colleague tells you that there are unfortunately no conjugate priors. As such, three possible solutions (of many) open to you are: (a) to use numerical integration to find the posterior distribution; (b) to use the Metropolis–Hastings algorithm; (c) to transform each of (α,β) so that they lie between $-\infty < \theta < \infty$ then use Random Walk Metropolis. Why can you not use vanilla Random Walk Metropolis for (α,β) here?

Problem 13.1.19 By using one of the three methods above, estimate the joint posterior distribution. Visualise the PDF of the joint posterior. How are α and β correlated here?

Problem 13.1.20 Construct 80% credible intervals for the parameters of the beta-binomial distribution.

Problem 13.1.21 Carry out appropriate posterior predictive checks using the new model. How well does this model fit the data?

Problem 13.2 The fairground revisited

You again find yourself in a fairground, and where there is a stall offering the chance to win money if you participate in a game. Before participating you watch a few other plays of the game (by other people in the crowd) to try to determine whether you want to play.

Problem 13.2.1 In the most boring version of the game, a woman flips a coin and you bet on its outcome. If the coin lands heads up, you win; if tails, you lose. Based on your knowledge of similar games (and knowledge that the game must be rigged for the woman to make a profit!) you assume that the coin must be biased towards tails. As such you decide to specify a prior on the probability of the coin falling heads up as $\theta \sim beta(2,5)$. Graph this function, and, using your knowledge of the beta distribution, determine the mean parameter value specified by this prior.

Problem 13.2.2 You watch the last 10 plays of the game, and the outcome is heads 3/10 times. Assuming a binomial likelihood, create a function that determines the likelihood for a given value of the probability of heads, θ. Hence or otherwise, determine the maximum likelihood estimate of θ.

Problem 13.2.3 Graph the likelihood × prior. From the graph approximately determine the MAP θ estimate value.

Problem 13.2.4 By using R's `integrate` function, find the denominator, and hence graph the posterior PDF.

Problem 13.2.5 Use your posterior to determine your break-even/fair price for participating in the game, assuming that you win £1 if the coin comes up heads, and nothing otherwise.

Problem 13.2.6 Another variant of the game is as follows. The woman flips a first coin: if it is tails you lose ($Y_i = 0$), and if it is heads you proceed to the next step. In this step, the woman flips another coin 10 times, and records the number of heads, Y_i, which equals your winnings. Explain why a reasonable choice for the likelihood might be:

$$L(\theta,\phi \mid Y_i) = \begin{cases} (1-\theta)+\theta(1-\phi)^{10}, & \text{if } Y_i = 0 \\ \theta \binom{10}{Y_i}\phi^{Y_i}(1-\phi)^{10-Y_i}, & \text{if } Y_i > 0 \end{cases} \qquad (13.24)$$

where θ and ϕ are the probabilities of the first and second coins falling heads up, and Y_i is the score on the game.

Problem 13.2.7 Using the above formula, write down the overall log-likelihood for a series of N observations for $Y_i = (Y_1, Y_2, ..., Y_N)$.

Problem 13.2.8 Using R's `optim` function, determine the maximum likelihood estimate of the parameters for $Y_i = (3,0,4,2,1,2,0,0,5,1)$. (*Hint 1*: Since R's `optim` function does minimisation by default, you will need to put a minus sign in front of the function to maximise it.)

Problem 13.2.9 Determine confidence intervals on your parameter estimates. (*Hint 1*: use the second derivative of the log-likelihood to estimate the Fischer information matrix, and hence determine the Cramér–Rao lower bound. *Hint 2*: use Mathematica.)

Problem 13.2.10 Assuming uniform priors for both θ and ϕ, create a function in R that calculates the un-normalised posterior (the numerator of Bayes' rule).

Problem 13.2.11 By implementing the Metropolis algorithm, estimate the posterior means of each parameter. (*Hint 1*: use a normal proposal distribution. *Hint 2*: use periodic boundary conditions on each parameter, so that a proposal off one side of the domain maps onto the other side.)

Problem 13.2.12 Find the 95% credible intervals for each parameter.

Problem 13.2.13 Using your posterior samples, determine the fair price of the game. (*Hint*: find the mean of the posterior predictive distribution.)

Problem 13.3 Malarial mosquitoes

Suppose that you work for the WHO and it is your job to research the behaviour of malaria-carrying mosquitoes. In particular, an important part of your research remit is to estimate the adult mosquito life span. The life span of an adult mosquito is a critical determinant of the severity of malaria, since the longer a mosquito lives, the greater the chance it has of (a) becoming infected by biting an infected human; (b) surviving the period where the malarial parasite undergoes a metamorphosis in the mosquito gut and migrates to the salivary glands; and (c) passing on the disease by biting an uninfected host.

Suppose you estimate the life span of mosquitoes by analysing the results of a mark–release–recapture field experiment. The experiment begins with the release of 1000 young adult mosquitoes (assumed to have an adult age of zero), each of which has been marked with a fluorescent dye. On each day (t) you attempt to collect mosquitoes using a large number of traps, and count the number of marked mosquitoes that you capture (X_t). The mosquitoes caught each day are then re-released unharmed. The experiment goes on for 15 days in total.

Since X_t is a count variable and you assume that the recapture of an individual marked mosquito is independent and identically distributed, you choose to use a Poisson model (as an approximation to the binomial since n is large):

$$X_t \sim Poisson(\lambda_t), \quad \lambda_t = 1000\exp(-\mu t)\psi, \tag{13.25}$$

where μ is the mortality hazard rate (assumed to be constant) and ψ is the daily recapture probability. You use a $\Gamma(2,20)$ prior for μ (which has a mean of 0.1), and a $beta(2,40)$ prior for ψ.

The data for the experiment is contained in the file RWM_mosquito.csv.

Problem 13.3.1 Using the data, create a function that returns the likelihood. (*Hint*: it is easiest to first write a function that accepts (μ,ψ) as an input, and outputs the mean on a day t.)

Problem 13.3.2 Find the maximum likelihood estimates of (μ,ψ). (*Hint 1*: this may be easier if you create a function that returns the log-likelihood, and maximise this instead. *Hint 2*: use R's optim function.)

Problem 13.3.3 Construct 95% confidence intervals for the parameters. (*Hint*: find the information matrix, and use it to find the Cramér–Rao lower bound. Then find approximate confidence intervals by using the central limit theorem.)

Problem 13.3.4 Write a function for the prior, and use this to create an expression for the un-normalised posterior.

Problem 13.3.5 Create a function that proposes a new point in the parameter space using a log-N proposal with mean at the current μ value, and a $beta(2+\psi,40-\psi)$ proposal for ψ. (*Hint*: use a log-$N(0.5(-\sigma^2 + 2\log(\mu)),\sigma)$, where μ is the current value of the parameter.)

Problem 13.3.6 Create a function that returns the ratio of the un-normalised posterior at the proposed step location, and compares it to the current position.

Problem 13.3.7 Create a Metropolis–Hastings accept–reject function.

Problem 13.3.8 Create a Metropolis–Hastings sampler by combining your proposal and accept–reject functions.

Problem 13.3.9 Use your sampler to estimate the posterior mean of μ and ψ for a sample size of 4000 (discard the first 50 observations.) (*Hint*: if possible, do this by running four chains in parallel.)

Problem 13.3.10 By numeric integration compute numerical estimates of the posterior means of μ and ψ. How do your sampler's estimates compare with the actual values? How do these compare to the MLEs?

Problem 13.3.11 Carry out appropriate posterior predictive checks to test the fit of the model. What do these suggest might be a more appropriate sampling distribution? (*Hint*: generate a single sample of recaptures for each value of (μ, ψ) using the Poisson sampling distribution. You only need to do this for about 200 sets of parameter values to get a good idea.)

Problem 13.3.12 An alternative model that incorporates age-dependent mortality is proposed where:

$$\lambda_t = 1000\exp(-\mu t^{\beta+1})\psi, \tag{13.26}$$

with $\beta \geq 0$. Assume that the prior for this parameter is given by $\beta \sim \exp(5)$. Using the same log-$\mathcal{N}$ proposal distribution as for μ, create a Random Walk Metropolis sampler for this new model. Use this sampler to find 80% credible intervals for the (μ, ψ, β) parameters.

Problem 13.3.13 Look at a scatter plot of μ against β. What does this tell you about parameter identification in this model?

14

Chapter contents

GIBBS SAMPLING

14⊙1 CHAPTER MISSION STATEMENT

This chapter introduces the reader to a powerful MCMC algorithm known as the Gibbs sampler, and explains its similarities and differences compared with the Metropolis algorithm introduced in Chapter 13.

14⊙2 CHAPTER GOALS

The Random Walk Metropolis algorithm introduced in Chapter 13 provides a powerful tool for doing MCMC. The simplicity of the Random Walk Metropolis algorithm is one of its greatest assets. It can be applied to a large swathe of problems. However, there is a cost to its generality – it can be slow to converge to the posterior distribution for more complex models. Furthermore, as we saw in Chapter 13, to ensure speedy convergence to the posterior, we must tune the proposal distribution for the Metropolis sampler for each new model we estimate.

The Metropolis algorithm is a type of rejection algorithm for generating dependent samples from the posterior distribution. By its nature, therefore, we tend to reject a large proportion of potential steps. This high rate of rejection can limit the algorithm's ability to explore posterior space. Would it not be better if, instead, we could have a sampler that always accepted a proposed step in posterior space? For a reasonably large set models, it turns out this is possible, if we use the *Gibbs sampler.*

But how do we step in parameter space to ensure that we do not reject any samples? Surely this requires us to be able to independently sample from the posterior density (which we know we can't)? It turns out that, while we often cannot calculate the posterior distribution itself, we may be able to calculate the *conditional* posterior density for one (or more) parameter(s). Furthermore, if we can independently sample from this conditional density, then we can accept all proposed steps. By accepting all steps, this should mean that we can explore posterior space at a faster rate.

Gibbs sampling works by exploiting coincidences of conditionality in posterior space. While this is not possible for all models, it nonetheless motivated the creation of the BUGS and JAGS languages for MCMC. In many analyses, it may not be possible to find, and independently sample from, conditional distributions for all parameters in the posterior. However, we can often do so for a subset of them. We can then use Gibbs sampling for this set of parameters, and an algorithm like Metropolis for the remaining ones. These combination samplers are, in fact, similar to what BUGS and JAGS use to allow them to be implemented in a range of circumstances.

Finally, before we proceed with Gibbs, a note of caution – while it may appear that this algorithm is always preferable to Random Walk Metropolis, this is not necessarily so. First, it requires that we can analytically calculate conditional densities, which is not possible for many problems. Second, Gibbs sampling may result in a slow exploration of posterior space when there is a significant correlation between parameter estimates. Furthermore, when we modify the basic Metropolis in Chapter 15 to create Hamiltonian Monte Carlo, we find that this type of sampler is typically much faster than Gibbs.

14○3 BACK TO PROSPECTING FOR IRON

Cast your mind back to the problem described in Section 13.4, where you are employed by a mining company that wants to map the amount of iron underneath a vast desert. As before, you are equipped with a machine which can measure the magnitude of the magnetic field beneath, where the magnetic field varies in proportion to the amount of iron. This time, we are surveying a different desert to before (see Figure 14.1), but the problem is still the same: your employers want a detailed map of the deposits underneath.

However, this time you are equipped with a computer linked to a satellite, which can scan the magnetic field under the desert along a given north–south or east–west direction from where you stand. Unfortunately, the satellite is faulty and is unable to return a direct map of the magnetic field below. However, based on its scan, it can return a random point along a north–south or east–west line, where the probability of sampling a particular spatial location is proportional to the amount of iron beneath it. The question is: How can we use this device to help us map the underground iron most efficiently?

One way is to ignore the faulty satellite and use the same method as we did in Chapter 13. There, we started at a random location in the desert and measured the magnetic field underneath it. We then used a bivariate normal distribution to pick a new (north, east) spot where we again measure the magnetic

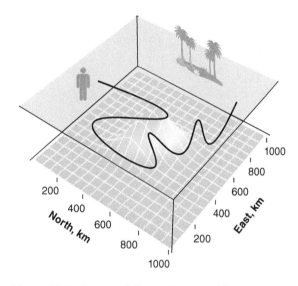

Figure 14.1 A map of the underground iron deposits. The lines show the directions that the satellite can scan along.

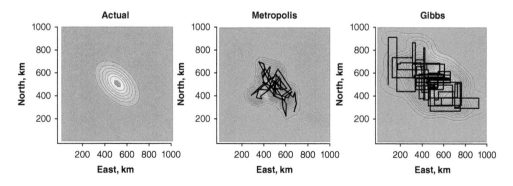

Figure 14.2 A contour map of the actual iron deposits (left), and reconstructed maps of deposits produced using the Metropolis (middle) and Gibbs algorithms (right). The black lines show the paths through the desert for a person using either method.

field. If the magnetic field is higher at our new spot, we move there. If the magnetic field is lower, we move there only probabilistically, where the probability of moving is given by the ratio of the new to old magnetic fields. If we use a list of our (north, east) locations over time as samples, then

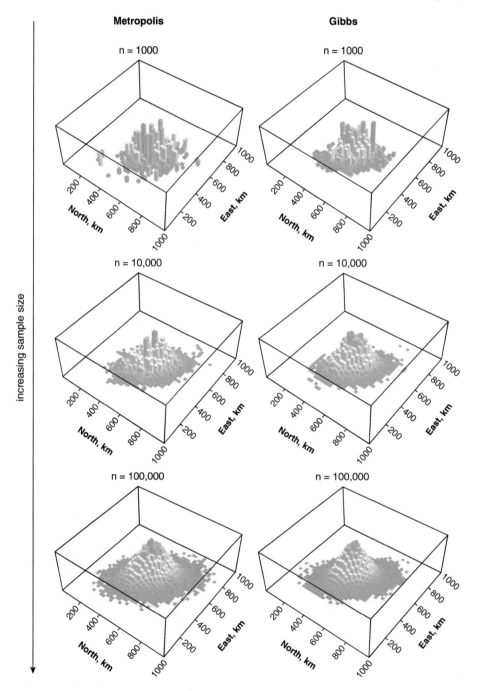

Figure 14.3   Histograms of samples produced by the Metropolis (left) and Gibbs (right) samplers across a range of sample sizes (increasing from top to bottom).

we can build up a map of the iron underneath, by considering their spatial density. This method amounts to using the Random Walk Metropolis sampler (see the middle panel of Figure 14.2).

A better way is to use the information from the satellite. If we start in a random location in the desert, we can use the satellite to determine our next sampling point in the east–west direction. We then move to the new point and use our satellite to determine a random point in the north–south direction and move there. We continue this process, alternating between moving to a random location in the east–west and then north–south directions. This method is the approach used by the Gibbs sampler (see the right-hand panel of Figure 14.2).

We notice two differences between the moves selected by these samplers. First, when using the Metropolis sampler, we often reject proposed steps and remain at our previous location in a given iteration. This contrasts with the Gibbs sampler, where we always move to a new spot in each iteration. Second, for the Metropolis sampler, we change both our north and east coordinates simultaneously (see the diagonal movement lines in the middle panel of Figure 14.2), whereas in the Gibbs case we move along only one direction at a time (see the horizontal and vertical lines in the right panel of Figure 14.2).

Which of the two methods – Random Walk Metropolis or Gibbs – is fastest? Reconstructions of the underground iron deposits for 1000, 10,000 and 100,000 iterations of each method are shown in Figure 14.3. After only 1000 iterations, the map produced by Gibbs sampling (top-right panel) is considerably closer to reality than Metropolis (top-left panel). After 10,000, some differences still persist, although Gibbs is less noisy. Finally, after 100,000 iterations, it is difficult to resolve a difference (bottom panels of Figure 14.3); both methods produce a fairly crisp map of the underground iron.

14○4 DEFINING THE GIBBS ALGORITHM

Now that we have some intuition for how Gibbs sampling works, we need to formally define it. In contrast to Metropolis, Gibbs sampling is only really valid for models with two or more parameters. So we use a model with three parameters, $\theta = (\theta_1, \theta_2, \theta_3)$, (with a data sample y) to describe the Gibbs algorithm. We assume that we cannot calculate the posterior distribution, but can determine exact expressions for the three conditional distributions: $p(\theta_1 | \theta_2, \theta_3, y)$, $p(\theta_2 | \theta_1, \theta_3, y)$ and $p(\theta_3 | \theta_1, \theta_2, y)$. Furthermore, we assume that these distributions are simple enough that we can generate independent samples from each of them.

For our example, the Gibbs algorithm consists of the following steps [14]: first, choose a random starting point $(\theta_1^0, \theta_2^0, \theta_3^0)$ using the same approach as for Metropolis. Then, in each subsequent iteration, do the following:

1   Choose a random parameter update ordering. In our example, in the first iteration we might have an order of $(\theta_3, \theta_2, \theta_1)$, then in the second we have $(\theta_1, \theta_3, \theta_2)$, and so on.
2   In the order determined in step 1, sample from the conditional posterior for each parameter using the most up-to-date parameters. So, for an ordering $(\theta_3, \theta_2, \theta_1)$ determined in step 1, we would first independently sample from $p(\theta_3^1 | \theta_1^0, \theta_2^0, y)$, then $p(\theta_2^1 | \theta_1^0, \theta_3^1, y)$ and finally $p(\theta_1^1 | \theta_2^1, \theta_3^1, y)$.

Notice that, in the second step, we use the most recent parameters (including those changed in the current iteration) to create the conditionals we then sample from. This process is repeated

An introduction to Gibbs sampling

until we determine our algorithm has converged, using the same multiple-chain $\hat{R}$ methodology we discussed in Section 13.9. We notice that for Gibbs there is no accept–reject step like that for the Metropolis algorithm – we accept all steps.

A subtlety of this method is that it can also be used in a slightly different way. Suppose that we can generate independent samples for the following alternative conditionals: $p(\theta_1,\theta_2 | \theta_3,\mathbf{y})$, $p(\theta_1,\theta_3 | \theta_2,\mathbf{y})$ and $p(\theta_2,\theta_3 | \theta_1,\mathbf{y})$. We could repeat the exact methodology above, except replacing the old univariate conditionals with these bivariate ones. Which of these methods should we prefer? We would like the one that is closest to independent sampling from the unconditional joint posterior. The first method samples from univariate conditionals, and thus updates just one parameter per step. However, the second method uses bivariate conditionals, and hence updates two parameters per step. The second is typically preferred since it is closer to the ideal of independently sampling from the three-dimensional unconditional posterior. Intuitively, there will typically be less correlation between consecutive samples for the bivariate sampler, since we change two parameters in each step. This decreased correlation means the effective sample size is higher for the second method.

Gibbs sampling of parameters in blocks can also be helpful if the parameters within the blocks are highly correlated with one another. By independently sampling the blocks, this allows us to mitigate against the risk of slow convergence of a correlated Gibbs sampler.

So why do we not always use a Gibbs sampler that samples from 2+ dimensional conditionals? Well, for the same reason we typically cannot sample independently from the posterior – constructing such a sampler may not be possible. In most applied settings, we are constrained by the maths of the problem, which can mean that block sampling a number of parameters is not possible. However, for circumstances that allow it, we typically prefer a block-updating Gibbs sampler to one that updates only a single parameter at a time.

14.4.1 Crime and punishment (unemployment)

Imagine that the posterior distribution for the unemployment (u) and crime levels (c) in a town is estimated to be a bivariate normal distribution of the form:

$$\begin{pmatrix} u \\ c \end{pmatrix} \sim N\left[\begin{pmatrix} a \\ b \end{pmatrix}, \begin{pmatrix} 1 & \rho \\ \rho & 1 \end{pmatrix} \right], \tag{14.1}$$

where all parameters are estimated from data and $\rho > 0$. In this example, we have assumed that we are lucky because we could estimate the posterior distribution analytically. Because we can sample independently from a bivariate normal we do not actually need to do MCMC, but nevertheless, we can use this example to illustrate the workings of Gibbs. Handily, the bivariate normal has simple conditional densities, which are each themselves normal (see the left-hand panel of Figure 14.4). We do not want to occupy ourselves with the mathematical derivation of these (see the chapter problem set), but they are given by:

$$u|c \sim N(a + \rho(c - b), \sqrt{1 - \rho^2})$$

$$c|u \sim N(b + \rho(u - a), \sqrt{1 - \rho^2}). \tag{14.2}$$

Since the right-hand sides of both the expressions in (14.2) are normal distributions, we can independently sample from them using statistical software's in-built random-number generators.

By alternating between sampling from each of these expressions, we can, therefore, sample from the posterior distribution.

Imagine that we start at some random location in parameter space, say (u^0, c^0), and then first update u^0 by sampling from:

$$u^1 \mid c^0 \sim N(a + \rho(c^0 - b), \sqrt{1 - \rho^2}).$$
(14.3)

This gives us u^1, which we use to characterise the conditional density given in expression (14.2). We then sample c^1 from this distribution:

$$c^1 \mid u^1 \sim N(b + \rho(u^1 - a), \sqrt{1 - \rho^2}).$$
(14.4)

We then repeat this process over and over, resulting in samples that recapitulate the true posterior distribution's shape after some time (see the middle and right-hand panels of Figure 14.4).

How to derive a Gibbs sampling routine in general

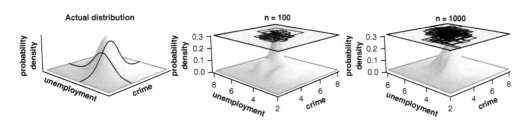

Figure 14.4 The actual posterior distribution for crime and unemployment (left), with distributions reconstructed from Gibbs sampling, for a sample size of 100 (middle) and 1000 (right). In the left-hand plot, the black lines illustrate the shape of the conditional densities. Above the middle and right-hand plots we show the paths followed by the Gibbs sampler over time.

14●5 GIBBS' EARTH: THE INTUITION BEHIND THE GIBBS ALGORITHM

Imagine that the earth's surface represents our posterior landscape, which we want to map. To do this we could do a random walk a la Metropolis, but if the proposal distribution is too narrow, then we would spend too long in the Sahara; alternatively, if the step size is too large we would get stuck in the Himalayas. This means it can take a long time for the Random Walk Metropolis sampler to explore the whole earth and converge on an accurate depiction of the landscape.

The Gibbs algorithm works by walking on the earth's surface, along lines of constant latitude or longitude. If we know what each of these transects looks like, then we can imagine reconstructing a picture of the earth using only these one-dimensional slices. Essentially this is what Gibbs sampling does. By taking samples from many different north–south or east–west slices, eventually, the algorithm can reconstruct an accurate picture of the whole.

Note that Gibbs sampling requires that we know what these slices along the earth's surface look like beforehand. This extra information that we impart to our sampler allows us to more speedily explore posterior space, but it is not without a cost – for many problems we do not know what these slices look like, and hence cannot implement Gibbs.

14.6 THE BENEFITS AND PROBLEMS WITH GIBBS AND RANDOM WALK METROPOLIS

Gibbs sampling can be great. If we can derive the conditional densities, and if these are relatively well behaved, then the rate of convergence to the posterior density is often faster than Random Walk Metropolis. Consider the crime and unemployment example, described in Section 14.4.1. If we use both the Gibbs sampler and Metropolis algorithms to explore the posterior surface, we find that the rate of convergence to the posterior is faster for Gibbs (see the top row of Figure 14.5). This is because Gibbs sampling – by accounting for the mathematical description of the entities involved – can generate more effective samples per iteration than Random Walk Metropolis. Nonetheless, after only a few hundred iterations, both sampling methods produce a sampling distribution that well approximates the posterior distribution.

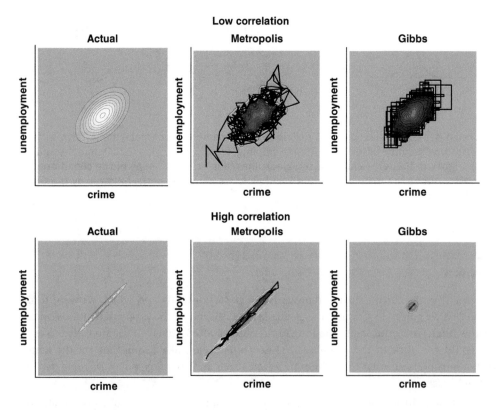

Figure 14.5 The actual distributions of crime and unemployment for two different towns (left panels), along with densities that have been estimated using Metropolis (middle) and Gibbs (right) sampling, each with a sample size of 1000. In the sampling plots the lines indicate the paths taken by the sampler over time.

Suppose that for a different town the correlation between our crime and unemployment variables is higher than the previous town so that our posterior is composed of a sharper diagonal ridge (see the bottom panels of Figure 14.5). Now we see a problem. After the same number of iterations as before, both sampling algorithms produce reconstructed distributions that look quite different to the actual distribution. In this case, it looks like the Random Walk Metropolis sampler has actually fared better than Gibbs.

So what is going on here? The problem here is that the underlying distribution's geometry – in other words, the sharpness of the ridge – is causing us to take far longer to explore the posterior space. For the Metropolis sampler, this is characterised by a high rejection rate, meaning that we cannot explore the central ridge efficiently. Whereas, for the Gibbs sampler, being forced to move in horizontal and vertical jumps means that we take a long time to explore the diagonally orientated distribution.

The performance of the two samplers worsens as the correlation between our variables increases. Both of these methods fail to work well for highly correlated distributions because the distribution's geometry is misaligned with the stepping directions of each sampler. This misalignment induces a high degree of autocorrelation in samples, resulting in a low effective sample size per iteration.

We would, thus, prefer a sampler that moves in accordance with the underlying distribution's shape. In this case, this would correspond to a sampler that moves mostly diagonally, in contrast to Gibbs' horizontal and vertical movements. By moving in this direction, we should avoid the high rate of rejection that we see for Random Walk Metropolis, and explore the posterior much more efficiently than Gibbs. Fear not! In Chapter 15, we introduce the Hamiltonian Monte Carlo sampler that satisfies these criteria.

14○7 A CHANGE OF PARAMETERS TO SPEED UP EXPLORATION

Another way to speed up sampling is to change variables for the underlying distribution so that the components are uncorrelated. In our crime and unemployment example, if $\rho = 0.5$ this equates to sampling from C and U defined as:

$$C = c - u$$

$$(14.5)$$

$$U = c + u.$$

This is equivalent to a rotation of the axes by 45 degrees clockwise (see Figure 14.6). Here C represents the difference between the crime level and unemployment, and U is their sum. The new variables are still jointly normally distributed, although they are now uncorrelated (see the chapter problem set for a full derivation). Since these variables are now uncorrelated, a Gibbs sampler in (C,U) parameter space fares much better (compare the middle and right-hand panels of Figure 14.6). These type of parameter transformations are what are known as *affine*, and actually underlie a class of algorithms known as *differential evolution* MCMC, which actually aim to be invariant to such changes of parameters.

While we have used a reparameterisation to speed up Gibbs sampling for this example, this concept is also relevant more generally. In particular, most sampling algorithms will have issues when parameters are highly correlated. Intuitively, this high correlation means that it

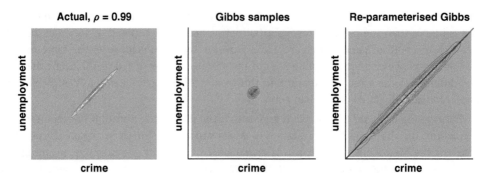

Figure 14.6 Using MCMC sampling to reconstruct a density (left) using simple Gibbs (left) and re-parameterised Gibbs (right). In the sampling plots the lines indicate the paths taken by the sampler over time.

is difficult to disentangle one variable's effects from another's. Whether we reconstruct the posterior by exact calculation, or use sampling to understand it, we are going to struggle to give separate meaning to highly correlated parameter estimates. The manifestation of this difficulty is parameters with a high uncertainty associated with their values. If you find that your sampler is struggling to converge, then 99% of the time this is not due to computational issues, but to your statistical model. (This is what Gelman calls his 'Folk Theorem' which we discuss in Chapter 16.) In this circumstance, it pays to think whether there is a way to change your model (often by a re-parameterisation) that reduces correlation in your parameters. Sometimes this may be difficult, but more often than not there is a solution.

14○8 CHAPTER SUMMARY

In this chapter, we introduced the Gibbs sampling algorithm, a type of dependent sampling routine that takes account of the particular mathematical structure of each problem. Using this information allows us to build up a picture of the unconditional posterior by iteratively drawing independent samples from the conditional distributions for each of the parameters.

But Gibbs sampling is not the solution to all our problems. First, it requires that we can calculate, and draw independent samples from, the conditional distributions of each parameter. In many situations, this will not be the case. Second, we have seen that correlated posterior geometries can make Gibbs sampling highly inefficient. To quote Charles Geyer [7]: 'If I had a nickel for every time someone had asked for help with slowly converging MCMC and the answer had been to stop using Gibbs, I would be rich.' Following Geyer's advice, we recommend switching to another sampling method if Gibbs sampling struggles. This is partly because another issue with Gibbs is that it forces us down a path where there is little remedy for the situation. This contrasts with the freedom of Metropolis (and Metropolis–Hastings), where at least we get to control the proposal distribution.

A problem with all the sampling algorithms we have considered thus far is that they do not adequately account for the geometry of the posterior distribution, in the way they step through parameter space. We saw in Section 14.7 that re-parameterising a model using our knowledge of posterior sampling can allow us to more efficiently sample from it. The question we now turn to is: Can we use the posterior geometry to speed up MCMC more generally? The answer is a resounding 'Yes – just use Hamiltonian Monte Carlo.' Accordingly, in Chapter 15 we discuss Hamiltonian Monte Carlo, the basis for the engine that powers Stan.

14○9 CHAPTER OUTCOMES

The reader should now be familiar with the following concepts:

- how Gibbs sampling works
- the benefits and costs of Gibbs sampling
- how highly correlated parameters make it difficult to do inference

14○10 PROBLEM SETS

Problem 14.1 The sensitivity and specificity of a test for a disease

Suppose that for a particular tropical disease no gold standard clinical test exists. Instead we have a test that is known to be imperfect, not always identifying the disease if the patient has it, and sometimes yielding false positives (patients that do not have the disease but test positive). However, by using this test in a clinical trial it is hoped that we can obtain better estimates for the test sensitivity (S, the proportion of disease-positive individuals who test positive) and specificity (C, the proportion of disease-negative individuals who test negative).

Table P14.1   Test outcomes versus true outcomes.

Test		Truth +	Truth −	
+		Y_1	$a - Y_1$	a
−		Y_2	$b - Y_2$	b
		$Y_1 + Y_2$	$N - (Y_1 + Y_2)$	N

To do this we can construct a table of the observed and latent data for the test outcomes (see Table P14.1). In the table a and b are the number of observed positive and negative results, respectively. Y_1 and Y_2 are latent variables that represent the gold standard – the true number of positive individuals out of a and b, respectively.

Problem 14.1.1 Write down an expression for the likelihood, supposing that the prevalence for the disease is π. (*Hint*: multiply together the likelihoods corresponding to each of the cells in Table P14.1.)

Problem 14.1.2 Assuming priors of the form $\pi \sim beta(\alpha_\psi, \beta_\pi)$, $S \sim beta(\alpha_S, \beta_S)$ and $C \sim beta(\alpha_C, \beta_C)$, it is possible to code up a Gibbs sampler for this problem [6] of the form:

$$Y_1 \mid a,\pi,S,C \sim binomial\left(a,\frac{\pi S}{\pi S+(1-\pi)(1-C)}\right),$$

$$Y_2 \mid b,\pi,S,C \sim binomial\left(b,\frac{\pi(1-S)}{\pi(1-S)+(1-\pi)C}\right),$$

$$\pi \mid a,b,Y_1,Y_2 \sim beta\left(Y_1+Y_2+\alpha_\pi,a+b-Y_1-Y_2+\beta_\pi\right),$$

(14.6)

$$S \mid Y_1,Y_2 \sim beta\left(Y_1+\alpha_S,Y_2+\beta_S\right),$$

$$C \mid a,b,Y_1,Y_2 \sim beta\left(b-Y_2+\alpha_C,a-Y_1+\beta_C\right).$$

Using the above expressions, code up a working Gibbs sampler.

Problem 14.1.3 Suppose that out of a sample of 100 people, 20 of those tested negative and 80 positive. Assuming uniform priors on π, S and C, use Gibbs sampling to generate posterior samples for π. What do you conclude?

Problem 14.1.4 Suppose that a previous study that compares the clinical test with a laboratory iron standard concludes that $S \sim beta(10,1)$ and $C \sim beta(10,1)$. Use Gibbs sampling to estimate the new posterior for π. Why does this look different to your previously estimated distribution?

Problem 14.1.5 Suppose a previous analysis concluded that $\pi \sim beta(1,10)$. Using this distribution as a prior, together with uniform priors on S and C, determine the posterior distributions for the test sensitivity and specificity, respectively. Why does the test appear to be quite specific, although it is unclear how sensitive it is?

Problem 14.1.6 Suppose that based on lab results you suppose that the test specificity $C \sim beta(10,1)$, and $\pi \sim beta(1,10)$, but the prior for S is still uniform. Explain the shape of the posterior for S now.

Problem 14.1.7 Now suppose that the sample size was 1000 people of which 200 tested positive. Using the same priors as the previous question, determine the posterior for S. What do you conclude about your test's sensitivity?

Problem 14.1.8 What do the previous results suggest is necessary to assess the sensitivity of a clinical test for a disease?

Problem 14.2 Coal mining disasters in the UK

The data in `gibbs_coal.csv` contain time series of the annual number of coal mining disasters in the UK from 1851 to 1961 [5]. In this section we will use Gibbs sampling to estimate the point in time when legislative and societal changes caused a reduction in coal mining disasters in the UK.

A model for the number of disasters D_t in a particular year t is:

$$D_t \sim \begin{cases} Poisson(\lambda_1), & \text{if } t \le n, \\ Poisson(\lambda_2), & \text{if } t > n, \end{cases} \tag{14.7}$$

where λ_1 and λ_2 are the early and late mean disaster rates in the UK, and n is the time where the change in rates occurred.

Problem 14.2.1 Graph the data over time. Around what year (n) does it appear the change in disaster rate occurred?

Problem 14.2.2 Assuming the same $\lambda_i \sim \Gamma(a,b)$ priors for $i = \{1,2\}$, and a discrete uniform prior for n between 1851 and 1861, determine an expression for the full (un-normalised) posterior density.

Problem 14.2.3 Determine the conditional distribution for λ_1 (namely, $p(\lambda_1 | x_{1:n}, n, a, b)$) by finding all those terms in the density that include λ_1, and removing the rest as constants of proportionality. (*Hint*: remember that a gamma prior is conjugate to a Poisson likelihood.)

Problem 14.2.4 Using your answer to the previous problem, write down the conditional distribution for λ_2.

Problem 14.2.5 By collecting the terms that depend on n, show that its conditional density can be written as:

$$p(n | x_{1:N}, \lambda_1, \lambda_2) \propto \lambda_1^{\sum_{t=1}^{n} x_t} e^{-n\lambda_1} \times \lambda_2^{\sum_{t=n+1}^{N} x_t} e^{-(N-n)\lambda_2}. \tag{14.8}$$

Problem 14.2.6 Write a function in R that calculates the un-normalised expression for $p(n | x_{1:N}, \lambda_1, \lambda_2)$ for a single value of n. (*Hint*: remember that the change point cannot occur at the last data point, and so return 0 for this case.)

Problem 14.2.7 Create a function that calculates the discrete probability distribution across all values of n. (*Hint*: remember, this must be a valid probability distribution.)

Problem 14.2.8 Create a function that independently samples from the discrete distribution for the n you calculate. (*Hint*: use the `sample` function.)

Problem 14.2.9 Write functions to independently sample from the conditional distributions for λ_1 and λ_2 that you previously determined.

Problem 14.2.10 Combine all three previously created sampling functions to create a working Gibbs sampler. Hence estimate the change point and its 95% central credible intervals.

Problem 14.2.11 Using your sampler, determine posterior median estimates for λ_1 and λ_2.

Problem 14.3 Bayesian networks

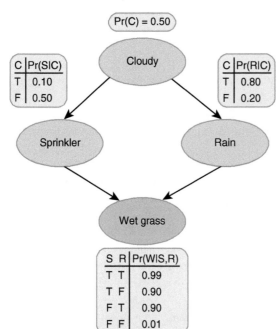

Suppose that when you leave your house in the morning you notice that the grass is wet. However, you do not know whether the grass is wet because of last night's rain, or because the sprinkler went on in the night. You want to determine the cause of the wet grass, because this affects whether you need to water your plants on your windowsill. The causal pathway of the grass being wet is shown in Figure P14.1, along with the probabilities of the states. Here 'cloudy' means that the night was completely overcast.

Problem 14.3.1 Show that the probability that it was cloudy last night conditional on the sprinkler being on, that it rained, and the grass being wet is approximately 0.444.

Problem 14.3.2 Show that the probability that it rained given that it was cloudy, the sprinkler was on, and the grass is wet is approximately 0.815.

Figure P14.1   A Bayesian network for the wet grass example.

Problem 14.3.3 The remaining (non-trivial) conditional probabilities are $p(c\,|-r,s,w) = 0.048$ and $p(r\,|-c,s,w) = 0.216$. Suppose that when we walk outside we see that the grass is wet, and we also know that the sprinkler went on last night (we were woken by its noise). Create a Gibbs sampler to determine the unconditional probability that it was cloudy. Then find the unconditional probability that it rained.

Problem 14.3.4 Using your Gibbs sampler, determine the joint probability that it was cloudy and it rained.

Problem 14.3.5 Visualise the path of your Gibbs sampler by creating a network graph showing the frequency of transitions between the four states. (*Hint 1*: first create an adjacency matrix by calculating the frequency of transitions between all states. *Hint 2*: to visualise the graph in R use the `iGraph` package.)

Problem 14.4 Proofs

Problem 14.4.1 Prove that the Gibbs sampler can be viewed as a case of Metropolis–Hastings.

Problem 14.4.2 For the bivariate normal density:

$$\begin{pmatrix} u \\ c \end{pmatrix} \sim N\left[\begin{pmatrix} a \\ b \end{pmatrix}, \begin{pmatrix} 1 & \rho \\ \rho & 1 \end{pmatrix}\right],$$

(14.9)

show that the conditional densities are of the form:

$$u\,|\,c \sim N(a + \rho(c - b), \sqrt{1 - \rho^2}),$$

$$c\,|\,u \sim N(b + \rho(u - a), \sqrt{1 - \rho^2}).$$

(14.10)

Problem 14.4.3 Show that the following changes of variables for a bivariate normal (with $\rho = 0.5$) as described in this chapter result in uncorrelated components:

$$C = c - u,$$

$$U = c + u.$$

(14.11)

15

Chapter contents

HAMILTONIAN
MONTE CARLO

CHAPTER MISSION STATEMENT

At the end of this chapter the reader will understand how Hamiltonian Monte Carlo works and how it can be used to efficiently sample from the posterior.

15⊙2 CHAPTER GOALS

In Chapter 13 we met the Random Walk Metropolis algorithm, which generates a sequence of dependent samples from the posterior. Random Walk Metropolis works by starting at a random location in parameter space. In each step we randomly choose a new direction and distance to step by sampling from a proposal distribution centred on our current location. If the value of the posterior density is greater at the new location we move there. If it is not, then we move there only *probabilistically*, with a probability given by the ratio of the new to old densities.

The Random Walk Metropolis algorithm is, as its name suggests, a kind of random walk through posterior space. It is random because we take no account of the underlying shape of the posterior when deciding where next to propose stepping. In Section 14.6 we saw that the arbitrary nature of the proposals used in Random Walk Metropolis results in a high rejection rate and, hence, inefficient exploration of the posterior distribution. If we imagine stepping through parameter space, then Random Walk Metropolis amounts to our doing it blindfolded. This stepping in the dark is scary, and inevitably it takes us a long time to explore the landscape.

A better approach is to remove the blindfold. Removing the blindfold does not, however, yield perfect vistas of the landscape in front of us; the air is thick with fog. However, we imagine we can see a few metres in each direction. This limited visibility nonetheless allows us to direct our stepping, and we preferentially step towards higher locations. We choose to step towards areas of high probability density, because these are the areas of posterior space where the bulk of probability mass is typically found. By using the local posterior geometry to determine where next to step, we can, therefore, much more efficiently explore the posterior density. This is exactly what *Hamiltonian Monte Carlo* (HMC) does, and is accountable for the considerable success of this method in recent years.

However, in HMC we must still set a typical stepping distance, in similar vein to Random Walk Metropolis. Determining this step length is crucial. Remember that we can see only a very limited distance around us at any point in time. It is this – localised – information that we use to guide our stepping. While it might appear that one direction is upwards, we might find that if we step too far, we actually overshoot a peak. In this case, based on our intuition, we would be best turning on our heels and walking back the way we came, in effect doing a U-turn. As you might expect, these about-face turns are inefficient – we do not want to take two steps forward and one step back.

The inefficiency of U-turns motivated the development of the so-called No-U-Turn Sampler (NUTS) [19], which powers Stan. We finish this chapter by discussing this magical device and how it can determine the right step length for any position in posterior space.

HAMILTONIAN MONTE CARLO AS A SLEDGE

Again, imagine that we are walking through posterior space. With perfect sight we could see the huge peaks and low-lying deserts stretching out to infinity. However, we do not have perfect sight; if we did, there would be no need to do sampling in the first place. Instead, imagine that there is a dense fog that limits our vision almost completely. A simple approach to exploration is to ignore what our eyes tell us, and just step in a random direction and distance, away from our current position. This random stepping is exactly what we do in Random Walk Metropolis, which we discussed in Chapter 13. However, as discussed previously (see Section 14.6), this directionless wandering comes at a cost: it can take us a large amount of time to explore posterior space. In particular, it takes us a long time to find those areas of high density and explore them efficiently. Clearly, Random Walk Metropolis is missing something – it does not take account of the posterior distribution's geometry when deciding where next to try stepping. For clarity, this does not mean that Random Walk Metropolis completely ignores the posterior geometry – if it did, then the sampling would be uniform over all parameter space. We know that Random Walk Metropolis uses an accept–reject rule that depends on the posterior density. In Section 13.6.4 we saw that this rule is tuned to perfection to allow us to accurately reproduce the posterior by sampling. Rather, what we argue here is that how we propose where to step next is inefficient in Random Walk Metropolis, since it does not take account of the posterior geometry.

We want to create a sampler which uses local geometric information to determine our proposed steps. To do this we move away from this vision of our stepping through posterior space, and instead imagine that we are passengers on a vehicle that moves through a related landscape (see Figure 15.1). This new landscape is similar to the posterior space, although everything is inverted: peaks become troughs and troughs are now peaks. Specifically, this space is the negative log of the posterior density (NLP), although do not worry about what this means for now. We imagine we are gliding over the frictionless surface of NLP space on a type of sledge. At any time, where we next move not only depends on our location, but also on our momentum. Our momentum is, in turn, determined partly by the gradient of NLP where we currently find ourselves. Dragged by gravity, if we had no momentum we would always tend to descend in NLP space (ascend in posterior space). However, our momentum also gives us enough forward motion to climb

The intuition behind the Hamiltonian Monte Carlo algorithm

upwards through the NLP landscape. Therefore the presence of this second variable – momentum – allows us to explore areas of low NLP (high posterior density) as well as high NLP (low posterior density). However, the effect of gravity should mean that we will spend more time in low areas and less in high-NLP regions, in good correspondence with our hopes for an ideal sampler.

It is important to remember that the physical analogy is really just a useful idea, not indicative of any underlying reality. In particular, the momentum of our sledge is purely a helper variable. It is useful because it allows us to reach and explore efficiently areas of parameter space that would otherwise be

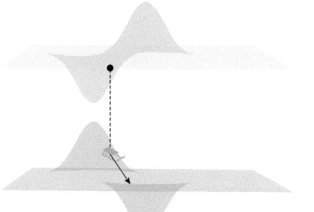

Figure 15.1 NLP space (bottom) is essentially the inverse of posterior space (top). By travelling around NLP space on a sledge we are more likely to visit areas of low NLP, which correspond to high posterior density.

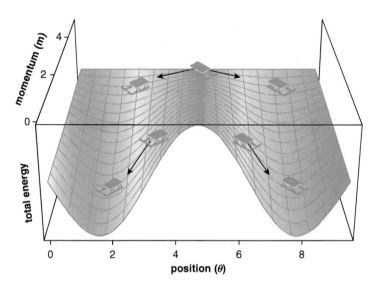

Figure 15.2 Two minima in NLP space (maxima in posterior space) become better connected if we allow our sledge to possess momentum.

hard to reach. As an example, two isolated peaks may be troublesome for some samplers but, by introducing momentum, it may become increasingly easier to get from one peak to the other (see Figure 15.2). This amounts to a reduction in multimodality that can cause slow exploration of the posterior.

However, the picture is not quite complete. As we have explained things, our initial state – location and momentum – would completely determine our future path. However, how should we select our initial state to ensure that we visit all of posterior space in exact accordance with its density? Without knowing what posterior space looks like, how can we ever hope to do this? The solution to this issue is to select, at each step, a random momentum from some proposal distribution. We use this momentum to determine the initial direction we move off in. In accordance with the laws of Newtonian physics in NLP space, we move in this direction for a specified distance, and then abruptly stop. We then compute the (un-normalised) posterior value at our new location and compare it to the original posterior height. To determine whether we accept this step or return to our previous location, we use an accept–reject rule much like for Random Walk Metropolis. The only difference here is that we also need to make a slight correction to the rule to account for our current and previous momenta (we delay going into these details until Section 15.7).

Don't worry if all of the algorithm's details just flew right over your head! In contrast to our previous MCMC samplers, HMC is a little bit more involved. However, as we shall hopefully demonstrate over the next few sections, it is no more difficult to understand.

15 O 4   NLP SPACE

In Hamiltonian Monte Carlo we use the physical analogy of a sledge moving over a frictionless terrain to help us visit those areas of high posterior density preferentially over lower regions.

But how do we design a terrain that allows this to happen? The simplest way would be to use the negative of the un-normalised posterior, since this means that troughs in this space would correspond to peaks in posterior space. Since gravity will tend to pull us towards the bottom of the landscape, by solving for the motion of our sledge we will inadvertently tend to visit areas of high posterior density.

For reasons that we do not want to go into here (statistical mechanics) we instead use the negative of the log of the un-normalised posterior density (which we term NLP):

$$NLP(\theta) = -\log[p(data \mid \theta) \times p(\theta)]. \tag{15.1}$$

We term the surface described by the function in expression (15.1) *NLP space*. By using the log transform this means that, technically, the landscape on which we move is slightly less curved than the un-normalised posterior space itself; the intuition remains the same, however – troughs in this space correspond to peaks in posterior space, and vice versa. Therefore, in the ensuing figures and discussion, we ignore this distinction. The important thing is that, because of the physical analogy, the sledge will tend to visit those areas of low NLP, which correspond to high posterior density (see Figure 15.3).

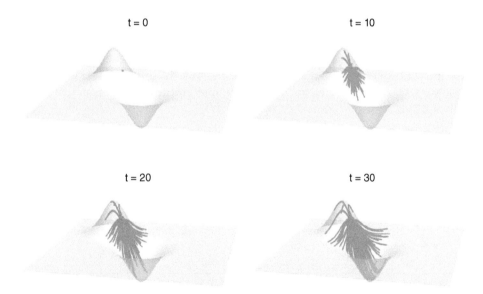

Figure 15.3   The path in NLP space of 100 sledges that are each assigned random initial momenta.

15○5   SOLVING FOR THE SLEDGE MOTION OVER NLP SPACE

If we had a sledge and a real frictionless terrain of the same dimensions and shape as the actual NLP space for our problem, then we could just shove the sledge (see Section 15.6 for how to do this properly) and follow its path. However, this is not usually the case, so we need to computationally solve for the path followed by the sledge over time. But how do we do this – particularly because the sledge moves in a space whose dimensionality typically exceeds that of everyday three-dimensional space?

Fortunately, the methods that we use to solve for the path of the sledge in any number of dimensions are the same as those that an engineer would use for three-dimensional space. This means that the number of dimensions does not affect the complexity of the methods that we use. But what are those methods? Technically, they involve objects known as *Hamiltonians,* which is just a fancy word for the total energy of the system. This is composed of the sum of the potential energy of the sledge, which depends on the location in parameter space (θ), and its kinetic energy, which depends on its momentum (m):

$$H(\theta,m) = \underbrace{U(\theta)}_{\text{potential energy}} + \underbrace{KE(m)}_{\text{kinetic energy}}. \tag{15.2}$$

The potential energy of the sledge is given by the negative of the log of the un-normalised posterior density:

$$U(\theta) = -\log\left[p(data\,|\,\theta) \times p(\theta)\right]. \tag{15.3}$$

While we would need to venture into statistical mechanics to understand why we choose this exact form for the potential energy, we can nonetheless appreciate the intuition that underpins it. As the posterior density increases, the potential energy decreases (becomes more negative) because we move towards a trough in NLP space. Intuitively, this is because there is less gravitational potential energy available to be converted into kinetic energy at troughs. Whereas at peaks in NLP space (troughs in posterior density space), if we give the sledge a gentle shove it will start to rapidly descend, with a corresponding increase in its kinetic energy. The potential energy at the top of hills is, therefore, greater (see Figure 15.4).

The kinetic energy term that we use is of the same form we encountered in high school physics and is proportional to the square of the sledge's momentum. With the Hamiltonian fully specified, we can then use standard methods to solve for the path of the sledge. Unfortunately, these methods are typically approximate in nature, since solving exactly for the path is too difficult.

HMC is insensitive to this approximation so long as the errors are not too large – the difference between the exact path of the sledge and the one that we estimate does not get too wide. To reduce the chance that this happens we use a class of approximation methods that is known as *symplectic,*

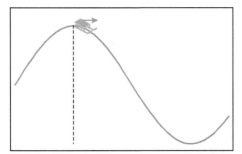 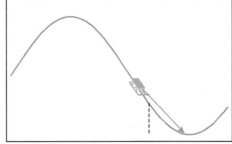

Figure 15.4 Potential energy (left) is converted into kinetic energy (right) as the sledge slides down a hill in NLP space so that the total energy remains constant.

of which the *leapfrog* algorithm is the most commonly employed. While we do not go into the details of the algorithm here, there is code in the chapter problem set that implements this routine (15.1.4). However, even this method is not foolproof – it can still fail to produce reasonable approximations in particular circumstances. It is this to which we next turn our attention.

15.5.1 Divergent iterations

Stan does its best to alert us of iterations where the approximate path diverges from the exact (true) path of the sledge, appropriately terming these *divergent iterations* (see Section 16.7.2). Are there characteristics of a posterior that make it more likely that the approximate sledge path will become separated from the true one? It turns out that, yes, there are.

To understand why these divergences occur, we need to understand a little about how the approximation methods work. Typically these methods break up the path of the sledge into discrete pieces over which the path is assumed to be a straight line (see the left-hand panel of Figure 15.5). If the length of these discrete pieces is sufficiently short, then the discrete approximate path closely follows the true curved path (see the right-panel of Figure 15.5).

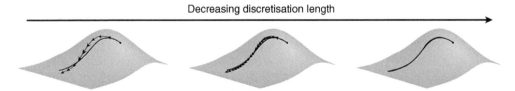

Decreasing discretisation length

Figure 15.5 As smaller discrete links (black arrows) are used to approximate the path of the sledge, the path becomes smoother and approaches the true path (black lines). In all cases, we show the first part of the path without arrows so that the true path can be seen.

However, if the curvature of the posterior is particularly sharp (see the right-hand panel of Figure 15.6), then the approximate path may be a poor estimate for the true one. In this context, the full path of the sledge may – as a consequence of a few faulty steps – diverge from the true path.

Why do we care about such divergences? Well, the reason is that, if they occur, we get an arbitrary reallocation of the posterior

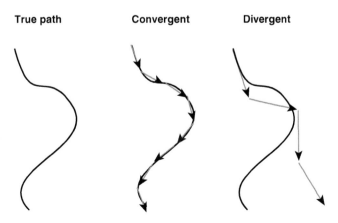

True path Convergent Divergent

Figure 15.6 Too much posterior curvature relative to the discretisation length can cause divergent paths.

probability mass around these points of divergence. Why does this matter? Because arbitrary is not in line with the shape of the actual posterior – it is by definition arbitrary!

Stan drops any iterations it deems to be divergent. The consequence of divergent iterations is therefore to bias the sampling distribution away from these points in posterior space. This matters because any posterior summary (mean, median, variance, and so on) will be incorrect. Just how incorrect depends on how much probability mass is located near the point(s) where divergences occur.

So we see that divergent iterations are always something to be concerned about, because they indicate that our MCMC algorithm is failing in some areas of posterior space. These failures are typically due to substantial local posterior curvature in these areas. How do we solve these issues? One way is to use a smaller step length (that is, the length of the discrete pieces of the path that are used to approximate the true path) to stimulate the path to reduce the approximation error in following the true path of the sledge (see Figure 15.6). The alternative way is to make a change to the model in an attempt to smooth out the posterior. While the discussion here has been fairly abstract, in Section 16.7.2 we include a more applied discussion of divergent iteration resolution.

HOW TO SHOVE THE SLEDGE

If we simply let the sledge move under gravity, it would eventually reach, then settle, in a trough in NLP space (corresponding to a peak in posterior space). However, while we want to bias our path in favour of regions of high posterior density, we still need to sample from regions of lower density, otherwise our sampling distribution will be too narrow. There is also the risk that if our sledge settles in one trough in NLP space, it will fail to reach other troughs in other parts of the landscape, resulting in a posterior that is biased away from certain peaks.

To avoid such problems we follow the path of our sledge for a predefined amount of time T (to be discussed in Section 15.10), then bring it instantaneously to rest, recording the position θ_1 at this point only if we accept this new location (see Section 15.7). We then give our sledge a shove of random strength in a randomly chosen direction. The usual way we do this is to select a new initial momentum of the sledge by independent sampling from a multivariate normal:

$$m \sim N(\mu, \Sigma). \tag{15.4}$$

We then solve for the path of the sledge for another length of time T as discussed in Section 15.5. At the end of this time, we again bring our sledge to rest and record the position θ_2 if we accept this new location, otherwise we return to θ_1 and record this location instead. By repeating this process – shoving, following and bringing to rest – a large number of times we build up a set of samples $(\theta_1, \theta_2, ..., \theta_p)$. However, as we indicated in passing, there is still one element of this process that is missing: the rule we use to determine whether we accept or reject each proposed location in parameter space. We turn our attention to this rule now.

15◯7 THE ACCEPTANCE PROBABILITY OF HMC

HMC is really a type of Metropolis algorithm, at its heart a rejection sampling algorithm. In each step, we randomly generate a proposed location in parameter space, then either accept or reject this location. The difference with Random Walk Metropolis is the way in which we generate the proposal in HMC. Whereas in Random Walk Metropolis we generate a proposed location by random sampling a location (typically from a normal distribution centred on our current location), in HMC we do something a little more complicated: we assign a random momentum to a fictitious sledge, and then solve for its motion as it slides through NLP space. Our proposal location is then given by the position of our sledge in parameter space after a predefined period of time T has elapsed.

As for Random Walk Metropolis, we need a rule to determine whether we accept a given proposal. Remember, this rule cannot be arbitrary – we need to design it so that (eventually) our sampling distribution will converge on the actual posterior. Fortunately, clever people have already done this work for us, so we accept a parameter θ_{t+1} with probability:

$$r = \frac{p(X \mid \theta_{t+1}) \times p(\theta_{t+1})}{p(X \mid \theta_t) \times p(\theta_t)} \times \frac{q(m')}{q(m)}, \tag{15.5}$$

where θ_t is our previous location in parameter space, m is the initial momentum of our sledge (that is, the value we sample at θ_t) and m' is the final momentum before we bring the sledge to rest. The function $q(m)$ is simply the probability density for whatever distribution was used to generate a random initial momentum. As discussed previously, the usual choice here is a multivariate normal distribution with mean zero and some covariance matrix (that is often diagonal).

How does our new acceptance probability compare with that from Random Walk Metropolis? The first part of the above expression is exactly the same as what we had before – it is just the ratio of the un-normalised posterior at the proposed location θ_{t+1} to that at θ_t. However, the second part of the expression is new. Is there an intuitive feel we can get for the purpose of this new part of our expression for r? To do so, we need to remember that the momentum proposal distribution we are using is a multivariate normal peaked at zero. This means that the acceptance probability is maximised at $m' = 0$, irrespective of the initial momentum m. But how can we get a small final momentum? We must have reached a peak in NLP space, corresponding to a trough in posterior space.

Hamiltonian dynamics of our sledge will naturally tend to make the sledge visit troughs in NLP space (corresponding to peaks in posterior space). Remember, this is the reason we used our physical analogy in the first place. However, we still need to ensure that we sample from each location in proportion to its height. If we do not, then we will get a sampler that is biased towards troughs in NLP space which correspond to peaks in posterior space. The function of the new term in expression (15.5) is to rebalance the path of our sampler towards those locations that would rarely be visited otherwise – the peaks in NLP space which correspond to the troughs in posterior space.

15○8 THE COMPLETE HMC ALGORITHM

Having surveyed the various elements of HMC, we are now in a position to describe the algorithm in its totality:

1   Select a random starting location θ_0 from some initial proposal distribution.
2   For $t = 1,2,...,n$ do the following:

- Generate a random initial momentum from a proposal distribution (for example, $m \sim N(\mu, \Sigma)$).
- Use the leapfrog algorithm to solve for the path of a sledge moving over NLP space for a time period T.
- After an amount of time T has elapsed, record the momentum of the sledge m' and its position in parameter space θ_{t+1}.
- Calculate

An
introduction
to Hamiltonian
Monte Carlo

$$r = \frac{p(X \mid \theta_{t+1}) \times p(\theta_{t+1})}{p(X \mid \theta_t) \times p(\theta_t)} \times \frac{q(m')}{q(m)}. \tag{15.6}$$

- Generate $u \sim U(0,1)$. If $r > u$ move to θ_{t+1}, otherwise remain at θ_t.

15○9　THE PERFORMANCE OF HMC VERSUS RANDOM WALK METROPOLIS AND GIBBS

Now that we have described the HMC algorithm, let's put it to use. Suppose that we want to sample from the posterior distribution:

$$\begin{pmatrix} X \\ Y \end{pmatrix} \sim N\left[\begin{pmatrix} 20 \\ 5 \end{pmatrix}, \begin{pmatrix} 2 & 0.8 \\ 0.8 & 0.5 \end{pmatrix} \right], \tag{15.7}$$

where, for example, (X,Y) could represent the daily returns of two different stocks. In this case, we assume that we know the posterior distribution (given above), so we simply use the value of the multivariate normal density at points in parameter space to calculate the ratios used in Random Walk Metropolis or HMC. If this were a Bayesian inference problem, the method would remain the same except that we would use the un-normalised posterior density.

In Figure 15.7 we compare the performance of 100 iterations of four sampling algorithms: Random Walk Metropolis, Gibbs, HMC and independent sampling. Random Walk Metropolis (top left) has relatively few accepted steps, and so is slow to traverse parameter space. Gibbs (top right) does a bit better, although, since it is constrained to move in either vertical or horizontal directions, it does not explore as fast as it might otherwise. The HMC sampler (bottom left) is, by contrast, unconstrained in its movement, and as a result explores the posterior mode efficiently. We finally include samples from an independent sampler (bottom right), to illustrate the gold standard; however, note that in practice we usually do not have access to such an efficient method.

15○10　OPTIMAL STEP LENGTH OF HMC: INTRODUCING THE 'NO-U-TURN SAMPLER'

We have, thus far, skirted over the issue of how long (T) to follow our sledge after we shove it. It should come as no surprise that, since HMC is really a type of Metropolis algorithm, choice of this algorithm parameter affects the rate at which our sampling distribution converges to posterior. Clearly, if T is short, then in each step we do not move far, and it will take us a long time to explore the posterior. Therefore, if we make T large, does this mean that the distances we travel in parameter space will be similarly large? It turns out to be a little more complex than

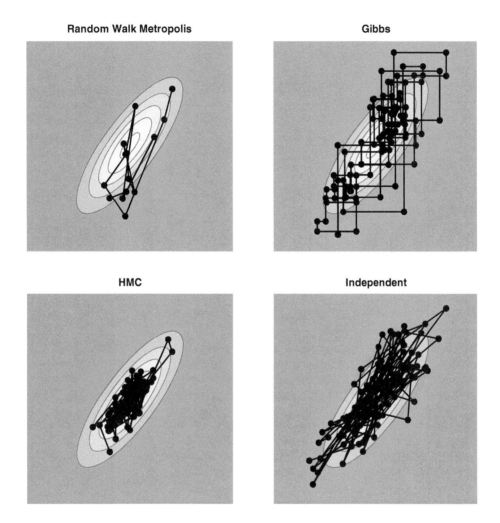

Figure 15.7 Showing the path taken by four different sampling algorithms from a bivariate normal distribution. In each case, 100 samples were drawn.

this reasoning suggests, because of the propensity of the sledge to loop round and retrace close to its original steps (see Figure 15.8).

The tendency of the sledge to perform such U-turns means that simulating the path of the sledge for longer periods can be an inefficient use of computational time. This is because some time is spent on simulating the path of the sledge when it is actually moving closer to its start point. This means that the rate of exploration of the posterior landscape is slower than would be the case if we chose a smaller T (see Figure 15.8).

One way to proceed would therefore be to tune T in preliminary runs of the HMC algorithm. By selecting a value of T that results in a high acceptance rate, we hope to ensure a fairly efficient running of the algorithm. However, it turns out that we can do slightly better.

The propensity of the sledge to do U-turns clearly depends on the geometry of the posterior itself. If the posterior is fairly curved, then the sledge will ascend hills, run out of momentum and

t = 0   t = 100

t = 200   t = 300

Figure 15.8   The sledge has the propensity to perform U-turns if followed for too long, meaning it can end up where it started. If, instead, we stopped the sledge after 100 time points, we would have a faster rate of exploration of parameter space.

U turns in posterior space: motivating the NUTS sampler

descend, perhaps returning the way it came. By contrast, if the posterior is flat, then such U-turns will not happen; the sledge will just continue on its way until time runs out. For highly curved posteriors, it is therefore preferable to use a relatively short T to negate the possibility of U-turns, whereas for flatter landscapes a longer T is preferable.

The situation is slightly more complex than this, however: a posterior will often be composed of a patchwork of curved and flat regions. This means that assigning a single global T value results in local inefficiencies: in curved regions T will be too long and the sledge will tend to do U-turns; in flat regions T will be too short, and so the rate of exploration of posterior space will be slower than optimal.

So what can we do? Ideally, we would allow T to vary along with our position in parameter space. By using a locally optimal T, we therefore hope to produce a sampler that avoids U-turns when the posterior is highly curved, and prevents early termination for flatter regions. But how can we do this without knowing the shape of the posterior itself – the very thing we are trying to understand by doing sampling in the first place?

Fortunately for us, some clever people have already done the work of creating such an efficient algorithm: Matthew Hoffman and Andrew Gelman call theirs the *No-U-Turn Sampler*, or (slightly unfortunately) NUTS for short [19]. The way it works is essentially by monitoring the distance between the starting location θ and the current position of the sledge $\tilde{\theta}$. If this distance increases during the next discrete step of the algorithm, then it terminates and we use the current position as our proposal location. The actual algorithm is more complex than this to ensure that we have detailed balance (see Section 13.6.3), although we do not wish to go into the details here. The best thing about this algorithm is that it is already implemented in Stan (see Chapter 16), and it is this sampler that is used by default when we run the software.

15●11 CHAPTER SUMMARY

With the end of this chapter we finish our run through the three algorithms that we discuss in this book: Random Walk Metropolis, the Gibbs sampler and Hamiltonian Monte Carlo. The order in which we met these samplers was chosen to correspond somewhat to their inherent complexity, and more or less reflects the temporal order in which these algorithms were developed. Random Walk Metropolis is simple to implement and places few requirements on our knowledge of the problem at hand. Its simplicity has an added benefit – generality. Random Walk Metropolis can be applied to virtually any problem when a likelihood can be calculated (for example, differential equations). However, while it is straightforward to code up Random Walk Metropolis, it can be slow to converge to the posterior – too slow for most interesting problems. Gibbs sampling requires that we know a little more about the problem at hand, particularly its geometry. By taking account of underlying geometric relationships between parameter sets, this algorithm is typically faster than Random Walk Metropolis. However, for many purposes, the maths required to derive the requisite conditional distributions can be demanding, and there are many circumstances where they do not exist. We have also seen that this algorithm is inefficient when large correlations exist between parameters, because the directions in which the sampler moves are not natural for the posterior geometry. HMC (and its recently developed, smarter cousin NUTS) is a version of the Metropolis algorithm that avoids some of these pitfalls by taking into account the posterior geometry when deciding where next to step. This means that the rate of convergence to the posterior can be orders of magnitude faster than for aforementioned methods.

In HMC we move in a space called the negative log posterior (NLP) space. This space is essentially the inverse of the posterior: peaks in NLP space correspond to troughs for the posterior and vice versa. We imagine that we slide over this frictionless NLP terrain on a sledge. Because of the physical analogy, the path that our sledge moves is towards the bottom of valleys in NLP space, corresponding to peaks in posterior space. The path that we follow will, therefore, automatically tend to propose locations with high posterior density, and hence the acceptance rate is typically much higher than for Random Walk Metropolis. This higher acceptance rate means that the algorithm explores posterior space more efficiently.

In each iteration of the HMC algorithm we solve for the path of the sledge across NLP space using Newton's laws of motion. Unfortunately, these equations are too hard to solve exactly, so we approximate the curved path, by breaking it up into a series of straight line segments. In order to achieve a good approximation to the exact path, these links must be short, meaning that many such straight steps are required to avoid the approximate path diverging from the exact one. However, it is possible that the curvature of the posterior at a particular point may be so extreme that tiny steps are required to avoid such a divergence. As we shall see in Chapter 16, Stan does its best to determine where such divergences occur and alerts us to their presence.

To increase the chance that we reach isolated NLP valleys, as well as climb its peaks, we periodically bring the sledge to rest and then give it a shove in a randomly chosen direction. This random initial value of the momentum is typically obtained by independent sampling from a multivariate normal distribution. The sledge is brought to rest after T time steps have elapsed. At the end of such a period, we record the position of the sledge in θ space along with its momentum. We then use a new version of the Metropolis accept–reject rule to determine whether we accept this new parameter value or return to the previous one. This rule ensures that we have asymptotic convergence of the sampling distribution to the posterior.

The time period T between consecutive measurements of the sledge's position affects the efficiency of the HMC sampler. If it is too short, then the sampler is slow to explore posterior space. If it is too long, then the sampler can become inefficient because it performs U-turns, meaning that the sledge moves over well-trodden turf. The No–U-Turn Sampler (NUTS) is an advancement on HMC that was developed to allow a locally optimal T to be determined at each position in parameter space.

Fortunately, NUTS is implemented in Stan, meaning that we are saved the nightmare of coding up the algorithm ourselves. However, it is important that we understand what is happening 'under the hood' in Stan (by reading this chapter) so that we do not encounter the many pitfalls of MCMC. While Stan obviates the need to code up the NUTS algorithm itself, to estimate our own models we must be conversational in Stan's own language. It is this challenge to which we turn in Chapter 16.

15○12 CHAPTER OUTCOMES

The reader should now be familiar with the following concepts:

- negative log posterior (NLP) space
- how a physical analogy – a sledge sliding down a frictionless NLP landscape – helps us speed up sampling
- what divergent iterations are, and how they are caused
- how the No-U-Turn Sampler (NUTS) yields locally adaptive time periods over which to simulate the sledge's motion using Newton's laws of motion

15○13 PROBLEM SETS

Problem 15.1 Cerebral malaria: coding up samplers

Suppose you work for the WHO researching malaria. In particular, it is your job to produce a model for the number of cases of cerebral malaria in a large country. Cerebral malaria is one of the most severe complications resulting from infection with *Plasmodium falciparum* malaria, and without treatment invariably causes death. However, even for patients receiving treatment there is still a significant chance of permanent cognitive impairment.

You decide to model the number of cases of cerebral malaria ($X = 5$) as being from a joint normal distribution along with the number of all malaria cases ($Y = 20$). The mean number of cases of cerebral malaria is μ_c, and the mean number of cases of all malaria is μ_t. If we assume an (improper) uniform prior distribution on these quantities and assume that the correlation between cerebral and total cases is known ($\rho = 0.8$) along with the variances, the posterior is:

$$\begin{pmatrix} \mu_t \\ \mu_c \end{pmatrix} \sim N\left[\begin{pmatrix} 20 \\ 5 \end{pmatrix}, \begin{pmatrix} 2 & 0.8 \\ 0.8 & 0.5 \end{pmatrix} \right], \tag{15.8}$$

where all quantities are measured in thousands.

Note that this example does not test your ability to do Bayesian inference (because we have already provided the exact form of the posterior distribution). Rather its purpose is to allow you to compare the performance of a number of different sampling algorithms.

Problem 15.1.1 Use your statistical software of choice to generate 100 independent samples of (μ_t, μ_c). Draw a scatter plot of your (μ_t, μ_c) samples, with lines connecting consecutive points. How close are the sample-estimated means to the true means? *Hint*: to do this in R you will need to use the MASS package:

```
library(MASS)
Sigma <- matrix(c(2,0.8,0.8,0.5),2,2)
mvrnorm(n = 100, c(20,5), Sigma)
```

Problem 15.1.2 Code up a Random Walk Metropolis sampler for this example. This is composed of the following steps:

1   Create a proposal function that takes the current value of $\theta = (\mu_t, \mu_c)$ and outputs a proposed value of these using a multivariate normal centred on the current estimates. (Here use a multivariate normal proposal with an identity covariance matrix.)

2   Create a function which takes as inputs $\theta^{current}$ and $\theta^{proposed}$, and outputs the ratio of the posteriors at the proposed value to the current one. *Hint*: to do this in R you will need to use the following to calculate the value of the posterior at (x, y):

```
library(mvtnorm)
Sigma <- matrix(c(2,0.8,0.8,0.5),2,2)
dmvnorm(c(x,y),c(20,5), Sigma)
```

3   Create an accept-reject function which takes as inputs $\theta^{current}$ and $\theta^{proposed}$, and then uses the above ratio function to find $r = \theta^{proposed} / \theta^{current}$; then compare r with a uniformly distributed random number u between 0 and 1. If $r > u$ then output $\theta^{proposed}$; otherwise output $\theta^{current}$.

4   Combine the proposal function along with the accept-reject function to make a function that takes as input $\theta^{current}$, proposes a new value of θ, and then, based on r, moves to that new point or stays in the current position.

5   Create a function called RWMetropolis that takes a starting value of θ and runs for n steps.

Use your RWMetropolis function to generate 100 samples from the posterior starting from $(\mu_t, \mu_c) = (10,5)$. Draw a line plot of your (μ_t, μ_c) samples. How do your estimates of the posterior mean from Random Walk Metropolis compare with the true values? Why is there a bias in your estimates, and how could this be corrected?

Problem 15.1.3 For your 100 samples, using Random Walk Metropolis calculate the percentage of accepted steps.

Problem 15.1.4 Create a function that calculates Gelman's $\hat{R}$ for each of (μ_t, μ_c) using:

$$\hat{R}(t) = \sqrt{\frac{W(t) + \frac{1}{t}(B(t) - W(t))}{W(t)}},$$ (15.9)

where:

$$W(t) = \frac{1}{m}\sum_{j=1}^{m} s(t)_j^2$$ (15.10)

measures the within-chain variance at time t averaged over m chains, and $s(t)_j^2$ is the sample variance of chain j. Also:

$$B(t) = \frac{t}{m-1}\sum_{j=1}^{m}(\overline{\theta(t)}_j - \overline{\theta(t)})^2$$ (15.11)

measures the between-chain variance at time t. Here $\overline{\theta(t)}_j$ is the average value of a parameter in chain j, and $\overline{\theta(t)}$ is the average value of a parameter across all chains. (*Hint 1*: first create two separate functions that calculate the within- and between-chain variance. *Hint 2*: you will obtain a value of $\hat{R}$ for each of (μ_t, μ_c).)

Problem 15.1.5 Start all eight chains at $(\mu_t, \mu_c) = (20, 5)$ and calculate $\hat{R}$ for a per chain sample size of 5. Does this mean we have reached convergence?

Problem 15.1.6 Using eight chains, calculate $\hat{R}$ for each of (μ_t, μ_c) for a sample size of 100. This time make sure to start your chains in overdispersed positions in parameter space. Use a random number from a multivariate normal centred on the posterior means with a covariance matrix of 40 times the identity matrix.

Problem 15.1.7 After approximately how many iterations does Random Walk Metropolis reach $\hat{R} < 1.1$?

Problem 15.1.8 The conditional distributions of each variable are given by:

$$\mu_t \sim N(20 + 1.6(\mu_c - 5), (1 - 0.8^2)2),$$

$$\mu_c \sim N(5 + 0.4(\mu_t - 20), (1 - 0.8^2)0.5).$$ (15.12)

Problem 15.1.9 Use your Gibbs sampler to draw 100 samples. Draw a scatter plot of your (μ_t, μ_c) samples with lines connecting consecutive points. Discarding the first 50 observations, how do the estimates of the mean of each parameter compare with their true values?

Problem 15.1.10 Generate 200 samples from each of your Random Walk Metropolis and Gibbs samplers. Discard the first 100 observations of each as warm-up. For each calculate the error in estimating the posterior mean of μ_t. Repeat this exercise 40 times, each time recording the error. How does their error compare to the independent sampler?

Problem 15.1.11 Repeat Problem 15.1.10 to obtain the average error in estimating the posterior mean of μ_t across a range of sample sizes from $n = 5$ to $n = 200$.

Problem 15.1.12 Using the results from the previous question, estimate the effective sample size for 150 observations of the Random Walk Metropolis and Gibbs samplers.

Problem 15.1.13 What do the above results tell you about the relative efficiency of each of the three samplers?

Problem 15.1.14 Code up a Hamiltonian Monte Carlo (HMC) sampler for this problem. (Alternatively, use the functions provided in the R file HMC_scripts.R adapted from [8].) Use a standard deviation of the momentum proposal distribution (normal) of 0.18, along with a step size $\epsilon = 0.18$ and $L = 10$ individual steps per iteration to simulate 100 samples from the posterior. How does the estimate of the mean compare with that from the independent, Random Walk Metropolis and Gibbs samplers?

Problem 15.1.15 What is the acceptance rate for HMC? How does this compare with Random Walk Metropolis?

Problem 15.1.16 Gibbs sampling has an acceptance rate of 100%. How can HMC be more efficient than Gibbs given that its acceptance rate is less than 100%?

Problem 15.1.17 You receive new data that results in a change in the posterior to:

$$\begin{pmatrix} \mu_t \\ \mu_c \end{pmatrix} \sim N \left[\begin{pmatrix} 20 \\ 5 \end{pmatrix}, \begin{pmatrix} 2 & 0.99 \\ 0.99 & 0.5 \end{pmatrix} \right].$$
(15.13)

Using your Random Walk Metropolis sampler, calculate $\hat{R}$ for eight chains, where each chain generates 100 samples.

Problem 15.1.18 Estimate the value of $\hat{R}$ for HMC on the posterior from the new data, for a sample size of 100. How does it compare to Random Walk Metropolis?

Problem 15.2 HMC and U-turns

The code in HMC_UTurn.R simulates Hamiltonian dynamics for a single particle on the distribution described in the previous question:

$$\begin{pmatrix} \mu_t \\ \mu_c \end{pmatrix} \sim N \left[\begin{pmatrix} 20 \\ 5 \end{pmatrix}, \begin{pmatrix} 2 & 0.8 \\ 0.8 & 0.5 \end{pmatrix} \right].$$
(15.14)

In this question we will see how the efficiency of HMC depends on the choice of the number of intermediate steps. In particular we investigate the propensity of a particle undergoing Newtonian dynamics to perform U-turns.

Problem 15.2.1 Simulate a single particle starting at $(20,5)$ for $L = 10$ steps with the parameters $\epsilon = 0.18$ (step size) and $\sigma = 0.18$ (momentum proposal distribution width). Plot the path in parameter space.

Problem 15.2.2 Now try $L = 20, 50, 100$ steps, again plotting the results. What do you notice about the paths?

Problem 15.2.3 Simulate 100 iterations of the particle starting at $(20,5)$, with each particle running for $L = 100$ steps. Examine the motion of the particle in one of the parameter dimensions, and hence determine an optimal number of steps for this distribution.

16

Chapter contents

STAN

16●1   CHAPTER MISSION STATEMENT

By the end of this chapter the reader will appreciate the benefits of using Stan to do Markov chain Monte Carlo (MCMC). They will also understand how to code up models in Stan's language and know what to do when things go wrong.

16●2   CHAPTER GOALS

Chapter 15 showed us the power of Hamiltonian Monte Carlo (HMC) compared to the older Random Walk Metropolis and Gibbs algorithms. However, this power comes at a cost of extra complexity. Furthermore, in HMC, as in Random Walk Metropolis, there is a need to tune the algorithm to ensure that it efficiently traverses posterior space. These two aspects can make implementing HMC foreboding, even for more experienced MCMCers. Fortunately, for many applications of Bayesian statistics, we do not need to: Stan [8] does the hard work for us.

Stan actually implements an improved version of HMC known as the No-U-Turn Sampler (NUTS) that self-tunes for maximal algorithmic efficiency. This makes Stan fast, really fast. All that the user needs to do is use the intuitive, and easy-to-learn, Stan language to code up their model, and Stan does the rest. The language is being constantly updated and improved, using some of the best minds in the business. In particular, the language is the brainchild of Andrew Gelman, one of the world's foremost Bayesians.

Stan is a probabilistic modelling language that implements black box MCMC that can be accessed through a variety of interfaces, including R, Python, the command line, Matlab, Stata, Mathematica and Julia. The R interface is known as RStan, and is probably the most popular of these. Its popularity means that it is well tested and supported, and so in this chapter we provide examples using this package. However, while we use RStan to call Stan, the underlying models are always written in the same Stan language, meaning that the example Stan programs that we provide in this chapter do not change across interfaces.

Stan programs are composed of a number of blocks, which are used to specify a model. While this variety may, at first, appear scary, having sections in compartments actually makes things a lot easier. In this chapter, we step individually through the different blocks, so that the reader learns their use and significance in an overall Stan program.

Stan supports a large range of data and parameter types, from continuous variables to arrays to covariance matrices and so on. In this chapter, we cover most of these and explain how to find out more if you are faced with a new type of data. Stan also comes pre-loaded with a wide assortment of probability distributions – both discrete and continuous. Also, even if a distribution of choice is not available, so long as you can code its log density, you can use it in Stan (see Section 16.6).

The Stan language is popular. This is important. When things go wrong with your Stan program – and they inevitably will at some point – the popularity of Stan means that there are ample resources to help you through. From very active user forums (staffed by Stan developers) to a thorough manual and numerous web case studies, Stan has got a lot of different ways to trouble-shoot. In this chapter, we walk the reader through these various ports and explain how to get the most from them. There are numerous other, less popular, MCMC packages, although they are not nearly as well supported as Stan. If you use one of these and get stuck, you are on your own for the most part. Our advice: use Stan!

The best way to get up and running with Stan is to code up example models. As such, this chapter is littered with example code in both R and Stan, which hopefully makes getting started a bit easier. However, we strongly encourage the reader to attempt to code up their respective models sooner rather than later. As with most things, we learn most rapidly when we step out of our comfort zone.

 ## WHY STAN, AND HOW TO GET IT?

This section explains in detail the benefits of Stan and how to download and start to use the software.

16.3.1 When to use black box MCMC rather than coding up the algorithms yourself

We have been introduced to three basic flavours of MCMC algorithms: Random Walk Metropolis, Gibbs and HMC. Each of these has its strengths and weaknesses. Random Walk Metropolis is simple to code and, as such, can be used in quite general settings. However, its generality comes at a cost – the algorithm is usually slow to converge, particularly for more complex models. Gibbs sampling can, at times, provide an increased rate of convergence, although it requires that we know the conditional distributions for parameters and can independently sample from them. HMC is a generalisation of Random Walk Metropolis that uses posterior geometry when deciding where to step next, and is usually much faster than the other two. However, to code up HMC we need to calculate the derivatives of the log density, which can be prohibitive for some classes of probability models, for example large systems of differential equations.

While the packages that implement variants of the three aforementioned algorithms are generally great, there will always be circumstances where they cannot be used. These circumstances can be due to the nature of the probability model or, sometimes, due to a mismatch in modelling software between elements of an analysis. It therefore pays to understand how these methods work so that they can be rewritten to suit different settings.

Furthermore, there are benefits to implementing these algorithms yourself; you learn much more about how they work by doing so. These benefits are realised when when you then go onto use so-called black box MCMC software, like Stan, BUGS and JAGS, since naive use of these languages can result in misleading results.

However, there are many circumstances where it pays to rely on the well-tested MCMC software produced by others. One of the benefits of using popular third-party software is that it may have fewer bugs than writing the MCMC algorithms yourself. Furthermore, the authors of these packages typically put a lot of thought into ensuring the implementation is efficient, meaning that they can be significantly faster than a custom implementation. An often-missed benefit of these packages is that they usually provide a raft of useful MCMC summary statistics. These metrics often allow a quick diagnosis of misbehaving chains and can point to issues with the underlying statistical model.

Overall, whether you decide to use a third-party MCMC implementation, or write one yourself, comes down to a number of factors: the time saved by relying on others' work, the convenience of the software to the problem at hand and the cost of learning a new programming language. As we said previously, there are definitely classes of problems that – at the moment – are not covered by packages, although, in the near future, the size of this class may shrink since the speed of software development in this area tends to be unusually fast. Re. the cost of learning a new language, we argue that some are easier to learn than others (see Section 16.3.2).

16.3.2 What is Stan?

Stan is an intuitive, yet sophisticated, probabilistic programming language that provides an interface to a recently proposed extension to HMC, known as NUTS [19, 8]. The idea is that you code up a model using Stan's syntax, and then Stan does the MCMC for you. But what exactly is the nature of the Stan language, and how does it compare with the popular BUGS and JAGS languages?

Stan is what is known as an *imperative* programming language. We will not go into the details of what this means, but will just say that most traditional programming languages like R, Python, Matlab, C++ and others tend to behave in this way, at least approximately so. This is not true for BUGS and JAGS, which are known as *declarative* languages. This distinction is important for two reasons: (1) we believe learning Stan is easier if you are familiar with other programming languages, and (2) partly because of its imperative nature, Stan is a type of Turing-complete language that basically means that it can be used to code up a larger swathe of models compared to BUGS and JAGS.

We also argue that even if you are already familiar with BUGS and JAGS, there are similarities between them and Stan (model blocks for one thing). This means that the learning curve for Stan is not steep for existent BUGS and JAGS users.

16.3.3 Why choose Stan?

There are a multitude of MCMC packages out there, so why do we suggest using Stan above all others? There are number of reasons for this, but the most important one is its popularity. While, on first glance, this might appear to be no more than suggesting users go with the status quo, there are very good reasons for choosing a popular piece of software. An important reason is that more popular software is usually better tested and, as a consequence, more bug-free. However, a more pressing reason is that Stan, because of its popularity, has a huge range of resources generated by users and developers. This is particularly relevant for MCMC, because inevitably there will be times when things go wrong: for example, your model does not compile, or your chains fail to converge. In these circumstances, it is important to know that there are places you can go to help solve your problem: the Stan manual, the user forum and the corpus of case studies produced for Stan are helpful sources here. Other MCMC software does not have this wealth of materials, and because of this, if you get stuck, you remain stuck. Even if the software has all the bells and whistles available from all the latest papers (although doubtful it would rival Stan), there is really no substitute for popularity. However, if you do not find the above reasoning sexy, there are a bunch of other reasons to use Stan:

- **Stan is fast.** In general, it is much faster than BUGS and JAGS in terms of the number of effective samples generated per second. This is partly a result of implementing an extension to HMC known as NUTS, but also because of other clever software quirks, like using algorithmic differentiation to evaluate derivatives, and because it uses good software design principles.

- **Learning Stan is easy.** As already described in Section 16.3.2, the imperative nature of the language means that it is similar to most other traditional programming languages. Also, the switch from BUGS or JAGS is not difficult because of the commonality between them.

- **Stan is more general than BUGS and JAGS.** We discussed in Section 16.3.2 that Stan is a Turing-complete language, and hence can be used to code a much wider class of problems than BUGS or JAGS.

- **Stan is written by smart people.** Specifically, it is the brainchild of Andrew Gelman, who is unequivocally the world's foremost Bayesian statistician. There are a load of other theoretical and applied statisticians working on the project, meaning that the language is frequently updated to include the latest methods, new data and parameter types as well as things that make it better.

- **The developers have translated examples from the leading textbooks in the field into Stan.** These include books that previously contained examples only in BUGS or JAGS (for example, the *BUGS book* [24]), making it easier to transition from these to Stan.

- **Recent books contain examples in Stan.** Following on from the previous case, many of the recent books written contain examples written in Stan, rather than BUGS or JAGS.

- **shinyStan makes inference fun.** OK, maybe we are a bit biased here, but the interactive nature of the shinyStan R package makes inference a lot easier and more of a pleasure than a chore. This is another reason why we suggest using R as opposed to one of the other statistical software packages which are available to us.

Overall, Stan makes our life easier. Not a convert yet? Well, that is what this chapter is for.

16.4 GETTING SET UP WITH STAN USING RSTAN

This section briefly describes how to get Stan set up on a computer. The reason for its brevity is mainly because there are detailed resources for this subject on the Stan website (http://mc-stan. org/). However, here we detail the basic steps for getting up and running using RStan, the R interface to the Stan language.

R. To begin with, since we are going to use R to call Stan, we need a newish version of it installed. To get this go to https://www.r-project.org/ and download the latest version for your particular system.

RStudio. Although not essential, we strongly suggest using RStudio to write, edit and run R code. It is great even if you do not use Stan. However, if you do, a particularly nice feature of this development environment is its capability to highlight Stan syntax as you write. To get RStudio go to https://www.rstudio.com/.

Toolchain. The Stan package relies on your computer having a few necessary tools to handle C++ files. Among other reasons this is because Stan code is, under the hood, actually translated into C++ code and compiled. The best way to get the requisite software for a Windows or Mac computer is to install RTools. The Stan website walks the user through this for both cases. If you are on a Linux computer, then you will need to install build-essential and a recent version of either g++ or clang++ compilers.

RStan. The only remaining thing that we need is the RStan package itself. This can be done from within R or RStudio, using the following commands:

```
install.packages('rstan',
                 repos = 'https://cloud.r-project.org/',
                 dependencies=TRUE)
```

You can speed up the installation by preceding the above with the optional command:

```
Sys.setenv(MAKEFLAGS = "-j4")
```

where you replace '4' in the above with the number of processors available on your computer.

16○5 OUR FIRST WORDS IN STAN

This section describes how to code up a basic Stan model. Since the backbone of typical Stan programs does not vary considerably, this section forms the basis for later, more complex models.

16.5.1 The main blocks of a Stan program

To explain the importance of each element of a typical Stan program, we introduce a simple example. Suppose that we want to infer the mean height, μ, in a population of interest. To carry out this inference we need some data, so suppose that we have recorded the height, Y_i (in metres), of 10 individuals drawn from that population. Further, suppose that the normal sampling model is appropriate given the multitude of different factors that affect the height of a person (see Section 3.5), that is:

$$Y_i \sim N(\mu, \sigma), \tag{16.1}$$

where σ is the standard deviation of the sampling distribution. To complete our specification of a Bayesian model we need priors, which we choose as:

$$\mu \sim N(1.5, 0.1)$$
$$\sigma \sim \Gamma(1,1) \tag{16.2}$$

The completed Stan program implementing the above model is shown in code block 1. Before we describe the importance of each of these blocks, we first take a moment to describe how best to write and save a Stan program:

```
data {
    real Y [10]; // heights for 10 people
}
parameters {
    real mu; // mean height in population
    real<lower=0> sigma; // sd of height distribution
}
model {
    for(i in 1:10) {
        Y[i] ~ normal(mu,sigma); // likelihood
    }
    mu ~ normal(1.5,0.1); // prior for mu
    sigma ~ gamma(1,1); // prior for sigma
}
```

Stan code 1   A simple Stan program.

Writing a Stan program

Stan programs can be written in a text editor and, as long as they are saved with a '.stan' ending (for example, aModel.stan), they can be executed. However, this is not best practice. Here, we suggest you write Stan models using RStudio or emacs. Both of these editors recognise Stan syntax and hence help to minimise errors while writing your models. To write a model in RStudio, you will need a fairly recent version of the software. You then must create a new text file, making sure to save it suffixed with .stan. The other option, emacs, has a bit of a steeper learning curve, although it has a great range of functionality that can speed up the model development process considerably.

How to write your first Stan program

We now describe the three most important blocks of a typical Stan program.

Data

```
data {
    real Y[10]; // heights for 10 people
}
```

The data block, as its name suggests, is used to declare all the data that you will pass to Stan (from R, Python or whatever other statistical software you use), which allow it to estimate your model. Stan is a strongly statically typed language, which basically means that you must declare the type of data or parameters which are used in your model. Also, if you declare a variable as one type, you cannot later convert it to another.

In the above we declare the variable Y – representing the heights of the 10 people – to be of type `real [10]`. This means that it is an array with 10 elements, each of which is an unbounded continuous variable. There are a range of different data types that can be declared, and we include only a handful of examples here:

- **real**<lower=0,upper=1> Z: a continuous variable bounded between 0 and 1
- **int**<lower=0> Z: a discrete variable that takes integer values with a minimum value of 0
- **int**<lower=0> Z[N]: an array of length *N*, where each element of the array is a discrete variable that takes integer values with a minimum value of 0
- **vector**[N] Z: a vector of continuous variables of length *N*
- **matrix**[3,3] Z: a 3 × 3 matrix of continuous variables
- **matrix**[3,3] Z[5,2]: a 5 × 2 array of 3 × 3 matrices

Among other types in the above, we introduced arrays, vectors and matrices. You may be wondering what the difference is between these three types. Vectors and matrices contain only elements of type real – that is, continuous variables – whereas arrays can contain data of any type. In the above, we show how to declare arrays of integers and matrices. So why ever use the more limited vector and matrix types? First, they can be used to do linear algebra, whereas arrays cannot. Second, some functions (for example, the multivariate normal distribution) use these types as inputs rather than arrays. Third, there are a few minor memory and speed benefits to using a matrix rather than a two-dimensional array, due to the way data are stored in memory.

You have probably also noticed that the Stan code has semi colons (;) at the end of each statement where something is assigned. This happens for data declarations and (as we soon see) for parameter declarations, and anywhere where you access an element of a data type and assign it to something else. One place they do not occur is at the start of any loops or conditional statements, where nothing is assigned. However, to be honest it is usually pretty obvious when and where these statements should occur. Hopefully the rest of this example will illustrate this.

You may also have noticed that we can use // to make comments that annotate the code and make it easier to understand. Use of comments is essential for reproducible research – both for yourself and for anyone else who tries to make sense of your work in the future. However, do not overuse comments. Put them only in places where it is not obvious what your code does. Overly commented code can be messy and hard to read.

Parameters

The next section of code we consider is the `parameters` block, where we declare all the parameters that we will infer in our model:

```
parameters {
    real mu; // mean height in population
    real<lower=0> sigma; // sd of height distribution
}
```

Here, we declared the mean height in the population, which is an unbounded continuous variable, and the standard deviation, which is a continuous non-negative variable. Note that we could have specified a lower bound of zero on mu here because it must be non-negative; however, parameter values near this bound are not approached in practice.

As with the data block, a range of data types are available to us here. These include the vector, matrix and array types that we discussed previously, but also more exotic entities, some of which we show below:

- **simplex**[K] Z: a vector of *K* non-negative continuous variables whose sum is 1; simplexes are useful for parameter vectors, whose elements represent probabilities
- **corr_matrix**[K] Z: a *K*× *K* dimensional correlation matrix (symmetric, positive definite matrix with unit diagonals, with all elements between –1 and 1)
- **ordered**[K] Z: a vector of *K* continuous elements where either $Z[1] > Z[2] > ... > Z[K]$ or $Z[1] < Z[2] < ... < Z[K]$

Notice that discrete parameters are missing from the above description. This is not a mistake. Stan currently does not support integer-valued parameters, directly at least. This is because the theory of HMC for discrete parameters is not yet sufficiently developed. However, the Stan development team are working on this, and hopefully at some point in the future this will be possible. While this might seem like a serious issue, since many models contain discrete parameters, it is possible to indirectly include discrete parameters by marginalising them out (see Section 16.6). This means that the vast majority of models that use discrete parameters can still be coded in Stan.

Model

The next part of a Stan program we discuss is the `model` code block, which is used to specify the likelihood and priors for a model (or, more generally, to increment the log probability):

```
model {
    for(i in 1:10) {
        Y[i] ~ normal(mu,sigma); // likelihood
    }
    mu ~ normal(1.5,0.1); // prior for mu
    sigma ~ gamma(1,1); // prior for sigma
}
```

Sampling statements

An important thing to notice about the above block is the use of so-called sampling statements written by ~. The term *sampling statement* is suggestive, and not to be taken literally [8]. In the above, we use a sampling statement for the individual elements of *Y*, because we assumed each height is drawn from a normal sampling distribution, $Y_i \sim N(\mu,\sigma)$. Similarly, we assumed that the parameters μ and σ are drawn from normal and gamma prior distributions.

However, do not think that Stan actually does the independent sampling that these statements seem to suggest. (If it could then we wouldn't need to do MCMC in the first place! See Chapter 12 if you can't remember why this is.) Remember that Stan essentially runs on HMC. HMC is an MCMC method that works in negative log posterior space. Because the overall posterior numerator is the product of a number of elements comprising the likelihood and prior:

$$p(\theta \mid X) \propto p(X \mid \theta) \times p(\theta)$$

$$= \prod_{i=1}^{N} p(X_i \mid \theta) \times p(\theta),$$

(16.3)

this means the overall log posterior is the sum of the individual log probability of each element in the likelihood and prior:

$$\log p(\theta \mid X) \propto \log p(X \mid \theta) + \log p(\theta)$$

(16.4)

$$= \sum_{i=1}^{N} \log p(X_i \mid \theta) + \log p(\theta).$$

Therefore, in HMC, all we need to do is evaluate the log probability of each of these elements and sum them together. This is exactly what the sampling statements (the ~) help us to do. For each step in the HMC, we get a new value of μ and σ and, hence, need to evaluate the (un-normalised, negative) log posterior density. So in each step Stan calculates a new log probability by starting with a value of 0 and incrementing it each time it encounters a ~ statement. So:

```
for(i in 1:10) {
    Y[i] ~ normal(mu,sigma);
}
```

increments the log probability by $\log(p(Y[i])) \propto -\frac{1}{2}\log(\sigma^2) - (Y[i] - \mu)^2 / 2\sigma^2$ for the heights of each of the $i = 1,...,10$ individuals. This is the normal density not including any constant terms – sampling statements throw away the constants as they are usually not needed. Another way to express the above sampling statement is by an alternative Stan notation:

```
for(i in 1:10) {
    target += normal_lpdf(Y[i]|mu,sigma);
}
```

which more transparently increments target – a container that holds the current value of the log posterior – by a log probability corresponding to the log of the normal density at a height of $Y[i]$. To be clear here, target statements are not actually the same as ~ ones, because target statements keep any constants in the log density. However, for the majority of cases the distinction does not matter. Stan programs with ~ statements are generally quicker, but if you want the actual log probability of the model you need to use target statements.

Why do we highlight the distinction between what ~ means statistically and what it means in the Stan language? This is because you may get errors that you think are bugs in Stan but are actually due to interpreting ~ statistically. Take the following excerpt from a Stan program:

```
parameters {
    real theta;
}
model {
    ....
    theta ~ uniform(0,1);
}
```

On first glance, it appears that the parameter `theta` should be constrained to lie between 0 and 1, because it has a continuous prior with those bounds. However, this is not the case. All the above sampling statement does is increment the log probability by an amount given by the log uniform density. This means that it is possible for `theta` to stray outside of the 0 and 1 bounds, and if you run this program you may actually see this for a few iterations. (Stan will output a statement of the form 'Log probability evaluates to log(0)...'.)

Vectorisation

There is actually a more efficient and compact way to write our original model that takes advantage of the inherent vectorised nature of sampling statements:

```
model {
    Y ~ normal(mu,sigma); // likelihood
    ....
}
```

where we have replaced the for loop that accesses each element of Y individually, by the above, where we use the array Y on the left-hand side. For more complex models, using vectorised code can amount to serious speed-ups in the MCMC because the code is better able to leverage the benefits of C++ when it is translated.

Probability distributions

Stan comes equipped with a range of useful probability distributions. We do not include all of these below because they are easily found in the Stan manual and are constantly being updated. However, here are a few of the more popular distributions:

*   **Discrete:** Bernoulli, binomial, Poisson, beta-binomial, negative-binomial, categorical, multinomial
*   **Continuous unbounded:** normal, skew-normal, Student-t, Cauchy, logistic
*   **Continuous bounded:** uniform, beta, log-normal, exponential, gamma, chi-squared, inv-chi-squared, Weibull, Wiener diffusion, Pareto
*   **Multivariate continuous:** normal, Student-t, Gaussian process
*   **Exotics:** Dirichlet, LKJ, Wishart and inv-Wishart, Von-Mises

It is also worth noting that Stan sometimes provides different parameterisations of the same probability distribution (see the binomial and binomial_logit distributions in the Stan manual, for example), which make life easier.

16.5.2 Executing a Stan program from R

Now that we understand the aforementioned data, parameters and model blocks of a Stan program, let's discuss how we execute a Stan program in R through RStan. Note that this section assumes that you have installed R, RStudio and RStan as described in Section 16.4. To get up and running, follow these steps:

1   Create a new folder that will contain our .stan file along with an R file that we will use to call Stan.
2   In RStudio create a new text file, and paste the code in `code block 1` into it. Save this file in the newly created folder as 'simple.stan' (when you do so, you should see that RStudio highlights code in line with Stan's syntax).
3   In RStudio create a new R Script file, and save it in the folder.
4   In RStudio change the working directory to be the same as the newly created folder. This can be done manually through the drop-downs at the top of the window or using a line of code that will look something like:

```
Setwd("~/folder name")
```

dependent on the folder structure on your computer.

5   In the R Script file, load the RStan package using:

```
library(rstan)
```

6   (Optional) Set up RStan to run in parallel on multiple processors (if your computer has them) with the following line in your R Script:

```
options(mc.cores = parallel::detectCores())
```

7   Create some fake height data in R using:

```
Y <- rnorm(10,1.5,0.2)
```

8   Compile and run the MCMC on your Stan program by the following line in your R Script:

```
fit <- stan('simple.stan',iter=200,chains=4,
             data=list(Y=Y))
```

The above translates your Stan model into C++ code and compiles it. (This step may take up to a few minutes on older computers.) It then runs the MCMC using 200 iterations across four chains. Using Rstan, we supply our data as a list. So the overall R Script should look something like this:

```
library(rstan)
options(mc.cores = parallel::detectCores())

Y <- rnorm(10,1.5,0.2)
fit <- stan('simple.stan',iter=200,chains=4,
             data=list(Y=Y))
```

16.5.3 Interpreting the results of a Stan MCMC run

Hopefully we have successfully run our first Stan model. How do we look at the results? There are a number of ways to do so, and here we begin with the simplest. We can look at summary statistics for our posterior samples using:

```
print(fit,probs = c(0.25,0.5,0.75))
```

where 'fit' is the object in which we saved the result of our Stan run previously. This should out-put results that look something like the following. The exact numbers will differ because they depend on the fake data that you created using rnorm in R, and because MCMC is stochastic. However, the structure should look similar.

```
## Print summary statistics
print(fit,probs = c (0.25, 0.5, 0.75))

## Inference for Stan model: StanJags_simpleNormal.
## 4 chains, each with iter=200; warmup=100; thin=1;
## post-warmup draws per chain=100, total post-warmup draws=400.
##
##          mean   se_mean    sd    25%    50%    75%   n_eff   Rhat
## mu       1.52     0.00   0.08   1.47   1.53   1.56    400    1.00
## sigma    0.27     0.02   0.09   0.28   0.32   0.38     31    1.09
## lp_ _    4.87     0.09   1.15   4.51   5.18   5.66    167    1.03
##
## Samples were drawn using NUTS(diag_e) at Wed Aug 17 00:31:27 2016.
## For each parameter, n_eff is a crude measure of effective sample size,
## and Rhat is the potential scale reduction factor on split chains (at
## convergence, Rhat=1).
##   The estimated Bayesian Fraction of Missing Information is a measure of
##   the efficiency of the sampler with values close to 1 being ideal.
##   For each chain, these estimates are
##   0.9 1.3 1 0.8
```

So what do all the parts of the above mean? Well, the top part just states that four chains were run for 200 iterations each. However, the first half of these chains were discarded as 'warm-up' (see Section 13.9.5), meaning that there are only 100 samples kept as posterior samples for each chain, resulting in $400 = 4 \times 100$ 'total post-warmup draws'. The table in the output contains summary statistics for the two parameters of our model (μ, σ) as well as for the log probability of the model 'lp__'. The last two columns of the table are convergence diagnostics for each parameter: n_eff is the number of effective samples and Rhat $= \hat{R}$. In this case, we see that $\hat{R} < 1.1$ for all our parameters, giving us some confidence that our posterior shape will not change much if we collect more samples. The first six columns of the table show summary measures for the posterior samples, including the mean (and its standard error), the standard deviation and the three quantiles we specified in our print(fit,probs=c(0.25,0.5,0.75)) statement. The last part of the output contains information on the sampling algorithm used (NUTS) and the estimated Bayesian Fraction of Missing Information (BFMI) for each chain. BFMI is a newly created criterion that measures the autocorrelation in energy distribution sampled by each chain, with values near 1 indi-cating efficient sampling [4].

How do we extract the posterior samples and then graph them?

```
library(ggplot2)
mu <- extract(fit,'mu')[[1]]
qplot(mu)
```

where *extract* is an RStan function that pulls out any parameter we desire from a Stan fit object. We have chosen to use the 'ggplot2' library to display a histogram of the data here.

shinyStan

If you are using R, there is another, more interactive (and hence fun!) way to view the results from a Stan run, using the shinyStan package. You can install this package from within R using:

```
install.packages('shinystan')
```

From there, it is simple to create a shinyStan object and launch the shinyStan application:

```
library(shinystan)
aFit <- as.shinystan(fit)
launch_shinystan(aFit)
```

Upon executing the above, your web browser should open up (you do not need to be connected to the Internet), and you should see an intro screen with options including DIAGNOSE, ESTIMATE and EXPLORE. DIAGNOSE allows you to view detailed MCMC diagnostic criteria by clicking through the various options, including convergence criteria such as $\hat{R}$, effective sample size, and divergent iterations. ESTIMATE provides tables and basic graphs of the parameters in your model. EXPLORE, among other things, allows you to create scatter plots of samples from each variable plotted against one another. This graph, in particular, can be useful in diagnosing issues with your MCMC (see Section 16.7.2).

16.5.4 The other blocks

The three code blocks that we have introduced thus far are typically essential in a Stan program (see Section 16.6 for a counter-example); however, there are other code blocks that help to make life even easier. In this section we describe these.

Generated quantities

The most widely useful of the other blocks is the `generated quantities` code block. One of the main uses of this section is to do posterior predictive checks of a model's fit (see Chapter 10). Once you know how this section works, you will find that it is much easier to do posterior predictive checks here rather than afterwards in R, Python, and so on. This section of a Stan program is executed once per sample, meaning that it does not typically pose a threat to efficiency (although it can significantly affect the memory used by Stan; see Section 16.5.5).

Let's use our heights example from the preceding sections to illustrate how we can use this code block to do a posterior predictive check. Suppose that we want to test whether our model can generate the extremes that we see in our data. In particular, we choose to count the fraction of posterior predictive samples – each of the same size as our original data – where the maximum or minimum of the simulated data is more extreme than the actual data. We do this using the following:

```
generated quantities{
    vector[10] lSimData;
    int aMax_indicator;
    int aMin_indicator;

    // Generate posterior predictive samples
    for(i in 1:10){
      lSimData[i] = normal_rng(mu,sigma);
    }

    // Compare with real data
    aMax_indicator = max(lSimData) > max(Y);
    aMin_indicator = min(lSimData) < min(Y);
}
```

The first part of this code just declares the variables we intend to use in this block. We then use our posterior samples of μ and σ to generate posterior predictive samples of the same length as the actual data. We then determine whether the maximum and minimum of the simulated data are more extreme than the real data, generating a variable equal to 1 if this is the case, and 0 otherwise.

Note that to generate random samples from a given distribution, we use the '_rng' suffix. So in the above, Y=normal_rng(mu,sigma) generates a single (pseudo-)independent sample from a normal distribution with a mean of mu and a standard deviation of sigma. This is completely different to Y ~ normal(mu,sigma), which means 'increment the overall log probability by an amount given by the log likelihood of a data point Y for a normal distribution with a mean of mu and standard deviation of sigma' (see Section 16.5.1 if you need to remind yourself about this).

If we run the whole program, including the generated quantities section at the bottom, we obtain results that look something like the following:

```
## Print summary statistics
print(fit,probs = c(0.25, 0.5, 0.75))
```

##	mean	se_mean	sd	25%	50%	75%	n_eff	Rhat
## mu	1.52	0.00	0.08	1.47	1.53	1.56	400	1.00
## sigma	0.34	0.02	0.09	0.28	0.32	0.38	31	1.09
## lSimData[1]	1.51	0.02	0.35	1.32	1.49	1.73	400	0.99

```
## lSimData[2]      1.56      0.02  0.37  1.32  1.54  1.81    400  0.99
## lSimData[3]      1.53      0.02  0.35  1.31  1.55  1.76    377  1.00
## lSimData[4]      1.53      0.02  0.33  1.31  1.54  1.76    400  1.02
## lSimData[5]      1.52      0.02  0.38  1.27  1.50  1.75    400  0.99
## lSimData[6]      1.52      0.02  0.36  1.30  1.53  1.77    400  1.00
## lSimData[7]      1.50      0.02  0.36  1.27  1.50  1.73    383  1.00
## lSimData[8]      1.54      0.02  0.35  1.33  1.53  1.76    337  0.99
## lSimData[9]      1.49      0.02  0.38  1.29  1.50  1.75    275  1.01
## lSimData[10]     1.51      0.02  0.36  1.30  1.52  1.73    400  1.03
## aMax_indicator   0.50      0.03  0.50  0.00  0.00  1.00    282  1.01
## aMin_indicator   0.40      0.04  0.49  0.00  0.00  1.00    196  1.01
## lp_ _            4.87      0.09  1.15  4.51  5.18  5.66    167  1.03
```

So we now have summary statistics for the posterior predictive data. In particular, we have the means of the two indicator variables which represent Bayesian p values (see Chapter 10). Therefore, using this posterior predictive check, we conclude that our model is a reasonable fit to the data, since the p values (the mean values of the indicator variable samples) are nowhere near 0 or 1.

Another use of this code block is to generate the requisite data for measuring a model's predictive performance. However, we leave a discussion of how to do this until Section 16.6.

Finally, another use we will mention but not discuss now is that the `generated quantities` block can be used to generate samples from parameters that interest us at a given level of a hierarchical model (see Chapter 17).

Functions

Code can be made more readable and less error prone if we define functions to carry out any frequently used operations. As an example, suppose that, together with the height of individuals in our sample, we also had their weight. Suppose that we believe that a reasonable model for the relationship between these two variables could be described by:

$$Y_i \sim N(\beta \log(X_i), \sigma), \tag{16.5}$$

where (X_i, Y_i) are the weight and height of individual i. While this model does not have repetitions, we might find it neater to use a function that calculates the mean of the normal:

```
functions{
   real covariateMean(real aX, real aBeta){
     return(aBeta * log(aX));
   }
}
```

where the first **real** before the function name declares that the function will return a continuous variable. The elements contained within parentheses tell the function that it will accept two reals – *aX* and *aBeta* – as inputs. The **return** statement then passes back the required value. Note that it is possible to declare variables in a Stan function; here, because the function is simple, we chose to calculate the value and return it in a single line. The whole Stan program then has the following form:

```
functions{
  real covariateMean(real aX, real aBeta){
    return(aBeta * log(aX));
  }
}
data {
    int N; // Number of people in sample
    real Y[N]; // Heights for N people
    real X[N]; // Weights for N people
}
parameters {
    real beta;
    real<lower=0> sigma; // sd of height pop distribution
}
model {
    for(i in 1:N){
        Y[i] ~ normal(covariateMean(X[i],beta),sigma);
    }
    beta ~ normal(0,1);
    sigma ~ gamma(1,1);
}
```

We have placed an $N(0,1)$ prior on the β parameter. Note that we have chosen to pass the sample size N as data to the Stan program. This is good practice since it allows the model to generalise to bigger samples and otherwise just neatens things up. Also note that functions must be declared at the top of a Stan program, otherwise the other blocks cannot find the requisite functions when they are executed. If you save this file in your working directory (again, making sure to save it as .stan), you can take it for a test drive. To do so, generate some fake data in R, then call Stan:

```
N <- 100
X <- rnorm(N,60,10)
beta <- 0.3
sigma <- 0.3
Y <- beta * log(X) + rnorm(N,0,sigma)

## Call Stan
fit <-stan('covariate.stan',iter=200,chains=4,
                data=list(Y=Y,X=X,N=N))
```

Hopefully you should get posterior samples whose mean is pretty close to the true value that was used to generate the fake data:

```
## Print summary statistics
print(fit,probs = c(0.25, 0.5, 0.75))

##          mean se_mean   sd  2.5%   25%   50%   75% 97.5% n_eff Rhat
## beta     0.30    0.00 0.01  0.28  0.29  0.30  0.30  0.31   400 1.00
## sigma    0.31    0.00 0.02  0.27  0.30  0.31  0.33  0.36    33 1.08
## lp__    65.78    0.09 0.96 63.15 65.37 66.02 66.46 66.79   113 1.03
```

Apart from helping you create more transparent and reliable code, functions also have another use – they can be used to allow sampling from any distribution whose log density can be written in Stan code. So, even if Stan does not have built-in functionality for a particular distribution, you can still use Stan to sample from it. See Section 16.6 for the recipe for this magic potion.

Transformed parameters

There are occasions when we want to generate samples for transformations of those parameters defined in the parameters block and, possibly, even sample from these transformed parameters. In our original heights example (no covariates), imagine that instead of setting priors on the standard deviation parameters – sigma – you wish to do so on the variance. However, you also want to generate samples for sigma. One way to do this is to use the transformed parameters block:

```
data {
    int N;
    real Y[N]; // heights for 10 people
}
parameters {
    real mu; // mean height in population
    real<lower=0>sigmaSq; // var of height pop distribution
}
transformed parameters{
  real sigma;
  sigma = sqrt(sigmaSq);
}
model {
    for(i in 1:N){
        Y[i] ~ normal(mu,sigma); // likelihood
    }
    mu ~ normal(1.5,0.1); // prior for mu
    sigmaSq ~ gamma(5,1); // prior for variance
}
```

where we have now declared a parameter sigmaSq in the parameters block which represents the variance of the sampling distribution; sigma, its standard deviation, is now declared in the `transformed parameters` block. Notice that we have set priors on `sigmaSq` in this program. Our results now contain posterior summaries for both of these parameters:

```
## Print summary statistics
print(fit,probs = c(0.25, 0.5, 0.75))
```

```
##             mean se_mean   sd  2.5%   25%   50%   75% 97.5% n_eff Rhat
## mu          1.50    0.00 0.03  1.43  1.48  1.50  1.51  1.55   400 1.00
## sigmaSq     0.10    0.00 0.01  0.07  0.08  0.09  0.13  0.13    90 1.03
## sigma       0.31    0.00 0.02  0.27  0.29  0.31  0.36  0.36    92 1.03
## lp_ _      61.48    0.08 0.96 59.36 61.34 62.11 62.73 62.73   156 1.03
```

Transformed data

The final code block is known as `transformed data`, and as its name suggests it can be used to make transformations to the data you pass to Stan. These transformations are carried out once at the beginning of the program, so it usually does not significantly affect the efficiency of execution (see Section 16.5.5). As a silly example, imagine that instead of fitting a model to the height data itself, we want our model to explain the squared deviation from the sample mean. One way to do this is to carry out the data transformation in Stan:

```
transformed data{
    vector[N] lSqDeviation;

    for(i in 1:N){
        lSqDeviation[i] = (Y[i] - mean(Y))^2;
    }
}
```

While data transforms can, of course, be carried out outside of Stan, sometimes it is convenient and neater to do these operations within the Stan script.

16.5.5 Efficiency and memory considerations for each block

When writing a Stan program, as with any other software, it is important to know where bottlenecks to efficiency are likely to occur. Further – particularly if you are running Stan on a laptop – it may also pay to be aware of the memory footprint of different parts of code. In this section, we briefly discuss each of these issues.

There is heterogeneity in the number of times that each block is executed in a typical Stan run:

- data - once at the beginning
- parameters - each time the log probability is evaluated
- model - each time the log probability is evaluated
- generated quantities - once per sample

- transformed data – once after the `data` block is executed
- transformed parameters – each time the log probability is evaluated

We have omitted the `functions` block from the above list since the frequency it is called depends on its use.

In the above, we see that there is considerable heterogeneity in the importance of each block for ensuring efficient MCMC. The log probability is evaluated each time the HMC/NUTS takes a step (multiple times per sample) and so causes the biggest bottlenecks for efficiency. Typically, the `model` block is the biggest drain on processor time, so it pays to optimise it.

The parameters that you declare in the `parameters` or `transformed parameters` blocks will have samples stored for each iteration. This can cause problems for memory, particularly if you use a large number of MCMC iterations or the parameters are multi-element objects like vectors, matrices or arrays. Similarly, we have experienced memory issues arising from the `generated quantities` block when doing posterior predictive checks with high-dimensional data. (If you generate simulated data, you will get one replicate per sample!) In these circumstances, it can pay to define variables locally in blocks of braces { }, which ensures that you will not obtain samples for these.

As an example, consider our posterior predictive check for the original model, where we compare the extremes of the simulated data with the actual maximum and minimum. We originally did this using:

```
generated quantities{
    vector[N] lSimData;
    int aMax_indicator;
    int aMin_indicator;

    // generate posterior predictive samples
    for(i in 1:N){
      lSimData[i] = normal_rng(mu,sigma);
    }

    // compare with real data
    aMax_indicator = max(lSimData) > max(Y);
    aMin_indicator = min(lSimData) < min(Y);
}
```

which kept the values of 10-element simulated data vector `lSimData` for each MCMC sample. While this might not be onerous for data with $N = 10$, it will be if we have data where $N = 1000$. An alternative way is to declare the vector that will hold the data in braces (indicating a local block):

```
generated quantities{
    int aMax_indicator;
    int aMin_indicator;
```

```
    // in local block generate
    // posterior predictive samples
    { vector[N] lSimData;
      for(i in 1:N){
        lSimData[i] = normal_rng(mu,sigma);
      }
      // compare with real data
      aMax_indicator = max(lSimData) > max(Y);
      aMin_indicator = min(lSimData) < min(Y);
    }
}
```

Now the output should not contain the simulated data itself but will have the two indicator variables:

```
## Print summary statistics
print(fit,probs = c(0.25, 0.5, 0.75))
```

```
##                       mean  se_mean  sd    25%   50%   75%   n_eff  Rhat
## mu                    1.52  0.00     0.08  1.47  1.53  1.56  400    1.00
## sigma                 0.34  0.02     0.09  0.28  0.32  0.38  31     1.09
## aMax_indicator  0.50  0.03           0.50  0.00  0.00  1.00  282    1.01
## aMin_indicator  0.40  0.04           0.49  0.00  0.00  1.00  196    1.01
## lp_ _                 4.87  0.09     1.15  4.51  5.18  5.66  167    1.03
```

16.5.6 Loops and conditional statements

Stan has the loops and conditional statements that most programming languages possess. This allows a large variety of models to be coded up in Stan. Here we illustrate two looping constructs that Stan allows: *for* and *while*.

For loops just iterate through the elements as suggested in the argument:

```
for(i in 1:10) {
    execute something;
}
```

So the above executes 10 times, once per each value of *i*. While loops are slightly different in that they are *conditional*; the number of times they execute depends on a condition being met. So:

```
int i = 0;
while(i < 10) {
    i = i + 1;
}
```

will execute where $i = 1,...,9$ at the start of the loop. The condition will fail to be met, however, when $i = 10$, and the loop will terminate.

Stan also allows conditional behaviour via *if* and *else* statements:

```
if(i < 2) {
    execute something;
} else if(i == 2) {
    execute another thing;
} else{
    execute that thing;
}
```

16 ○ 6 ESSENTIAL STAN READING

This section introduces the reader to a wide, and somewhat unconnected, range of tricks that we have found useful in writing Stan programs. Even if you find no immediate use for these ideas, we believe that it nonetheless helps to be aware of them.

Accessing elements using indices

Often we need to access elements of a given data or parameter object. For a vector or array, this is straightforward using the square brackets notation in Stan, for example:

```
vector[N] X;
real aTemp;
...
// access first element of vector
aTemp = X[1];
```

This holds even for more complex arrays, where each element is a structured object:

```
corr_matrix[K] X[N];
corr_matrix[K] aTemp;
...
// access third element of array where individual elements correspond to
correlation matrices
aTemp = X[3];
```

For multi-index arrays and matrices, the process is no more difficult except that we now need to specify multiple indices within the square brackets:

```
simplex[K] X[N,L];
simplex[K] aTemp;
...
aTemp = X[3,5];
```

If you want to pull out several elements of multi-element objects, this is also straightforward:

```
real X[4];
int indices[3];
real Y[3];

X = (2,3,5,7);
indices = (4,1,2);

// yields Y = (7,2,3)
Y = X[indices];
```

Passing ragged arrays to Stan

Suppose that you have individual data for three studies of individuals' heights. In particular, imagine that you have the following data in R, and you want to generate a separate estimate of the mean population height for each of the three cases:

```
X.1 <- c(1.53,1.67,1.52)
X.2 <- c(1.75,1.62,1.87,1.95)
X.3 <- c(1.25,1.75)
```

What is the best way to pass this data to Stan? A nice trick is to combine all data into one long data vector. We then create helper arrays in R that indicate the size of each data set and its starting position in the long array:

```
Y <- c(1.53,1.67,1.52,1.75,1.62,1.87,1.95,1.25,1.75)
S <- c(3,4,2) // sample sizes of each study
index <- c(1,4,8) // start position of each study
```

Next we create a Stan program that analyses each of the studies separately – allowing estimates of the mean and standard deviation for each individual study to be obtained:

```
data {
    int N; // number of samples across all studies
    int K; // number of studies
    real Y[N]; // heights for N all people
    int S[K]; // sample sizes of each study
    int index[K]; // start position of each study
}
parameters {
    real mu[K]; // mean height in population
    real<lower=0> sigma[K]; // sd of height pop distribution
}
model {
    // likelihood
    for(i in 1:K){
        // select relevant elements for each study
```

```
        Y[index[i]:(index[i]+S[i]-1)] ~ normal(mu[i],sigma[i]);
    }
    mu ~ normal(1.5,0.1);// prior for each mu
    sigma ~ gamma(1,1); // prior for each sigma
}
```

where the above code has used the vectorised nature of the sampling statements to write the likelihood and priors compactly. The above yields the following results:

```
## Print summary statistics
print(fit,probs = c(0.25, 0.5, 0.75))

##             mean se_mean    sd   2.5%   25%   50%   75% 97.5% n_eff Rhat
## mu[1]       1.54    0.00  0.06   1.42  1.51  1.55  1.58  1.65   308 1.01
## mu[2]       1.62    0.01  0.10   1.41  1.55  1.62  1.69  1.80   331 1.00
## mu[3]       1.50    0.00  0.10   1.31  1.44  1.50  1.57  1.67   400 1.00
## sigma[1]    0.16    0.02  0.14   0.05  0.08  0.13  0.19  0.59    61 1.08
## sigma[2]    0.33    0.02  0.21   0.12  0.19  0.27  0.38  0.99   110 1.02
## sigma[3]    0.53    0.04  0.47   0.14  0.26  0.38  0.56  2.09   111 1.02
## lp_ _       2.34    0.18  1.80  -2.14  1.41  2.65  3.67  4.99   100 1.03
```

You may notice when you run the above code that you get a warning of 'divergent iterations'. While we will cover what this means in Section 16.7.2, we note briefly here that it can cause a bias in the results. Seeing as the problem here is quite minor because we have only a few divergent iterations, we can actually solve it by calling Stan as follows:

```
fit <-stan('multipleStudies.stan',
            data=list(Y=Y,N=N,K=K,S=S,index=index),
            iter=200,chains=4,control=
            list(adapt_delta=0.95,stepsize=0.01))
```

This should sort the problem. See Section 16.7.2 for further explanation of why this works.

An alternative way to estimate this type of model is to pass an array which identifies the group to which each observation belongs:

```
data {
    int N; // number of samples across all studies
    int K; // number of studies
    real Y[N]; // heights for N all people
    int groups[N]; // id of each observation
}
parameters {
    real mu[K]; // mean height in population
    real<lower=0> sigma[K]; //sd of height pop distribution
}
```

```
model {
  // likelihood
  for(i in 1:K){
    // select relevant mean and sd for each study
    Y[i] ~ normal(mu[groups[i]],sigma[groups[i]]);
  }
  mu ~ normal(1.5,0.1); // prior for each mu
  sigma ~ gamma(1,1); // prior for each sigma
}
```

where groups (= 1,1,1,...,2,2,2,...,3,3,3...) is the array containing this information. Here, rather than selecting the data that corresponds to each parameter set, we do the reverse – select the parameters which correspond to each data point.

Using Stan to generate independent samples

Sometimes it is helpful to use Stan as a tool to generate independent samples from a distribution of interest. This may be useful for posterior predictive checking or, alternatively, because we want to know how a given Stan distribution behaves. Suppose that we want to know what independent samples from the Stan neg_binomial_2 distribution look like. To do this, we leverage the power of the generated quantities block and create a bare-bones Stan program of the following form:

```
data{
  real mu;
  real kappa;
}
model{
}
generated quantities {
  int Y;
  Y = neg_binomial_2_rng(mu,kappa);
}
```

where we supply the desired mu and kappa of this distribution as data inputs. Notice that we have to suffix the distribution with '_rng' because we want to generate independent samples from it. Also notice that the above model does not contain a parameters block. Therefore, to execute this program we need to slightly alter the way we call it from R:

```
fit <- stan('bareBones.stan',data=list(mu=10,kappa=5),
            algorithm='Fixed_param',iter=4000,chains=1)
```

where we have generated 4000 independent samples from this distribution with a mean of mu=10 and kappa=5. As before, we can extract the independent samples and graph them:

```
Y <- extract(fit,'Y')[[1]]
qplot(Y) + geom_histogram(binwidth
= 2)
```

```
## 'stat bin()' using 'bins = 30'.
Pick better value with 'binwidth'.
```

Translate and compile a model for later use

It would be good to avoid having to re-compile models each time that we want to reuse them. Fortunately, Stan has a number of ways of doing just this. The simplest is to use the following option:

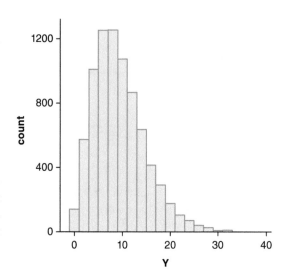

```
rstan_options(auto_write= TRUE)
```

This ensures a compiled version of the Stan model is written to the hard disk in the same directory as the .stan file. An alternative way forward is to store your model as an instance of 'stanmodel', which can be used later for MCMC in the same R session:

```
aModel <- stan_model('example.stan')
fit <- sampling(aModel,iter=400,data=list(Y=Y),chains=4)
```

Custom probability density functions: no problem with Stan

Suppose that we have a variable X that we believe follows the distribution:

$$\frac{\sqrt{2}}{\pi\left((x-\mu)^4+1\right)}, \tag{16.6}$$

where $-\infty < x < \infty$, which for $\mu = 2$ looks like:

```
curve((sqrt(2)/pi)*1/(1+(x-2)⁴),
-5,5)
```

Coding up a bespoke probability density in Stan

Unfortunately, this probability density function is not available in Stan. (Which isn't really that surprising since we invented it.) So what can we do? Well, it turns out we can still use Stan for inference by writing a function that returns the log density for each value of μ (just the log of the above). We then use this log density value to increment the overall log density:

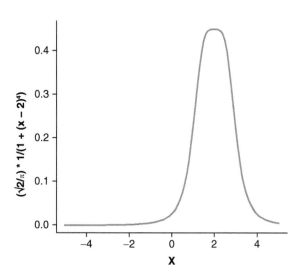

```
functions{
  real example_lpdf(real aX, real aMu){
    return(log(sqrt(2)/( pi() * (1 + (aX - aMu)^4))));
  }
}
data {
  int N;
  real X[N];
}
parameters{
  real mu;
}
model {
  for(i in 1:N){
    X[i] ~ example(mu);
  }
  mu ~ normal(0,2);
}
```

where we have specified a $\mu \sim N(0,2)$ prior. In the above, we have suffixed our custom log probability density function definition with '_lpdf'. This tells Stan to regard this function as a typical log probability density function, which we can use along with a '~' statement resulting in the following:

```
N<- 4
X <- c(-1.5,2.2,0.1,-0.4)
fit <- stan('StanJags_customPDF.stan',iter=200,chains=4,data=list(N=N,X=X))
print(fit,probs = c(0.25, 0.5, 0.75))
```

```
##          mean   se_mean    sd    25%     50%     75%   n_eff   Rhat
## mu      -0.18     0.03   0.54  -0.57   -0.25    0.23    291     1
## lp_ _   -8.47     0.04   0.67  -8.56   -8.23   -8.07    255     1
```

To use this functionality for any density, we must define our data as the function's first input and all parameters after this, so:

```
real normalCustom_lpdf(real aX, real aMu, real aSigma)
```

would implement a log density function that we call using

```
X ~ normalCustom(mu, sigma);
```

or alternatively using

```
target += normalCustom_lpdf(X|mu, sigma);
```

Let's prove this works for a distribution that exists in R and Stan – the normal. The Stan model can be written as follows:

```
functions{
  real normalCustom_lpdf(real aX, real aMu, real aSigma){
    return(-log(aSigma) - 1/(2*aSigma^2)*(aX-aMu)^2);
  }
}
data {
  int N;
  real X[N];
}
parameters {
  real mu;
  real<lower=0> sigma;
}
model {
  for(i in 1:N){
    X[i] ~ normalCustom(mu, sigma);
  }
  mu ~ normal(0,2);
  sigma ~ lognormal(0,1);
}
```

where we have assigned normal and log-N priors on mu and sigma, respectively. Now we generate some fake data with $X \sim N(3,5)$ and fit the model:

```
N <- 1000
X <- rnorm(N,3,5)
fit <- stan('customNormal.stan',iter=200,chains=4,
              data=list(N=N,X=X))
print(fit,probs= c(0.25,0.5,0.75))
```

```
##          mean se_mean   sd     25%       50%       75% n_eff Rhat
## mu       2.82    0.02 0.17    2.71      2.80      2.94    87 1.03
## sigma    4.88    0.01 0.11    4.81      4.88      4.95   400 1.00
## lp_ _ -2088.85    0.12 1.06 -2089.39 -2088.50 -2088.08    81 1.05
```

which works pretty well here since mu and sigma are close to their actual values.

So the moral here is that – so long as you can write a function in Stan that returns the log density of a distribution – you can use Stan to sample from it.

Calculating WAIC, LOO-CV and other measures

Often we want to estimate the predictive performance of a model to compare it with others in order to choose between competing hypotheses. In Chapter 10 we discussed various alternative metrics and advocated, where possible, that researchers should repeatedly partition their data into training and test sets (that is, use explicit cross-validation). The training sets are used to fit the model, and the test sets to estimate their out-of-sample predictive capability. However, there are circumstances where repeated partitioning is not feasible due to the computational cost of estimating a model. In these cases, we can use WAIC and estimates of LOO-CV to measure the out-of-sample predictive capability of a model. In this section, we show how to estimate a model's predictive capability using cross-validation, WAIC and LOO-CV through an example. Suppose that we generate some fake data from a Student-*t* distribution (see Section 8.4.7):

```
N <- 10000
## Student-t with nu=5
X <- rt(N,5)
```

We then fit two models to the data – one uses a normal sampling distribution and the other assumes a Student-*t* sampling distribution. Here we know the Student-*t* distribution should perform better since we used it to generate our data, and hence we use this toy problem to illustrate how cross-validation, WAIC and LOO-CV can be calculated.

WAIC and LOO-CV

We start by considering WAIC and LOO-CV since these are more easily handled than explicit cross-validation. These methods require that we calculate the log-likelihood for each data point across all posterior samples (see Chapter 10). This is straightforward to handle using the generated quantities block. We illustrate this for the normal model first:

```
generated quantities{
  vector[N] logLikelihood;
  for(i in 1:N){
    logLikelihood[i] = normal_lpdf(X[i]|mu,sigma);
  }
}
```

In the above, we iterate across all *N* elements in our data sample and record the log-likelihood for these. Furthermore, this loop is undertaken for each posterior sample of (mu, sigma), and hence a matrix of log-likelihoods is obtained overall.

The Student-*t* model is similar, although we have an extra nu parameter in its log density function:

```
generated quantities{
  vector[N] logLikelihood;
  for(i in 1:N){
    logLikelihood[i] = student_t_lpdf(X[i]|nu,mu,sigma);
  }
}
```

We set the following priors for both models, $mu \sim N(0,1)$ and $sigma \sim \log\text{-}N(0,1)$, and $nu \sim \log\text{-}N(0,1)$ for the degrees of freedom parameter for the Student-*t* model.

To calculate WAIC we use the excellent loo package [40]. Since we have saved the log-likelihood for each model, this is actually quite easy to do:

```
library(loo)
fit1 <- stan('normal.stan',iter=200,chains=4,data=list(N=N,X=X))
logLikelihood1 <- extract_log_lik(fit1,'logLikelihood')
WAIC1 <- waic(logLikelihood1)
print(WAIC1)

## Computed from 400 by 10000 log-likelihood matrix
##
##                      Estimate     SE
## elpd_waic            -17002.7  133.0
## p_waic                    4.0    0.7
## waic                  34005.4  266.0


fit2 <- stan('StudentT.stan',iter=200,chains=4,data=list(N=N,X=X))
logLikelihood2 <- extract_log_lik(fit2,'logLikelihood')
WAIC2 <- waic(logLikelihood2)
print(WAIC2)

## Computed from 400 by 10000 log-likelihood matrix
##
##                      Estimate     SE
## elpd_waic            -16467.8   94.3
## p_waic                    2.9    0.1
## waic                  32935.7  188.6
```

We see that the Student-*t* model has a higher estimated expected log pointwise predictive density (*elpd* = –16,467.8, which, times –2, corresponds to a lower WAIC). However, to determine whether this difference represents anything other than sampling error, we compare these two models in the correct – pairwise – way using:

```
compare(WAIC1,WAIC2)

## elpd_diff              se
##     534.9            76.8
```

from the same package, and we see that the difference in *elpd* is much greater than the standard error. This suggests that there is a significant difference in performance between these two models, and we prefer the Student-*t* model. But how do we determine whether the difference is significant? One way is to calculate a *z* score and compare with a standard normal:

$$Pr\left(z \geq \frac{534.9}{76.8}\right) \approx 10^{-12}. \tag{16.7}$$

While we are not in general fond of Frequentist hypothesis tests, this is the current state of the art here. In this case, it indicates that there is basically zero probability of this difference occurring if both models are equally predictive.

The same package allows us to estimate *elpd* via LOO-CV without doing explicit cross-validation. This proceeds as before except we substitute loo → waic:

```
LOO1 <- loo(logLikelihood1)
print(LOO1)

## Computed from 400 by 10000 log-likelihood matrix
##
##             Estimate       SE
## elpd_loo    -17002.7    133.0
## p_loo            4.0      0.7
## looic        34005.4    266.0
##
## All Pareto k estimates OK (k < 0.5)

LOO2 <- loo(logLikelihood2)
print(LOO2)

## Computed from 400 by 10000 log-likelihood matrix
##
##             Estimate       SE
## elpd_loo    -16467.8     94.3
## p_loo            2.9      0.1
## looic        32935.6    188.6
##
## All Pareto k estimates OK (k < 0.5)

compare(LOO1,LOO2)

## elpd_diff               se
##     534.9             76.8
```

This produces similar estimates of *elpd* as for the WAIC in this case. In both cases, we find that the estimated *elpd* is greater for the Student-*t* model than for the normal one, as expected.

In general, we prefer the LOO-CV measure since it represents a better approximation to the out-of-sample predictive capability of our model. However, it is important to note that it is not uncommon to get warnings about either the 'p_waic exceeding ...' or 'Pareto k estimates exceeding...'. While we refer the interested reader to the details of the loo paper itself [40], we mention here that it is important to take heed of these warnings. These warnings typically indicate that one or more of the approximations used to estimate these criteria are likely violated, and hence inferences about model performance cannot be trusted. In these cases, it may be better to use explicit cross-validation, to which we turn our attention now.

Explicit cross-validation

We recommend that, where possible, the reader should use explicit cross-validation to estimate a model's out-of-sample predictive performance. The reason for this recommendation is twofold:

first, the aforementioned WAIC and LOO-CV methods can fail to produce reasonable estimates of out-of-sample predictive error if one or more of a number of conditions are not met; second, explicit cross-validation allows us to manually select a test set that may better represent the model's eventual use.

Using a poorly chosen partitioning can lead to very inadequate measures of a model's performance, so we recommend thinking carefully here. If the model will be used to predict batches of new data, then perhaps a K-Fold cross-validation scheme is best. Alternatively, if the unit of interest is a single data point, then perhaps a leave-one-out cross-validation scheme is best. (Time series and hierarchically structured data can be a bit tricky here.)

Lacking any preference for an explicit cross-validation scheme, we suggest using K-Fold cross-validation since it is less computationally onerous than leave-one-out cross-validation. In K-Fold cross-validation, the data are repeatedly partitioned into training and test sets. The process continues until each data point has been included once (and once only) in a test set.

We continue the previous example, but now show how to estimate model performance on a test set for the normal model:

```
data {
   int NTest;
   int NTrain;
   real XTrain[NTrain];
   real XTest[NTest];
}
parameters {
   real mu;
   real<lower=0>sigma;
}
model {
   XTrain ~ normal(mu,sigma);
   mu ~ normal(0,1);
   sigma ~ lognormal(0,1);
}
generated quantities{
   vector[NTest] logLikelihood;
   for(i in 1:NTest){
      logLikelihood[i] = normal_lpdf(XTest[i]|mu,sigma);
   }
}
```

where we fit the model on the training set XTrain and calculate the log probability on the test set XTest. To do K-Fold cross-validation we use the brilliant Caret R package (which is our favourite library for machine learning) to generate equally sized randomised test sets, where each data point features once, and once only, in each test set [22]:

```
library(caret)
testIndices <- createFolds(X, k = 5, list = TRUE,
                           returnTrain = FALSE)
```

where we have specified five folds. We then create an R function to handle the repeated training and testing of a given model, and calculate the *elpd* for each of the test sets:

```
library(loo)
kFold <- function(aModel,testIndices,X){
  numFolds <- length(testIndices)

  ## calculate expected log pointwise predictive density
  lPointLogLikelihoodTotal <- vector()

  for(i in 1:numFolds){
    XTest <- X[testIndices[[i]]]
    XTrain <- X[-testIndices[[i]]]
    fit <- sampling(aModel,iter=200,chains=4, data=list(NTest=2000,NTrain=8000,
                    XTrain=XTrain,XTest=XTest))
    logLikelihood1 <- extract_log_lik(fit,'logLikelihood')
    lPointLogLikelihood1 <- colMeans(logLikelihood1)
    lPointLogLikelihoodTotal <- c(lPointLogLikelihoodTotal,
                                  lPointLogLikelihood1)
  }
  return(lPointLogLikelihoodTotal)
}
```

which we then use to compare the normal and Student-*t* models:

```
Model1 <- stan_model('Normal_kFolds.stan')
Model2 <- stan_model('StudentT_kFolds.stan')

lELPD1 <- kFold(Model1,testIndices,X)
lELPD2 <- kFold(Model2,testIndices,X)

sum(lELPD1)

## [1] -16836.58

sum(lELPD2)

## [1] -16431.44

difference <- sum(lELPD2) - sum(lELPD1)
sd <- sqrt(1000)*sd(lELPD2 - lELPD1)
pvalue <- 1- pnorm(difference/sd)
print(pvalue)

## [1] 0
```

noting that again the Student-*t* distribution performs better than the normal distribution. (Above, we calculate the standard deviation on the difference in log pointwise predictive density to calculate a *z* score.) We also note the similarity in estimates compared with the more approximate WAIC and LOO-CV methods described above, which is reassuring.

Jacobians: when do we need these?

Suppose that we have a uniformly distributed variable, θ, and draw samples for it:

```
library(ggplot2)

theta <- runif(100000)
qplot(theta)
```

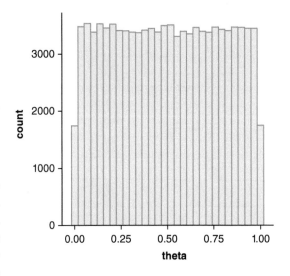

Then we square the samples. What does the distribution of θ^2 look like?

```
qplot(theta^2)
```

This is definitely not uniform. Whenever we apply a non-linear transform to a variable, its probability distribution is stretched in some areas and squashed in others. The correct way to mathematically determine how this stretching manifests is known as the *Jacobian* transform.

In Stan, we are required to manually specify this Jacobian if we ever sample from a transformed parameter. As an example [8],[1] imagine we have some binary data $Y = (0,0,1,0)$ that represents the outcomes of some sort of test – where individual data points can be either a success (1) or failure (0). We model each outcome as a Bernoulli distribution (see Section 8.4.1) and use the following Stan model:

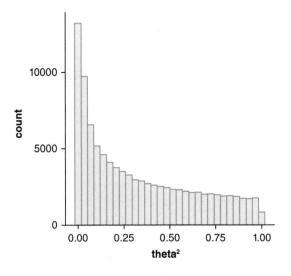

```
data {
  int<lower=0>N;
  int<lower=0, upper=1> Y[N];
}
parameters {
```

---

[1]Inspired by Bob Carpenter's example: http://mc-stan.org/documentation/case-studies/mle-params.html.

```
    real alpha;
}
transformed parameters{
    real<lower=0,upper=1> theta;
    theta = inv_logit(alpha);
}
model {
    for (n in 1:N){
        Y[n] ~ bernoulli(theta);
    }
    theta ~ uniform(0, 1);
}
```

This specifies `alpha` as our parameter, which represents the log odds of success, and `theta` as a transformed parameter. If we run this model, we get a warning from Stan:

```
DIAGNOSTIC(S)FROM PARSER:
Warning (non-fatal):
Left-hand side of sampling statement (~) may contain a non-linear transform
of a parameter or local variable.
If so, you need to call increment_log_prob() with the log absolute determinant
of the Jacobian of the transform.
Left-hand-side of sampling statement:
        theta ~ uniform(...)
```

This indicates that we are sampling from a transformation of the `alpha` parameter and need to add a term that corresponds to a Jacobian term. Before we change our model, let's look at our posterior summaries:

```
## Print summary statistics
print(fit,probs = c(0.25, 0.5, 0.75))

##           mean se_mean   sd   2.5%    25%    50%    75% 97.5% n_eff Rhat
## alpha  -1.57    0.10 1.49  -5.17  -2.45  -1.52  -0.55   0.98   222 1.00
## theta   0.25    0.01 0.20   0.01   0.08   0.18   0.37   0.73   304 1.00
## lp_ _  -2.90    0.06 0.83   5.35  -3.12  -2.54  -2.34  -2.25   174 1.01
```

Here we have a posterior mean of `theta` – the probability of success – being 0.25. However, we know that since the uniform prior is actually a *beta*(1,1) distribution, the posterior is a *beta*(1+1,1+4−1) = *beta*(2,4) distribution (see Chapter 9). This has a mean of $\bar{\theta} = \frac{2}{2+4} \approx 0.33$, which is not what we obtained.

The reason we obtained this bias is because we failed to account for our change of variables. In particular, since we set a prior on a transformation of alpha, we got a bias in our posterior samples. How do we correct this? We first have to calculate the Jacobian. For $\alpha = \text{logit}(\theta)$ we find that the density satisfies:

$$p(\alpha) = p(\theta) \left| \frac{d}{d\alpha} \text{logit}^{-1}(\alpha) \right|,$$ (16.8)

where the second term on the right-hand side is the Jacobian. The inverse logit function is actually the sigmoid function yielding a Jacobian equal to:

$$\left| \frac{d}{d\alpha} \text{logit}^{-1}(\alpha) \right| = \frac{d}{d\alpha} \frac{1}{1+\exp(-\alpha)}$$

$$= \text{logit}^{-1}(\alpha) \times (1 - \text{logit}^{-1}(\alpha))$$ (16.9)

$$= \theta \times (1 - \theta),$$

which we log and then use to increment the log probability in a line in our model block:

```
model {
    for (n in 1:N) {
        Y[n] ~ bernoulli(theta);
    }
    theta ~ uniform(0, 1);
    target += log(theta) + log(1-theta);
}
```

which, when we run the new Stan program and look at the posterior summaries, gives:

```
## Print summary statistics
print(fit,probs = c(0.25, 0.5, 0.75))
```

```
##            mean se_mean   sd   2.5%   25%    50%    75% 97.5% n_eff Rhat
## alpha -0.90     0.06 1.07 -2.96 -1.59 -0.91 -0.26  1.29   373    1
## theta  0.33     0.01 0.20  0.05  0.17  0.29  0.44  0.78   391    1
## lp_ _ -4.50     0.06 0.93 -7.23 -4.77 -4.12 -3.90 -3.82   234    1
```

in accordance with the analytic mean.

Knowing when you need to use a Jacobian can seem confusing at first. However, it is not if you know the following rule:

> Use a Jacobian when you transform a parameter and then sample it, but not when you sample a parameter and then transform it.

So if, instead, we use the model:

```
data {
    int<lower=0> N;
    int<lower=0, upper=1> Y[N];
}
parameters {
```

```
  real<lower=0,upper=1> theta;
}
transformed parameters{
  real alpha;
  alpha = logit(theta);
}
model {
  for (n in 1:N){
    Y[n] ~ bernoulli(theta);
  }
  theta ~ uniform(0, 1);
}
```

there is no need for a Jacobian term because we have defined `theta` as a parameter (which we sample from) and `alpha` as the transformed one. So here we get the correct posterior summaries:

```
## Print summary statistics
print(fit,probs = c(0.25, 0.5, 0.75))

##          mean se_mean   sd  2.5%   25%   50%   75% 97.5% n_eff Rhat
## alpha  -0.92    0.07  1.1 -3.22 -1.61 -0.84 -0.17  1.16   241 1.01
## theta   0.33    0.01  0.2  0.04  0.17  0.30  0.46  0.76   230 1.01
## lp_ _  -4.53    0.07  0.9 -6.83 -4.83 -4.21 -3.88 -3.82   191 1.02
```

Marginalising out discrete parameters

Stan does not directly allow discrete parameters. This is because currently the theory of how to extend HMC to these circumstances is not well developed. While in the future it may be possible to directly include discrete parameters in Stan, fortunately it is still possible to indirectly use them by marginalising them out of the joint log density. This amounts to summing the joint density over all possible values of the discrete parameter θ:

$$p(\beta) = \sum_{i=1}^{k} p(\beta, \theta_i). \tag{16.10}$$

However, we must do so on the log probability scale because this is what Stan uses:

$$\log p(\beta) = \log \sum_{i=1}^{k} p(\beta, \theta_i)$$

$$= \log \sum_{i=1}^{k} \exp(\log p(\beta, \theta_i)) \tag{16.11}$$

$$= \text{log\_sum\_exp}_{i=1}^{K}(\log p(\beta, \theta_i)).$$

We obtained the second line of (16.11) from the first by using $\exp(\log(x)) = x$. To reiterate, we need expression (16.11) because Stan uses $\log p$, not p itself. The last line uses the definition of a function available in Stan:

$$\text{log\_sum\_exp}_{i=1}^K \alpha = \log \sum_{i=1}^{k} \exp(\alpha), \tag{16.12}$$

which makes life easier for us with discrete models. Note the Stan function is equivalent to the expression (16.11), but is computed in a way that makes it more numerically stable (since the exponential of the log probabilities can be tiny).

So how do we implement discrete models in Stan itself? Let's consider an example. Suppose that we have two coins in our pocket. One is heavily biased towards tails and the other is heavily biased towards heads. In each experiment, we pull out a coin at random – not observing which coin it is – and throw it 10 times, recording the total number of heads, X. We run the same experiment 20 times, each time recording the total number of heads. Suppose that we want to infer the (unobserved) identity of the coin in each experiment as well as the probabilities of throwing a heads for each of the two coins.

On first glance, the above model seems problematic because the identity of the coin in each experiment can be one of two possible states – tails- or heads-biased – and hence is discrete. We can write down this model in statistical form:

$$s_n \sim discrete - uniform(1,2)$$

// tails-biased

if $(s_n = 1)$

$$X_n \sim \mathcal{B}(10, \theta_1) \tag{16.13}$$

// heads-biased (s=2)

else

$$X_n \sim \mathcal{B}(10, \theta_2),$$

where $\theta_1 < 0.5 < \theta_2$. The key to writing this model in Stan is finding a way to calculate the log posterior density, lp. If we can find the log density, then we can simply use:

```
target += logProb;
```

and run Stan as per usual. We start by considering each of the studies individually and assume that both coins are equally likely a priori. The probability of each coin type s for a single experiment where we throw X heads out of 10 throws is then:

$$0.5 \times \text{binomial\_pmf}(X \mid 10, theta[s]), \tag{16.14}$$

where $theta[s]$ is the probability of heads for coin type $s \in [1,2]$ and binomial_pmf is the binomial probability mass function. In Stan, we want the log probability and hence use instead:

```
log(0.5) + binomial_lpmf(X|N,theta[s]);
```

where binomial_lpmf is the log probability mass for a binomial distribution. In our Stan program, we store the log probability for each coin type s in a 1 × 2 vector for each experiment.

This amounts to storing all the results in a 20 × 2 matrix, *lp*, where a single row corresponds to an individual experiment:

```
transformed parameters{
   real<lower=0,upper=1> theta[2];
   matrix[nStudy,2] lp;

   for(n in 1:nStudy){
     for(s in 1:2){
       lp[n,s] = log(0.5) + binomial_lpmf(X[n]|N,theta[s]);
     }
   }
}
```

We then marginalise out the discrete coin type *s* from the joint density by summing over it using log_sum_exp. Once it is marginalised, we then increment the log probability by this amount:

```
model {
   for(n in 1:nStudy){
     target += log_sum_exp(lp[n]);
   }
}
```

In this case, we actually find it easier to make use of Stan's logit formulation of the binomial, where we pass an unconstrained real parameter to the distribution. Writing the entire program now:

```
data {
   int<lower=1> nStudy; // num studies
   int<lower=1> N; // samples per study
   int<lower=0, upper=N> X[nStudy]; // number successes
}
parameters {
   ordered[2] alpha;
}
transformed parameters{
   real<lower=0,upper=1> theta[2];
   matrix[nStudy,2] lp;

   for(i in 1:2){
     theta[i] = inv_logit(alpha[i]);
   }
   for(n in 1:nStudy){
     for(s in 1:2){
       lp[n,s] = log(0.5) +
                   binomial_logit_lpmf(X[n]|N,alpha[s]);
     }
   }
}
```

```
model {
  for(n in 1:nStudy){
    target += log_sum_exp(lp[n]);
  }
}
generated quantities{
  real pstate[nStudy];
  for(n in 1:nStudy){
    pstate[n] = exp(lp[n,1])/(exp(lp[n,1]) + exp(lp[n,2]));
  }
}
```

where we have used the Stan type *ordered* to ensure that one of the coin probabilities (obtained by transforming the alpha variable using the inverse logit transform) is always larger than the other. In the model block, we iterate through the individual studies and increment the log probability by an amount determined by marginalising the joint log density over the variable that corresponds to the status of an individual coin. So the idea is that – in each step of Stan – we sample a value for alpha (then transformed to get theta), then we use these values to calculate the log probability of each coin state *s*. We then marginalise *s* out of the joint log density and update the total overall log probability accordingly.

We use the generated quantities block to estimate the probabilities of state *s* = 1 in experiment *n* by averaging over all *L* posterior draws:

$$q(s = 1 \mid X[n]) \approx \frac{1}{L} \sum_{i=1}^{L} q(s = 1, \text{alpha}[s = 1] \mid X[n]), \tag{16.15}$$

where $q(.)$ is the un-normalised posterior density. The averaging over all posterior draws is necessary to obtain the marginal un-normalised density for coin type (where alpha, and hence the coin bias, have been averaged out of the joint density). To normalise the posterior density, we therefore divide the above by the sum of the un-normalised probability across both states:

$$Pr(s = 1 \mid X[n]) = \frac{q(s = 1 \mid X[n])}{q(s = 1 \mid X[n]) + q(s = 2 \mid X[n])}. \tag{16.16}$$

In the Stan code, we use the log density and so need to take the exponent of each term. A more numerically stable (but slightly more opaque) way to write the above in Stan is as follows:

```
generated quantities{
  real pstate[nStudy];
  for(n in 1:nStudy){
    pstate[n] = exp(lp[n,1] - log_sum_exp(lp[n]));
  }
}
```

This only requires that we take the exponential once. We now generate some fake data in R assuming that $\theta_1 = 0.1$ and $\theta_2 = 0.9$:

```
nStudy <- 20
N <- 10
Z <- matrix(nrow = N,ncol = nStudy)
theta <- c(0.1,0.9)
state <- vector(length=nStudy)

for(i in 1:nStudy){
  if(runif(1)<0.5){
    Z[,i] <- rbinom(N,1,theta[1])
    state[i] <- 1
  } else{
    Z[,i] <- rbinom(N,1,theta[2])
    state[i] <- 0
  }
}
X <- colSums(Z)
```

and pass this data to our Stan program:

```
fit <- stan('discreteCoins.stan',iter=200,chains=4,
            data=list(X=X,N=N,nStudy=nStudy))
print(fit,probs = c(0.2,0.5,0.75),c('theta','pstate'))
```

```
##                mean   se_mean    sd    20%    50%    75%   n_eff   Rhat
## theta[1]       0.09    0.00    0.03   0.06   0.08   0.10     93   1.02
## theta[2]       0.90    0.00    0.04   0.87   0.91   0.93    400   1.00
## pstate[1]      0.00    0.00    0.00   0.00   0.00   0.00    151   1.01
## pstate[2]      1.00    0.00    0.00   1.00   1.00   1.00    301   1.00
## pstate[3]      1.00    0.00    0.00   1.00   1.00   1.00    391   1.00
## pstate[4]      1.00    0.00    0.00   1.00   1.00   1.00    301   1.00
## pstate[5]      1.00    0.00    0.00   1.00   1.00   1.00    391   1.00
## pstate[6]      1.00    0.00    0.00   1.00   1.00   1.00    337   1.00
## pstate[7]      0.00    0.00    0.00   0.00   0.00   0.00    135   1.01
## pstate[8]      0.00    0.00    0.00   0.00   0.00   0.00    151   1.01
## pstate[9]      1.00    0.00    0.00   1.00   1.00   1.00    301   1.00
## pstate[10]     0.00    0.00    0.00   0.00   0.00   0.00    151   1.01
## pstate[11]     0.00    0.00    0.00   0.00   0.00   0.00    151   1.01
## pstate[12]     1.00    0.00    0.00   1.00   1.00   1.00    337   1.00
## pstate[13]     1.00    0.00    0.00   1.00   1.00   1.00    301   1.00
## pstate[14]     1.00    0.00    0.00   1.00   1.00   1.00    337   1.00
## pstate[15]     0.00    0.00    0.00   0.00   0.00   0.00    135   1.01
## pstate[16]     0.00    0.00    0.00   0.00   0.00   0.00    135   1.01
## pstate[17]     0.04    0.01    0.10   0.00   0.00   0.02    272   1.01
## pstate[18]     1.00    0.00    0.00   1.00   1.00   1.00    391   1.00
## pstate[19]     1.00    0.00    0.00   1.00   1.00   1.00    337   1.00
## pstate[20]     1.00    0.00    0.00   1.00   1.00   1.00    301   1.00
```

where we see the model has correctly inferred the probabilities of throwing heads for each coin as well as the correct coin type in each experiment:

```
## predict state 1 if prob>0.5
state_est <- ifelse(colMeans(extract(fit,'pstate')[[1]])>0.5,1,0)
sum(abs(state_est - state))
```

```
## [1] 0
```

WHAT TO DO WHEN THINGS GO WRONG

Rarely in life do things run entirely smoothly. This is particularly true with statistical modelling. However, this is only part of the problem in statistics. The other part of the problem is recognising that something is actually wrong. In this section, we describe how to see and interpret the ample warning signs that Stan provides us with. Broadly, there are two categories of errors: coding errors and sampling issues. Coding errors are, in general, easier to diagnose and typically can be resolved fairly quickly. Sampling issues can be trickier since their resolution is typically quite problem specific. However, once you have got a few models under your belt you should start to understand the source of these issues. At the heart of sampling issues is a principle that Gelman refers to as his *folk theorem*: A problem with MCMC is usually a problem with the model, not the sampling algorithm. If you remember this dictum you will save time fiddling with MCMC parameters and find yourself spending more time thinking about what really matters – the statistical model. We divide the following sections into coding errors and sampling issues because diagnosis and solution differ quite considerably between the two.

In the last sections of this chapter, we consider how to get further help should you need it. Fortunately, Stan has excellent resources, and we explain how to make best use of them.

16.7.1 Coding errors

Stan is pretty good at telling you when you make a mistake with code. Suppose that we are missing a semicolon at the end of a statement:

```
data {
  int N;
  real X[N]
}
```

If we try to run this model we get the following message:

```
fit <- stan('aModel.stan',data=list(N=N,X=X),iter=200,chains=4)
```

```
## SYNTAX ERROR, MESSAGE(S) FROM PARSER:
##
## ERROR at line 4
##
```

```
## 2:              int N;
## 3:              real X[N]
## 4:        }
##            ^
## 5:
##
## PARSER EXPECTED: ";"
```

We read at the end that our parser expected a semicolon but did not find one.

Another common error that we find ourselves making is illustrated by the following:

```
generated quantities{
  vector[N] XPred;

  for(i in 1:N){
    XPred[i] <- normal(mu,sigma);
  }
}
```

which looks OK on first glance but produces an error:

```
## SYNTAX ERROR, MESSAGE(S) FROM PARSER:
##
## No matches for:
## normal(real, real)
## Function normal not found.
## Function normal not found.
```

This seems puzzling at first because we have actually defined `sigma` to be a `real<lower=0>` variable. The issue here is that we actually want to replace `normal` with `normal_rng` because we want to generate independent samples from this distribution, not increment the log probability.

Stan is, in general, quite informative about the root cause of most coding errors. However, there will be circumstances when the warning messages produced may not necessarily shed too much light on a problem. In these cases, we recommend consulting the Stan manual and user forum. If you still have trouble finding a solution, then consider asking a question on the Stan user forum, although before you do, try to recreate the simplest possible model that replicates the error. This process is highly informative in itself, but also helps others to most rapidly find the source of any problems.

Debugging through fake data simulations

Another class of coding problems is subtler. They may not produce any error messages and can go unnoticed unless we actively search for them. One of the most powerful methods in this search is to use fake data simulations. In this method, we generate simulated data from a statistical process whose parameters we know for certain. We then compare our MCMC-estimated parameter values with the true parameter values. While there may be statistical reasons for discrepancies here (see Section 16.7.2), coding errors can also cause differences between the estimated and actual data.

As an example, imagine we are again estimating the height of individuals in three separate populations, in a similar vein to that in Section 16.6. We start by generating fake data from three populations of known means:

```
mu <- c(1.3,1.6,2.1)
Y <- vector()
S <- vector(length=3)
K <- 3
for(i in 1:3){
   S[i] <- rpois(1,10)
   X <- rnorm(S[i],mu[i],0.1)
   Y <- c(Y,X)
}
index <- c(1,1+cumsum(S))[-4]
N <- length(Y)
```

As before, the index contains the starting position of each series and S holds the number of individuals in each sample.

We then write our model:

```
data {
   int N; // number of samples across all studies
   int K; // number of studies
   real Y[N]; // heights for N all people
   int S[K]; // sample sizes of each study
   int index[K]; // start position of each study
}
parameters {
   real mu[K]; // mean height in population
   real<lower=0> sigma[K]; //sd of height pop distribution
}
model {
   for(i in 1:(K-1)){
       Y[index[i]:(index[i]+S[i]-1)] ~ normal(mu[i],sigma[i]);
   }
   mu ~ normal(1.5,0.8);
   sigma ~ gamma(1,1);
}
```

and run the Stan model from R – it compiles; no errors here, we think. However, on printing the results we find the following:

```
print(fit,probs = c(0.25,0.5,0.75))
##              mean  se_mean   sd    25%   50%    75%  n_eff  Rhat
## mu[1]        1.28     0.00  0.04   1.26  1.28   1.31    400  1.00
## mu[2]        1.58     0.00  0.03   1.56  1.58   1.59    301  0.99
```

## mu[3]	1.45	0.08	0.77	0.94	1.38	1.98	104	1.00
## sigma[1]	0.12	0.00	0.03	0.10	0.12	0.14	210	1.03
## sigma[2]	0.07	0.00	0.02	0.06	0.06	0.08	192	1.01
## sigma[3]	1.24	0.12	1.15	0.37	0.99	1.81	97	1.05
## lp_ _	29.98	0.18	1.94	28.86	30.38	31.37	110	1.05

The first two means are well replicated in our data, but the latter one is not. Why is this? It is because we failed to notice the K-1 in the for loop declaration – it should say for(i in 1:K). We change this, rerun the model and print the results:

```
print(fit,probs = c(0.25,0.5,0.75))
```

##	mean	se_mean	sd	20%	50%	75%	n_eff	Rhat
## mu[1]	1.29	0.00	0.04	1.26	1.29	1.31	400	1.00
## mu[2]	1.58	0.00	0.03	1.56	1.58	1.60	400	1.00
## mu[3]	2.07	0.00	0.03	2.05	2.07	2.09	291	1.01
## sigma[1]	0.12	0.00	0.03	0.10	0.11	0.13	143	1.02
## sigma[2]	0.07	0.00	0.02	0.06	0.07	0.08	99	1.04
## sigma[3]	0.12	0.00	0.03	0.10	0.11	0.13	143	1.01
## lp_ _	50.46	0.14	1.71	49.48	50.81	51.72	154	1.01

We see that the posterior summary statistics are now in much better accordance with the true values.

Debugging by print

Another useful tool in debugging is the use of the **print** statement:

```
real X;
X = 1.0;
print(X);
```

This prints the value of a given variable to the output. This tool can be particularly useful when you want to determine the value of an element of a vector that is assigned in some sort of loop.

16.7.2 Sampling issues

Another class of problems has to do with issues with the MCMC sampling. These problems are, in general, trickier to resolve than coding problems. However, we believe that if you understand the basis of the issues that we introduce in this section, you will know how to diagnose this type of problem, should it appear. An important idea to always keep in mind is Gelman's folk theorem – that issues with sampling are usually due to problems with the model, not the sampling algorithm. Further, it is important to remember that any MCMC sampling algorithm, Stan or otherwise, is approximate in nature. The quality of the approximation hinges crucially on our ability to recognise and deal with any issues that arise. Stan is very good at pointing out these issues, but it is our responsibility to act on them. Ignore the warning signs at your own peril!

The real power of fake data

The following examples make clear the importance of using fake data simulation in applied research. In each of the cases, we simulate data from a statistical process whose parameters we know for certain. In doing so, we can test the limits of knowability using our models. If we did not go first through the exercise and, instead, started to analyse our real data straight away, we would not necessarily understand the reason for slow convergence, divergent iterations, and so on. Fake data simulation is thus a prerequisite for all dᵃta analyses. The exercise of generating fake data may seem annoying at times – particularly for hierarchical models – but there is always a considerable improvement to your knowledge about the system at hand if you do so.

Fake data generation can also be useful before we receive data, for example when designing a physical experiment. By simulating data from an entirely known process, we learn how much data are necessary to achieve a given level of accuracy in parameter estimates, and can adjust our experimental design accordingly.

Slow convergence indicated by $\hat{R} > 1.1$

You may notice that one or more of your parameters has a value of $\hat{R} > 1.1$. This is always something to be concerned about. It means that there is some area of posterior space that has not been adequately explored. Further, you cannot assume that since all of your 'important' parameters have $\hat{R} > 1.1$, you can forget about the few that have not converged. Parameter estimates depend on one another, so it is entirely possible that exploring a new area of parameter space for one 'unimportant' parameter may lead to exploration of new areas for an 'important' one. These *epistatic* interactions[2] mean that we must be confident that our nuisance parameters have converged.

So why are some models slow to converge? Generally, it means that the posterior is not very curved in some areas of parameter space, meaning that the posterior has long tails. These extended tails mean that MCMC samplers take much longer to explore the posterior space and, as a result, convergence is slow. The lack of curvature can also make it difficult to separate the effect of one parameter from another one; that is, there is an identification issue. Poor identification can be caused by a wide variety of reasons: inadequate data, uninformative priors and ill-conceived models are common causes. However, common to all of these causes is the idea that the data provides insufficient information to tease apart the effect of one parameter from another.

For example, suppose we generate 10 data points from a Student-t distribution with $v = 3$, $\sigma = 1$ and $\mu = 2$:

```
N <- 10
X <- rt(N, df=3)*1 + 2
```

If we fit the same distribution to this data in Stan using the following code:

```
model {
  X ~ student_t(nu,mu,sigma);
}
```

---

[2]This term is borrowed from genetics, where it means that one gene's effect can depend on whether other genes are present.

where we have not specified priors on the three parameters, then this means that Stan will place (improper) uniform priors on all of these. If we pass the data to Stan, and run the full Stan model, we obtain the following results:

```
print(fit,probs = c(0.5))
```

```
##                  mean       se_mean          sd          50% n_eff       Rhat
## mu      2.690000e+00 6.000000e-02 8.000000e-02 2.670000e+00 2      2888.53
## sigma 8.400000e-01 8.000000e-02 1.200000e-01 8.100000e-01 2      9678.73
## nu      7.647104e+15 5.083569e+15 7.207292e+15 6.379618e+15 2    922459.78
## lp_ _  2.676100e+02 1.563500e+02 2.216600e+02 2.731300e+02 2   1314147.11
```

and we see that the values of $\hat{R}$ are a long way from 1.

So what is the problem? The issue here is that the current data does not provide enough information to estimate the parameters of the Student-t distribution. So if we generate more data – say 1000 data points – we then get much faster convergence:

```
N <- 1000
X <- rt(N, df=3)*1 + 2
fit   <-   stan('studentT_withPriors.stan',   data=list(N=N,X=X),iter=200,
chains=4)
print(fit,probs = c(0.5))
```

```
##              mean  se_mean    sd      50%  n_eff  Rhat
## mu           1.96     0.00  0.03     1.96    400  1.00
## sigma        0.97     0.00  0.03     0.97    256  1.00
## nu           3.39     0.02  0.33     3.36    179  1.00
## lp_ _    -1130.90     0.08  1.03 -1130.62    153  1.02
```

However, in most real-life examples we do not have the luxury of simply collecting more data – at least as easily as we did here. So we need another way of putting more information into the system to allow our parameters to be identified. One way forward is to use weakly informative priors (see Section 5.6.1):

```
model {
    X ~ student_t(nu,mu,sigma);
    mu ~ normal(0,10);
    sigma ~ lognormal(0,1);
    nu ~ lognormal(0,1);
}
```

While these priors have quite a gentle curvature, this added information is sufficient to identify the parameters:

```
print(fit,probs = c(0.5))
```

```
##              mean  se_mean    sd      50%  n_eff  Rhat
## mu           2.00     0.00  0.04     2.01    400  1.01
## sigma        1.05     0.00  0.04     1.05    256  1.01
## nu           3.14     0.02  0.27     3.12    145  1.01
## lp_ _    -1237.91     0.09  1.08 -1237.54    153  1.03
```

Increasing the number of MCMC samples will facilitate convergence to the posterior. However, in many circumstances the rate of convergence is so low that we have to run our samplers for an inordinate amount of time to adequately explore posterior space. Furthermore, we argue that this does not really address the cause of the problem; your time would be better spent trying to diagnose the reasons behind slow convergence. Remember, Gelman's folk theorem states that problems with MCMC sampling are usually due to problems with the underlying model, not the sampling algorithm. As a rule of thumb, we recommend that if, after a few thousand iterations (obviously this depends a bit on model complexity) the NUTS sampler has not converged, then we should consider making changes to the model.

Divergent iterations

Suppose that we work as economists for the government of a small country. Part of our job is to estimate the length of time that typical paper currency remains in domestic circulation before becoming lost, broken or travelling abroad. Furthermore, suppose that the governmental mint that print the notes does not include the date of printing on the currency, making it hard to accurately estimate the age of a given note. However, the mint can add a marking to the note that shows up under UV light.

To estimate the life span of currency, we decide to create an experiment where we release 3000 marked notes into circulation. As is the case in many countries, the central bank has a physical bank where individuals can go and exchange coins for notes (or vice versa) or exchange foreign currency for domestic. The workers in the bank have a UV machine that allows them to determine whether a given note is marked. The idea behind our experiment is to monitor the returns of marked bank notes over time as a way of determining their life span in circulation. If notes leave circulation quickly, there will be a corresponding rapid decline in the numbers of marked notes collected in the central bank. If notes last a long time, then there should not be too much change in the numbers of notes collected over time.

We choose to model the number of notes Y_t collected in year t as having a binomial sampling distribution:

$$Y_t \sim \mathcal{B}(3000, \psi \exp(-\mu \times t^\beta)), \tag{16.17}$$

where ψ is the probability that a single note is collected in a given year and μ is a parameter that – along with β – determines the life span of notes. We expect that, as notes age, their probability of leaving circulation increases, at a rate whose magnitude is modulated by β.

We code up the above model in Stan, choosing to use Stan's default uniform priors on all parameters (which are improper for μ and β):

▶

What are divergent transitions and what to do about them?

```
data {
    int N;
    int Y[N];
    int numReleased;
}
parameters {
    real<lower=0,upper=1> psi;
    real<lower=0> mu;
```

```
    real<lower=0> beta;
}
model {
    for(t in 1:N)
        Y[t] ~ binomial(numReleased,psi * exp(-mu*(t^beta)));
}
```

We suppose that we will collect 10 years' worth of data. To determine how easily the parameters of our model can be estimated, we generate fake data where we assume a constant rate of note 'mortality', $\beta = 1$:

```
numReleased <- 3000
psi <- 0.01
mu <- 0.1
N <- 10
Y <- vector(length=N)

for(i in 1:N){
    Y[i] <- rbinom(1,numReleased,psi*exp(-mu*i))
}
```

We run Stan (with 2000 iterations across each of eight chains) using the fake data we generated and get the following warning message:

```
## WARNING: Warning messages:
## 1: There were 203 divergent transitions after warmup.
## Increasing adapt_delta above 0.8 may help.
## 2: Examine the pairs() plot to diagnose sampling problems
```

This indicates that the sampler experienced 203 divergent iterations. (You may need to run the above Stan model a few times to generate a comparable number of divergent iterations.) What does this mean, and is it something to worry about?

Divergent iterations occur when the methods used to approximate the path of our fictitious particle in parameter space produce paths that are poor approximations to the exact solution (see Section 15.5.1). NUTS is able to determine if these divergences likely occur and terminates the simulation of the particle – for this particular iteration of the sampler – early. The number of divergent iterations reported is then the total number of these divergent iterations (after warm-up) that occur. So what causes divergent iterations? The most usual cause is having step sizes (that is, the length of the discrete pieces of the path that are used to approximate the true path) that are too large relative to the posterior curvature in certain areas of parameter space. Taking steps that are too big results in a crude approximation to the exact path of our particle and we get a divergence (see Chapter 15).

Divergent iterations are definitely something to worry about. Since NUTS terminates early for these iterations, this causes a bias away from this area of parameter space. This bias means that we do not explore posterior space fully and our posterior summaries will not faithfully reproduce the exact posterior properties.

But why do some models or data produce divergent errors and others do not? Remember that NUTS self-tunes to find a step size which results in an efficient global exploration of posterior space. However, for some models, there may be areas of high posterior curvature which mean that the globally optimum step size is too large. So if a model has a wide variation in the amount of posterior curvature, it is ripe for divergent iterations.

So looking at our bank note example, why do we get divergences? The best way to diagnose this is either through use of shinyStan or, as we show below, through the *pairs* function:

pairs(fit)

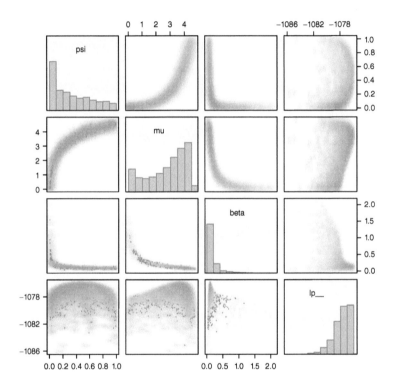

On the plot any samples with divergent iterations are shown as red points. From this we see that there are quite distinct regions where divergent iterations occur. For example, in the plots of mu against beta, we see that many divergent iterations occur in the 'neck' region of the posterior samples. This makes sense because, in this region, small changes in either parameter can strongly affect the behaviour of the model – the posterior is highly curved in this region, and small step sizes are warranted. By contrast, in the tails of this scatter plot, large changes in either mu or beta (mu in bottom right and beta in top left) change fairly little about the model's behaviour. Here, the resultant posterior density is more gently curved, and large step sizes make most sense. Therefore, a step size that is globally optimal may fail to be appropriate in these two regions. In the tails, the exploration of posterior space is inefficient; in the neck, the step sizes are too large and we get divergent iterations.

How can we deal with these divergent iterations? As a first step we can try decreasing the step size and increasing the target acceptance rate of NUTS. Both of these have the effect of tuning down the global step size of the sampler, which should help to mitigate against divergent iterations. To do this we make the following call to Stan in R:

```
fit<-stan('aModel.stan',data=list(N=N,Y=X, numReleased=numReleased),iter=2000,
          chains=8, control=list(adapt_delta=0.95,stepsize=0.01))
```

The resultant pairs plots should now be devoid of divergent iterations.

In more serious cases it may not be possible to entirely eliminate divergent iterations by modifying the target acceptance rate and step size of the sampler. As a rule of thumb, we say that if changing a target acceptance rate to 0.99 does not remove divergent iterations, then we need to think carefully about their cause. This is another example of Gelman's folk theorem in action. Often a re-parameterised model may be available that will avoid some of the issues that result in divergent iterations or slow convergence (the two often go hand in hand).

An alternative way to avoid divergent iterations is to use priors that give less weight for certain regions of parameter space, which have wildly different optimal step sizes. This makes the specification of a single, global, step size less suboptimal. In the above example, we could use a prior for beta that gives most weight around beta = 1, if we believe that there is not a strong effect of bank note age on whether a note leaves circulation.

Tree depth exceeding maximum

In some circumstances, the posterior may have considerable curvature, resulting in NUTS using small step sizes. These small step sizes can mean that it takes the sampler a long time to explore posterior space. A small step size can cause NUTS to hit what is known as the *maximum tree depth*. While we were deliberately fairly shallow in our discussion of NUTS in Chapter 15, we can nonetheless describe the significance of this. Essentially, this means that NUTS cannot as effectively determine the optimal number of steps for a given position in parameter space (to travel as far as possible without doing a U-turn) with resultant inefficiencies in the sampler. These inefficiencies in themselves are not problematic for inferences, but they often go hand in hand with slow convergence or divergent iterations. As before, we suggest attempting to get to the bottom of the problems rather than side stepping them by changing NUTS parameters manually.

 HOW TO GET FURTHER HELP

It has been a challenge to write this chapter to include enough commonly encountered Stan issues without the book becoming a more boring version of *War and Peace*. Inevitably, we have had to leave out cases in order to save space. However, it was never a goal of ours to write a fully comprehensive guide to Stan. There are a few reasons for this: (1) Bayesian inference issues tend to be quite problem specific, meaning that there are as many issues as there are models. (2) The existing documentation – both the case studies on the Stan website and the Stan manual – contain thorough examples. (3) The Stan user forum is a great place to troubleshoot.

If you experience a problem with your model (as inevitably you will), we encourage you to first attempt to find the cause of your issues using similar methods to those described in this chapter. In particular, we suggest attempting to reproduce the issue using the simplest version of your model possible. This is often best done with fake data so that you can see how characteristics of the data affect the occurrence of the issue. Reproducing issues with simpler models is often very informative in itself, and this may illuminate you sufficiently to be able to proceed without outside help. However, there will be circumstances when you fail to understand the causes of, or potential solutions to, a particular issue. Fortunately, the Stan documentation is quite extensive; the manual, case studies and user forum are three essential resources.

There will be times, however, when, despite your best efforts, you are unable to solve a given issue. In these circumstances, you can consider asking a question on the Stan user forum. But before you do so, it pays to create a simple example model that reproduces the same issues. When you post, be sure to include your code, and potentially data, and try to make your question as succinct and clear as possible. The development team at Stan are usually very good at responding, although this depends on the day of the week and other factors, as well as the quality of your question!

CHAPTER SUMMARY

In this chapter, we introduced Stan as a language for doing efficient MCMC sampling. We believe that it is by far the best tool out there currently, and hope that the examples contained in this chapter have convinced you of some of its benefits.

We also covered some of the more common issues that users of Stan will encounter. These fall into two groups: coding errors and sampling issues. Coding errors are usually relatively simple to handle and can be diagnosed by intelligent use of fake data and print statements. Gelman's folk theorem states that sampling issues are almost invariably due to problems with the underlying statistical model, not the sampling algorithm. We cannot advocate this view strongly enough – do not waste too much time fiddling with NUTS's sampling parameters. If you are having trouble with convergence or divergent iterations, take a good hard look at your model. The best way to do this is by fitting your model to fake data which has been simulated from a process whose parameter values you know. By comparing your model estimates with the true parameter values, you can determine whether you need more data, or need to use more informative priors or, finally, to re-parameterise the model. Failing that, fortunately Stan has considerable resources to consult if you do run into a problem you cannot solve on your own.

Now that we have introduced Stan, we are in a good position to tackle hierarchical models. In the final part of the book we introduce this concept and show its usefulness in a wide range of real-life settings.

16 ○ 10 CHAPTER OUTCOMES

The reader should now be familiar with the following concepts:

- how to write basic Stan models and call these from R
- how to do posterior predictive checks using the `generated quantities` block
- how to troubleshoot when things go wrong with your Stan model
- the fact that most problems with MCMC sampling are due to problems with the underlying model, not the sampling algorithm (Gelman's folk theorem)

16○11 PROBLEM SETS

Problem 16.1 Discoveries data revisited

The file `evaluation_discoveries.csv` contains data on the numbers of 'great' inventions and scientific discoveries (X_t) in each year from 1860 to 1959 [1]. In this question you will develop a model to explain the variation in scientific inventions over time. The simplest model here is to assume that (a) one discovery is independent of all others, and (b) the rate of occurrence of discoveries is the same in all years (λ). Since the data are discrete, these assumptions suggest the use of a Poisson likelihood:

$$X_t \sim Poisson(\lambda). \hspace{3cm} (16.18)$$

Problem 16.1.1 Open a text editor and create a file called `discoveries.stan` in your working directory. In the file create three `parameter` blocks:

```
data {
}
parameters {
}
model {
}
```

Problem 16.1.2 Fill in the `data` and `parameter` blocks for the above model.

Problem 16.1.3 Using a $log\text{-}N(2,1)$ prior for λ, code up the `model` block, making sure to save your file afterwards.

Problem 16.1.4 Open your statistical software (R, Python, Matlab, and so on) and load any packages necessary to use Stan. (*Hint*: in R this is done by using `library(rstan)`; in Python this is done using `import pystan`.)

Problem 16.1.5 Load the data into your software and then put it into a structure that can be passed to Stan. (*Hint*: in R create a list of the data; in Python create a dictionary where the 'key' for each variable is the desired variable name.)

Problem 16.1.6 Run your model using Stan, with four chains, each with a sample size of 1000, and a warm-up of 500 samples. Set `seed=1` to allow for reproducibility of your results. Store your result in an object called `fit`.

Problem 16.1.7 Diagnose whether your model has converged by printing `fit`.

Problem 16.1.8 For your sample what is the equivalent number of samples for an independent sampler?

Problem 16.1.9 Find the central posterior 80% credible interval for λ.

Problem 16.1.10 Draw a histogram of your posterior samples for λ.

Problem 16.1.11 Load the `evaluation_discoveries.csv` data and graph it. What does this suggest about our model's assumptions?

Problem 16.1.12 Create a `generated quantities` block in your Stan file, and use it to sample from the posterior predictive distribution. Then carry out appropriate posterior predictive checks to evaluate your model. (*Hint*: use the `poisson_rng` function to generate independent samples from your lambda.)

Problem 16.1.13 A more robust sampling distribution is a negative binomial model:

$$X_i \sim NB(\mu, \kappa), \tag{16.19}$$

where μ is the mean number of discoveries per year, and $var(X) = \mu + \mu^2 / \kappa$. Here κ measures the degree of overdispersion of your model; specifically if κ increases then overdispersion decreases.

Write a new stan file called `discoveries_negbin.stan` that uses this new sampling model. (*Hint*: use the Stan manual section on discrete distributions to search for the correct negative binomial function name; be careful – there are two different parameterisations of this function available in Stan.) Assume that we are using the following priors:

$$\mu \sim log\text{-}\mathcal{N}(2,1) \,,$$

$$\tag{16.20}$$

$$\kappa \sim log\text{-}\mathcal{N}(2,1) \,.$$

Draw 1000 samples across four chains for your new model. Has it converged to the posterior?

Problem 16.1.14 Carry out posterior predictive checks on the new model. What do you conclude about the use of a negative binomial here versus the simpler Poisson?

Problem 16.1.15 Find the central posterior 80% credible interval for the mean rate of discoveries μ from the negative binomial model. How does it compare with your results from the Poisson model? Why is this the case?

Problem 16.1.16 Calculate the autocorrelation in the residuals between the actual and simulated data series. What do these suggest about our current model?

Problem 16.1.17 Following on from the above, suggest an alternative model formulation.

Problem 16.2 Hungover holiday regressions

The data in file `stan_hangover.csv` contains a series of Google Trends estimates of the search traffic volume for the term 'hangover cure' in the UK between February 2012 and January 2016. The idea behind this problem is to determine how much more hung over people are in the 'holiday season', defined here as the period between 10 December and 7 January, than on average for the rest of the year.

Problem 16.2.1 Graph the search volume over time, and try to observe the uplift in search volume around the holiday season.

Problem 16.2.2 The variable *holiday* is a type of indicator variable that takes the value 1 if the given week is all holiday season, 0 if it contains none of it, and $0 < X < 1$ for a week that contains a fraction X of days that fall in the holiday season. Graph this variable over time so that you understand how it works.

Problem 16.2.3 A simple linear regression is proposed of the form:

$$V_t \sim N(\beta_0 + \beta_1 h_t, \sigma), \tag{16.21}$$

where V_t is the search volume in week t and h_t is the holiday season indicator variable. Interpret β_0 and β_1 and explain how these can be used to estimate the increased percentage of hangovers in the holiday season.

Problem 16.2.4 Assuming $\beta_i \sim N(0,50)$ and $\sigma \sim half\text{-}N(0,10)$ priors, write a Stan model to estimate the percentage increase in hangoverness over the holiday period.

Problem 16.3 Coding up a bespoke probability density

In the file `stan_survival.csv` there is data for a variable Y that we believe comes from a probability distribution:

$$p(Y) = \frac{\sqrt[3]{b}}{\Gamma(\frac{4}{3})} \exp(-bY^3), \tag{16.22}$$

where $b > 0$ is a parameter of interest. In this question we are going to write a Stan program to estimate the parameter b even though this distribution is not among Stan's implemented distributions.

Problem 16.3.1 Explain what is meant by the following statement in Stan:

```
theta ~ beta(1,1);
```

In particular, explain why this is essentially equivalent to the following:

```
target += beta_lpdf(theta|1,1);
```

where `target` is a Stan variable that stores the overall log probability, and `+=` increments `target` by an amount corresponding to the right-hand side.

Problem 16.3.2 Work out by hand an expression for the log probability of the density in expression (16.22).

Problem 16.3.3 Write a Stan function that for a given value of y and b calculates the log probability (ignoring any constant terms). *Hint*: Stan functions are declared as follows:

```
functions{
  real anExample(real a, real b){
    ...
    return(something);
  }
}
```

where in this example the function takes two reals as inputs and outputs something of type real.

Problem 16.3.4 Use your previously created function to write a Stan program that estimates b, and then use it to do so with the y series contained within `stan_survival.csv`. (*Hint:* Stan functions must be declared at the top of a Stan program.)

Problem 16.4 Is a tumour benign or malignant?

Suppose that if a tumour is benign the result of a clinical test for the disease for individual i is $X_i \sim \mathcal{B}(20, \theta_b)$, whereas if the tumour is malignant $X_i \sim \mathcal{B}(20, \theta_m)$, where $\theta_b < \theta_m$. Suppose that we collect data on 10 patients' scores on this clinical test, $X = \{4, 18, 6, 4, 5, 6, 4, 6, 16, 7\}$, and would like to infer the disease status for each individual, as well as the parameters (θ_b, θ_m).

Problem 16.4.1 Write down in pseudo-code the full model, where we suppose that we use uniform priors on (θ_b, θ_m) and discrete uniform priors on the disease status s_i of individual i.

Problem 16.4.2 Assuming that $s_i \in [1, 2]$ is the disease status of each individual (1 corresponding to a benign growth, and 2 to a malignant one), use the `transformed parameters` block to calculate the log probability of each individual's data. (*Hint:* this will be a 10×2 matrix, where the 2 corresponds to two possible disease statuses for each individual.)

Problem 16.4.3 The disease status of each individual $s_i \in [1, 2]$ is a discrete variable, and because Stan does not support discrete parameters directly it is not as straightforward to code up these problems as for continuous parameter problems. The way to do this is by marginalising out s_i from the joint distribution:

$$p(\theta_b, \theta_m \mid X) = \sum_{s_1=1}^{2} p(\theta_b, \theta_m, s_1 \mid X), \tag{16.23}$$

where we have illustrated this for the disease status of individual 1. This then allows us to find an expression for the posterior density which we log to give `lp`, and then use `target+=lp` to increment the log probability. However, because we do this on the log-density scale we instead do the following:

$$\log p(\theta_b, \theta_m \mid X) = \log \sum_{s_1=1}^{2} p(\theta_b, \theta_m, s_1 \mid X)$$

$$= \log \sum_{s_1=1}^{2} \exp(\log p(\theta_b, \theta_m, s_1 \mid X)) \tag{16.24}$$

$$= \text{log\_sum\_exp}_{s_1=1}^{2}(\log p(\theta_b, \theta_m, s_1 \mid X)),$$

where `log_sum_exp(.)` (a function available in Stan) is defined as:

$$\text{log\_sum\_exp}_{i=1}^{K}\alpha = \log\sum_{i=1}^{K}\exp(\alpha), \tag{16.25}$$

and is a numerically more stable way of doing the above calculation. Using this knowledge, write a full Stan model that implements this marginalisation, and use it to estimate θ_b and θ_m. (*Hint:* use the `binomial_logit_lpmf(X[i]|N,alpha[s])` function in Stan and define **ordered**`[2]` `alpha`, then transform from the unconstrained alpha to theta using `inv_logit`.)

Problem 16.4.4 We use the `generated quantities` block to estimate the probabilities of state $s = 1$ in each different experiment by averaging over all L posterior draws:

$$q(s = 1 | X) \approx \frac{1}{L}\sum_{i=1}^{L} q(s = 1, alpha[s = 1] | X), \tag{16.26}$$

where $q(.)$ is the unnormalised posterior density. The averaging over all posterior draws is necessary to marginalise out the alpha parameter. To normalise the posterior density we therefore divide the above by the sum of the un-normalised probability across both states:

$$Pr(s = 1 | X) = \frac{q(s = 1 | X)}{q(s = 1 | X) + q(s = 2 | X)}. \tag{16.27}$$

Using the above knowledge, add a `generated quantities` block to your Stan model that does this, and hence estimate the probability that each individual's tumour is benign.

Problem 16.4.5 An alternative way to code this problem is to derive a Gibbs sampler. As a first step in this process, write out the full joint posterior numerator. (*Hint:* now use a slightly altered definition of $s_i \in [0,1]$, where 1 indicates a benign tumour for individual i.)

Problem 16.4.6 By removing those terms that do not depend on θ_b, derive the conditional distribution $\theta_b | \theta_m, S, X$. Hence write down $\theta_m | \theta_b, S, X$.

Problem 16.4.7 Show that the distribution for $s_i | s_{-i}, \theta_b, \theta_m, X$ can be written as:

$$s_i | s_{-i}, \theta_b, \theta_m, X \sim Ber\left(\frac{1}{1 + \left[\frac{\theta_m/(1-\theta_m)}{\theta_b/(1-\theta_b)}\right]^{X_i}\left[\frac{1-\theta_m}{1-\theta_b}\right]^{20}}\right). \tag{16.28}$$

Problem 16.4.8 Using your three derived conditional distributions, create a Gibbs sampler in R, and use it to estimate $(\theta_b, \theta_m, s_1, ..., s_{10})$.

Problem 16.5 How many times did I flip the coin?

Suppose that I have a coin and that θ denotes the probability of its landing heads up. In each experiment I flip the coin N times, where N is unknown to the observer, and record the number of heads obtained, Y. I repeat the experiment 10 times, each time flipping the coin the same N times, and record $Y = \{9,7,11,10,10,9,8,11,9,11\}$ heads.

Problem 16.5.1 Write down an expression for the likelihood, stating any assumptions you make.

Problem 16.5.2 Suppose that the maximum number of times the coin could be flipped is 20, and that all other (allowed) values we regard a priori as equally probable. Further suppose that, based on previous coin flipping fun, we specify a prior $\theta \sim beta(7,2)$. Write down the model as a whole (namely, the likelihood and the priors):

$$Y_i \sim \mathcal{B}(N,\theta),$$

$$N \sim discrete\text{-}uniform(11,20), \tag{16.29}$$

$$\theta \sim beta(7,2).$$

Problem 16.5.3 This problem can be coded in Stan by marginalising out the discrete parameter N. The key to doing this is to write down an expression for the log probability for each result Y_i conditional on an assumed value of N, and θ. Explain why this can be written in Stan as:

```
log(0.1) + binomial_lpmf(Y[i]|N[s],theta);
```

where `N[s]` is the sth element of a vector $\boldsymbol{N}$ containing all possible values for this variable.

Problem 16.5.4 In the `transformed parameters` block, write code that calculates the log probability for each experiment and each possible value of N.

Problem 16.5.5 Write a Stan program to estimate θ. (*Hint*: in the `model` block use `target+= log_sum_exp(lp)` to marginalise out N and increment the log probability.)

Problem 16.5.6 Use the `generated quantities` block to estimate the probabilities of each state.

Problem 16.5.7 An alternative way to estimate N and θ is to derive a Gibbs sampler for this problem. To do this, first show that the joint (un-normalised) posterior distribution can be written as:

$$p(\theta,N\,|\,Y) \propto \left[\prod_{i=1}^{k} \binom{N}{Y_i} \theta^{Y_i}(1-\theta)^{N-Y_i} \right] \theta^{\alpha-1}(1-\theta^{\beta-1}), \tag{16.30}$$

where $K = 10$ and $(\alpha,\beta) = (7,2)$ are the parameters of the prior distribution for θ.

Problem 16.5.8 Derive the conditional distribution $\theta\,|\,N,Y$. (*Hint*: remove all parts of the joint distribution that do not explicitly depend on θ.)

Problem 16.5.9 Write an R function that independently samples from the conditional distribution $\theta\,|\,N,Y$.

Problem 16.5.10 Show that the conditional probability mass function $N|\theta,Y$ can be written as:

$$p(N|\theta,Y) \propto \left[\prod_{i=1}^{k}\binom{N}{Y_i}\right](1-\theta)^{NK}.$$ (16.31)

Problem 16.5.11 Using the previously derived expression, write a function that calculates the un-normalised conditional $N|\theta,Y$ for $N=11,...,20$, which when normalised can be used to sample a value for N. (*Hint*: use the `sample` function in R.)

Problem 16.5.12 Write a working Gibbs sampler using your two previously created functions, and use this to estimate the probability distribution over θ and N.

Problem 16.5.13 Compare the rate of convergence in the mean of N sampled via Gibbs with that estimated from the $p(N)$ distribution that you sampled in HMC. Why is the rate of convergence so much faster for HMC? (*Hint*: this is not due to the standard benefits of HMC that were extolled in this chapter.)

PART V

HIERARCHICAL MODELS AND REGRESSION

PART V MISSION STATEMENT

This part introduces the reader to hierarchical models. We shall see that hierarchical thinking can be applied to a range of different settings, including regression models, and often yields results that are preferable to more traditional modelling frameworks. While we argue that hierarchical models actually simplify many analyses, it can be harder to efficiently sample from them. In this context Stan's lightning-fast speed is a key weapon in the data scientist's toolbox, and here we show how to use this language to sample from a number of different hierarchical models. Along the way we shall cover how best to specify, estimate and test linear and generalised linear regression models – themselves ubiquitous tools in the social and physical sciences.

PART V GOALS

In real life we are often required to analyse data that is structured in some hierarchical way. For example, we might collect data on individual students' SAT scores. These individuals belong to particular classes within particular schools within particular states. We expect that individuals in different classes may not perform equivalently in the SATs due to variation in teaching and peers. Further, we might believe that individuals in separate schools will obtain different scores in the SATs due to variation in school quality and the local neighbourhood. Finally, individuals from two different states may experience different curricula and live in varying geographies, both of which might affect how they fare on tests. Implicit to this example is the supposition that individuals in the same class are more similar than individuals in the same school (not in the same class) which, in turn, are more similar than two randomly chosen individuals from the same state. We would like to estimate a model that accounts for the within-group similarity, yet allows for a gradation of differences between groups in accordance with the hierarchical structure of the data. Hierarchical Bayesian models do just this. They bridge a gap between methods that estimate a separate model for each individual group and a 'pooled' model where we allow for no inter-group differences. Furthermore, the position where hierarchical models lie on this spectrum is not specified by the analyst – the data determines it!

By making more sensible assumptions about the data-generating process, hierarchical models produce more reliable estimates that are less sensitive to outliers. While hierarchical models may appear, at first, to be more complex than non-hierarchical equivalents, they are actually, in a way, simpler. Since the parameters across different groups are related to one another in hierarchical models, their effective model complexity is less than 'heterogeneous' models that estimate separate models for each group. As a consequence, hierarchical models produce the best forecasts – an example use is Nate Silver's correct prediction of the 2008 US presidential election results.

Hierarchical models make it easier to specify a more realistic model, yet do pose some difficulties to estimation. Like many non-hierarchical models, this class of models is typically too complex for exact inference, and so is best handled by MCMC. However, it is generally easier to specify an unidentified model in hierarchical settings. By Gelman's folk theorem we thus find that pathologies with sampling (divergent iterations, slow convergence, and so on) occur more frequently in hierarchical models. We therefore need to use all the good practices we learned in Chapter 16 to avoid these pitfalls, fake data simulation being particularly important.

An important use of hierarchical models is in regression, where the data can often be structured in nature. Fortunately, in the Bayesian paradigm there is really no difference between regression and many other types of model that we have already covered. However, there are some techniques and ideas that are worth discussing, so we devote the latter two chapters of this part to this purpose – Chapter 18 to linear regression and Chapter 19 to generalised linear models.

17

Chapter contents

HIERARCHICAL
MODELS

17⊙1   CHAPTER MISSION STATEMENT

This chapter introduces the concept of hierarchical models, and describes the benefits of this framework over more traditional 'non-hierarchical' models. We also explain how best to specify and estimate these types of models.

17⊙2   CHAPTER GOALS

Suppose that we want to estimate the average decrement to life expectancy for an individual due to smoking one year during their teens. To do so, we conduct a meta-analysis, where we use the results of all previously published studies to produce an overall estimate of the effect of smoking. While we may believe that each of the studies follows good experimental and statistical protocol, there will no doubt be differences between the studies. For example, the research in each study will likely be carried out by unique teams, and the clinical methodology may also vary. One way to proceed is to take the raw data and apply a common statistical procedure to each individual data sample, to produce separate study-level estimates of the effect of smoking. We might even consider simply averaging these estimates to produce an overall estimate across all groups. We could then use graphs to describe the variation in estimates, and hope to find consensus estimates by visual inspection of the plots.

However, this approach does not give us exactly what we want – a single posterior distribution representing the estimated effect of smoking that combines the evidence from all of the previous studies. Only when we have this object will our result truly represent the synthesis of all information available to us. Most importantly, unless we have an overall posterior we will not have a proper gauge of uncertainty.

One way to generate an overall posterior would be to combine the raw data from the various studies, and estimate a model with a set of parameters that are fixed across the individual studies. By fixing the parameters and pooling the data, we arrive at 'overall' effect estimates. However, while we superficially obtain cross-study estimates of the effect of smoking on life span, the estimates will not be worth their weight in cigarettes. This is because the assumptions that underlie a pooled model are inappropriate here. By crudely pooling our data from all the previous studies, we implicitly assume that the methods used to generate each data set were the same. But we know from reading the individual studies that the methods they used differ. Clearly, pooling the data from all the previous studies together in an uninformed matter will not suffice – this will lead to an understatement of the uncertainty involved in the data-generating process.

Hierarchical models walk a line between the two extremes we just discussed: a heterogeneous model, where we estimate a separate model for each study; and a fully pooled one, where we estimate a model where the parameters are the same across all studies. Hierarchical models assume that the methods used to generate the data in each study are related to one another, but, crucially, not the same. How similar, you ask? Well, one of the beautiful things about a hierarchical approach is that the data determines the degree of similarity, not the analyst. The other benefit of this framework is that it can produce an overall estimate of the effect of interest – in our present case, the average effect on life expectancy for smoking for a single year during the teenage years. And unlike the fully pooled estimates, the hierarchical posterior distribution will reflect the true uncertainty across all studies.

Hierarchical models may appear complex due to the statistical models that we are required to use. However, one can actually view hierarchical models simpler than approaches where we estimate a different model for each group (the 'heterogeneous' framework). An additional benefit of the hierarchical approach is that because we, in effect, partially pool data across groups, we often achieve more precise estimates of quantities of interest at the group level. Additionally, because of the greater statistical power that comes from pooling data, these estimates are generally more robust to extreme observations.

In this chapter we use Stan to estimate two different hierarchical models, since we believe that the benefits and consequences of the hierarchical framework are best demonstrated through examples. Using Stan also means that we can mostly forget about the relatively complex statistical distributions involved in these models, and focus on what matters – analysing the data.

17 ⃝ 3 THE SPECTRUM FROM FULLY POOLED TO HETEROGENEOUS MODELS

Suppose that we work for a state education authority and have the scores on a standardised mathematics test for randomly selected students (of the same age) from 100 schools in the region. For simplicity's sake, we assume that the scores are continuous, and can be either positive (for a good student) or negative (for a student that spends too much time playing *Candy Crush*). We want to estimate the mean test score for a randomly selected pupil within the region.

What is a hierarchical model?

17.3.1 Fully pooled model

Starting out, we decide to forget about the school which a student belongs to, and plot the aggregate data (see Figure 17.1). Looking at the graph in Figure 17.1, we model the test scores as being normally distributed:

$$S_{ij} \sim N(\mu, \sigma) \tag{17.1}$$

where S_{ij} is the test score for individual i who goes to school j with an overall (that is, across all schools) mean of μ and standard deviation σ. We code up this model in Stan to allow us to estimate the posterior distributions for μ and σ:

```
data{
  int N;
  real X[N];
}


parameters{
  real mu;
  real<lower=0> sigma;
}
```

```
model{
  for(i in 1:N)
    X[i] ~ normal(mu,sigma);
  mu ~ normal(50,20);
  sigma ~ lognormal(1,1);
}
```

Pooled versus
heterogeneous
coefficients
versus
hierarchical
models

where we have used weakly informative priors for μ and σ (see Section 5.6.1). This results in a posterior distribution for the mean score μ as shown in the left-hand panel of Figure 17.3. We seem contented – we estimated the mean test score and have an uncertainty in our estimate – so we are done, right? However, remember from Chapter 10 that we cannot rest until we have subjected our model to posterior predictive checks (PPCs), to check that our model adequately describes the data.

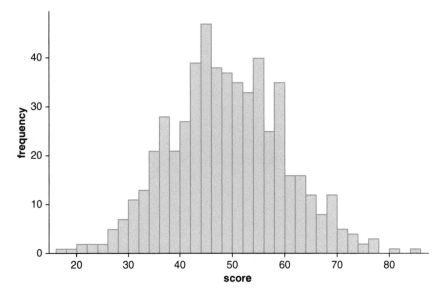

Figure 17.1 The count of test scores for students across all schools. The data sample comprises the results of 550 students.

The distributions of test scores for each individual school are shown in Figure 17.2. One way to test our model is to compare the performance of the worst school with data that has been simulated from the posterior distribution. To do this we use the generated quantities code block:

```
generated quantities{
  real XSim[N];
  real logLikelihood[N];

  for(i in 1:N){
    XSim[i] = normal_rng(mu,sigma);
    logLikelihood[i] = normal_lpdf(X[i]|mu,sigma);
  }
}
```

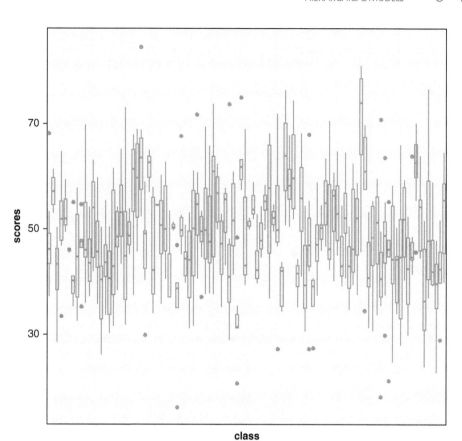

Figure 17.2   The distribution of test scores for fictitious students, grouped by school. The upper and lower fences indicate the 75% and 25% quantiles of the data, and the middle bar shows the median test score. The upper and lower whiskers indicate 1.5 times the interquartile range from the upper and lower fences, respectively. The points indicate outliers. The overall data sample comprises the results of 550 students.

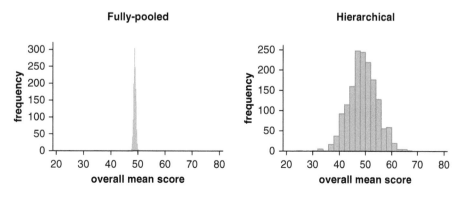

Figure 17.3   Posterior samples for the overall mean test score for the fully pooled model (left), and for the hierarchical model (right).

where we have simulated test scores for all *N* individuals in our data set. We then find the worst school in the simulated data, and compare its mean test score with the school that actually did the worst in the real data (see the left-hand panel of Figure 17.4). Unfortunately, in none of the simulations was the simulated data as extreme as the real test scores – our model is clearly deficient.

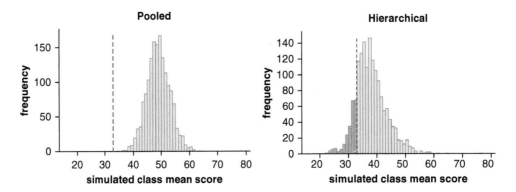

Figure 17.4   Left: simulated mean test scores for the worst-performing schools using the pooled model. Right: the same but using the hierarchical model. In both cases the dashed line indicates the mean of the school with the lowest test scores in the real data. If the simulated data are lower than the actual data, the bars are coloured grey; otherwise red.

17.3.2 Heterogeneous model

Examining Figure 17.2 again, we see there is considerable variation in test scores between schools. Perhaps it would be better if we used a model that accounted for this heterogeneity? We now decide to use a model that estimates separate means and standard deviations for each of the schools. The Stan code for this model is the following:

```
data{
    int K; // number of schools
    int N; // total number of observations
    real X[N]; // observations
    int school[N]; // index 1-100 with identity of school to which individual belongs
}

parameters{
    real mu[K];
    real<lower=0> sigma[K];
}

model{
    for(i in 1:N){
        X[i] ~ normal(mu[school[i]],sigma[school[i]]);
    }
    mu ~ normal(50,10);
    sigma ~ lognormal(1,1);
}
```

where `school` is an index ranging from 1 to 100 which indicates the school each student belongs to (see Section 16.6). Using this model we obtain estimates of the mean test scores shown in Figure 17.5 (the heterogeneous estimates).

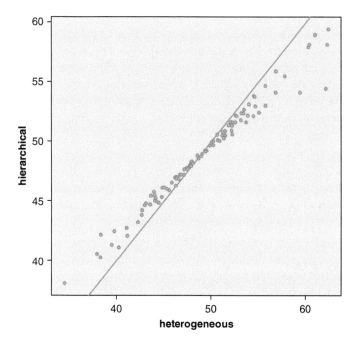

Figure 17.5 Posterior estimates of the mean test scores for each school using the heterogeneous and hierarchical models. The line is the $y = x$ line. The points indicate the posterior means.

It is not clear how to apply the same PPC to this heterogeneous parameter model. Since we have allowed there to be separate means (and standard deviations) for each of the schools, this model will likely overfit the data. This means that, if we compare the mean test scores for simulated and real data for our worst-performing school, we will surely (and somewhat artificially) find these to be in good correspondence.

Even if we forget about the problems inherent with applying the previous PPC, we still have issues. In particular, how can we draw conclusions about the overall mean test score, since all we have is a bunch of school-level estimates? While with the fully pooled model our overall posterior distribution was too narrow, at least it represented something we were actually trying to estimate in the first place.

17.3.3 Hierarchical model

The heterogeneous model accounted for differences between the schools by estimating separate models for each of the schools, but this meant we were unable to make statements about the population as a whole. The fully pooled model (where we assumed the parameters were fixed across all schools) allowed us to estimate the overall mean test score, although, by ignoring the school-level grouping of the data, the overall estimate had insufficient uncertainty associated with it. We would like a model framework that lies somewhere between these two extremes. It should account for the hierarchical structure of the data, but still allow us to make inferences about the overall population. When we have such a framework we hope to have a better handle on the uncertainty in our estimates than that obtained from the fully pooled model.

Hierarchical models are such an invention. In a hierarchical model we assume that the individual school means are, in some way, related to one another. This relation, or *dependence* as it is called in statistics, is because the schools are from the same state. While the individual students in the schools will be different, they will likely come from similar types of families – with similar incomes, parental education, and so on. Also, the state's education policy will likely constrain the pedagogical practices of the teachers, and will naturally result in similar test score performance across different schools.

By the same reasoning, however, we cannot conclude that the schools will be exactly the same. For a start, the schools have different teachers. Anyone who has been to school knows that teacher quality varies, and that this partly determines student performance on tests. Further, the student composition will vary. Some schools may be composed of students from families with slightly higher parental education than others, for example.

In a hierarchical model, we therefore assume that the mean test scores in each school can differ, but that these means are related to one another. In particular, we assume that the μ_i (representing the mean test score for school i) is determined from a state-level distribution of means:

$$\mu_i \sim N(\bar{\mu}, \bar{\sigma}), \tag{17.2}$$

where we have chosen to specify the state-level distribution as another normal distribution, where $\bar{\mu}$ is the average of the mean test scores across all schools in the state, and $\bar{\sigma}$ determines the spread of school means around the overall state-level mean.

The above relation is really just a type of prior, except where the prior distribution's inputs are parameters $(\bar{\mu}, \bar{\sigma})$, not numbers as before. According to the Bayesian paradigm, these inputs are also set priors (sometimes called *hyper-priors* since they are specified for parameters that determine priors for other parameters). This results in a Stan file of the following form:

```
data{
  int K;
  int N;
  real X[N];
  int school[N];
}

parameters{
  real mu[K];
  real<lower=0> sigma[K];
  real mu_bar;
  real<lower=0> sigma_bar;
}
```

```
model{
  for(i in 1:N){
    X[i] ~ normal(mu[school[i]],sigma[school[i]]);
  }

  // priors
  mu ~ normal(mu_bar,sigma_bar);
  // assume heterogeneous standard deviations across schools
  sigma ~ lognormal(1,1);

  // hyper-priors
  mu_bar ~ normal(50,5);
  sigma_bar ~ lognormal(-1,1);
}
```

We want to use this model to estimate the mean test score for a randomly selected student in the state. Because $\bar{\mu}$ is the average of the school means, it will naturally have lower uncertainty associated with it than the quantity we actually want – the mean test score of an individual taken from a randomly chosen school. To get this quantity we use the generated quantities code block:

```
generated quantities{
  real mu_average;
  mu_average = normal_rng(mu_bar,sigma_bar);
}
```

where mu_average is the mean test score in a hypothetical school (different from the other 99 for which we have data). The resultant posterior is considerably wider than the fully pooled equivalent, so is better able to account for the variation in school quality that is evident in the data (see Figure 17.3). Because of this greater variation in estimates the hierarchical model produces simulated means that are much closer to the actual means for the worst-performing school (Figure 17.4). Therefore, by accounting for the hierarchies in the data, we have more confidence that the posterior distribution we estimate from this new approach truly represents the uncertainty seen in the data.

17.3.4 The additional benefits of hierarchical models

It is noticeable from Figure 17.5 that the estimates of the school-level mean test scores obtained from the hierarchical model are shifted versus their heterogeneous equivalents. In general, the hierarchical estimates are shifted towards the overall average. Further, the schools with the most extreme parameter estimates are shifted the most. This type of behaviour is common for hierarchical models, and is known as 'shrinkage towards the mean'. This is a desirable by-product of using hierarchical models, because it takes probability mass away from the outlier estimates, which often have higher uncertainties associated with them, and reallocates it towards those points with lower uncertainty. This means that hierarchical models are naturally more robust than heterogeneous models and, because they are less likely to overfit the data, they perform better on out-of-sample prediction.

An additional benefit of hierarchical models is that, because they partially pool data across groups, the sample size is essentially greater than for the heterogeneous model, where an independent model is fitted for each group. This increased sample size means that we typically achieve higher precision for group-level estimates in hierarchical models.

In short, hierarchical models are a great thing to use. They combine the best bits of both the fully pooled and heterogeneous models, without bringing along any of their flaws. Additionally, the data decides where estimates should locate on the spectrum between these two extremes. If the data from each group looks similar, then we end up nearer the fully pooled estimates. Alternatively, if the data varies considerably by group, the hierarchical estimates will be closer to the heterogeneous ones.

The benefits of hierarchical models grow as the number of groups increases, and when the data are sparser for each group. Typically, this type of approach works best when there are more than, say, 10 groups. Too few groups and there just is not enough data to reach an overall consensus.

What are the benefits of hierarchical models?

The only downside of hierarchical models is that we have to be even more careful than before to ensure that we can disentangle the effects of the various parameters in our model: it is much easier for our model to become unidentified. This means that fake data simulation is even more crucial for hierarchical models (see Sections 16.7.2 and 17.6).

17○4 NON-CENTRED PARAMETERISATIONS IN HIERARCHICAL MODELS

In Section 17.3 we used priors of the form:

$$\theta_i \sim \mathcal{N}(\bar{\theta}, \sigma_\theta), \tag{17.3}$$

where i corresponds to an individual group in our sample, $\bar{\theta}$ is the population-level mean, and σ_θ determines the spread of individual group parameter values about this mean. The Stan code that we used to estimate this type of model was of the following form:

```
model {
    ...
    theta ~ normal(theta_bar, sigma_theta);
    theta_bar ~ normal(a, b);
}
```

This seemed to work OK, although it turns out that there is a better way to sample from such models. This is due to the dependence structure in the prior, and the way in which the HMC and NUTS samplers work. Both algorithms optimise their step sizes to result in a high acceptance rate for the proposed steps. This optimisation is done at the global level. By *global* we mean across all points in the posterior landscape. Inevitably, by striving for a globally optimal step size, we end up with a step size that is locally suboptimal: in places where the posterior is flat, it is optimal to use long strides; in other locations where there is significant posterior curvature, we want to step smaller distances to allow us to efficiently explore the posterior density. This means that there will be locations where the step size is too short (and we spend too long in that area), and others where it is too long (and we fail to properly explore an area of interest). The manifestation of suboptimum local step sizes is that our sampler can be slow to converge to the posterior.

So why is this a problem for hierarchical priors like the ones we specified in expression (17.3)? The issue is that for some values of $\bar{\theta}$ it is optimal to take short steps in some of the θ_i parameter dimensions, whereas for others a longer step length is preferable. This dependence in the posterior makes it hard to choose a global step size that allows efficient exploration in both of these regimes. Sometimes this dependence is so extreme that it also causes pathologies with the sampling, which manifest in the form of divergent iterations (see Sections 15.5.1 and 16.7.2). This occurs because the posterior curvature in some regions of parameter space can be extreme, and requires a very fine approximation scheme to adequately approximate the true path of our sledge.

So what can we do? One solution is to allow stepping distance to be determined by the local posterior curvature. This is the approach taken by a recently proposed MCMC method known as Riemannian Monte Carlo (RMC) [3], which uses the second derivative of the log posterior to measure curvature. This approach will yield more effective samples per iteration; however, the computational burden of determining the second derivative may limit its practical use. So, while we may get more effective samples per iteration, the individual iterations may take so long that we get fewer effective samples per second.

Does this mean that we cannot use hierarchical priors? No. It turns out that we can sample efficiently from these types of model, so long as we re-parameterise them using what is known as a *non-centred* parameterisation [8]. To do this we use a helper parameter, θ_i^{raw}, along with the following prior structure:

$$\theta_i^{\text{raw}} \sim N(0,1),$$

$$\bar{\theta} \sim N(a,b).$$

(17.4)

We then set:

$$\theta_i = \bar{\theta} + \theta_i^{\text{raw}} \times \sigma_\theta.$$

(17.5)

What prior for θ_i is implied by the above? It is the same as before, $\theta_i \sim N(\bar{\theta}, \sigma_\theta)$. So why do we do this? Because this type of prior structure results in lower dependence between $\bar{\theta}$ and θ_i^{raw}. This means that the optimal step length for θ_i^{raw} is less sensitive to $\bar{\theta}$ than it was for θ_i in the original model, and that the locally optimal step length for θ_i^{raw} will tend to be closer to the global optimum. We can now explore the posterior much more efficiently than before.

So how do we code up such models in Stan? The following is a straightforward way to do this:

```
parameters{
  real theta_raw;
  real theta_bar;
  real<lower=0> sigma_theta;
  ...
}
```

```
transformed parameters{
  real theta[K];
  for(i in 1:K)
    theta[i] = theta_bar + theta_raw * sigma_theta;
}


model{
  ...
  theta_raw ~ normal(0,1);
  theta_bar ~ normal(a,b);
}
```

What are non-centred parameterisations and why are they useful?

The methods used to obtain non-centred parameterisations depend on the specific model; however, the basic principle is similar to the above. We advise the interested reader to consult the Stan manual for more examples of these reformulated models.

17 ⊙ 5   CASE STUDY: FORECASTING THE RESULT OF THE UK'S REFERENDUM ON EU MEMBERSHIP

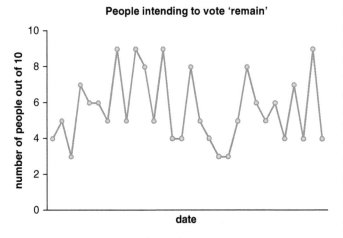

People intending to vote 'remain'

Figure 17.6 The numbers of individuals intending to vote 'remain' in a referendum about the UK's membership in the EU, across 30 different polls. In each case the polls comprised 10 individuals.

In this example we use a hierarchical model to analyse political poll data. In particular, we imagine a dystopian future where the UK decides to hold a referendum about its membership in the EU. We work for an independent think tank, and want to predict the outcome of the election using data from 30 recent polls, each comprising 10 individuals (see Figure 17.6). These polls were conducted by a number of different polling agencies, with differing methodologies used to select their samples. Note that, as per many other examples in this book, the data here is fake.

In this context it seems reasonable to use a binomial sampling model for the number of people X_i intending to vote 'remain' in poll i (see Section 8.4.2):

$$X_i \sim \mathcal{B}(N,\theta), \tag{17.6}$$

where $N = 10$ is the sample size of each poll, and θ is the probability that a randomly chosen individual intends to vote 'remain'.

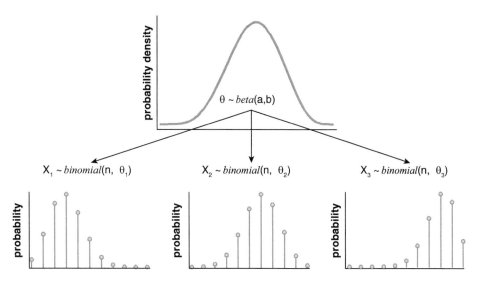

Figure 17.7 The structure of the hierarchical model used to explain the polling data. Since each poll used different methodologies to select its sample, the probability that a randomly chosen individual intends to vote 'remain' varies in each case. For poll i this parameter θ_i is determined by drawing a value from a population-level distribution (shown as the top plot). In turn, the value of θ_i that is sampled characterises a probability distribution for the numbers of individuals intending to vote 'remain' in that sample (bottom panels). In the example cases shown, $0 < \theta_1 < \theta_2 < \theta_3 < 1$.

If we use the binomial likelihood given in expression (17.6) this amounts to pooling the data across all 30 studies. However, we know that the polls were conducted by a number of agencies, each with their own sampling methodology (for example, the way in which they chose their sample and the exact interview process). It therefore seems restrictive to assume a θ value that is common to all the polls. Instead, we allow this probability to vary by poll, and assume that each θ_i is drawn from some population-level distribution (see Figure 17.7):

$$\theta_i \sim beta(a,b), \quad\quad\quad (17.7)$$

where a and b are parameters that characterise this distribution (see the upper panel of Figure 17.7). Since (a, b) are parameters, in Bayesian inference, we must assign them priors. It is actually easier to set priors on the transformed parameters:[1]

$$a = \alpha \times \kappa,$$
$$\quad\quad\quad (17.8)$$
$$b = (1-\alpha) \times \kappa,$$

where $0 \le \alpha \le 1$ measures the overall probability that an individual intends to vote 'remain', and $\kappa \ge 1$ represents our confidence in this value. We use the following Stan code to implement this model:

---

[1]This parameterisation comes from the Baseball case study at http://mc-stan.org/documentation/case-studies.

```
data {
  int K;
  int Y[K];
  int N[K];
}
parameters {
  real<lower=0, upper=1> alpha;
  real<lower=1> kappa;
  vector<lower=0, upper=1>[K] theta;
}

model {
  for (i in 1:K){
    Y[i] ~ binomial(N[i],theta[i]);// Likelihood
  }
  // prior
  theta ~ beta(alpha * kappa, (1 - alpha) * kappa);

  // hyper-priors
  kappa ~ pareto(1, 0.3);
  alpha ~ beta(5,5);
}
```

We specify a *pareto(1,.)* distribution as a prior for κ, since this has support only for $\kappa \geq 1$, and a beta prior (see Section 8.5.1) for α, where we specify most weight towards $\alpha = \frac{1}{2}$, corresponding to an equal split of remainers and leavers in the population.

The purpose of this model was to estimate the proportion of individuals that will vote 'remain' in the final poll – the EU referendum itself. To do this we follow two steps: independently sample (α, κ) from their posteriors, and then sample $\theta \sim beta(\alpha\kappa, (1-\alpha)\kappa)$. We use the generated quantities code block in Stan to do this:

```
generated quantities{
  real<lower=0,upper=1> aTheta;

  aTheta = beta_rng(alpha * kappa, (1 - alpha) * kappa);
}
```

This results in the posterior shown in Figure 17.8. Seeing this, we lose our lunch – it looks very possible that the UK will vote to leave the EU! (We actually used the above approach with real data in the weeks running up to the real EU referendum and obtained a similarly close forecast, which was echoed in the eventual result in the UK where 'remain' scored 48% versus 52% for 'leave'.)

17⦿6 THE IMPORTANCE OF FAKE DATA SIMULATION FOR COMPLEX MODELS

Before applying any model to real data, it is crucial to test it on fake data (see Section 16.7.2). This is for a number of reasons: first, to ensure that the code you have written is not wrong and,

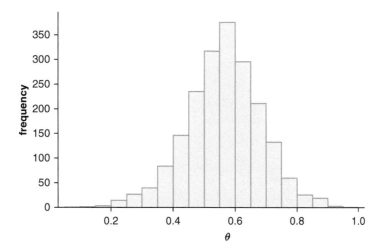

Figure 17.8 The forecasted proportion of people intending to vote 'remain' in the EU referendum. Note that this was estimated using fictitious data.

second, to ensure that your model is identified. Usually, coding errors are spotted relatively easily, even when using real data, because the results are nonsensical. However, without using fake data, it is difficult to determine whether a parameter is unidentified because of the model's structure (including choice of priors), or due to a lack of data.

Consider again the EU referendum example introduced in Section 17.5, and suppose that we want to estimate the hierarchical model we described. Suppose that we want to determine the number of polls required to accurately estimate the proportion of individuals θ intending to vote to remain in the EU. To do this we generate fake data for κ separate polls, each comprising a sample of 10 individuals, assuming that the data in each poll is generated from a single θ value. We then examine how close the estimated population proportion is to the true value of θ. Of course, we could have allowed θ to vary according to some overall distribution. However, we only want to get a feel for how much data we need, so we use the simpler case where this parameter is fixed.

In the R code below we generate fake data from five polls, assuming $\theta = 0.35$, and then estimate the previously defined model using Stan:

```
K <- 5 ## number of polls
aN <- 10 ## number of individuals in each poll
theta <- 0.35
Y <- rbinom(K,aN,theta)
N <- rep(aN,K)

aModel <- stan_model('Hierarchical_eu.stan')
fit <- sampling(aModel,data=list(N=N,K=K,Y=Y), iter=400,chains=4)
```

The resultant posterior is shown in the left-hand panel of Figure 17.9 where there are $K = 5$ polls. This indicates that it is hard to draw any conclusions about the overall proportion θ. There are two ways to remedy this situation: either collect more data or use more prior information. Both of these actions inject more information into the system, and hence allow more precise estimates to be obtained.

We repeat the above exercise now using data from $\kappa = 30$ polls (see the right-hand panel of Figure 17.9). There is now a much better resolution for the overall proportion θ; parameter identification now appears possible.

This exercise is useful and worth doing before we obtain or analyse the data from the real polls, because it shows us the limits of our model. In this case it tells us that in order to be confident in our estimates, we need about 30 polls' worth of data. When only five polls are completed, we can report our estimates, but it will be difficult to draw conclusions about the underlying proportion θ with so little data.

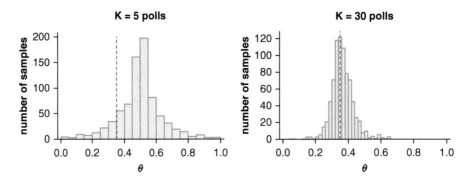

Figure 17.9 Samples from the posterior distributions for the overall proportion of individuals intending to vote 'remain' for (left) 5 polls and (right) 30 polls of fake data. In both cases $\theta = 0.35$ across all the polls (dashed line), and each poll was composed of 10 individuals.

Fake data simulation is also useful when trying to determine the reasons why it takes MCMC algorithms a long time to converge. Slow convergence is always due to a posterior distribution having fat tails, meaning there is insufficient curvature in the posterior to precisely identify parameters. This can be for a number of reasons: using a poorly conceived model, using priors that are too broad, or having insufficient data. By generating data from a set of parameters whose values you know, it is possible to determine how collecting more data, or specifying priors encompassing more information, will result in faster convergence.

17⦿7   CHAPTER SUMMARY

Nowadays data that is structured or grouped in some way is more common than ever. This is particularly true for longitudinal data, where information is collected for the same group of individuals over time. Here, there will be dependence between the data produced by the same individuals at different points in time. To model this relatedness we want the parameters of a model to depend on one another. This is exactly what happens in hierarchical models.

In hierarchical models the concept of a prior is extended to encompass a number of different levels (which has led some to call these multilevel models, although this is sometimes used to mean something altogether different). In these models the line between prior and likelihood is more blurry, and as we shall see in the following chapters it is possible for data to directly enter one or more of these levels.

Hierarchical models typically cause shrinkage of individual estimates towards the overall group mean. This is because, in these models, data are shared across individuals within the same group, and hence the individual estimates converge to the overall consensus. Much like we trust committees to arrive at better decisions than individuals, hierarchical models tend to outperform the array of separate individual-level models that are often used instead.

The benefits of hierarchical models increase along with the number of groups, and the sparser the data are within each group. In this circumstance there is much to be gained by pooling together the data in an intelligent way. This is because, by pooling the data, in effect we increase the sample size, which leads to increases in the statistical power (the probability of detecting an effect if it exists). This means that the group-level estimates are typically more precise than those obtained from a non-hierarchical model.

In all analyses it is essential to use fake data simulation before you begin to analyse real data. It is tempting to start the 'real' analysis rather than waste time working with fake data. In our experience, for all but the simplest of models, testing on simulated data saves considerable time, frustration and embarrassment. On more than one occasion, we have presented results that more reflected the inadequacies of the model than real insights into the data itself. Save yourself this embarrassment – do fake data simulation before you start modelling the real thing.

Hierarchical models provide a richer framework than that available for non-hierarchical models. Their nuances become even more crucial when the data and settings are more complex. In Chapters 18 and 19 we shall encounter circumstances when hierarchical models confer considerable opportunities compared to their simpler cousins.

17◉8 CHAPTER OUTCOMES

The reader should now be familiar with the following concepts:

- fully pooled and heterogeneous coefficient models
- how hierarchical models sit somewhere along a spectrum between the two above extremes
- the benefits of a hierarchical approach: shrinkage towards the grand mean, lower group-level variances, and a better quantification of overall uncertainty
- the added importance of fake data simulation for hierarchical models

17◉9 PROBLEM SETS

Problem 17.1 A meta-analysis of beta blocker trials

Table P17.1 shows the results of some of the 22 trials included in a meta-analysis of clinical trial data on the effect of beta-blockers on reducing the risk of myocardial infarction [3]. The file `hierarchical_betaBlocker.csv` contains the full data set.

Table P17.1 The data from the original study.

Study	Mortality: Treated	Mortality: Control
1	3/38	3/39
2	7/114	14/116
3	5/69	11/93
4	102/1533	127/1520
⋮		
20	32/209	40/218
21	27/391	43/364
22	22/680	39/647

The aim of this meta-analysis is to determine a robust estimate of the effect of beta-blockers by pooling information from a range of previous studies (this problem has been adapted from Splegelhalter et al. [9]).

Problem 17.1.1 Start by assuming that the numbers of deaths in the control $\left(r_i^c\right)$ and treated $\left(r_i^t\right)$ groups for each trial are given by binomial distributions of the form:

$$r_i^c \sim \mathcal{B}(p_i^c, n_i^c),$$

$$r_i^t \sim \mathcal{B}(p_i^t, n_i^t),$$
(17.9)

where (n_i^t, n_i^c) are the numbers of individuals in the treatment and control data sets, respectively. Further assume that the probabilities of mortality in the treatment and control data sets are given by:

$$\mathrm{logit}(p_i^c) = \mu_i,$$

$$\mathrm{logit}(p_i^t) = \mu_i + \delta_i,$$
(17.10)

where:

$$\mathrm{logit}(x) = \log\left(\frac{x}{1-x}\right),$$
(17.11)

and we expect $\delta_i < 0$ if the beta-blockers have the desired effect. We assume the following diffuse priors for the parameters:

$$\mu_i \sim \mathcal{N}(0,10),$$

$$\delta_i \sim \mathcal{N}(0,10).$$
(17.12)

Estimate the posteriors for δ_i for the above model using Stan, or otherwise. Note that for this model there is no interdependence between the studies. (*Hint*: use the Stan `binomial_logit` function.)

Problem 17.1.2 An alternative framework is a hierarchical model where we assume there to be a common overarching distribution across trials such that $\delta_i \sim \mathcal{N}(d, \sigma)$. By assuming the following priors on these parameters estimate this model:

$$d \sim \mathcal{N}(0,10),$$

$$\sigma \sim Cauchy(0,2.5), \quad \text{for } \sigma \geq 0.$$
(17.13)

Estimate the posteriors for δ_i using Stan. How do these estimates compare to the non-hierarchical model?

Problem 17.1.3 Using the hierarchical model, estimate the cross-study effect of the beta-blockers. (*Hint*: use the `generated quantities` code block.)

Problem 17.1.4 For an out-of-sample trial suppose we know that $\mu_i = -2.5$. Using the cross-study estimates for δ, estimate the reduction in probability for a patient taking the beta-blockers.

Problem 17.1.5 Estimate a model with a single, constant value of δ and μ across all trials. Graph the posterior for δ, and compare it with the cross-study hierarchical model estimate.

Problem 17.1.6 Carry out appropriate posterior predictive checks on the homogeneous and hierarchical models, and hence conclude the preferred modelling choice.

Problem 17.2 I can't get no sleep

The data are from a study described in Belenky et al. [2] that measured the effect of sleep deprivation on cognitive performance. There were 18 subjects chosen from a population of interest (lorry drivers) who were restricted to 3 hours of sleep during the trial. On each day of the experiment their reaction time to a visual stimulus was measured. The data for this example is contained within `evaluation_sleepstudy.csv`, consisting of three variables, *Reaction*, *Days* and *Subject ID*, which measure the reaction time of a given subject on a particular day.

A simple model that explains the variation in reaction times is a linear regression model of the form:

$$R(t) \sim N(\alpha + \beta t, \sigma), \tag{17.14}$$

where $R(t)$ is the reaction time on day t of the experiment across all observations.

Problem 17.2.1 Assuming $N(0,250)$ priors on both α and β, code up the above model in Stan. Use it to generate 1000 samples per chain, across four chains. Has the sampling algorithm converged?

Problem 17.2.2 Plot the posterior samples for α and β. What is the relationship between the two variables, and why?

Problem 17.2.3 By using the `generated quantities` code block or otherwise, generate samples from the posterior predictive distribution. By overlaying the real time series for each individual on a graph of the posterior predictive, comment on the fit of the model to data.

Problem 17.2.4 Fit a model with separate (α, β) for each individual in the data set. Use separate and independent $N(0,250)$ priors for the parameters. Again use 1000 samples per chain over four chains.

Problem 17.2.5 Compute the posterior mean estimates of the β parameters for the new heterogeneous parameters model. How do these compare to the single β estimate obtained for the homogeneous model?

Problem 17.2.6 Using the `generated quantities` code block or otherwise, generate samples from the posterior predictive distribution. By comparing individual subject data to the posterior predictive samples, comment on the fit of the new model.

Problem 17.2.7 Partition the data into two subsets: a training set (of subjects 1–17) and a testing set (of subject 18 only). By fitting both the heterogeneous and homogeneous coefficients models to the training sets, compare the performance of each model on predicting the test set data.

Problem 17.2.8 Alternatively, we can fit a hierarchical model to the data which (hopefully) captures some of the best elements of each of the aforementioned models. Fit such a model in Stan using normal priors for α_i and β_i and appropriate priors on the hyper-parameters of these distributions.

Problem 17.2.9 Graph the posterior distribution for β for another individual (not in the original data set). How does this distribution compare to the value of β obtained from the homogeneous coefficient model?

Problem 17.3 Hierarchical ODEs: bacterial cell population growth

The file `hierarchical_ode.csv` contains data for five replicates of an experiment in which bacterial cell population numbers were measured over time. The following model for bacterial population size is proposed to explain the data:

$$\frac{dN}{dt} = \alpha N(1 - \beta N). \tag{17.15}$$

However, measurement of bacterial cell numbers is subject to random, uncorrelated measurement error:

$$N^*(t) \sim N(N(t), \sigma), \tag{17.16}$$

where $N^*(t)$ is the measured number of cells, and $N(t)$ is the true population size. Finally, we suppose that the initial number of bacterial cells is unknown, and hence must be estimated.

Further we assume the following priors:

$$\alpha \sim N(0,2),$$

$$\beta \sim N(0,2),$$

$$\sigma \sim Cauchy(0,1), \tag{17.17}$$

$$N(0) \sim N(5,2),$$

where all parameters have a lower value of 0.

Problem 17.3.1 Write a Stan function that returns dN/dt. *Hint 1*: this will need to be done within the `functions` block at the top of the Stan file. *Hint 2*: the function must have a structure:

```
real[] bacteria_deriv(real t, real[] y, real[] theta, real[] x_r, int[] x_i)
```

where the variables x_i and x_r are not used here, but nonetheless need to be defined:

```
transformed data {
  real x_r[0];
  int x_i[0];
}
```

Problem 17.3.2 Estimate a model where the parameters (α, β) are assumed to be the same across all experimental replicates.

Problem 17.3.3 By graphing the data or otherwise, comment on the assumption of a common (α, β) across all replicates.

Problem 17.3.4 Now estimate a model that estimates separate values for (α, β) across all replicates. Graph the posterior distribution for each parameter.

Problem 17.3.5 Estimate a hierarchical model assuming the following priors:

$$\alpha \sim \Gamma(a,b),$$
$$\beta \sim \Gamma(c,d),$$
$$a \sim N(20,5),$$
$$b \sim N(40,5),$$
$$c \sim N(10,3),$$
$$d \sim N(100,5).$$

$$(17.18)$$

Compare your estimates of (α, β) with those from the completely heterogeneous model.

Problem 17.3.6 Estimate the overall (α, β) for the hierarchical model. How do these compare to the pooled model estimates?

Problem 17.3.7 By holding out one of your data sets, compare the predictive performance of each model.

Problem 17.4 Bowel cancer model selection

The file `hierarchical_cancer.csv` contains (fictitious) data on the population size of a given county (N) and the number of bowel cancer cases in that county (X). In this question we aim to build a model to estimate the underlying rate of cancer occurrence λ.

Problem 17.4.1 A simple model is to assume that cancer occurrence is an independent event, and hence we use the model:

$$X_i \sim Poisson(N_i\lambda),$$

$$(17.19)$$

where N_i is the population in county i, and X_i is the number of cases of bowel cancer in the same county. Write a model in Stan to estimate the underlying rate of bowel cancer occurrence (λ), where we assume a prior of the form $\lambda \sim N(0.5, 0.5)$.

Problem 17.4.2 Using the `generated quantities` block record the estimated log-likelihood of each data point, for each posterior sample of λ.

Problem 17.4.3 By using Stan's `optimizing` function to obtain the MAP estimate of λ, estimate the expected log pointwise predictive density (*elpd*) via a deviance information criterion (DIC) method:

$$\widehat{elpd} = \log p(X \mid \hat{\theta}_{\text{Bayes}}) - 2var_{s=1}^{S} \log p(X \mid \theta_{s}) \qquad (17.20)$$

where $var_{s=1}^{S} \log p(X \mid \theta_{s})$ is the variance in log-likelihood for all data points across S posterior draws. (*Hint*: the latter part of the formula requires that we estimate the model by sampling.)

Problem 17.4.4 Estimate *elpd* using the Akaike information criterion (AIC) method. (*Hint*: use Stan's `optimizing` function where the Stan file has had the prior commented out, to achieve the maximum likelihood estimate of the log-likelihood.)

Problem 17.4.5 Either manually or using the `loo` package in R, estimate *elpd* by a Watanabe–Akaike information criterion (WAIC) method. If you choose the manual method, this can be done with the formula:

$$\widehat{elpd} = \underbrace{\sum_{i=1}^{N} \log\left(\frac{1}{S}\sum_{s=1}^{S} p(X_i \mid \theta_s)\right)}_{\text{log pointwise predictive density}} - p_{\text{WAIC}}, \qquad (17.21)$$

where:

$$p_{\text{WAIC}} = \sum_{i=1}^{N} var_{s=1}^{S}\left[\log\left(X_i \mid \theta_s\right)\right]. \qquad (17.22)$$

Problem 17.4.6 By partitioning the data into 10 folds of training and testing sets (where one data point occurs in each testing set once only), estimate the out-of-sample predictive capability of the model. (*Hint 1*: in R use the `Caret` package's `createFolds` to create 10 non-overlapping folds. *Hint 2*: adjust your Stan program to calculate the log-likelihood on the test set.)

Problem 17.4.7 A colleague suggests fitting a negative binomial sampling model to the data, in case overdispersion exists. Using a $\kappa \sim log\text{-}N(0, 0.5)$ prior on the dispersion parameter, change your Stan model to use this distribution, and estimate the out-of-sample predictive density using any of the previous methods. Which model do you prefer? (*Hint*: use Stan's `neg_binomial_2` function to increment the log probability.)

Problem 17.4.8 A straightforward way to estimate the marginal likelihood is to use:

$$p(X) \approx \frac{1}{S}\sum_{s=1}^{S} p(X \mid \theta_s),$$ (17.23)

where $\theta_s \sim p(\theta)$. Either using Stan's generated quantities block or otherwise, estimate the marginal likelihood of the Poisson model. (*Hint*: if you use Stan then you need to use log_sum_exp to marginalise the sampled log probabilities.)

Problem 17.4.9 Estimate the marginal likelihood of the negative binomial model, and hence estimate the log Bayes factor. Which model do you prefer?

18

Chapter contents

LINEAR REGRESSION MODELS

CHAPTER MISSION STATEMENT

In this chapter we discuss Bayesian linear regression. In particular, we examine the use and benefits of hierarchical models in the context of regression, where the benefits of this approach become even more apparent.

 CHAPTER GOALS

Regression is a ubiquitous tool across the physical and social sciences, where it is used to try to untangle cause and effect in a range of settings. Regression is used to determine the nature of relationships between sets of variables. For example, to determine how the weight of an individual is affected by their height. In linear regression the dependent variable (in the example, height) is modelled as being equal to a linear combination of coefficients and independent variables (here there is a single factor, weight). The dependent variable depends on other factors not included in the regression, typically because we do not have data for these inputs. In our example, the height of an individual is determined by an individual's genetics, diet, and so on. This means that the dependent variable is not perfectly determined by the variables that we include and, hence, there is variation about the value predicted by the regression model. In the Bayesian approach to regression we specify a sampling distribution to describe this variation, which is often chosen to be a normal distribution. In Bayesian approaches we then place priors on the regression coefficients. In our weight and height example, this amounts to specifying a prior on the strength of covariance between these two variables. As for a number of other analyses, the Bayesian approach to regression will typically produce results that look similar to those obtained from a Frequentist approach, particularly if vaguely informative priors are used.

However, the Bayesian method really distinguishes itself when model complexity increases. This is most evident when we consider data that is hierarchically grouped in some way. While hierarchical models do exist in Frequentist frameworks (often called Random Effects or Mixed Effects models), the Bayesian method makes it substantially easier to extend a model to incorporate more realistic assumptions about the data-generating process. This is particularly true when we use Stan for the analysis, and the example we use in this chapter – examining the determinants of high school education scores in England – is accordingly estimated using this tool.

In Bayesian hierarchical regression prior knowledge and data can be incorporated in the model at every level of the hierarchy. This freedom means we can estimate models that are a much better approximation to real life than non-hierarchical approaches. Unsurprisingly, hierarchical models typically outperform other approaches. Most notably, Nate Silver used Bayesian hierarchical regression models to correctly predict the outcome of the 2008 US presidential election [32].

This chapter is less theoretical and more applied than those previous. This is because we have already covered most of the requisite theory (particularly in Chapter 17), but also because we believe that the nuances of Bayesian regression are best illustrated through applied examples.

 EXAMPLE: HIGH SCHOOL TEST SCORES IN ENGLAND

Unlike many of the preceding chapters, the data we analyse here is real. It consists of data collected by the Department for Education in England and contains measures of high school test performance collected over the academic year 2015–2016. The variable of key interest to us is the percentage of students achieving C or above (or equivalent) in their maths and English GCSEs (standardised tests taken by pupils typically at 16 years of age) for each school where data was available (3458 in total; see Figure 18.1). For each school we also have data on the percentage of female students, the percentage of students receiving free school meals, and the percentage of students for whom English is not a first language. For all schools we also know which local education authority (LEA) they belong to. LEAs are responsible for managing education provision for schools within a given region. Since decisions made by LEAs (choice of curriculum, allocation of funds, and so on) may have an impact on the performance of students, we want our eventual model to allow us to determine the influence of LEAs on test performance.

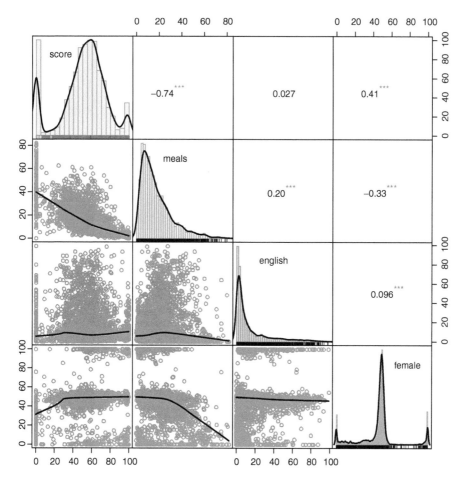

Figure 18.1   The data from 3458 schools in England collected for the academic year of 2015-2016. 'scores' is the percentage of pupils achieving grades A*-C, or equivalent, at GCSE; 'meals' is the percentage of students who take free school meals; 'english' is the percentage of students with English *not* as a first language; 'female' is the percentage of female students in the school. The numbers in the upper diagonal cells indicate the correlation between the variables, and *** indicates that the correlation is significant at the 1% level. The diagonal plots show the marginal distributions of each variable, and the lower-off-diagonal plots show the bivariate relationships between variables, with a local regression line added.

18⊙4 POOLED MODEL

The most basic model to describe test scores is a linear regression of the form:

$$score_{ij} \sim \mathcal{N}\left(\alpha + \beta_m meals_{ij} + \beta_e english_{ij} + \beta_f female_{ij}, \sigma\right),$$

(18.1)

where 'score' represents the percentage of students achieving a C or higher at GCSE in English and maths for school i within a local education authority j. Here we have chosen a normal likelihood for computational ease, although we recognise that this is less than ideal, given that the dependent variable is bounded between 0% and 100%. This model assumes that the effect of each of the independent factors on test scores is fixed across all LEAs. So, for example, an incremental increase in the proportion of female students has the same average effect on test scores for a school in LEA A as it does for another in LEA B.

This model can be coded up in a straightforward way in Stan:

```
data{
  int N;
  real score[N];
  real meals[N];
  real female[N];
  real english[N];
}
parameters{
  real alpha;
  real beta_m;
  real beta_f;
  real beta_e;
  real<lower=0> sigma;
}
model{
  for(i in 1:N){
    score[i] ~ normal(alpha + beta_m*meals[i] +
            beta_f*female[i] + beta_e*english[i],sigma);
  }
  // Priors
  alpha ~ normal(50,10);
  beta_m ~ normal(0,1);
  beta_f ~ normal(0,1);
  beta_e ~ normal(0,1);
  sigma ~ normal(0,2);
}
```

where we have set fairly uninformative priors on each of the effect sizes, and a vaguely informative prior for α:

```
## Print summary statistics
print(fit,probs = c(0.25, 0.5, 0.75))
```

```
##                mean se_mean    sd       25%       50%       75% n_eff Rhat
## alpha         61.21    0.04  0.85     60.59     61.25     61.81   557 1.00
## beta_m        -1.25    0.00  0.02     -1.26     -1.25     -1.24   567 1.00
## beta_f         0.19    0.00  0.01      0.18      0.19      0.20   657 1.00
## beta_e         0.20    0.00  0.01      0.19      0.20      0.21   138 1.03
## sigma         15.18    0.01  0.18     15.06     15.18     15.31   476 1.00
## lp__       -11189.23    0.09  1.51 -11190.05 -11188.97 -11188.06   281 1.01
```

So it appears that schools with a higher proportion of students taking free school meals perform considerably worse on tests. Schools with more female students do a bit better. Finally (and perhaps controversially for UK Independence Party supporters), schools comprising more students with English as a second language fare slightly better too. It should not surprise us that schools where large proportions of students take meals do worse on exams since these students likely come from impoverished backgrounds, often from broken families, with a low level of parental education. It should also not surprise us that the effect size we estimate for school meals (more than a percentage point decrease in test scores for a one-point increase in the proportion of students taking free school meals, on average) is the largest out of the three variables we consider, since in Figure 18.1 we see a strong negative correlation between the percentage of students taking free school meals and the test scores.

While the results of this model would be similar to those from a Frequentist analysis, it is much more straightforward to extend this model. Suppose, for example, we want to use the more robust Student-*t* distribution for our likelihood. All we need to change in Stan is:

```
parameters{
   ...
   real<lower=0> nu;
}
model{
   for(i in 1:N){
      score[i] ~ student_t(nu,alpha + beta_m*meals[i] +
            beta_f*female[i] + beta_e*english[i],sigma);
   }
   ...
   nu ~ ...
}
```

To re-estimate the model using a Frequentist method would require a large change to our code. With Stan we need only to add three short lines!

18○5 INTERACTIONS

Suppose that we believe that the impact of having more students for whom English is not their first language may depend on the school's gender composition. As such, we estimate an equation of the form:

$$\text{score}_{ij} \sim \mathcal{N}\left(\alpha + \beta_m \text{meals}_{ij} + \beta_e \text{english}_{ij} + \beta_f \text{female}_{ij} + \delta \text{english}_{ij} \text{female}_{ij}, \sigma\right). \tag{18.2}$$

We can use expression (18.2) to calculate the average score for a school with a 1% higher rate of pupils with English not as their first language:

$$\overline{score}_{ij}' = \alpha + \beta_m meals_{ij} + \beta_e(english_{ij} + 1) + \beta_f female_{ij} + \delta(english_{ij} + 1)female_{ij}$$

$$= \overline{score}_{ij} + \beta_e + \delta female_{ij},$$

(18.3)

where $\overline{score}_{ij}$ is the average score for a school with a 1% lower rate of pupils with English not as a first language. So by including an interaction term, δ, in the model, the effect of an increase in English is modulated by the proportion of females in the school. The strength of this interaction effect is given by δ.

Estimating this model in Stan is straightforward and requires only a modest change to the model block (also a declaration of delta in the parameters block):

```
for(i in 1:N){
    score[i] ~ normal(alpha + beta_m*meals[i] + beta_f*female[i] +
        beta_e*english[i] + delta*english[i]*female[i],sigma);
}
...
delta ~ normal(0,1);
```

where we have set a fairly uninformative prior on the interaction parameter. The results of running this adapted model are as follows:

```
## Print summary statistics
print(fit,probs = c(0.25, 0.5, 0.75))
```

```
##                 mean se_mean     sd       25%         50%         75% n_eff   Rhat
## alpha        58.1492  0.0422 1.0443   57.4413     58.1598     58.8274   614 1.0045
## beta_m       -1.2281  0.0006 0.0198   -1.2405     -1.2282     -1.2152  1008 0.9990
## beta_f        0.2526  0.0007 0.0185    0.2405      0.2525      0.2648   615 1.0061
## beta_e        0.3313  0.0014 0.0330    0.3100      0.3324      0.3525   587 1.0074
## delta        -0.0028  0.0000 0.0006   -0.0032     -0.0028     -0.0024   590 1.0071
## sigma        15.1356  0.0060 0.1807   15.0083     15.1304     15.2569   897 1.0009
## lp_ _     -11179.9470  0.0737 1.7705 -11180.8926 -11179.6117 -11178.6395   577 1.0044
```

So the positive effect of having English as a second language is slightly diminished if a school has a higher proportion of female students. Specifically, a one-point increase in the percentage of females in the school leads to a 3/1000 of a percentage point decrease in the effect of having more students with English as a second language.

We note that the estimated posteriors for coefficients are all fairly narrow. Perhaps too narrow. Are we really confident that a 1% increase in the percentage of pupils that have free school meals lowers test scores by $1.21 \leq \beta_m \leq 1.24\%$ (25–75% credible interval) on average? Something is probably amiss (see Section 18.7).

HETEROGENEOUS COEFFICIENT MODEL

The assumption that the provision of free school meals has the same effect across all of England is highly suspect. Schools, and the regions they belong to, vary in quality of education provision. As an example, there may be a different effect size based on whether the school is located in an urban or rural area. Fortunately for each school, we know which LEA it belongs to. There are 152 LEAs in England, which are the local councils responsible for education provision in their jurisdiction.

A crude way to use this data is to estimate separate models for each LEA, and hence use a regression equation of the form:

$$\text{score}_{ij} \sim \mathcal{N}\left(\alpha_j + \beta_{m,j}\text{meals}_{ij} + \beta_{e,j}\text{english}_{ij} + \beta_{f,j}\text{female}_{ij}, \sigma_j\right), \tag{18.4}$$

where the j subscript for each of the parameters indicates the effect size for LEA j, and we assign independent priors for the set of parameters for each LEA. This amounts to estimating a separate model for each LEA.

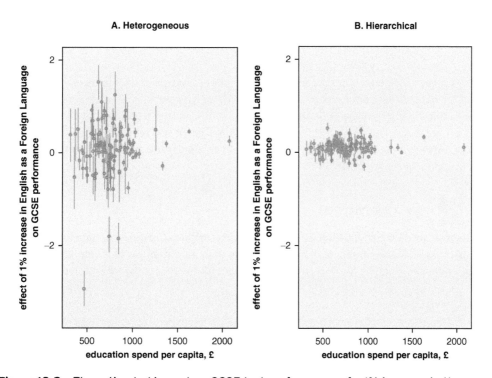

Figure 18.2 The estimated impact on GCSE test performance of a 1% increase in the proportion of students with English not as a first language for each LEA, as a function of per capita education spend for the heterogeneous (left) and hierarchical models (right). The points indicate posterior median estimates, and the upper and lower whiskers show the 75% and 25% posterior quantiles.

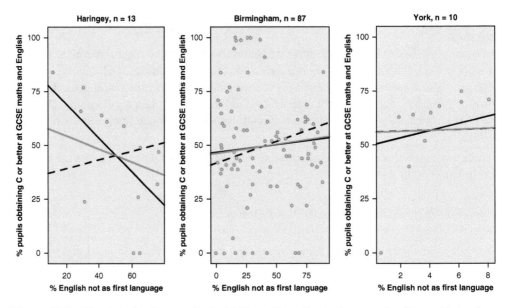

Figure 18.3   The data for three selected LEAs with estimated regression lines obtained from the heterogeneous model (black lines), the hierarchical model (red lines) and the fully pooled model (dashed black lines). In all cases the lines are constrained to go through the sample mean of the data for that LEA.

Unlike for the fully pooled case, we now have estimates of the effect sizes for each LEA. Because each LEA has differing amounts of data (one LEA has data for only three schools!), there is considerable variation in the estimates across the LEAs. Consider the estimates of the effect of having more students with English not as a first language on test scores (see Figure 18.2). This includes a strongly negative effect for Haringey ($n = 13$ schools) and a strongly positive effect for York ($n = 10$ schools; Figure 18.3).

18○7 HIERARCHICAL MODEL

A better way to allow for LEA-level variation in the effect sizes is to estimate a hierarchical model. In this framework the parameters for each LEA are drawn from an overarching 'England-level' distribution. For example, for the effect of free school meals, we use the following priors:

$$\beta_{m,j} \sim N(\bar{\beta}_m, \sigma_m), \tag{18.5}$$

where $\bar{\beta}_m$ is the average effect of free school meals across all of England, and σ_m measures the variation in individual LEA effects about this mean. This type of model can be implemented in Stan as follows:

```
data{
  int N;
  real score[N];
  int LEA[N]; // a vector with LEA groups 1-152
```

```
  real meals[N];
  real female[N];
  real english[N];
  int numLEA;
}

parameters{
  real alpha[numLEA];
  real beta_m[numLEA];
  real beta_f[numLEA];
  real beta_e[numLEA];
  real<lower=0> sigma[numLEA];
  real alpha_top;
  real<lower=0> alpha_sigma;
  real beta_m_top;
  real<lower=0> beta_m_sigma;
  real beta_f_top;
  real<lower=0> beta_f_sigma;
  real beta_e_top;
  real<lower=0> beta_e_sigma;
}
model{
  for(i in 1:N){
    int aLEA;
    aLEA = LEA[i];
    score[i] ~ normal(alpha[aLEA] + beta_m[aLEA]*meals[i] +
        beta_f[aLEA]*female[i] +
        beta_e[aLEA]*english[i],sigma[aLEA]);
  }
  // Priors
  alpha ~ normal(alpha_top,alpha_sigma);
  beta_m ~ normal(beta_m_top,beta_m_sigma);
  beta_f ~ normal(beta_f_top,beta_f_sigma);
  beta_e ~ normal(beta_e_top,beta_e_sigma);
  sigma ~ normal(0,2);

  // Hyper-priors
  alpha_top ~ normal(50,10);
  beta_m_top ~ normal(0,1);
  beta_f_top ~ normal(0,1);
  beta_e_top ~ normal(0,1);
  alpha_sigma ~ normal(0,1);
  beta_m_sigma ~ normal(0,1);
  beta_f_sigma ~ normal(0,1);
  beta_e_sigma ~ normal(0,1);
  }
```

```
generated quantities{
  real alpha_overall;
  real beta_m_overall;
  real beta_f_overall;
  real beta_e_overall;

  alpha_overall = normal_rng(alpha_top,alpha_sigma);
  beta_m_overall = normal_rng(beta_m_top,beta_m_sigma);
  beta_f_overall = normal_rng(beta_f_top,beta_f_sigma);
  beta_e_overall = normal_rng(beta_f_top,beta_f_sigma);
}
```

Here we have assigned hierarchical priors for each of the regression parameters (for simplicity we assume independent standard deviations for each of the LEAs). We use the `generated quantities` block to produce overall estimates of the effect sizes for a randomly selected LEA, by independent sampling from the respective priors. We need this step because the 'top'-suffixed parameters represent means of effect sizes, and hence would yield overly confident estimates at the LEA level.

Running the above model we obtain the following results for the overall effect sizes:

```
## Print summary statistics
print(fit,probs = c(0.25, 0.5, 0.75))
```

```
##                   mean  se_mean    sd    25%    50%    75%  n_eff  Rhat
## alpha_overall    68.71     0.12  4.55  65.65  68.68  71.67   1384     1
## beta_m_overall   -1.51     0.01  0.42  -1.79  -1.52  -1.22   1600     1
## beta_f_overall    0.15     0.00  0.03   0.13   0.15   0.16    866     1
## beta_e_overall    0.15     0.00  0.03   0.13   0.15   0.16    713     1
```

The posterior distributions for the effect sizes are now wider than those that we found previously (particularly for the effect of free school meals) using the non-hierarchical model. This increased uncertainty seems warranted given the heterogeneous nature of the individual LEAs. However, the overall picture is similar: schools with a higher proportion of students who get free school meals perform much worse on GCSEs; those with a higher proportion of females do slightly better; and similarly those schools with a greater proportion of students with English as a second language also score marginally higher.

Even though there is more uncertainty in the overall estimates of the effect sizes versus the fully pooled model, there is reduced variance in the posterior distributions for each LEA compared with the heterogeneous coefficient model (see Figure 18.2). This is because in the hierarchical model we partially pool information across LEAs. In effect, this partial pooling of information raises the sample size for each LEA, resulting in a reduction in variance of the estimates.

It is also evident that the individual effect size estimates are reweighted towards the overall grand mean. In Figure 18.3 we show how the hierarchical estimates of the effect of not having English as a first language (red lines) lie between the position of the heterogeneous estimates (black lines) and the grand mean (dashed black line). This reduction in individual heterogeneity is desired as it reduces the leverage of individual extrema on the overall inferences, increasing their robustness. The degree to which the heterogeneous estimates are moved to form the hierarchical estimates depends on the amount of data available for that group. For example, for Birmingham ($n = 87$ schools) the hierarchical estimates lie close to the heterogeneous estimates because there is considerable data.

18◎8 INCORPORATING LEA-LEVEL DATA

Suppose that we want to assess how policy changes at the LEA level affect the test scores of students in a randomly selected school within that LEA. In particular, we might hope that increases in education spending by LEAs would lead to better student performance. Here is an example of a model that accounts for this LEA-level variable:

$$\text{score}_{ij} \sim N\left(\alpha_j + \beta_{m,j}\text{meals}_{ij} + \beta_{e,j}\text{english}_{ij} + \beta_{f,j}\text{female}_{ij}, \sigma_j\right)$$

$$\alpha_j \sim N\left(\bar{\alpha} + \beta_{epc}\text{education}_j, \sigma_\alpha\right)$$

(18.6)

where we model the score of school i within LEA j, and education$_j$ is the per capita education spending for that LEA. As before, we allow there to be LEA-specific effects of free school meals, English as a foreign language and female students. However, we now allow the per capita expenditure on education services for each LEA to influence test scores, with an effect size given by β_{epc}. We can implement this in Stan as follows (data block same as on P460–461):

```
parameters{
  real alpha_raw[numLEA];
  real beta_m[numLEA];
  real beta_f[numLEA];
  real beta_e[numLEA];
  real<lower=0> sigma[numLEA];
  real alpha_top;
  real<lower=0> alpha_sigma;
  real beta_m_top;
  real<lower=0> beta_m_sigma;
  real beta_f_top;
  real<lower=0> beta_f_sigma;
  real beta_e_top;
  real<lower=0> beta_e_sigma;
  real beta_epc;
}
transformed parameters{
  real alpha[numLEA];
  for(i in 1:numLEA){
    alpha[i] = alpha_sigma * alpha_raw[i] + alpha_top
        + beta_epc*education[i];
  }
}
```

```
model{
  for(i in 1:N){
    int aLEA;
    aLEA = LEA[i];
    score[i] ~ normal(alpha[aLEA] + beta_m[aLEA]*meals[i]
        + beta_f[aLEA]*female[i] + beta_e[aLEA]*english[i],sigma[aLEA]);
  }
  // priors
  alpha_raw ~ normal(0,1);
  beta_m ~ normal(beta_m_top,beta_m_sigma);
  beta_f ~ normal(beta_f_top,beta_f_sigma);
  beta_e ~ normal(beta_e_top,beta_e_sigma);
  sigma ~ normal(0,2);

  // Hyper-priors
  alpha_top ~ normal(50,10);
  beta_m_top ~ normal(0,1);
  beta_f_top ~ normal(0,1);
  beta_e_top ~ normal(0,1);
  alpha_sigma ~ normal(0,1);
  beta_m_sigma ~ normal(0,1);
  beta_f_sigma ~ normal(0,1);
  beta_e_sigma ~ normal(0,1);
  beta_epc ~ normal(0,1);
}
```

In this code we used what is known as a non-centred parameterisation of a statistical model (see Section 17.4), which is a technique used to speed up convergence to the posterior distribution (see Section 16.7.2). In this parameterisation we can generate a prior distribution of the form we specified in the previous expression by first sampling a parameter alpha_raw that is assigned a standard normal prior, then multiplying this by sigma_alpha and adding on a mean in the transformed parameters block. While mathematically this is equivalent to the prior given in the bottom line of (18.6), by sampling from alpha_raw rather than alpha itself, the optimal step size of our NUTS algorithm no longer depends as strongly on population-level parameters. This results in faster exploration of the posterior distribution, and a lower risk of divergent iterations.

Unfortunately, it appears that spending at the LEA level does not strongly affect the test score performance of students (Figure 18.4). This could be for a number of reasons. Perhaps the test score of a student reflects the education that they have received throughout their childhood. Thus, using the latest LEA spending figures (as we have done here), may neglect the integrative effect of education spending. We might also expect that the effect of changes to LEA education funding depends heavily on the way in which this money is spent. For example, increasing the number of teachers (resulting in fewer students per teacher) may be effective, but building new sports facilities may not. However, these results do seem to hint that determining the effect of regional education spending on test scores may not be as straightforward as hoped.

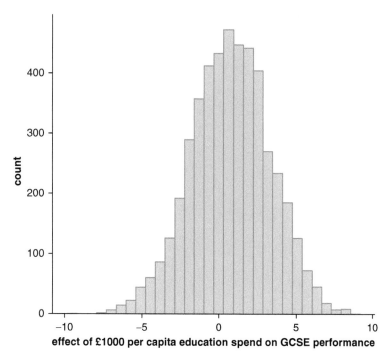

Figure 18.4 Posterior samples for the estimated effect of a £1K increase in education spending per capita for a randomly selected LEA on GCSE performance, as estimated by the hierarchical model described by the likelihood and prior in (18.6).

18〇9 CHAPTER SUMMARY

This chapter has provided a whistle-stop tour of Bayesian regression models. These models in their simplest (non-hierarchical) flavour produce results that are often similar to Frequentist approaches, particularly when there is abundant data available to inform parameter estimates. However, we still prefer the Bayesian approach because of the creativity it provides in model testing through posterior predictive checks.

Where the Bayesian approach really shines is when the data are structured in some way. Multilevel models allow the analyst to include relevant information at the most appropriate level of the data hierarchy and, as a result, often provide the best predictions. The quality of data that is collected will likely improve over time, meaning that the prevalence and importance of these models are set to increase.

Hierarchical linear regression models, like the hierarchical models we introduced in Chapter 17, partially pool data across groups in an intelligent way. This information sharing means that parameter estimates for each group tend to have lower uncertainty associated with them than is obtained by estimating a separate model for each group (as is the case for the heterogeneous coefficients model). Also, the group-level estimates for hierarchical models tend to be closer to the grand mean than equivalent estimates from the heterogeneous coefficients model. This is particularly evident for those groups with few observations, and where the estimates are particularly extreme.

This reduction in the heterogeneity of group-level estimates is desirable since it increases the robustness of the model, meaning it will generalise better to out-of-sample data.

In the next chapter we discuss the next logical extension of the Bayesian methodology, to handle generalised linear models, where it is no longer suitable to assume that the dependent variable is unbounded and continuous. However, somewhat unlike Frequentist approaches, the Bayesian method extends naturally to these new circumstances, without a notable increase in model complexity or much of a change in the methods used to estimate the model. Also, fortunately, we can use the same hierarchical modelling approaches to build multilevel models with generalised linear models, meaning that we can again leverage the power of the Bayesian approach.

18○10 CHAPTER OUTCOMES

The reader should now be familiar with the following concepts:

- the Bayesian approach to linear regression
- the benefits of a hierarchical linear regression model over approaches where we pool the data, or estimate a separate model for each group of individuals
- how multilevel models allow data to be incorporated at the most relevant level of a hierarchy

18○11 PROBLEM SETS

Problem 18.1 Crime and punishment

The data in `linearRegression_crimePunishment.csv` contains the murder rate per capita and the rate of automobile crimes per 100,000 individuals (both on the log scale) in the 10 US states that have changed their legislation on capital punishment since 1960 (in all cases the states abolished capital punishment). We also include a dummy variable (*law*) that is 1 if the state allows capital punishment in that year, and 0 otherwise. The crime data are from http://www. disastercenter.com.

Problem 18.1.1 Graph the data and comment on any trends.

Problem 18.1.2 A simple model for murder rates is of the form:

$$murder_{i,t} \sim N\left(\alpha + \beta\, penalty_{i,t} + \gamma car_{i,t}, \sigma\right), \tag{18.7}$$

where we assume that the effect of having the death penalty is given by β, which is assumed to be the same across all states. We include $car_{i,t}$, a measure of crimes on automobiles, as an independent variable to proxy for the contemporaneous underlying level of crime. Estimate this model and hence determine whether the death penalty acts as a deterrent to murder.

Problem 18.1.3 An alternative model allows there to be state-level effects:

$$murder_{i,t} \sim N\left(\alpha_i + \beta_i penalty_{i,t} + \gamma_i car_{i,t}, \sigma_i\right), \tag{18.8}$$

where we assume that $\alpha_i \sim N(\bar{\alpha}, \sigma_\alpha)$, $\beta_i \sim N(\bar{\beta}, \sigma_\beta)$ and $\gamma_i \sim N(\bar{\gamma}, \sigma_\gamma)$ (we assume fully heterogeneous estimates for σ). Estimate the above model and compare the results with the homogeneous coefficients model.

Problem 18.1.4 Compare the predictive fit of the models using the estimated leave-one-out cross-validation from the `loo` package. Which of the three models do you prefer? Hence conclude whether the death penalty acts as a deterrent to murder.

Problem 18.1.5 Critically evaluate the best-performing model and hence any conclusions that can be drawn from this analysis.

19

Chapter contents

GENERALISED LINEAR MODELS AND OTHER ANIMALS

19 ⊙ 1   CHAPTER MISSION STATEMENT

This chapter introduces the Bayesian approach to generalised linear models, which are used in situations when the dependent variable is not constrained to be continuous and unbounded. The chapter also discusses the important topic of how to estimate models with discrete parameters in Stan.

19 ⊙ 2   CHAPTER GOALS

We often want to build models to describe a real-life behaviour that cannot be summarised using a continuous unbounded metric. As an example, we might model the occurrence of disease outbreaks in a particular geographic region. This variable of interest is constrained: the count of disease outbreaks must be a non-negative integer. As per standard linear regression we may want to use information from covariates, such as the quality of water sanitation in an area, to help explain some of the variation in disease outbreak count. Such independent variables are often, in contrast to the dependent variable, unconstrained. We therefore need a way to allow changes in an unconstrained factor to affect the dependent variable on an appropriately constrained scale. This is the motivation behind *generalised linear models* (GLMs). In these models, the mean of a sampling distribution is modelled as a function of linear combination of coefficients and independent variables. This linearity in independent factors is what accounts for the word *linear* in the GLM name.

GLMs are incredibly flexible beasts. They basically provide a way to test the effect of potential causative agents (the independent variables) on an outcome (the dependent variable), regardless of what sort of scale the latter is measured on. So, whether the dependent variable is a binary outcome, a count variable, a waiting time or almost whatever, we can still try to explain its variation using other variables. Basically, GLMs allow us to do regression analyses in almost any circumstance we can think of.

Fortunately, GLMs are really no different from linear regression, except that we are more constrained in our choice of likelihood. Whereas linear models typically assume a normal likelihood (or sometimes a Student-*t*), GLMs require a likelihood that is appropriate to the nature of the particular dependent variable. So, for a binary outcome variable we might choose a Bernoulli likelihood along with something known as a *link* function (here an example might be a logit function) that allows us to map continuous changes in independent factors to an interval between zero and one (the scale of the probability variable that characterises the Bernoulli distribution). However, once this choice has been made, we are free to analyse our models in similar fashion to linear regression models.

Like linear regression models, the Bayesian approach really inspires when the data are hierarchically structured in some way. In this circumstance we are free to use information at each level of the hierarchy to better explain our data. Like their linear model counterparts, these multilevel GLMs are usually the best in class. Their predictive performance on out-of-sample data is usually better, and they provide a richer explanation of the data-generating process than non-hierarchical equivalents. In summary, these types of models are great!

We are nearly done in our exposition of Bayesian analysis through Stan. However, there is one remaining gap in our knowledge that limits our ability to estimate a wide class of models in Stan. Currently, we cannot explicitly include discrete parameters in Stan models. This is because the Hamiltonian Monte Carlo (HMC; really the No-U-Turn Sampler (NUTS)), which is the algorithm that Stan implements, is not yet extended to deal with discrete parameters. While this might seem like a major blow to Stan, in practice it is not limiting as there is a solution to this issue. By marginalising out the discrete variables from the joint probability distribution (which we met in Chapter 3), we can still estimate these types of models in Stan. Although we had a short discussion about this topic in Chapter 16, we wish to spend a little more time here to consolidate our understanding.

The process of marginalisation may seem a little opaque at first, and an extra difficulty when considering the use of Stan as your primary MCMC engine, but there actually are real benefits of this approach. While we do not want to go into the details here, a result known as the Rao–Blackwell theorem means that marginalising out discrete parameters can often significantly speed up sampling convergence.

As in the linear regression chapter, we explain the use of GLMs and discrete parameter models through examples. We believe this is the best way to cover the material, particularly since the theory has largely been covered in preceding chapters.

19○3 EXAMPLE: ELECTORAL PARTICIPATION IN EUROPEAN COUNTRIES

The data that we use to illustrate the GLM approach comes from the European Social Survey. Our data consists of individual voter electoral participation data (that we represent by a variable called 'vote') derived from surveys conducted in 25 countries in Europe in 2012. This variable is a binary indicator equal to 0 if the individual did not vote in the last national election and 1 if they did (see Figure 19.1 for a map of the aggregated data).

To explain the individual voter preferences, we use three variables: whether participants stated they belonged to a religion (rlgblg), their gender (gender = 1 for male, 0 for female) and their age (age). The simplest model assumes that the effect of each of these variables on voter participation is the same across all countries included in our sample. What sort of model should we use here? This, at first, does not appear simple since the dependent variable is binary, and we want to determine the impact of the independent variables (that are not all binary indicators).

One solution is to model the dependent variable as the outcome of a Bernoulli process:

$$\text{vote}_{ij} \sim Ber(\theta_{ij}), \tag{19.1}$$

where $0 \le \theta_{ij} \le 1$ is the probability that individual i in country j voted in the last national election. In our GLM we allow this probability parameter to be a function of the other independent variables:

$$\theta_{ij} = \Lambda\left(\alpha + \beta_g \text{gender}_{ij} + \beta_a \text{age}_{ij} + \beta_r \text{rlgblg}_{ij}\right), \tag{19.2}$$

Figure 19.1 A map showing the percentage of sampled individuals who voted in the last general election. See Figure 19.3 for the percentage who answered that they belonged to a religious group in the survey.

where $\Lambda(.)$ is a function whose output is constrained to lie between 0 and 1. Here we use the logistic sigmoid that has this property:

$$\Lambda(x) = \frac{1}{1+e^{-x}},$$

$\hspace{11.5cm}$ (19.3)

whose graph is shown in Figure 19.2. This function $\Lambda(.)$ is an example of a link function in generalised linear modelling.[1] This is because it links linear combinations of predictors with the mean of the outcome variable.

---

[1]More commonly the term *link* is used to refer to the inverse of such a transformation. In this context this would be logit(.). However, for our purposes we find it easier to buck the trend.

The full likelihood for the model can be written as follows:

$$\text{vote}_{ij} \sim Ber\Big(\Lambda\big(\alpha + \beta_g \text{gender}_{ij} + \beta_a \text{age}_{ij} + \beta_r \text{rlgblg}_{ij}\big)\Big). \tag{19.4}$$

Since none of the βs have a j subscript this model assumes that the effects of each of the independent variables are the same across all countries. This is an example of a pooled model. This model can be coded up in Stan as follows:

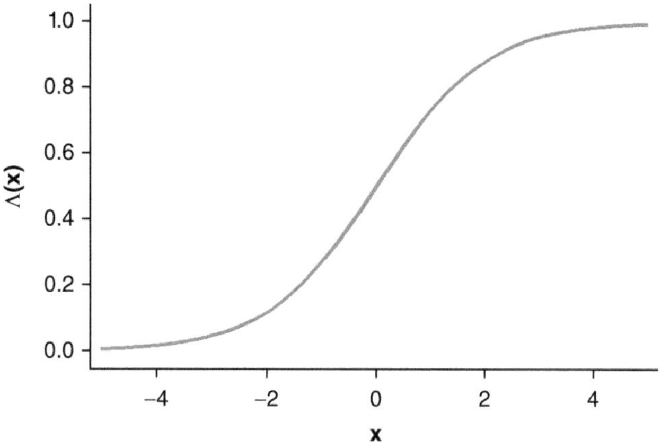

```
data{
    int N;
    int vote[N];
    int rlgblg[N];
    real age[N];
    int gender[N];
}
parameters{
    real alpha;
    real beta_g;
    real beta_a;
    real beta_r;
}
model{
    // likelihood
    for(i in 1:N){
        vote[i] ~ bernoulli_logit(alpha + beta_g * gender[i] + beta_a * age[i]
                    + beta_r * rlgblg[i]);
    }
    // priors
    alpha ~ normal(0,1);
    beta_g ~ normal(0,1);
    beta_a ~ normal(0,1);
    beta_r ~ normal(0,1);
}
```

Figure 19.2 The logistic function used to convert an unbounded variable (x) to a bounded one ($\Lambda(x)$).

where `bernoulli_logit(.)` is Stan's shorthand way of estimating the model written in the equation above. The results from estimating the above model are shown below:

```
## Print summary statistics
print(fit,probs = c(0.25, 0.5, 0.75))
```

	mean	se_mean	sd	25%	50%	75%	n_eff	Rhat
alpha	0.20	0	0.03	0.18	0.20	0.22	637	1.01
beta_g	0.12	0	0.02	0.10	0.12	0.13	660	1.01
beta_a	0.02	0	0.00	0.02	0.02	0.02	1011	1.00
beta_r	0.04	0	0.02	0.03	0.04	0.06	583	1.00

So we estimate that women are, on average, less likely to vote than men (gender is 1 for men, 0 for women), older people are more likely to vote, and people who belong to a religion are marginally more likely to participate in elections.

The various countries that comprise our sample have diverse societies, meaning it is unlikely that the effects of the aforementioned variables are the same in each. One way to allow for such variation is to estimate a separate model for each country, which can be written as:

$$\text{vote}_{ij} \sim Ber\left(\Lambda\left(\alpha_j + \beta_{g,j}\text{gender}_{ij} + \beta_{a,j}\text{age}_{ij} + \beta_{r,j}\text{rlgblg}_{ij}\right)\right), \tag{19.5}$$

where the j subscript on each of the parameters allows there to be different effect sizes for each of the countries in our data set. If we assign independent priors for all of these country-level parameters, this is equivalent to estimating a separate model for each country. This type of model can be coded up in Stan using the following:

```
data{
    int N;
    int K;
    int vote[N];
    int country[N];
    int rlgblg[N];
    real age[N];
    int gender[N];
}
parameters{
    real alpha[K];
    real beta_g[K];
    real beta_a[K];
    real beta_r[K];
}
model{
    for(i in 1:N){
        int aCountry;
        aCountry = country[i];
        vote[i] ~ bernoulli_logit(alpha[aCountry] + beta_g[aCountry] *
                    gender[i] + beta_a[aCountry] * age[i] + beta_r[aCountry] *
                    rlgblg[i]);
    }
    // implicitly places independent priors for each j
    alpha ~ normal(0,1);
    beta_g ~ normal(0,1);
    beta_a ~ normal(0,1);
    beta_r ~ normal(0,1);
}
```

Estimating the above model, we obtain the results shown in the left-hand panel of Figure 19.4. We see that there is considerable cross-country heterogeneity in our estimates of the effect of being male on electoral participation. Whereas for most countries there is a positive effect of being male on the probability of voting, for Estonia the effect is strongly negative (women are about 10% more likely to vote, on average).

However, we feel that estimating entirely separate models for each of the countries is missing a trick. Is there some information that could be shared across the different countries to help produce better inferences? We now consider a hierarchical model, which is similar to the previous model except that we now allow dependence between the individual country-level parameters. So, for example, considering the effect of gender on voting preferences, we might choose a normal 'Europe-level' model of the form:

$$\beta_{g,i} \sim N\left(\bar{\beta}_g, \sigma_g\right), \tag{19.6}$$

where $\bar{\beta}_g$ and σ_g are the mean and standard deviation in the effect sizes in our sample of countries. We omit the full Stan model here for brevity because the general structure is similar

Figure 19.3 A map showing the percentage of sampled individuals who voted in the last general elections who answered that they belonged to a religious group.

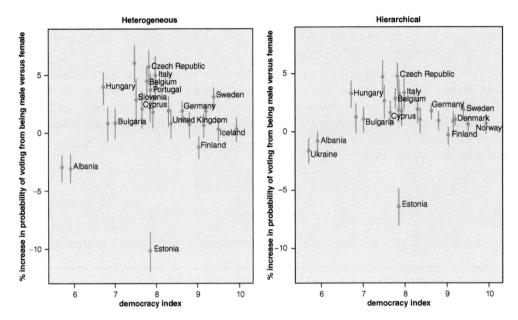

Figure 19.4   The country-level estimates of the effect of being male (as opposed to female) on the probability that an individual voted in the last election from the heterogeneous model (left) and the hierarchical model (right) as a function of the democracy index of each country. The democracy index is a measure created by *The Economist*, and measures state of democracy in each country (low values indicate a poorly functioning democracy). Here we use values from this index for 2012. The estimates of the effect size assume that each individual belongs to a religious group, and are at the mean age we find in the data.

to the hierarchical model we encountered in Chapter 18. However, we note that the individual country-level estimates are generally closer towards the grand mean than their heterogeneous model equivalents (see the right-hand panel of Figure 19.4). There is also lower uncertainty in the individual estimates obtained from the hierarchical model since we are, in effect, pooling information from across the different countries.

19.3.1 Multilevel interactions

Suppose that we believe that the effect gender has on an individual's electoral participation depends on the society they belong to. Looking at the correlation between our estimates and the democracy index in Figure 19.3 we might hypothesise that as a nation becomes more democratic, males are even more likely to vote. In other words, in a highly democratic country the gap between the electoral participation rates of men and women (with men voting more often) is greater than for a less democratic country. The simplest way to encode such an effect would be by including an interaction term between gender and democracy in our likelihood:

$$\text{vote}_{ij} \sim Ber\left(\Lambda\left(\alpha_j + \beta_{g,j}\text{gender}_{ij} + \delta_g\text{gender}_{ij}\text{democracy}_j + \beta_{a,j}\text{age}_{ij} + \beta_{r,j}\text{rlgblg}_{ij}\right)\right), \tag{19.7}$$

where democracy$_j$ is measured at the country level, meaning that we estimate a single parameter δ_g that quantifies the strength of this interaction. However, do we believe that the effect of a changing democratic landscape is independent of the society in question? In other words, do we think that the effect of an improved democratic rule is exactly the same for all countries? Of course not. Countries within Europe have diverse cultures, and it would be naive to expect a unimodal response to societal transition.

A better way to capture the interaction between democracy and gender would be to consider a higher level of abstraction. In particular, we suppose a system of the form:

$$\text{vote}_{ij} \sim Ber\left(\Lambda\left(\alpha_j + \beta_{g,j}\text{gender}_{ij} + \beta_{a,j}\text{age}_{ij} + \beta_{r,j}\text{rlgblg}_{ij}\right)\right)$$

$$\beta_{g,j} \sim N(\alpha + \delta_g\text{democracy}_j, \sigma),$$

(19.8)

where the bottom line in (19.8) indicates there is an average effect of size δ_g, which quantifies the impact of gender on electoral participation across all Europe. However, importantly, this formulation allows there to be individual country variation in the strength of this interaction. This means that the above model is less restrictive than the aforementioned non-hierarchical one.

To estimate this model in Stan, we use a non-centred parameterisation to reduce the risk of divergent iterations (see Section 18.8):

```
data{
    int N;
    int K;
    int vote[N];
    int country[N];
    int rlgblg[N];
    real age[N];
    int gender[N];

    // country-level variables
    real democracy[K];
}
parameters{
    real alpha_raw[K];
    real beta_g_raw[K];
    real beta_r_raw[K];
    real beta_a_raw[K];
    real alpha_top;
    real<lower=0>alpha_sigma;
    real beta_g_top;
    real<lower=0>beta_g_sigma;
    real beta_a_top;
    real<lower=0>beta_a_sigma;
```

```
    real beta_r_top;
    real<lower=0>beta_r_sigma;
    real delta;
}
transformed parameters{
    real alpha[K];
    real beta_g[K];
    real beta_r[K];
    real beta_a[K];
    for(i in 1:K){
        alpha[i] = alpha_top + alpha_sigma * alpha_raw[i];
        beta_g[i] = beta_g_top + delta * democracy[i] + beta_g_sigma *
                    beta_g_raw[i];
        beta_r[i] = beta_r_top + beta_r_sigma * beta_r_raw[i];
        beta_a[i] = beta_a_top + beta_a_sigma * beta_a_raw[i];
    }
}
model{
    for(i in 1:N){
        int aCountry;
        aCountry = country[i];
        vote[i] ~ bernoulli_logit(alpha[aCountry] + beta_g[aCountry] * gender[i] +
                    beta_a[aCountry] * age[i] + beta_r[aCountry] * rlgblg[i]);
    }
    // priors
    alpha_raw ~ normal(0,1);
    beta_g_raw ~ normal(0,1);
    beta_r_raw ~ normal(0,1);
    beta_a_raw ~ normal(0,1);

    // hyper-priors
    alpha_top ~ normal(0,1);
    alpha_sigma ~ normal(0,1);
    beta_g_top ~ normal(0,1);
    beta_g_sigma ~ normal(0,1);
    beta_a_top ~ normal(0,1);
    beta_a_sigma ~ normal(0,1);
    beta_r_top ~ normal(0,1);
    beta_r_sigma ~ normal(0,1);
}
generated quantities{
    real alpha_overall;
    real beta_g_overall;
    real beta_a_overall;
    real beta_r_overall;
```

```
  alpha_overall = normal_rng(alpha_top,alpha_sigma);
  beta_g_overall = normal_rng(beta_g_top,beta_g_sigma);
  beta_a_overall = normal_rng(beta_a_top,beta_a_sigma);
  beta_r_overall = normal_rng(beta_r_top,beta_r_sigma);
}
```

The above produces the following results:

```
## Print summary statistics
print(fit,probs = c(0.25, 0.5, 0.75))
```

##		mean	se_mean	sd	25%	50%	75%	97.5%	n_eff	Rhat
##	delta	0.07	0.05	-0.02	0.03	0.06	0.10	261	0.99	
##	alpha_overall	1.21	0.71	-0.33	0.79	1.25	1.65	400	1.00	
##	beta_g_overall	0.09	0.17	-0.29	-0.02	0.10	0.20	329	1.01	
##	beta_r_overall	0.16	0.32	-0.52	-0.04	0.16	0.38	339	1.00	
##	beta_a_overall	0.4	0.29	-0.07	0.29	0.46	0.66	370	0.99	

So overall we find that the only reliable indicator of whether an individual will vote is their age. Presumably, there is so much variation in the impact of gender or religion on electoral participation across countries that we do not estimate an overall effect that differs from zero. The interaction of gender and democracy is also estimated to be relatively weak.

19.3.2 Comparing the predictive fit of each of the models

Suppose that we want to determine which of the four models provides the best predictions on voter participation. Ideally, we would do this by repeatedly partitioning our data into training and testing sets (see Chapter 10 for the theory and Chapter 16 for the implementation), using the former to fit our model and the latter to evaluate its predictive fit. However, the aforementioned models are fairly complex and the data set is also quite large, meaning that it will be impractical to use explicit cross-validation here because of the computational burden involved. Instead, we evaluate the predictive capability of the model on within-sample data, and then try to correct for any potential overfit.

Here we use the loo package for R to estimate the leave-one-out cross-validation predictive capability of each of the models (see Chapter 10). To use this method we need only to store the log probability of each data point for each posterior sample from our parameters. We do this using the generated quantities block. So for all models but the pooled one, this can be done using the following (the pooled code is simpler because we do not allow variation in the parameters for each country):

```
generated quantities{
  real logLikelihood[N];

  for(i in 1:N){
    int aCountry;
    aCountry = country[i];
```

```
logLikelihood[i] = bernoulli_logit_lpmf(vote[i]|alpha[aCountry] +
                   beta_g[aCountry] * gender[i] + beta_a[aCountry] * age[i] +
                   beta_r[aCountry] * rlgblg[i]);
    }
}
```

Table 19.1   The estimated expected log predictive density for the four models of voter participation. This metric is a measure of a model's fit to data, with higher values indicating a better fit.

Model	Expected log predictive density	Standard error
Pooled	−22,637.8	108.9
Heterogeneous	−21,463.2	112.4
Hierarchical	−21,457.7	111.6
Multilevel interaction	−21,457.0	111.5

The results of using the loo package for each of the models are shown in Table 19.1. This package outputs estimates of the expected log predictive density for an out-of-sample data point, along with standard errors associated with these estimates (see Chapter 10). Our analysis indicates that the multilevel model fits the data best, followed by the hierarchical model, then the heterogeneous one. Unsurprisingly the pooled model is least able to explain the variation in the dependent variable. However, taking the uncertainty into account (using the compare function from loo), we find no real difference between the hierarchical and multilevel interaction models, although both of these are better than the other two.

19●4   DISCRETE PARAMETER MODELS IN STAN

Although we discussed discrete models in Stan in Chapter 16, we now spend a little more time on this subject to consolidate our thinking on this topic. HMC and its faster cousin NUTS are truly excellent strings in the data scientist's bow. These samplers are best explained by using a physical analogy. Here we imagine a sledge sliding over a smooth landscape that is related to posterior space. By design this landscape (negative log posterior space) means our sledge (whose position relates to samples for the parameters) will more often visit areas of high density (see Chapter 15 for a more complete discussion of HMC). This results in more accepted proposals than are possible for Random Walk Metropolis. The Achilles heel of the physical analogy is that it requires parameter space to be continuous, otherwise we have difficulty describing the motion of our sledge over the space with Newtonian mechanics.[2] This might seem like a severe roadblock to using Stan to estimate a model with discrete parameters, but there is a neat and, as it turns out, efficient way to do this in Stan. It involves marginalising out the discrete parameters.

How to code up a model with discrete parameters in Stan

What do we mean by 'marginalising out' here? Suppose that we have a two-dimensional probability distribution $p(\beta_i, \theta)$ where the $\beta_i \in \{\beta_1, \beta_2, ..., \beta_K\}$ is discrete parameter with K possible

[2]However, recent research by Akihiko Nishimura et al. into HMC suggests ways to extend this sampling algorithm to discrete parameter spaces (see https://arxiv.org/abs/1705.08510).

values, and θ is continuous. We can actually remove the joint probability's dependence on the discrete parameter by summing over all possible values of β_i:

$$p(\theta) = \sum_{i=1}^{k} p(\beta_i, \theta),$$ (19.9)

leaving a marginal density $p(\theta)$ that is only a function of a continuous parameter θ.

If we can carry out such a marginalisation in Stan, this means that we can then proceed as usual, since our posterior will only be a function of continuous parameters and HMC will work. However, there is a slight complication, because – remember – Stan actually deals in the log of the (un-normalised) posterior density as its preferred currency. So we need to do something akin to the following mathematical operation:

$$\log p(\theta) = \log \sum_{i=1}^{k} \exp(\log p(\beta_i, \theta)),$$ (19.10)

where the left-hand side of expression (19.10) is the marginalised log posterior. On the right-hand side of this expression we must take the exponent of the log probability to convert it into a probability. However, if we explicitly code up expression (19.10) in Stan, we would suffer from issues of numerical instability, since the probabilities themselves can be very small. Handily, Stan has a function that avoids such computational instability, and obviates our need to code things up ourselves. This function can be used to rewrite expression (19.10) as:

$$\log p(\theta) = \log\_sum\_exp_{i=1}^{K}(\log p(\beta_i, \theta)),$$ (19.11)

where we choose not to specify the exact functional form of $\log\_sum\_exp_{i=1}^{K}$ since it is unnecessary here, but we note that the result of using either expression (19.10) or (19.11) is the same.

19.4.1 Example: how many times was the coin flipped?

To provide an example of how to code up a model involving discrete parameters in Stan, we imagine a coin where θ denotes the probability of its landing heads up. In each repetition of the experiment, the coin is flipped exactly N times, where N is unknown to us. Suppose that the experiment is repeated 10 times, and the following numbers of heads are obtained, $Y = \{9,7,11,10,10,9,8,11,9,11\}$. We use a binomial distribution to describe the number of heads obtained in each replicate:

$$Y_i \sim \mathcal{B}(N, \theta),$$ (19.12)

where N and θ are the same across all repetitions. Suppose that we know that the maximum number of times the coin is flipped in a single replicate is 20, and we believe that all feasible values of N are equally likely. Also, imagine that from our previous coin-flipping experience we believe that the coin is biased towards heads. We quantify these beliefs using the following priors:

$$\theta \sim beta(7,2)$$
(19.13)
$$N \sim discrete-uniform(11,20),$$

where 11 is the minimum number of flips possible, since this equals the maximum count of heads that we see in our data. The key to writing this model in Stan is deriving an expression for the (un-normalised) log posterior probability that is devoid of any explicit reference to N. To do this we first write the log posterior probability for all the data (the following is vectorised):

```
log(0.1) + binomial_lpmf(Y|N[s],theta);
```

where `binomial_lpmf` is the log probability for a binomial distribution for our vector of counts `Y`, and `N[s]` is the number of total throws for each experimental repetition. Here s indexes an array `int N[10]` that contains all integer values of N between 11 and 20. The `log(0.1)` term here is due to the discrete uniform prior we place on N: because there are 10 possible values of N, the individual probability is 0.1. When we use Stan we deal with the log probability, meaning that we log this value and add it onto the likelihood term (we add it because the log of a product is a sum of logs).

In our Stan code we record the log posterior probability for each possible value of s in a vector:

```
transformed parameters{
  vector[10] lp;
  for(s in 1:10){
    lp[s] = log(0.1) + binomial_lpmf(Y|N[s],theta);
  }
}
```

We then marginalise out any dependence on s in the `model` block and increment the overall log probability by this amount:

```
model{
  target += log_sum_exp(lp);
  theta ~ beta(7,2);
}
```

The whole model can therefore be written in Stan as follows:

```
data{
  int K;
  int Y[K];
}
transformed data{
  int N[10];
  for(s in 1:10){
    N[s] = 10 + s;
  }
}
parameters{
  real<lower=0,upper=1> theta;
}
transformed parameters{
  vector[10] lp;
  for(s in 1:10){
```

```
        lp[s] = log(0.1) + binomial_lpmf(Y|N[s],theta);
    }
}
model{
    target += log_sum_exp(lp);
    theta ~ beta(7,2);
}
```

where `int N` is not defined as a parameter in the model, but created as a data object in the `transformed data` block. The results of estimating the above model are as follows:

```
## Print summary statistics
print(fit, pars = 'theta', probs = c(0.25, 0.5, 0.75))
##          mean  se_mean    sd  2.5%   25%   50%   75%  97.5%  n_eff  Rhat
## theta  0.78     0.00  0.09  0.57  0.73  0.80  0.85   0.90    669     1
```

Our posterior here largely reflects our prior beliefs that the coin is biased towards heads. This makes intuitive sense because there is little information in the data to suggest which values of θ are more likely.

Estimating this model gives us a posterior for θ, but how can we obtain a posterior for N? On first glances this appears tricky since we deliberately avoid including N as a parameter in the model. However, we can calculate the un-normalised probability for any particular value of N by marginalising θ out of the un-normalised posterior probability:

$$q(N = 11|Y) \approx \frac{1}{L}\sum_{i=1}^{L} q(N = 11, \theta_i | Y), \tag{19.14}$$

where $q(N = 11|Y)$ is the un-normalised posterior probability of $N = 11$, and L is the number of posterior samples. How do we convert this un-normalised probability into a valid probability distribution? Since the distribution is a discrete function of N we just sum all the possible un-normalised probabilities, then normalise using this value:

$$Pr(N = 11|Y) = \frac{q(N = 11|Y)}{\sum_{N=11}^{20} q(N = i|Y)}. \tag{19.15}$$

How do we do this in Stan? This is straightforward if we use the `generated quantities` block:

```
generated quantities {
    simplex[10] pState;
    pState = exp(lp - log_sum_exp(lp));
}
```

where we remember that `lp` is a 10-dimensional vector with each entry corresponding to the un-normalised posterior probability of a particular value of $N = \{11,12,...,20\}$. We also remember that `log_sum_exp(lp)` determines the log of the marginalised un-normalised posterior probability (the denominator of expression (19.15)). So the term `lp - log_sum_exp(lp)` just

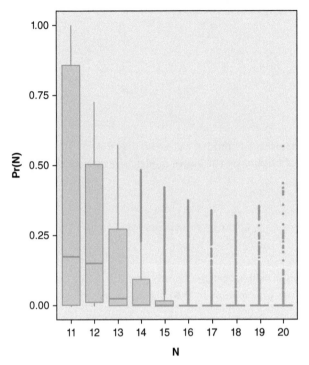

Figure 19.5 The estimated posterior probabilities for the number of times. The coin was flipped. The upper and lower fences indicate the 75% and 25% quantiles of the data, and the middle bar shows the median test score. The upper and lower whiskers indicate 1.5 times the interquartile range from the upper and lower fences, respectively. The points indicate outliers.

amounts to determining the log of the normalised posterior probability for each value of N (because a minus in logs corresponds to a division in levels). Using this code, we generate the posterior shown in Figure 19.5. Since we have estimated that the coin is biased towards heads, the posterior distribution for N gives highest weight to $N = 11$ since this corresponds to the maximum number of heads that we observe in the data.

 **CHAPTER SUMMARY**

This chapter extended the idea of multilevel regression models to encompass more general situations, where the dependent variable is no longer an unconstrained continuous variable. These generalised linear models (GLMs) are incredibly flexible tools for trying to bind cause and effect in the social and physical sciences. They allow us to estimate models where the dependent variable represents a count, a binary or multi-outcome result, a waiting time, a probability vector, and so on. The only limitation we have with these types of models is finding an appropriate likelihood. However, so long as we can find or construct such a likelihood, we can estimate our model.

As in the previous chapter we saw how the Bayesian paradigm allows us to straightforwardly build models that account for the hierarchical structure of the data. The line between prior and likelihood is blurred in these types of models, as priors for lower-level parameters can be informed by data at the group level. This provides a flexibility that means that these models tend to perform better than their non-hierarchical equivalents, because they can more realistically represent a given data-generating process.

We also saw how we can use Stan to estimate models with discrete parameters through marginalisation. While it may seem like an extra step to estimate these models in Stan, as opposed to JAGS or BUGS, the marginalised models are, in general, much more efficient to sample from than the full joint distributions. This increased efficiency means that the rate of convergence of the sampling algorithm to the posterior distribution will be considerably faster. We also saw that, even though we marginalise discrete parameters out of the log probability in Stan, we can still estimate their posterior distribution using the `generated quantities` block. To do so we estimate the un-normalised probability of each discrete state. We then normalise this quantity to produce the posterior probability by dividing through by the sum of the un-normalised probabilities across all discrete states.

More generally, we have now come to the end of our tour through Bayesland. This will no doubt be sad times for you all. If pathetic fallacy is not a fallacy, there will be torrents of rain smashing against your window panes. But do we have any advice to lighten the mood and help you in your own analysis quest? In order of importance, we now list what we think are key steps to becoming a Bayes master.

1   **Spend a long time visualising your data before you start modelling.** There are no hard rules to follow here, unfortunately, and achieving the right visualisation for your data can be an arduous process. Try to be creative. Do not just follow what you or others have done in the past. That said, it is still worth trying to inform yourself about what others have done to produce creative and illuminating visualisations of data. A great book on the subject by the master of graphics, Edward Tufte, is *The Visual Display of Quantitative Information* [39].

2   **When building a model, start simple and build up complexity as needed.** Here, posterior predictive checks are your best friend as they typically are good (if chosen correctly) at hinting at a model's inadequacies. Good visualisations help us to pick sensible posterior predictive checks.

3   **Read articles and books on statistical inference from a range of sources.** You have started with this one (a good choice, we hope), but there are certainly large gains to be had by being polygamous here. See Section 1.11 for a list of such books.

4   **If you use statistics in your work, take the opportunity to present your results to your colleagues.** The process of writing the presentation, collecting one's thoughts and getting feedback is really valuable and inevitably results in a higher quality of work.

5   **When in doubt use hierarchical models.** As you can probably tell from the propaganda of the last part of this book, we truly believe in the power of these models, and think they are an indispensable tool in the data scientist's toolkit.

19○6   CHAPTER OUTCOMES

The reader should now be familiar with the following concepts:

- what a generalised linear model is and how it can be used to do regression in more general settings than linear models
- the power of multilevel hierarchical models where data can be used as inputs to priors at a range of different levels of a hierarchy
- how to estimate models in Stan with discrete parameters through marginalisation, and how to estimate the posteriors for these parameters using Stan's `generated quantities` code block

19○7   PROBLEM SETS

Problem 19.1 Seatbelts

The file `glm_seatbelts.csv` contains data on the monthly total of car drivers killed (on a $\log_{10}$ scale) in Great Britain between January 1969 and December 1984 (see `https://stat.ethz.ch/R-manual/R-devel/library/datasets/html/UKDriverDeaths.html`). It also contains a measure of petrol prices over the same period, as well as a variable that represents the month on a scale of 1–12.

During the period for which the data runs there was a change in the law that meant it became a legal requirement to wear seatbelts in cars. In this question we are going to estimate when this event occurred by examining the data.

Problem 19.1.1 Plot the data. Can you see by eye when the legislation was likely enacted?

Problem 19.1.2 A model is proposed of the form:

$$deaths(t) \sim N\left(\alpha + \beta\,petrol(t) + \sum_{i=1}^{11} \delta_i D(i,t) + \gamma(t,s), \sigma\right), \tag{19.16}$$

where:

$$\gamma = \begin{cases} 0, & \text{if } t < s, \\ \gamma_0, & \text{if } t \geq s, \end{cases} \tag{19.17}$$

and $\gamma_0 < 0$ represents the effect of the seatbelt legislation on the numbers of car drivers killed after some implementation date s; $D(i,t)$ is a dummy variable for month i equal to 1 if and only if the date t corresponds to that month, and equal to 0 otherwise.

Implement the above model in Stan, and hence estimate the effect that the seatbelt legislation had on car driver deaths.

Problem 19.1.3 Using the `generated quantities` block, estimate the date when the legislation was enacted.

Problem 19.2 Model choice for a meta-analysis

Suppose that the data contained in `GLM_metaAnalysis.csv` contains the (fictitious) result of 20 trials of a new drug. In each trial 10 patients with a particular disorder are treated with the drug, and the data records the number of individuals cured in each trial.

Problem 19.2.1 Graph the data across all 20 trials. What does this suggest about a potential model to explain the data?

Problem 19.2.2 Suppose that we have two models that we could use to describe the data:

$$X_i \sim \mathcal{B}(10,\theta), \tag{19.18}$$

or

$$X_i \sim beta\text{-}binomial(10,a,b), \tag{19.19}$$

where X_i is the number of successes in trial $i \in [1,20]$. Write two Stan programs to fit each of the above models to the data, and use the estimated LOO-CV (use the `loo` package in R) to choose between the above models. (Assign $\theta \sim beta(1,1)$ and $a,b \sim N(2,5)$ for priors for each model, where a and b are constrained to be positive.)

Problem 19.2.3 An alternative way to choose between these models is to use Bayes factors. Rather than determine the marginal likelihoods explicitly, this can actually be done in Stan by allowing a discrete model choice parameter $s \in \{1,2\}$ that dictates which model to use. Code up this model in Stan, and by examining the posterior distribution for $Pr(s)$ determine which sampling distribution fits the data best. (*Hint*: assign equal probability to each model a priori and marginalise out s to obtain the log probability.)

Problem 19.2.4 An alternative approach is to use the binomial likelihood, but use a hierarchical model where each θ_i is drawn from some population-level distribution. Comment on whether you would prefer this approach or the beta-binomial model. (*Hint*: do not estimate the hierarchical model.)

Problem 19.3 Terrorism

In this question we will investigate the link between the incidence of terrorism and a country's level of income. The data in `glm_terrorism.csv` contains for 100 countries (those for which the latest data was available) the following series:

- *count*: the number of acts of terrorism perpetrated in each country from 2012 to 2015, as compiled by START [7].
- *gdp*: the gross domestic product of each country in 2015, as compiled by the World Bank.
- *population*: the population of each country in 2015, as compiled by the World Bank.
- *gdpPerCapita*: the GDP per capita in each country.
- *religion*, *ethnic*, *language*: measures of fractionalisation with respect to each of these measures, obtained from `http://www.anderson.ucla.edu/faculty_pages/romain.wacziarg`.
- *law* and *corruption*: measures of the rule of law and corruption (actually an inverse measure), as compiled by the World Bank in its 2016 *World Governance Indicators* report.
- *democracy* and *autocracy*: indicators of democracy and autocracy respectively from the polity4 database.
- *region* and *region_numeric*: the region to which a country belongs out of Asia, Europe, Middle East and North Africa, Sub-Saharan Africa, South America and North America.

Problem 19.3.1 Graph the data. What does this tell you about the processes?

Problem 19.3.2 A simple model for the terrorism count is:

$$count_i \sim Poisson(\alpha + \beta_1 population_i + \beta_2 gdpPerCapita_i), \qquad (19.20)$$

where i corresponds to one of the countries in our data set. Code up this model in Stan, and use it to obtain estimates of the effect of a country's income level on the incidence of terrorism.

Problem 19.3.3 Now include *corruption*, *religion* and *ethnic* as further variables in the above generalised linear model. What is the impact of each of these variables on the terrorism count?

Problem 19.3.4 Conduct posterior predictive checks to assess the applicability of the model to the data. What do these tests suggest? Use this information to formulate an improved model and use it to determine the effect of economic development on terrorism.

Problem 19.4 Eurovision

The file `Eurovision.csv` contains historical data on the outcome of the Eurovision song contest from 1976 to 2015 for the 20 countries which have featured most consistently in the finals throughout the years. Along with the results from the contest, we also include data on the distance between pairs of countries, whether those countries share a common language, and if one was ever colonised by the other. In this question we ask you to develop a model to help explain the way in which countries award points to one another. Choice of the model's structure, the covariates to include, and the way in which the model is tested should be decided upon by you. How far you wish to go with this analysis is up to you, but could take the form of a project.

Problem 19.5 More terrorism (harder)

The file `terrorism.csv` contains historical pairwise counts of terrorist attacks perpetrated by citizens of an origin country against a target country, compiled by Alan Krueger (see `http://krueger.princeton.edu/pages/`) and assembled from the US State Department's annual list of significant international terrorist incidences (PGT). In this question we ask you to develop a model to explain the incidence of such attacks using data on the attributes of each country (the origin and target). Choice of the model's structure, the covariates to include, and the way in which the model is tested should be decided upon by you. How far you wish to go with this analysis is up to you, but could take the form of a project.

BIBLIOGRAPHY*

1   Bergland, G. D. (1969). A guided tour of the fast Fourier transform. *Spectrum, 6*(7), 41–52.

2   Bernardo, J. M. (1979). Reference posterior distributions for Bayesian inference. *Journal of the Royal Statistical Society. Series B (Methodological), 41*(2), 113–147.

3   Betancourt, M. (2013). A general metric for Riemannian manifold Hamiltonian Monte Carlo. In Nielsen, F. & Barbaresco, F. (Eds.), *Geometric science of information* (pp. 327–334). Berlin: Springer.

4   Betancourt, M. (2016). Diagnosing suboptimal cotangent disintegrations in Hamiltonian Monte Carlo. *arXiv preprint arXiv:1604.00695.*

5   Blei, D. M., Ng, A. Y., & Jordan, M. I. (2003). Latent Dirichlet allocation. *Journal of Machine Learning Research, 3,* 993–1022.

6   Bolstad, W. M. (2007). *Introduction to Bayesian statistics* (2nd ed.). Hoboken, NJ: John Wiley & Sons.

7   Brooks, S., Gelman, A., Jones, G., & Meng, X.-L. (Eds.). (2011). *Handbook of Markov chain Monte Carlo.* Boca Raton, FL: Chapman & Hall/CRC Press.

8   Carpenter, B., Gelman, A., Hoffman, M., Lee, D., Goodrich, B., Betancourt, M., et al. (2016). Stan: A probabilistic programming language. *Journal of Statistical Software, 76*(1).

9   Casella, G. (1985). An introduction to empirical Bayes data analysis. *The American Statistician, 39*(2), 83–87.

10 Chib, S., & Greenberg, E. (1995). Understanding the Metropolis-Hastings algorithm. *The American Statistician, 49*(4), 327–335.

11 Epstein, J. M. (2008). Why model? *Journal of Artificial Societies and Social Simulation, 11*(4), 12.

12 Gebali, F. (2008). Reducible Markov chains. In *Analysis of computer and communication networks* (pp. 1–32). New York: Springer.

13 Gelman, A. (2006). Prior distributions for variance parameters in hierarchical models (comment on article by Browne and Draper). *Bayesian Analysis, 1*(3), 515–534.

14 Gelman, A., Carlin, J. B., Stern, H. S., Dunson, D. B., Vehtari, A., & Rubin, D. B. (2013). *Bayesian data analysis* (3rd ed.). Boca Raton, FL: CRC Press.

15 Gelman, A., Hwang, J., & Vehtari, A. (2014). Understanding predictive information criteria for Bayesian models. *Statistics and Computing, 24*(6), 997–1016.

16 Gelman, A., & Rubin, D. B. (1992). Inference from iterative simulation using multiple sequences. *Statistical Science, 7*(4), 457–472.

*Problem sets bibliography appears on p. 491.

17   Gill, J. (2007). *Bayesian methods: A social and behavioral sciences approach* (2nd ed.). Boca Raton, FL: Chapman & Hall/CRC Press.

18   Hanea, A. M., & Nane, G. F. (2013). The asymptotic distribution of the determinant of a random correlation matrix. *arXiv preprint arXiv:1309.7268.*

19   Hoffman, M. D., & Gelman, A. (2014). The No-U-Turn Sampler: Adaptively setting path lengths in Hamiltonian Monte Carlo. *Journal of Machine Learning Research, 15*(1), 1593–1623.

20   Ioannidis, J. P. A. (2005). Why most published research findings are false. *PLoS Medicine, 2*(8), e124.

21   Kahneman, D. (2011). *Thinking, fast and slow.* New York: Farrar, Straus and Giroux.

22   Kuhn, M. (with Wing, J., Weston, S., Williams, A., Keefer, C., & Engelhardt, A). (2012). *caret: Classification and regression training* (R package version 5.15-044).

23   Lewandowski, D., Kurowicka, D., & Joe, H. (2009). Generating random correlation matrices based on vines and extended onion method. *Journal of Multivariate Analysis, 100*(9), 1989–2001.

24   Lunn, D., Jackson, C., Best, N., Thomas, A., & Spiegelhalter, D. (2012). *The BUGS book: A practical introduction to Bayesian analysis.* Boca Raton, FL: CRC Press.

25   Mandelbrot, B. B., & Hudson, R. L. (2008). *Misbehaviour of markets.* New York: Basic Books.

26   McGrayne, S. B. (2011). *The theory that would not die: How Bayes' rule cracked the enigma code, hunted down Russian submarines, and emerged triumphant from two centuries of controversy.* New Haven, CT: Yale University Press.

27   Mimno, D., & Blei, D. (2011). Bayesian checking for topic models. In *Proceedings of the conference on empirical methods in natural language processing* (pp. 227–237). Stroudsburg, PA: Association for Computational Linguistics.

28   Neal, R. M. (2001). Annealed importance sampling. *Statistics and Computing, 11*(2), 125–139.

29   R Core Team. (2014). *R: A language and environment for statistical computing.* Vienna: R Foundation for Statistical Computing.

30   Roberts, G. O., Gelman, A., & Gilks, W. R. (1997). Weak convergence and optimal scaling of random walk Metropolis algorithms. *Annals of Applied Probability, 7*(1), 110–120.

31   Rosenthal, J. S. (2011). Optimal proposal distributions and adaptive MCMC. In S. Brooks, A. Gelman, G. Jones, & X.-L. Meng (Eds.), *Handbook of Markov chain Monte Carlo* (pp. 93–112). Boca Raton, FL: Chapman & Hall/CRC Press.

32   Silver, N. (2012). *The signal and the noise: The art and science of prediction.* New York: Penguin.

33   Spiegelhalter, D. J., Best, N. G., Carlin, B. P., & Van Der Linde, A. (2002). Bayesian measures of model complexity and fit. *Journal of the Royal Statistical Society: Series B (Statistical Methodology), 64*(4), 583–639.

34   Stan Development Team. (2014). Stan: A C++ library for probability and sampling (Version 2.5.0).

35   Stewart, W., & Stewart, S. (2014). Teaching Markov chain Monte Carlo: Revealing the basic ideas behind the algorithm. *PRIMUS, 24*(1), 25–45.

36   Taleb, N. N. (2010). *The black swan: The impact of the highly improbable fragility* (Vol. 2). New York: Random House.

37   Tegmark, M. (2014). *Our mathematical universe: My quest for the ultimate nature of reality.* New York: Knopf.

38   Tokuda, T., Goodrich, B., Mechelen, I. V., Gelman, A., & Tuerlinckx, F. (2011). *Visualizing distributions of covariance matrices.* New York: Columbia University Press.

39   Tufte, E. (2001). *The visual display of quantitative information.* Cheshire, CT: Graphics Press.

40   Vehtari, A., Gelman, A., & Gabry, J. (2015). Efficient implementation of leave-one-out cross-validation and WAIC for evaluating fitted Bayesian models. *arXiv preprint arXiv:1507.04544.*

PROBLEM SETS

Bibliography

1   Delury, G. E. (1975). *The World Almanac and Book of Facts.* World Almanac Books.

2   Belenky, G., Wesensten, N. J., Thorne, D. R, Thomas, M. L., Sing, H. C., Redmond, D. P., Russo, M. B., & Balkin, T. J. (2003). Patterns of performance degradation and restoration during sleep restriction and subsequent recovery: A sleep dose-response study. *Journal of Sleep Research, 12*(1):1–12.

3   Carlin, J. B. (1992). Meta-analysis for 2×2 tables: A Bayesian approach. *Statistics in Medicine, 11*(2):141–158.

4   Gelman, A. (2008). Objections to Bayesian statistics. *Bayesian Analysis, 3*(3):445–449.

5   Jarrett, R. G. (1979). A note on the intervals between coal-mining disasters. *Biometrika, 66*(1):191–193.

6   Joseph, L., Gyorkos, T. W., & Coupal, L. (1995). Bayesian estimation of disease prevalence and the parameters of diagnostic tests in the absence of a gold standard. *American Journal of Epidemiology, 141*(3):263–272.

7   National Consortium for the Study of Terrorism and Responses to Terrorism (START) (2016). Global terrorism database.

8   Neal, R. M. (2011). MCMC using Hamiltonian dynamics. In Brooks, S., Gelman, A., Jones, G. L., & Xiao-Li Meng, X.-L. (Eds.), *Handbook of Markov Chain Monte Carlo* (pp. 113–162). Chapman & Hall/CRC.

9   Spiegelhalter, D. J., Best, N. G., Carlin, B. P., & Van Der Linde, A. (2002). Bayesian measures of model complexity and fit. *Journal of the Royal Statistical Society: Series B, 64*(4):583–639.

10   Thall, P. F., & Vail, S. C. (1990). Some covariance models for longitudinal count data with overdispersion. *Biometrics, 46*(3):657–671.

INDEX